Y0-BCR-878

Reference Library of

BLACK

AMERICA

Reference Library of
BLACK AMERICA

VOLUME
II

Edited by
Jessie Carney Smith
Joseph M. Palmisano

Distributed exclusively by:

African American Publications
Proteus Enterprises

Staff

Jessie Carney Smith and Joseph M. Palmisano, *Editors*
Patrick J. Politano, *Assistant Editor*
William Harmer, Ashyia N. Henderson, Brian J. Koski, Gloria Lam, Jeffrey Lehman, Allison McClintic Marion, Mark F. Mikula, David G. Oblender, Rebecca Parks, Shirelle Phelps, Kathleen Romig, *Contributing Staff*
Linda S. Hubbard, *Managing Editor, Multicultural Team*

Maria Franklin, *Permissions Manager*
Margaret Chamberlain, *Permissions Specialist*
Keasha Jack-Lyles and Shalice Shah-Caldwell, *Permissions Associates*

Justine H. Carson, *Manager, Vocabulary Development and Indexer*
Rebecca Abbott Forgette, *Indexing Specialist*

Mary Beth Trimper, *Production Director*
Wendy Blurton, *Senior Buyer*
Cynthia Baldwin, *Product Design Manager*
Gary Popiela, *Graphic Artist*
Barbara J. Yarrow, *Imaging/Multimedia Manager*
Randy Bassett, *Image Database Supervisor*
Pamela A. Reed, *Imaging Coordinator*
Robert Duncan, *Imaging Specialist*
Christine O'Bryan, *Desktop Publisher*

Victoria B. Cariappa, *Research Manager*
Barbara McNeil, *Research Specialists*
Patricia Tsune Ballard, *Research Associate*

While every effort has been made to ensure the reliability of the information presented in this publication, Gale Group does not guarantee the accuracy of the data contained herein. Gale accepts no payment for listing, and inclusion in the publication of any organization, agency, institution, publication, service, or individual does not imply endorsement of the editors or publisher. Errors brought to the attention of the publisher and verified to the satisfaction of the publisher will be corrected in future editions.

This publication is a creative work fully protected by all applicable copyright laws, as well as by misappropriation, trade secret, unfair competition, and other applicable laws. The authors and editors of this work have added value to the underlying factual material herein through one or more of the following: unique and original selection, coordination, expression, arrangement, and classification of the information. All rights to this publication will be vigorously defended. No part of this book may be reproduced in any form without permission in writing from the publisher, except by a reviewer who wishes to quote brief passages or entries in connection with a review written for inclusion in a magazine or newspaper.

Copyright © 2000
Gale Group, Inc.
27500 Drake Road
Farmington Hills, MI 48331-3535

ISBN 0-7876-4363-7 (set)
ISBN 0-7876-4364-5 (volume 1)
ISBN 0-7876-4365-3 (volume 2)
ISBN 0-7876-4366-1 (volume 3)
ISBN 0-7876-4367-X (volume 4)
ISBN 0-7876-4368-8 (volume 5)

Printed in the United States of America

10 9 8 7 6 5 4 3 2 1

Advisory Board

Emily M. Belcher
African American Studies Bibliographer and General and Humanities Reference Librarian, Firestone Library,
Princeton University

Karen L. Jefferson
Head of Archives and Special Collections, Robert W. Woodruff Library, Atlanta University Center

Marjorie Lusko
Adult Services Coordinator, Oak Park Public Library

Wilson J. Moses
Professor of History and Fellow of the Institute for Arts and Humanistic Studies,
The Pennsylvania State University

Guthrie P. Ramsey Jr.
Assistant Professor of Music, University of Pennsylvania

Mark A. Reid
Professor of English, University of Florida-Gainesville

Charles E. Sykes
Director, African American Arts Institute, Indiana University

Contributors

Donald F. Amerman, Jr.
Editorial Consultant, A & M Editorial Services

Stephen W. Angell
Associate Professor of Religion, Florida A & M University

Calvert Bean
Associate Editor, *International Dictionary of Black Composers*

Lean'tin Laverne Bracks
Editorial Consultant

Rose M. Brewer
Morse Alumni Distinguished Teaching Professor of Afro-American and African Studies, University of Minnesota-Minneapolis

Christopher A. Brooks
Professor of African American Studies, Virginia Commonwealth University

Paulette Coleman
General Officer, African Methodist Episcopal Church

DeWitt S. Dykes, Jr.
Professor of History, Oakland University

James Gallert
Vice President, Jazz Alliance of Michigan

Joseph Guy
Jazz and Touring Coordinator, Southern Arts Federation

Tracey Desirnaí Hicks
Membership and Volunteer Services Coordinator,
Charles H. Wright Museum of African American History

Phyllis J. Jackson
Assistant Professor of Art and Art History, Pomona College

Kristine Krapp
Editor, *Notable Black American Scientists* and *Black Firsts in Science and Technology*

Kevin C. Kretschmer
Reference Librarian, Blazer Library, Kentucky State University

Bernadette Meier
Editorial Consultant

Hollis F. Price, Jr.
Professor of Economics, Tennessee State University

Guthrie P. Ramsey Jr.
Assistant Professor of Music, University of Pennsylvania

Houston B. Roberson
Assistant Professor of History, University of the South

Gil L. Robertson IV
Founder, The Robertson Treatment

Audrey Y. Williams
Professor of Management, Zicklin School of Business, Baruch College, City University of New York

Raymond A. Winbush
Director, Race Relations Institute, Fisk University
Benjamin Hooks Professor of Social Justice, Fisk University

Michael D. Woodard
President, Woodard & Associates

Linda T. Wynn
Assistant Director of State Programs, Tennessee Historical Commission
Adjunct Professor, Department of History, Fisk University

Contents

◆ **VOLUME 1**

Introduction xiii

1 Chronology 1

2 African American Firsts 85

**3 Significant Documents in African
American History** 111

4 African American Landmarks 179

Appendix **A-1**

African American Recipients of
Selected Awards A-1

African American Federal Judges A-16

African American Olympic Medalists A-20

Index **A-29**

◆ **VOLUME 2**

Introduction xiii

5 Africa and the Black Diaspora **225**

A Brief History of Africa 225

The Modern Day People of Africa 229

Black People in the Western Hemisphere 236

Country Profiles 240

6 Africans in America: 1600 to 1900 . . . . **317**

Exploration and the First Settlements in the
Americas 317

Slavery in Colonial America: 1619–1787 317

African American Status in the New
Republic 321

Expansion of Slavery 325

Anti-Slavery Movements 328

The Compromise of 1850 329

Civil War 331

Reconstruction 333

The Advent of Independent African
American Institutions 334

African American Status after
Reconstruction 336

Figures of the Past 337

7 Civil Rights **343**

Early Rights Movements 343

Civil Rights during the Reconstruction
Period 344

Civil Rights in the Early Twentieth Century 345

Civil Rights during the Mid- to Late
Twentieth Century 345

Civil Rights Activists 350

Federal and State Civil Rights Agencies 371

Civil Rights Statistics 375

8 Black Nationalism **377**

The Ideology of Black Nationalism 377

Early Black Nationalism in the United
States 378

Black Nationalism in the Twentieth
Century 380

Black Nationalists and Pan-African
Theorists 384

9 National Organizations **395**

A Brief History 395

National Organization Leaders 400

National Organizations 418

10 Law **447**

The Legal Status of African Americans:
1790–1883 447

African Americans and the Criminal Justice
System 451

African Americans in the Federal Courts 452

African Americans on the U.S. Supreme
Court 454

Major Federal Legislation 455

Major U.S. Supreme Court Decisions 457

Attorneys, Judges, and Legal Scholars 475

Criminal Justice Statistics 490

Appendix **A-1**

African American Recipients of

Selected Awards A-1
African American Federal Judges A-16
African American Olympic Medalists A-20
Index **A-29**

◆ VOLUME 3

Introduction xiii

⑪ Politics **491**
Race, Politics, and Government 491
Congressional Black Caucus Members
    (106th Congress) 496
Government Officials 498
Political Statistics 542

⑫ Population **543**
The Size of the African American
    Population 543
Regional Distribution 544
African American Towns and Settlements 546
Contemporary Demographic
    Characteristics 548
Population Projections for the Twenty-first
    Century 549
Population Statistics 551

⑬ Employment and Income **557**
Employment Trends 557
Factors in Employment and
    Unemployment Levels 557
Federal Government Response to
    Employment Discrimination 559
Income and Poverty Trends 560
Federal and State Programs that Address
    Poverty 562
Status of African Americans 563
Employment and Income Statistics 567

⑭ Entrepreneurship **575**
Colonial Entrepreneurship Efforts by
    African Americans 575
Pre-Civil War Entrepreneurship in the
    African American Community 575
Post-Civil War Entrepreneurship in the
    African American Community 576
African American Entrepreneurs in the
    Early Twentieth Century 576
Post-Civil Rights Era Assistance to African
    American Businesses 579
Recent Economic Trends 580
Entrepreneurs and Business Executives 582

⑮ The Family **595**
Family Structure and Stability 595
Marriage 600
Gay/Lesbian/Bisexuality/Transgender
    Issues 602
Fertility and Births 603

Children 604
Health 605
Life Expectancy 609
Social Activists 611
Family Statistics 614

⑯ Education **621**
Educational Opportunities in Colonial
    America 621
African American Educational Institutions
    in the Nineteenth Century 621
Philanthropy and Education 625
African American Education in the
    Twentieth Century 626
Current Educational Trends 629
Administrators, Educators, and Scholars 632
Historically and Predominantly African
    American Colleges and Universities 650
Research Institutions 658
African Americans Holding Endowed
    University Chairs, Chairs of Excellence,
    or Chaired Professorships (1999) 663
Education Statistics 668

⑰ Religion **671**
Origins and History of African American
    Religious Traditions 671
African American Female Religious
    Leadership 674
African American Churches during
    Reconstruction 674
African American Churches in the
    Twentieth Century 676
Evolving Trends among African American
    Churches 678
African American Denominations 684
Religious Leaders 692
Religious Statistics 707

⑱ Literature **709**
African American Writers of Colonial
    America 709
African American Literature during the
    Antebellum Period 709
The "New Negro" Movement 710
The Harlem Renaissance 710
African American Writers in the Mid-
    Twentieth Century 711
The Black Arts Movement 712
African American Literature of the Late
    Twentieth Century 713
Novelists, Poets, and Playwrights 714

Appendix **A-1**
African American Recipients of
    Selected Awards A-1
African American Federal Judges A-16
African American Olympic Medalists A-20

Index A-29

◆ **VOLUME 4**
Introduction xiii

19 Media **749**
  Book Publishers 749
  Newspaper and Magazine Publishers 753
  Broadcasting 755
  African American Media in Cyberspace 761
  Publishing, Radio, and Television
      Professionals 762
  Print and Broadcast Media 787

20 Film and Television **829**
  African Americans in Film 829
  African Americans in Television 835
  Filmography of Selected Feature Films
      and Documentaries 838
  Actors, Filmmakers, and Film and
      Television Executives 856

21 Drama, Comedy, and Dance **877**
  The Origins of African American
      Performance Art 877
  Minstrelsy 878
  Reclaiming the Black Image: 1890 to 1920 879
  African American Dramatic Theater in the
      Twentieth Century 880
  African American Musicals in the Twentieth
      Century 883
  African American Comedy in the Twentieth
      Century 885
  African American Dance in the Twentieth
      Century 887
  Stage Actors, Comedians, Choreographers,
      and Dancers 890

22 Classical Music **921**
  Black Musicians in Early America 921
  Classical Music in the Twentieth Century 923
  Studies in African American Music 924
  Classical Music Composers, Conductors,
      Instrumentalists, and Singers 925

23 Sacred Music Traditions **957**
  Early Influences of African American
      Sacred Music 957
  The Emergence of Spirituals in the
      Nineteenth Century 958
  The Rise of Gospel Music in the Twentieth
      Century 960
  Sacred Music Composers, Musicians, and
      Singers 964

Appendix **A-1**
African American Recipients of
    Selected Awards A-1

African American Federal Judges A-16
African American Olympic Medalists A-20
Index **A-29**

◆ **VOLUME 5**
Introduction xiii

24 Blues and Jazz **973**
  The Blues Tradition 973
  The Jazz Tradition 976
  Women in Blues and Jazz 984
  The Future of Blues and Jazz 985
  Blues and Jazz Composers, Musicians, and
      Singers 985

25 Popular Music **1035**
  The Rise of Rhythm and Blues 1035
  "Crossovers" into Country Music 1038
  Sweet Soul Music and Social Revolution 1039
  Psychedelic Soul to Disco 1042
  Rap: From Subculture to Mass Appeal 1043
  New Directions: From Nuevo Soul to Pop-
      Hip Hop 1045
  Popular Music Composers, Musicians, and
      Singers 1046

26 Visual and Applied Arts **1087**
  The African Roots of African American Art ... 1087
  The Formation of an Arts Tradition 1088
  The African Legacy Endures in Colonial
      America 1088
  Rise of the Professional Artists 1089
  African American Arts in the Twentieth
      Century 1091
  Arts-Related Support Professions 1097
  Exhibiting African American Art 1097
  Visual and Applied Artists 1099
  Museums and Galleries Exhibiting African
      American Art 1128

27 Science and Technology **1137**
  Early African American Inventors 1137
  Early African American Scientists 1139
  African Americans in Medicine 1140
  African Americans in Air and Space 1142
  Modern Contributions to Science and
      Technology 1144
  Popular African American Internet Sites 1146
  Engineers, Mathematicians, Inventors,
      Physicians, and Scientists 1150

28 Sports **1169**
  Baseball 1169
  Football 1170
  Boxing 1171
  Basketball 1173
  Other Sports 1175
  Women in Sports 1177

Athletes, Coaches, and Sports Executives 1178

29 Military **1205**
The Colonial Period 1205
The Revolutionary War (1775–1783) 1205
The War of 1812 (1812–1815) 1206
The Civil War (1861–1865) 1206
The Indian Campaigns (1866–1890) 1209
The Spanish-American War (1898) 1210
World War I (1914–1918) 1213
The Interwar Years (1919–1940) 1215
World War II (1941–1945) 1215
The Desegregation of the Military (1946–
   1949) 1221
The Korean War (1950–1953) 1222

The Vietnam War (1964–1973) 1224
Military Participation in the 1970s and
   1980s 1225
The Persian Gulf War (1991) 1226
The Military Moving into the New
   Millennium 1226
Outstanding Military Figures 1227
Military Statistics 1244

Appendix **A-1**
African American Recipients of
   Selected Awards A-1
African American Federal Judges A-16
African American Olympic Medalists A-20
Index **A-29**

Introduction

The *Reference Library of Black America* is based on the eighth edition of *The African American Alamanac*, first published in 1967 as *The Negro Almanac* and subsequently cited by *Library Journal*, in conjunction with the American Library Association, as "Outstanding Reference Source." It offers a comprehensive and accurate survey of black culture in the United States and around the world.

New Features in This Edition

All material was extensively reviewed by the editors and a board of prominent advisors and, where appropriate, updated and/or expanded; in many instances completely new topics were added to the existing essays. As a result, most chapters have been rewritten and focus on issues facing African Americans as we enter a new millenium.

African American women and their significant contributions have been given greater emphasis in the reference work than ever before. Examples of this expanded coverage include: speeches and writings of Sojourner Truth, Ida B. Wells-Barnett, Mary McLeod Bethune, and Barbara Jordan (Chapter 3); genetic evidence of a link between Sally Hemings and Thomas Jefferson (Chapter 6); biographical profiles of historic female activists of the black nationalist and civil rights movements (Chapters 8 and 9); female leadership in African American churches (Chapter 17); prominent women artists in the musical fields of gospel, blues, and jazz (Chapters 23, 24, and 25); and the increasing presence of female athletes in professional sports (Chapter 28).

The tremendous impact of the Internet is also reflected in the content of the *Reference Library of Black America*. Many entry listings in such sections as "National Organizations" (Chapter 9); "Historically and Predominantly African American Colleges and Universities" and "Research Institutions" (Chapter 16); "African American Media in Cyberspace" and "Magazines and Journals" (Chapter 19); "Museums and Galleries Exhibiting African American Art" (Chapter 26); and "Popular African American Internet Sites" (Chapter 27) now include website addresses. In addition, the promising effects of information technology on the African American community are discussed in "Entrepreneurship" (Chapter 14), "Media" (Chapter 19), and "Science and Technology" (Chapter 27).

Important African American towns and settlements are described for the first time in "African American Landmarks" (Chapter 4) and "Population" (Chapter 12). Included are listings of such historic sites as Nicodemus, Kansas; Boley, Oklahoma; the Sea Islands in South Carolina and Georgia; and Eatonville, Florida. In addition, expanded, up-to-date profiles of African and Western Hemisphere nations are offered in "Africa and the Black Diaspora" (Chapter 5).

Two new chapters have been added that significantly enhance the broad coverage of the *Reference Library of Black America:*

- "Film and Television" (Chapter 20) offers an overview of African Americans in the film and television industries, a selected filmography of more than two hundred films and documentaries depicting African American themes and issues, and biographical profiles of actors, filmmakers, and industry executives both current and historical.

- "Sacred Music Traditions" (Chapter 23) provides an essay that thoroughly describes the important periods and styles of African American sacred music, as well as concise biographical profiles of notable sacred music composers, musicians, and singers.

Approximately thirty new statistical charts compiled by the Bureau of the Census for the *Statistical Abstract of the United States* appear in pertinent chapters. Finally, a completely revised name and keyword index provides improved access to the contents of the *Reference Library of Black America.*

Content and Arrangement

Information in this edition of the *Reference Library of Black America* appears in 29 subject chapters. Many chapters open with an essay focusing on historical developments or the contributions of African Americans to the subject area, followed by concise biographical profiles of selected individuals. Although the listees featured here represent only a small portion of the African American community, they embody excellence and diversity in their respective fields of endeavor. Where an individual has made a significant contribution in more than one area, his or her biographical profile appears in the subject area for which he or she is best known.

Nearly seven hundred photographs, illustrations, maps, and statistical charts aid the reader in understanding the topics and people covered in the reference work. An expanded appendix contains the names and contributions of African American recipients of selected awards and honors.

⑤

Africa and the Black Diaspora

◆ A Brief History of Africa ◆ The Modern Day People of Africa
◆ Black People in the Western Hemisphere ◆ Country Profiles
by Donald F. Amerman, Jr.

According to renowned Kenyan scholar Dr. Ali Mazrui and author of *The Africans: A Triple Heritage* (1986), modern Africa has been heavily influenced by three main forces—indigenous traditions, the tenets of Islam, and Western culture including Christianity—with both positive and negative results. Among the benefits are a strong sense of continuity and regard for heritage, moral order, and membership in the global village. However, the mingling of such dynamic and divergent threads has caused a clash of cultures with an aftermath of "inefficiency, mismanagement, corruption, and decay of the infrastructure."

◆ A BRIEF HISTORY OF AFRICA

Archaeologists have come to believe that early humans, called *Hominidae*, originated in Africa some eight million years ago and migrated to other continents. Throughout much of the continent there flourished, 15 million to 25 million years ago, a number of families of Dryopithecine apes widely believed to be the forerunners of both humans and more recent ape species. Members of the genus *Australopithecus*, remains of which have been found in southern Africa, are the earliest known hominids and are believed to have developed about eight million years ago. Intermediary forms of human beings—*Homo habilis* and *Homo erectus*—ranged over large portions of the African continent before and during the Pleistocene age. The earliest forms of *Homo sapiens*, the species of modern man, began to appear about one-half a million years ago.

By the time of the Middle Stone Age, three distinct groups of people had evolved in Africa—Bushmanoid, Pygmoid, and Negroid. Only a few Bushmen, as well as a limited number of related Hottentot people, are still found in parts of the southwest portion of the continent, and a few isolated Pygmy groups have survived, mainly in the Congo forests. However, it was the Negroid group that became dominant on the continent. Thus, a number of distinct African races had developed by the close of the Pleistocene period.

The unification of the kingdom of Egypt, a civilization then in its infancy, occurred about 3000 BC. For the next three millennia, Egypt flourished along the Nile, giving rise to some of the most impressive accomplishments of early civilization. These accomplishments include the Pyramids of Giza and the Lighthouse of Alexandria, both of which are included among the Seven Wonders of the Ancient World. The construction by early man of such mammoth building projects as the Pyramids and the Sphinx continues to inspire wonder in today's visitors to these sites. The ancient Egyptians managed to cultivate much of the desert countryside of Egypt through innovative methods of irrigation until most of North Africa fell under Roman control in 146 BC.

Additional sophisticated societies began to develop in sub-Saharan Africa, among them the Kush, which flourished in Nubia, south of Egypt, between 700 BC and 200 AD. Others included the ancient Ghana, Kanem, Mali, Songhai, and the Haissa states. In the Congo, the kingdoms of Lunda, Lula, Bushong, and Kongo were founded, probably between the sixteenth and eighteenth centuries. On the Guinea Coast, the city states of Benin, Ite, Oyo, Ashanti, and Yoruba date back to the fifteenth century. These states traded extensively in gold, ivory, salt, and livestock.

Western Africa was home to the earliest trading empires. Between the fifth and eleventh centuries AD, the empire of Ghana dominated trade in the Sahara region in slaves, gold, and kola nuts. Along the shores of Lake Chad, the empire of Kanem-Bornu developed contemporaneously with Ghana, flourishing there until the seventeenth century. Of the Muslim empires that developed in western Africa, the greatest by far was the Mali, which was dominant from about 1250 to 1400 AD. Succeeding the Mali empire was the Songhai empire of Gao, which flourished throughout most of the fifteenth and sixteenth centuries.

Beginning in the seventh century AD, most of northern Africa fell to Arab invaders, who quickly established the newly founded religion of Islam in African. To control the conquered areas, the Muslims imposed an Islamic governmental structure called the caliphate, which remained in force until the thirteenth century. Muslim traders then became aware of Africa's largely untapped potential in natural resources. By the ninth century, Muslim merchants from North Africa began to trade regularly with the peoples of West Africa, at first exchanging North African salt for gold from West Africa. The merchant class in West Africa was the first major group in the region to fall under the spell of Islam. The West African merchants were soon joined in their conversion to Islam by tribal leaders. Arab traders first began to set up trading outposts along the East African coast in the twelfth century. These coastal trading centers became part of an intricate trading network that linked Arabia with the markets of China and Southeast Asia.

Trade with Europe began around the fifteenth century, with the slave trade playing an important role. An estimated ten to thirty million people were sold into slavery by the mid-nineteenth century. The slave trade had a devastating effect upon the local societies from which the slaves were drawn and Africa as a whole. Slave traders knew well that growers in the Americas and elsewhere wanted the youngest and strongest to work their fields, so it was those individuals for whom they hunted, leaving the older and weaker behind. The interior of Africa was first exposed to Europeans in the eighteenth century by missionaries, traders, and adventurers.

Although the British government declared the slave trade illegal in 1807, such human commerce continued to some degree through most of the nineteenth century. Some African territories, stung by the British ban on the slave trade, turned to other European nations to continue such trading. When the British fleet was deployed along the coast of West Africa to enforce that country's ban on the slave trade, slave traders simply shifted their operations to areas not under surveillance. Slaves were even shipped from East African ports to the Americas.

A Senegalese Muslim transcribes from the Koran (Global Learning, Inc.).

Until the middle of the nineteenth century, the European colonial presence in Africa was confined largely to British and Dutch settlers in South Africa. However, with the opening of the Suez Canal in 1869 and the contemporaneous discovery of diamonds in South Africa, European interest in Africa's natural wealth and strategic location increased exponentially. European powers rushed to seize as big a chunk of the continent for themselves as possible. In the final two decades of the nineteenth century, Britain, France, Belgium, Germany, and Portugal scrambled to either conquer African territory or negotiate agreements with African leaders that allowed for mutual control. Only Ethiopia and Liberia escaped European colonization. Germany, however, lost its African territories after World War I.

Although the colonial powers varied to some degree in their treatment of African colonies, almost all did relatively little to improve the quality of life for their African subjects. They concentrated instead on finding more efficient ways to extract raw materials from the colonies or selling European products to them. European rule in Africa proved short-lived. In 1922, Egypt was granted independence from Britain. North Africa became a major arena of World War II, and after the collapse of France, much of French North Africa was occupied in 1942 by Anglo-American forces. There followed a series of strategic battles between Allied and Axis forces across the sweep of North Africa.

As the tide of nationalism swept across Africa in the mid-twentieth century, the colonial powers, drained by World War II, proved unable to resist. In 1957 the Gold Coast won its independence from Britain and was renamed Ghana. The following year, France gave Guinea its freedom. Over the next few years, Britain and France granted independence to almost all of their other colonies in Africa.

The road to independence for Portugal's African colonies proved a good deal more torturous than most of the territories under British and French control. It took a revolution at home and years of guerrilla warfare in Africa to gain independence for the Portuguese colonies of Angola and Mozambique. Even France and Britain experienced some difficulties in extricating themselves from their colonial holdings in Africa. France was forced to endure a long and costly war with nationalists in Algeria before finally agreeing to independence for the colony in 1962. A unilateral declaration of independence by the white minority of Southern Rhodesia in 1965 led to a 15-year standoff between the colony and Britain. The situation was finally resolved in 1980, when agreement was reached to establish the multiracial nation of Zimbabwe. Africa's last colony, Southwest Africa, was granted independence as Namibia in late 1988, after 73 years of South African control.

The collapse of communism in Eastern Europe and the end of the Cold War had a profound effect on Africa. In the years since independence, many of the new African nations, almost all of which could be classified as developing countries, chose socialist systems, selecting the Soviet Union as their model for economic and political development. Embracing the notion of centrally-planned economies, many of these countries developed into single-party dictatorships. Almost all African countries in the socialist sphere closely aligned themselves with the Soviet Union, which provided for substantial military and economic assistance. When the Soviet Union disintegrated in the early 1990s, many socialist African states were left without a major source of support. Socialism quickly fell into disfavor, with most countries in Africa turning to Western Europe and the United States for help. To curry favor in Western capitals and also in the hope of reinvigorating their failing economies, many of these African nations took aggressive steps to install market mechanisms.

The collapse of the Soviet Union and most of its client states cut off much of the financial support for revolutionary movements in such African countries as Angola and Mozambique. With the Soviets and their allies largely out of the picture, the United States gradually withdrew its support for many African countries' opposition to these Soviet-financed wars of liberation. Among the countries torn apart by these continuing internal struggles was Somalia, which fell into anarchy as multiple warlords battled each other for effective control of the country. In 1992 the United Nations was forced to send nearly 30,000 troops into the country in an effort to restore order.

The early 1990s witnessed the collapse of several dictatorial African regimes as the forces of democratization swept across the continent. The socialist leadership of Benin was forced out, the dictator of Mali was overthrown, and Zambian President Kenneth Kaunda was defeated in 1991. Three years later, Malawi's dictator, Hastings Banda, also met defeat at the polls. In other quarters, chaos still reigned—Angola continued to be torn apart by civil war, and ethnic warfare in Rwanda took a staggering toll in human lives. A shaky peace took hold in Liberia after a bloody civil war, only to be shattered in 1998 by a resumption of internal strife.

Undoubtedly, the brightest news from Africa in the final decade of the twentieth century was the end of apartheid in South Africa and the country's first all-race, multiparty elections in 1994. Long-time political prisoner Nelson Mandela was elected president in those historic elections.

Prominent African Nationalist Movements

The faces of African nationalism are many and, although most first emerged in the twentieth century, some were well established even earlier. In the late nineteenth century, the Afrikaner nationalism movement was born, fanned by the radical Afrikaner nationalist mythology of Stephen Jacobus Du Toit in his newspaper *Die Afrikaanse Patriot*. Du Toit, founder of the rabidly anti-British Afrikaner Bond, an organization dedicated to driving the British out of South Africa, told his followers that the Afrikaners, also known as Boers, were God's chosen people. The Afrikaners' defeat at the hands of the British in the Boer War in 1902 helped to fuel nationalism among the Afrikaners.

The troubled relationship between South Africa's Afrikaners and the British continued. The two divided over the issue of racial segregation between 1910 and 1939. During both World War I and World War II, many in the Afrikaner community opposed any support of Britain against Germany. Between 1924 and 1933, the National Party, led by Prime Minister J.B.M. Hertzog, promoted bilingualism (English and Afrikaans) in South Africa. Aligning itself with the Dutch Reformed Church, the Afrikaner nationalist movement was steadfast in its opposition to race mixing in South Africa. Three years after the end of World War II, the National Party, led by Daniel Malan, won a stunning victory and immediately imposed the policy of racial separation known as apartheid. Afrikaner nationalism continued strong until the late 1970s when it became apparent that Afrikaners could not contain the rising nationalism of the country's black African majority.

The major force for nationalism among South Africa's black majority, the African National Congress (ANC),

U.S. President Bill Clinton greets South African President Nelson Mandela at a press conference in Cape Town, South Africa (Archive Photos, Inc.).

was founded in 1912 as a nonviolent civil rights organization dedicated to the promotion of black African interests. Drawing largely from the country's middle class, the ANC first worked for change through constitutional means. In a 1940 attempt to revitalize the organization, President Alfred B. Xuma began recruiting new members including Nelson Mandela, Oliver Tambo, and Walter Sisulu. Membership in the ANC swelled substantially in the 1950s after the imposition of apartheid. In the late 1950s, members of the ANC who felt that the country belonged only to black Africans broke away from the organization and formed the Pan-Africanist Congress (PAC). PAC's program of mass demonstrations led in 1960 to the Sharpeville Massacre. The government responded by banning all black political organizations including the PAC and the ANC.

In 1961 elements within the ANC set up a military wing called Umkhonto we Sizwe, which launched a program of sabotage against the government. The unrest that followed led to the arrests of Mandela and Sisulu, both of whom were sentenced to life in prison. Tambo left the country to set up an external wing of the ANC. A 1976 revolt in Soweto reinvigorated languishing black nationalist sentiments in South Africa, leading to an increase in the ANC's membership rolls. In 1990 the government lifted its ban on black political organizations, allowing the ANC once again to operate out in the open. The government also freed Mandela from prison in 1990, setting in motion feverish politicking that led to all-race elections in 1994. In that election, Mandela was elected the country's first president. Three years later, Mandela stepped down as the leader of the ANC.

A strong believer in African liberation, Kwame Nkrumah led Britain's West African colony of Gold Coast to independence as Ghana in 1957. The son of a goldsmith, Nkrumah was born in Nkroful in the Gold Coast. He was trained as a teacher and in 1935 went to the United States to continue his studies. While studying in England in 1945, he helped to organize the fifth Pan-African Congress, which drew together African intellectuals and leaders from all over the continent. Returning to Gold Coast in 1947, he became general secretary of the United Gold Coast Convention, but abandoned it two years later to organize the more radical Convention People's Party. Imprisoned briefly in 1950 for his involvement in a campaign of nonviolent protests, he was released to form a government after the CPP swept the colony's elections in 1951. After leading the colony to independence as Ghana in 1957, Nkrumah was instrumental in the founding of the Organization of African Unity in 1963. The following year, he formed a one-party government at home and named himself president for life. He was overthrown by the Ghanaian military in 1966 and spent the rest of his years in exile, dying in Bucharest, Romania, in 1972.

The nationalist movement in Kenya, which won its independence from Britain in 1963, was led by Jomo Kenyatta, a Kikuyu born in Gatundu in the 1890s. Educated by missionaries, Kenyatta moved to Nairobi in the early 1920s and joined the Kikuyu Central Association, eventually assuming the editorship of the KCA's newspaper. Kenyatta traveled to England in 1929 and 1931 to press, unsuccessfully, KCA demands for the return of Kikuyu land lost to Europeans. For the next fifteen years, Kenyatta studied throughout Europe, publishing a number of articles about his native Kenya and the difficulties of its people under colonial rule. His book *Facing Mount Kenya* explored Kikuyu tribal society and the effects of colonialism. In 1945 Kenyatta helped to organize the fifth Pan-African Congress in London. In June 1947 he became president of the Kenya African Union (KAU), a political organization formed a few years earlier. Kenyatta led KAU's unsuccessful campaign for Kenya's self-government under African leadership. Although Kenyatta professed to oppose the use of violence in achieving African nationalist goals, colonial authorities linked him to the Mau Mau terrorist network of the early 1950s and jailed him for nearly nine years. Assuming the leadership of the Kenya African National Union (KANU) shortly after his release from prison, Kenyatta led his party to victory in May 1963 elections, which were held in advance of independence. He led his country to independence in December of 1963 and was elected president of the Republic of Kenya a year later.

◆ THE MODERN DAY PEOPLE OF AFRICA

Geography

The second largest continent on the globe, Africa is bisected by the equator and bordered to the west by the Atlantic Ocean and to the east by the Indian Ocean. Roughly the shape of an inverted triangle—with a large bulge on its northwestern end and a small horn on its eastern tip—it contains 52 countries and six islands that together make up about twenty percent of the world's land mass or 11.5 million square miles.

Africa is essentially a huge plateau divided naturally into two sections. Northern Africa, a culturally and historically Mediterranean region, includes the Sahara desert—the world's largest expanse of desert, coming close to the size of the United States. Sub-Saharan, or so-called "Black Africa," also contains some desert land, but is mainly tropical, with rain forests clustered around the equator; vast savanna grasslands covering more than thirty percent of continent and surrounding the rain forests on the north, east, and south; some mountainous regions; and rivers and lakes that formed from the natural uplifting of the plateau's surface.

Notable geographical marvels in Africa include Mts. Kenya and Kilimanjaro (the latter of whose highest peak is one of the tallest in the world); the rivers Niger, Senegal, Congo, Zambezi (home of the mile-wide Victoria Falls, one of the world's seven natural wonders), Orange, Limpopo, Malawi, and Nile (the longest river in the world); lakes Tanganyika, Albert, Rudolf, and Victoria (the second largest freshwater body in the world); and the Libyan, Nubian, and Kalahari deserts.

Economics/Natural Resources

A mineral-rich continent, Africa is a prime source of copper, diamonds, gold, manganese, oil, uranium, zinc, and several other deposits. The equatorial forests produce ebony, teak, and rosewood, while cash crops include bananas, cocoa, coffee, cloves, cotton, sisal, sugar cane, tobacco, yams, and all kinds of nuts including cashews and groundnuts. In fact, agriculture has formed the basis of most African economies for centuries. Despite such a wealth of resources, many African nations rank among the poorest in the world. Tribal and political wars, illiteracy, droughts, lack of technological prowess, and the commonality of corruption among government officials all contribute to the weak economy encountered in much of the continent.

Though Africa does have booming urban and industrial centers—for example, Johannesburg, South Africa; Lagos, Nigeria; Dakar, Senegal; Harare, Zimbabwe—the continent is better known to visitors for the national parks and reserves of East and southern Africa. Wildlife concentrations in these locations vary but include antelope, impala, Thompson's gazelles, and wildebeests; buffalo, hippos, and rhinos; elephants; giraffes; zebras; crocodiles; a variety of bird species; hyenas, jackals, and wild dogs; cheetahs, jaguars, leopards, lions, and tigers.

Kenya, located in East Africa, is one of the oldest and most popular game-viewing destinations for safari-seek-

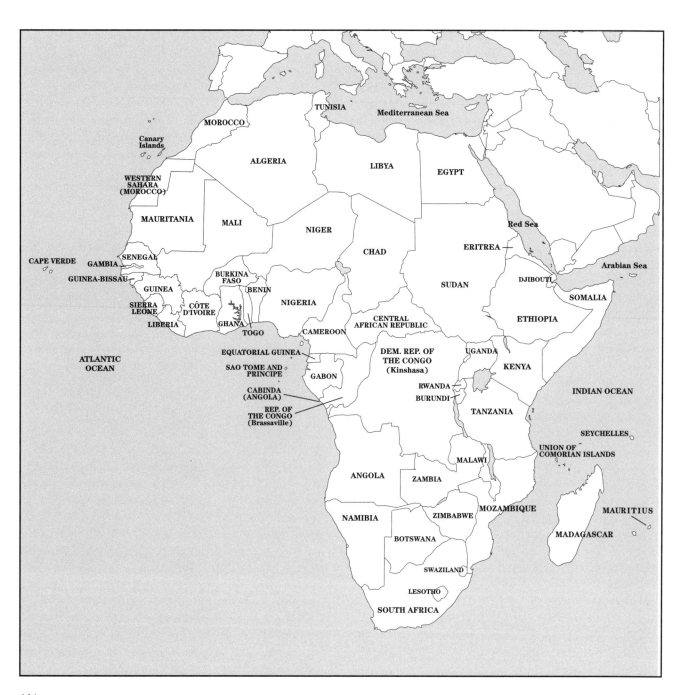

Africa

ing tourists. The Samburu National Reserve, Lake Nakuru (also known as the "pink lake" because of an abundance of flamingos), Masai Mara National Reserve, and Amboseli are all favored spots. Nearby, Tanzania offers Lake Manyara National Park, Serengeti National Park, and Ngorongoro Crater (a natural amphitheatre that was formed by the collapse of a volcano). Uganda features Bwindi Forest, home of the Buhoma Gorilla Camp. In the southern region of Africa, South Africa contains ostrich farms; Kruger National Park, one of the continent's largest reserves; Cango Caves; and

Kirstenbosch Botanical Gardens. Zimbabwe contributes man-made Lake Kariba, a permanent water source for monkeys, warthogs, waterbuck, and other species including birds; Hwange, a game reserve filled with more than 107 species; and the Zambezi Nature Sanctuary and Crocodile Farm.

Population

The African population is most heavily concentrated in Nigeria; southern Ghana; along the Gulf of Guinea;

Mount Kilimanjaro in Tanzania (Cory Langley).

Benin and Togo; the Nile Valley; in northern Sudan; the East Africa highlands of Ethiopia, Kenya, and Tanzania; eastern Democratic Republic of the Congo; the eastern and southern coasts; and the inland High Veld of South Africa. The desert and mountain regions are largely uninhabited.

In recent years the population of African has grown rapidly. In 1950 the total population was estimated at 281 million, but by 1990 the population had reached 817 million, making it the third most populous continent on the planet. No African nation has developed an effective population control program, and such practices as having multiple wives and early marriages continue. By the year 2020, the population of sub-Saharan Africa alone is expected to reach 1.2 billion.

Until recently, almost ninety percent of Africa's population lived in rural areas. African cities with populations exceeding one million include Accra, Ghana; Addis Ababa, Ethiopia; Cape Town and Johannesburg, South Africa; Cairo, Egypt; Maputo, Mozambique; Ibadan and Lagos, Nigeria; and Congo-Kinshasa. In addition to indigenous Africans, about five million people are of predominantly European descent and one million are of Asian descent.

During a 1959 archaeological expedition in Olduvai Gorge, Tanzania, Kenyan-born anthropologist L.S.B. Leakey and his wife Mary discovered a skull of a species thought to date back more than two million years called *Australopithecus boisei, Zinjanthropus*, or "Nutcracker Man" in popular vernacular. Within the next ten years they also unearthed *Homo habilis*, also estimated to date between 1.5 to 2 million years ago, and *Kenyapithecus africanus*. Fossils of early hominoids resembling man have been found in Ethiopia, Kenya, and South Africa by other scientists. The remains are believed to be predecessors of our own human species *Homo sapiens*.

Language

The diversity of Africa's people is underscored by the existence of more than 2,000 languages and dialects including Africanized forms of English, French, and Portuguese. Some fifty major languages are spoken by groups of one million or more people. The major language groups include Arabic (spoken mainly in north Africa), Fula, Hausa, Lingala, Malinke, Nguni (which includes SiNdebele, Xhosa, and Zulu), SeTwana-SeSotho, Swahili, and Yoruba.

Namibian men mining for diamonds in southern Africa (Laure Communications).

"African-language" names are often derived from the names of the ethnic tribes that speak them. For example, Zulu is spoken primarily by Zulus, and Kibondi is the language of the Bondi tribe. Swahili, the most widely spoken language on the continent, is the only one that breaks the pattern. A commercial language originally used among traders and business people, it evolved from Portuguese, Arabic, and Bantu.

As many languages were never translated into written form, Africa acquired a very long and rich oral tradition. In many cases, the oral tradition was the only method of passing literature and history from generation to generation in ancient times. After the fourteenth century, the use of Arabic by educated Muslim blacks was extensive, and some oral literature was subsequently reduced to a more permanent written form. But in spite of the Arab influence, the oral heritage of Africans remained strong, serving not only as an educational device, but as a guide for the administration of government and the conduct of religious ceremonies.

A wealth of proverbs from African culture have survived through the generations. Some of the more popular ones are: if you want to know the end, look at the beginning; when one door closes, another one opens; if we stand tall it is because we stand on the backs of those who came before us; two men in a burning house must not stop to argue; where you sit when you are old shows where you stood in youth; you must live within your sacred truth; the one who asks questions doesn't lose his way; if you plant turnips you will not harvest grapes; god makes three requests of his children: do the best you can, where you are, with what you have now; you must act as if it is impossible to fail; some would be great drinkers but they haven't got the wine; some great eaters but they haven't got the food.

Literature

It is impossible to consider the literature of Africa without including the great body of oral literature for which the continent is so famous. The relationship between oral and written literature is complex and not easily analyzed. It certainly is not simply a matter of evolution that brings us from the oral tradition to the commitment of some of these tales to the written word. In fact, the oral tradition is alive and well today in many small villages throughout Africa.

Of all the arts, literature—both oral and written—is probably the one most highly esteemed in African tradition. Literature for our purposes must be considered to include not just novels and short stories but folk tales, myths, legends, proverbs, and poetry. Much of the folklore of Africa is available only in the oral form. One of the best examples of oral literature is the epic of *Sundiata*, founder of the West African kingdom of Mali in the thirteenth century. However, written literature is not without its own rich history in Africa. For centuries, written literature in Amharic, Arabic, Hausa, and Swahili has existed and, more recently, there has been a sharp increase in African literature written in the languages of the European colonial powers.

The West Coast of Africa, with its long tradition as a breeding ground for the arts, is home to some of the most important of today's African writers. Among these, Nigerian Chinua Achebe, author of *Man of the People*, the story of a newly independent African state strangely reminiscent of his own country, rails against corruption and the cult of personality. All of his work, which includes *Things Fall Apart*, *Arrow of God*, and *No Longer at Ease*, voices a concern for the loss of native culture in the flood of imported European values. Other Nigerian writers making a name for themselves include Cyprian Ekwensi, Amos Tutuola, and Oruora Nzekwu. In Nzekwu's *Blade Among the Boys*, the clash between his native Ibo religion and imported Christian ideals causes confusion in the life of a sensitive young man.

Most of the best-known literature out of South Africa during the twentieth century has come from white authors uneasy about their country's racist policies. William Plomer's *Turbott Wolfe*, published in 1925 well before the imposition of apartheid, argued for a mixing of white and black blood in South Africa to prevent a future in which the country's whites dominated the country. Probably the best-known of the anti-apartheid novels is Alan Paton's *Cry, the Beloved Country*. Other South African authors such as Doris Lessing, Dan Jacobson, and Nadine Gordimer have elevated this literature of protest to a new level of excellence. Gordimer received the Nobel Prize for Literature in 1991, following fellow Africans Wole Soyinka of Nigeria in 1986, and Naguib Mahfouz of Egypt in 1988.

Other of Africa's best-known authors include Cameroon's Mongo Beti; Ghana's Ayi Kwei Armah and J.E. Casely-Hayford; Kenya's Ngugi wa Thiong'o; Lesotho's Thomas Mofolo; Nigeria's Ken Saro-Wiwa; Senegal's Sembène Ousmane and Lèopold Sédar Senghor; Somali's Nuruddin Farah; South Africa's Bessie Head, Ezekiel Mphahlele, and Lewis Nkosi; Uganda's Okot p'Bitek; and Zimbabwe's Dennis Brutus.

Unfortunately for journalists, freedom of the press is a scarce commodity in much of Africa, with many of those who dare to report the truth about government corruption or abuse of human rights being forced into exile or constantly threatened and harassed if they stay. For that reason, many Africans learn more about their neighbors—both locally and continentally—through Western media. But among Africa's most courageous and well-respected journalists are Liberia's Kenneth Y. Best and Isaac Bantu, Ghana's Ben Ephson, and South Africa's Percy Qoboza.

Film

Film is a relatively new art form to Africa, but it has been embraced eagerly as yet another medium through which to tell the many stories of the continent. Perhaps more than any other section of the continent, West Africa, particularly the former French-speaking colonies, has been drawn to the production of motion pictures. Among West Africa's leading filmmakers are Senegal's Ousmane Sembè:ne and Moussa Touré, Burkina Faso's Idrissa Ouédraogo, Drissa Touré, Gaston Kaboré, and Dani Kouyaté, and Mali's Cheik Oumar Sissoko and Abdoulaye Ascofare. From Cameroon have come the motion pictures of Jean-Marie Teno and Bassek Ba Kkobhio, while Côte d'Ivoire has produced the films of Roger Gneon M'Bala.

The former English-speaking colonies of Africa have managed to turn out a large number of well-received films as well. Among the more successful filmmakers in this group are Moses Adejumo, Afolabi Adesanya, Awala Bayo, and Fred Chagu of Nigeria, John Akomfrah of Ghana, Simon Bright of Zimbabwe, and Barry Feinberg, Athol Fugard, and Peter Goldsmid of South Africa.

There was a sharp jump in the number of Africans engaged in filmmaking between 1980 and 1990. Another significant change has been the increasing involvement of African women in motion pictures. The major political changes in South Africa over the last decade have helped to open that market to a much wider range of "alternative" films and videos than was possible before.

In 1993, the films coming out of Africa were few in number but notable in quality. Among them, *Samba Traore*, directed by Idrissa Ouédraogo, employed an age-old plot line quite effectively: the flight of a young criminal to avoid punishment for his crime. Burundian director Leonce Ngabo cooperated with French and Swiss filmmakers in the production of *Gito the Ungrateful*, the tale of a youth searching for his identity. Director Roger Gneon M'Bala of the Côte d'Ivoire explored the subject of religion in his *In the Name of Christ*. One of the few notable African films of 1994 was *Le Ballon d'or*, directed by Cheik Boukouré of Guinea, which related the story of a young boy's dream of becoming a world-class soccer player.

Some of the most impressive African films of 1995 came from the tiny West African country of Burkina Faso. These included Drissa Touré's *Haramuya*, Dani Kouyaté's *Keita, Voice of the Griot*, and Idrissa Ouédraogo's *Africa, My Africa*. From Cameroon came *The Great White of Lambarene*, an African evaluation of missionary/doctor/philosopher/musician Albert Schweitzer. Also from Cameroon came one of the best African films of 1996: *Clando*, the story of a young foe of a repressive African regime who emigrates illegally to Germany. Burkina Faso's film community produced some of the most notable motion pictures of 1997. Foremost among these were Idrissa Ouédraogo's *Kini and Adams*, which told the story of the relationship between two poor farmers, and Gaston Kaboré's *Buud Yam*, the tale of a young man's quest to find medicine for his ailing foster sister. Stirring up controversy in 1997 was Guinea's *Dakan*, director Mohamed Camara's exploration of homosexuality, the first African motion picture to tackle the subject.

Music

Despite the Western stereotype that associates the beating of tribal drums with the whole of traditional music, African music is incredibly diverse and reflective of the vast array of peoples, cultures, and traditions. Confined to localities, some of the world's greatest and most unheralded musicians—many self-taught—play to crowds in Africa. In the past few decades, "cross-over" artists have breached the boundaries of their homeland to win acclaim and fans in the United States and Europe. The irony is that these so-called "African superstars" may not even be stars in their own countries, let alone on the rest of the continent.

Nonetheless, such contemporary American musical forms as blues and jazz have been heavily influenced by African styles and polyrhythms carried over by slaves. In fact, the African lute evolved into the modern-day guitar. Guitars form the basis of *benga* music (popular in Kenya); *juju* (a Nigerian music also replete with talking drums and vocal call and response); palm wine music (an acoustic form popular in regions of West Africa, where palm wine is a favorite elixir); highlife (a jazzy, complex West African dance music punctuated by horns); and *soukous* (derived by the French word for "shake," a peppy dance form originating mainly in Congo-Brazzaville and Congo-Kinshasa). Percussion-based music includes: *apala* (a street-form emergent from Islamic music); *mbalax* (a modern dance style popularized in Senegal); and *jit* (a Zimbabwean hybrid of traditional *chimurenga* guitar, disco-style drum beats, highlife, and *soukous*). *Kora* features a 21-string harp, *kwela* incorporates a penny whistle, and *mbira* got its moniker from the Zimbabwean name for a finger piano. Cameroonians may jive to *makossa* while those in Sierre Leone pop their fingers to milo jazz and Cape Verdeans release their troubles with the deep blues of *morna*. South Africans may party to *mbaquanga* on one night and get spiritual with the choral vocals of *mbube* the next. Permutations of once solely African music include *salsa* (Spanish folk music combined with African drums and Cuban rhythms), *soca* (African music with a heady dose of English and Latin folk music), and *zouk* (a mix of French, African, and Guadeloupian music).

Some of Africa's biggest artists, "cross-over" or otherwise, include Angola's Kuenda Bonga (a political-minded singer-songwriter) and Ruy Mingas (a famous Portugeuse-African vocalist and current minister of culture of that country); Burkino Faso's Farafina (a group led by *balafon* virtuoso Mahama Konaté); Cape Verde's Cesaria Evora ("The Barefoot Diva"); Congo-Kinshasa's Mbilia Bel (one of Africa's most successful female singers), 4 Etoiles (featuring *soukous* guitarist Syran Mbenza), Ricardo Lemvo & Makina Loca (an Afro-Latino vocalist), Les Bantous (a *rhumba* band), Tabu Ley (a *soukous* master), Sam Mangwana (known as "Le Pigeon," since his travels and music have produced mixtures of Cuban, Portuguese-African, and Caribbean rhythms), Tshala Muana ("Queen of Mutuashi, a dance form), Papa Wemba (one of the world's greatest singers), and Zap Mama (an all-female group led by poet Marie Daulne); Gabon's Pierre Akendengue (a blind singer, guitarist, poet, and playwright); Guinea's Bembeya Jazz National (featuring Sekou "Diamond Fingers" Diabate); Mali's Toumani Diabate (considered the world's greatest *kora* player), Oumou Sangare (the country's favorite female "praise singer"), and Ali Farka Toure ("The Bluesman of Mali"); Nigeria's King Sunny Ade ("The King of Juju") and Fela Anikulapo Kuti (an outspoken social critic, pianist, saxophonist, and singer); Senegal's Baaba Maal (known as "The Nightingale" because of his clear high-pitched voice), Youssou N'Dour (produces an exciting blend of mbalax, reggae, jazz, and calypso music), and Orchestre Baobab de Dakar; Sierre Leone's Abdul Tee-Jay (a London-based studio guitarist adept at several forms including highlife, *soukous*, *makossa*, and *soca*); South Africa's Ladysmith Black Mambazo (an a capella group led by tenor vocalist Joseph Shabalala), Mahlathini (legendary, deep-voiced "King of the Groaners"), the Mahotella Queens (*mbaqanga* mavens), Miriam Makeba ("The Empress of African Song"), Hugh Masekela (trumpet and flugelhorn playing jazz legend), West Nkosi (multi-talented musician, arranger, producer, and bandleader), and The Soul Brothers (one of the nation's biggest-selling groups); Tanzania's Zuhura Swaleh (a female *taarab* singer); and Zimbabwe's Thomas Mapfumo (credited with having created *chimurenga*, or liberation music) and Stella Chiweshe ("The Queen of Mbira").

Family

Family is the social backbone of Africa. Within most African cultures, family impacts all realms of everyday living, both politically and economically. Familial obligations are not restricted to just immediate family; tribal conflict notwithstanding, in Africa each individual is regarded as a dear cousin. In fact, the Western method of breaking familial relationships down to degrees—e.g., first cousin, great-great grandfather twice removed—is virtually nonexistent. Either two people are related or not; and more often then not, without even looking, those individuals will find ties. This unique kinship is inclusive of ancestors. The dead are forever remembered among the living, and the elderly are held with a special regard. Rather than being hidden away or considered burdens, older Africans are viewed as storehouses of wisdom and are a welcome part of society. Women, too, are highly esteemed in much of African tradition, particularly in the agri-based cultures. Often women, not men, are heads of households.

Among Africans, marriage represents a union of two families, not just a bride and groom. Parents and extended family members offer emotional support to a couple throughout their marriage. The bonding of families begins when a man obtains formal permission to marry a prospective bride. In some cultures, bride prices or dowries are still negotiated as are pre-arranged marriages. In true oral tradition, Africans often deliver the news of their upcoming nuptials by word of mouth. Any offspring are extremely valued, and additions to the family are cause for celebration.

Health

Diseases that have been successfully monitored and controlled in Western nations—diphtheria, measles, pertussis, poliomyelitis, tetanus, and tuberculosis—continue to be a problem in many parts of Africa. Diarrhea and tuberculosis account for one-half of all deaths in children. In addition, the fatal yet curable, indigenous sleeping sickness, or African Trypanosomiasis (spread by tsetse flies that carry a parasite, the trypanosome, from human to human), has become a surging epidemic in the Sudan and may spread to the Congo and the Central African Republic. By no coincidence, these three countries have recently undergone civil warfare and tremendous political upheaval.

The emergence of Acquired Immune Deficiency Syndrome (AIDS) has had a devastating effect on the continent as well. In 1998, 66 percent of the AIDS cases in the world were found in Africa, of which 530,000 were babies born infected. The demographic impact of AIDS is most immediate and serious in two geographic areas: Central-Austral Africa and West Africa, specifically in the country of Côte d'Ivoire. In both regions, falling life expectancy and increasing infant and child mortality have already been observed. Given the high proportion of the population already infected—up to thirty percent of young adults in some urban areas—and the high mortality resulting from the disease, a further impact over the next two decades is inevitable in these areas. The impact may eventually become as serious in several other geographical areas, but this will depend foremost on whether the spread of HIV can be contained.

In the mid-1990s, Ebola outbreaks wreaked havoc in the Democratic Republic of the Congo, Liberia, Gabon, and the Ivory Coast. Spread through contact with bodily fluids, the virus is hardy and can survive on moist surfaces such as bodies or food for long periods. The deadly virus disintegrates the membranous linings of blood vessels and organs, usually leading to heart and other organ failure. Each eruption of the modern-day plague has warranted strict quarantines. Ebola is one of most contagious and lethal viruses known to mankind, and the international scientific community has come together in trying to locate the sources of contamination in hopes of bringing an end to a virus whose newer strains have increased the fatality rate of the afflicted from 80 percent to 97 percent since earlier outbreaks dating back to the 1970s in the Sudan and former Zaire.

Senegalese microbiologist Soulyemane Mboup and other African researchers have made significant contributions to the fight against AIDS. While Mboup is credited as one of the discoverers of the HIV–2 virus, other African scientists seem to have developed a method of using interferon, an immune system-enhancing protein, to alleviate the symptoms of both Ebola and AIDS. In some cases, researchers have claimed to completely eradicate the presence of these diseases in affected patients.

Food shortages caused by drought and civil conflicts continue to cause mass starvation and malnutrition in Ethiopia, Somalia, Mozambique, as well as in parts of western Africa. In the late 1980s and into the 1990s, the international community has joined forces to try to alleviate the situation by sending food and aid to the needy and even resorting to peacekeeping military personnel in situations caused by ongoing civil disturbances.

The practice of female circumcision or genital mutilation—one of many varying rites of passage performed in parts of Africa—has been denounced by Western society as the harbinger of medical problems for women later in life including the inability to walk, chronic infections, and difficult childbirth. While an African and Western effort to stamp out the sometimes fatal ritual is growing, many others decry what they deem to be cultural interference. Tradition holds that the surgery preserves the chastity of those upon whom it is performed.

Medicine and medical advice are often dispensed by traditional healers in Africa, often referred to as "witch doctors" by skeptical Westerners. Diviners and healers treat mental disorders as well as physical ones. They also provide advice for resolving social disputes.

Cuisine

Food plays a large role in African traditions, customs, and beliefs. Africans make liberal use of fresh, locally grown foods in their cooking. Papayas, coconuts, avocados, mangos, guavas, and other "exotic" fruits are abundant and, along with other fruits and vegetables, are eaten much more liberally than in the United States, and many, such as yams and cassava root, are used as staples. For example maize, cassava, and plantains are often dried and ground into flour. Legumes are also prevalent in African meals. Particularly in the coastal nations, seafood, including shark, is frequently eaten fresh, dried, or smoked. Bat, beef, chicken, goat, monkey, pigeons, and pork are just some of the meats that can be found in different regions. Most Africans enjoy very spicy, hot food. An African pepper that goes by many names *pilli-pilli, piri-piri, and beri-beri* is frequently used. Much hotter than cayenne pepper, *pilli-pilli* does more than increase the palatability of a meal. Similar to garlic, pepper is thought to enhance the body's immune system. Coconut flesh is incorporated into many dishes as is coconut milk, which is also imbibed as a refreshing beverage. African beer, wine, and liquor, both homemade and commercial, are available.

In many African cultures, food is served in one large common bowl; diners then eat with their hands, thus reinforcing the idea of community.

◆ BLACK PEOPLE IN THE WESTERN HEMISPHERE

The Caribbean and Latin American regions of the New World were the first areas of the Western Hemisphere to be settled by African immigrants, some of whom may have arrived in the Americas on the maiden voyage of Christopher Columbus in 1492. Free blacks, many of whom were natives of Spain and Portugal, traveled with Columbus and other early Spanish and Portuguese explorers on voyages to the Americas. This first trickle of blacks of African ancestry into the New World was soon followed by a flood of enslaved Africans who were brought to work on European settlements.

The very earliest blacks to settle in the Americas included Pedro Alonso Niño, a navigator on the first voyage of Columbus to the New World, and a group of black settlers who joined with Spanish explorer Nicolás

San women of the Kalahari Desert gathering edible roots in Botswana (Laure Communications).

de Ovando to establish the first Western settlement on Hispaniola. Some of the blacks accompanying Spanish explorers on their missions to the Americas were indeed slaves, as was the case with Nuflo de Olano, who was present when Vasco Nuñez de Balboa first sighted the Pacific Ocean in 1513. Blacks also were present in the expeditions of both Hernán Cortés and Francisco Pizarro.

Among the so-called Iberian blacks was Estevanico, a survivor of Pánfilo de Narváez's ill-fated 1527 expedition to Florida. On an eight-year overland trip, he made his way with three other survivors to Mexico City, learning a number of Native American languages along the way. He was later killed in a confrontation with members of the Zuñi tribe in what is now New Mexico. Juan Valiente, a black slave of the Spaniards, fought so valiantly with his masters against the Araucanian people of Chile in the 1540s that he was rewarded with his freedom and an estate near Santiago.

As the number of Spanish settlements in the New World grew quickly, so too did the demand for manpower to work the estates of the new settlers. In 1518, Spain's King Charles I gave his approval to the move-

Central African woman prepares a meal for her family (United Nations).

ment of slaves directly from Africa to the American colonies. The Spanish crown controlled the slave trade, selling the right to import slaves to merchants willing to pay the price. The Portuguese, who were busily settling the vastness of Brazil, had begun bringing slaves from Africa by the 1530s.

From the time that the slave trade into the Americas was launched by the Spanish and Portuguese in the early 1500s until its abolition in the latter half of the nineteenth century, an estimated ten to thirty million Africans were sold into slavery in the New World. Almost half of that number, or 47 percent, were put into service in the Caribbean and the Guianas of northeastern South America. Brazil took roughly 38 percent of the slaves, while North America took only about 4.5 percent of the total.

The number of slaves brought into the Spanish and Portuguese colonies of the Americas varied substantially according to the needs of the colony. New Spain, as Mexico was then known, imported about 120,000 African slaves between 1519 and 1650, or about 1,000 slaves a year, most of whom were pressed into service in the colony's mines. Between 1650 and 1810, the number of slaves imported each year was cut almost in half, as

more Native Americans became available to work the mines.

Most of the early black population in Latin America and the Caribbean was involved in domestic service or farm labor. Perhaps one-fifth of the black population found work as street vendors, artisans, sailors, miners, and wet nurses. Throughout the Spanish and Portuguese colonies, a number of masters voluntarily set their slaves free, while others encouraged their slaves to purchase their freedom on a sort of installment plan called *coartación*. Life for the slaves of the New World, however, was generally harsh and unpleasant, and the frustration over the elusiveness of freedom sometimes boiled over into unrest and even outright revolt. Such was the case in the colony now known as Haiti, where nearly 500,000 slaves led by François Toussaint L'Ouverture revolted in 1791, throwing off British and Spanish control. In 1801, Toussaint L'Ouverture conquered Santo Domingo, which had been ceded by Spain to France in 1795, and thus he governed the entire island. Following a hard-fought resistance to French colonial ambitions in the Western Hemisphere, Toussaint L'Ouverture struck a peace treaty with Napoleon in 1802.

South America

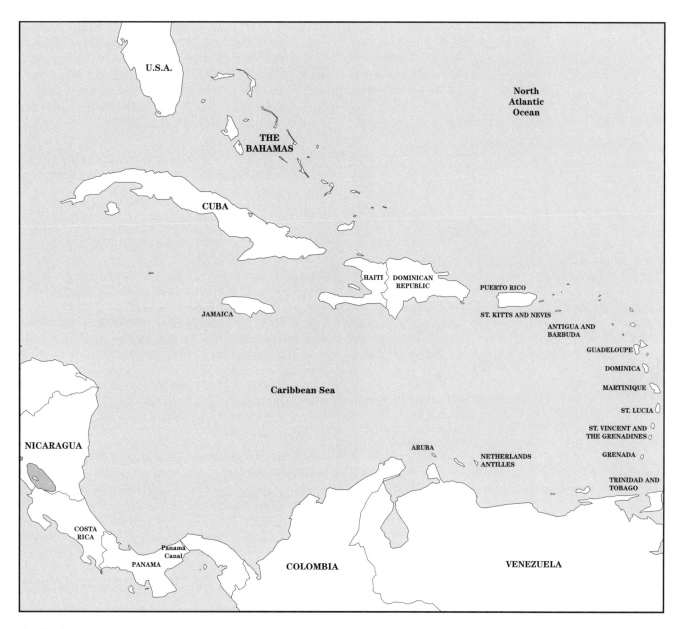

The Caribbean

Today on many islands of the Caribbean, persons of African descent make up the majority of the population; on Barbados and Jamaica, blacks are the overwhelming majority. In other areas, notably on the continental mainland from Mexico south to Argentina, blacks have been largely absorbed into the mainstream of the population. In South America, the black population consists of a mixture of many different cultures: Africans and Indians, known as *zambos;* Caucasians and American Indians, known as *mestizos;* and those who are a mixture of white and black are, as in the United States, referred to as *mulattos.*

Similar to the blacks who live today in the Caribbean and Latin American regions, most of the black popula-

tion of the United States is descended from African slaves who were brought into North America to work on plantations and farms, particularly in the southern part of the country. Most of these slaves arrived in the United States between 1700 and the early 1800s, although slavery continued into the second half of the nineteenth century. Although slaves were found in all 13 of the original British colonies as well as French Louisiana and the Spanish colony of Florida, the need for slave manpower in the North decreased sharply after the American Revolution. In the South, which was heavily agricultural, slaves remained a highly valued commodity.

On the eve of the Civil War in 1860, blacks in the South numbered about four million, making up approximately one-third of the total population of the region. At the same time, there were about half a million free blacks living throughout the United States, slightly more than half of them in the South. The free black population was a powerful force working for the abolition of slavery in this country. In 1997 African Americans in the United States numbered 32.3 million, accounting for 12.0 percent of the total population.

In recent years, the Caribbean basin has been a major source of black immigration into the United States, with immigrants primarily from Jamaica and Haiti entering the country in search of work. In 1980 the Mariel boatlift brought a significant amount of Cuban refugees to the United States. More recently, thousands of Haitians have attempted, with little success, to emigrate to the United States, since the September of 1991 coup that ousted President Jean-Bertrand Aristide, who was later reinstated with the aid of the U.S. government. Efforts by the United States to foster economic recovery in Haiti have been largely unsuccessful, and attempts to nurture the fledgling democracy, thus far, have yielded limited results.

◆ COUNTRY PROFILES

Africa

Algeria

Official name: Democratic and Popular Republic of Algeria
Independence: July 5, 1962
Area: 919,595 sq. mi.
Form of government: Multiparty republic
Capital: Algiers
International relations: UN, OAU, Arab League
Currency: Dinar
Income: (per capita US$) 2,060 (1991)
Population: (1998 estimate) 30 million
Ethnic divisions: Arab and Berber
Religious groups: Sunni Islam
Languages spoken: Arabic (official), Berber dialects, French
Literacy: 61.6% (1995)
Exports: Petroleum products
Imports: Food; machinery; iron and steel
Primary trade partners: France, Italy, United States, Spain, Germany

Since the period of 5 BC, the area that makes up what is now Algeria has been populated by indigenous tribes who have been progressively pushed back from the coast by invaders. As a result, the country's boundaries have shifted during various stages of the conquests. Nearly all Algerians are Muslim of Arab, Berber, or mixed stock.

French colonization began in 1830 and continued until 1954, when the indigenous population staged a revolt. The revolution was launched by a small group of nationalists who called themselves the National Liberation Front (FLN). Negotiations led to a cease-fire signed by France and the FLN on March 18, 1962; France then declared Algeria independent on July 3.

Mohammed Ben Bella became Algeria's first postindependence president, only to be ousted three years later by Col. Boume'dienne. After he died, Chadi Benjadid became the head of state. In 1991, Algeria held its first free election after thirty years of a one-party system, and the National Liberation Front was defeated by the fundamentalist Islamic Salvation Front (FIS) in the first round of voting for the National Assembly. When it appeared clear that the fundamentalist group would win a majority in the second round of voting scheduled for January 1992, the government and army intervened to cancel the elections. Mohammed Boudiaf, a former dissident in the FLN, was installed as president of the ruling State Supreme Council. In May 1992, Boudiaf was assassinated, allegedly by an FIS gunman while delivering a speech in Annaba, continuing the ongoing conflict between the government and the fundamentalist Muslims of the FIS. Algeria has since been in a declared state of emergency.

In 1994, Liamine Zeroual became president and greatly increased the power of that office through constitutional changes approved by voters. The conflict with religious extremists and the FIS continued as both groups boycotted the next round of elections in 1997. This move allowed the military government to consolidate its hold on power as the level of violence in the country, as evidenced by the bloody Ramadan massacres and random killings of that same year.

Angola

Official name: Republic of Angola
Independence: November 11, 1975
Area: 481,353 sq. mi.
Form of Government: Multiparty republic
Capital: Luanda
International relations: UN, OAU, EU
Currency: Kwanza
Income: (per capita US$) 750 (1990)
Population: (1998 estimate) 10.9 million
Ethnic divisions: Ovimbundu 37.2%, Mbundu 21.6%, Kongo 13.2%, Luimbe-Nganguela 5.4%, Nyaneka-Humbe 5.4%, Chokwe 4.2%, Luvale 3.4%, others 9.6%
Religious groups: Roman Catholic, Protestant, traditional belief
Languages spoken: Portuguese (official), tribal languages and dialects
Literacy: 63% (1995)

Exports: Crude oil, petroleum-based products, coffee, diamonds

Imports: Consumer goods, capital goods, transport equipment

Primary trade partners: Portugal, United States, Brazil, Germany, France

Angola's boundaries were formally established by the Berlin West Africa Congress of 1884–1885. Following World War II, Portuguese interest in colonizing Angola increased, leading to the establishment of a strict and harsh colonial rule.

Discontent over Portuguese unwillingness to concede eventual independence led to the formation of the Popular Movement for the Liberation of Angola (MPLA), the National Front for the Liberation of Angola (FNLA), and the National Union for the Total Independence of Angola (UNITA). In January 1975, the Portuguese and the three liberation movements worked out a complicated agreement—the Alvor Accord—that provided for a transitional government composed of all three groups and for elections in preparation for independence in November of 1975.

The departure of the Portuguese in late 1975 left Angola in the midst of a fierce struggle for power between the three divided liberation movements. Fueling the civil war was the involvement of such foreign powers as the United States, South Africa, the Soviet Union, and Cuba. South African troops, encouraged by the United States, which backed the FNLA-UNITA alliance, actually invaded Angola but were repelled. The Marxist MPLA was finally able to establish control of the country under Augustinho Neto who ruled as the newly independent country's first president until his death in 1979. Neto was succeeded by José Eduardo Dos Santos, but the MPLA government, weakened by continuing South African incursions into Angolan territory and its own inflexible economic policies, had lost territory in the south of the country to UNITA by the early 1980s.

By the late 1980s, the embattled MPLA government was forced to abandon some of its most stridently Marxist economic policies, which opened the door to more cordial relations with Western countries. Hope for a lasting peace increased in 1991, when peace accords were signed between the MPLA and UNITA. However, war again erupted the following year, when UNITA refused to acknowledge its defeat in multiparty elections. The struggle between MPLA and UNITA for control of Angola continued into the late 1990s.

In 1997, a plan to install a government of national unity had to be abandoned when Jonas Savimbi, leader of UNITA, refused to come to Luanda because he feared for his life. Savimbi also balked at proposals that he

Two Angolan women walking along their village (Cory Langley).

surrender UNITA's control over most of the country's diamond business, arguing that the MPLA controlled all of Angola's lucrative oil trade. In 1998, escalating political and military tension between the Angolan government and UNITA again threatened to flare into a full-scale civil war. With the possibility of the civil war turning into a broader regional conflict, Angola's recovery from years of conflict could be further postponed.

Angolans are almost entirely Bantu of various ethnic subgroupings. The Ovimbundu subgroup in central and southeastern Angola is the largest, consisting of about 37 percent of the population. The Kongo, concentrated in the northwest but also living in areas adjacent to the Congo as well as Cabinda, constitute about 13 percent. The Mbundu, about 22 percent of the population, are concentrated in the area around Luanda and out toward the east.

Benin
Official name: Republic of Benin
Independence: August 1, 1960
Area: 43,483 sq. mi.
Form of government: Multiparty
Capital: Cotonou (de facto), Porto-Novo (official)
International relations: UN, OAU, EU
Currency: CFA franc
Income: (per capita US$) 370 (1995)
Population: (1998 estimate) 6.1 million
Ethnic divisions: Fon, Adja, Bariba, Yoruba
Religious groups: Traditional belief 62%, Christian 23%, Muslim 12%, other 3%

Vendors selling their wares at a market in Benin (Cory Langley).

Languages spoken: French (official), Fon
Literacy: 37% (1991)
Exports: Coffee, cocoa beans, cotton, palm products, crude oil
Imports: Manufactured goods, food products, machinery
Primary trade partners: India, France, Portugal, Thailand, Italy

During the precolonial era, Benin was a collection of small principalities, the most powerful of which was the Fon Kingdom of Dahomey. By the seventeenth and eighteenth centuries, the Portuguese and other Europeans established trading posts along the coast. From these posts thousands of slaves were shipped to the New World, primarily to Brazil and the Caribbean. This part of West Africa became known as the Slave Coast.

In 1892, the King of Dahomey was subjugated, and the country organized as the French protectorate of Dahomey. It remained a French colony until independence in 1960, when the name was changed to the Republic of Dahomey, and Hubert Maga became president. Three years later, he was overthrown by military commanders. Mathieu Kérékou took over in 1975. In the same year, the name of the country was changed to the People's Republic of Benin. When the government re-

verted to civilian control in 1980, Kérékou was reelected president of the republic. Facing formidable internal dissent, Kérékou in 1989 abandoned his Marxist-Leninist ideology. A new constitution, adopted in 1990, laid the groundwork for the establishment of a multiparty republic. Nicéphore Soglo defeated Kérékou in presidential elections in 1991, Benin's first free ballot in thirty years. Although the country's economy improved under Soglo, his personal popularity declined, and he was defeated by Kérékou in 1996 presidential elections. In his second term Kérékou has largely abandoned his socialist vision, instead pursuing policies of economic liberalization.

The population of Benin comprises about twenty sociocultural groups. Four groups—the Fon, Aja (who are related), Bariba, and Yoruba—account for more than half of the population.

Botswana

Official name: Republic of Botswana
Independence: September 30, 1966
Area: 231,804 sq. mi.
Form of government: Multiparty
Capital: Gaberone

International relations: UN, OAC, Commonwealth, EU

Currency: Pula

Income: (per capita US$) 2,800 (1994)

Population: (1998 estimate) 1.5 million

Ethnic divisions: Tswana 75%, Kalanga, Kgalagadi, Yei, Herero, Mbukushu, Basarwa (Bushmen), Khoi (Hottentots), and whites about 25%

Religious groups: Traditional belief 50%, Christianity 50%

Languages spoken: English (official), SeTswana

Literacy: 70% (1995)

Exports: Meat, diamonds, copper, nickel

Imports: Machinery and transport equipment, food, chemical products

Primary trade partners: South Korea, Zimbabwe, United States, United Kingdom

Europeans made first contact with the area in the early nineteenth century. In the last quarter of the century, hostilities broke out between the Botswana and the Afrikaners from South Africa (Transvaal). Following appeals by the Botswana for assistance, the British government in 1885 proclaimed "Bechuanaland" to be under British protection. In 1909, despite South African pressure, inhabitants of Bechuanaland, Basutoland (now Lesotho), and Swaziland demanded and received British agreement that they not be included in the proposed Union of South Africa.

In June 1964, the British government accepted proposals for a form of self-government for Botswana that would lead to independence. Botswana became independent on September 30, 1966, and Seretse Khama was installed as the prime minister after the Bechuanaland Democratic Party (BDP) won majority votes. The country was later named Botswana, and upon Khama's death in 1980, Quett Ketumile Joni Masire assumed the presidency, an office to which he was reelected three times. Constitutional reforms in 1994–1995 allowed more political parties to participate in the government and greatly reduced the power of the central government. However, the retirement of President Masire and the orderly succession of his vice president, Festus Mogae, to the presidency in 1998 appeared to extend the BDP's firm grip on power.

Since winning independence, Botswana has maintained a nonaligned foreign policy. Although it opposed the former racist policies of neighboring South Africa, Botswana maintained close economic ties. Large deposits of diamonds have been discovered in Botswana in recent years, making the country one of the world's major producers of the valuable gemstone.

Some 75 percent of the country's population is made up of the Tswana tribe (Botswana), which is divided into eight subgroups: Bamangwate, Bakwena, Batawana, Bangwaketse, Bakgatla, Bamalete, Barolong,

Three high school girls walk down the street in Gaborne, Botswana (Laure Communications).

and Batlokwa. The Kalanga, Herero, Bushmen (Basarwa), Yei, and Kgalagadi are minorities.

Burkina Faso (formerly Upper Volta)

Official name: Republic of Burkina Faso

Independence: August 5, 1960

Area: 105,869 sq. mi.

Form of government: Multiparty

Capital: Ouagadougou

International relations: UN, OAU, EU

Currency: CFA franc

Income: (per capita US$) 230 (1995)

Population: (1998) 11.3 million

Ethnic divisions: Mossi, Bobo, Mande, Fulani

Religious groups: Traditional belief 45%, Muslim 43%, Christian 12%

Languages spoken: French (official), More, other tribal languages

Literacy: 18.2% (1995)

Exports: Cotton, petroleum, live animals

Imports: Capital equipment, food products, raw materials

Primary trade partners: Côte d'Ivoire, France, Nigeria, Japan

Until the end of the nineteenth century, the history of Burkina Faso was dominated by the Mossi, who are believed to have come from central or eastern Africa in the eleventh century. When the French arrived and claimed the area in 1896, the Mossi resisted but were defeated when their capital at Ouagadougou was captured. After World War II, the Mossi renewed their pressure for separate territorial status, and Upper Volta became an autonomous republic in the French Community on December 11, 1958. It achieved independence on August 5, 1960, under President Maurice Yaméogo. Austerity measures imposed by the Yaméogo government at the end of 1965 led to a confrontation between the nation's trade unions and the government. In the opening days of 1966, power was seized by General Sangoulé

Women grinding food products with mortar and pestle in Yako, Burkina Faso (David Johnson).

Lamizana, the army chief of staff. He named himself president and suspended the constitution. In 1980, Lamizana was ousted in a bloodless coup, which was followed by two more coups over the next three years. In August 1984, one year after the coup that brought Captain Thomas Sankara to power as head of the National Revolutionary Council, the country's name was changed from Upper Volta to Burkina Faso.

Sankara was overthrown and executed in an October 1987 coup led by Blaise Campaoré. In 1990, Campaoré introduced some democratic reforms and the following year was reelected. His party won a legislative majority in May 1992 legislative elections. During the mid-1990s, Burkina Faso actively supported revolutionary movements in Gambia and Liberia, alienating it from its neighbors and most Western powers. However, in 1998 Burkina Faso hosted the African Cup of Nations soccer tournament, Africa's biggest sporting event. The nation received favorable international media coverage for its efforts.

The majority of the population belong to two major West African cultural groups, the Voltaic and the Mande. The Voltaic are far more numerous and include the Mossi, which make up about one-half of the population. The Mossi are still bound by the traditions of the emperor, the Mogho Naba, who holds court in Ouagadougou. Burkina Faso is one of the poorest nations in the world, with most inhabitants subsisting on agriculture and animal husbandry.

Burundi
Official name: Republic of Burundi
Independence: July 1, 1962
Area: 10,747 sq. mi.
Form of government: Military
Capital: Bujumbura
International relations: UN, OAU, EU

Currency: Burundi franc
Income: (per capita US$) 160 (1995)
Population: (1998 estimate) 6 million
Ethnic divisions: Hutu 85%, Tutsi 14%, Twa 1%
Religious groups: Christian 79%, traditional belief 19%, Muslim 2%
Languages spoken: Rundi and French (both official), Swahili
Literacy: 35.3% (1995)
Exports: Coffee, cotton, animal hides
Imports: Machinery, transport equipment, food, petroleum products
Primary trade partners: Belgium, Luxembourg, France, Germany, United States

Prior to the arrival of Europeans, Burundi was a kingdom with a highly stratified, feudal social structure. Rulers were drawn from princely dynastic families or *ganwa*, from whom a king or *mwami* was chosen. A *mwami* continued to rule even after independence was granted.

European explorers and missionaries began making brief visits to the area as early as 1858. However, Burundi did not come under European administration until the 1890s, when it became part of German East Africa. In 1916 Belgian troops occupied the country, and the League of Nations mandated it to Belgium in 1923 as part of the Territory of Ruanda-Urundi, now the nations of Rwanda and Burundi. Burundi became independent on July 1, 1962. Just ten years after independence, an abortive coup d'état provoked brutal massacres, claiming the lives of more than 100,000 people.

Burundi's population is made up of three ethnic groups—Hutu, Tutsi, and Twa. Hutus, who make up 85 percent of the population, are primarily farmers whose Bantu-speaking ancestors migrated into Burundi 800 to 1,000 years ago. The Tutsi, who make up 14 percent of the population, are a pastoral people who migrated from Ethiopia several hundred years later. Years of dispute with neighboring Rwanda have continued into the 1990s. Ethnic conflict between the Hutus and Tutsis has led to many atrocities, most notably an explosion of violence in 1993 that claimed tens of thousands of lives and displaced nearly three-quarters of a million Burundians, both Tutsi and Hutu. A military coup in 1996 changed nothing as the violence continued in the late 1990s, despite offers of mediation by the United States and massive humanitarian aid.

Cameroon
Official name: Republic of Cameroon
Independence: January 1, 1960
Area: 183,568 sq. mi.
Form of government: Multiparty
Capital: Yaoundé

International Relations: EU, OAU, UN
Currency: CFA franc
Income: (per capita US$) 650 (1995)
Population: (1998 estimate) 15 million
Ethnic divisions: More than 200 groups
Religious groups: Christian, Muslim, traditional belief
Languages spoken: English and French (official), more
     than 200 tribal languages
Literacy: 63.4% (1995)
Exports: Crude oil, bananas, cocoa, coffee, cotton
Imports: Semifinished goods, food products, equipment
Primary trade partners: Belgium, Luxembourg, France,
     Netherlands, Italy, United States

The earliest inhabitants of Cameroon were probably Pygmies, who still inhabit the southern forests. However, Bantu-speaking people were among the first to invade Cameroon from equatorial Africa, settling in the south and later in the west. The Muslim Fulani from the Niger basin arrived in the eleventh and nineteenth centuries and settled in the north. Europeans first made contact with the area in the 1500s. For the next three centuries, Spanish, Dutch, and British traders visited the area.

In July of 1884, Germany, the United Kingdom, and France each attempted to annex the area. A 1919 declaration divided Cameroon between the United Kingdom and France, with the larger, eastern area under France. In December of 1958, the French trusteeship was ended, and French Cameroon became the Republic of Cameroon on January 1, 1960.

The Republic of Cameroon consisted of a federal system integrating the French-controlled south and the British-controlled north under the leadership of its first president, Ahmadou Ahidjo. The country depends heavily on foreign capital and has been faced with internal problems, both ethnic and social, under the leadership of Ahidjo's successor, Paul Biya. Despite sometimes violent confrontations between the nation's political parties, Biya was reelected in 1997 presidential elections, which were boycotted by the three main opposition parties. Despite recent health problems, relative economic prosperity and strong-arm tactics against opponents have enabled Biya to withstand both international and domestic opposition.

Cameroon has about two hundred tribal groups and clans, speaking at least as many languages and dialects.

Cape Verde
Official name: Republic of Cape Verde
Independence: July 5, 1975
Area: 1,555 sq. mi.
Form of government: Multiparty
Capital: Praia
International relations: UN, OAU.

Cameroonian ceremonial mask adorned by the people of the Kilum Mountain Rainforest (David Johnson).

Currency: Escudo
Income: (per capita US$) 960 (1995)
Population: (1998 estimate) 400,000
Ethnic divisions: Creole (mixed African and Portuguese),
     African, European
Religious groups: Roman Catholic, Protestant
Languages spoken: Portuguese (official), Crioulo
     (national)
Literacy: 71.6% (1991)
Exports: Fish products, vegetable products
Imports: Food products, transport equipment
Primary trade partners: Portugal, Netherlands, Germany, France

Located in the north Atlantic Ocean, the Cape Verde archipelago remained uninhabited until the Portuguese visited it in 1456 and African slaves were brought to the islands to work on Portuguese plantations. As a result, Cape Verdeans have mixed African and Portuguese origins.

In 1951 Portugal changed Cape Verde's status from a colony to an overseas province. In 1956, the African Party for the Independence of Guinea-Bissau and Cape Verde (PAIGC) was organized to bring about improvement in economic, social, and political conditions in Cape Verde and Portuguese Guinea. The PAIGC began an armed rebellion against Portugal in 1961. Acts of sabotage eventually grew into a war in Portuguese Guinea that pitted 10,000 Soviet Bloc-supported PAIGC soldiers against 35,000 Portuguese and African troops.

In December of 1974, the PAIGC and Portugal signed an agreement providing for a transitional government composed of Portuguese and Cape Verdeans. On June 30, 1975, Cape Verdeans elected a National Assembly, which received the instruments of independence from Portugal on July 5, 1975. After winning independence, the country voted for a union with Guinea-Bissau. In 1980, the link ended when João Vieira seized power in Guinea-Bissau. The PAIGC was dissolved and replaced by PAICV (African Party for the Independence of Cape Verde). Pedro Pires, Cape Verde's prime minister and a prominent nationalist, was elected president in 1986. Under him, Cape Verde followed a socialist path with programs of nationalization and agrarian reform. In the country's first free presidential elections made possible by political reforms, Antonio Mascarenhas Monteiro was elected in 1991. A new constitution, firmly establishing the country's new multiparty system, was adopted the following year. In 1996, Mascarenhas was reelected president to another five-year term.

The official language is Portuguese. However, most Cape Verdeans speak a Creole dialect, Crioulo, which consists of archaic Portuguese modified through contact with African and other European languages. Leading contemporary Afro-Cape Verdeans include Cesaria Evora, an internationally renowned singer.

Central African Republic
Official name: République Centrafricaine
Independence: August 13, 1960
Area: 240,535 sq. mi.
Form of government: Multiparty system
Capital: Bangui
International relations: EU, OAU, UN
Currency: CFA franc
Income: (per capita US$) 340 (1995)
Population: (1998 estimate) 3.4 million
Ethnic divisions: More than 80 groups including Baya, Banda, Sara, Mandja, Mboum, Ngbandi, M'Baka
Religious groups: Traditional belief 24%, Protestant 25%, Roman Catholic 25%, Muslim 15%, Other 11%
Languages spoken: French (official), Sango (national)
Literacy: 60% (1995)
Exports: Coffee, cotton, diamonds
Imports: Food products, transport equipment, chemical products
Primary trade partners: Belgium, Luxembourg, France, Japan, Cameroon, United States

The first Europeans to settle in the area that is now the Central African Republic were the French who established an outpost at Bangu. United with Chad in 1906, the outpost formed the Oubangui-Chari-Chad colony.

In 1910 it became one of the four territories of the Federation of French Equatorial Africa, along with Chad, Congo (Brazzaville), and Gabon. However, a constitutional referendum of September 1958 dissolved the federation. The nation became an autonomous republic within the newly established French Community on December 1, 1958, and acceded to complete independence as the Central African Republic on August 13, 1960. The first president and the founder of the Central African Republic was Bathelemy Boganda.

Boganda's successor, David Dacko, was overthrown in 1966 by Gen. Jean-Badel Bokassa, who embarked on a reign of terror, proclaiming himself emperor. A 1981 coup d'état put Dacko back in power. Gen. André Kolingba succeeded Dacko, and a multiparty state was established in 1991. The results of multiparty legislative and presidential elections, held in October 1992, were thrown out by the country's supreme court, which cited multiple irregularities. In September 1993 elections, Ange-Felix Patassé was elected president, succeeding Kolingba who released Bokassa from prison as one of his last official acts. Patassé was at odds with the military for much of the 1990s, and French troops were needed to put down military mutinies in the late 1990s. In early 1998, the United Nations sent an all-African peacekeeping force to the Central Africa Republic to enforce the so-called Bangui Accords of 1997, which called for an armistice and new elections.

The Central African Republic is made up of more than eighty ethnic groups, each with its own language. About seventy percent of the population comprises Baya-Mandjia and Banda, with approximately seven percent M'Baka. Sango, the language of a small group along the Oubangui River, is the national language spoken by the majority of Central Africans. The country is one of the poorest nations in Africa, with a high mortality rate and widespread malnutrition and illiteracy.

Chad
Official name: Republic of Chad
Independence: August 11, 1960
Area: 495,755 sq. mi.
Form of government: Multiparty
Capital: N'Djamena.
International relations: EU, OAU, UN
Currency: CFA franc
Income: (per capita US$) 180 (1995)
Population: (1998 estimate) 7.4 million

Ethnic divisions: More than 200 groups including Sara, Toubou (Gourane), Arab, Fulbe, Kotoko, Hausa, Kanembou, Bagirmi, Boulala, Zaghawa, Hadjerai, and Maba

Religious groups: Muslim, Christian, traditional beliefs

Languages spoken: French and Arabic (official); 200 tribal languages

Literacy: 48.1% (1995)

Exports: Cotton, diamonds, petroleum products, wood

Imports: Petroleum products, pharmaceuticals, machinery, transport equipment, chemicals

Primary trade partners: France, Portugal, Cameroon, Germany, Belgium, Luxembourg

The region that is now Chad was known to Middle Eastern traders and geographers as far back as the late Middle Ages. Since then, Chad has served as a crossroads for the Muslim peoples of the desert and savannah regions and the animist Bantu tribes of the tropical forests.

The Sao people populated the Chari River basin for thousands of years, but their relatively weak chiefdoms were overtaken by the powerful chiefs of what were to become the Kanem-Bornu and Baguirmi kingdoms. At their peak, these two kingdoms and the kingdom of Ouaddai controlled a good part of what is now Chad, as well as parts of Nigeria and Sudan.

The French first made contact with the region in 1891. The first major colonial battle for Chad was fought in 1900 between the French major Lamy and the African leader Rabah. Although the French won that battle, they did not declare the territory for themselves until 1911, and thereafter armed clashes between colonial troops and local bands continued for many years. Although Chad joined the French colonies of Gabon, Oubangui-Charo, and Moyen Congo to form the Federation of French Equatorial Africa in 1910, Chad did not have colonial status until 1920.

In 1959, the territory of French Equatorial Africa was dissolved, and four states—Gabon, the Central African Republic, Congo (Brazzaville), and Chad—became autonomous members of the French Community. In 1960 Chad became an independent nation under its first president, François Tombalbaye. He was faced with the pressure of resolving the ongoing conflict between the Muslim north and the black south and responded by instituting authoritarian rule. Backed by Libya, FRONAT (Front de Libération Nationale) guerrillas of the north gained power, naming Goukouni Oueddei as head of state. In 1982, he was succeeded by Hisséne Habré, but civil war broke out one year later.

In 1990, Habré was ousted by a rebel group with Libyan support. Rebel leader Idriss Déby assumed the presidency. In January 1992, the Déby government

claimed to have put down an uprising by forces loyal to Habré. An understanding was reached in 1994, ending the long-standing battle between the government and Habré forces. In mid-1996 elections under a newly adopted democratic constitution, Déby was elected president. After several postponements, Déby's party dominated legislative elections in 1997. Though Déby's defeated opponents claimed electoral fraud, international observers declared the elections free and fair.

Chad is made up of more than two hundred ethnic groups. Those in the north and east are generally Muslim, while most southerners are animists and Christians. Ethnic and religious divisions continue to run deep in Chad. The government continues to face armed resistance from rebels in the south demanding regional autonomy, and in 1998 Amnesty International charged the government with arbitrarily killing civilians from the south.

Comoros

Official name: Federal Islamic Republic of the Comoros

Independence: July 6, 1975

Area: 838 sq. mi.

Form of government: Multiparty

Capital: Moroni

International relations: EU, OAU, UN

Currency: CFA franc

Income: (per capita US$) 470 (1995)

Population: (1998) 546,000

Ethnic divisions: Antalote, Cafre, Makoa, Oimatsaha, Sakalava

Religious groups: Sunni Muslim 98%, Roman Catholic 2%

Languages spoken: Comorian, Arabic, French

Literacy: 57% (1995)

Exports: Cloves, vanilla, ylang ylang

Imports: Rice, petroleum products, vehicles, meat, fish

Primary trade partners: France, Germany, Pakistan, United States, United Arab Emirates

Located off the northwestern coast of Madagascar, Portuguese explorers visited the archipelago in 1505. In 1843, the sultan of Mayotte was persuaded to relinquish the island of Mayotte to the French. By 1912 France had established colonial rule over the additional islands of Grande Comore, Anjouan, and Mohéli and placed them under the administration of the governor general of Madagascar. After World War II, the islands became a French overseas territory and were represented in France's National Assembly. On July 6, 1975, the Comorian Parliament passed a resolution declaring unilateral independence. However, the deputies of Mayotte abstained; it remains under French administration. As a result, the Comorian government has effective control over only Grande Comore, Anjouan, and Mohéli. This was followed by a extended period of political upheaval in Comoros including a series of political insurrections and coup d'états.

In 1996, Mohamed Taki Abdulkarim was elected president and unveiled a new constitution extending the powers of the president and making Islam the state religion. In 1997 the islands of Anjouan and Mohéli announced their intention to secede: in light of the relatively high standard of living enjoyed by Mayotte, they wished to return to French administration. After initially affirming its willingness to reincorporate the islands, France urged the Organization of African Unity (OAU) to find a peaceful settlement to the conflict. The OAU later worked out a framework agreement whereby the islands would have their own government within a new entity to be named the Union of Comorian Islands, which would have a separate administration. At an April 1999 peace conference in Madagascar, representatives of Grand Comore, Mohéli , and the Comoros government signed the agreement; the Anjouan delegation did not. Shortly afterwards, army officers took over the Comoros Republic in an apparent coup.

The Comorians inhabiting the islands of Grande Comore, Anjouan, and Mohéli (about 86 percent of the population) share African-Arab origins. Islam is the dominant religion, but a substantial minority of the citizens of Mayotte (the Mahorais) are Catholic and have been influenced strongly by French culture. The most common language is Shikomoro, a Swahili dialect. French and Malagasy are also spoken.

Congo (Brazzaville)

Official name: Republic of the Congo
Independence: August 15, 1960
Area: 132,000 sq. mi.
Form of government: Multiparty
Capital: Brazzaville
International relations: EU, OAU, UN
Currency: CFA franc
Income: (per capita US$) 680 (1995)
Population: (1998) 2.7 million
Ethnic divisions: 15 main groups, 75 subgroups; largest groups are Kongo 51.5%, Teke 17.3%, and Mboshi 11.5%
Religious groups: Traditional belief 33%, Christian 65%, Muslim 2%
Languages spoken: French (official), Lingala, Kikongo
Literacy: 74.9% (1995)
Exports: Crude petroleum, diamonds, wood
Imports: Machinery, transport equipment, consumer products, chemicals, fuels, beverages, tobacco
Primary trade partners: France, United States, Netherlands, Italy

The early history of the Congo is believed to have focused on three tribal kingdoms—the Kongo, the Loango, and the Teke. Established in the fourth century,

Ntore dancers from the Republic of the Congo (National Museum of African Art).

the Kongo was a highly centralized kingdom that later developed a close commercial relationship with the Portuguese, who were the first Europeans to explore the area.

With the development of the slave trade, the Portuguese turned their attention from the Kongo Kingdom to the Loango Kingdom. By the time the slave trade was abolished in the 1800s, the Loango Kingdom had been reduced to many small, independent groups. The Teke Kingdom of the interior, which had sold slaves to the Loango Kingdom, ended its independence in 1883, when the Teke king concluded a treaty with Pierre Savorgnan de Brazza, placing the Teke lands and people under French protection. The area then became known as Middle Congo.

In 1910, Middle Congo became part of French Equatorial Africa, which also included Gabon, the Central African Republic, and Chad. A constitutional referendum in September 1958 replaced the Federation of French Equatorial Africa with the French Community. Middle Congo, under the name Republic of the Congo, and the three other territories of French Equatorial Africa became fully autonomous members within the French Community. On April 15, 1960, it became an independent nation but retained close, formal bonds with the community.

President Fulbert Youlou instituted a dictatorship for the first three years following independence and then was succeeded by a revolutionary government headed by Alphonse Massamba-Debat. In 1968 the military seized control of the nation under Gen. Marien Ngouabi, who declared the Congo a republic to be governed under a one-party system. Assassinated in 1977, Ngouabi was succeeded as president by General Joachim Yhombi-Opango. Two years later, Yhombi-Opango was succeeded by Denis Sassou-Nguesso, who was reelected to the presidency in 1984 and 1989.

The 1990s brought increasing dissatisfaction with the Sassou-Nguesso regime, which was forced in 1992 to adopt a new constitution, making the country a multiparty democracy. In August 1992, Sassou-Nguesso lost in presidential elections to Pascal Lissouba, but the latter's government was soon plagued by accusations of ethnic favoritism. Clashes between various private militias exploded into civil war, killing between 6,000 and 10,000 people and largely destroying Brazzaville. Many of the country's citizens rallied behind opposition forces led by Sassou-Nguesso who, with considerable Angolan assistance, overthrew Lissouba in late 1997. Continuing to maintain power, Sassou-Nguesso has promised national reconciliation, a return to civilian rule, and a professional military.

Congo (Kinshasa)

Official name: Democratic Republic of the Congo
Independence: June 30, 1960
Area: 905,568 sq. mi.
Form of government: Republic
Capital: Kinshasa
International relations: OAU, UN
Currency: New Congo
Income: (per capita US$) 150 (1996)
Population: (1998) 49 million
Ethnic divisions: 250 tribal groups
Religious groups: Roman Catholic 50%, Protestant 20%, Muslim 10%, Kimbanguist 10%, other syncretic sects and traditional beliefs 10%
Languages spoken: French, Lingala, Swahili, Kingwana (a variant), Kikongo, Tshiluba
Literacy: 77.3% (1995)
Exports: Copper, coffee, diamonds, cobalt, crude oil
Imports: Consumer goods, foodstuffs, raw materials
Primary trade partners: Belgium, France, United States, South Africa, Japan

The area that is now the Democratic Republic of the Congo or Congo-Kinshasa is believed to have been populated as early as 10,000 years ago. An influx of peoples arrived in the seventh and eighth centuries, when Bantu people from present-day Nigeria settled, bringing with them knowledge of the manufacture and use of metals. In 1482 the Portuguese arrived at the mouth of the Congo River. They found an organized society—the Bakongo Kingdom—that included parts of

present-day Congo-Brazzaville, Congo-Kinshasa, and Angola. The Portuguese named the area Congo. At the Berlin Conference of 1885, King Leopold's claim to the greater part of the Zaire River basin was recognized. The Congo Free State remained his personal possession until he ceded it to the Belgian State in 1907, when it was renamed the Belgian Congo.

Following riots in Leopoldville in 1958, Belgian King Bedouin announced that the colony could look forward to independence. Roundtable conferences were convened at Brussels in January 1960, and Belgium granted independence on June 30, 1960. Parliamentary elections were held in April of 1960. The Congolese National Movement (MNC) obtained a majority of the seats, and Patrice Lumumba was named prime minister. After much maneuvering, the leader of the Alliance of the Bakongo (ABAKO) Party, Joseph Kasavubu, was named president.

Chaos started right after independence. Moise Tshombe, premier of Katanga Province, declared Katanga (rich with copper) independent. Belgian military intervened and, soon after, U.N. troops arrived to help normalize the situation. Meanwhile, Lumumba was assassinated. Tshombe served as prime minister until 1965, when Joseph Mobutu organized a coup d'état. While amassing great personal riches, Mobutu managed to bring resource-rich Congo-Kinshasa (then known as Zaire) to the brink of bankruptcy during the more than thirty years that he held power. The country's increasingly fragile economy and pressures from a sharp influx in refugees all contributed to growing dissatisfaction with Mobutu's regime.

Anti-Mobutu guerrilla fighter Laurent-Désiré Kabila, leader of the Alliance of Democratic Forces for the Liberation of Congo, led rebel forces in seizing large portions of the country in the fall of 1996. In May 1997, as rebels neared Kinshasa, Mobutu stepped down and fled the capital, later dying in exile. The rebels took control of the country, which they renamed the Democratic Republic of the Congo. Kabila's regime has faced heavy criticism from the international community, who suspect that his troops were responsible for the disappearance and assumed massacre of thousands of Hutu refugees. In addition, the political favoritism exhibited by Kabila has led to serious civil strife that threatens to spark a broad regional conflict beyond Congo-Kinshasa's borders.

As many as 250 ethnic groups in the Democratic Republic of the Congo have been distinguished and named. The largest group, the Kongo, may include as many as 2.5 million persons. Other socially and numerically important groups are the Luba, Lunda, Bashi, and Mongo. Some groups, including the aboriginal Pygmies, occupy isolated ecological niches and number only a few thousand.

Approximately seven hundred local languages and dialects are spoken; four serve as official languages. Lingala developed along the Congo River in the 1880s, in response to the need for a common commercial language. Swahili, introduced into the country by Arabs and especially the Zanzibari Swahilis during the nineteenth century slaving operations, is spoken extensively in the eastern half of the country. Kikongo is used primarily in the area between Kinshasa and the Atlantic Ocean, as well as in parts of Congo and Angola. Tshiluba is spoken primarily by the tribal groups of the south-central Democratic Republic of the Congo.

Côte d' Ivoire (Ivory Coast)

Official name: Republic of Côte d'Ivoire (Ivory Coast)
Independence: August 7, 1960
Area: 124,502 sq. mi.
Form of government: Multiparty
Capital: Abidjan
International relations: EU, OAU, UN
Currency: CFA franc
Income: (per capita US$) 668 (1995)
Population: (1998) 15 million
Ethnic divisions: More than 60 groups
Religious groups: Muslim, traditional belief, Christian
Languages spoken: French (official), tribal dialects
Literacy: 40.1% (1995)
Exports: Cocoa, cocoa butter, coffee, petroleum products, wood
Imports: Food, petroleum, transport equipment, plastics, paper, pharmaceuticals, electrical equipment
Primary trade partners: France, Nigeria, United States, Netherlands, Germany, Italy, Ghana

The French made their initial contact with Côte d'Ivoire in 1637, when missionaries landed at Assinie near the Gold Coast (now Ghana) border. However, these early contacts were limited. In 1843 and 1844, France signed treaties with the kings of the Grand Bassam and Assinie regions, placing their territories under a French protectorate. French explorers, missionaries, trading companies, and soldiers gradually extended the area under French control until 1893, when Côte d'Ivoire was officially made a French colony.

In December of 1958, Côte d'Ivoire became an autonomous republic within the French Community. Côte d'Ivoire became independent on August 7, 1960. Félix Houphouëatt-Boigny led the country under a one-party system. He maintained strong ties with Europe, which helped bring about rapid development and economic stability. In October 1990, Houphouëatt-Boigny was elected to his seventh term as president in the country's first multiparty elections. He died in 1993 and was succeeded by Henri Konan Bédié, head of the National Assembly. Bédié was again elected to office in 1995 elections that were boycotted by opposition parties protesting the government's political restrictions. Continuing the policies of his predecessor, Bédié has helped build a nation of political stability and limited economic prosperity. At the same time, he has maintained a neocolonial dependence on France and blocked effective democratic reforms.

Côte d'Ivoire's more than sixty ethnic groups usually are classified into seven principal divisions—Akan, Krou, Lagoon, Nuclear Mande, Peripheral Mande, Senoufo, and Lobi. The Baoule in the Akan division is probably the largest single subgroup, with perhaps twenty percent of the overall population. The Bete in the Krou division and the Senoufo in the north are the second and third-largest groups, with roughly 18 and 15 percent of the national population, respectively.

Djibouti

Official name: Republic of Djibouti
Independence: June 27, 1977
Area: 8,494 sq. mi.
Form of government: Multiparty
Capital: Djibouti
International relations: Arab League, EU, OAU, UN
Currency: Djibouti franc
Income: (per capita US$) 835 (1994)
Population: (1998) 441,000
Ethnic divisions: Somalis (Issas), Afar, French, Arab, Ethiopian, Italian
Religious groups: Muslim 94%, Christian 6%
Languages spoken: French (official), Somali, Afar, Arabic
Literacy: 46.2% (1987)
Exports: Cereals, coffee, leather and skins, tea
Imports: Food, beverages, tobacco, machinery, petroleum products, apparel
Primary trade partners: France, Ethiopia, Somalia, Italy

The region, which now makes up the Republic of Djibouti, was first settled by the French in 1862 as a result of growing French interest in British activity in Egypt. In 1884 France expanded its protectorate to include the shores of the Gulf of Tadjourah and the hinterland, designating the area French Somaliland. The boundaries of the protectorate, marked out in 1897 by France and Emperor Manelik II of Ethiopia, were affirmed further by agreements with Emperor Haile Selassie I in 1945 and 1954.

In July of 1967, a directive from Paris formally changed the name of the territory to the French Territory of Afars and Issas. In 1975 the French government began to accommodate increasingly insistent demands for independence. In June of 1976, the territory's citizenship law, which had favored the Afar minority, was revised to

Djiboutian women sitting beneath a tree in northeast Africa (Laure Communications).

Egyptian family standing beside a building (Cory Langley).

reflect more closely the weight of the Issa Somali majority. In a May of 1977 referendum the electorate voted for independence, and the Republic of Djibouti was inaugurated on June 27, 1977. Independence was followed by a republican form of government.

Since independence, the country has been led by Hassan Gouled Aptidon, the republic's first and only president. Beginning in the 1980s, however, Gouled's tenure was marred by political repression, ethnic hostilities, and serious international debt. Opposition to the Gouled government sparked a sizeable Afar resistance movement in the 1990s; negotiations with the government led to a comprehensive treaty in December 1994. When Gouled had to leave the country from December 1995 until February 1996 to seek medical treatment in France, a destabilizing struggle for succession ensued. Upon his return, he suspended the civil rights of prominent opposition leaders and restated his intention to remain in office until his term expires in 1999.

The indigenous population of the Republic of Djibouti is divided between the majority Somalis (predominantly of the Issa tribe with minority Ishaak and Gadaboursi representation) and the Afars and Danakils.

Egypt

Official name: Arab Republic of Egypt
Independence: February 28, 1922
Area: 386,662 sq. mi
Form of government: Presidential republic
Capital: Cairo
International relations: Arab League, OAU, UN
Currency: Egyptian pound
Income: (per capita US$) 1,140 (1996)
Population: (1998) 65 million
Ethnic divisions: Egyptian, Bedouin Arab, Nubian
Religious groups: Sunni Muslim 94%, Coptic Christian
Languages spoken: Arabic (official), English
Literacy: 51.4% (1995)
Exports: Crude oil, petroleum products, cotton yarn, raw cotton, textiles, chemicals
Imports: Machinery and equipment, food products, fertilizer, wood products, durable goods
Primary trade partners: United States, Japan

Egypt has endured as a unified state for more than 5,000 years, and archaeological evidence indicates that a developed Egyptian society has existed much longer. In about 3100 BC, Egypt was united under a ruler known as Mena, or Menes, who inaugurated the thirty pharaonic dynasties into which Egypt's ancient history is divided—the Old and Middle Kingdoms and the New Empire.

In 525 BC, the Persians dethroned the last pharaoh of the 26th dynasty. The country remained a Persian province until the conquest of Alexander the Great in 332 BC. After Alexander's death in 323 BC, the Macedonian commander, Ptolemy, established personal control over Egypt, assuming the title of pharaoh in 304 BC. The Ptolemaic line ended in 30 BC with the suicide of Queen Cleopatra. The Emperor Augustus then established direct Roman control over Egypt, initiating almost seven centuries of Roman and Byzantine rule.

Egypt was invaded and conquered by Arab forces in 642 AD and a process of Arabization and Islamization ensued. The French arrived in Egypt in 1798 until an Anglo-Ottoman invasion force drove out the French in 1801. Following a period of chaos, the Albanian Muhammad Ali obtained control of the country.

In 1882 the British occupied Egypt and declared a formal protectorate over Egypt on December 18, 1914. In deference to growing nationalist feelings, Britain unilaterally declared Egyptian independence on February 28, 1922. King Faud I ruled after independence until 1952, when he was overthrown by Gamal Abdel Nasser. Upon Nasser's death, Anwar el-Sadat took over the leadership until he was assassinated in 1981 and succeeded by Hosni Mubarak.

The Mubarak government has come under increasing fire from Muslim fundamentalists who in 1992 began launching violent attacks against tourists, Coptic Christians, and government officials. Shortly before parliamentary elections in 1995, Mubarak accused the opposition Muslim Brotherhood of aiding and abetting some of the Muslim fundamentalist groups. A number of members of the Muslim Brotherhood were arrested and imprisoned. Mubarak's National Democratic Party won an overwhelming victory in the parliamentary balloting. Since that time, Egypt has refused to release any of the religious zealots, and violence against tourists and Coptic Christians has increased. Yet, Mubarak's continued reliance on the military and his ban on Islamist political opposition threatens his regime's stability, particularly when ordinary Egyptians continue to face economic hardship.

The Egyptian population is fairly homogenous—Mediterranean and Arab influences appear in the north, as well as some mixing in the south with the Nubians of northern Sudan. Ethnic minorities include a small number of Bedouin Arab nomads dispersed in the eastern and western deserts and in the Sinai, as well as some 50,000 to 200,000 Nubians clustered along the Nile in Upper Egypt.

Eritrea

Official name: State of Eritrea
Independence: May 27, 1993
Area: 46,842 sq. mi
Form of government: Transitional government
Capital: Asmara
International relations: OAU, UN
Currency: Eritrean nafka
Population: (1998) 3.8 million
Ethnic divisions: Tigrinya 50%, Tigre and Kunama 40%, other 10%
Religious groups: Muslim 50%, Monophysite Christian 50%
Languages spoken: Tigrinya, Tigre, Afar, English, Arabic
Literacy: 51.4% (1995)
Exports: Livestock, sorghum, textiles
Imports: Processed goods, machinery, petroleum
Primary trade partners: Ethiopia, Italy, Saudi Arabia, United Kingdom, United States, Yemen

Eritrea was an integral part of the kingdom of Aksum and has shared its destiny with Ethiopia. Islamic colonists became established in the coastal area and dominate the region until the later half of the nineteenth century, when Egyptians settled in the area. Founded in 1890 by the Italians, the colony of Eritrea was annexed by Ethiopia after World War II. For years the Eritrian People's Liberation Forum waged a struggle for independence that was eventually won on May 25, 1993.

Since independence, neighboring Sudan and Eritrea have frequently swapped charges that one was helping opposition groups seeking the overthrow of the other's government. This growing enmity resulted in a severing of diplomatic relations between the two in December 1994. In 1996 Eritrea skirmished briefly with both Djibouti over a contested border and with Yemen over ownership of a collection of small Red Sea Islands. Perhaps most seriously though, armed conflict with Ethiopia erupted again in June 1998. The immediate cause of the fighting was again a disputed border, but tensions over trade issues had been building for months. Despite efforts by the United States, the Organization of African Unity, and neighboring African countries to resolve the conflict diplomatically, both sides continued to arm themselves.

Equatorial Guinea

Official name: Republic of Equatorial Guinea
Independence: October 12, 1968
Area: 10,831 sq. mi.
Form of government: Multiparty
Capital: Malabo
International relations: EU, OAU, UN
Currency: CFA franc
Income: (per capita US$) 700 (1996)
Population: (1997) 442,516
Ethnic divisions: Fang 80%, Bubi 15%, other 5%
Religious groups: Roman Catholic 98%, Protestant, traditional belief
Languages spoken: Spanish (official), Fang, Bubi, pidgin, English, French, other tribal languages
Literacy: 78.5% (1995)
Exports: Coffee, timber, cacao beans

Men accompanied by camels in Agordat, Eritrea (Cory Langley).

Imports: Petroleum, food, beverages, clothing, machinery
Primary trade partners: Spain, Cameroon, Nigeria, United States

The first inhabitants of the region that is now Equatorial Guinea are believed to have been Pygmies, of whom only isolated pockets remain in northern Rio Muni. Bantu migrations between the seventeenth and nineteenth centuries brought the coastal tribes and the Fang people to the area.

The Portuguese, seeking a route to India, landed on the island of Bioko in 1471. The Portuguese retained control until 1778, when the island and adjacent islets were ceded to Spain. From 1827 to 1843, Britain established a base on the island to combat the slave trade. Conflicting claims to the mainland were settled in 1900 by the Treaty of Paris.

In 1959 the Spanish territory of the Gulf of Guinea was established. In 1963 the name of the country was changed to Equatorial Guinea. In March 1968 under pressure from Equatoguinean nationalists and the United Nations, Spain announced that it would grant independence to Equatorial Guinea. In September 1968, Macias Macías Nguema was elected first president of Equatorial Guinea, and independence was granted in October. A military coup occurred in 1979 deposing Nguema, who was put to death for "crimes against humanity." Lieutenant Colonel Teodoro Obiang Nguema Mbasogo, leader of the coup that brought down Nguema, succeeded him as president. Although Obiang's government made a show of various political reforms over the past few decades, outside observers remain harshly critical of the regime's repressive policies. In addition, Obiang's government has been sharply criticized for the mishandling of the national economy including the oil boom of the 1990s.

The majority of the Equatoguinean people are of Bantu origin. The largest tribe, the Fang, constitute eighty percent of the population and are divided into about 67 clans. Those to the north of Rio Benito on Rio Muni speak Fang-Ntumu, and those to the south speak Fang-Okak, two mutually intelligible dialects. The Bubi, who form 15 percent of the population, are indigenous to Bioko Island. In addition, several coastal tribes exist, who are sometimes referred to as "Playeros," and include the Ndowes, Bujebas, Balengues, and Bengas on the mainland and small islands, and Fernandinos, a Creole community, on Bioko. These groups comprise five percent of the population.

A mosque in Axum, Ethiopia (Cory Langley).

Ethiopia

Official name: Federal Democratic Republic of Ethiopia
Area: 435,186 sq. mi.
Form of government: Federal republic
Capital: Addis Ababa
International relations: EU, IMF, OAU, UN
Currency: Birr
Income: (per capita US$) 100 (1996)
Population: (1998) 57 million
Ethnic divisions: Oromo 40%, Amhara and Tigre 32%, other 28%
Religious groups: Muslim 45%, Ethiopian Orthodox Christian 40%, traditional beliefs 15%
Languages spoken: Amharic (official), Tigrinya, Orominga, Arabic, English
Literacy: 35% (1991)
Exports: Coffee, hides and skins, live animals
Imports: Capital goods, consumer goods, fuel
Primary trade partners: United States, Germany, Italy, Saudi Arabia, Japan

Ethiopia is the oldest independent country in Africa and one of the oldest in the world. Herodotus, the Greek historian of the fifth century BC, describes ancient Ethiopia in his writings, and the Old Testament of the Bible records the Queen of Sheba's visit to Jerusalem. Missionaries from Egypt and Syria introduced Christianity in the fourth century AD Europeans did not make contact with Ethiopia until the Portuguese in 1493.

In 1930, Haile Selassie was crowned emperor. His reign was interrupted in 1936 when Italian fascist forces invaded and occupied Ethiopia. The emperor was eventually forced into exile in England despite his plea to the League of Nations for intervention. Five years later, the Italians were defeated by British and Ethiopian forces, and the emperor returned to the throne. After a period of civil unrest, which began in February 1974, the aging Haile Selassie was deposed on September 13, 1974. After deposing Selasie, the military, led by Col. Mariam Haile Mengistu, took over the government and nationalized nearly all the country's economic institutions.

Discontent had been spreading throughout Ethiopian urban elites, and an escalating series of mutinies in the armed forced, demonstrations, and strikes led to the seizure of state power by the armed forces coordinating committee, which later became the Provisional Military Administrative Council (PMAC). The PMAC formally declared its intent to remake Ethiopia into a socialist state. It finally destroyed its opposition in a program of mass arrests and executions known as the "red terror," which lasted from November 1977 to March 1978. An estimated 10,000 people, mostly in Addis Ababa, were killed by government forces. Mengistu's failure to respond to growing national problems—droughts, civil war with Eritrea and Tigray, and declining Soviet aid—ended his rule. Early in 1991, he was forced into exile in Zimbabwe by forces of the Ethiopian People's Revolutionary Democratic Front (EPRDF), led by Meles Zenawi.

In 1994, the economy stagnated, the government's heavy regulation of commerce discouraged agricultural production and food distribution, and famine threatened Ethiopia. International assistance saved many lives, however, and in 1995 the government finally established a process for returning nationalized land to private control. This redistribution of land appeared to improve Ethiopia's agricultural fortunes: the country enjoyed good harvests in both 1996 and 1997.

In the mid-1990s, Ethiopia also witnessed significant political achievements: delegates to a new legislative body, the Council of People's Representatives, were elected; and a new constitution giving special rights to several ethnic rights was also adopted. The name of the country was officially changed to the Federal Democratic Republic of Ethiopia in August 1995—the same month that Meles Zenawi was elected prime minister by the new legislature. However, the late 1990s were marked by ethnic strife and violent raids carried out by soldiers discharged at the end of Ethiopia's long civil war. In 1998 a border dispute with neighboring Eritrea threatened to end Ethiopia's peaceful recovery from years of warfare.

Ethiopia's population is highly diverse. Most of its people speak a Semitic or Cushitic language. The Amhara, Tigreans, and Oromo make up more than three-fourths of the population, but there are more than forty different ethnic groups within Ethiopia.

Gabon
Official name: Gabonese Republic
Independence: August 17, 1960
Area: 103,348 sq. mi.
Form of government: Multiparty republic
Capital: Libreville
International relations: EU, OAU, UN
Currency: CFA franc
Income: (per capita US$) 5070 (1996)
Population: (1998) 1.2 million
Ethnic divisions: Fang, Myene, Bapounou, Eschira, Bandjabi, Beteke/Obamba
Religious groups: Christian, Muslim, traditional belief
Languages spoken: French (official), Fang, Myene, Bateke, Bapounou/Eschira, Bandjabi
Literacy: 63.3% (1995)

Exports: Crude petroleum, manganese, uranium
Imports: Foodstuffs, chemicals, petroleum products, consumer goods
Primary trade partners: United States, France, Japan, Germany

Gabon's first European visitors were Portuguese traders who arrived in the fifteenth century. The coast became a center of the slave trade. Dutch, British, and French traders later came in the sixteenth century. France assumed the status of protector by signing treaties with Gabonese coastal chiefs in 1839 and 1841. In 1910 Gabon became one of the four territories of French Equatorial Africa, a federation that survived until 1959. The territories became independent in 1960 as the Central African Republic, Chad, Congo (Brazzaville), and Gabon, which was led by Léon M'ba after independence. Upon his death in 1967, Albert Bongo took over as head of state. Reelected in 1973, 1979, and 1986, Bongo faced growing opposition inside Gabon as the 1990s began. The Bongo administration moved toward establishment of a multiparty system, but early attempts in 1990 were rejected by opposition parties that charged Bongo's regime with fraud. A constitution adopted in 1991 formalized the multiparty system, and in the first elections under the new system in December 1993, Bongo received 51.5 percent of the presidential vote. Unrest soon broke out in reaction to these widely regarded fraudulent elections. This led to mediation and all opposition parties being brought into the government. In 1996, a new constitution was approved by voters adding a senate to the legislature.

Almost all Gabonese are of Bantu origin. Gabon has at least forty tribal groups, with separate languages and cultures; the largest group is the Fang. Other tribes include the Myene, Bandjabi, Eshira, Bapounou, Bateke/Obamba, and Okande.

Gambia
Official name: Republic of The Gambia
Independence: February 18, 1965
Area; 4,361 sq. mi.
Form of government: Multiparty
Capital: Banjul
International relations: Commonwealth, EU, OAU, UN
Currency: Dalasi
Income: (per capita US$) 330 (1995)
Population: (1997) 1.3 million
Ethnic divisions: Mandinka 36.1%, Fula 16.8%, Wolof 13.4%, Jola 9.2%, Serahuli 7.3%, other 1.4%
Religious groups: Muslim 85%, Christian traditional belief
Languages spoken: English (official), Mandinka, Wolof, Fula, other tribal languages
Literacy: 38.6% (1995)
Exports: Groundnuts, fish, cotton lint

Imports: Foodstuffs, consumer goods, raw materials, fuel
Primary trade partners: United Kingdom, United States, Japan

Gambia was once part of the Empire of Ghana and the Kingdom of Songhai. When the Portuguese visited in the fifteenth century, it was part of the Kingdom of Mali. By the sixteenth century, Portuguese slave traders and gold seekers had settled and had sold exclusive trade rights on the Gambia River to English merchants. During the late seventeenth century and throughout the eighteenth century, England and France struggled continuously for political and commercial supremacy in the regions of the Senegal and Gambia Rivers.

In 1807 slave trading was abolished throughout the British Empire, and the British tried unsuccessfully to end the slave traffic in Gambia. An 1889 agreement with France established the present boundaries, and Gambia became a British Crown colony. Gambia achieved independence on February 18, 1965, as a constitutional monarchy within the British Commonwealth. In 1970 Gambia became a republic. Several attempts were made to establish a post-independence union with Senegal. A contingent of Senegalese soldiers were stationed in Gambia, but the arrangement soured. Coupled with mounting economic problems, the confederation collapsed in 1989, although a new friendship treaty between the two countries was signed in 1991. Sir Dawda K. Jawara, who had led the country since independence in 1965, was overthrown by the military in July 1994. The leaders of the coup set up a provisional ruling council headed by Yayeh Jammeh. Pressured to restore democracy, Jammeh adopted a new constitution in August 1996 that was widely criticized for the restrictions imposed on opposition parties. Jammeh retired from the military and ran successfully for president in September 1996.

Ghana

Official name: Republic of Ghana
Independence: March 6, 1957
Area: 92,100 sq. mi.
Form of government: Constitutional democracy
Capital: Accra
International relations: Commonwealth, EU, OAU, UN
Currency: Cedi
Income: (per capita US$) 360 (1996)
Population: (1997) 18.5 million
Ethnic divisions: Akan, Ewe, Ga
Religious groups: Christian 43%, traditional belief 38%, Muslim 12%, other 8%
Languages spoken: English (official), Akan 44%, Mole-Dagbani 16%, Ewe 13%, Ga-Adangbe 8%
Literacy: 64.5% (1995)
Exports: Cocoa, diamonds, gold, manganese ore, wood

Imports: Petroleum, consumer goods, capital equipment
Primary trade partners: Germany, United Kingdom, United States, Japan

The first contact between Europe and the Gold Coast dates to 1470 when a party of Portuguese arrived. For the next three centuries, the English, Danes, Dutch, Germans, and Portuguese controlled various parts of the coastal areas. In 1821 the British government took control of the British trading forts on the Gold Coast. In 1844 Fanti chiefs in the area signed an agreement with the British. Between 1826 and 1900 the British fought a series of campaigns against the Ashantis, whose kingdom was located inland. By 1902, the British had succeeded in colonizing the Ashanti region.

On March 6, 1957, the United Kingdom relinquished its control over the Colony of the Gold Coast and Ashanti, the Northern Territories Protectorate, and British Togoland. The Gold Coast and the former British Togoland merged to form what is now Ghana. Focusing on anti-imperialism and pan-Africanism, Ghana became a model for the whole continent. Kwame Nkrumah, which had led Ghana to independence, was idolized throughout the continent. However, in the years that followed, Nkrumah turned increasingly dictatorial. In 1966 he was overthrown and went into exile in nearby Guinea. When Jerry Rawlings, who had masterminded two successfuly coups in 1979 and 1981, became head of state in 1982, he promised to return the country to pluralism. In 1992 he was elected to the presidency in a multiparty election and won reelection in 1996. With an improved economic and political climate, the appointment of Kofi Annan to head the United Nations in 1997, and President Clinton's historic 1998 visit, Ghana's prominence among African nations has been restored.

Most Ghanaians descend from migrating tribes that probably came down the Volta River valley in the thirteenth century. Ethnically, Ghana is divided into small groups speaking more than fifty languages and dialects. Among the more important linguistic groups are the Akans, which include the Fantis along the coast and the Ashantis in the forest region north of the coast; the Guans, on the plains of the Volta River; the Ga and Ewe-speaking peoples of the south and southeast; and the Moshi-Dagomba-speaking tribes of the northern and upper regions.

Guinea

Official name: Republic of Guinea
Independence: October 2, 1958
Area: 94,927 sq. mi.
Form of government: Republic
Capital: Conakry
International relations: EU, OAU, UN
Currency: Syli

Income: (per capita US$) 580 (1996)
Population: (1998) 7.5 million
Ethnic divisions: Foulah, Malinke, Soussou, 15 smaller groups
Religious groups: Muslim 85%, Christian 8%, traditional belief 7%
Languages spoken: French (official), tribal languages
Literacy: 36% (1995)
Exports: Agricultural products, minerals, bauxite, coffee
Imports: Petroleum products, metals, machinery, transport equipment, foodstuffs, textiles
Primary trade partners: United States, Belgium, France, Côte d'Ivoire, Ireland

The empires of Ghana, Mali, and Songhai spanned the period from about the tenth to the fifteenth centuries. French military penetration into the area began in the mid-nineteenth century. By signing treaties with the French in the 1880s, Guinea's Malinke leader, Samory Toure, secured a free hand to expand eastward. In 1890 he allied himself with the Toucouleur Empire and Kingdom of Sikasso and tried to expel the French from the area. However, he was defeated in 1898, and France gained control of Guinea and the Ivory Coast (now Côte d'Ivoire).

Guinea became an independent republic in 1958 and voted against entering the French community. Se'kou Touré was the first president until his death in 1984. Shortly after his death, the interim government was ousted in a military coup led by Colonel Lansana Conté, who became president and leader of the Military Committee for National Rectification. He took ambitious steps to democratize the nation and dismantle the existing socialist state. In 1993 Conté was elected president in the country's first multiparty elections. A military mutiny in 1996 took some sixty lives before the president was able to negotiate a truce with his troops. In an attempt to restore confidence in his ability to improve the financial situation of the country, Conté appointed an economist, Sidya Touré, to the office of prime minister that same year.

Guinea consists of four main ethnic groups—Peuls (Foulah or Foulani), who inhabit the mountainous Fouta Djallon; Malinkes (or Mandingos), in the savannah regions; Soussous in the coastal areas; and Forestal tribes in the forest regions.

Guinea-Bissau

Official name: Republic of Guinea-Bissau
Independence: September 24, 1973
Area: 13,946 sq. mi.
Form of government: Multiparty
Capital: Bissau
International relations: EU, OAU, UN
Currency: Guinea peso

Income: (per capita US$) 250 (1996)
Population: (1998) 1.2 million
Ethnic divisions: Balanta 27%, Fula 23%, Mandinka 12%, Manjaco 11%, Papel 10%, Biafada 3%, Mancanha 3%, Bijago 3%
Religious groups: Traditional belief 65%, Muslim 30%, Christian 5%
Languages spoken: Portuguese (official); Criolo, tribal languages
Literacy: 54.9% (1995)
Exports: Coconuts, fish, groundnuts
Imports: Foodstuffs, transportation equipment, petroleum products
Primary trade partners: Portugal, Spain, Senegal, Netherlands

The rivers of Guinea and the islands of Cape Verde were one of the first areas in Africa explored by the Portuguese in the fifteenth century. Portugal claimed Portuguese Guinea in 1446. In 1630 a "captaincy-general" of Portuguese Guinea was established to administer the territory. With the assistance of local tribes, the Portuguese entered the slave trade, exporting large numbers of Africans to the New World through Cape Verde. The slave trade declined in the nineteenth century, and Bissau, originally founded as a fort in 1765, became the major commercial center.

In 1956 the African Party for the Independence of Guinea and Cape Verde (PAIGC) was organized by Amilcar Cabral and Raphael Barbosa. Despite the presence of more than 30,000 Portuguese troops, the PAIGC exercised influence over much of the country; the Portuguese were increasingly confined to their garrisons and larger towns. The PAIGC National Assembly declared the independence of Guinea-Bissau on December 24, 1973, the same year that PAIGC leader Amilcar Cabral was assassinated by the Portuguese secret police. Portugal granted *de jure* independence on September 19, 1974, when the United States recognized the new nation. Luís de Almeida Cabral, Amilcar's brother, became president of Guinea-Bissau and Cape Verde. Cape Verde later broke away from Guinea-Bissau and its leader, João Bernardo Vieira, who had overthrown Cabral in November 1980.

Vieira, who survived a coup attempt in November 1985, was elected to five-year terms as president in 1984, 1989, and 1994. However, his administration was criticized for entrenched corruption. During a five-month civil war in 1998, rebel forces seized most of the country and part of Bissau. In November 1998, Vieira agreed to a peace accord that called for new elections and the disarmament of the presidential guard. After the presidential guard refused to disarm though, a breakaway army faction drove Vieira from office in May 1999.

The population of Guinea-Bissau comprises several diverse tribal groups, each with its own language, customs, and social organization. The Fula and Mandinka tribes in the north and northeast of the country are mostly Muslim. Other important tribal groups are the Balanta and Papel, living in the southern coastal regions, and the Manjaco and Mancanha, occupying the central and northern coastal areas.

Kenya

Official name: Republic of Kenya
Independence: December 12, 1963
Area: 224,960 sq. mi.
Form of government: Multiparty
Capital: Nairobi
International relations: Commonwealth, EU, OAU, UN
Currency: Kenyan shilling
Income:(per capita US$) 340 (1996)
Population: (1998) 28.3 million
Ethnic divisions: Kikuyu 21%, Luhya 14%, Luo 13%, Kalenjin 11%, Kamba 11%, Kisii 6%, Meru 5%. Non-Africans 1%
Religious groups: Traditional belief 26%, Protestant 38%, Roman Catholic 28%, Muslim 6%
Languages spoken: Swahili (official), English, tribal languages
Literacy: 78.1% (1995)
Exports: Coffee, hides and skins, petroleum products, soda ash, tea
Imports: Machinery and transport equipment, petroleum and petroleum products, iron, steel
Primary trade partners: European Union countries, United States, African countries

The Cushitic-speaking people, who occupied the area that is now Kenya around 1000 BC, were known to have maintained contact with Arab traders during the first century AD. Arab and Persian settlements were founded along the coast as early as the eighth century AD. By then, Bantu and Nilotic peoples also had moved into the area. The Arabs were followed by the Portuguese in 1498, by Islamic control under the Imam of Oman in the 1600s, and by British influence in the nineteenth century. In 1885 European powers first partitioned East Africa into spheres of influence. In 1895 the British government established the East African Protectorate.

From October 1952 to December 1959, Kenya was under a state of emergency, arising from the Mau Mau rebellion against British colonial rule. The first direct elections for Africans to the legislative council took place in 1957, and then Kenya became fully independent on December 12, 1963. Jomo Kenyatta, a member of the predominant Kikuyu tribe and head of the Kenya African National Union, became Kenya's first president. He adopted a moderate, pro-Western policy and pursued

Masai warriors wearing traditional costumes at a Kenyan wedding in the Amboseli Game Reserve (Global Learning, Inc.).

capitalism internally, allowing Kenya to achieve a higher level of economic prosperity than its neighbors. Kenyatta died in 1978 and was succeeded by Daniel arap Moi, who in his first few years as president pursued a populist course. However, in 1982, the constitution was modified to make the country a one-party state. Mounting opposition to his repressive rule through the 1980s put increasing pressure on Moi, who in December 1991 agreed to legalize opposition political parties. Moi was reelected in 1992, although he continued to be the target of criticism from opposition parties, upset by cumbersome restrictions on their activities. In December 1997 Moi was again returned to office, leading to widespread violence and continual accusations of corruption, ethnic favoritism, and human rights abuses.

Lesotho

Official name: Kingdom of Lesotho
Independence: October 4, 1966
Area: 11,718 sq. mi.
Form of government: Constitutional monarchy
Capital: Maseru
International relations: Commonwealth, EU, OAU, UN
Currency: Maloti
Income: (per capita US$) 485 (1990)
Population: (1998) 2.1 million
Ethnic divisions: Basotho, Nguni
Religious groups: Roman Catholic, Lesotho Evangelical, Anglican
Languages spoken: English (official), Sesotho
Literacy: 71.4% (1995)
Exports: Diamonds, live animals, mohair, wool, wheat
Imports: Maize, building materials, apparel, vehicles, machinery, medicine
Primary trade partners: South Africa, Asia, United States

Until the end of the sixteenth century, Basutoland, now Lesotho, was sparsely populated by bushmen

(Qhuaique). Between the sixteenth and nineteenth centuries, refugees from surrounding areas gradually formed the Basotho ethnic group. In 1818 Moshoeshoe I, consolidated various Basotho groupings and became king. During his reign from 1823 to 1870, a series of wars with South Africa resulted in the loss of extensive lands, now known as the "Lost Territory." Moshoeshoe appealed to Queen Victoria for assistance, and in 1868 the country was placed under British protection.

In 1955, the Basutoland Council asked that it be empowered to legislate on internal affairs and, in 1959, a new constitution gave Basutoland its first elected legislature. On October 4, 1966, the new Kingdom of Lesotho attained full independence. Three years later, Leabua Jonathan became the head of state and embarked on repressing internal opposition. Years later, when he appeared to be losing the presidential elections, he seized power in order to retain his leadership. In 1986 Jonathan was overthrown by the military. On an interim basis, executive, and legislative powers were vested in King Moshoeshoe II, although most powers were exercised by a military council. Moshoeshoe II was exiled in March 1990 and replaced by his son, who was enthroned as Letsie III. After Letsie came under increasing criticism from leaders of neighboring states, he abdicated in 1995 and returned the crown to his father, Moshoeshoe II. The following year, Moshoeshoe was killed in an auto accident, and Letsie III returned to the throne.

Liberia

Official name: Republic of Liberia
Independence: July 26, 1847
Area: 43,000 sq. mi.
Form of government: Republic
Capital: Monrovia
International relations: EU, OAU, UN
Currency: Liberian dollar
Income: (per capita US$) 250 (1990)
Population: (1998 estimate) 2.8 million
Ethnic divisions: 5% descendants of freed American slaves, 95% indigenous tribes (the largest of which are Kpelle, Bassa, Gio, Kru, Grebo, Mano, Krahn, Gola, Gbandi, Loma, Kissi, Vai, Mandingo, and Belle)
Religious groups: Christian, Traditional belief, Muslim
Languages spoken: English (official), more than 20 tribal languages of the Niger-Congo language group
Literacy: 38.3% (1995)
Exports: Cocoa, coffee, diamonds, iron ore, rubber, wood
Imports: Mineral fuels, chemicals, transportation equipment, foodstuffs
Primary trade partners: United States, European Union countries, Japan

It is believed that the forebears of many present-day Liberians migrated into the area from the north and east between the twelfth and seventeenth centuries. Portuguese explorers visited Liberia's coast in 1461, and during the next three hundred years, European merchants and coastal Africans engaged in trade.

The history of modern Liberia dates from 1816, when the American Colonization Society, a private organization, was given a charter by the United States Congress to send freed slaves to the west coast of Africa. The United States government, under President James Monroe, provided funds and assisted in negotiations with native chiefs for the ceding of land for this purpose. The first settlers landed at the site of Monrovia in 1822. In 1838 the settlers united to form the Commonwealth of Liberia, under a governor appointed by the American Colonization Society.

In 1847 Liberia became Africa's first independent republic. The republic's first one hundred years have been described as a "century of survival" due to attempts by neighboring colonial powers, particularly France and Britain, to encroach on Liberia. Independence gave power to the black elite of American origin and technically excluded the indigenous population, creating social tension. In 1980 Sargent Samuel Doe and his Council of Popular Redemption came to power in a bloody coup. Doe leaned on the Soviet Union and established himself as a dictator. He was killed, however, during an insurrection led by the National Patriotic Front, a rebel group led by Charles Taylor. Taylor's group pitted itself against the Liberian army, a monitoring group from the Economic Community of West African States (ECOWAS), and the United Liberation Movement of Liberia for Democracy (ULIMO), a group made up of former Doe allies. Several attempts at ending the civil war were unsuccessful, and the strife continued well into the 1990s. Finally in 1997 a program to disarm warring factions was declared a success. In July of that year, Taylor was elected president by a landslide. He has worked to rebuild the nation's economy, shattered by years of civil war.

Libya

Official name: Socialist People's Libyan Arab Jamahiriya
Independence: December 24, 1951
Area: 679,536 sq. mi.
Form of government: Military
Capital: Tripoli
International relations: Arab League, OAU, UN
Currency: Libyan dinar
Income: (per capita US$) 6,060 (1990)
Population: (1997) 5.7 million
Ethnic divisions: Arab and Arab/Berber 80%, Berber 15%, Touareg and Tebous Arab
Religious groups: Sunni Muslim 97%, other 3%
Languages spoken: Arabic

Literacy: 76.2% (1995)

Exports: Crude oil, refined petroleum products, natural gas

Imports: Machinery, transportation equipment, food

Primary trade partners: Italy, Germany, Spain, United Kingdom, Turkey, Greece

In the seventh century AD, Arabs conquered the area that is now Libya. In the following centuries, most of the inhabitants adopted Islam and the Arabic language and culture. The Ottoman Turks then conquered the country in the sixteenth century. Libya remained part of their empire—although, at times, virtually autonomous—until Italy invaded in 1911 and, after years of resistance, incorporated Libya as its colony.

King Idris I, Emir of Cyrenaica, led a Libyan resistance to Italian occupation between the two world wars. Under the terms of the 1947 peace treaty with the Allies, Italy relinquished all claims to Libya. On November 21, 1949, the United Nations General Assembly passed a resolution stating that Libya should become independent before January 1, 1952. Libya declared its independence on December 24, 1951.

In a military coup of 1969, King Idris was overthrown by Muammar al-Qaddafi, who nationalized all the petroleum resources and embarked on a program of support for international terrorism against the Western countries. Some of Qaddafi's activities have also created friction with neighboring countries and, in 1986, the United States bombed Tripoli and Benghazi. Five years later, during the Persian Gulf War, Libya opposed Iraq's seizure of Kuwait as well as the use of force against Iraq by the United States and its allies. In 1992, the United Nations imposed sanctions against Libya for its refusal to extradite two suspects in the 1988 bombing of Pan Am Flight 103 over Scotland. Those sanctions were lifted in 1999, when Libya turned the suspects over to the UN for trial by a Scottish court. Despite five unsuccessful coup attempts and considerable international animosity, Qaddafi remains firmly in office as leader of Libya.

Madagascar

Official name: Republic of Madagascar

Independence: June 26, 1960

Area: 226,658 sq. mi.

Form of government: Republic

Capital: Antananarivo

International relations: EU, OAU, UN

Currency: Malagasy franc

Income:(per capita US$) 300 (1996)

Population: (1998) 14.5 million

Ethnic divisions: 18 Malagasy tribes, small groups of Comorian, French, Indian, and Chinese

Religious groups: Traditional belief, Christian, Muslim

Languages spoken: Malagasy (official), French (official)

Literacy: 80.2% (1995)

Exports: Coffee, cloves, crude petroleum, sugar, vanilla

Imports: Intermediate manufactured goods, capital goods, petroleum, food

Primary trade partners: France, United States, Germany, Japan

Located east of the African mainland in the Indian Ocean, Madagascar is home to people who arrived from Africa and Asia during the first five centuries AD. Three major kingdoms ruled the island—Betsimisaraka, Merina, and Sakalava. In the seventh century AD, Arabs established trading posts in the coastal areas of what is now Madagascar. Portuguese sighted the island in the sixteenth century and, in the late seventeenth century, the French established trading posts along the east coast.

In the 1790s, the Merina rulers succeeded in establishing hegemony over the major part of the island including the coast. The Merina ruler and the British governor of Mauritius concluded a treaty abolishing the slave trade, which had been important in Madagascar's economy and, in return, the island received British military assistance. British influence remained strong for several decades. The British accepted the imposition of a French protectorate over Madagascar in 1885. France established control by military force in 1895, and the Merina monarchy was abolished. The Malagasy Republic was proclaimed on October 14, 1958, as an autonomous state within the French Community. A period of provisional government ended with the adoption of a constitution in 1959 and full independence in 1960.

Madagascar pursued a moderate policy after independence, and collaboration with France continued until 1972 when a military coup installed a socialist government headed by General Gabriel Ramanantsoa. Ramanantsoa, who aligned his government with the East Bloc, was ousted and replaced by Lieutenant Commander Didier Ratsiraka in 1975. Late that year, the country was renamed the Democratic Republic of Madagascar. Through the 1980s and into the early 1990s, Ratsiraka's government faced growing opposition and, in August 1991, the government promised to make democratic reforms. A year later a new constitution was approved by popular vote. Ratsiraka was defeated by Albert Zafy in a presidential runoff election in 1993. Zafy was impeached in 1996 for failure to reach agreement with the International Monetary Fund on the Malagasy franc's exchange rate, stepped down in October 1996, and ran unsuccessfully against Ratsiraka for the presidency in December 1996.

Madagascar's population is predominantly of Asian and African origin. The largest groups are the

Vendors selling their wares in Madagascar (Cory Langley).

Betsimisaraka (one million), the Tsimihety (500,000), and the Sakalava (500,000).

Malawi
Official name: Republic of Malawi
Independence: July 6, 1964
Area: 45,747 sq. mi.
Form of government: Multiparty
Capital: Lilongwe
International relations: EU, OAU, UN
Currency: Kwacha
 Income: (per capita US$) 220 (1996)
Population: (1998) 9.8 million
Ethnic divisions: Chewa, Nyanja, Tumbuka, Yao, Lomwe, Sena, Tonga, Ngoni Asians
Religious groups: Protestant, Roman Catholic, Muslim, traditional belief
Languages spoken: Chicewa and English (official), tribal languages
Literacy: 56.4% (1995)
Exports: Cotton, groundnuts, sugar, tea, tobacco
Imports: Food, petroleum products, semimanufactured goods, transportation equipment
Primary trade partners: United States, United Kingdom, South Africa

Hominid remains and stone implements dating back more than 1 million years, have been identified in Malawi. Early humans are believed to have inhabited the area surrounding Lake Malawi 50,000 to 60,000 years ago.

Malawi derives its name from the Maravi, a Bantu people who came from the southern Congo about six hundred years ago. By the sixteenth century, the two divisions of the tribe had established a kingdom stretching from north of today's Nkhotakota to the Zambezi River in the south and from Lake Malawi in the east to the Luangwa River in Zambia in the west.

The Portuguese first reached the area in the sixteenth century. David Livingston reached the shore of Lake Malawi in 1859. By 1878 a number of traders, mostly from Scotland, formed the African Lakes Company to supply goods and services to the missionaries. In 1891 the British established the Nyasaland Protectorate. Nyasaland joined with Northern and Southern Rhodesia in 1953 to form the Federation of Rhodesia and Nyasaland.

Throughout the 1950s, pressures were exerted within Nyasaland for independence. In July 1958, Dr. H. Kamazu Banda returned to the country after a long stay in the United States (where he had obtained his medical degree at Meharry Medical College in 1937), the United

Men mending their fishing nets in Malawi (Cory Langley).

Kingdom, and Ghana. He assumed leadership of the Nyasaland African Congress, which later became the Malawi Congress Party (MCP). In 1959 Banda was sent to Gwele Prison for his political activities but was released in 1960.

On April 15, 1961, the MCP won an overwhelming victory in elections for a new legislative council. In a second constitutional conference in London in November of 1962, the British government agreed to give Nyasaland self-governing status the following year. Dr. Banda became prime minister on February 1, 1963, although the British still controlled Malawi's financial security and judicial systems. The Federation of Rhodesia and Nyasaland was dissolved on December 31, 1963, and Malawi became fully independent on July 6, 1964. Two years later, Malawi adopted a new constitution and became a republic with Dr. Banda as its first president. In 1994, in the country's first multiparty elections, Bakili Muluzi, leader of the United Democratic Front and a former cabinet minister, defeated Banda. Muluzi freed political prisoners and closed three prisons. In 1995 Banda and a top aide went on trial for the 1983 murders of four government officials: both were acquitted in December 1995.

The Chewas constitute ninety percent of the population of the central region; the Nyanja tribe predominates in the south and the Tumbuka in the north. In addition, significant numbers of the Tongas live in the north; Ngonis—an offshoot of the Zulus who came from South Africa in the early 1800s—live in the lower northern and lower central regions; and the Yao, who are mostly Muslim, live along the southeastern border with Mozambique.

Mali
Official name: Republic of Mali
Independence: September 22, 1960
Area: 478,767 sq. mi.
Form of government: Multiparty republic
Capital: Bamako
International relations: EU, OAU, UN
Currency: CFA franc
Population: (1998) 10.1 million
Ethnic divisions: Mande (Bambara or Bamana, Malinke, Sarakole) 50%, Peul 17% Voltaic 12%, Songhai 6%, Tuareg and Moor 10%, other 5%
Religious groups: Islam 90%, traditional belief 10%
Languages spoken: French (official), Bambara (spoken by about 80% of the population)
Literacy: 31% (1995)
Exports: Cotton, groundnuts, live animals, gold
Imports: Machinery and equipment, food, construction material
Primary trade partners: France, France Zone countries, European Union countries

Mali is the cultural heir to succession of ancient African empires—Ghana, Malinke, and Songhai—that occupied the West African savanna. The Ghana empire, dominated by the Soninke people and centered in the area along the Malian-Mauritanian frontier, was a powerful trading state from about 700 to 1075 AD. The Malinke kingdom of Mali, from which the republic takes its name, had its origins on the upper Niger River in the eleventh century. Expanding rapidly in the thirteenth century under the leadership of Soundiata Keita, it reached its height about 1325, when it conquered Timbuktu and Gao. The Songhai empire expanded its power from its center in Gao during the period of 1465 to 1530. At its peak under Askia Mohammad I, it encompassed the Hausa states as far as Kano (in present-day Nigeria) and much of the territory that had belonged to the Mali Empire in the west. It was destroyed by a Moroccan invasion in 1591.

French military penetration of the area began around 1880. A French civilian governor of Soudan (the French name for the area) was appointed in 1893, but resistance to French control was not abrogated until 1898 when the Malinke warrior, Samory Toure, was defeated after seven years of war. In January 1959, Soudan joined

A Malian street scene (Cory Langley).

Senegal to form the Mali Federation, which became fully independent within the French Community on June 20, 1960. The federation collapsed on August 20, 1960, when Senegal seceded. On September 22, Soudan proclaimed itself the Republic of Mali and withdrew from the French Community.

The first head of state—Modibo Keita—followed a socialist orientation and gradually increased his authoritarian leadership. In 1968, the Military Committee of National Liberation coup overthrew Keita's government and set up a ruling junta led by Lieutenant Moussa Traoré. Although the Traoré government did little to advance the country's economy, Traoré was returned to office in 1979 and 1985. However, a military coup in March 1991 deposed Traoré. In January 1992 a new constitution was adopted and Alpha Oumar Kounaré was elected president in multiparty elections in April 1992. He was reelected to office in May 1997.

Mali's population consists of diverse sub-Saharan ethnic groups, sharing similar historic, cultural, and religious traditions. Exceptions are the Tuaregs and Moors, desert nomads, who are related to the North African Berbers.

Mauritania
Official name: Islamic Republic of Mauritania
Independence: November 28, 1960
Area: 397,995 sq. mi.
Form of government: Republic
Capital: Nouakchott
International relations: Arab League, EU, OAU, UN
Currency: Ouguiya
Income: (per capita US$) 470 (1996)
Population: (1998) 2.5 million
Ethnic divisions: Arab-Berber, Arab-Berber-Negroid, Negroid
Religious groups: Muslim
Languages spoken: Hassaniya Arabic (national), French (official), Pular, Wolof, and Soninke
Literacy: 37.7% (1995)
Exports: Fish, gypsum, iron ore
Imports: Foodstuffs, consumer goods, petroleum products, capital goods
Primary trade partners: Japan, Italy, Algeria, China, United States

Archaeological evidence suggests that Berber and Negroid Mauritanians lived beside one another before the spread of the desert drove them southward. Migration of these people increased during the third and fourth centuries AD, when Berber groups arrived seeking pasture land for their herds and safety from political unrest and war in the north. The Berbers established a loose confederation, called the Sanhadja, and trading towns to facilitate the trade of gold, ivory, and slaves.

In the tenth century, conquests by warriors of the Soudanese Kingdom of Ghana broke up the Berber confederation. In the eleventh century, the conquest of the Western Sahara regions by a Berber tribe decimated the Ghanaian kingdom and firmly established Islam throughout Mauritania. However, these people were defeated by Arab invaders in the sixteenth century.

French military penetration of Mauritania began early in the twentieth century. However, the area did not come under French control until about 1934. Until independence, the French governed the country largely by relying on the authority of the tribal chiefs, some of whom, such as the Emirs of Trarza and Adrar, had considerable authority. Under French occupation, slavery was legally abolished.

Mauritania became a French colony in 1920. The Islamic Republic of Mauritania was proclaimed in November 1958. Mauritania became independent on November 28, 1960, and withdrew from the French Community in 1966.

Mokhtar Ould Daddah, leader of the Mauritian People's Party was the first head of state, but a series of coups took place: the first, in 1978, replaced Daddah with Col. Moustabpha Ould Mohammed Salek, who was then replaced by Prime Minister Mohammed Khouma Ould Haidalla. In 1984, another coup, this one led by Haidalla deputy Maawiya Ould Sid'Ahmed Taya, unseated Haidalla. Under increasing pressure to democratize, Taya in 1991 adopted a new constitution creating a multiparty state. In a disputed January 1992 election, Taya was chosen executive president. Even though important U.S. aid has been cut off due to a poor human rights record and allegations of slave trading, Taya was returned to office in 1996.

Moors, heterogeneous groups of Arab-Berber people who speak Hassaniya dialects, make up an estimated

Nomadic family of Mauritania (Laure Communications).

three-quarters of the population and are traditionally nomadic pastoralists. The country's black population—the Toucouleur, Soninke, Bambara, and Wolof—are mainly cultivators and are concentrated along the Senegal River.

Mauritius
Official name: Republic of Mauritius
Independence: March 12, 1968
Area: 788 sq. mi.
Form of government: Multiparty
Capital: Port Louis
International relations: Commonwealth, EU, OAU, UN
Currency: Rupee
Income: (per capita US$) 3790 (1996)
Population: (1998) 1.2 million
Ethnic divisions: Indo-Mauritian 68%, Creole 27%, Sino-Mauritian 3%, Franco-Mauritian 2%
Religious groups: Hindu, Muslim, Christian, Buddhist
Languages spoken: English (official), Creole, French, Hindi, Urdu, Hakka, Bhojpuri
Literacy: 82.9% (1995)
Exports: Garments, molasses, sugar, tea, textiles
Imports: Manufactured goods, capital equipment, foodstuffs, petroleum products, chemicals

Primary trade partners: European Union countries, United States, South Africa

Portuguese sailors first visited Mauritius in the early sixteenth century, although the island was known to Arabs and Malays much earlier. Dutch sailors, who named the island in honor of Prince Maurice of Nassau, established a small colony in 1638, but abandoned it in 1710. The French claimed Mauritius in 1715, renaming it Ile de France. In 1810 Mauritius was captured by the British, whose possession of the island was confirmed four years later by the Treaty of Paris. After slavery was abolished in 1835, indentured laborers from India brought an additional cultural influence to the island. Mauritius achieved independence on March 12, 1968. Sir Seewoosagur Ramgoolam, head of the Mauritius Labor Party (MLP), led the country for the first 14 years of independence. The opposition Mauritian Military Movement (MMM), under the leadership of Aneerood Jugnauth, came to power in 1982. Pushed from power in an internal MMM struggle, Jugnauth formed a new opposition party, the Mauritian Socialist Movement (MSM). The MSM joined with the MLP in 1983 to win a parliamentary majority. The MSM-MLP coalition was again victorious in both 1987 and 1991. In 1992, the country became a republic, and Cassam Uteem was elected president by the national assembly. In December 1995, Jugnauth was replaced as prime minister by Navin Ramgoolam, son of Seewoosagur Ramgoolam.

Twenty-seven percent of Mauritians are of mixed European and African descent, tracing their origins to the plantation owners and slaves who were the first to exploit the island's potential for growing sugar. Descendants of the Indian immigrants constitute 68 percent of the population and are the principal laborers in the sugar industry.

Mayotte (Mahoré)

Independence: n/a (overseas territory of France)
Area: 144 sq. mi.
Form of government: Represented in French National Assembly
Capital: Mamoudzou
Currency: French franc
Income: (per capita US$) 600 (1997 estimate)
Population: (1998 estimate) 115,000
Religious groups: Muslim 99%; remainder Christian (mostly Roman Catholic)
Languages spoken: Mahorian (a Swahili dialect), French
Exports: Coconut, sugar cane, vanilla, ylang-ylang
Imports: Building materials, machinery, transportation equipment, metals, chemicals, apparel
Primary trade partners: France, Southeast Asian countries

Part of the Comoros archipelago, Mayotte shares its history with the Comoros Federal Islamic Republic. When Comoros declared independence in 1975, Mayotte voted to remain an overseas territory of France. Although Comoros has since claimed Mayotte, the French have promised the islanders that they may remain French citizens for as long as they wish. Both the United Nations and the Organization of African Unity, however, have recognized Mayotte as part of the Comoros.

Morocco

Official name: Kingdom of Morocco
Independence: March 2, 1956
Area: 172,414 sq. mi.
Form of government: Monarchy
Capital: Rabat
International relations: Arab League, UN
Currency: Dirham
Income: (per capita US$) 1,360 (1995)
Population: (1998) 29.1 million
Ethnic divisions: Arab-Berber
Religious groups: Sunni Muslim
Languages spoken: Arabic (official), French, Berber dialects
Literacy: 43.7% (1995)

Classic Arab architecture serves as an entranceway to Fez, Morocco (Cory Langley).

Exports: Phosphates and phosphoric acid, citrus fruits, clothing, fertilizers, preserved fish, vegetables
Imports: Food products
Primary trade partners: France, Spain, other European Union countries

Arab forces began occupying Morocco in the seventh century AD, bringing with them Arab civilization and Islam. Morocco's location and resources led to early competition among Europeans in Africa, beginning with successful Portuguese efforts to control the Atlantic coast in the fifteenth century. France showed a strong interest in Morocco as early as 1830. The Treaty of Fez (1912) made Morocco a protectorate of France. By the same treaty, Spain assumed the role of protecting power over the northern and southern (Saharan) zones. The Kingdom of Morocco recovered its political independence from France on March 2, 1956, and by agreements with Spain in 1956 and 1958.

Morocco's claim to sovereignty over the Western Sahara, also known as Spanish Sahara, is based largely on the historical argument of traditional loyalty of the Saharan tribal leaders to the Moroccan sultan as spiritual leader and ruler. The International Court of Justice, to which the issue was referred, delivered its opinion in 1975 that while historical ties exist between the inhabitants of the Western Sahara and Morocco, they are insufficient to establish Moroccan sovereignty.

Morocco, however, exerted pressure on Spain in 1974 and 1975 to relinquish the Western Sahara. When the Spanish left the territory in 1976, they ceded the northern two-thirds to Morocco and the southern one-third to Mauritania. However, the disposition of the territory was disputed by the Polisario Front, a nationalist guerrilla organization. Polisario declared the territory an independent nation. All claimants skirmished over the territory for years, until a cease-fire was declared in 1991. The dispute, however, continued to simmer late in the 1990s. In 1998 the United Nations scheduled a referendum for self-determination for Western Sahara, which is currently occupied by UN peacekeeping forces.

King Hassan II ruled Morocco from 1961 until his death in July 1999. Although he offered strong support for the Arab cause during the 1967 war with Israel, Hassan was identified by Arab extremists as soft on Israel, and several attempts were made on his life. In the late 1990s, Islamic extremists forced Hassan to create a new parliamentary body. Upon his death, Hassan's son, Mohamed VI, assumed the throne.

Mozambique

Official name: Republic of Mozambique
Independence: June 25, 1975
Area: 309,496 sq. mi.
Form of government: Multiparty
Capital: Maputo
International relations: EU, OAU, UN
Currency: Meticai
Income: (per capita US$) 100 (1996)
Population: (1998) 18.6 million
Ethnic divisions: Makua, Tsonga, Makonde, and other tribal groups
Religious groups: Traditional belief 50%, Muslim 30%, Christian 15%
Languages spoken: Portuguese (official), tribal languages
Literacy: 40.1% (1995)
Exports: Cotton, molasses, nuts, sugar, tea
Imports: Food, apparel, farm equipment, petroleum
Primary trade partners: South Africa, Spain, United States, United Kingdom

Mozambique's first inhabitants were Bushmanoid hunters and gatherers, ancestors of the Khoisani peoples. During the first four centuries AD, waves of Bantu-speaking peoples migrated from the north through the Zambezi River Valley and then gradually into the plateau and coastal areas. When Portuguese explorers reached Mozambique in 1498, Arab trading settlements had existed along the coast for several centuries. Later, traders and prospectors penetrated the hinterland seeking gold and slaves.

After World War II, while many European nations were granting independence to their colonies, Portugal clung to the concept that Mozambique and other Portuguese possessions were "overseas provinces." In 1962 several Mozambican anti-Portuguese political groups formed the Front for Liberation of Mozambique (FRELIMO) that in September, 1964, initiated an armed campaign against Portuguese colonial rule. After ten years of sporadic warfare and major political changes in Portugal, Mozambique became independent on June 25, 1975.

Samora Machel led Frelimo to independence in 1975, and immediately faced civil war with RENAMO (Mozambique National Resistance). More than 600,000 were killed in the civil war; farms, roads, railways were destroyed; and half of the population was dislocated. After Samora was killed in an air crash, Joaquím Chissano became head of state. A cease-fire was reached with RENAMO in 1992, and the country's first multiparty elections were held in October 1994. Chissano was elected president, and FRELIMO, his party, won 129 of 250 assembly seats. A United Nations peacekeeping force, which had been deployed in December 1992, was withdrawn from Mozambique in early 1995. Privatization of industries has led to massive foreign investment by international corporations and the World Bank.

The ten major ethnic groups living in Mozambique are divided into subgroups with diverse languages, dialects, cultures, and history; the largest are the Majua and Tsonga.

Namibia

Official name: Republic of Namibia
Independence: March 21, 1990
Area: 318,260 sq. mi.
Form of government: Multiparty
Capital: Windhoek
International relations: OAU, UN
Currency: Namibian dollar
Income: (per capita US$) $2,040 (1996)
Population: (1998) 1.6 million
Ethnic divisions: Black 87%; white 6%; mixed race 7%
Religious groups: Predominantly Christian, traditional belief
Languages spoken: English (official), Afrikaans, German, tribal languages
Literacy: 38% (1995)
Exports: Diamonds, gold, copper, cattle, fish
Imports: Foodstuffs, petroleum, machinery and equipment
Primary trade partners: South Africa, Switzerland, Germany, United States

Herero women and man wearing traditional costumes congregate at a fair in Namibia (Laure Communications).

In 1878 the United Kingdom annexed Walvis Bay on behalf of Cape Colony, and the area was incorporated into the Cape of Good Hope in 1884. In 1883, a German trader, Adolf Luderitz, claimed the remainder of the coastal region after negotiations with a local chief. German administration ended during World War I, when the territory was occupied by South African forces in 1915.

On December 17, 1920, South Africa undertook the administration of South West Africa under the terms of Article 22 of the Covenant of the League of Nations and a mandate agreement confirmed by the League Council. The mandate agreement gave South Africa full power of administration and legislation over the territory as an integral part of South Africa. During the 1960s, as other African nations gained independence, pressure mounted on South Africa to do so in South West Africa.

In 1966 the United Nations General Assembly revoked South Africa's mandate. Also in 1966, the South West Africa People's Organization (SWAPO) began guerrilla attacks on Namibia, infiltrating the territory from bases in Zambia. In a 1971 advisory opinion, the International Court of Justice upheld United Nation authority over Namibia, determining that the South African pres-

ence in Namibia was illegal and that South Africa, therefore, was obligated to withdraw its administration from Namibia immediately. In 1977 the United Nations approved Security Council Resolution 435 that called for the holding of elections in Namibia under U.N. supervision and the cessation of hostile acts by all parties. South Africa agreed to cooperate in achieving implementation of Resolution 435. Nevertheless, in December 1978, in defiance of the U.N. proposal, it unilaterally held elections in Namibia that were boycotted by SWAPO and other political parties.

Intense discussions between the concerned parties continued during the 1978–1988 period. In May 1988, a U.S. mediation team brought negotiators from Angola, Cuba, and South Africa and observers from the Soviet Union together in London. On April 1, the Republic of South Africa agreed to withdraw its troops. Implementation of Resolution 435 officially began on April 1, 1989. The elections held November 7–11, 1989, were certified as free and fair by the special representative, with SWAPO taking 57 percent of the vote; the Democratic Turnhalle Alliance, the principal opposition party, received 29 percent of the vote. By February 9, 1990, the constituent assembly had drafted and adopted a constitution. March 21 of that same year was set as the date for independence. SWAPO's Sam Nujoma won elections, and he became the first head of state in 1990. For the next four years, until February 1994, South Africa continued to administer a small Namibian enclave containing the nation's major seaport, Walvis Bay. In 1994 elections, SWAPO won 53 of 72 seats in the National Assembly. However, dissatisfaction with SWAPO and Nujoma has increased. The international community has criticized Nujoma's plans to run for a third term as president (which the constitution does not permit) as well as his government's lavish spending habits. Meanwhile, Namibia's strong labor unions have prevented significant cuts in the large state bureaucracy.

Namibia is one of the least populated countries in Africa. Namibia's indigenous Africans are of diverse linguistic and ethnic origins. The principal groups are the Ovambo, Kavango, Herero/Himba, Damara, mixed race ("Colored" and Rehoboth Baster), white (Afrikaner, German and Portuguese), Nama, Caprivian (Lozi), Bushman, and Tswana. The minority white population is primarily of South African, British, and German descent. Approximately sixty percent of the white population speaks Afrikaans (a variation of Dutch), thirty percent German, and ten percent English.

Niger

Official name: Republic of Niger
Independence: August 3, 1960
Area: 489,200 sq. mi.
Form of government: Transitional
Capital: Niamey
International relations: EU, OAU, UN
Currency: CFA franc
Income: (per capita US$) 210 (1996)
Population: (1998) 9.7 million
Ethnic divisions: Hausa 56%, Djerma 22%, Fulani 8.5% Tuareg 8%, Beri Beri (Kanouri) 4.3% Arab, Toubou, and Gourmantche 1.2%
Religious groups: Muslim, traditional belief, and Christians
Languages spoken: French (official), Hausa, Djerma
Literacy: 13.6% (1995)
Exports: Uranium ore, live animals, uranium
Imports: Consumer goods, machinery, vehicles, petroleum
Primary trade partners: France, Nigeria, Italy, Côte d'Ivoire

Considerable evidence indicates that about 600,000 years ago humans inhabited what has since become the desolate Sahara of northern Niger. Niger was an important economic crossroads, and the empires of Songhei, Mali, Gao, Kanem, and Bornu, as well as a number of Hausa states, claimed control over portions of the area.

A minaret in Agadez, Niger (United Nations).

During recent centuries, the nomadic Taureg formed large confederations, pushed southward and, siding with various Hausa states, clashed with the Fulani empire of Sokoto, which had gained control of much of the Hausa territory in the late eighteenth century. In the nineteenth century, the first European explorers reached the area searching for the mouth of the Niger River.

Although French efforts at colonization began before 1900, dissident ethnic groups, especially the desert Taureg, were not defeated until 1922. On December 4, 1958, after the establishment of the Fifth French Republic, Niger became an autonomous state within the French Community. Following full independence on August 3, 1960, however, membership was allowed to lapse. Hamani Diori was overthrown in a military coup and replaced by Col. Seyni Kountché as president. Thirteen years later Ali Saibou succeeded him. More recently, Ibrahim Barré Mainassara in July 1996 was confirmed in elections as president, a post he had assumed in January of 1996 after ousting Mahamane Ousmane.

The two largest ethnic groups in Niger are the Hausa, who also constitute the major ethnic group in northern Nigeria, and the Djerma-Songhai. Both groups are farmers who live in the arable, southern tier. The rest of the population consists of nomadic or semi-nomadic livestock-raising peoples, which include the Fulani, Tuareg, Kanouri, and Toubou.

Nigeria

Official name: Federal Republic of Nigeria
Independence: October 1, 1960
Area: 356,670 sq. mi.
Form of government: Military
Capital: Abuja
International relations: Commonwealth, EU, OAU, UN
Currency: Naira
Income: (per capita US$) 280 (1996)
Population: (1997) 110.5 million
Ethnic divisions: 250 tribal groups; the largest are Hausa-Fulani, Ibo, and Yoruba
Religious groups: Muslim, Christian, traditional belief
Languages spoken: English (official), Hausa, Ibo, Yoruba
Literacy: 57.1% (1995)
Exports: Petroleum, cocoa, rubber
Imports: Machinery and equipment, manufactured goods, food
Primary trade partners: United States, European Union countries, Japan

Evidence shows that more than 2,000 years ago the Nok people, who lived in what is now the Plateau state, worked iron and produced sophisticated terra cotta sculpture. In the centuries that followed, the Hausa kingdom and the Bornu empire near Lake Chad, prospered as important terminals of north-south trade between North African Berbers and forest people who exchanged slaves, ivory, and kola nuts for salt, glass beads, coral, cloth, weapons, brass rods, and cowrie shells used as currency. In the southwest, the Uoruba kingdom of Oyo, which was founded about 1400 and reached its height between the seventeenth and nineteenth centuries, attained a high level of political organization and extended as far as modern Togo. In the south central part of present-day Nigeria, as early as the fifteenth century, the kingdom of Benin had developed an efficient army, an elaborate ceremonial court, and artisans whose works in ivory, wood, bronze, and brass are prized throughout the world today.

Between the seventeenth and nineteenth centuries, European traders established coastal ports for the increasing traffic in slaves destined for the Americas. In 1855 British claims to a sphere of influence in that area received international recognition, and, in the following year, the Royal Niger Company was chartered. In 1900 the company's territory came under the control of the British government. In 1914, the area was formally united as the "Colony and Protectorate of Nigeria." Nigeria was granted full independence on October 1, 1960, as a federation of three regions.

Since independence, Nigeria has faced numerous coups. The Ibos tried to secede and tension between various ethnic groups increased, while the country began a rapid economic development based on oil production. Yakubu Gowon, who had managed to stay in power, was overthrown in 1976 by Mohammed Murtala, followed by Gen. Olusegun Obasanjo. A return to civilian rule came in 1979 under Shehu Shagari; however the military returned in 1984 under Mohammed Buhari and then again under Maj. Gen. Ibrahim Babangida. Defense Minister Sani Abacha ascended to power on November 17, 1993: his government was internationally denounced for widespread human rights abuses including numerous executions. Under increasing domestic and international pressure, Abacha promised to implement a new constitution (drafted by a constitutional commission in 1995) following presidential elections in October 1998. However, Abacha died of a heart attack in June 1998. His successor, Gen. Abdulsalam Abubakar, met with several opposition and foreign diplomats, promised to respect the election timetable, and released many political prisoners. Following riots due to the death of famed political prisoner Moshood Abiola, Abubakar announced a new transition program that called for the military's withdrawal in May 1999.

The most populous country in Africa, Nigeria accounts for one-quarter of sub-Saharan Africa's people. The dominant ethnic group in the northern two-thirds of the country is the Hausa-Fulani, most of whom are Muslims. Other major ethnic groups of the north are the Nupe, Tiv, and Kanuri. The Yoruba people are predominant in the southwest. About half of the Yorubas are Christian and half are Muslim. The predominately Catholic Ibos are the largest ethnic group in the southeast, with the Efik, Ibibio, and Ijaw comprising a substantial segment of the population in that area as well.

Reúnion

Independence: n/a (overseas department of France)
Area: 968 sq. mi.
Form of government: Represented in French National Assembly
Capital: Saint Denis
Currency: French franc
Population: (1998) 692,204
Ethnic divisions: Intermixed African, French, Malagasy, Chinese, Pakistani, and Indian ancestry
Religious groups: Roman Catholic 94%
Languages spoken: French (official), Creole
Exports: Sugar
Imports: Rice and petroleum products
Primary trade partners: France

The island of Reúnion, located in the Indian Ocean, remained uninhabited until 1654, when the French East

India Company established bases and brought in slaves from Africa and Madagascar. France governed the island as a colony until 1946, when it was granted department status. In 1974 France changed Reúnion's status to that of administrative region. Reúnion sends five directly elected representatives to the French National Assembly and three indirectly elected representatives to the Senate. Although groups have occasionally called for the island's independence, the proposals have generally received little support from of Réunion citizens who are well aware of the economic advantages gained through territorial ties to France.

The population of Reúnion is of mixed African, French, Indian, and Chinese origin.

Rwanda

Official name: Republic of Rwanda
Independence: July 1, 1962
Area: 10,169 sq. mi.
Form of government: Multiparty
Capital: Kigali
International relations: OAU, UN
Currency: Rwandan franc
Income: (per capita US$) 200 (1996)
Population: (1998) 8 million
Ethnic divisions: Hutu 90%, Tutsi 9%, Twa 1%
Religious groups: Christian, traditional belief, Muslim
Languages spoken: French, Kinyarwanda
Literacy: 60.5%
Exports: Coffee, tea, tin
Imports: Textiles, food, machinery and equipment, petroleum products
Primary trade partners: Germany, Belgium, United States, United Kingdom

Hutu's farmed the area that is now Rwanda until the fifteenth century when Tutsi herders settled in the area. In 1899 the court of Mwami submitted to a German protectorate with resistance. Belgian troops from the Congo occupied Rwanda in 1916 and, after World War I, the League of Nations mandated Rwanda and its southern neighbor, Burundi, to Belgium as the Territory of Ruanda-Urundi. Following World War II, Ruanda-Urundi became a United Nations trust territory with Belgium as the administering authority. The Party of the Hutu Emancipation Movement (PARMEHUTU) won an overwhelming victory in a U.N. supervised referendum.

The PARMEHUTU government, formed as a result of the September 1961 election, was granted internal autonomy by Belgium on January 1, 1962. A United Nations General Assembly resolution terminated the Belgian trusteeship and granted full independence to Rwanda (and Burundi) effective July 1, 1962. Gregiore Kayibanda, leader of the PARMEHUTU Party, became Rwanda's first elected president.

While ethnic clashes continued with neighboring Burundi, Gen. Juvenal Habyarimana, who had been a military head of state, returned to power in the presidential elections of 1978 and 1983 (having been the only candidate in both). In 1994, shortly after ending peace talks with the Tutsi-backed Rwandan Patriotic Front (RPF), President Habyarimana and Burundian President Cyprien Ntaryamira were killed together when their plane was shot down near Kigali. Rwanda exploded in ethnic violence, and the Hutu-dominated Rwandan army went on a rampage, reportedly killing between 500,000 and 1 million Rwandans, mostly Tutsis and Hutus sympathetic to the Tutsi cause. Forces of the RPF and the Rwandan army soon were in a full-blown civil war. A cease-fire was established in July 1994, and a government backed by the RPF was installed in Kigali. Promises of amnesty failed to convince many of the Hutus who had fled into the former Zaire (now the Democratic Republic of the Congo) to return.

Regional instability continued to threaten Rwanda's recovery, as exhibited by the renewed fighting along the Democratic Republic of the Congo border in mid-1998. Many Tutsi on both sides of the border aided Laurent-Désiré Kabila to oust then-Zaire's President Mobutu. But Kabila, facing pressure within his own country, purged his military of Rwandan and Congolese Tutsi in 1997. This breach of trust, combined with the continuing agitation of Hutu refugees in Congo, led Rwanda's government to support an armed rebellion against Kabila's government in the Democratic Republic of the Congo during 1998.

The indigenous population consists of three ethnic groups. The Tutsi (14 percent) are a pastoral people of Nilotic origin. The Hutus, who comprise the majority of the population (85 percent), are farmers of Bantu origin. The Twa pygmies (1 percent) are thought to be the remnants of the earliest settlers of the region.

Saint Helena

Independence: n/a (dependent territory of the United Kingdom)
Area: 47 sq. mi.
Capital: Jamestown
Currency: Saint Helena pound
Population: (1998 estimate) 7,091
Ethnic divisions: African descent, white
Religious groups: Anglican majority, Baptist, Seventh-Day Adventist, and Roman Catholic
Languages spoken: English
Literacy: 97%
Exports: Fish, handicrafts
Imports: Food, beverages, tobacco, fuel, building materials, vehicles and parts
Primary trade partners: South Africa, United Kingdom

The islands of Saint Helena, Ascension, and Tristan da Cunha lie about one-third of the way from Africa to South America in the South Atlantic Ocean. The islands remained uninhabited until they were first explored by the Portuguese navigator, João de Nova, in 1502. In 1659, the British East India Company established a settlement on Saint Helena and in 1673 was granted a charter to govern the island. Napoleon was exiled to Saint Helena from 1815 until his death in 1821.

São Tomé and Príncipe

Official name: Democratic Republic of São Tomé and Príncipe
Independence: July 12, 1975
Area: 371 sq. mi.
Form of government: Multiparty
Capital: São Tomé
International relations: EU, OAU, UN
Currency: Dobra
Income: (per capita US$) 330 (1996)
Population: (1998) 160,000
Ethnic divisions: Mixed African, Portuguese-African
Religious groups: Christian 80%
Languages spoken: Portuguese (official), Fang
Literacy: 57.4% (1995)
Exports: Cocoa, coffee, cinchona bark, copra, palm kernels
Imports: Machinery and electrical equipment, food, petroleum
Primary trade partners: Netherlands, Germany, Portugal, Japan

These uninhabited islands were first visited by Portuguese navigators between 1469 and 1472. The first successful settlement of São Tomé was established in 1493. Príncipe was settled in 1500. By the mid-1500s, with the help of slave labor, the Portuguese settlers had turned the islands into Africa's foremost exporter of sugar. São Tomé and Príncipe were taken over and administered by the Portuguese crown in 1522 and 1573, respectively. By 1908 São Tomé had become the world's largest producer of cocoa, still the country's most important crop.

The rocas system, which gave the plantation managers a high degree of authority, led to abuses against the African farm workers. Although Portugal officially abolished slavery in 1876, the practice of forced paid labor continued. Sporadic labor unrest and dissatisfaction continued well into the twentieth century, culminating in an outbreak of riots in 1953 in which several hundred African laborers were killed.

By the late 1950s, a small group of São Tomés had formed the Movement for the Liberation of São Tomé and Príncipe (MLSTP). In 1974 Portuguese representatives met with the MLSTP in Algiers and worked out an agreement for the transfer of sovereignty. After a period of transition, São Tomé and Príncipe achieved independence on July 12, 1975, choosing as its first president the MLSTP Secretary General Manuel Pinto da Costa. Four years after independence, da Costa consolidated his power by eliminating the position of prime minister and assuming those duties himself. He served until 1991, when Miguel Trovoada was elected as president. A coup by military officers on August 15, 1995, removed Trovoada from office, but only briefly. He was reinstated as president seven days later, after he agreed to amnesty for the officers engineering the coup. In 1996 he was reelected to a five-year term.

São Tomé and Príncipe's population consists of people descended from groups that have migrated to the islands since 1485. Six groups are identifiable: mestizo, of mixed-blood, descendants of African slaves brought to the islands during the early years of settlement from Benin, Gabon, Congo, and Angola; Anglares, reputedly descendants of Angolan slaves who survived on a 1540 shipwreck and now earn their livelihood fishing; Forros, descendants of freed slaves; Servicais, contract laborers from Angola, Mozambique, and Cape Verde, living temporarily on the islands; Tongas, children of servicais born on the islands; and Europeans, primarily Portuguese.

Senegal

Official name: Republic of Senegal
Independence: August 20, 1960
Area: 75,749 sq. mi.
Form of government: Multiparty
Capital: Dakar
International relations: EU, OAU, UN
Currency: CFA franc
Income: (per capita US$) 600 (1996)
Population: (1998) 10.4 million
Ethnic divisions: Wolof 36%, Fulani (Peulh) and Toucouleur 26%, Serer 17%, Diola, Mandingo, others 21%
Religious groups: Muslim 92%, traditional belief 6%, Christian 2%
Languages spoken: French (official), Solof, Pulaar, Diola, Mandingo
Literacy: 66.9% (1995)
Exports: Fish, groundnuts, petroleum, phosphates
Imports: Food and beverages, consumer goods, capital goods, petroleum
Primary trade partners: European Union countries, Nigeria, Côte d'Ivoire

Archaeological findings throughout the area indicate that Senegal was inhabited in prehistoric times. Islam established itself in the Senegal River valley during the eleventh century. In the thirteenth and fourteenth centuries, the area came under the influence of the great Mandingo empires to the east, during which the Jolof

Slave fortress at Goree Island off the coast of Senegal (Corbis Corporation [Bellevue]).

empire of Senegal was founded. The Empire comprised the states of Cayor, Baol, Oualo, Sine, and Soloum until the sixteenth century, when they revolted for independence.

The Portuguese were the first Europeans to trade in Senegal, arriving in the fifteenth century. They were soon followed by the Dutch and French. During the nineteenth century, the French gradually established control over the interior regions and administered them as a protectorate until 1920, and as a colony thereafter.

In January of 1959, Senegal and the French Soudan merged to form the Mali Federation, which became fully independent on June 20, 1960. Due to internal political difficulties, the federation broke up on August 20, 1960; Senegal and Soudan (renamed the Republic of Mali) each proclaimed separate independence. Leopold Sedar Senghor, an internationally renowned poet, politician, and statesman, was elected Senegal's first president in August of 1960. Senghor guided the nation and instituted a multiparty system in 1976. Senghor stepped down in 1980, naming Abdou Diouf, prime minister since 1970, as his successor. Senegal joined with Gambia in 1982 to form the confederation of Senegambia, headed by Diouf. The confederation collapsed at the end of the 1980s, although the two countries in 1991 signed a new treaty of cooperation. Over time the Senegalese public became increasingly disenchanted with Diouf and his Socialist Party's grip on power. In 1991 Diouf initiated electoral reforms, though the changes failed to satisfy opposition leaders. Diouf was again elected to a seven-year term as president in 1993. Pres. Bill Clinton's 1998 visit to Senegal signaled a greater U.S. interest in the country.

Seychelles
Official name: Republic of Seychelles
Independence: June 29, 1976
Area: 171 sq. mi.

Form of government: Republic
Capital: Victoria
International relations: EU, OAU, UN
Currency: Rupee
Income: (per capita US$) 6,720 (1996)
Population (1998): 79,000
Ethnic divisions: Creole (mixture of Asian, African, and European)
Religious groups: Roman Catholic 90%, Anglican 8%, other 2%
Languages spoken: Creole, English, French
Literacy: 85% (1991)
Exports: Cinnamon bark, copra, fish
Imports: Manufactured goods, food, petroleum products
Primary trade partners: France, United Kingdom, Singapore, South Africa

In 1742 the French governor of Mauritius, sent an expedition to the islands. A second expedition in 1756 reasserted formal possession by France. The Seychelles islands were captured and freed several times during the French Revolution and the Napoleonic wars, then passed officially to the British under the Treaty of Paris in 1814. Negotiations with the British resulted in an agreement by which Seychelles became a sovereign republic on June 29, 1976. After independence Seychelles had a multiparty government, but one year later Albert René instituted his People's Progressive Front as the only party. Despite several coup attempts during the 1980s, René was able to hold onto power, and in 1991, the government turned toward a multiparty state. René was elected to a fourth term in 1993. Since then, René has begun to implement a number of free-market reforms, promoting the islands as a center for offshore banking. In addition, several national industries have been privatized.

Most Seychellois are descendants of early French settlers and the African slaves brought to the Seychelles in the nineteenth century by the British, who freed them from slave ships on the East African coast. Indians and Chinese account for the other permanent inhabitants.

Sierra Leone
Official name: Republic of Sierra Leone
Independence: April 27, 1961
Area: 27,699 sq. mi.
Form of government: Multiparty
Capital: Freetown
International relations: Commonwealth, EU, OAU, UN
Currency: Leone
Income: (per capita US$) 200 (1996)
Population: (1998) 5.1 million
Ethnic divisions: Temne 30%, Mende 29%, Creole 2%
Religious groups: Muslim 60%, Animist 30%, Christian 10%

Languages spoken: English (official), Krio (lingua franca), Temne, Mende, other tribal languages
Literacy: 31.4% (1995)
Exports: Bauxite, cocoa, coffee, diamonds, rutile
Imports: Foodstuffs, machinery and equipment, fuels
Primary trade partners: United States, European Union countries, Japan, China

Sierra Leone was one of the first West African British colonies. Foreign settlement did not occur for another two centuries, when the British laid plans for a refuge within the British Empire for freed slaves. In 1787 the site of Freetown received the first four hundred freedmen from Great Britain. Disease and hostility from the indigenous people almost eliminated this first group. Five years later, however, another group of settlers, 1,000 freed slaves who had fled from the United States to Nova Scotia during the American Revolution, arrived under the auspices of the newly formed British Sierra Leone Company. In 1800 about 550 blacks arrived from Jamaica via Nova Scotia; these were the maroons, escaped slaves who maintained their independence in the mountains of Jamaica.

The 1951 constitution provided the framework for decolonization. Independence came in April 1961, and Sierra Leone became a parliamentary system within the British Commonwealth. In April 1971, it adopted a republican constitution, cutting the link to the British monarchy but remaining with the Commonwealth. Siaka Stevens, who fought for government control of the country's major resources, namely iron and diamonds, led the country until his retirement in November 1985. He was succeeded as president in January 1986 by Major General Joseph Saidu Momoh. Guerrillas spilling over into Sierra Leone from the Liberian civil war captured some border towns in 1991. These border skirmishes eventually evolved into a civil war within Sierra Leone. Momoh was ousted by a military coup in April 1992 and was replaced by Captain Valentine Strasser. Strasser, criticized for the brutality of his regime, was removed from office in a 1996 bloodless coup. Ahmed Tehan Kabbah was elected president in late February 1996. A military junta deposed Kabbah in May 1997, but he was restored to office in March 1998. However, fighting between the government and rebel forces continued into the new millennium.

Eighteen ethnic groups make up the indigenous population of Sierra Leone. The Temne in the north and the Mende in the south are the largest. About 60,000 are Creoles, descendants of black settlers from Great Britain or North America.

Somalia
Official name: Somalia Democratic Republic

Independence: July 1, 1960
Area: 246,282 sq. mi.
Form of government: Anarchy
Capital: Mogadishu
International relations: OAU, UN
Currency: Somalian shilling
Income:(per capita US$) 150 (1990)
Population: (1998): 6.8 million
Ethnic divisions: Somali 98.8%, Arab and Asian 1.2%
Religious groups: Muslim
Languages spoken: Somali
Literacy: 24.1% (1995)
Exports: Bananas, fish, hides, live animals
Imports: Petroleum products, food, livestock, fertilizer, machinery, textiles
Primary trade partners: Saudi Arabia, Italy, United States, Germany

The British East India Company's desire for unrestricted harbor facilities led to the conclusion of treaties with the sultan of Tajura as early as 1840. It was not until 1886, however, that the British gained control over northern Somalia through treaties with various Somali chiefs. The boundary between Ethiopia and British Somaliland was established in 1897 through treaty negotiations between British negotiators and King Menellik.

In 1855, Italy obtained commercial advantages in the area from the sultan of Zanzibar and in 1889 concluded agreements with the sultans of Obbia and Caluula, who placed their territories under Italy's protection. Between 1897 and 1908, Italy made agreements with the Ethiopians and the British that marked out the boundaries of Italian Somaliland. In June 1940, Italian troops overran British Somaliland and drove out the British garrison. In 1941 British forces began operations against the Italian East African Empire and quickly brought the greater part of the Italian Somaliland under British control.

From 1941 to 1950, while Somalia was under British military administration, transition toward self-government had begun. Elections for the Legislative Assembly were held in February 1960. The protectorate became independent on June 26, 1960; five days later, on July 1, it joined Italian Somaliland to form the Somali Republic. Gen. Mohammed Siad Barre led a military coup in 1969 and established a Marxist political system. Years later Barre concentrated power in his own family and clan. In 1991 he was toppled, but opposing factions continued fighting for power. After years of civil war and severe drought, the United Nations, with U.S. leadership, introduced forces into Somalia in late 1992 in an attempt to restore order and feed the country's many starving inhabitants. Attempts failed in the late 1990s to gather hundreds of warring clan leaders in an effort to hammer

Somali women dressed in traditional costumes performing with the National Theater Company in Mogadishu (Laure Communications).

out some sort of truce. Pakistani forces took over the leadership of the UN mission, which finally retreated in March 1995. The situation remains chaotic as the new millennium begins.

The Somali people are herders and farmers. The largest group in the country is the Somali, who are nomadic or seminomadic herders. The remaining population consists of Jiiddu, Tunni, and Maay.

South Africa

Official name: Republic of South Africa
Independence: May 31, 1910
Area: 510,125 sq. mi.
Form of government: Multiparty
Capital: Pretoria
International relations: OAU, UN
Currency: Rand
Income: (per capita US$) 3,360 (1996)
Population: (1998) 42.8 million
Ethnic divisions: Black 75%; white 14%; "colored" (mixed race) 8%; Asian (Indian) 3%.
Religious groups: Christian, traditional belief, Hindu, Muslim, Jewish

Languages spoken: English and Afrikaans (official), Zulu, Xhosa, Luvenda, North and South SeSotho, SeTswana, other tribal languages.
Literacy: 81.8% (1995)
Exports: Diamonds, gold
Imports: Machinery, transportation and electrical equipment, chemicals, plastics, rubber, paper, textiles
Primary trade partners: United Kingdom, United States, Italy, Japan, Germany

Of the present inhabitants of South Africa, the earliest were Bushmen and Hottentots who are members of the Khoisan language group. In 1488, the Portuguese were the first Europeans to reach the Cape of Good Hope. Permanent white settlement began when the Dutch East India Company established a provisioning station in 1652. In subsequent decades, French Huguenot refugees, Dutch, and Germans settled in the Cape area to form the Afrikaner segment of the modern population.

Britain seized the Cape of Good Hope at the end of the eighteenth century. Partly to escape British political rule and preserve cultural hegemony, many Afrikaner farmers (Boers) undertook a northern migration (the "Great Trek") beginning in 1836. This movement brought

Fishermen gathering their nets in Hout Bay, South Africa (Laure Communications).

them into contact with several African groups, the most formidable of which were the Zulu. Under their powerful leader, Shaka (1787–1828), the Zulu conquered most of the territory between the Drakensberg Mountains and the sea (now Natal). The Zulu were defeated at the Battle of Blood River in 1838.

The independent Boer republics of the Transvaal (the South African Republic) and the Orange Free State were created in 1852 and 1854. Following the two Boer wars from 1880 to 1881 and 1899 to 1902, British forces conquered the Boer republics and incorporated them into the British Empire. A strong resurgence of Afrikaner nationalism in the 1940s and 1950s led to a decision, through a 1960 referendum among whites, to give up dominion status and establish a republic. The republic was established on May 31, 1961. The National Party extended racial segregation, or the policy of apartheid, through passage of a number of legislative acts. In the 1960s and the 1970s, other laws were passed to further restrict every black African.

The African National Congress (ANC), a predominantly black South African political and paramilitary organization founded in 1912, is the oldest organization opposing legalized racism and white rule in South Afri-

ca. It was banned by the South African government from 1960 to 1990, operating underground and in exile.

In December 1988, under great international pressure, the government commuted the death sentences of the Sharpeville Six, who were convicted of murder for their presence in a crowd that killed a black township official. President F. W. de Klerk took several steps beginning in 1989 to demonstrate his commitment to ending apartheid including the release of ANC leader Nelson Mandela, imprisoned in 1962 and sentenced to life in 1964 for treason and sabotage, and other political prisoners and detainees; and unbanning the ANC and 32 other anti-apartheid organizations. The tide of social and political changes instigated by de Klerk led to a new constitution and eventually multiparty elections in April 1994 that put Mandela in power as the first black African president of the nation. In April 1996, the Truth and Reconciliation Commission (TRC), the body responsible for investigating crimes committed during the apartheid era in South Africa, began its hearings. Despite misgivings about both its impartiality and its effectiveness, most observers agree that the TRC, which continued to work past its original 18-month deadline, has helped reconcile the new South Africa with its past.

In late 1997 Mandela retired as head of the ANC and was replaced by Thabo Mbeki. Mandela, who announced in 1996 he would not seek a second term as president, had groomed Mbeki to succeed him. Mbeki won the 1999 election, and the ANC was able to form a coalition to give it a two-thirds majority, which is necessary to amend the constitution.

South Africa's apartheid classification system, which ended in the early 1990s, divided the nation's population into four major racial categories—Africans (blacks), whites, "coloreds," and Asians. The Africans, who comprise 72 percent of the population, are mainly descendants of the Sotho and Nguni peoples, who migrated southward centuries ago. The largest African ethnic groups are the Zulu (nearly 6 million) and Xhosa (about 5.8 million). The white population consists primarily of descendants of Dutch, French, English, and German settlers, with smaller mixtures of other European peoples, and constitutes about 14 percent of the total population. "Coloreds" are mostly descendants of indigenous peoples and the earliest European and Malay settlers in the area. "Coloreds" comprise 9 percent of the population and live primarily in Cape Province. Asians, mainly descendants of the Indian workers brought to South Africa in the mid-nineteenth century to work as indentured laborers on sugar estates in Natal, constitute about 3 percent of the population.

Sudan

Official name: Republic of the Sudan
Independence: January 1, 1956
Area: 967,500 sq. mi.
Form of government: Transitional
Capital: Khartoum
International relations: Arab League, EU, OAU, UN
Currency: Sudanese pound
Income: (per capita US$) 860 (1996)
Population: (1998) 33.6 million
Ethnic divisions: Arab, black
Religious groups: Islam, traditional belief (southern Sudan), Christian
Languages spoken: Arabic (official), English, tribal languages
Literacy: 46.1% (1995)
Exports: Cotton, groundnuts, sorghum
Imports: Foodstuffs, petroleum products, manufactured goods, pharmaceuticals, chemicals
Primary trade partners: European Union countries, Saudi Arabia, United States

From the beginning of the Christian era until 1820, Sudan existed as a collection of small, independent states. In 1881 a religious leader named Mohammed Ahmed ibn Abdalla proclaimed himself the Mahdi, or "expected one," and began to unify tribes in western and central Sudan. The Mahdi led a nationalist revolt culminating in the fall of Khartoum in 1885. He died shortly thereafter, but his state survived until overwhelmed by Anglo-Egyptian forces in 1898; in 1899 Sudan was proclaimed a condominium under Anglo-Egyptian administration. In February 1953, the United Kingdom and Egypt concluded an agreement providing for Sudanese self-government. Sudan achieved independence on January 1, 1956. In 1969 Col. Gaafar Muhammad al-Nimeiry, leading a group of army officers, seized power and set up government under a revolutionary council. Elected president in 1972, Nimeiry first turned to the Soviet Union and Libya for support. However, after several coup attempts, allegedly backed by Libya and local communists, Nimeiry turned to Egypt and the West for assistance. Nimeiry was elected to a third term as president in 1983 but was removed from office two years later in a bloodless coup. After a year of military rule, Sadiq al-Mahdi was elected prime minister. Mahdi's regime was toppled in June 1989 by a military coup led by Omar Hassan al-Bashir. In 1993 Bashir took some steps toward establishment of a multiparty state, most of which were dismissed as cosmetic by the opposition. In 1996 Bashir and his party swept presidential and legislative elections. Meanwhile, a civil war continued to rage between the Arab peoples of the north and the black Africans in the south of Sudan.

Swaziland

Official name: Kingdom of Swaziland
Independence: September 6, 1968
Area: 6,704 sq. mi.
Form of government: Monarchy
Capital: Mbabane
International relations: Commonwealth, EU, OAU, UN
Currency: Lilangeni
Income: (per capita US$) 1,130 (1996)
Population: (1998) 966,000
Ethnic divisions: Swazi, some Zulu
Religious groups: Christian and indigenous belief
Languages spoken: English, siSwati (both official)
Literacy: 76.7% (1995)
Exports: Asbestos, citrus, sugar, wood pulp, cotton yarn
Imports: Motor vehicles, machinery, transportation equipment, petroleum products, foodstuffs, chemicals
Primary trade partners: South Africa, European Union countries, Canada, Switzerland, United Kingdom

The people of the present Swazi nation migrated south before the sixteenth century to what is now Mozambique. After a series of conflicts with people living in the area that is now Maputo, the Swazi settled in northern Zululand in about 1750. Unable to match the growing Zulu strength there, the Swazis moved gradually northward in the early 1800s and established themselves in the area of modern Swaziland. The Swazi

An intricately carved drum in Swaziland (Cory Langley).

consolidated their hold in this area under several able leaders. The most important of these was Mswati, from whom the Swazi derive their name. Under his leadership in the 1840s, the Swazi expanded their territory to the northwest and stabilized the southern frontier with the Zulus.

The first Swazi contact with the British came early in Mswati's reign when he asked the British agent general in South Africa for assistance against Zulu raids into Swaziland. Agreements made between the British and the Transvaal (South Africa) governments in 1881 and 1884 provided that Swaziland should be independent. In 1903 Britain formally took over the administration of Swaziland.

Sobhuza II became head of the Swazi Nation in 1921. By the 1960s, political activity intensified, partly in response to events elsewhere in Africa. Several political parties were formed that agitated for independence. The traditional Swazi leaders, including King Sobhuza and his council, formed the Imbokodvo National Movement. In 1966 the British agreed to hold talks on a new constitution. The constitutional committee, consisting of representatives of the king and of the Swazi National Council, other political parties, and the British govern-

ment agreed on a constitutional monarchy for Swaziland, with self-government to follow parliamentary elections in 1967. Swaziland became independent on September 6, 1968. In 1973 Sobhuza II repealed the constitution, dissolved the political parties, and assumed full power until his death in 1982. Mswati III became king in 1986.

In 1993, Mswati III called for Swaziland's first general election in twenty years, though he retained a great deal of political power; pro-democratic forces viewed the elections as inadequate. More recently Swaziland has been affected by waves of general strikes, most of them organized by the Swazi Federation of Trade Unions (SFTU). The last major strike, in early 1996, led to the formation of a Constitutional Review Commission, which Mswati promised would deliver several democratic reforms. But Mswati limited membership on the commission to his own appointees, prompting the SFTU and its allies to reject the commission and call for further strikes.

Tanzania

Official name: United Republic of Tanzania
Independence: December 9, 1961
Area: 364,900 sq. mi.
Form of government: Multiparty
Capital: Dar es Salaam
International relations: Commonwealth, EU, OAU, UN
Currency: Tanzanian shilling
Income:(per capita US$) 190 (1996)
Population: (1998) 30.6 million
Ethnic divisions: More than 120 groups
Religious groups: Muslim 35%, traditional belief 35%, Christian 30%
Languages spoken: Swahili (official), English
Literacy: 67.8% (1995)
Exports: Cashews, coffee, cloves, cotton, diamonds, sisal, tea
Imports: Manufactured goods, crude oil, cotton piece goods, foodstuffs
Primary trade partners: Germany, United Kingdom, Japan, United States

The area that is now Tanzania is believed to have been inhabited originally by ethnic groups using a click-tongue language similar to that of southern Africa's Bushmen and Hottentots. Although remnants of these early tribes still exist, most were gradually displaced by Bantu farmers migrating form the west and south and by Nilotes and related Northern peoples.

The coastal area first felt the impact of foreign influence as early as the eighth century. By the twelfth century, traders and immigrants came from as far away as Persia (now Iran) and India. The Portuguese navigator, Vasco da Gama, first visited the East African coast in 1498 on his voyage to India and by 1506 the Portu-

A Tanzanian street scene (Cory Langley).

guese claimed control over the entire coast. This control was nominal, however, for the Portuguese did not attempt to colonize the area or explore the interior. By the early eighteenth century, Arabs from Oman had assisted the indigenous coastal dwellers in driving out the Portuguese from the area north of the Ruvuma River. They established their own garrisons at Zanzibar, Pemba, and Kilwa and carried on a lucrative trade in slaves and ivory.

German colonial interests were first advanced in 1884. Karl Peters, who formed the Society for German Colonization, concluded a series of treaties by which tribal chiefs in the interior accepted German protection. In 1886 and 1890, Anglo-German agreements were negotiated that delineated the British and German spheres of influence in the interior of East Africa. In 1891 the German government took over direct administration of the territory from the German East Africa Company and appointed a governor with headquarters at Dar es Salaam. German colonial administration provided African resistance, culminating in the Maji Maji rebellion of 1905 to 1907. German colonial domination of Tanganyika ended with World War I. Control of most of the territory passed to the United Kingdom under a League of Nations mandate.

In the following years, Tanganyika moved gradually toward self-government and independence. In 1954 Julius K. Nyerere, a schoolteacher educated abroad, organized the Tanganyika African Union (UANU). In May 1961, Tanganyika became autonomous, and Nyerere became prime minister under a new constitution. Full independence was achieved on December 9, 1961. On April 26, 1964, Tanganyika united with Zanzibar to form the United Republic of Tanganyika and Zanzibar, renamed the United Republic of Tanzania on October 29, 1964. Nyerere in November 1985 became one of the few leaders on the continent to retire peacefully. He was succeeded by Ali Hassan Mwinyi as president. Opposi-

tion parties were legalized in 1992, paving the way for Tanzania's first multiparty elections in October 1995. The Revolutionary Party's Benjamin Mkapa was elected president and his party won the majority of the seats in the National Assembly. Continuing strife in countries bordering Tanzania fueled a surge in the flow of refugees into the country during the mid-1990s. In 1997, Tanzania began a repatriation plan to return the refugees to their homelands.

Tanzania's population consists of more than 120 ethnic groups, of which only the Sukuma has more than one million members. The majority of Tanzanians, including such large tribes as the Sukuma and the Nyamwezi, are of Bantu stock. Groups of Nilotic or related origin include the nomadic Masai and the Luo, both of which are found in greater numbers in neighboring Kenya. Two small groups speak languages of the Khoisan family peculiar to the Bushman and Hottentot peoples. Cushitic-speaking peoples, originally from the Ethiopian highlands, reside in a few areas of Tanzania.

Togo

Official name: Republic of Togo
Independence: April 27, 1960
Area: 21,925 sq. mi.
Form of government: Republic
Capital: Lomé
International relations: EU, OAU, UN
Currency: CFA franc
Income:(per capita US$) 340 (1996)
Population: (1998) 4.9 million
Ethnic divisions: Ewe, Mina, Kabye, Cotocoli, Moba
Religious groups: Animist 50%, Christian 35%, Muslim 15%
Languages spoken: French (official), Ewe, Mina, Kabye
Literacy: 51.7% (1995)
Exports: Cocoa, coffee, phosphates
Imports: Machinery and equipment, consumer goods, food, chemical products
Primary trade partners: African France Zone countries, United States

The Ewe people first moved into the area that is now Togo from the Niger River Valley between the twelfth and fourteenth centuries. During the fifteenth and sixteenth centuries, Portuguese explorers and traders visited the coast. For the next two hundred years, the coastal region was a major raiding center for Europeans in search of slaves, earning Togo and the surrounding region the name "the Slave Coast."

In a 1884 treaty signed at Togoville, Germany declared a protectorate over the area. In 1914 Togoland was invaded by French and British forces and fell after a brief resistance. Following the war, Togoland became a League of Nations mandate divided for administrative

A broom vendor on a city street in Togo (Cory Langley).

purposes between France and the United Kingdom. By statute in 1955, French Togo became an autonomous republic within the French Union. In 1957 the residents of British Togoland voted to join the Gold Coast as part of the new independent nation of Ghana. On April 27, 1960, Togo severed its juridical ties with France, shed its United Nations trusteeship status, and became fully independent. The first president—Sylvanus Olympia— was overthrown three years after independence. Nicholas Grunitzky headed the government for a short period and, in 1976, Col. Gnassingbé Eyadéma seized power and instituted a one-party state. Reelected in 1979 and 1986, Eyadéma in August 1991 agreed to share power with a transitional government until multiparty elections could be scheduled. Though troops loyal to Eyadéma reportedly tried repeatedly to overthrow the interim regime, Eyadéma was reelected in multiparty elections in 1993.

Since 1994 the Togolese economy has seen a partial recovery. But the current political scene is less promising: in 1997 Eyadéma's government blocked the creation of an independent electoral commission and, after military harassment of opposition leaders marred the 1998 presidential campaign, Eyadéma's claim to have won reelection for another five years led to opposition protests and rioting.

Togo's population is composed of about 21 ethnic groups. The two major ones are the Ewe in the south and the Kabye in the north.

Tunisia
Official name: Republic of Tunisia
Independence: March 20, 1956
Area: 63,170 sq. mi.
Form of government: Republic
Capital: Tunis
International relations: OAU, UN
Currency: Dinar
Income: (per capita US$) 2,140 (1996)
Population: (1998) 9.4 million
Ethnic divisions: Arab 98%, Berber 1%, European 1%
Religious groups: Muslim 99%, Christian and Jewish less than 1%
Languages spoken: Arabic (official), French
Literacy: 66.7% (1995)
Exports: Hydrocarbons, agricultural products, phosphates, chemicals
Imports: Industrials goods and equipment, hydrocarbons, foodstuffs, consumer goods
Primary trade partners: European Union countries, Southwest Asian countries, Algeria, India, United States

Tunisians are descended mainly from indigenous Berber tribes and from Arab tribes that migrated to North Africa during the seventh century AD. Recorded history in Tunisia begins with the arrival of Phoenicians, who founded Carthage and other North African settlements. In the seventh century, the Muslim conquest transformed North Africa and Tunisia became a center of Arab culture until its assimilation in the Turkish Ottoman Empire in the sixteenth century. In 1881 France established a protectorate there, only to see a rise of nationalism lead to Tunisia's independence in 1956.

One year after independence, Habib Bourguiba deposed the president and instituted a socialist system, later declaring himself president for life. In late 1987, Bourguiba was declared senile, and he was replaced as president by Prime Minister Zine al-Abidine Ben Ali, who took steps to democratize the country. In April 1989 elections, Ben Ali was elected to a full term as president. In 1994 he ran unopposed for president and was reelected. Ben Ali continued to crack down on growing Muslim fundamentalism throughout the 1990s.

Uganda
Official name: Republic of Uganda
Independence: October 9, 1962
Area: 93,104 sq. mi.
Form of government: Republic

Tunisian women walking together (Cory Langley).

Capital: Kampala

International relations: Commonwealth, EU, OAU, UN

Currency: Ugandan shilling

Income: (per capita US$) 310 (1996)

Population: (1998) 22.2 million

Ethnic divisions: Baganda, Iteso, Basoga, Banyaruanda, Bakiga, Bagisu

Religious groups: Christian (majority), Muslim, traditional belief

Languages spoken: English (official), Luganda, Swahili, other Bantu and Nilotic languages

Literacy:48% (1991)

Exports: Coffee, copper, cotton, tea

Imports: Petroleum products, machinery, cotton piece goods, metals, transportation equipment, food

Primary trade partners: United States, Kenya, United Kingdom, France, Italy

Arab traders moving inland from Indian Ocean coastal enclaves reached the interior of Uganda in the 1830s and found several African kingdoms, including the Buganda kingdom, that had well-developed political institutions dating back several centuries.

In 1888 control of the emerging British sphere of interest in East Africa was assigned by royal charter to the Imperial British East Africa Company, an arrangement strengthened in 1890 by an Anglo-German agreement confirming British dominance over Kenya and Uganda. In 1894 the Kingdom of Uganda was placed under a formal British protectorate. The British protectorate period began to change formally in 1955, when constitutional changes leading to Uganda's independence were adopted. The first general elections in Uganda were held in 1961, and the British government granted internal self-government to Uganda on March 1, 1962, with Benedicto Kiwanuka as the first prime minister.

In February of 1966, Prime Minister Milton Obote suspended the constitution, assumed all government powers, and removed the president and vice president. On January 25, 1971, Obote's government was ousted in a military coup led by armed forces commander Idi Amin Dada. Amin declared himself president, dissolved the parliament, and amended the constitution to give himself absolute power. Idi Amin's eight-year rule produced economic decline, social disintegration, and massive human rights violations. In 1978 Tanzanian forces pushed back an incursion by Amin's troops. Backed by Ugandan exiles, Tanzanian forces waged a war of liberation against Amin. On April 11, 1979, the Ugandan capital was captured, and Amin and his remaining forces fled. There followed a chaotic year or so, during which three provisional presidents led the shattered country. In December 1980, Obote was once again elected to the presidency and then overthrown by military coup. The military regime that followed was short-lived. In January 1986, National Resistance Army leader Yoweri Museveni seized power. Museveni, most recently elected president in 1996 in the country's first presidential elections in 16 years, has done much to nurse Uganda's economy back to health.

Bantu, Nilotic, and Nilo-Hamitic peoples constitute most of Uganda's population. The Bantu are the most numerous and include the Baganda, with more than one million members. The Nilo-Hamitic Iteso is the second-largest group, followed by the Banyankole and Basoga, both of Bantu extraction.

Zambia

Official name: Republic of Zambia
Independence: October 24, 1964
Area: 290,586 sq. mi.
Form of government: Republic
Capital: Lusaka
International relations: OAU, UN
Currency: Zambian kwacha
Income: (per capita US$) 370 (1996)
Population: (1998) 9.5 million
Ethnic divisions: More than 70 tribal groups
Religious groups: Christian, indigenous belief, Muslim
Languages spoken: English (official), about 70 local
    languages and dialects including Bemba, Tonga,
    Nyanja, Lozi, Luvale, Ndembu (Lundu), and Kaonde
Literacy: 78.2% (1995)
Exports: Copper, zinc, cobalt, lead, tobacco
Imports: Machinery, transportation equipment, chemi-
    cals, fuels, manufactured goods, foodstuffs
Primary trade partners: European Union countries, Ja-
    pan, South Africa, United States

About 2,000 years ago, the indigenous hunter-gatherer occupants of Zambia began to be displaced or absorbed by more advanced migrating tribes. By the fifteenth century, the major waves of Bantu-speaking immigrants arrived, with the greatest influx occurring between the late seventeenth and early nineteenth centuries. These groups came primarily from the Luba and Lunda tribes of southern Zaire and northern Angola but were joined in the nineteenth century by Ngoni peoples from the south. By the latter part of that century, the various peoples of Zambia were largely established in the areas they currently occupy.

Except for an occasional Portuguese explorer, the area lay untouched by Europeans for centuries, until the mid-nineteenth century, when it was penetrated by

European explorers, missionaries, and traders. In 1888 Northern and Southern Rhodesia were proclaimed a British sphere of influence. In 1953 both Rhodesias were joined with Nyasaland to form the Federation of Rhodesia and Nyasaland.

Northern Rhodesia was the center of much of the turmoil and crises that characterized the federation in its last years. At the core of the controversy were insistent African demands for greater participation in government. A two-stage election held in October and December 1962 resulted in an African majority in the Legislative Council. The council passed resolutions calling for Northern Rhodesia's secession from the federation and demanding full internal self-government. On December 31, 1963, the federation was dissolved, and Northern Rhodesia became the Republic of Zambia on October 24, 1964. Led by Kenneth Kaunda for nearly thirty years, the country in 1991 held its first multiparty elections. Frederick Chiluba, leader of the Movement for Multiparty Democracy, defeated Kaunda by a wide margin. In 1996 a new constitution prevented Kaunda from running for president, as it introduced a provision that a candidate's parents must be Zambian-born. (Kaunda's parents were Malawian). Chiluba's party easily won elections that same year, amidst widespread student riots and widespread popular dissent.

Zambia's population comprises more than seventy Bantu-speaking tribes. Some tribes are small, and only two have enough people to constitute at least ten percent of the population.

Zimbabwe

Official name: Republic of Zimbabwe
Independence: April 18, 1980
Area: 150,804 sq. mi.
Form of government: Republic
Capital: Harare
International relations: OAU, UN
Currency: Zimbabwe dollar
Income: (per capita US$) 670 (1996)
Population: (1998) 11 million
Ethnic divisions: Shona 80%, Ndebele 19%
Religious groups: Syncretic 50% (part Christian, part
    traditional belief), Christian 25%, traditional beliefs
    24%, Hindu and Muslim less than 1%
Languages spoken: English (official), Shona, Sindebele
Literacy: 85.1% (1995)
Exports: Tobacco, minerals, cotton, maize
Imports: Machinery, transportation equipment, manu-
    factured goods, chemicals, fuels
Primary trade partners: United Kingdom, Germany, South
    Africa, United States, Japan

Archaeologists have found Stone Age implements and pebble tools in several areas of Zimbabwe, suggest-

Victoria Falls, Zimbabwe (Cory Langley).

ing human habitation for many centuries. The ruins of stone buildings also provide evidence of early civilization.

In the sixteenth century, the Portuguese were the first Europeans to attempt colonization of south-central Africa, but the hinterland lay virtually untouched by Europeans until the arrival of explorers, missionaries, and traders some three hundred years later. In 1888, the area that became Southern and Northern Rhodesia was proclaimed a British sphere of influence. The British South Africa Company was chartered in 1889, and the settlement of Salisbury (now Harare) was established in 1890.

In 1895 the territory was formally named Rhodesia. In 1923 Southern Rhodesia's white settlers were given the choice of being incorporated into the Union of South Africa or becoming a separate entity within the British Empire. The settlers rejected incorporation, and Southern Rhodesia was formally annexed by the United Kingdom. In September 1953, Southern Rhodesia was joined with the British protectorates of Northern Rhodesia and Nyasaland. The federation was dissolved at the end of 1963 after much crisis and turmoil with Northern Rhodesia and Nyasaland became the independent states of Zambia and Malawi in 1964.

Although prepared to grant independence to Rhodesia, the United Kingdom insisted that the authorities at Salisbury first demonstrate their intention to move toward eventual majority rule. Desiring to keep their dominant position, the white Rhodesians refused to give such assurance. On November 11, 1965, after lengthy and unsuccessful negotiations with the British government, Prime Minister Ian Smith issued a Unilateral Declaration of Independence (UDI) from the United Kingdom. The British government considered the UDI unconstitutional and illegal, but made clear that it would not use force to end the rebellion. The British government imposed unilateral economic sanctions on Rhodesia and requested other nations to do the same. On December 16, 1966, the United Nations Security Council, for the first time in its history, imposed mandatory economic sanctions on a state.

In the early 1970s, informal attempts at settlement were renewed between the United Kingdom and the Rhodesia administration. In 1974 the major African nationalist groups—the Zimbabwe African People's Union (ZAPU) and the Zimbabwe African National Union (ZANU), which split away from ZAPU in 1963—were united into the "Patriotic Front" and combined their military forces. In 1976 the Smith government agreed in principle to majority rule and to a meeting in Geneva with black nationalist leaders. Blacks represented at the Geneva meeting included ZAPU leader Joshua Nkomo, ZANU leader Robert Mugabe, UANC chairman Bishop Abel Muzorewa, and former ZANU leader, the Rev. Ndabaningi Sithole. However, the meeting failed.

On March 3, 1978, the Smith administration signed an internal settlement agreement in Salisbury with Bishop Muzorewa, Rev. Sithole, and Chief Jeremiah Chirau. The agreement provided for qualified majority rule and elections with universal suffrage. Following elections in April 1979, in which his UANC part won a majority, Bishop Muzorewa assumed office on June 1, becoming Zimbabwe's first black prime minister. However, the installation of the new black majority government did not end the guerrilla conflict that had claimed more than 20,000 lives.

The British and the African parties began deliberations on a Rhodesian settlement in London on September 10, 1979. On December 21, the parties signed an agreement calling for a cease-fire, new elections, a transition period under British rule, and a new constitution implementing majority rule while protecting minority rights. The elections were supervised by the British government. Robert Mugabe's ZANU Party won an absolute majority and was asked to form Zimbabwe's first government. The British government formally granted independence to Zimbabwe on April 18, 1980. In 1985 Mugabe's party won by a landslide in the country's first general election since independence. He was reelected in 1990 and 1996.

Zimbabwe's population is divided into two major language groups, which are subdivided into several tribal groups. The Mashona (Shona speakers), who constitute about eighty percent of the population, have lived in the area the longest and are the majority language groups. The Matabele (Sindebele speakers), representing about 19 percent of the population and entered in the southwest near Bulawayo, arrived within the last 150 years. An offshoot of the South African Zulu group, they had maintained control over the Mashona until the white occupation of Rhodesia.

Western Hemisphere

Anguilla
Independence: n/a (dependent territory of the United Kingdom)
Area: 91 sq. km.
Form of government: British dependency
Capital: The Valley
Currency: East Caribbean dollar
Population: (1998) 11,000
Ethnic divisions: Black

Religious groups: Anglican 40%, Methodist 33%, Seventh-Day Adventist 7%, Baptist 5%, Roman Catholic 3%, other 12%
Languages spoken: English
Exports: Fish, lobster
Imports: Food, textiles, furniture, motor vehicles, and fuel
Primary trade partners: Canada, the United Kingdom, and the United States

According to legend, this slender island, named in Spanish for the eel its shape suggests, got that name from no less a figure than Christopher Columbus, who is said to have sailed through this area of the Caribbean on one of his early voyages of discovery at the end of the fifteenth century. Some historians dismiss this story as fanciful and contend that the French were the first Europeans to visit these shores. Whatever the story, it is certain that the first colonial settlement was established by the British in 1650. Unlike many other islands in the region, Anguilla remained under the power of the British for the entire colonial period.

The British settlers quickly established farms on the island, although these agricultural holdings were less expansive than the plantation-size holdings found on some of the other Caribbean islands held by the British. This was because the island itself was relatively small and its soil less fertile than on other British-held islands. To work these farms, however, the British imported slaves. Because the island was small, the British decided in the early nineteenth century to link its colonial administration with that of Saint Christopher, better known as Saint Kitts, and Nevis, both of which lie to the south of Anguilla. The three-island colony's local administration was located on Saint Kitts, the largest of the islands.

The British abolished slavery in all of its colonial holdings in 1834, but most of the former slaves continued to work in farming or fishing for many years thereafter. In time, the harvesting of salt emerged as another major occupation for the former slaves. One of the slave traditions that lives on in contemporary celebrations is known as the "jollification." In this observance, Anguillans of both sexes dressed as field workers parade together to a location where a field is planted. Songs of Afro-Caribbean origins are sung as they proceed along their route and begin their field work.

In the late 1960s, as Saint Kitts and Nevis clamored for their independence from Britain, Anguillans decided their future would be brighter if they became a separate dependent territory tied to Britain. In 1967 the island issued a unilateral declaration of independence from Saint Kitts and Nevis, triggering a mini-invasion by British troops to quell the rebellion. In the early 1970s, the island was accorded the British crown colony status that it sought.

Antigua and Barbuda

Independence: November 1, 1981
Area: 171 sq. mi.
Form of government: Autonomous member of the United Kingdom
Capital: St. John's
International relations: UN, OAS, CARICOM
Currency: East Caribbean dollar
Income: (per capita US$) 6,800 (1999)
Population: (1999) 64,006
Ethnic divisions: Black, some British and Portuguese
Religious groups: Principally Anglican, with evangelical Protestant and Roman Catholic minorities.
Languages spoken: English (official), regional dialects
Literacy: 90% (1997)
Exports: Petroleum products, manufactures, food and live animals, machinery, transport equipment
Imports: Food and live animals, machinery and transport equipment, manufactures, chemicals, oil
Primary trade partners: United States, United Kingdom, Canada, numerous Caribbean nations

Christopher Columbus first visited the islands of Antigua and Barbuda in 1493. Missionaries attempted to settle on the island, but were hindered by the fierce Carib Indians, who inhabited the islands, and the absence of natural freshwater springs. In 1632 the British successfully established a colony. Sir Christopher Codrington established the first large sugar estate in Antigua in 1674, bringing slaves from Africa's west coast to work the plantations. Although Antiguan slaves were emancipated in 1834, they remained bound to their plantation owners. Economic opportunities for the new freemen were limited by a lack of surplus farming land, no access to credit, and an economy built on agriculture rather than manufacturing.

The majority of modern-day Antiguans are descended from the African slaves imported by the British to work the island's sugar plantations. Although the sugar estates were extremely profitable for both their owners and Britain, generating more wealth in the 1780s than all of Britain's New England colonies combined, life for the island's slaves was very harsh indeed. The harshness of life and work on the sugar plantations led to slave riots including one in 1831, just three years before the British ended slavery on the island.

Led by Chief Minister Vere Cornwall Bird, Sr., Antigua began to push for independence in the late 1960s. There was a separate push by Barbudans for their independence, but neither the Antiguan nor the British government supported this movement. Antigua and Barbuda became a single, fully independent nation in 1981. Antigua and Barbuda entered the twenty-first century ruled by its black majority.

Argentina

Official Name: Republic of Argentina
Independence: July 9, 1816
Area: 1,072,156 sq. mi.
Form of government: Presidential republic
Capital: Buenos Aires
International relations: GATT, UN, UNCTAD
Currency: Peso
Income: (per capita US$) 8,370 (1996)
Population: (1999 estimate) 36.2 million
Ethnic divisions: European descendents 85%, mestizo and other 15%
Religious groups: Roman Catholic
Languages spoken: Spanish (official), English
Literacy: 96.2% (1995)
Exports: Iron ore, livestock, petroleum, meat, wheat
Imports: Machinery and equipment, chemicals, metals, fuels and lubricants, agricultural products
Primary trade partners: United States, Brazil, Germany, Italy, Japan

Though traditionally known for its early Spanish and nineteenth-century Italian and German heritage, Argentina had a large black population during much of the colonial and independence periods. Today the Afro-Argentine population is estimated at a few thousand.

The first slaves were brought into Argentina in the final two decades of the sixteenth century. By 1680 nearly 23,000 slaves had been imported legally, although those brought into the country illegally would certainly swell that figure considerably. Most of the slaves brought into Argentina originated in what is now the Congo and Angola. Although the local government banned the importation of slaves in 1813, illegal trade in slaves continued for nearly thirty more years until a treaty with Britain in 1840 finally cut off this commerce in human cargo. As in most of the Americas, the slaves brought into Argentina were employed as farm workers or domestic servants. Ownership of one or more slaves was considered a status symbol among Argentina's ranchers.

Until relatively recently, Argentina's African heritage has received little attention, due perhaps in part to the scarcity of Afro-Argentines. The limited number of blacks in the country have allowed the country's historians and sociologists to indulge in a bit of revisionism, insisting that blacks are of little historical relevance in Argentina. Regrettably, racist attitudes are not uncommon in modern-day Argentina. When the country's soccer team has faced opposing teams made up largely of blacks, headlines in the sports pages have sometimes referred to these opponents in a derogatory and decidedly racist manner. A handful of contemporary scholars have attempted to preserve the history of the African contributions to the development of Argentina.

Aruba

Independence: (Autonomous part of Netherlands)

Area: 75 sq. mi

Form of government: Autonomous part of the Netherlands

Capital: Oranjestad

Currency: Aruba florin

Income: (per capita US$) 18,000 (1994)

Population: 68,031

Ethnic divisions: Mixed European and Carib Indian 85%, black 15%

Religious groups: Roman Catholic, Protestant, Jewish

Languages spoken: Papiamento, English, Dutch, Spanish

Literacy: above 90%

Exports: Refined petroleum products

Imports: Crude oil

Primary trade partners: Venezuela, Netherlands, United States

Aruba is one of the few Caribbean islands whose people are still largely descended from an original indigenous population. More than 85 percent of Arubans are of mixed Arawak Indian and European ancestry. A majority of the remaining 15 percent are black immigrants from other Caribbean islands who have come to Aruba to fill some of the many available jobs in thriving tourist and oil industries.

The island's arid climate and relatively barren soil prevented the development of any major agricultural cultivation on Aruba. This lack of large-scale farming helps to explain the absence of any significant slave heritage on the island. When the first oil refineries began to spring up on Aruba in the 1930s, workers, many of them black, were imported from other islands in the Caribbean.

Though their numbers are relatively small, particularly when viewed against the backdrop of the Caribbean as a whole, the blacks of Aruba have made significant contributions to the island's culture in the relatively short time they have been present on the island. Papiamento, the local language, draws on elements of several European languages, the native Arawak tongue, and several African dialects.

Bahamas

Official Name: Commonwealth of the Bahamas

Independence: July 10, 1973

Area: 5,382 sq. mi

Form of Government: Independent state under British sovereignty

Capital: Nassau

International relations: CARICOM, EU, OAS, UN

Currency: Bahamian dollar

Income: (per capita US$) 12,440 (1995)

Population: (1998) 280,000

Ethnic divisions: Black 85%, European 15%

Religious groups: Baptist, Anglican, Roman Catholic, Methodist

Languages spoken: English, Creole

Literacy: 98.2% (1995)

Exports: Pharmaceuticals, shellfish, salt, cement, rum, aragonite, cascarilla bark, tomatoes, and citrus.

Imports: Foodstuffs, meat, motor vehicles, oil, animal feed, petroleum products, clothing, machinery, and appliances.

Primary trade partners: United States, Canada, EU members

Christopher Columbus first visited the islands of the Bahamas in 1492, when he landed in the Western Hemisphere, either at Long Bay, Samana Cay, San Salvador Island, or one of a number of other islands. In 1647 the first permanent European settlement was founded. In 1717 the islands became a British crown colony. Most of these British colonists were not large landowners, so African slavery developed more slowly in the Bahamas than in several nearby islands. But it did develop, and over time blacks came to dominate the islands, accounting today for about 85 percent of the total population.

Britain's abolition of slavery in all its territories set free some 10,000 former slaves scattered across the Bahamas. Under the terms of the British edict ending slavery in 1834, the newly freed slaves were apprenticed to their former owners and required to remain with those owners as apprentices for a period of four years. Many of the former slaves continued to pursue occupations in farming and fishing, even after their apprenticeships had ended. Eventually a black middle class developed on the islands as individual blacks managed to obtain a higher education and enter such professions as doctors, lawyers, and educators.

Eighty-five percent of Bahamians are of African descent. Many of their ancestors arrived in the Bahamas when it was a staging area for the slave trade and when Bermuda forced out free blacks and slaves. Later, black slaves were brought into the islands by the thousands of British loyalists who fled the American colonies during the Revolutionary War.

The twentieth-century boom in South Florida and the promise of better-paying jobs lured many black Bahamians to the United States, despite the racial discrimination they encountered upon their arrival. A psychological and cultural barrier developed between those Bahamians who left their homeland in an attempt to better themselves and those who chose to remain in the islands. A similar division was seen between those who were attracted to Nassau and the more rapidly developing islands and those who opted for the quiet life on the outer islands.

Bahamian musicians adorned in celebratory costumes performing in the streets (Cory Langley).

The Bahamas were granted self-government through a series of constitutional and political steps, culminating in independence on July 10, 1973. The Progressive Liberal Party led the Bahamas to independence and remained in power until the early 1990s. In August 1992, the Free National Movement (FNM) won parliamentary elections, and its leader, Hubert Ingraham, became prime minister. In March 1997 elections, Ingraham and the FNM were reelected.

Barbados

Independence: November 30, 1966
Area: 166 sq. mi.
Form of government: Independent state under British sovereignty
Capital: Bridgetown
International relations: CARICOM, EU, OAS, UN
Currency: Barbados dollar
Income: (per capita US$) 6,590 (1995)
Population: (1997) 258,756
Ethnic divisions: Black 80%, mixed 16%, European 4%
Religious groups: Anglican 70%, Roman Catholic, Methodist, Baptist and Moravian
Languages spoken: English
Literacy: 97.4% (1995)

Exports: Fish, sugar, rum, chemicals, fuel
Imports: Consumer goods, machinery, foodstuffs, construction materials, chemicals, fuel
Primary trade partners: United States, United Kingdom, Trinidad and Tobago

It should hardly come as a surprise that Barbados is considered the most British of the Caribbean islands. For more than three hundred years, the island was under the control of the British, whose institutions became firmly entrenched in the Barbadian culture and economy. The first British colonists arrived in 1627, bringing with them ten slaves of African ancestry. The slave population remained relatively limited for the first few years, as most colonists were unable to afford to purchase slave labor and instead worked the land themselves or with the help of indentured servants from Europe. Although the number of slaves on the island was small, their role in the island's economy was pivotal. African slaves, along with some of the native Amerindian people who had been enslaved, were forced to handle the most challenging tasks by their owners.

With the rise of the sugar industry, beginning in the 1640s, Barbados became more heavily involved in the slave trade. Between 1645 and 1685, the number of

African slaves on the island skyrocketed from about 5,700 to nearly 60,000. By 1700, the slave population on Barbados was estimated at close to 135,000. Drawn mostly from West Africa, these slaves spoke a variety of languages and represented a staggering number of ethnic groups including the Fon, Fante, Ga, Asante, and Yoruba peoples. By the early eighteenth century, many of the European-born indentured servants who had carried much of the workload in the colony's early years began leaving Barbados in waves. This aggravated the problem of racial imbalance, worrying the white landowners and resulting in tough, new regulations to control the slave population.

Despite the imposition of strong regulations to prevent unrest among the huge slave population, Barbados experienced three major slave rebellions in 1649, 1675, and 1692. Colonial justice was harsh. Rebellious slaves were tortured in an attempt to get them to name confederates. Of those captured and tried, most were sentenced to be executed, often by somewhat barbarous methods including being burned alive. Little slave resistance was recorded in the eighteenth century, but the British Parliament's 1807 ban on the international slave trade, the Haitian Revolution that brought blacks to power, and the visits of abolitionists to the island culminated in the so-called Easter Rebellion in 1816. As many as 1,000 slaves were killed in the fighting, nearly 150 were executed after the rebellion was put down, and another 120 slaves or so were deported from the island. So shaken by the uprising was the British government that it pressured Barbadian colonists to relax their hold on the slave population. In 1833, the British Parliament voted to end slavery in all British territories.

From 1958 to 1962, Barbados was one of ten members of the West Indies Federation. Barbados negotiated its own independence at a constitutional conference with the United Kingdom in June 1966. The country attained self-rule on November 30, 1966. Since that time, Barbados has been a member of the British Commonwealth of Nations and has assumed a leadership role in the Caribbean Community (CARICOM). Owen Arthur, a member of the Barbados Labour Party, assumed the prime ministership in 1994, after former Prime Minister Erskine Sandiford lost a vote of confidence in the National Assembly. Leading contemporary Afro-Barbadians include George Lamming, a novelist, critic, essayist, and educator.

Ethnically, the population of Barbados is 80 percent African, 16 percent mixed, and 4 percent European.

Belize

Independence: September 21, 1981
Area: 8,867 sq. mi.

Form of government: Independent state under British sovereignty
Capital: Belmopan
International relations: CARICOM, EU, UN
Currency: Belize dollar
Income: (per capita US$) 2,880 (1996)
Population: (1998) 230,000
Ethnic divisions: Creole, black, mestizo, Amerindian
Religious groups: Roman Catholic, Anglican, Methodist, Muslim, Buddhist
Languages spoken: English (official), Spanish, Mayan
Literacy: 91.2% (1995)
Exports: Bananas, citrus fruit, sugar, wood, apparel
Imports: Machinery and transportation equipment, food, manufactured goods, fuels, chemicals
Primary trade partners: United States, United Kingdom, Mexico

Belize, known until 1973 as British Honduras, is the only country in Central America in which blacks have made up a majority of the population throughout the twentieth century. The country did not achieve full independence until September 21, 1981. Originally peopled largely by a succession of native American peoples, including the Maya, Belize passed between British and Spanish control throughout the seventeenth century. A treaty between the two countries in 1765 maintained Spain's claim to the land but recognized the British right to maintain coastal settlements for the harvesting of logwood, which was valued for its use in producing dyes. As the British log harvesting efforts expanded, slaves were brought in from Africa and other British colonies in the Caribbean to assist with the effort.

Once the presence of the British wood-harvesting enclave had been established by treaty, the woodcutters graduated from cutting logwood and began to go after mahogany. The nature of this work had a profound effect on slave life in the colony. Trusted slaves roamed the forests of the land, often with little or no supervision, hunting for mahogany trees to be felled. Once found, these slaves known as huntsmen reported to axmen, a team of slaves that would then cut down the trees. Although the slaves employed in mahogany harvesting enjoyed somewhat more freedom to range through the rain forest, the treatment of these slaves overall was not noticeably more humane than that accorded slaves involved in agriculture.

The British established the colony of British Honduras in 1840; it became a crown colony in 1862. Self-government was granted in January 1964. The official name of the territory was changed from British Honduras to Belize in June of 1973, and full independence was granted on September 21, 1981, with George C. Price of the People's United Party installed as the head of government. In December 1984 elections, voters elected

Manuel Esquivel prime minister. Five years later, Price was again elected prime minister, a post that was recaptured by Esquivel in 1993 elections. Leading contemporary Afro-Belizeans include Zee Edgell, a writer who has concentrated her writings on the Belizean independence movement, the nation's multi-ethnic traditions, and the lives of women in Belize.

Most Belizeans are of multiracial descent. Nearly 40 to 45 percent of the population is of African ancestry; more than 25 percent is of mixed local Indian and European descent (mestizo). Another one-fifth of the population is composed of Carib, Mayan, or other Amerindian ethnic groups.

Bermuda

Independence: n/a (parliamentary British colony with internal government since 1620)
Area: 20.6 sq. mi.
Form of government: Semi-autonomous British colony
Capital: Hamilton
Currency: Bermuda dollar
Income: (per capita US$) 17,000 (1987)
Population: (1998) 62,569
Ethnic divisions: Black 61%, white and other 39%
Religious groups: Anglican 37%, Protestant 21%, Roman Catholic 14%, other 28%
Languages spoken: English
Literacy: 98%
Exports: Bananas, coffee, cotton, tobacco
Imports: Agricultural products, machinery, transportation equipment, pharmaceuticals
Primary trade partners: United Kingdom, United States

Located in the Atlantic Ocean about 650 miles east of North Carolina, Bermuda is relatively isolated. The first Europeans to visit Bermuda were Spanish explorers in 1503. In 1609 a group of British explorers became stranded on the islands and their reports aroused great interest about the islands in England. In 1612 British colonists arrived and founded the town of Saint George, the oldest, continuously inhabited English-speaking settlement in the Western Hemisphere.

Slaves from Africa were brought to Bermuda soon after the colony began. Although the island's soil and area were ill-suited for large-scale farming, the slaves were put to work as fishermen, tradesmen, and, to a limited extent, as field hands. The slaves of Bermuda rose up against their masters on several occasions, most notably in 1730, after which the accused ringleader, Sarah Bassett, was burned at the stake. Thirty years later, between six hundred and seven hundred slaves were accused of plotting a large-scale rebellion. A number of those were tried and subsequently executed. The slave trade was outlawed in Bermuda in 1807, and all slaves were freed in 1834.

Unfortunately for the newly freed slaves of the island nation, employment opportunities in the tobacco, shipbuilding, and salt mining industries, all of which had been mainstays of the Bermudian economy, began to shrink dramatically as those industries themselves started to end. The island economy got a temporary shot in the arm during the U.S. Civil War when Union ships blockaded the ports of the Confederacy. Southern importers arranged to have their incoming goods off-loaded at Bermuda and then smuggled through the blockade in smaller ships. However, with the end of the war, this temporary economy boost disappeared. Bermudians, with an area of less than 21 square miles, turned to small-scale agricultural ventures to produce income. The cultivation of onions, potatoes, and Easter lilies eventually proved so successful and profitable that indentured servants had to be brought in from Portugal to help handle part of the workload.

For most of its first three hundred years, the government of Bermuda was composed exclusively of wealthy white landowners or appointees of the British Crown. Not until 1963 were the protests of black Bermudians heeded and universal adult suffrage introduced. Landowners still had an edge, however, as the law provided them each with two votes. A new constitution in 1868 gave the locally elected government complete control over Bermuda's affairs. Sentiment against independence for Bermuda remains strong, as reflected in the most recent referendum on the issue; 73 percent voted against independence in 1995.

Nearly two-thirds of the Bermudians are of African descent. An estimated 7,000 U.S. citizens live on the island; approximately 2,800 of them are military personnel and their dependents.

Bolivia

Official Name: Republic of Bolivia
Independence: August 6, 1825
Area: 424,166 sq. mi.
Form of government: Presidential republic
Capital: La Paz
International relations: LAIA, OAS, UN
Currency: Boliviano
Income: (per capita US$) 830 (1995)
Population: (1998) 7.8 million
Ethnic divisions: Quechua 30%, mestizo 30%, Aymara 25%, other 15%
Religious groups: Roman Catholic
Languages spoken: Spanish (official), Quechua (official), Aymara (official)
Literacy: 83.1% (1995)
Exports: Copper, gold, zinc, natural gas, jewelry
Imports: Capital goods, chemicals, petroleum

Primary trade partners: United States, Argentina, Brazil, Japan

Although blacks make up only about two percent of Bolivia's population, their history extends back to the first half of the sixteenth century when the first slaves were brought into the country. These blacks were imported from Peru to help supplement the labor of the indigenous native American population, many of whom had succumbed to diseases introduced by European settlers. The African origins of these slaves is the subject of debate, with some contending that they came from an area of the West African coast between the Senegal and Niger rivers, while others maintain they were brought from Angola. This question of the earliest Afro-Bolivians' origins is unlikely ever to be resolved, since Spain maintained no West African trading centers and thus drew slaves from a wide area and also because the record keeping of those moving the slaves left much to be desired. Frequently there was an assumption that the slaves came from an area close to their port of embarkation in Africa, but often this was not the case.

The slaves of African origin brought into Bolivia did not fare well at high elevations and under the stressful working conditions of the mines. By 1554 most of the African slaves had been replaced in the country's silver mines by indigenous labor. The blacks were then put into other lines of work, including as domestic servants. Some were even apprenticed to artisans skilled in the crafting of silver and other metals. The majority of the black slaves were moved to rural areas and pressed into service as cultivators of crops to feed the country's growing population. Within Bolivia, many of the black slaves eventually mixed with other ethnic groups. Children of mixed African and European ancestry were sometimes classified as mulattos, while those of African and native American descent were called zambos. Calculating the African or African-mixed population in Bolivia's past because of the haphazard manner in which records were kept.

Although their numbers were few, Afro-Bolivians joined the country's struggle to win its independence from Spain. Independence was achieved in 1825, and soon thereafter the country's founding constitution called for the emancipation of all its slaves. However, not all blacks and native Americans in bondage were set free. As of 1831, the country's constitution contained a "free-womb" statute that decreed that no one born after independence could be considered a slave, but continued to recognize those previously in bondage as slaves. Complete liberation of the slaves did not come until 1851.

Never particularly active on the political front, Afro-Bolivians have had some impact on contemporary culture, given their dwindling numbers. In the early 1980s, a group of students from Coroico, Nor Yungas, formed a dance troupe to preserve some of the original Afro-Bolivian dance forms of the region. Called the Grupo Afroboliviano, the troupe performed throughout the country, helping to create an awareness among their countrymen of the distinct Afro-Bolivian culture. This, in turn, has sparked a number of efforts to preserve this culture.

Brazil

Official Name: Federative Republic of Brazil

Independence: September 7, 1822

Area: 3.3 million sq. mi.

Form of government: Presidential republic

Capital: Brasilia

International relations: LAIA, OAS, UN

Currency: Cruzeiro

Income: (per capita US$) 4,640 (1996)

Population: (1998) 169.8 million

Ethnic divisions: Portuguese, black, Indian (principally Tupi and Guarani linguistic stock), Italian, German, Japanese

Religious groups: Christian 93%, other 7%

Languages spoken: Portuguese (official), Spanish, English, French

Literacy: 83.3% (1995)

Exports: Coffee, iron ore, soybean, steel, sugar, footwear

Imports: Crude oil, capital goods, chemical products, foodstuffs

Primary trade partners: European Union countries, United States, Japan

Brazil was formally claimed in 1500 by the Portuguese and was ruled from Lisbon as a colony until 1808. Brazil successfully declared independence on September 7, 1922. Four major groups make up the Brazilian population: indigenous Indians of Tupi and Guarani language stock; the Portuguese; Africans brought to Brazil as slaves; and various European and Asian immigrant groups that have settled in Brazil since the mid-nineteenth century.

Slavery was introduced into Brazil in the 1530s and expanded greatly when sugar became important. It grew rapidly between 1580 and 1640, when Spain controlled the country. Estimates of the total number of slaves brought to Brazil varies from six million to twenty million. Slavery did not finally end in Brazil until 1888. Though slavery in Brazil was often extremely brutal, and the death rate of blacks on sugar, coffee, and cotton plantations was enormous, large numbers of Africans achieved freedom. About 25 percent of Brazil's blacks were free during slavery.

During the nineteenth century, free blacks intermarried so rapidly that their numbers fell from about 400,000 in 1800 to 20,000 by 1888, when slavery was finally

Brazilian vendor selling food along the beaches of Rio de Janiero (Cory Langley).

abolished. Free blacks enjoyed full legal equality during both the period of slavery and after it was abolished.

In Brazil, slaves who served masters in cities were often allowed to seek part-time and temporary employment elsewhere. They were able to read and write and develop employable skills. Blacks became important to the development and economy of the country, and some became prominent in public life. Black Brazilian Nilo Pecanha served as vice president and briefly as president of Brazil in the first decade of this century. Blacks also achieved fame in Brazil's intellectual and artistic life.

In the early twentieth century, a new black consciousness emerged in response to the appearance of a number of Afro-Brazilian publications. Also springing up during this period were a number of organizations that aspired to right some of the wrongs faced by the nation's black population. White Brazilians in the years following the abolition of slavery embarked on a policy of "whitening" the country's population through intermixing with Afro-Brazilians. The Brazilian program of "branqueamento" was based on the notion that the presence of European blood in an individual was suffi-

cient to make him or her white. It was against the discrimination and poverty stemming from this racist policy that the Afro-Brazilian organizations fought in the early twentieth century.

The black population of Brazil is the largest in the Americas. Only Nigeria in Africa has a larger population of blacks. The African influences on both the population and the culture of Brazil are all-pervasive. Perhaps no single event better illustrates the scope of the African contribution to Brazilian life than Carnival. However, behind the laughter and goodwill of this annual four-day celebration, the truth is somewhat less reassuring for those who would assume that racism is long dead in Brazil. In fact, Brazilians of African descent lack clout on both the political and the economic level. Afro-Brazilians lag behind their fellow countrymen in terms of education, housing, employment, and health. Activists within the Afro-Brazilian community continue the struggle to achieve complete equality for everyone in the country, regardless of race. Leading contemporary Afro-Brazilians include: musicians Jorge Benjor, Carlinhos Brown, Gilberto Gil, husband and wife duo Airto Moreira and Flora Purim, and Milton Nascimento; literary figure Abdias do Nascimento; and internationally recognized sports figure Pelé.

Canada

Independence: July 1, 1867

Area: 3.8 million sq. mi.

Form of government: Independent state with British sovereignty

Capital: Ottawa

International relations: Commonwealth, NATO, OECD, UN

Currency: Canadian dollar

Income: (per capita US$) 19,330 (1996)

Population: (1998) 30.7 million

Ethnic divisions: European of mostly English or French origin, indigenous peoples, black

Religious groups: Roman Catholic, United Church

Languages spoken: English (official), French (official)

Literacy: 96.6% (1995)

Exports: Manufactured goods, minerals

Imports: Crude oil, chemicals, motor vehicles and parts, durable goods, computers, telecommunications equipment

Primary trade partners: United States, Japan, United Kingdom, Germany, France

Blacks make up a tiny portion—only about two percent—of Canada's total population, but their contributions to the country's founding and its history far outweigh their meager numbers. Africans are believed to have participated in a number of the early exploratory missions to the country. Legend holds that one of the crew members on Jacques Cartier's expedition was an African. However, it is known for certain that a Mathieu de Coste (sometimes rendered as da Costa) served the governor of Acadia as an interpreter to the local Micmac indigenous peoples. Early records indicated that the first slave brought directly to Canada from Africa was a child, brought to Quebec in 1628 by Englishman David Kirke and sold to a local resident upon Kirke's departure the following year. The child was baptized Olivier Le Jeune in May 1633. According to records, he died in 1654.

Between 1628 and the British conquest of 1759, New France imported 1,132 slaves of African origin. Most of these slaves came from the French West Indies or the British colonies elsewhere in North America. A governor of New France had petitioned Paris to permit a trade in African slaves but was turned down, so there was no direct importation of slaves from Africa. The number of slaves living in the British-held colonies of Canada was relatively small until the time of the American Revolution. Loyalists fleeing the new American republic brought with them some 2,000 black slaves. About 1,200 of that number went to the Maritimes including New Brunswick, Nova Scotia, and Prince Edward Island. Of the remaining 800, about 300 went to Lower Canada, as Quebec was then known, and 500 went to Upper Canada (Ontario). Even more influential in Canada's development was the arrival of some 3,500 free black Loyalists, who fled to Canada following the American Revolution. Most of these black Loyalists settled in Nova Scotia and New Brunswick.

Slave codes were more severe in the British-held territories than in New France, where slaves could marry, own property, and maintain parental rights. However, the British were not to sustain slavery for long. London had divided Canada into two governments, Upper Canada and Lower Canada. The governor of Upper Canada, Colonel James Simcoe, an ardent abolitionist, induced the area's legislature to pass laws forbidding importation of slaves and freeing every slave born in the area by the age of 25. As a result, slavery in Upper Canada soon collapsed.

Similar legislation was not enacted in Lower Canada. However, by 1800 the courts, through complex legal decisions, established the principle that a slave could leave his master whenever he wished. In the Maritime Provinces, courts also acted to eliminate slavery in fact if not in theory. Slavery was formally abolished in Canada in 1833.

Meanwhile, starting slowly in the eighteenth century, Canada was becoming a haven for slaves fleeing across her southern borders. Slaves who had served with the British in the American War for Independence came to Halifax from New York in large numbers in 1782 and 1783. Though many were to migrate to Freetown on the West Coast of Africa, others stayed. In 1826, Canada defied the United States and formally refused to return fugitive slaves. In 1829 the legislature of Lower Canada announced that every slave that entered the province was immediately free, a declaration that gave impetus to the Underground Railroad and stimulated moves for resettlement by blacks in Canada.

The passage of the Fugitive Slave Act in 1850 meant that any escaped slave who remained in the United States was to be returned to his owner. Within a year after passage of the law, some 10,000 slaves arrived in Canada, welcomed by a majority of Canadians who provided communities and services for them.

African Americans were accepted into the mainstream of Canadian life, were allowed to choose separate or integrated schools, and were elected to local office and served as officers in the Canadian Army. Black laborers contributed substantially to the expansion of the Canadian Pacific Railroad, as immigrants from Eastern and Southern Europe were to contribute to the development of railroads in the United States. Black skilled laborers were much in demand. By 1861, at the outbreak of the Civil War in the United States, there were 50,000 blacks in Canada. However, after the Civil War, feelings of fear among white Canadians led to discrimination in employment and schools. Many African Americans re-emigrated to the United States, feeling that, with slavery outlawed there, a bright future awaited them. By 1871 the black population of Canada dipped to about 20,000.

Canada, the most sparsely populated country in the world with 1.5 persons per square mile, has become a haven for so many refugees that it has earned awards for outstanding achievement from human rights organizations. In fact, so many immigrants from Asia, Africa, the Caribbean and elsewhere have moved to Canada, that the established British-Caucasian population has expressed fears it will become extinct (assimilated) within one hundred years. Toronto alone has become one of the world's most cosmopolitan cities with more than one hundred cultural or ethnic groups.

Cayman Islands

Independence: n/a (dependent territory of the United Kingdom)
Area: 260 sq. km.
Form of government: British colony
Capital: George Town
Currency: Cayman dollar
Income: (per capita US$) 11,000
Population: (1998) 38,000
Ethnic divisions: 40% mixed, 20% white, 40% black

Religious groups: United Church (Presbyterian and Congregational), Anglican, Baptist, Roman Catholic, Church of God, other Protestant denominations
Languages spoken: English
Exports: Farm products, wood, shellfish

During his fourth visit to the Caribbean in 1503, Christopher Columbus sighted these islands and dubbed them Las Tortugas for the large number of sea turtles he saw in the area. Later in the sixteenth century, Europeans passing through the area began calling the islands Las Caymanas, the Carib Amerindian term for crocodiles. However, it is believed that it was the island's many iguanas, rather than real crocodiles, that inspired this name change. In any case, apart from brief visits to pick up fresh water and turtle meat, Europeans had little to do with these islands until the middle of the seventeenth century when the first European settlement was made. The earliest settlements on the islands were made by a rather disreputable blend of characters including pirates, army deserters, debtors, and shipwrecked sailors. Under the Treaty of Madrid, the Caymans came under British control in 1670. It was more than sixty years before the British established their first permanent settlement, made up largely of planters who had previously been located on Jamaica. Because of this relationship between Jamaica and the Caymans, the islands were considered dependencies of the former until 1962.

These earliest of British settlers first imported African slaves into the islands, using them largely as domestic servants, fishermen, and subsistence farmers. The islands, not particularly fertile, were never considered an ideal setting for farming, so the large-scale agricultural undertakings the planters had enjoyed in Jamaica could not be duplicated in the Caymans. The absence of a plantation-type system and the relative proximity within which the planters and the newly imported slaves lived led in time to a good deal of intermarriage between the two groups. Nearly half of the population of the Caymans today is made up of islanders of mixed European and African descent. As elsewhere throughout the British territories, slavery was abolished in 1834.

When Jamaica won its independence in 1962, the Caymans became a directly held colony of Britain. Under the new arrangements with the United Kingdom, the islanders were given a new constitution and a larger measure of control over their internal affairs. A tourist board launched in 1966 proved extremely successful in attracting tourists to the islands. By 1994, more than one million tourists, close to seventy percent of them from the United States, were visiting the islands annually. Another major source of income for the Caymans came from offshore banking. Shortly after its change in status with Jamaica, Cayman Islanders enacted new legisla-

tion to encourage company registration, offshore banking, and trust-company formation in the islands. Today, more than five hundred banks do business in the Caymans, and the companies registered there number in the thousands. Prospering under existing conditions, islanders have made no major push for independence.

Chile

Official name: Republic of Chile
Independence: September 18, 1810
Area: 292,257 sq. mi.
Form of government: Presidential republic
Capital: Santiago
International relations: LAIA, OAS, UN
Currency: Peso
Income: (per capita US$) 5,150 (1996)
Population: (1998) 14.8 million
Ethnic divisions: European and European-Native American 95%
Religious groups: Roman Catholic 89%, Protestant 11%
Languages spoken: Spanish
Literacy: 95.2% (1995)
Exports: Almonds, copper, gold, grapes, nitrate, silver, sulfur
Imports: Capital goods, spare parts, raw materials, petroleum, foodstuffs
Primary trade partners: European Union countries, United States, Japan, Argentina, Brazil

Africans first came to Chile with the expedition of Spanish explorer Diego de Almagro in 1536. Some served the expedition as slaves, while others served as soldiers. One such member of the expedition was Juan Valiente, a slave from Mexico who was permitted to join Almagro as a soldier. He later distinguished himself in battle and in time rose to captain of the expedition's infantry. The earliest slaves brought into Chile were used to supplement the labors of indigenous workers in construction, farming, and the mining of gold. Relatively hard-strapped for money, Chile could not afford to import large numbers of slaves.

Despite the economic limits on the importation of slaves, the country's black population, both free and slave, grew fairly dramatically during the final three decades of the sixteenth century. From a population of 7,000 among a total Chilean population of 624,000, the number of blacks surged by 1590 to a total of 20,000, among an overall population of 586,000. Both in the rural countryside and in Chile's growing cities, free and slave blacks found livelihoods. In the cities, most black slaves worked as domestic servants, while outside the cities, they toiled as miners, sheepherders, and cowboys. Free blacks drove coaches, made saddles, and reportedly even served as executioners. Even though the colonial Spanish law accorded blacks the lowest status possible, local authorities often saw fit to circumvent the Spanish crown and gave some slaves positions with supervisory responsibility. A select number of black slaves so distinguished themselves as soldiers that they received land grants. Juan Valiente, the slave from Mexico who served the Almagro expedition as a soldier, became the first black in the Americas known to receive such a land grant.

At about the same time, Chileans first declared their independence from Spain in 1810, talk of an abolition of slavery began to surface. It was not until 1823, however, that Chile became the first Spanish American republic to totally abolish slavery. Since the time of emancipation, the influence of the Afro-Chilean on the country's culture and development seems to have virtually disappeared. Unlike what has happened in many neighboring countries, there has been no Afro-Chilean cultural revival nor any organized involvement in politics by Afro-Chileans. The Chilean census of 1940 revealed a population of only 1,000 blacks and 3,000 mulattos. Some observers and scholars of the Chilean social scene suggest that continuing intermarriage and intermixing have combined to virtually wipe out the black population of the country.

Colombia

Official Name: Republic of Colombia
Independence: July 20, 1810
Area: 440,831 sq. mi.
Form of government: Presidential republic
Capital: Bogota
International relations: LAIA, OAS, UN
Currency: Colombian peso
Income: (per capita US$) 2,280 (1996)
Population: (1998) 38.6 million
Ethnic divisions: Mestizo 58%, white 20%, mulatto 14%, black 4%, mixed black-Indian 3%, Indian 1%
Religious groups: Roman Catholic 95%
Languages spoken: Spanish
Literacy: 91.3% (1995)
Exports: Coffee, emeralds, petroleum, silver, flowers
Imports: Industrial equipment, transportation equipment, consumer goods, chemicals, paper goods
Primary trade partners: United States, European Union countries, Brazil, Japan

The diversity of ethnic origins in Colombia results from the intermixture of indigenous Indians, Spanish colonists, and African slaves. In 1549 the area was established as a Spanish colony with the capital at Bogota. In 1717 Bogota became the capital of the viceroyalty of New Granada, which included what is now Venezuela, Ecuador, and Panama. On July 20, 1810, the citizens of Bogota created the first representative council to defy Spanish authority. Total independence

was proclaimed in 1813, and in 1819 the Republic of Greater Colombia was formed.

The African contributions to the population and culture of Colombia are many and varied. The high rate of intermarriage has resulted in a racially diverse population with close to seventy percent of its people classified as mestizos. The terminology used to refer to people of African ancestry or of mixed ancestry is somewhat complicated. The term black, or "negro" in Spanish, is common but avoided by many Colombians because of its sometimes disparaging connotations. More common are the terms "moreno" (brown) and "gente de color" (colored people). In the rural area of the country near the Pacific coast, some of the people of African ancestry refer to themselves as "libres," or free people, terminology that dates back to colonial times. Some people refer to blacks as "costenos" since many of the country's coastal residents are Afro-Colombians.

African slaves were first imported into communities along the northern coast of New Granada, a portion of which later became Colombia, in the 1520s. The port of Cartagena on the Caribbean coast developed into the principal slave trading port. The slaves brought into New Granada were used mostly in mining gold, although some saw service as domestic servants and farmworkers. The supply of native Americans, who had first been pressed into service in the mines, was rapidly being depleted, and the importation of African slaves was deemed necessary to keep the mines operating.

Even during the years of slavery, there was a considerable amount of intermarriage and intermixing between the peoples of colonial New Granada. It is estimated that by the 1770s about sixty percent of the population was classified as "free people of color." As in most territories where slaves were held, masters sometimes decided to set some or all of their slaves free, which turned out often to be a mixed blessing for those who could not find work on their own. Colombia won its independence in 1819, but slavery was not officially abolished until 1851. In the late twentieth century, Colombia's black population was concentrated in three main areas of the country: the upper central portion of the Cauca Valley, which is heavily planted in sugar cane; the Pacific coast; and the Caribbean coastal region. In the 1990s, Pledad Corboda de Castro became the first black woman to be elected to the Colombian Senate in the 1990s. In 1993 she wrote a law instituting equal rights for Afro-Colombians. Other leading contemporary Afro-Colombians include Totó la Momposina, a singer, dancer, and performer of traditional rhythms, and Manuel Zapata Olivella, a writer, physician, anthropologist, diplomat, and leading intellectual and artist of twentieth-century Latin America.

Costa Rica

Official Name: Republic of Costa Rica
Independence: September 15, 1821
Area 19,714 sq. mi.
Form of government: Presidential republic
Capital: San José
International relations: CACMO, OAS, UN
Currency: Colon
Income: (per capita US$) 2,620 (1996)
Population: (1998) 3.6 million
Ethnic divisions: European (including a few mestizos) 97%, black 2%, indigenous 1%
Religious groups: Roman Catholic 95%
Languages spoken: Spanish, Jamaican dialect of English spoken around Puerto Limon
Literacy: 94.8% (1995)
Exports: Bananas, cocoa, sugar, timber
Imports: Raw materials, consumer goods, capital equipment
Primary trade partners: United States, Germany, Mexico

In 1502, on his fourth and last voyage to the New World, Christopher Columbus made the first European landfall in the area. Settlement of Costa Rica began in 1522. In 1821 Costa Rica joined other Central American provinces in a joint declaration of independence from Spain. Unlike most of their Central American neighbors, Costa Ricans are largely of European rather than mestizo descent, and Spain is the primary country of origin. The indigenous population today numbers no more than 25,000. Blacks, descendants of nineteenth-century Jamaican immigrant workers, constitute a significant English-speaking minority of about 30,000 concentrated around the Caribbean port city of Limon.

The greatest influx of slaves into Costa Rica began during the late 1700s when Spanish colonists began importing slaves from neighboring colonies and directly from Africa to replace the dwindling labor force of indigenous Amerindian peoples, many of whom had contracted and died from diseases introduced by Europeans. The census of 1801, the first to provide figures on the black population, reported that 17 percent of the colony's population was made up of blacks or those of mixed-black descent, including mulattos, the result of black-white intermixing, and zambos of black and Amerindian descent.

More significant than the earlier importation of slaves was the movement to what is now Costa Rica by a substantial number of free black laborers from the islands of the Caribbean, particularly Jamaica. This wave of immigrants began arriving in the late nineteenth century and came to help build the railroad designed to carry coffee from the country's interior to ports along its Atlantic Coast. When this construction project had been completed, many of these West Indian laborers stayed on and took work in the banana plantations of the United Fruit Company. Since the majority of these workers had come from English-speaking islands in the Caribbean and continued to speak English among themselves after coming to Costa Rica, they were considered more valuable employees by United Fruit managers, most of whom were English-speaking as well. In the 1920s, when the banana plantations of eastern Costa Rica experienced problems, United Fruit began concentrating on production from western Costa Rica. Most West Indian blacks, whose population was concentrated along the Atlantic coast, showed little interest in relocating westward. Additionally, the government of Costa Rica, feeling the effects of the worldwide Great Depression, enacted laws giving preferential treatment to Costa Rican nationals. Since most of the West Indian workers had never become citizens, they were left without the agricultural work to which they were accustomed. Many moved into cities to make a living. This gradual disintegration of the black coastal enclaves helped to speed black assimilation into the local culture.

Despite a small elite of black intellectuals, the average Afro-Costa Rican in the late twentieth century was poor and worked in subsistence farming or as a wage laborer. Although there was some organized effort by the elite to achieve equality for the country's blacks, few Afro-Costa Ricans ever have achieved political power. The population of blacks in Costa Rica in the early 1990s was estimated at about 64,000, or two percent of the country's population. Leading contemporary Afro-Costa Ricans include Quince Duncan, a writer of West Indian descent.

Cuba

Official name: Republic of Cuba
Independence: May 20, 1902
Area: 42,803 sq. mi.
Form of government: Socialist military
Capital: Havana
International relations: CELA, UN
Currency: Cuban peso
Income: (per capita US$) 1,480 (1996)
Population: (1998) 11.1 million
Ethnic divisions: Spanish-African mixture
Religious groups: Nonreligious 55%, Christian 43%, traditional belief 2%
Languages spoken: Spanish
Literacy: 95.7% (1995)
Exports: Chromium, nickel, sugar
Imports: Petroleum, food, machinery, chemicals
Primary trade partners: Russia, China, Canada, Spain, Mexico

Cuba is a multi-racial society with a population of mainly Spanish and African origins. When Columbus

Cuban vendor selling postcards in Havana (Cory Langley).

first visited the island in 1492, he found it inhabited by three native American groups: the Ciboneys, Guanahuatabeys, and Taino Arawaks. As Spain developed its colonial empire in the Western Hemisphere, Havana became an important commercial seaport. Settlers eventually moved inland, devoting themselves mainly to sugar cane and tobacco farming. As the native Indian population died out, African slaves were imported to work on the plantations, the first such shipment arriving in 1526. These first slaves were used largely to work the island's sugar and coffee plantations. A 1774 census counted 96,000 whites, 31,000 free blacks, and 44,000 slaves in Cuba.

The slave trade grew rapidly during the final third of the eighteenth century and the first quarter of the nineteenth century. Among the factors contributing to this dramatic growth were the collapse of the sugar trade out of Haiti following its revolution and Spain's decision to allow Cuba to trade with the outside world. By the early nineteenth century, the slave population of Cuba was estimated at more than a million individuals. Most of the indigenous population had fallen victim to disease or died in conflict with European settlers, so that left the Spaniards and the slaves of African ancestry

as the two main population groups within Cuba. Relations between the two groups were at times strained. In 1812, Jose Antonio Aponte, a free black working as a carpenter in Havana, plotted a conspiracy to overthrow colonial rule and abolish slavery. A major factor militating against social advancement by blacks in Cuba was the fear of an uprising by slaves such as had occurred in Haiti. The impact of this phobia is best illustrated by the colonists' savage repression of the so-called Ladder Conspiracy in 1844. In its wake, colonial authorities, widely supported by the European population, executed thousands of blacks and mulattos.

Blacks were allowed to form councils called "cabildos." At first these groups were set up to correspond to the various sections of Africa from which the slaves had originally come. In time, the councils evolved into all-African organizations, accepting members who had originated in all parts of the continent. Eventually, these cabildos developed into the twentieth century clubs and mutual aid societies.

Afro-Cubans played a crucial role in the country's fight for independence from Spain, beginning with the Ten Years' War that began in 1868.. The rebels' 1866 constitution declared that all residents of the republic who took up arms against the Spanish were to be considered free. Following that lead, the rebels' Central Assembly of Representatives proclaimed the abolition of slavery. However, the underlying fear of blacks felt by most white Cubans was exploited by Spanish forces to plant seeds of doubt in the minds of rebel leaders. Rebels were asked to consider the true intentions of blacks who rose through the ranks of the rebel military. Again, visions of a Haiti-type insurrection arose. The resulting divisions among rebel forces led eventually to the failure of their push for independence. The treaty with Spain ending the Ten Years' War provided for freedom only for the blacks who had fought in the revolution. A subsequent uprising, dubbed the Little War of 1879–1880, was discredited in the Spanish press as being racist in nature because many of its leaders were black. Although colonial authorities abolished slavery in 1880, they replaced it with a system called "patronato," under which former slaves were apprenticed to their owners for a period of eight years. In 1886, the system of patronato was ended prematurely, bringing freedom to all.

During the twentieth century, Fidel Castro, who seized power in 1959, transformed Cuba into a socialist nation with the aid of the Soviet Union. Castro became a champion of anti-colonialism, which made him popular in third world countries struggling for independence. The collapse of the Soviet Union and the loss of its extensive aid to Cuba have exacerbated the island's economic difficulties. This, along with the politically repressive nature of the Castro regime, continues to prompt many Cubans to attempt to flee their country. Leading contemporary Afro-Cubans include: musical performers Alfredo "Chocolate" Armenteros, Rubén González, Pablo Milanés, Lázaro Ros, and Jesús (Chucho) Valdés; artists María Magdalena Campos-Pons and Manuel Mendive; film director Gloria Rolando; and literary figures Marcelino Arozarena, Nancy Morejón, and Excilia Saldaña.

Dominica

Official name: Commonwealth of Dominica
Independence: November 3, 1978
Area: 290 sq. mi.
Form of government: Parliamentary republic
Capital: Roseau
International relations: CARICOM, Commonwealth, OAS, UN
Currency: East Caribbean dollar
Income: (per capita US$) 3,120 (1996)
Population: (1998) 66,633
Ethnic divisions: Black, Carib Indian
Religious groups: Roman Catholic 80%, Church of England, other Protestant denominations
Languages spoken: English (official), a French patois is widely spoken
Literacy: 94.1% (1995)
Exports: Citrus fruit, cocoa, coconuts
Imports: Manufactured goods, machinery and equipment, food, chemicals
Primary trade partners: United Kingdom, CARICOM countries, Italy, United States

Dominica was first visited by Europeans on Columbus's second voyage in 1493. Spanish ships frequently landed on Dominica during the sixteenth century but failed to establish a stronghold on the island. In 1635 France claimed Dominica. As part of the 1763 Treaty of Paris that ended the Seven Years' War being fought in Europe, North America, and India, the island became a British possession.

In 1763 the British established a legislative assembly, representing only the white population. In 1831, reflecting a liberalization of official British racial attitudes, the "Brown Privilege Bill" conferred political and social rights on nonwhites. Three blacks were elected to the Legislative Assembly the following year, and by 1838 the recently enfranchised blacks dominated that body. Most black legislators were smallholders or merchants, who held economic and social views diametrically opposed to the interests of the small, wealthy English planter class. Reacting to a perceived threat, the planters lobbied for more direct British rule. In 1865, after much agitation and tension, the colonial office replaced the elective assembly with one in which half of the members were appointed.

The power of the black population progressively eroded until all political rights for the vast majority of the population were effectively curtailed. On November 3, 1978, the Commonwealth of Dominica was granted independence by the United Kingdom. Almost all 81,000 Dominicans are descendants of African slaves imported by planters in the eighteenth century.

In 1980 Mary Eugenia Charles became the first woman to come to power in the Caribbean as well as the only black woman to lead an independent nation. Her longevity and determination earned her the nickname "The Iron Lady of the Caribbean." Trained as a lawyer, Charles rose through the ranks of government, spending most of her career in politics. After serving three terms as prime minister, she was succeeded in 1995 by Edison C. James.

Dominican Republic

Independence: February 27, 1844
Area: 18,815 sq. mi.
Form of government: Presidential republic

Capital: Santo Domingo
International relations: CARICOM, OAS, UN
Currency: Dominican peso
Income: (per capita US$) 1,650 (1990)
Population: (1998) 8 million
Ethnic divisions: Mixed 73%, black 11%
Religious groups: Roman Catholic 95%
Languages spoken: Spanish
Literacy: 82.1% (1995)
Exports: Gold, silver, sugar cane, coffee
Imports: Foodstuffs, petroleum, cotton, chemicals, pharmaceuticals
Primary trade partners: United States, European Union countries, Puerto Rico

The island of Hispaniola, of which the Dominican Republic forms the eastern two-thirds and Haiti the remainder, was originally occupied by members of the Taino tribe when Columbus and his companions landed there in 1492. Brutal colonial conditions reduced the Taino population from an estimated one million to about two hundred in only fifty years.

Santo Domingo, as the territory was known under Spanish rule, has long been considered the "cradle of blackness in the Americas" because it served as the port of entry for the first slaves traded to the Western Hemisphere. Beginning shortly after the first visit of Columbus, the slave trade brought in waves of Christianized blacks, known as "ladinos," and "bosales," as blacks imported directly from Africa were known. At first these slaves were put to work in the country's gold mines. However, these soon gave out, and efforts were undertaken to cultivate sugar cane on a large scale. Once the sugar business had been successfully established, after a period of fits and starts, progressively more slaves were brought in to work the fields.

From early in the colony's history, blacks outnumbered whites by a significant margin. In 1542, only fifty years after the first visit of Columbus, the population was made up of 30,000 blacks, 6,000 whites, and only 200 Tainos. By the close of the sixteenth century, blacks represented 61 percent of the total population, followed by whites at 23 percent and mulattos at 15 percent. Eventually, sugar cultivation's position as the colony's main cash crop was overtaken by livestock raising and the cultivation of ginger. These changes had a number of effects on the slave population, among those the fact that fewer slaves were needed to raise livestock than were needed in the cultivation of sugar cane. The reduction in the need for slave labor was timely, because the late sixteenth and early seventeenth centuries saw the loss of a significant number of slaves to disease.

Living conditions for the slaves of Santo Domingo were harsh. The colonial powers, worried by the possibility of a large-scale uprising by blacks, enacted a system of laws that closely regulated every aspect of the lives of slaves. These laws, however, failed to altogether eliminate slave revolts, of which several occurred in the early years of the colony. In the wake of the Haitian Revolution, Toussaint L'Ouverture, a former Haitian slave who had become a military leader, seized control of Santo Domingo, bringing all of Hispaniola under his control. He abolished slavery throughout Santo Domingo. The following year French soldiers invaded, taking control of Santo Domingo for France, which retained control until the War of Reconquest in 1809. Under French rule, slavery was reinstated. The War of Reconquest, plotted by creoles with the support of the Spanish governor of nearby Puerto Rico, returned Santo Domingo to Spanish control. In 1822, Haitian President Jean-Pierre Boyer seized the colony and maintained control for the next 22 years. Once again, slavery was abolished in Santo Domingo. Independence from Haiti was finally achieved in 1844.

One of the dominant figures in twentieth-century Dominican Republic history was dictator Rafael Trujillo, who ruled the country with an iron hand for more than thirty years. After Trujillo's dictatorship ended in a 1961 assassination, Joaquín Balaguer took over as president and instituted a police state. In 1962, former exile Juan Bosch was elected president in the country's first free elections in four decades. Criticized for being too soft on communism, Bosch was deposed in September 1963 and replaced by a three-man civilian junta. When pro-Bosch elements in the military rebelled against the government, U.S. forces intervened. Voters in 1966 returned Balaguer to the presidency. He won reelection easily in 1970 and 1974. However, in 1978 elections, Balaguer was unseated by Silvestre Antonio Guzmán. In July 1982 Salvador Jorge Blanco was elected to succeed him. Balaguer was returned to the presidency in 1986 elections. He was reelected in 1990 and 1994, but agreed to serve only two years of the last term to which he was elected after charges of election fraud. In 1996 Leonel Fernández Reyna was elected president.

Leading contemporary Afro-Dominicans include literary figures Manuel del Cabral and Blas Jiménez and musicians Juan Luis Guerra and Johnny Ventura.

Ecuador

Official name: Republic of Ecuador
Area: 105,037 sq. mi.
Form of government: Presidential republic
Capital: Quito
International relations: LAIA, OAS, UN
Currency: Sucre
Income: (per capita US$) 1,630 (1996)

Improvised housing in Santo Domingo, Dominican Republic (United Nations).

Population (1998) 12.3 million

Ethnic divisions: Mestizo 55%, indigenous peoples 25%, Spanish 10%, black 10%

Religious groups: Roman Catholic

Languages spoken: Spanish (official)

Literacy: 90.1% (1995)

Exports: Coffee, cocoa, gold, petroleum, shrimp

Imports: Transportation equipment, consumer goods, vehicles, machinery, chemicals

Primary trade partners: United States, European Union countries, Central and South American countries, Caribbean countries

Together with Colombia, its neighbor to the north, and Panama, Ecuador shares a region that makes up the so-called Pacific Lowlands Black Culture. This region stretches from Panama's Darién province in the north through Colombia's Cauca Valley on to Esmeraldas province in Ecuador in the south. The Pacific coastal area stretching through the three countries developed its high concentration of Afro-Hispanics through the migration patterns of blacks and a tradition of racial intermixing that began in colonial times. Although the three-nation Pacific coastal area is notable for its size, blacks historically settled in all three major geographi-

cal areas of Ecuador: the Pacific coast, the Amazon lowlands in the eastern part of the country, and the highlands.

As in much of Latin America, Ecuador's Spanish colonial rulers followed a policy of racial and cultural whitening, encouraging widespread racial mixing as a logical avenue to reach that goal. Even in the late twentieth century, remnants of that philosophy can be found in Ecuador. So deeply ingrained is the policy of whitening that even some black groups strongly advocate greater cultural and racial blending.

African slaves were first brought to Ecuador in the middle of the sixteenth century. Most were pressed into service as farm workers in portions of the colony where Indian labor was either scarce or nonexistent. An enclave of blacks grew up in the northwest coastal province of Esmeraldas, after a small party of slaves being transported by ship between Panama and Peru escaped and settled in the area. The escaped slaves mixed freely with the Indians of the region, and the resulting zambos of mixed black and Indian blood came to dominate this region. Although some blacks who joined in the fight for Ecuador's independence from Spain were freed in return for their war efforts, an official proclamation ending slavery did not come until 1851. Even so, an involuntary form of slavery survived until 1894.

Leading contemporary Afro-Ecuadorians include literary figures Nelson Estupiñán Bass and Antonio Preciado Bedoya.

El Salvador

Official name: Republic of El Salvador
Independence: September 15, 1821
Area: 8,124 sq. mi.
Form of government: Presidential republic
Capital: San Salvador
International relations: CACM, OAS, UN
Currency: Colon
Income: (per capita US$) 1,800 (1996)
Population (1998) 5.8 million
Ethnic divisions: Mestizo 94%, indigenous peoples, 5%, white 1%
Religious groups: Roman Catholic 75%, other 25%
Languages spoken: Spanish, Nahuatl, English
Literacy: 71.5% (1995)
Exports: Coffee, sugar cane, shrimp
Imports: Raw materials, consumer goods, capital goods
Primary trade partners: United States, Guatemala, Germany, Mexico

In the final days of the twentieth century, the black population of El Salvador was negligible, the lowest proportion of African-descended residents to be found anywhere in Central America. During the colonial period, some African slaves were imported by El Salvador's Spanish rulers to help fill labor shortages created by the wholesale exportation of the indigenous Amerindian peoples to South America and Mexico. However, Central America's needs for slave labor was not as great as in other of Spain's New World colonies, largely because the mines in the region produced relatively modest yields and large-scale agriculture was virtually nonexistent. Without the profits from such enterprises, most landowners in El Salvador could ill afford the cost of importing African slaves, particularly since in most cases the available Amerindian labors were sufficient to fill their needs.

By the early 1800s the number of slaves was so low that it was difficult to find residents who identified themselves as having African roots. Between the low number of slaves and the high rate of intermixing between European, indigenous, and the few blacks in the colony, it had become virtually impossible to distinguish between those with African blood and the mestizos of mixed European and Indian ancestry. By 1824, the Central American Federation, from which the countries of Costa Rica, El Salvador, Guatemala, Honduras, and Nicaragua were eventually formed, had won its independence from Spain. Because the number of slaves

throughout the area was small, particularly when compared with other territories in the New World, abolition of slavery was achieved without a great deal of trauma on all parties involved.

French Guiana

Independence: n/a (overseas department of France since 1946)
Area: 33,399 sq. mi.
Capital: Cayenne
Currency: French franc
Population: (1998 estimate) 162,547
Ethnic divisions: African and Afro-European 66%, European 18%, Asian Indian, Chinese, Amerindian, Brazilian 16%
Religious groups: Roman Catholic, Protestant sects, Hindu, traditional African belief
Languages spoken: French (official)
Exports: Shrimp, fish, timber, gold
Primary trade partners: France

The first European visitor to what is now French Guiana was Christopher Columbus, who stopped off there during the course of his third voyage to the New World. Struck the beauty of the region, he wrote glowingly of its wonders. His writings later inspired other European explorers to visit the area, many of whom were convinced that the mythical Eldorado, the golden city, was to be found within the territory's interior. The French first visited the area in 1604, looking not only for gold but for territory that could be claimed for their country. It was not until 1652 that the first slaves were brought into Guiana. Because the colony was fairly sparsely settled, the slave population grew very slowly. By 1765, Guiana's slave population totaled only about 5,700. Sixty-five years later, in 1830, it reaches its peak of just over 19,000.

Although most of the African slaves had come from tropical climates themselves, many fell victim to tropical diseases in Guiana. Others fled their masters in the more heavily settled coastal zone and escaped into the interior where they reverted to a lifestyle as hunter-gatherers, much as they had done in their home countries. Although French attempts to establish agricultural plantations in Guiana failed, the colonial powers were undaunted in their determination to develop the territory. The abolition of slavery in 1848 sounded the death knell for Guiana's two main industries—lumber and sugar—collapsed. To give the colony a raison d'être, the French decided to transform Guiana into a penal colony. Between 1852 and 1939, France shipped more than 70,000 prisoners to the colony. Tropical diseases, including malaria and yellow fever, took an enormous toll on the prisoners, claiming the lives of nearly ninety percent of them.

Among the notable French Guianans of African descent, Félix Eboué stands out for his significant contributions as an adviser to General Charles de Gaulle during World War II. Born in 1884, Eboué was the descendant of African slaves. He first distinguished himself through his reforms of the French colonial administration. Poet Léon-Gontran Damas is the country's most famous writer. In the late twentieth century, a number of elements of the Afro-Guianan community were actively seeking to revive and preserve black culture in the country.

Grenada

Independence: February 7, 1974
Area: 131 sq. mi.
Form of government: Independent within British sovereignty
Capital: Saint George
International relations: CARICOM, EU, OAS, UN
Currency: East Caribbean dollar
Income: (per capita US$) 2,980 (1996)
Population: (1998) 95,535
Ethnic divisions: Black, some Asian Indian, European, Arawak/Carib Indian
Religious groups: Roman Catholic 63%, Church of England, other Protestant denominations
Languages spoken: English (official), some vestigial French patois
Literacy: 97.8% (1995)
Exports: Banana, cocoa, coffee, coconuts, apparel
Imports: Food, manufactured goods, machinery, chemicals
Primary trade partners: United Kingdom, Netherlands, Trinidad and Tobago

Similar to the rest of the West Indies, Grenada was originally settled to cultivate sugar, which was grown on estates using slave labor. Most of Grenada's population is of African descent; little trace of the early Arawak and Carib Indians remains.

Columbus first visited Grenada in 1498. Grenada remained uncolonized for more than one hundred years after the first visit by Europeans, and British efforts to settle the island were unsuccessful. In 1650 a French company purchased Grenada from the British and established a small settlement. By 1753, the island's population was dominated by slaves, who numbered close to 12,000, against a total of 1,262 whites and 179 free blacks. Most of the free blacks were of mixed European-African descent, the result of intermixing between the island's French planters and their slaves. The island remained under French control until captured by the British more than a century later during the Seven Years War. Slavery was outlawed in 1833, the same year Grenada was made part of the British Windward Islands

Administration. In 1958 the Windward Islands Administration dissolved. Grenada became an associated state on March 3, 1967, but sought full independence, which the British government granted on February 7, 1974.

The New Jewel movement led by Maurice Bishop assumed power in 1979. He was overthrown and killed in 1983 when Bernard Coard took over the country. The United States, along with forces from other English-speaking Caribbean countries invaded to restore order. The country was then governed by an interim advisory council until parliamentary elections in December 1984. Those elections established Herbert A. Blaize as Grenada's new prime minister. After Blaize's death, Nicholas Brathwaite was elected prime minister. Brathwaite's popularity plummeted in the wake of an economic slowdown in the early 1990s, and he announced he would resign as prime minister in 1995. He was succeeded by George Brizan in February 1995, who in late June 1995 turned over power to Keith Mitchell, established as prime minister in parliamentary elections earlier that month.

The island faced new economic troubles in the mid-1990s when the banana crop failed and an infestation of mealybugs severely damaged the cocoa crop. Grenada is one of four former English colonies in the Caribbean considering the formation of a federation to ease financial pressures on all member countries. The others countries discussing joining in this federation are Dominica, St. Lucia, and St. Vincent and the Grenadines. One of the major success stories in Grenada during the 1990s has been the growth experienced by the island's tourism industry. Grenada has proved particularly popular with divers, snorkelers, and sailors in recent years. Also a major player in the island's economy is the spice industry, which continues to turn in a strong performance. The island produces more spices per square mile than anywhere else on earth.

Guadeloupe

Independence: n/a (overseas department of France)
Area: 660 sq. mi.
Capital: Basse-Terre
Income: (per capita US$) $7,700 (1996)
Population: (1998) 416,000
Ethnic divisions: Afro-European, European, Afro-Asian, Asian
Religious groups: Roman Catholic, Hindu, and traditional African belief
Languages spoken: French, creole
Literacy: 89% (1995)
Exports: Bananas, rum, sugar cane
Imports: Fuel, vehicles, consumer goods
Primary trade partners: France, Martinique

Columbus sighted Guadeloupe in 1493. The area was permanently settled by the French in the seventeenth century. The first slaves were brought from Africa to work the plantations around 1650, and the first slave rebellion occurred in 1656. Guadeloupe was poorly administered in its early days and was a dependency of Martinique until 1775.

The slaves of Guadeloupe were slow to react to news of the French Revolution. The French abolition of slavery less than five years later was not preceded by any major uprisings on the island, although a handful of minor revolts did occur. Two members of the French Republican Convention, who brought the abolition decree to Guadeloupe, also recruited freed slaves to help drive out British invaders, who had occupied the island while France was preoccupied with its revolution at home. In the wake of the rout of British occupying forces, many white landowners and merchants sympathetic to the British cause were executed or exiled. As a result, the white ruling class was considerably weakened and depleted in numbers. In the years following the British occupation of the island, whites made up only about 10 percent of the population, compared to about 33 percent in 1735. As the white population was weakened, the black merchant class gained strength. Blacks and those of mixed African and European descent were welcomed into the colony's military.

A number of black soldiers in 1802 revolted against troops sent to the Caribbean by Napoleon Bonaparte to reinstitute slavery. Their resistance was quickly overcome, and France reimposed a particularly brutal brand of enslavement on its islands for the next 46 years. By 1835, 13 years before abolition, free blacks on the island outnumbers whites by a margin of 19,000 to 12,000. In the wake of Britain's ban on slavery in its Caribbean colonies, attempts were made in the French island to make slavery less dehumanizing, as if indeed that were possible. The hope was that by so doing the institution of slavery could be preserved. Despite legislated measures to give slaves some basic rights, the effort was a failure, since individual slave owners were free to deal with their slaves as they wished.

Most Guadeloupeans are of mixed Afro-European and Afro-Indian ancestry (descendants of laborers brought over from India during the ninteenth century). Several thousand metropolitan French reside there, including civil servants, business people, and their dependents. Leading contemporary Afro-Guadeloupeans include literary figures Jean Louis Baghio'o, Maryse Condé, and Simone Schwartz-Bart.

Guatemala
Official name: Republic of Guatemala
Independence: September 15, 1821
Area: 42,042 sq. mi.
Form of government: Presidential republic
Capital: Guatemala City
International relations: CACM, OAS, UN
Currency: Quetzal
Income: (per capita US$) 1,450 (1996)
Population: (1998) 12 million
Ethnic divisions: Mestizo, Native American, black
Religious groups: Christian, traditional Mayan
Languages spoken: Spanish (official)
Literacy: 55.6% (1991)
Exports: Coffee, sugar, bananas, cardamom, beef
Imports: Fuel and petroleum products, machinery, grain, fertilizer, vehicles
Primary trade partners: United States, El Salvador, Mexico, Germany

Although blacks make up a very small percentages of Guatemala's population, there are traces of African influence to be found in the Central American country. Among these are a popular folk dance called the marimba, based on rhythms and steps brought to the country by African slaves.

Beginning in the first half of the sixteenth century, steps were taken by Guatemalan whites to limit the number of blacks allowed into the colony. The heavy concentrations of Amerindian indigenous peoples provided an adequate labor supply for most of Guatemala, thus reducing the need for the importation of African slaves. The Guatemalan town of Tianguey enacted an ordinance in 1537 prohibiting the entry of blacks or those of mixed-black ancestry without express permission from town officials. The aim was to prevent any intermixing with the indigenous peoples of the area. Even in the twentieth century, the country's government has attempted to legislate against immigration by blacks. Guatemala's 1945 constitution official bans "immigration of individuals of the black race."

Guyana
Official name: Cooperative Republic of Guyana
Independence: May 26, 1966
Area: 83,000 sq. mi.
Form of government: Multiparty
Capital: Georgetown
International relations: CARICOM, Commonwealth, EU, UN
Currency: Guyana dollar
Income: (per capita US$) 860 (1996)
Population: (1998) 708,000
Ethnic divisions: Asian Indian 49.6%, African 30.4%, mixed 14.1%, European and Chinese 0.5%
Religious groups: Christian 50%, Hindu 33%, Muslim 9%
Languages spoken: English, Guyanese Creole, Amerindian dialects

Literacy: 98.1% (1995)

Exports: Bauxite, gold, sugar, rice, sugar

Imports: Manufactured goods, machinery, petroleum, food

Primary trade partners: United Kingdom, United States, Trinidad and Tobago, Italy

Guiana was the name given the area sighted by Columbus in 1498, comprising modern Guyana, Suriname, French Guiana, and parts of Brazil and Venezuela. The Dutch settled in Guyana in the late sixteenth century. Dutch control ended when the British became the de facto rulers in 1796. In 1815 the colonies of Essequibo, Demerara, and Berbice were officially ceded to the British by the Congress of Vienna and, in 1831, were consolidated as British Guiana.

Slave revolts, such as the one in 1763 led by Guyana's national hero, Cuffy, stressed the desire to obtain basic rights and were underscored by a willingness to compromise. Following the abolition of slavery in 1834, indentured workers were brought primarily from India but also from Portugal and China. A scheme in 1862 to bring black workers from the United States was unsuccessful.

Independence was achieved in 1966, and Guyana became a republic on February 23, 1970, the anniversary of the Cuffy slave rebellion. Between 1968 and 1972 Guyana was ruled by the PNC party. In 1975. Guyana gained unfortunate international recognition after a religious cult in Jonestown was led into mass suicide by its leader, Jim Jones.

Although the black population of Guyana trails that of the Indo-Guyanese, who make up slightly more than fifty percent of the population and a sharply higher percentage in the late twentieth century government, the African influences upon the country's culture are significant. Blacks played a major role in the development of modern-day Guyana, from the mid-seventeenth century when the first African slaves were sold to Dutch planters through the early years after independence, when the country was ruled by authoritarian black governments. Forbes Burnham, an Afro-Guyanese led the country from 1968 until 1985. When Burnham died in office in 1985, he was succeeded by Desmond Hoyte, who held office until 1992. In the country's first free elections since 1964, Cheddi Jagan, the first leader of the country after independence, was again voted into office. Jagan died suddenly in office in January 1997 and was succeeded by his widow, Janet, who in December 1997 won the presidency on her own. Other influential Afro-Guyanese include literary figures Martin Carter and Theodore Wilson Harris.

Haiti

Official name: Republic of Haiti

Independence: January 1, 1804

Area: 10,714 sq. mi.

Form of government: Multiparty

Capital: Port-au-Prince

International relations: CARICOM, EU, OAS, UN

Currency: Gourde

Income: (per capita US$) 360 (1996)

Population: (1998) 6.8 million

Ethnic Group: Blacks 95%, mulatto and European 5%

Religious groups: Roman Catholic 80%, Protestant 10%, traditional (voodoo) practices 10%

Languages spoken: French (official), Creole

Literacy: 45% (1995)

Exports: Coffee, cotton, sugar, light manufactured goods

Imports: Machinery, manufactured goods, food and beverages, petroleum products, chemical

Primary trade partners: United States, European Union countries, Central and South American countries

Columbus first visited the Island of Hispaniola in 1492. In 1697 Spain ceded the western third of Hispaniola to France. During this period, slaves were brought from Africa to work the sugar cane and coffee plantations. Several decades later, a major revolt erupted—white French planters, African slaves, and free mulattoes (some of whom owned slaves) clashed over issues of rights, land, and labor, as the forces of France, Britain, and Spain manipulated the conflict. At first the slaves and mulattoes shared the goals of the French revolution in opposition to the royalist French planters, but with time a coalition of planters and mulattoes arose in opposition to the slaves.

Toussaint L'Ouverture became the leader of the revolutionary slave forces, which by mid-1790s consisted of a disciplined group of four thousand mostly ex-slaves. He successfully waged a campaign against the British. At the height of L'Ouverture's power and influence in 1796, Gen. Rigaud, who led the mulatto forces, sought to reimpose slavery on the black islanders. L'Ouverture quickly achieved victory, captured Santo Domingo, and by 1801 had virtual control of the Spanish part of the island. In 1802, a French expeditionary force was sent to reestablish French control of the island. Following a hard-fought resistance to French colonial ambitions in the Western Hemisphere, Toussaint L'Ouverture struck a peace treaty with Napoleon. However, L'Ouverture was tricked, captured, and sent to France where he died on April 7, 1803, under inhumane conditions.

In the wake of its victorious struggle for independence, Haiti became a model for much of the black world. However, it was not long before the black-ruled country began to face enormous pressure, both from within the country and abroad. The country's new rulers were ill-prepared for the responsibility of leading a nation, thus keeping the country in a state of instability.

It had no other country to which it could turn for either moral or financial support, because it was regarded as an outcast in a world that was largely controlled by whites. The very idea of slaves overthrowing their masters to seize control of a country was frightening to most white-controlled governments. The country was in ruins in the wake of its battle to banish the French, and Dessalines made a critical error when he pressed all Haitians who were not in the military into agricultural service on some of the surviving plantations. Further exacerbating problems for the new black republic was the growing enmity that developed between the country's black majority and the mulatto elite. After the death of Dessalines, control of the island was split between the blacks, who held the northern part of Haiti, and the mulattos, who were in control of the South.

In the twentieth century, the country languished under nearly thirty years of despotic rule by the Duvalier family. François Duvalier was elected president in 1957; in the 1960s he declared himself president for life. Upon his death in 1971, he was succeeded by his son, Jean-Claude. During this period, much of the Western world, including the United States, cut off foreign assistance to Haiti to express its collective unhappiness over the political situation there. In the 1980s, popular dissatisfaction with the Duvalier rule grew stronger, and early in 1986 the young Duvalier was forced to flee the country. A politically tumultuous period followed, with one corrupt leader quickly succeeding another, until the election in December 1990 of Jean-Bertrand Aristide. Only eight months after his inauguration in February 1991, Aristide was ousted in a coup led by Brigadier General Raoul Cedras. Following Aristide's ouster, thousands of Haitians attempted to emigrate to the United States, with little success. In 1994, U.S. forces took control and Aristide was returned to power. He handed power over to Rene Preval, his hand-picked successor, in December 1995. The country was in an economic and political shambles into the late 1990s.

Almost 95 percent of the Haitians are of black African descent; the rest of the population are mostly of mixed African-Caucasian ancestry (mulattos). Leading contemporary Afro-Haitians include: Manno Charlemagne, a protest singer and politician; Franck Etienne, a poet, playwright, novelist, teacher, and politician; and literary figure Paulette Poujol-Oriol.

Honduras
Official name: Republic of Honduras
Independence: September 15, 1821
Area: 43,433 sq. mi.
Form of government: Republic
Capital: Tegucigalpa
Currency: Lempira

Income: (per capita US$) 660 (1996)
Population: (1998) 5.9 million
Ethnic divisions: Mestizo 90%, indigenous peoples 7%, black 2%, white 1%
Religious groups: Roman Catholic
Languages spoken: Spanish
Literacy: 72.7% (1995)
Exports: Bananas, coffee, shrimp, lobsters, minerals, lumber
Imports: Machinery and transportation equipment, chemical products, manufactured goods, fuel and oil
Primary trade partners: United States, Germany, Mexico, Guatemala, Belgium

The first shipment of African slaves—a group of 165—arrived in Honduras in 1540. About five years later, the number of slaves within the colony had risen to 5,000, most of them brought in to replace Indian workers who had been claimed by disease. Most of these Africans were employed as domestic servants or laborers on small farms that were cultivated solely to produce food for consumption within the colony. The absence of plantation-scale farming and mines kept the region's slave population from growing dramatically. The black population grew more after Honduras won independence, when a large number of West Indian blacks of mixed African and Carib Indian ancestry arrived in the country. Up to 5,000 of these newly arrived immigrants known as Garifuna relocated from the Caribbean island of Saint Vincent to the island of Roatán, off the coast of Honduras, at the end of the eighteenth century. Over time most of these Garifuna moved to the mainland.

Another influx of black slaves arrived in Honduras in the 1830s, when a group of white settlers from the Cayman Islands, fearful about their fate if Britain's plans to abolish slavery materialized, began settling in the Honduran Bay Islands. A number of these white Cayman Islanders brought their slaves with them. By the mid-nineteenth century, about seven hundred blacks from the Cayman Islands had moved to this island group, once again outnumbering the white population. When U.S. fruit companies established vast plantations in the eastern portion of the country, both the black Cayman Islanders and many of the Garifuna went to work for them. The new employment opportunities offered by the fruit estates eventually attracted further black immigration from throughout the Caribbean.

Jamaica
Independence: August 6, 1962
Area: 4,244 sq. mi.
Form of government: Independent under British sovereignty
Capital: Kingston

Linstead market in Jamaica.

International relations: CARICOM, EU, OAS, UN
Currency: Jamaican dollar
Income: (per capita US$) 1,740 (1996)
Population: (1998) 2.6 million.
Ethnic divisions: African 76.3%, Afro-European 15.1%, Chinese and Afro-Chinese 1.2%, Asian Indian and Afro-Asian Indian 3.4%, European 3.2%
Religious groups: Anglican, Baptist and other Protestant denominations, Roman Catholic
Languages spoken: English, Creole
Literacy: 85% (1995)
Exports: Bauxite
Imports: Machinery, transportation equipment, construction materials, fuel, food, chemicals
Primary trade partners: United States, United Kingdom, Japan, Mexico

Jamaica was first visited in 1494 by Christopher Columbus and settled by the Spanish during the early sixteenth century. In 1650s British forces seized the island and in 1670 gained formal possession under the Treaty of Madrid.

Sugar and slavery were important elements in Jamaica's history and development. By the early 1830s, the affairs of the colony were dominated by the island's white minority. As international pressure for an end to slavery began to build, events within Jamaica made clear that the days of slavery were numbered. In 1832, in a revolt known as the Baptist War, more than 20,000 slaves rose up in an effort to break the bonds of slavery. So expansive and violent was this insurrection that it caught the attention of the world outside Jamaica. Conjuring up images of a slave revolution, such as had occurred in Haiti about thirty years earlier, the Jamaican uprising hastened action in Britain's Parliament to abolish slavery. The vote that came in August 1833 freed more than 300,000 slaves in Jamaica. However, provisions of emancipation provided for a gradual transition from bondage to complete freedom. For most slaves, this meant a lengthy period of apprenticeship to their former masters. With the abolition of slavery, the settlers were forced to recruit other sources of cheap labor, resorting to the importation of Asian Indian and Chinese farm hands.

In 1958 Jamaica joined nine other British territories in the West Indies Federation, but withdrew when, in a 1961 referendum, Jamaican voters rejected membership. Jamaica gained independence from the United Kingdom in 1962, but remained a member of the Commonwealth. In the country's first election following independence, Alexander Bustamante, a leader of the Labor Party, was elected prime minister. Bustamante retired five years later and passed power to Hugh Shearer. After a number of years under the Jamaican Labor party, the 1972 elections put Michael Norman Manley in power. Manley, who steered the country toward socialism, served until 1980, when voters selected Edward Seaga as prime minister. In 1989 voters returned Manley to the prime ministership, but he stepped down in March 1992 because of ill health. His successor, Percival J. Patterson, handily won reelection in 1993.

A new phenomenon has become particularly apparent in Jamaica, a country that has lost nearly thirty percent of its population to the United States. Though prevalent in all countries that experience heavy emigration, tens of thousands of Jamaican parents have gone abroad, leaving behind children whom they hope to one day be able to summon. The youngsters have acquired the nickname "barrel children" from the barrels filled with goodies—food, clothing, and photographs—the parents send back whenever possible. Though these children have not actually been abandoned, they are often passed from relative to relative or to friends or strangers. Highly at risk, the children are often susceptible to abuse from their supposed benefactors, many drop out of school, and some get into trouble with the law.

Leading contemporary Afro-Jamaicans include novelist and sociologist Erna Brodber, painter and sculptor

Everald Brown, reggae musician Jimmy Cliff, novelist and playwright John Hearne, and poet and music producer Mutabaruka.

Martinique

Independence: n/a (overseas department of France)
Area: 425 sq. mi.
Capital: Fort-de-France
Currency: French franc
Population: (1998) 407,000
Ethnic divisions: Afro-European, Afro-Indian, European
Religious groups: Roman Catholic 95%, Baptist, Seventh-day Adventist, Jehovah Witness, Pentecostal, Hindu, traditional African belief 5%
Languages spoken: French
Exports: Bananas, pineapples, sugar cane, petroleum products
Imports: Meat, vegetables, grain
Primary trade partners: France, United Kingdom, Guadeloupe, Italy

Christopher Columbus first visited Martinique in 1502 on his fourth voyage to the New World. The island's indigenous Carib Indian population was largely decimated by disease in the wake of Columbus's visit. The area was permanently settled by the French in the seventeenth century. Except for three short periods of British occupation, Martinique has been a French possession since 1635.

As sugar plantations sprang up on Martinique, the need for slave labor grew quickly, particularly since the island's indigenous Carib Indians had been all but wiped out by disease introduced by the first European visitors. The island's population in 1789 was estimated at 12,000 whites, 65,000 slaves, and 5,000 free blacks. In 1848, less than sixty years later, the slave population had moved up by only about 12 percent to 73,000, while the total of free blacks had soared by almost 700 percent. The white population, meanwhile, had shrunk to about 9,000. In the spring of 1848, the slaves of Martinique staged a large-scale revolt that precipitated abolition of slavery in the French colonies one month later.

The island witnessed a number of dramatic changes during the twentieth century. The political realm, once large restricted to Martinique's white minority, began to open up to those of African ancestry. In 1945 black poet and intellectual Aimé Césaire was elected as a Martinican deputy to the French parliament. In addition to his continuing involvement in the politics of his country, Césaire was instrumental in jump-starting the country's cultural renewal with his book of poetry *Cahier d'un retour au pays natal* (Notebook of a Return to My Native Land) published in 1947. A strong supporter of Martinique's existing status as an overseas department of France, Césaire has fallen out of favor with some of Martinique's young intellectuals for his failure to call for independence from France.

About 95 percent of the people of Martinique are of Afro-European or Afro-European-Indian descent. The rest are traditional white planter families, commonly referred to as békdés or creoles, and a sizable number of metropolitan French work in administration and business. Leading contemporary Afro-Martinicians include literary figures Aimé Césaire, Patrick Chamoiseau, Raphaëatl Confiant, and Joseph Zobel.

Mexico

Official name: The United Mexican States
Independence: September 16, 1821
Area: 758,452 sq. mi.
Form of government: Federal republic
Capital: Mexico City
International relations: LAIA, SELA, UN
Currency: Mexican peso
Income: (per capita US$) 3,591 (1996)
Population: (1998) 98.6 million
Ethnic divisions: Mestizo 60%, Mesoamerican 30%, others 10%
Religious groups: Roman Catholic
Languages spoken: Spanish
Literacy: 89.6% (1995)
Exports: Coffee, copper, cotton, petroleum, silver, sugar, sulfur
Imports: Metalworking machinery, steel mill products, agricultural machinery, electrical equipment, aircraft, auto parts
Primary trade partners: United States, Japan, European Union countries

When Hernán Cortes stepped ashore in Mexico in 1519, he was accompanied by a free black named Juan Garrido, who later participated in the Spanish toppling of Tenochtitlán, the Aztec capital. By the middle of the sixteenth century, it is estimated that there were almost 150,000 black slaves in the country. One of the earlier slaves, Estevanico, is credited with opening up the northern interior lands—of what is now New Mexico and Arizona—to Spanish conquest. During the sixteenth and seventeenth centuries, black Mexicans were believed to have outnumbered whites by a ratio of two to one. However, both groups were vastly outnumbered by the indigenous peoples of Mexico.

Beginning in the early part of the eighteenth century, the country's Afro-Mexican population started to decline, in part because of new Spanish restrictions on the slave trade. Although the imported African slaves proved more resistant to many of the European-borne diseases than the indigenous peoples, many did succumb to foreign diseases including tuberculosis, yellow fever, and syphilis. Some of the enslaved blacks were simply worked to death. Furthermore, many of the African slaves brought into the colony intermixed with indigenous peoples and whites. The reasons for this large-scale intermixing was twofold: the Spaniards purposely limited the number of female slaves they brought into Mexico, and the prevailing caste system gave individuals with a lighter skin color a higher standing. In 1829 Mexico abolished slavery in all its states except Texas, allowing it to remain there to pacify the United States. As slavery in the United States moved westward into Texas, Mexico became a haven for escaped slaves who slipped into the heart of the country and blended with the population.

Some 100,000 blacks, about 0.5 percent of the population, live in Mexico today, mostly in the port cities of Veracruz and Acapulco. Blacks in lesser numbers live in Mexico City and in border cities across the Rio Grande River from Texas.

Montserrat

Independence: n/a (dependent territory of the United Kingdom)
Area: 100 sq. km.
Capital: Plymouth
International relations: CARICOM
Currency: East Caribbean dollar
Income: (per capita US$) 4,380 (1995)
Population: (1998) 12,771
Ethnic divisions: Black, European
Religious groups: Anglican, Methodist, Roman Catholic, Pentecostal, Seventh-Day Adventist, other Christian denominations
Languages spoken: English
Literacy: 97.7% (1995)
Exports: Electronic equipment, plastic bags, apparel
Imports: Machinery and transportation equipment, foodstuffs, manufactured goods, fuels
Primary trade partners: United States, United Kingdom

When the Leeward Islands (Antigua, Anguilla, Barbuda, Montserrat, Nevis, and Saint Kitts) were first visited by Christopher Columbus in 1493, they were inhabited by Carib Indians. Montserrat was first colonized in 1632 by English settlers who moved to the island from nearby Saint Kitts and Nevis. The island's first slaves were believed to have arrived in Montserrat in 1651. By the early 1670s there were about 1,000 slaves on the island, a figure that jumped to nearly 6,000 by 1729. At that time blacks outnumbered whites by about five to one.

The lives of slaves on Montserrat were closely regulated. Colonial laws prohibited slaves from becoming masons, shinglers, sawyers, tailors, coopers, or smiths. Furthermore, blacks were forbidden to plant indigo, ginger, cocoa, cotton, or coffee, the main cash crops of the region, although they could grow vegetables for their own use in small gardens. These restrictions ensured that few slaves would ever be able to make and set aside enough money to purchase their freedom. In 1768 and 1770, the island's whites were alarmed by rumors of planned slave revolts. Neither rumored uprising, however, actually took place.

Throughout the 18th century, the British and French warred for possession of Montserrat, which was finally confirmed as a British possession by the Treaty of Versailles (1783). By the early 19th century, Montserrat had a plantation economy, but the abolition of slavery in 1834, the elimination of the apprentice system, the declining market for sugar, and a series of natural disasters brought the downfall of the sugar estates.

Today, most of Montserrat's population is an intermixture of European settlers and the descendants of West African slaves. In 1997 the 3,000-foot Soufriere Hills volcano erupted repeatedly, causing widespread devastation to property and virtually collapsing the island's economy. More than two-thirds of the country's residents sought shelter off the island.

Netherlands Antilles

Independence: n/a (autonomous part of the Kingdom of the Netherlands)
Area: 309 sq. mi.
Capital: Willemstad
International relations: CARICOM
Currency: Guilder or florin
Income: (per capita US$) 10,000 (1992)
Population: (1998) 206,000
Ethnic divisions: Black 85%, European, Carib Indian
Religious groups: Roman Catholic, Protestant
Languages spoken: Papiamento, English, Dutch, Spanish
Literacy: 98% (1981)
Exports: Petroleum products
Imports: Petroleum, consumer goods, capital goods
Primary trade partners: Venezuela, United States

The Spanish first landed in Curaçao in 1499, and in 1527 they took possession of Curaçao, Bonaire, and Aruba. So poor was the soil on most of the islands that the Spanish called them *islas inutiles*, capturing many of the native Arawak Indians and then transporting them to nearby Spanish islands to work on plantations. In 1634, the three islands were passed to the Netherlands, where they have remained except for two short periods of British rule during the Napoleonic Wars.

The islands' rich salt deposits, particularly off the coasts of Saint Maarten, Bonaire, and Curaçao, were perhaps the main reason the Dutch had sought to gain their control. However, the mining of salt was both a difficult and labor-intensive job, and there were not nearly enough Dutch colonists willing to do it. The

Dutch decided to import African slaves to handle the workload. The first boatloads of slaves, mostly from the Congo and Angola, arrived in Curaçao in 1639. The Dutch West India Company, which handled the slave trading responsibilities for the Netherlands, increased dramatically in size during this period, becoming the second largest slave-trading power in the Atlantic by the 1640s. By 1700 the slave population on Curaçao and Bonaire totaled 4,000 with another 1,000 slaves split between Saint Eustatius and Saint Maarten. A century later, between them Saint Maarten and Saint Eustatius were home to some 9,000 slaves. Both Curaçao and Bonaire had experienced similar increases, although no exact figures from 1800 are available for those islands. Slavery was abolished in 1863.

Today, some forty nationalities are represented in the Netherlands Antilles and Aruba. The people of the Netherlands Antilles are primarily are African or mixed African-European descent.

Nicaragua

Official name: Republic of Nicaragua
Independence: September 15, 1821
Area: 49,998 sq. mi.
Form of government: Presidential republic
Capital: Managua
International relations: CACM, OAS, UN
Currency: Cordoba
Income: (per capita US$) 440 (1996)
Population: (1998) 4.6 million
Ethnic divisions: Mestizo 69%, white 17%, black 9%, indigenous peoples 5%
Religious groups: Roman Catholic 85%
Languages spoken: Spanish
Literacy: 66% (1995)
Exports: Bananas, coffee, gold, meat, sugar
Imports: Consumer goods, machinery and equipment, petroleum products
Primary trade partners: United States, Central American countries, Venezuela, Japan, Canada, Germany

Christopher Columbus first visited what is now Nicaragua in 1502 on his last voyage to the Americas. It was, however, not until Balboa's discovery of the Pacific in 1513 that Spanish efforts to settle the area began in earnest. Because the economy could neither support nor did it require large-scale slave labor, early Spanish colonists brought relatively few African slaves to what is now Nicaragua. However, the early 1600s saw the development of an English enclave along the territory's desolate Atlantic Coast, known as the Mosquito Coast. By the middle of the seventeenth century, these English settlers had begun to import slaves into their enclave to work the area's plantations and assist in harvesting coastal timber. A century later when Britain was forced

to abandon its Mosquito Coast protectorate, most of the blacks remained, creating black Creole villages, such as Pearl Lagoon and Bluefields. So far were these communities from the center of Spanish power in Managua that the blacks enjoyed considerable local autonomy. The abolition of slavery in the British colonies of the Caribbean in the early 1830s set off a new wave of immigration into the Mosquito Coast as the newly freed slaves joined the free blacks on the Nicaraguan coast. Nicaragua did not win its independence from Spain until 1838.

Today, Nicaragua's population is comprised of mestizos (69%), whites (17%), blacks (9%), and indigenous peoples (5%).

Panama

Official name: Republic of Panama
Independence: November 3, 1903
Area: 29,157 sq. mi.
Form of government: Presidential republic
Capital: Panama City
International relations: OAU, UN
Currency: Balboa
Income: (per capita US$) 3,080 (1996)
Population: (1998) 2.7 million
Ethnic divisions: Mestizo 70%, West Indian 14%, white 10%, Indian 6%
Religious groups: Roman Catholic 85%, Protestant (Evangelical) 15%
Languages spoken: Spanish (official), English, Indian languages
Literacy: 90.8% (1995)
Exports: Cocoa, coffee, bananas, apparel
Imports: Capital goods, crude oil, foodstuffs, consumer goods
Primary trade partners: United States, European Union countries, Central American and Caribbean countries

Prior to the arrival of Europeans, Panama was inhabited by Amerindian groups. By 1519 the Spanish had established settlements, killing or enslaving much of the indigenous Indian population. Africans were brought in to replace the Indian slave workforce. Panama was a part of Colombia from the time of independence in 1821 until it broke away as a separate country in 1903.

One of the most dramatic forces of change in Panama has been the construction of the Panama Canal connecting the Atlantic and the Pacific Oceans. Supported by the United States, which desperately wanted to build the canal, Panama seceded from Colombia. Two weeks later the United States and the newly independent Panama signed a treaty permitting the United States to build the canal and enjoy control over a five-mile stretch of Panamanian territory on either side of the waterway. Panama's existing black population was soon increased dramatically as West Indians arrived by the thousands to help in the massive construction project. Working and living conditions for blacks involved in the project were harsh, particularly since many of the American supervisors overseeing the project were natives of the U.S. South. Segregated living arrangements were put in place by these supervisors. Discrimination against blacks and other Panamanians working on the canal was blatant. They were paid less than Spaniards and Italians who had been imported into Panama to perform the same level of manual labor on the project.

Today, most Panamanians are of mixed parentage—Spanish, Indian, or black.

Paraguay

Official name: Republic of Paraguay
Independence: May 14, 1811
Area: 157,048 sq. mi.
Form of government: Republic
Capital: Asunción
International relations: LAIA, UN
Currency: Guarani
Income: (per capita US$) 1,950 (1996)
Population: (1998) 5.3 million
Ethnic divisions: Mestizo 95%, other 5%
Religious groups: Roman Catholic 90%, Protestant 10%
Languages spoken: Spanish (official)
Literacy: 92.1% (1995)
Exports: Cotton, soybeans, timber, vegetable oils, meat products, coffee
Imports: Capital goods, foodstuffs, consumer goods, raw materials
Primary trade partners: European Union countries, Brazil, Argentina, United States, Japan

Since early colonial times, people of African descent, most of them brought into the territory as slaves, have played a significant role in the development of Paraguay and its culture. Because the colony lacked the wealth of natural resources of many of its neighbors in South America and also because the indigenous peoples of the region could be pressed into service, the number of slaves imported was on a smaller scale than elsewhere. The nature of the work to which the early African (and Indian) slaves were put was not much different in nature than in other Spanish colonies of the region: farm work, livestock raising, and domestic service. In later years, some blacks were employed for more specialized tasks including road construction and repair and the smelting of iron. As of 1650, surviving records indicate, the African slave population totaled 15,000 out of a total population of 250,000. However, unlike other Spanish-held territories where the slave population continued to grow strongly into the nineteenth century, by 1782 Paraguay's African slaves had dropped to less than 11,000 in number.

A system unique to Paraguay called *amparo* provided that any freed slave who could not pay tribute to the Spanish crown was turned over to the protective custody of the local government or religious orders. Under conditions much like slavery, many of these newly freed slaves were settled into all-black communities and compelled to work for their custodians. In Paraguay's battle for independence from Spain, it was unnecessary to draft the services of Afro-Paraguayans, free or slave. Thus when independence was achieved in 1811, colonial officials were under no obligation to begin freeing slaves in payments for their military services. It was not until 1869 that the government finally ordered the total abolition of slavery.

Estimates of the modern-day population of blacks in Paraguay are difficult to obtain, although some have suggested they account for as much as 3.5 percent of the total population of 5.3 million, or about 186,000.

Peru

Official name: Republic of Peru
Independence: July 28, 1821
Area: 494,210 sq. mi.
Form of government: Republic
Capital: Lima
International relations: LAIA, UN
Currency: Nuevo sol
Income: (per capita US$) 2,510 (1996)
Population: (1998) 25.6 million
Ethnic divisions: Indigenous peoples 45%, mestizo 37%, white 15%, other 3%
Religious groups: Roman Catholic 95%, other 5%
Languages spoken: Spanish (official)
Literacy: 88.8% (1995)
Exports: Copper, zinc, fishmeal, crude petroleum
Imports: Machinery, transportation equipment, foodstuffs, iron and steel
Primary trade partners: United States, Colombia, Japan, Germany

To most, Peru is perhaps best known as the home of the Incas, whose rich culture was developed in the mountain strongholds of the Andes. Most students today are also familiar with the Spanish conquistadors who sought out the Incas' riches in gold and silver and toppled their sophisticated empire in the process. What few recognize is the very real contribution made to Peru's conquest and its subsequent development by African slaves and their descendants. Among the best known of the early blacks involved in the conquest of the Incan Empire was Juan Valiente, a slave serving under Diego de Almagro, who himself accompanied Francisco Pizarro into Peru in 1524. For his services, Valiente was eventually rewarded with a land grant and a number of Indians who were required to pay tribute to him. Strangely, Valiente, despite his new found fortune, remained a slave until his death. As his military superiors negotiated with his master for Valiente's freedom, he was killed in an engagement against local Araucanian Indians at Tucapel.

In Peru's early colonial period, relatively few African slaves were imported, since the bulk of the available work was in the mines high in the mountains, an environment for which the colonial authorities thought the Africans ill-suited. Furthermore, there was plenty of Indian labor available for this work. As the country's arid coastal plain was gradually irrigated and put under cultivation, the need for African slaves grew. Obtaining slaves was a monumental challenge, as they had to be shipped from the west coast of Africa, across the Atlantic, around treacherous Cape Horn at the southern tip of South America, and north along the Pacific Coast to Panama, where they were unloaded. So arduous was the voyage that many slaves did not survive. For those importing the slaves, the cost of this trade was very high indeed. However, well into the seventeenth century, Peru's demands for slaves from Africa remained strong. During the campaign of Argentine José de San Martin for Peru's independence in the 1820s, he tried to entice African slaves into military service with promises of freedom for those who joined him. In fact, for most black slaves in Peru, it was not until 1854 that slavery was officially abolished.

Today, blacks comprise a very small percentage of Peru's population. Leading contemporary Afro-Peruvians include composer, vocalist, and ethnomusicologist Susana Baca and writer, university professor, and journalist Gregorio Martínez.

Puerto Rico

Independence: n/a (commonwealth associated with the
    United States)
Area: 3,459 sq. mi.
Capital: San Juan
Currency: U.S. dollar
Income: (per capita US$) 6,760
Population: (1997) 3.8 million
Ethnic division: Mixed, black, Indian, whites
Religious groups: Roman Catholic 85%, Protestant de-
    nominations and other 15%
Literacy: 90% (1993)
Languages spoken: Spanish (official), English

First visited by Columbus in 1493 on his second voyage to the New World, Puerto Rico was soon conquered by Spaniard Ponce de Leon, who was appointed governor of the island in 1509. (It is interesting to note that several African slaves accompanied Columbus on his 1493 visit to the island.) The indigenous Carib Indians, almost all of whom were utilized by the Spaniards

as plantation laborers, were eventually wiped out by diseases and harsh treatment and replaced by African slaves.

When Spain authorized Puerto Rico's slave trade in 1510, a number of free blacks from Seville immigrated to the island in search of broader opportunities. For the most part, these were *ladinos*, as Christianized blacks were known, who sought jobs as domestic servants or mine workers. Free blacks outnumbered slaves for most of the island's history. The island's population, according to the 1845 census, included 216,083 whites, 175,000 free blacks, and 51,265 black slaves. Slavery on the island was completely abolished on March 22, 1873. Fifteen years later, Puerto Rico gained its independence from Spain and became a protectorate of the United States, as a result of the Spanish-American War.

Many Puerto Ricans today are of mixed black and Spanish ancestry. For the most part, the original Indian inhabitants of the island were exterminated in the sixteenth century. Leading contemporary Afro-Puerto Ricans include literary figures Isabelo Zenón Cruz, Angela María Dávila, and Ana Lydia Vega.

Saint Kitts and Nevis

Official name: Federation of Saint Kitts and Nevis
Independence: September 19, 1983
Area: Saint Kitts, (68 sq. mi.); Nevis, (36 sq. mi.)
Form of government: Constitutional monarchy
Capital: Basseterre
International relations: CARICOM, EU, OAS, UN
Currency: East Caribbean dollar
Income: (per capita US$) 6,050 (1996)
Population: (1998) 43,000
Ethnic divisions: Black, some British
Religious groups: Principally Anglican, with evangelical
    Protestant and Roman Catholic minorities
Languages spoken: English
Literacy: 97.3% (1995)
Exports: Machinery, foodstuffs, electronics, beverages,
    tobacco, sugar cane
Imports: Machinery, manufactured goods, foodstuffs, fuel
Primary trade partners: United States, United Kingdom,
    CARICOM countries, Canada, Japan

Christopher Columbus first visited the islands in 1493 on his second voyage to the area. Although some historians have suggested that Columbus named the larger island San Cristobal (Saint Christopher) in his own honor or for his patron saint, the name actually was given to the island by Spanish sailors. The island's nickname, Saint Kitts, comes from English sailors' slang for Saint Christopher. In 1624, Saint Christopher became England's first settlement in the West Indies, and it was from there that colonists spread to other islands in the region. In 1624 the French colonized part of the island. However, it was ceded entirely to Britain by the Treaty of Utrecht in 1713.

By the 1660s, approximately one-half of the Saint Kitts' population of 6,000 was black. Over the next one hundred years, the ratio changed dramatically, so that by the final quarter of the eighteenth century, the island had ten times as many blacks as whites. The only real industry on both Saint Kitts and Nevis was sugar. It was also the central reason for the high concentration of slaves, most of whom were essential for working the sugar cane fields. In 1834, as in most English colonies, slavery was abolished. There followed a mandatory four-year apprenticeship during which the newly freed slaves were obligated to continue to work for their former masters for a small salary. Little changed for most blacks on the islands, as they continued to toil in the sugar fields of their former masters, even after the end of their apprenticeships. However, they now were obligated to pay for housing and their food on the same estates on which they had once been slaves. Many of the islands' blacks left the islands in search of better work elsewhere.

The Federation of Saint Kitts and Nevis attained full independence on September 19, 1983. Today, blacks comprise the largest percentage of Saint Kitts and Nevis's population.

Saint Lucia
Independence: February 22, 1979
Area: 238 sq. mi.
Form of government: Independent state within British Commonwealth (parliamentary democracy)
Capital: Castries
International relations: CARICOM, EU, OAS, UN
Currency: East Caribbean dollar
Income: (per capita US$) 3,790 (1996)
Population: (1997) 152,000
Ethnic divisions: Black 90.3%, mixed 5.5%, Asian Indian 3.2%, Caucasian 0.8%
Religious groups: Roman Catholic 90%, Church of England 3%, other 7%
Languages spoken: English (official), French patois
Literacy: 81.7% (1995)
Exports: Bananas, coconuts, cacao, apparel
Imports: Manufactured goods, machinery, transportation equipment, foodstuffs, chemical
Primary trade partners: United Kingdom, United States, CARICOM countries

The timing of the first European visit to the lushly beautiful island of Saint Lucia has been the subject of debate for some time. Many islanders believe the story, perhaps apocryphal, that Christopher Columbus discovered the island on December 13, 1502, the feast day of Saint Lucy. Whatever the truth about its first European

visitor and the timing of the visit, it is known that Europeans were unable to gain a foothold on Saint Lucia until the middle of the seventeenth century because of the native Carib Indians' fierce resistance. Once European settlement began, the Spanish, British, and French squabbled over who had claimed the island first. The Spanish failed to press their claim, but the British and the French continued to fight over Saint Lucia until 1814, during which time the island changed hands seven times. This competition for control of the island impeded large-scale development of plantations on Saint Lucia.

French planters are believed to have imported the first African slaves to Saint Lucia in about 1763, a relatively late start for the slave trade, when compared to other French and British colonies in the region. During the years of slavery, the local patois, a mixture of African dialects and French, developed. It is still spoken throughout the island today. When the island officially became a British territory in 1814, this already entrenched French-based patois made it difficult for the British colonists to communicate with the island's blacks. When slavery was abolished throughout the British colonies in 1834, more than 13,000 slaves on Saint Lucia were freed. Most of the newly freed blacks fled their masters' plantations and carved out tiny farms of their own.

Saint Lucia became an independent state within the British Commonwealth on February 22, 1979. Today, visitors from the United States, Canada, and Europe have been attracted by the island's multicultural heritage—Saint Lucia is now inhabited mainly by people of African and mixed African-European descent, with small Caucasian and Asian Indian minorities.

Saint Vincent and the Grenadines
Independence: October 27, 1979
Area: 150 sq. mi.
Form of government: Independent within British Commonwealth (constitutional monarchy)
Capital: Kingstown
International relations: CARICOM, EU, OAS, UN
Currency: East Caribbean dollar
Income: (per capita US$) 2,190 (1996)
Population: (1998) 119,818
Ethnic division: Blacks, whites, Asian Indians, Carib Indians
Religious groups: Anglican, Methodist, Roman Catholic, Seventh-Day Adventist
Languages spoken: English (official), French patois
Literacy: 82% (1994)
Exports: Bananas, coconuts, cotton, tennis racquets
Imports: Foodstuffs, machinery and equipment, chemicals, fuels

Primary trade partners: United Kingdom, United States, CARICOM countries

Similar to Saint Lucia, its neighbor to the north, Saint Vincent and the Grenadines, a chain of Caribbean islands, saw no permanent European settlement until the seventeenth century. The Carib Indians, then occupying the islands, fiercely resisted European attempts to colonize. A group of African slaves who survived the sinking of a Dutch slave ship on which they were being transported were the first outsiders allowed by the Caribs to settle on the islands. A treaty between the Caribs and Europeans in the early 1700s finally opened the way for European settlement. The first Europeans to gain a foothold on the islands were the French, who managed to coexist relatively peacefully with the Caribs. When the British moved into the islands and began competing with French planters to see who could carve out the larger plantations, friction with the Caribs was inevitable. After a Carib revolt late in the eighteenth century, British colonial authorities captured more than 5,000 Caribs and exiled them off British Honduras. This stripped the islands of much of their free blacks, most of whom had lived among the Caribs. The blacks remaining in the islands were mostly slaves.

In the early nineteenth century, a massive volcanic eruption caused widespread devastation on Saint Vincent, wiping out much of the island's coffee and cacao crops. When slavery was abolished in 1834, many of the newly freed slaves decided to try to carve out small farms for themselves. White plantation owners were forced to import Portuguese and Asian Indian indentured servants to work in the island's sugar cane fields. As the sugar industry began to slump in the final quarter of the nineteenth century, the government opted to turn over more land to small farmers. Well into the twentieth century, the majority of the island's residents were engaged in small-scale agriculture, a prescription for a precarious economy given agriculture's vulnerability to the vagaries of nature.

The islands were granted full autonomy in 1969 and achieved full independence in 1979.

Suriname

Official name: Republic of Suriname
Independence: November 25, 1975
Area: 63,037 sq. mi.
Form of government: Constitutional republic
Capital: Paramaribo
International relations: CARICOM, EU, OAS, UN
Currency: Surinam guilder
Income: (per capita US$) 3,150 (1995)
Population: (1997) 424,569

Ethnic divisions: Hindustani (Asian Indian) 37%, Creole 31%, Javanese 15%, Bush Negro 10%, Amerindians 3%, Chinese 1.7%
Religious groups: Hindu, Muslim, Roman Catholic, Dutch Reformed, Moravian, and several other Christian groups
Languages spoken: Dutch (official) English, Sranang Tongo (a Creole language), Hindustani, Javanese
Literacy: 93% (1997)
Exports: Bananas, bauxite, citrus, coffee, cocoa, sugar cane
Imports: Capital equipment, petroleum, foodstuffs, cotton, consumer goods
Primary trade partners: Norway, United States, Netherlands, Trinidad and Tobago

Columbus first sighted the Suriname coast in 1498, and Spain claimed the area in 1593. Suriname became a Dutch colony in 1667. However, the new colony, Dutch Guiana, did not thrive. The colony experienced frequent uprisings by the slave population, which was often treated with extraordinary cruelty. Many of the slaves fled to the interior, where they resumed a West African culture and established the six major Bush Negro tribes in existence today: the Ndjuka and the Saramaka, the two largest groups, and the Paramaka, Aluki, Swinti, and Matawai.

Well into the eighteenth century, the territory was unique in its high percentage of African-born slaves—by the mid-1750s, about one-third of Dutch Guiana's slaves had arrived from Africa. Among the factors contributing to this phenomenon were a high mortality rate among the slaves and the need to keep importing slaves at a fast pace, in part to replace some who had escaped. Suriname experienced less in the way of violent slave revolts, such as those common throughout much of the New World—the most common form of protest among Suriname slaves was escape.

The maroons, as the runaway slaves were called, were not the only ones to take a stand against slavery, however. Although Dutch Guiana saw less of the slave violence common to slave-holding New World colonies, there was a notable uprising in 1832, when much of the colony's capital was put to the torch by slaves. In 1860 virtually the entire slave population of the colony escaped to uninhabited parts of the colony. Bowing to these growing pressures, the Netherlands abolished slavery in 1863.

Starting in 1951, Suriname began to acquire an increasing measure of autonomy from the Netherlands. On December 15, 1954, Suriname became an autonomous part of the Kingdom of the Netherlands and gained independence on November 25, 1975. Désiré Bourtese led a military coup in 1980 and instituted a socialist state. A separate challenge to the government came from a guerrilla movement under the leadership of Ronny Brunswijk. The Surinamese Liberation Army (SLA), also known as the Maroon or Bush Negro insurgency, began operating in the northeast in July 1986. It struck against various economic targets including the Suriname Aluminium Company. The government responded with repression and the killing of civilians suspected of supporting the insurgency.

Political upheaval continued in spite of the elections held in 1987. International pressure eventually prevailed, and the military relinquished its control of the government. Ronald Venetiaan was elected president in 1991, followed by Jules Wijdenbosch in 1996. These elections marked the first time in independent Suriname's history that one democratically elected government passed peacefully to another.

Trinidad and Tobago

Official name: Republic of Trinidad and Tobago
Independence: August 31, 1962
Area: 1,980 sq. mi.
Form of government: Constitutional republic
Capital: Port-of-Spain
International relations: CARICOM, Commonwealth, EU, OAS, UN
Currency: Trinidad/Tobago dollar
Income: (per capita US$) 4,210 (1995)
Population: (1998) 1.1 million
Ethnic divisions: (1988): Black 43%, Asian Indian 40%, mixed 14%, other 3%
Religious groups: Roman Catholic 39%, Hindu 25.0%, Anglican 14.7%, other Christian denominations 14.4%, Muslim 6.9%
Languages spoken: English (official), Hindi, French
Exports: Natural asphalt, petroleum, chemicals, steel products, fertilizer, sugar, cocoa, coffee
Imports: Machinery, transportation equipment, consumer goods, foodstuffs
Primary trade partners: United States, CARICOM countries, Venezuela, Central and South American countries, European Union countries

The island of Trinidad was first visited by Columbus in 1498 on his third voyage to the Western Hemisphere. The Spanish made the first successful attempt to colonize Trinidad in 1592. Trinidad continued under Spanish rule until it was captured by the British in 1797. Africans were brought to the islands during the eighteenth century to provide labor on the sugar cane plantations. Following the abolition of slavery, Indian and Chinese labor was imported.

Trinidad was ceded formally to the United Kingdom in 1802 and the island of Tobago was ceded to the United Kingdom in 1814. In 1888, Trinidad and Tobago emerged to form a single colony. In 1958 the United Kingdom established the autonomous Federation of the West Indies. Jamaica withdrew in 1961, and when Trinidad and Tobago followed, the federation collapsed. Trinidad and Tobago obtained full independence and joined the Commonwealth in 1962.

Eric Williams became prime minister at independence and held that position until he died in 1981. Williams was succeeded by George Chambers, who had served as his agriculture minister. Chambers was succeeded in 1996 by Arthur Napoleon Robinson. During an abortive coup attempt in July 1990, Robinson and other government officials were held hostage by a group of more than one hundred Muslim militants. In December of that year, Patrick Manning was elected prime minister. Black-led since 1956, the two-island nation elected its first Asian Indian prime minister, Basdeo Panday, in 1996.

A major center of African culture in the Caribbean, Trinidad and Tobago gave birth to calypso and steelpan, as the music of the steel drum is known locally. The country's annual Carnival festival is but one of the nation's many celebrations of music and dance. Leading contemporary Afro-Trinidadians include calypso singer Mighty Sparrow, visual artist/novelist Valerie Belgrave, and literary figures Rafael de Boissiere, Dionne Brand, Merle Hodge, and Earl Lovelace.

Turks and Caicos Islands

Independence: n/a (dependent territory of the United Kingdom)
Area: 166 sq. mi.
Capital: Grand Turk
Currency: U.S. dollar
Population: (1998) 16,000
Ethnic divisions: Black
Religious groups: Baptist 41.2%, Methodist 18.9%, Anglican 18.3%, Seventh-Day Adventist 1.7%
Languages spoken: English (official)
Exports: Conch, lobster, fish

Two groups of islands in the Atlantic southeast of the Bahamas, the Turks and Caicos were valued by early British settlers for their salt flats, which for hundreds of years were the economic mainstay of the islands. In 1678 English settlers who had come to the islands by way of Bermuda began importing African slaves to work the salt flats. Of this arduous work, Mary Prince, a female slave, wrote in *The History of Mary Prince, A West Indian Slave* (1831): "We . . . worked through the heat of the day; the sun flaming upon our hands like fire, and raising salt blisters in those parts which were not completely covered. Our feet and legs, from standing in the salt water for so many hours, soon became full of

Trinidadian and Tobagonian musicians playing traditional steel drums (Susan D. Rock).

dreadful boils, which eat down in some cases to the very bone, afflicting the sufferers with great torment. . . . Oh that Turk's Island was a horrible place!"

Although slavery was abolished on the islands in 1834, as in most of Britain's New World colonies, life remained extremely difficult for the newly emancipated slaves, for the salt trade remained the islands' only major business for decades to come. It was not until well into the twentieth century that the black majority of the Turks and Caicos managed to acquire any degree of political power. After nearly fifty years of control from the Bahamas, from 1799 to 1848, the islands were granted their own local government, but it was controlled firmly by the white minority. This period of local autonomy lasted until 1873.

Between 1874 and 1959, the Turks and Caicos islands were administered as a dependency of Jamaica. In 1962 the islands became a separate colony. In 1985 Norman B. Saunders, the chief minister and two other ministers caused a scandal when they were arrested in Florida on drug charges and later charged, convicted, and jailed. One year later, the ministerial government ended when other ministers were found guilty of "unconstitutional behavior." The islands remain a crown colony.

Uruguay

Official name: Oriental Republic of Uruguay

Independence: August 25, 1828

Area: 68,037 sq. mi.

Form of government: Republic

Capital: Montevideo

International relations: LAIA, OAS, UN

Currency: Uruguayan peso

Income: (per capita US$) 5,680 (1996)

Population: (1998) 3.3 million.

Ethnic divisions: European descent 86%, mestizo 8%, black 6%

Religious groups: Roman Catholic 66%

Languages spoken: Spanish

Literacy: 97.3% (1995)

Exports: Woolen textiles, beef and other animal products, leather, rice

Imports: Machinery and equipment, vehicles, minerals, plastics

Primary trade partners: Brazil, Argentina, United States, China, Nigeria, Italy

The first Africans arrived in what is now Uruguay as early as 1534 in the company of Spanish explorers. These slaves, most of whom were *ladinos*, as Christianized slaves were known in Spain, joined their masters in the exploration of the Rio de la Plata. By the end of the sixteenth century, Spain was importing increasingly larger numbers of its slaves from Angola in southwestern Africa. Most of the slaves destined for use in the New World were shipped to either Mexico or Cartagena, in what is now Colombia, for transshipment to other Spanish colonies throughout the region. The lengthy voyage of the slave ships from Angola to both Mexico and Cartagena took a tremendous toll on their human cargoes, and many slaves died before reaching their destination. The Spanish began shipping some of their slaves to Buenos Aires on the Rio de la Plata in the southeast of South America. By the end of the seventeenth century, the Spanish discovered that Montevideo, also on the Rio de la Plata but 120 miles closer to the Atlantic, had a fine natural harbor. A settlement was begun there in 1724 and before long much of the slave trade to the region had moved from Buenos Aires to Montevideo, the future capital of Uruguay.

Although the numbers of African slaves imported through Montevideo were impressively high, many of these did not remain in Uruguay, but were shipped into other territories in the region where the demand for slave labor was strong. Within what is now Uruguay, there were little in the way of major mining or agricultural enterprises, and most slaves who remained there toiled as domestic servants. The bulk of the slaves in Uruguay remained in the capital of Montevideo. An end to slavery came in fits and starts during the 1840s. Although freed, many slaves continued to work for their former masters under conditions not far removed from slavery itself. Uruguay's National Statistics Institute conducted a study in the latter half of the 1990s that found about six percent of Uruguayans identify themselves as black.

Venezuela

Official name: Republic of Venezuela
Independence: July 5, 1811
Area: 352,144 sq. mi.
Form of government: Presidential republic
Capital: Caracas
International relations: LAIA, OAS, UN
Currency: Bolivar
Income: (per capita US$) 3,020 (1996)
Population: (1998) 22.8 million.
Ethnic divisions: Spanish, Italian, Portuguese, Amerindian, black
Religious groups: Roman Catholic 96%
Languages spoken: Spanish (official), Indian dialects
Literacy: 91.1% (1995)
Exports: Coffee, cocoa, cotton, sugar cane, tobacco, steel, chemicals, manufactured goods

Imports: Raw materials, machinery and equipment, transportation equipment
Primary trade partners: United States, Japan, Germany, Netherlands

In the sixteenth and seventeenth centuries, Caracas was a major center for the importation of slaves. In the early nineteenth century, blacks and mulattos comprised more than half of the population of the Captaincy General of Caracas, as Venezuela was known at that time. In the latter stages of Venezuela's fight for independence from Spain, Simón Bolivar made extensive use of blacks, mulattos, and zambos, admitting them to the ranks of his rebel army. These blacks played a critical role in the defeat of colonists loyal to Spain. By 1821, Venezuela had been largely wrested from Spain's control.

As early as 1819 Bolivar had called for the abolition of slavery, but he was overruled by a coalition of rebel leaders. Several attempts to loosen the bonds of Venezuelan slaves were undertaken, but little real change was effected in the institution. It was not until 1854 that the country's slaves were finally emancipated.

Today, about 900,000 of Venezuela's 17 million people are black, and another 500,000 are zambos of mixed African and Indian descent. Blacks remain a significant element of the country's population because of its proximity to the Caribbean and employment opportunities that have been available in this oil-rich nation.

Virgin Islands, British

Independence: n/a (dependent territory of United Kingdom)
Area: 59 sq. mi.
Capital: Road Town
Population: (1998) 19,000
Ethnic divisions: Black 90%, remainder white and Asian
Religious groups: Protestant 86% Methodist 45%, Anglican 21%, Church of God 7%, Roman Catholic 6%, Seventh-Day Adventist 5%, Baptist 4%, Jehovah's Witnesses 2%, other 6%
Languages spoken: English (official)
Exports: Bananas, citrus fruit, coconut, sugar, petroleum products

Initially visited by Christopher Columbus in 1493, the Virgin Islands (an archipelago of 74 islands) is now divided into two distinct clusters—British Virgin Islands (six main islands, nearly forty islets) and U.S. Virgin Islands (three main islands, 65 islets). Great Britain obtained title to the islands and islets in 1666 and, until 1960, administered them as part of the Leeward Islands. At present, the government is headed by a Crown-appointed administrator who is assisted by both executive and legislative councils.

During the latter half of the seventeenth century, British settlers discovered that the islands would support the cultivation of both cotton and sugar. However, to work the fields it was necessary to import slave labor from Africa. Life for the slaves in the British islands was particularly harsh, with inhumane penalties exacted for relatively minor infractions of the rules. A slave who refused his master's orders could have part of his body cut off or his nose split. In 1790 slaves in Tortola revolted after rumors spread that Britain had abolished slavery but local slaveowners were withholding freedom. Although Britain abolished the slave trade in 1808, full emancipation did not come for Virgin Island slaves until 1834. Slavery was replaced by a four-year apprenticeship program, under which all slaves were required to remain in the custody of their former masters.

Today, almost the entire population is of African descent.

Virgin Islands, United States

Independence: n/a (territory of the United States)
Area: 133 sq. mi.
Capital: Charlotte Amalie
Currency: U.S. dollar
Population: (1998) 118,000
Ethnic divisions: Black
Religious groups: Baptist, 42%, Roman Catholic 34%, Episcopalian 17%, other 7%
Languages spoken: English (official), Spanish, Creole
Exports: Petroleum products, rum

The United States Virgin Islands—the largest of which are the islands of Saint Croix, Saint John, and Saint Thomas—were originally settled by the Danish West India Company. Saint Thomas was the first to be colonized in 1672; in 1683 Saint John was colonized; and by 1733, Saint Croix had been acquired from France. Some twenty years later, the holdings of the company were taken over by the Danish crown, which then reconstituted them as the Danish West Indies.

As in the neighboring British Virgin Islands, the Danish West Indies was found to be ideally suited for the cultivation of sugar cane and cotton. The first shipment of African slaves, numbering 103, arrived in Saint Thomas in 1673. The island had some 160 plantations and more than 3,000 slaves by 1715, only 42 years later. The island of Saint John witnessed a major slave uprising in 1733. The life of slaves in the islands was a harsh one indeed, but in the months preceding the Saint John revolt, their situation had been made even more difficult when the island was hit by a drought and two hurricanes. The actual revolt was set off by the passage in September 1733 of a set of harsh new regulations governing slaves. Slave leaders captured the island's only fort and managed to hold it for six months. Slaves in the Danish islands finally won their freedom in 1848.

The United States bought the territory from Denmark in 1917 for some $25 million and granted citizenship to its inhabitants ten years later. In 1931 its administration was transferred from the United States Navy to the Department of the Interior. The first black governor, William H. Hastie, was appointed in 1946. Melvin Evans, appointed governor in 1969, two years later became the first black governor to be elected. He served until 1975 when islanders elected Cyril E. King as their new governor. King died three years later and was succeeded by his lieutenant governor, Juan Luis, who was reelected governor in 1982. Elected governor in 1986 and reelected in 1990 was Alexander Farrelly who was succeeded by Roy Schneider after the 1994 elections.

6

Africans in America: 1600 to 1900

◆ Exploration and the First Settlements in the Americas
◆ Slavery in Colonial America: 1619–1787 ◆ African American Status in the New Republic
◆ Expansion of Slavery ◆ Anti–Slavery Movements ◆ The Compromise of 1850 ◆ Civil War
◆ Reconstruction ◆ The Advent of Independent African American Institutions
◆ African American Status after Reconstruction ◆ Figures of the Past
by Houston B. Roberson

◆ EXPLORATION AND THE FIRST SETTLEMENTS IN THE AMERICAS

The presence of the first Africans in the Americas is a point of contention among historians. Some scholars assert that Africans established contact with the Americas prior to the Europeans, arguing from archeological, anthropological, botanical, and linguistic evidence that Africans were present in pre-Columbian America; the work of Ivan Van Sertima is notable in this regard. Others mark the advent of the African presence as coinciding with the presence of the Europeans. Pedro Alonzo Niño, an explorer and companion to Christopher Columbus on his exploratory journey of 1492, appears to have been African; and it is known that an African named Estevanico accompanied the Spanish explorers Panfilo de Narvaez and Alvar Nuñez Cabeza de Vaca on trips throughout the American Southwest during the 1500s. Several other European explorers, including Vasco Nuñez de Balboa and Hernán Cortés, also had African members in their parties.

In 1496 Santo Domingo was established as the first permanent European settlement in the Americas. Indigenous Carib Indians were at first used as laborers; however, they were ill-suited to the rigors of the European system of slavery and died in large numbers from either disease or the constant pressure of forced labor. Portuguese explorers first visited the west coast of Africa in the fifteenth century and found that slave

trading was an established institution. West Africans had for some time sold each other to Arabic traders from North Africa. By the early sixteenth century the Portuguese and Spanish were supplying newly established colonies in the Americas with African slave labor and, by the seventeenth century, several other European nations had entered the trade. African slaves proved to be a relatively cheap and inexhaustible source of labor and, from about 1501, they were increasingly used as slaves, replacing the dwindling indigenous labor pool.

◆ SLAVERY IN COLONIAL AMERICA: 1619–1787

The Emergence of Slave Status

Twenty Africans accompanied the Europeans who landed at Jamestown, Virginia, in 1619. These people were not slaves but indentured servants and, upon completing their contracts, they were free to enjoy the liberties and privileges of the "free laboring class." By 1650 there were about three hundred Africans in the American colonies, most of whom were indentured servants, and some of whom eventually became property holders and active citizens. The first African American born in the colonies, William Tucker, shared with the other settlers the common birthright of freedom. The slave Anthony Johnson apparently became free about 1622 and had by 1651 amassed enough wealth to import five servants of his own, for which he obtained two hundred and fifty acres from the colonial government; the African American carpenter Richard Johnson imported two white servants in 1654 and received one hundred acres.

It is unclear when the first African slaves arrived in the North American colonies. From the 1640s Africans were increasingly regarded as chattel (or persons regarded as fixed items of personal property). In 1641 Massachusetts became the first state to make perpetual bondage legal, and the institution gradually spread among the original thirteen colonies. Rhode Island had an antislavery ordinance, but this was openly violated, and only Pennsylvania maintained a sustained opposition to slavery. By the 1650s Africans were commonly sold for life and, in 1661, the Virginia House of Burgesses formally recognized the institution of African slavery. The erosion of African indentured servitude in Maryland was finalized with the slave law of 1663, which stated specifically that "All negroes or other slaves within the province, [and] all negroes to be hereafter imported, shall serve *durante vita.*"

As white indentured servitude gradually disappeared from the colonial labor market, the flow of African labor into the colonies was accelerated, and planters rigidly institutionalized the perpetual servitude of Africans. One practical reason for this system was that slaves of African origin could be more easily detected than whites should they escape. Among the common rationalizations for the enslavement of Africans was reference to their non-Christian status: it was asserted that Africans were primitive and savage and fit for nothing better than a life of unbroken labor. Even after African Americans became Christianized, their slave status was not altered; in 1667 the Virginia legislature enacted a statute that proclaimed that "baptism doth not alter the condition of the person as to his bondage or freedom."

The Trans-Atlantic Slave Trade

The Dutch West Indies Company began to provide slave labor to the American colonies in 1621. By the late seventeenth century the Royal African Company, an English company whose most profitable commodity was slaves, began to exert powerful influence within the English court and parliament. The British government in turn exerted great pressure upon the American colonies to develop attitudes and laws that would support a slave economy. The influence of the Royal African Company contributed to William Penn's decision to overrule the objections of fellow Quakers and permit slavery in Pennsylvania. The company also drew the shipping industry of New England into the slave trade. By the time the Royal African Company lost its monopoly on the West African slave trade in 1696, the sea captains of New England were participating in the massive slave incursions into Africa.

The majority of Africans who were transported to the Americas as slaves came from the area comprising the modern nations of Senegal, Gambia, Guinea, Sierra Leone, Liberia, Burkina Faso, Ivory Coast, Ghana, Togo, Benin, Nigeria, Cameroon, Gabon, the Republic of the Congo, and the Democratic Republic of the Congo. The number of Africans who reached the Americas is estimated at between ten and twenty million. About six hundred thousand Africans were brought during the sixteenth century, two million in the seventeenth century, five million in the eighteenth century; and three million in the nineteenth century. In addition to those who reached the Americas must be added the enormous number who died in passage. It is estimated that 15 percent of those who were shipped to the Americas died of disease on the overcrowded boats of the "Middle Passage," and that another 30 percent died during the brutal training period faced in the West Indies before shipment to the American mainland.

Slavery Expansion in Colonial America

The colonies of New England played a principal role in the slave trade, despite their having little local need for slave labor. By 1700, African Americans of New England numbered only one thousand among a population of ninety thousand. In the mid-Atlantic colonies, the population comprised a larger percentage, as small slaveholdings employed slaves as farm laborers, domestics, and craftsmen. In New York, slaves comprised 12 percent of the population during the mid-eighteenth century. The Quakers of Pennsylvania protested that slavery violated the principles of Christianity and the rights of man and passed laws prohibiting the slave trade in 1688, 1693, and 1696, but the British parliament overruled these statutes in 1712.

Most slaves, however, lived in the South. The Southern colonies were divided between the tobacco producing provinces of Virginia, Maryland, and North Carolina, and the huge rice and indigo plantations now comprising the Carolinas and Georgia. Tobacco tended to be grown on family farms around the Chesapeake Bay area and, because of this fact, the slave population was not as concentrated as it was on the plantations further to the south.

The growth of a plantation economy and the concentration of a large number of African Americans in the Southern states led first Virginia (1636) and then the other states to form all white militias. The terror of slave uprisings led the slaveholders to institute ever harsher slave codes. Ultimately, a slave could not own anything, carry a weapon, or even leave his plantation without a written pass. Murder, rape, arson, and even lesser of-

With slave traders and buyers gathered, a group of Africans disembarks from a slave ship (The Library of Congress).

fenses were punishable by death; small offenses were commonly punished by whipping, maiming, and branding. In the area where ninety percent of colonial African Americans lived, a slave had no rights to defend himself against a white and, as far north as Virginia, it was impossible for a white to be convicted for the murder of a slave.

The Maiden Lane slave revolt in New York City in 1712 and the public paranoia over the alleged slave conspiracy of 1741 led to the development of slave codes that were in some cases as severe as those in the South, but in general the North was a relatively less oppressive environment. In Pennsylvania the Quakers allowed African Americans a relative degree of freedom, and in New England the slave codes tended to reflect Old Testament law, maintaining the legal status of slaves as persons with certain limited rights.

Maroon Communities Arise throughout the Americas

The African experience of *marronage* or *cimarronaje* (i.e., escape from slavery), its survivors, and their descendants in the New World reflects an important part of the African diaspora in the Americas. However, little has been documented about this aspect of history.

For more than four centuries, thousands of enslaved Africans managed to escape from plantations and mines of European colonizers throughout the Americas, seeking their freedom in the wilderness. Between the early sixteenth and late nineteenth centuries, maroons challenged the colonial powers and violently resisted enslavement, striking hard at the foundation of the plantation economy of the Western Hemisphere.

In remote areas throughout the United States, the Caribbean, Central America, and South America, maroon communities emerged as free and independent societies that oftentimes forced colonial governments to sign treaties and pacts guaranteeing their freedom, land, and political autonomy. These communities emerged as an integration of African, Native American, and European cultural elements. After centuries of struggle, survival, assimilation, and adaptation, these maroon communities were able to develop a unique sense of identity and history, contributing in many ways to the shape of the Western Hemisphere.

Today, descendants of some of the original maroon communities live in Oklahoma and Seminole communities in Texas, as well as Mexico, Jamaica, Suriname, French Guyana, Colombia, and the Bahamas.

Military Service before and during the Revolutionary War

Records of King William's War (1689–1697) relate that the first to fall in Massachusetts was "an Naygro of Colo. Tyng," slain at Falmouth. During Queen Anne's War (1702–1713), African Americans were drafted and sent to fight the French and the Indians when white colonists failed to provide the number of requisitioned men. Many armed African Americans fought at Fort William Henry in New York. Slaves sought freedom as their payment for fighting, and those who were already free sought the wider benefits of land and cash payments. The colony of Virginia ended its policy of excluding African Americans from the militia by 1723, and in 1747 the South Carolina Company made slaves eligible for enlistment in the territorial militia according to a quota system in which a 3:1 ratio was maintained between whites and blacks, thus abating the white's fears of insurrection. African Americans also fought for the British in the French and Indian War.

African American Patriots

In the years leading to the Revolutionary War, it became apparent that, despite the growth of slavery, at least some African Americans were willing to fight alongside white Americans. On March 5, 1770, an Afri-

Blacks were commonly sold at slave auctions (Corbis Corporation [Bellevue]).

can American named Crispus Attucks was one of the first men killed in the Revolutionary War, when British troops fired on a crowd of protesters in the Boston Massacre. Many African American minutemen fought at the defense of Concord Bridge: among them were Lemuel Haynes, a gifted speaker and later a prominent Congregationalist minister, and Peter Salem, who had received his freedom to enlist. Other figures of the Revolutionary War include Pomp Blackman, Caesar Ferrit, and his son John, Prince Estabrook (who was wounded at Lexington), Samuel Craft, and Primas Black and Epheram Blackman (who were members of Ethan Allen's Green Mountain Boys).

The Move to Disarm African Americans

A major issue during the Revolutionary War was whether African American slaves, and even freemen, should be permitted to bear arms. On May 29, 1775, the Massachusetts Committee of Safety, in a move which reflected their desire to strengthen ties with Southern states, proclaimed that the enlistment of slaves "was inconsistent with the principles that are to be supported, and reflect[ed] dishonor on the colony." On July 9, 1775, Horatio Gates, the adjutant general of the Conti-

nental Army, issued from General Washington's headquarters the order that recruiting officers should not accept "any stroller, Negro, or vagabond."

The enormous slave populations of certain Southern states meant that many whites lived in perpetual fear of slave uprisings. In South Carolina slaves outnumbered whites, and in Georgia the population was above forty percent slaves. To minimize the risk of slaves arming themselves, Edward Rutledge of South Carolina introduced a measure in the Continental Congress to discharge all African Americans (whether free or enslaved) from the Continental Army. Although the proposal was rejected, General George Washington's own council of war decided to terminate all African American enlistment two weeks later, and on October 13, 1775, Continental Congress passed the law. Colonial generals such as John Thomas argued that African Americans soldiered as well as whites and had already "proved themselves brave" in action, but their protests went unheeded. At the close of 1775, it was extremely difficult for African Americans to join the revolutionary forces at any level.

However, on November 7, 1775, the British made a political move that forced the Continental Army to

Crispus Attucks (The Library of Congress)

often armed. African Americans were often enlisted for longer terms than whites and, by the latter years of the war, many of the most seasoned veterans were African American troops.

◆ AFRICAN AMERICAN STATUS IN THE NEW REPUBLIC

Slaves and Freemen after the Revolution

At the end of the war about five thousand African Americans had been emancipated through military service. In the following years the Northern states abolished slavery: Vermont in 1777, Massachusetts in 1783, Connecticut and Rhode Island in 1784, New York in 1785, New Jersey in 1786, and Pennsylvania in 1789. In the mid-Atlantic state of Virginia, Thomas Jefferson convinced the state legislature to allow slaveowners to manumit their slaves in 1783. In 1790 there were 757,208 African Americans comprising 19 percent of the population of the United States: 697,681 were slave, and 59,527 were free. During this time the free population faced many of the same restrictions as the slave population: they could not walk on the streets after dark, travel between towns without a pass, or own weapons. There was also the danger of being captured and enslaved, whether one was free or not.

The large number of Southern slaves that had responded to the British Army's call to duty and escaped to the British lines, on the other hand, met a more disheartening fate. Fighting against the colonies in exchange for their freedom, most of these slaves were returned to their slaveowners after the defeat of Great Britain. In other cases, they were shipped to various British-controlled colonies to continue a miserable life of slavery.

The United States Constitution

The U.S. Constitution, drafted in 1787 and ratified in 1788, provided fundamental political principles for the nation. Key among these principles were the belief that all people share a fundamental equality, that they possess certain unalienable rights, and that government derives its power from the people. But African Americans were not afforded the rights and privileges of the Constitution. At the time, it was generally believed by whites that people of African descent were racially inferior and incapable of being assimilated into society. It was also widely believed that they were not citizens of the new republic. Article I, section 2 of the Constitution specified that all persons who are not free shall be counted as three-fifths a person for the sake of tax purposes, and article I, section 9 authorized the continued importation of slaves until 1808.

reverse its policy. Lord Dunmore, the governor of Virginia, issued a proclamation that stated, " I do hereby declare all indentured servants, Negroes, or others free, that are able and willing to bear arms, they joining his Majesty's troops, as soon as may be, for the more speedily reducing this Colony to a proper dignity." As the leaders of the impending revolution realized the consequences of the wholesale enlistment of slaves in the British Army, they brought an end to their racially exclusionary policy. Local militias that were formerly unable to fill their muster rolls enlisted free African Americans and won the reluctant acceptance of slave owners as slaves were substituted for those white men who bought their way out of service. As the war progressed, slaveowners were compensated for the enlistment of slaves who were then made free. During the course of the Revolution, many colonies granted freedom to slaves in return for military service. Rhode Island passed the first slave enlistment act on February 2, 1778, raising a regiment that participated gallantly in many important battles. In 1780 Maryland became the only Southern state to enroll slave troops, while South Carolina and Georgia refused altogether to even arm their slaves. While slave conscripts were at first assigned to combat support, in the heat of battle they were

Following the war, many enslaved Africans who had fled to British lines during the American Revolution were shipped to various British-controlled, slaveholding colonies (The Library of Congress).

Slavery in the New Nation

In 1793 Eli Whitney invented the cotton gin, which separated cotton from cotton fiber, led to a subsequent increase in the consumption of cotton, and heightened the demand for slaves in the cotton-producing states. In 1800 there were more than 893,600 African slaves in the United States; by 1810 there were over 1,191,300. Although the slave trade was technically discontinued in 1808, it is estimated that from that date until 1860 more than 250,000 slaves were illegally imported; furthermore, nothing prohibited slaves from being bartered, and the breeding of slaves for sale became a specialized business. Some of the largest slave trading firms in the nation were located in Maryland, Virginia, and the District of Columbia. Such was the expansion of slavery that, between 1800 and 1859, the population of Mississippi grew from 3,489 slaves and 5,179 whites to 309,878 slaves and 295,718 whites, respectively.

By the mid-eighteenth century, three-fourths of the cotton produced in the world came from the United States, and profits from cotton were so great that vast plantations were hacked from the wilderness, allowing armies of slaves to work the fields. By mid-century the states of Georgia, Alabama, Mississippi, and Louisiana annually produced 1,726,349 bales of cotton, 48 million pounds of rice, and 226,098,000 pounds of sugar. With the outbreak of the Civil War, there were nearly four million slaves in the United States, and nearly three-fourths of them worked in cotton agriculture.

Slave Life

Slavery was by its very nature a brutal and exploitative business, and the average slave lived a terribly grim life. The more fortunate slaves tended to work on family-sized farms or had positions as house servants.

Besides cotton production, African American slaves also cultivated rice (Index Stock Imagery).

Whatever one's surroundings, much of one's fortune depended upon the kindness of the master. On the larger plantations slaves were divided between house and field hands. The former group was charged with such assorted tasks as caring for the grounds and garden of the house, maintenance of the rigs and appliances, house cleaning, and caring for the master's children. House servants were frequently allowed to practice trades, such as smithery, masonry, and tailoring; some even became skilled musicians and doctors. Body slaves served their masters as valets and personal messengers, and from this intimacy real friendships sometimes developed.

But house servants were in a sense aristocrats among slaves. Their daily lives had little in common with those of the faceless masses of field hands who confronted the brutal monotony of sowing and reaping without respite or prospect of change. On larger plantations with 25 or more slaves, the only contact between field hands and whites occurred through the overseer, who often employed cruel and vicious brutality to maintain control. Many planters felt that the largest profits were made by working a slave to death in eight or ten years and then buying a new one. Even tenderhearted masters often had little contact with their field workers, and so long as the overseer returned a profit, no questions were asked. In many places slaves were given no free time at all, but were forced to work fourteen or fifteen hours a day. Louisiana was the only state with a law regarding the amount of work that could be demanded of a slave—the law permitted a slave to be worked 21 hours every day.

Most slaves could only expect to live with the bare necessities of shelter, clothing, and food. Shelter often consisted of a cramped, windowless, mud-floored shack in which a large family was expected to live; clothing was basic in design and made of course materials; and food was often limited to a bucket of rice or corn per week with no meat. The only break in the routine occurred on such holidays as Christmas, though in some cases slaves were able to hunt, fish, or garden in the hours after work.

Miscegenation

The history of the United States is replete with stories of enslaved African America female slaves being forced into sexual liaisons with their masters and bearing children who were often denied their rightful legal inheritances. In such cities as Charleston, South Carolina, Mobile, Alabama, and New Orleans, Louisiana, there was widespread intermixture between white men and African American women. In New Orleans, as some historians have demonstrated, the practice of young white men maintaining young black women in concubinage was so common as almost to gain social acceptability. However, white fathers varied in accepting responsibility for their black children. Some sold them outright into slavery, while others provided them with money, land, and manumission. Census data indicates that on the eve of the Civil War, of the approximately 3.9 million African American slaves, more that 411,000 were counted as mulatto. The actual figure was almost certainly higher because census takers strictly went by the physical features that they observed and judged as mixed race. It is therefore likely that mulattos with predominately African American features were not counted.

Perhaps the most famous, troubling, and enduring miscegenation narrative is the story of Sally Hemings, whose own birth was the product of a slave-master relationship, and Thomas Jefferson, author of the Declaration of Independence and third president of the United States. Despite the fear of race mixing that he expressed in his *Notes on Virginia*, recent DNA evidence suggests with almost absolute certainty that Jefferson, possibly his brother, Randolph, or one of Randolph's six sons, fathered at least one child with Sally Hemings, one of Jefferson's many slaves. Oral tradition among African American members of Jefferson's family has insisted for generations that they were biological descendants of Thomas Jefferson. Most historians chose to believe the white Jefferson descendants who have steadfastly denied that Jefferson or his kin would have fathered one of Hemings's children without any special provision for them. Only recently, after genetics tests erased any reasonable doubts, have most historians begun to reconsider their position on this issue. (The descendants of Sally Hemings were finally allowed to attend the Jefferson family reunion at Monticello, the historic home of Thomas Jefferson, in May 1999. Though the Hemings descendants were not formally admitted into the Monticello Association, the family organization agreed to further examine the DNA test results as well as other evidence provided.)

This saga illuminates the difficulty and struggle enslaved African American women faced as victims who, whether the relationship was consensual or forced, ultimately had no freedom over their bodies and no power of securing protection and security for their progeny beyond whatever was deemed appropriate by the slave-master fathers. Interestingly, the scientific confirmation of the Jefferson-Hemings relationship comes at a time when white members and black members of a few American families are beginning to confront their past familial relationship and forge some level of recognition of past exploitation as a means of possible future reconciliation within their families.

Slave Naming Practices

Slaves had purposeful naming practices that were distinctively different from those of their masters. Most slaves were able to choose the names of their children, usually naming their sons after fathers and daughters after female relatives other than their mother, in order to help identify kin relationships and keep track of which cousins one should not marry. (Slaves followed marriage rules that prohibited marrying one's cousin, even though many planters and free African Americans did not.)

Generally, many slaves used English or European names for themselves and their children to satisfy the preferences of masters. Yet, many Africans kept alive their sense of cultural independence and roots by choosing English equivalents of African names or English names that sounded similar to African names. Still, some African slaves used African names all their lives.

In addition to given or first names, slaves could also have surnames distinctive from those of their owners, although owners were usually unaware of the surnames. Normally, slaves chose a surname that represented or

Slaves standing outside their quarters in South Carolina (The Library of Congress).

identified the first slave owner of the earliest born-in-Africa ancestor who came to North America as a slave. The surname would then be handed down over the generations to help track relations and lineage. Though many slaves had their own surnames or "titles," many did not. After the end of slavery, those who already possessed surnames revealed them, while others chose one for the first time. During and immediately after the Civil War, government agencies often insisted that slaves have surnames to enroll in their programs or receive government benefits. Those whose family had been owned by members of the same family for several generations might have the same last name as the last owner, although the name was originally chosen to identify a more distant owner within the same family. Those who were aware of a slave family surname extending over two or more generations were likely to keep it in order to feel connected with ancestors, even if the name was one associated with a disliked master. Some persons changed names several times to avoid the possibility of reenslavement. Even after a name was chosen, it was often recorded differently at various times, due to the low level of literacy and variations in spelling.

The Denmark Vesey Conspiracy

The mistreatment of slaves in the years after the Revolution led to an atmosphere of suspicion and terror. Masters lived in constant fear of uprisings, and much time was given over to surveillance. Although organized rebellions were rare, there were many instances of angry slaves burning dwellings and murdering their masters. Slave codes became increasingly strict, but no amount of regulation could dissipate the anger of the slaves nor the guilt and unease that many slave owners experienced.

In 1800 an African American named Denmark Vesey purchased his freedom and, from about 1817, he planned a slave revolt in Charleston, South Carolina. The revolt was scheduled to begin on July 14, 1822. With the help of five other African Americans, as many as nine thousand slaves were recruited before their plans were uncovered. As word of the revolt began to leak out, Vesey was forced to move the date forward to June 16; again word was leaked. The state militia was mustered, and an intense investigation of the plot was begun. Some135 slaves were arrested during the course of the investigation; 97 were bound over for trial; 45 were transported out of the country; and Vesey and 34 others were hanged. As news of the conspiracy spread, Southern states further tightened their slave codes.

◆ EXPANSION OF SLAVERY

Slavery in the Northwest Territory

In the early seventeenth century the French began to settle in what comprises present-day Illinois, Indiana, Michigan, Ohio, and Wisconsin, and part of Minnesota. The British began to settle in the area during the mid-eighteenth century; and, in July of 1787, Congress passed the Northwest Ordinance, which established a government for the Northwest Territory and provided terms under which states could be formed for entrance into the Union. The ordinance also contained controversial provisions: one prohibited slavery and involuntary servitude in the territory, and the other provided for the return of fugitive slaves to the states from which they had escaped. The European farmers who had brought slaves into the territory were angered by the clause prohibiting slavery, and Congress was petitioned for its repeal. The prohibition against slavery was practically circumvented when the Illinois and Indiana territories established a system of indentured servitude under which any person owning slaves could bring them into the region and place them under lifetime indenture. The restrictions placed on these servants were much like the slave codes of the Southern colonies—indentured servants could not travel alone without a pass or attend public gatherings independently.

The Missouri Compromise

In April of 1803 the United States paid $15 million for the Louisiana Territory, an area comprising the entire Mississippi drainage basin, which had been settled by the French in the late seventeenth century. Many Southerners hoped to extend slavery into the vast new territory, and it was widely expected that Missouri would be admitted to the Union as a slave state. A series of heated debates erupted over the extension of slavery in the region, and in 1819 the House of Representatives introduced legislation authorizing statehood for Missouri while prohibiting the further introduction of slavery into the new state. This drew angry protest from pro-slavery supporters. The controversy was further escalated by two events: Alabama was admitted to the Union as a slave state in 1819, making the total number of slave and free states equal, and Maine applied for statehood in 1820. Between 1820–1821 the Missouri Compromise was reached, admitting Missouri to the Union as a slave state with a slave population of almost 10,000, and Maine as a free state, with the understanding that the future expansion of slavery would be prohibited above the latitude of 36° 33'N.

Texas and the Mexican-American War

The territory comprising Texas was part of the Louisiana Territory when the United States purchased it in 1803, but, by 1819, it had become part of Mexico. Mexico provided land grants to American settlers (many of whom brought their slaves with them), and soon Americans outnumbered the Mexicans of the region. In 1836, Texas declared its independence from Mexico and requested annexation to the United States. The possibility of another slave state entering the Union stirred fresh debate. On March 1, 1845, President John Tyler signed the joint resolution of Congress to admit Texas as a slave state; the voters of Texas supported the action, and Texas became a slave state on December 29, 1845. In 1846, Mexican and American troops clashed in Texas, and the United States declared war on the Republic of Mexico. The war ended in 1848 with the Treaty of Guadalupe Hidalgo, whereby Mexico relinquished its claims to Texas and the United States acquired all of the land extending to the Pacific Ocean.

The Wilmot Proviso

In 1846 David Wilmot, a Democrat from Pennsylvania, introduced an amendment to a bill appropriating $2

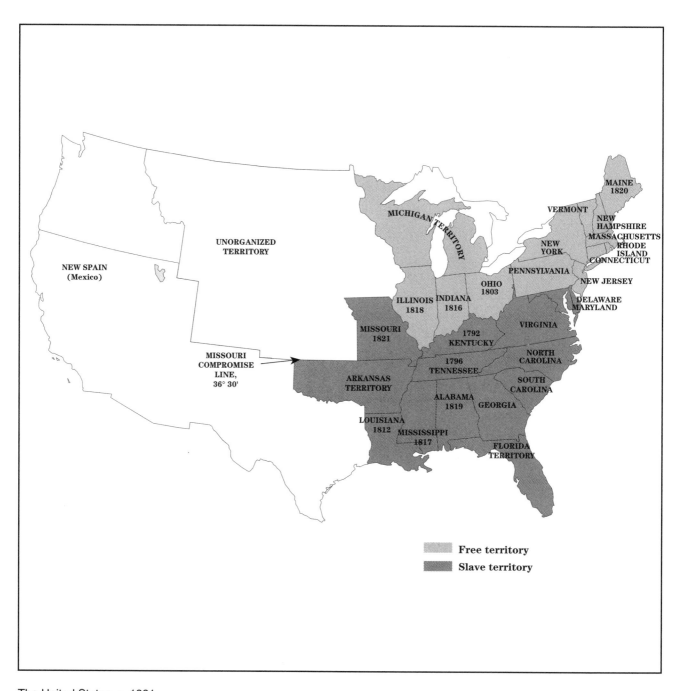

The United States, c. 1821.

million for President James Polk to use in negotiating a territorial settlement with Mexico; the amendment stipulated that none of the newly acquired land would be open to slavery. Although the amendment received strong support from Northern Democrats and was passed by the House of Representatives, the Senate adjourned without voting on it. During the next session of Congress a new bill providing $3 million for territorial settlement was introduced. Wilmot again proposed an amendment prohibiting the expansion of slavery into the newly acquired territory. The bill was passed by the House of Representatives, but the Senate drew up a new bill excluding the Wilmot Proviso.

Fugitive Slave Laws

Tensions between Northern and Southern politicians continued to mount over the issue of fugitive slaves. Article IV, Section 2 of the Constitution authorized the return of fugitive slaves and provided procedures for recovery, and in 1793 the Fugitive Slave Act was passed. In Northern states that strongly opposed slavery, "per-

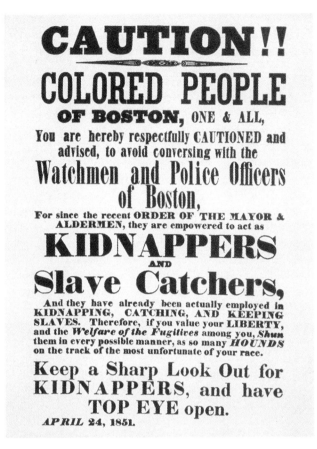

$200 Reward.

RANAWAY from the subscriber, on the night of Thursday, the 30th of September.

FIVE NEGRO SLAVES,

To-wit: one Negro man, his wife, and three children.

The man is a black negro, full height, very erect, his face a little thin. He is about forty years of age, and calls himself *Washington Reed*, and is known by the name of Washington. He is probably well dressed, possibly takes with him an ivory headed cane, and is of good address. Several of his teeth are gone.

Mary, his wife, is about thirty years of age, a bright mulatto woman, and quite stout and strong.

The oldest of the children is a boy, of the name of FIELDING, twelve years of age, a dark mulatto, with heavy eyelids. He probably wore a new cloth cap.

MATILDA, the second child, is a girl, six years of age, rather a dark mulatto, but a bright and smart looking child.

MALCOLM, the youngest, is a boy, four years old, a lighter mulatto than the last, and about equally as bright. He probably also wore a cloth cap. If examined, he will be found to have a swelling at the navel.

Washington and Mary have lived at or near St. Louis, with the subscriber, for about 15 years.

It is supposed that they are making their way to Chicago, and that a white man accompanies them, that they will travel chiefly at night, and most probably in a covered wagon.

A reward of $150 will be paid for their apprehension, so that I can get them, if taken within one hundred miles of St. Louis, and $200 if taken beyond that, and secured so that I can get them, and other reasonable additional charges, if delivered to the subscriber, or to THOMAS ALLEN, Esq., at St. Louis, Mo. The above negroes, for the last few years, have been in possession of Thomas Allen, Esq., of St. Louis.

WM. RUSSELL.

ST. LOUIS, Oct. 1, 1847.

An 1847 handbill offering a reward for the return of runaway slaves to their owner (The Library of Congress).

Handbill warning African Americans—both enslaved and free—of the ever-present danger of slave catchers and kidnappers (The Library of Congress).

sonal liberty" laws were passed in order to undermine federal law; liberty laws placed the burden of proof on masters in cases concerning alleged fugitive slaves. Such a law was enacted in Pennsylvania in 1826, requiring state certification before alleged fugitives could be returned. When Edward Prigg, a professional slave catcher, attempted to capture a fugitive slave residing in the state, he was arrested on kidnapping charges for failing to acquire necessary certification. The Supreme Court ruled in *Prigg v. Pennsylvania* (1842) that the state's law could not interfere with federal action regarding fugitives and the right of slaveholders to recover property; it also found that states would not be obligated to enforce federal fugitive slave statutes. This led abolitionists to seize upon the idea of not enforcing federal statutes. Following the court's decision several Northern states enacted even more radical personal liberty laws prohibiting the enforcement of the Fugitive Slave Act.

Free African Americans in the South Before 1865

While the majority of the African American population was enslaved before 1865, a sizable number of African Americans were free. The quality of freedom that African Americans experienced before 1865 generally conformed to the following trajectory: they had a fairly high legal status during the colonial period that was strengthened during the American Revolution, but, almost immediately afterwards, it began to deteriorate. Most notably, the 1790 Alien and Naturalization Act

passed under the newly enacted U. S. Constitution disallowed African Americans from becoming citizens and so denied them the federal protections that whites enjoyed.

By the end of the eighteenth century, most Northern states had either abolished slavery or began programs for gradual emancipation. Slavery had been excluded from the Northwest Territory and, ironically, the American Revolution, with its philosophy of egalitarianism, led to some African Americans gaining their freedom even as other African Americans were increasingly enslaved. Of course, some enslaved African Americans achieved freedom through escape to the North.

In 1790, it is estimated that there were 59,000 free African Americans (i.e., 27,000 in the North and 32,000 in the South). By 1830, there were approximately 319,000 free African Americans and by 1860, they numbered about 488,000—46 percent of whom lived in the North. Free African Americans were concentrated in the following areas: the tidewater counties of Virginia and Maryland; the Piedmont region of Virginia and North Carolina, the Southern cities of Baltimore, Washington,

Charleston, Mobile, and New Orleans. It is perhaps more accurate to refer to this group of people as non-enslaved African Americans because they faced a myriad of restrictions. In many instances, their freedom of movement was restricted to the county or state in which they lived, they had to carry passes or certificates of freedom, they were barred from certain professions and rarely permitted to vote, and, though they were required to pay local taxes, could not send their children to public schools. Despite these circumscriptions, free African Americans found ways to be productive members of society. Perhaps their greatest advantage over enslaved African Americans was that they possessed more control over their bodies and their labor. They worked in most trades but especially the building, clothing, and food production industries. In fact, U.S. Census taken between 1820 and 1860 indicate that African Americans were involved in fifty different kinds of occupations.

◆ ANTI-SLAVERY MOVEMENTS

Quakers and Mennonites

The early opposition to slavery was generally based on religious beliefs; Christian ethics were seen as incompatible with slavery. Quakers (or the Society of Friends) and Mennonites were two of first groups to oppose the practice in the United States. Quakers and Mennonites settled mainly in Pennsylvania, though also in the South, and advocated simple living, modest dress, and nonviolence. In 1652 the Quakers passed a resolution against lifetime indenture, and in 1688 the Mennonites did the same. With the continued rise of slavery in the South, many Quakers protested and moved north into Indiana and Ohio.

The Free African Society

In 1787 the Free African Society was organized in Philadelphia by two African Americans, the Rev. Richard Allen and Absalom Jones; Adams later founded the Bethel African Methodist Church, and Jones became the rector of a Protestant Episcopal Church. The society was an important model for political consciousness and economic organization for African Americans throughout the country. It provided economic and medical aid, advocated abolition, and maintained channels of communication with African Americans in the South. Similar to the many other African American organizations that followed, the society was rooted in religious principles. Throughout the nineteenth century, a number of mutual aid societies also sprung up in African American communities of the eastern seaboard, providing loans, insurance, and various other economic and social services to their members and the larger community.

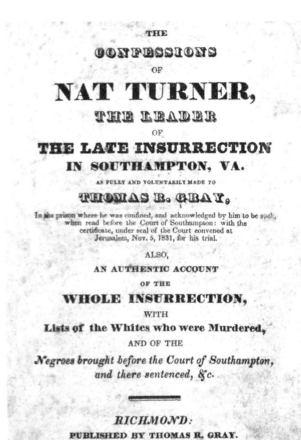

In *The Confessions of Nat Turner,* the slave rebel describes the 1831 uprising in Southampton, Virginia (The Library of Congress).

American Colonization Society

In 1816 the American Colonization Society was organized in Washington, DC, with the objective of encouraging the repatriation of African Americans to Africa. While the idea of returning free African Americans was motivated in part by humanitarian intent, the society was rather moderate in its opposition to slavery. Support for the society came in part from those who feared the possibility of a large, free African American population in the United States.

Congress issued a charter to the society for the transportation of freed slaves to the west coast of Africa, provided funds, and assisted in negotiations with African chiefs who ceded the land that comprised what became Liberia. While Northerners contributed support and donations to the society, Southern patrols threatened freedmen into emigrating. In 1822 the first settlers landed at the site on the western coast of Africa, which was later named Monrovia after President James Monroe. In 1838 the Commonwealth of Liberia was formed and placed under the administration of a governor appointed by the society.

Abolition Societies Formed in Philadelphia and New York

The earliest abolition societies were the Pennsylvania Society for Promoting the Abolition of Slavery, formed in Philadelphia in 1775, and the New York Manumission Society, formed in the city in 1785. Prior to the 1830s a number of anti-slavery societies arose in both the North and the South, and during the 1830s and 1840s numerous abolitionist organizations arose alongside the women's rights organizations as part of the general social reform movement. The American Anti-Slavery Society was formed in Philadelphia in 1833, and after attending one of its meetings, the Quaker abolitionist Lucretia Coffin Mott formed the Philadelphia Female Anti-Slavery Society with the assistance of Elizabeth Cady Stanton. Mott and her husband, James, were active in the Underground Railroad and various other anti-slavery activities, and James served as a delegate to the World Anti-Slavery Convention.

The press served as the primary tool of the anti-slavery movement. In 1827, the journalists Samuel Cornish and John Russwurm launched *Freedom's Journal*, the first African American owned and edited newspaper; in 1831, William Lloyd Garrison published the first issue of *Liberator*; and other anti-slavery papers followed, including *Anti-Slavery Record*; the *Emancipator*; *Human Rights*; and the *North Star*, launched by Frederick Douglass.

While many of the anti-slavery organizations were dominated by whites, African American leaders played an important role in the abolition movement. Some of the most notable leaders were Alexander Crummell, Frederick Douglass, Sarah Mapp Douglass, Charlotte Forten, Henry Highland Garnet, Sojourner Truth, and David Walker. Most of these leaders were committed to cooperative relations with whites and opposed separatist doctrines, while some of the more militant abolitionists (i.e., Garnet and Walker) stressed the conditional necessity of violence in the struggle against slavery.

In the South the activities of the abolition movement only hardened the resolve of the slaveholding class to maintain the system of slavery. Depending upon the circumstances, Southern justification of slavery continued along several lines: it was an economic necessity, a means of converting African pagans to Christianity, and a means of controlling an inferior race.

The Underground Railroad Transports Slaves to Freedom

A vast network of individuals and groups developed throughout the country to assist African Americans in escaping from slavery, reaching its height between 1835 and 1865. Abolitionists and free blacks provided "stations," food, shelter, and financial assistance, while experienced "conductors," who were often themselves runaway slaves, led thousands of "passengers" to freedom in the Northern states, Canada, and Mexico. Two of the most famous conductors were Josiah Henson and Harriet Tubman.

Most of the movement occurred at night, with passengers hiding in the barns and homes of sympathetic whites and blacks during the day. Because of the extreme secrecy required to maintain its operation, the precise number of slaves freed by the railroad is unknown. However, its very existence instilled fear in Southern slaveowners and served to further motivate Northern abolitionists in their cause to end slavery.

Nat Turner

In February of 1831, Nat Turner, a slave in Southampton County, Virginia, began to plan a slave revolt, and on August 22, Turner and his co-conspirators killed Turner's master and family. Within 24 hours about sixty whites in the county had been killed. Turner was captured on October 30 and hung on November 11. The incident contributed to the increasing paranoia of Southern society.

Free Labor and Free Soil Movements

Radical Democrats and members of the Whig party who opposed slavery united to form a new political party in Buffalo, New York, in 1848. The party adopted a platform supporting free labor and free soil in response to feelings among Northerners that slavery restricted the freedom of Northern workers to contract for work and should therefore be excluded from the developing regions of the West. Southerners wanted the freedom to expand westward and take their slaves with them. Sen. John C. Calhoun of South Carolina and other Southern delegates maintained that both Congress and the territorial legislatures lacked the authority to restrict the expansion of slavery into the territories. The control of Northern states over the national government led these men to consider secession from the Union.

◆ THE COMPROMISE OF 1850

As the debate over the admission of new Western states continued, Southerners argued that the South should be given guarantees of equal positioning in the territories. In 1850 Sen. Henry Clay proposed a compromise in which California would be admitted as a free state, the new territories of New Mexico and Utah

Among these twelve members of the Pennsylvania Abolition Society was William Lloyd Garrison (bottom right).

would be organized, slavery would be abolished in the District of Columbia, more forceful fugitive slave legislation would be enacted, and the Texas war debt would be resolved. At the time the compromise was hailed by many as the solution to the debate over slavery.

Dred Scott v. Sandford

The slavery debate presented supporters and opponents of the institution with two very important questions: how should fugitives from slavery be treated in jurisdictions where slavery was illegal, and should a slave brought into a free state by his master be viewed as free? The first question was partially addressed by Article IV, Section 2 of the Constitution and by the Fugitive Slave Acts of 1793 and 1850; however the second question had not as yet been addressed. During the 1830s and 1840s a slave by the name of Dred Scott accompanied his master, a surgeon in the U.S. Army on numerous trips to military posts around the country including the free states of Illinois and the territory of Wisconsin. In 1846 Scott sued his master for his freedom, asserting that his sojourns in free jurisdictions made him free. After numerous delays, trials, and retrials, the case reached the Supreme Court in 1856. The court

responded with nine separate opinions, and Chief Justice Roger Brook Taney delivered the deciding opinion. The ruling was both complex and controversial: the Missouri Compromise of 1820 was ruled unconstitutional on the grounds that Congress did not have authority to limit the expansion of slavery; slavery was found to be legal in the territories until the citizens voted for or against it; and Africans and their descendants were found to be ineligible for citizenship in the United States as the framers of the Constitution had not viewed Africans as citizens. Since African Americans were not viewed by the court as citizens, they could not file suit. Despite the finality of the court's decision, the issue of slavery remained unresolved.

John Brown and Harpers Ferry

On October 16, 1859 a white, visionary abolitionist named John Brown led a band of 21 men (five of whom were African Americans) in the seizure of the federal arsenal at Harpers Ferry. After holding the site for several hours, Brown and his followers were captured by federal troops under the command of Robert E. Lee. Southerners were outraged by Brown's actions, interpreting them as symptomatic of a willingness among

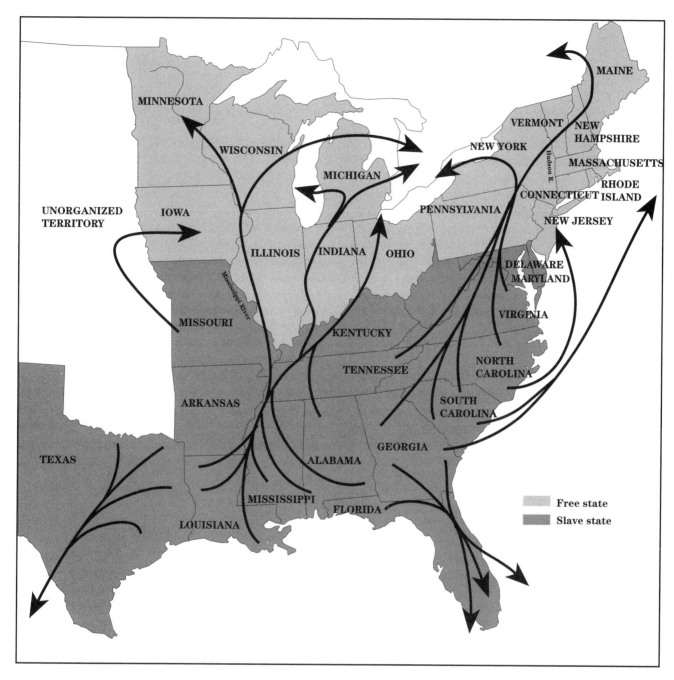

Underground Railroad routes traveled by African Americans to escape slavery in the South.

Northerners to attempt the forcible overthrow of slavery. In December of 1859, Brown was hanged alongside Dangerfield Newby, a runaway slave; John A. Copeland of Carolina; Sheridan Leary, a harness maker and freedman; and Shields Gree, a sailor from South Carolina.

◆ CIVIL WAR

In 1860 Abraham Lincoln, a Northern Republican, was elected president amid continuing polarization over the issue of slavery. Lincoln had voiced opposition to

the expansion of slavery in the past, and with his election Southerners became even more fearful of an ideological assault on state's rights and the abolition of slavery nationwide. In 1860 a delegation from South Carolina voted unanimously for the repeal of the state's 1788 ratification of the Constitution and the severing of all relations with the Union; Georgia, Florida, Alabama, Mississippi, Louisiana, and Texas soon followed. In February of 1861, the seven states drew up a constitution and elected Jefferson Davis as president of the Confederate States of America. As Northern leaders

These African Americans were believed to have traveled on the Underground Railroad in order to escape slavery in the South (The Library of Congress).

sought a means of preserving the nation, Southern troops seized federal installations, post offices, and customs houses, and in April of 1861 Confederate forces took one of the last Union holds in the South—Fort Sumter in Charleston Harbor, South Carolina. Lincoln was forced to retaliate.

African American Soldiers in the Civil War

From the beginning of the war African Americans engaged in the fighting, although Lincoln at first refused to officially employ them in the Union Army. By 1862 Lincoln concluded that the use of African American soldiers was a necessity. An estimated 180,000 African American soldiers served in the Union Army and another 20,000 served in its Navy; however, not all of those African Americans who participated in the war fought on the Union side. There are no accurate records of how many African American soldiers fought for the South, but their numbers grew as white Southerners became more desperate.

Lincoln faced a dilemma in that if he issued an order of universal emancipation, as the abolitionists encouraged him to do, he risked alienating the border states

that remained supportive of the Union: these were Delaware, Maryland, Kentucky, and Missouri. In a letter to Horace Greeley, Lincoln stated:

> "If I could save the Union without freeing any slave, I would do it; if I could save it by freeing all the slaves, I would do it; and if I could save it by freeing some and leaving others alone, I would also do that. What I do about slavery and the colored race, I do because I believe it helps save the Union. . . ."

During the summer of 1862, Lincoln began to feel that the emancipation of the slaves would be necessary to realizing victory over the South, and on January 1, 1863 he issued the Emancipation Proclamation, freeing slaves in those states that had seceded from the Union. Because the proclamation did not apply to the areas under occupation by Union forces, 800,000 slaves remained unaffected by its provisions. He dared not alienate the slave-owning border states on the Union side, especially in light of the growing antipathy toward African Americans in many Northern cities. In the Draft Riots of July 13–16, 1863, huge mobs of whites in New York City (angry over the provisions of the Conscription Act)

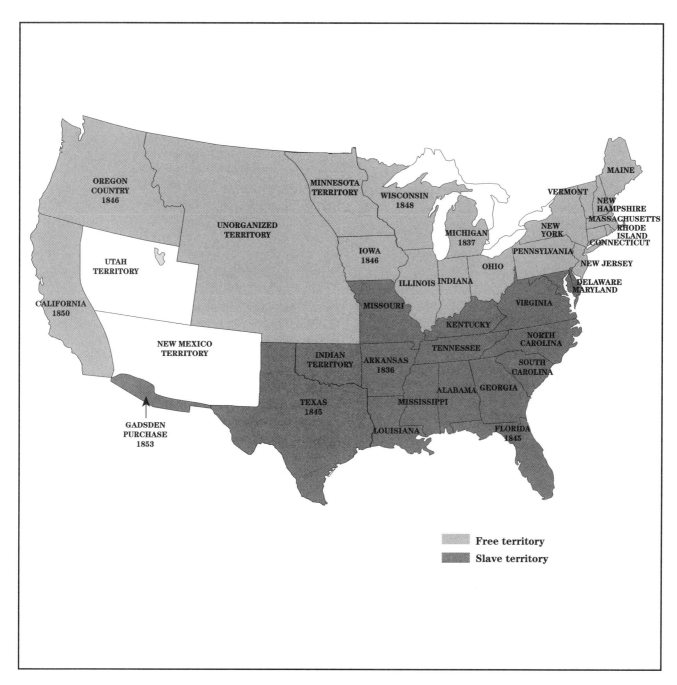

The United States, c. 1850.

attacked blacks and abolitionists, destroying property and viciously beating many to death.

The Civil War lasted from April of 1861 to April 1865, and at the end more than 360,000 Union soldiers and 258,000 Confederate solders were dead. By the end of the war 21 African Americans had received the Medal of Honor, and indeterminate numbers of others had made sacrifices for the cause. On December 18, 1865, the Thirteenth Amendment of the Constitution was ratified, formally abolishing slavery in the United States.

◆ RECONSTRUCTION

Civil Rights and Reconstruction Acts

On March 3, 1865, Congress enacted the first of several acts that set up and empowered the Bureau of Refugees, Freedmen and Abandoned Lands (or the Freedmen's Bureau). The organization provided former slaves with basic health and educational services and administered land that had been abandoned during the war. In 1866 Congress passed the Civil Rights Act, in which a number of personal liberties were outlined, including the right to make contracts, sue or be sued, own and sell property, and receive the equal benefit of the law. The Reconstruction Act of 1867 outlined the terms under which the Southern states might re-enter the Union—one of these terms required each state to call a convention to draft a new state constitution that would guarantee voting rights for all races. President Johnson vetoed the bill, but Radical Republicans in Congress were able to muster the necessary two-thirds majority needed to override the veto. In addition to abolishing slavery, most new constitutions abolished property qualifications for voting and imprisonment for debt. The state constitutions drawn up in 1867 and 1868 were the most progressive the South had known.

During Reconstruction, more than two hundred African Americans held various public offices. South Carolina had two lieutenant governors, Alonzo J. Ransier and Richard H. Gleaves. Jonathan Jasper Wright, the first African American elected to the Pennsylvania bar, traveled to the South and, in 1870, was elected to South Carolina's Supreme Court. Between 1870 and 1901, twenty African Americans served in the U. S. House of Representatives and two African Americans, Hiram R. Revels and Blanche K. Bruce, represented Mississippi in the U. S. Senate. When Bruce's senate term ended, no other African American would be elected to the U. S. Senate until 1966, when Massachusetts elected Republican Edward Brooke.

◆ THE ADVENT OF INDEPENDENT AFRICAN AMERICAN INSTITUTIONS

African Americans' notions of what emancipation entitled contrasted sharply with that of most white Americans. For most whites, it was simply a moment that led to the absence of legalized slavery with few, if any, tacit implications for equality or justice for their erstwhile bondsmen. For African Americans, emancipation was a period of time when African Americans sought to construct the contours of their newly won liberty. It required conscious and intentional acts of self-determination, and, therefore, occasioned a movement to seek political, economic, and social justice and equality. African Americans, therefore, enjoyed their greatest successes in areas where defining freedom was least dependent upon white control or approval—the family, independent African American churches, and African American colleges.

Family

Though denied the rights and protections of legal marriage, African Americans formed strong familial bonds during slavery. Emancipation allowed some African Americans, forcibly separated during slavery, to rejoin their families; and it permitted African Americans who had been living together as husband and wife to marry legally. Census reports in several Southern states, including Alabama, South Carolina and Virginia, suggest that by 1870 the proportions of blacks married and involved in family life was comparable to that of whites. Stable family life therefore helped provide an anchor for African Americans in their struggle to live meaningful lives.

Independent African American Churches

Postbellum African American churches functioned not only to meet spiritual yearnings, but also social, economic, and political needs. The churches of African Americans, therefore, helped institutionalize strategies for surviving in an oppressive society. Called the "cultural womb" of the African American community, the church influenced almost all African American institutions and organizations from providing a training ground for musicians and musical forms to founding banks to the more traditional role of instilling moral sensibility. Some historians claim that, collectively, African American churches should be viewed as a "nation within a nation" because these churches played an important political role in the community, as the only "arena of social life in which Negroes could aspire to become leaders . . ." The religious vision and initiative that established these churches were part of an emancipation movement that relied upon African American churches to provide not only spiritual nourishment and moral leadership, but also to serve as a forum to address community concerns.

African American ministers played a crucial role in helping to establish independent churches. As important symbols who presided over the rites of passage—baptisms, marriages and deaths—ministers were intimately involved in the lives of church members. Ministers participated in helping the Freedmen's Bureau teach newly freed men and women to read and write, find housing and jobs, and even choose new family names. Often they were the best-educated members of their congregations. Most African American preachers had to learn to balance seeking power and opportunity for their congregation with allaying whites' fears of blacks organizing or galvanizing their resources. On the one hand, ministers were in the best position, as respected members of the community, to advocate a liberal interpretation of emancipation. On the other hand, because they had so much power over other African Americans, their very presence posed a threat to white supremacy. African American clergy, therefore, learned the art of negotiating with whites in power.

African Americans gathering for a watch night meeting on the night before the Emancipation Proclamation takes effect (The Library of Congress).

Being too outspoken could cost them their lives; capitulating too much to white authority could eclipse their congregations' freedom.

Between roughly 1865 and the early 1900s, seven major independent African American denominations were founded: the African Methodist Episcopal Church (A.M.E.); the African Methodist Episcopal Church Zion (A.M.E.Z.); the Christian Methodist Episcopal Church (C.M.E.); the National Baptist Convention, USA, Inc; National Baptist Convention of America Unincorporated; the Progressive National Baptist Convention; and The Church of God in Christ (C.O.G.I.C.). Though some African Americans chose to remain in white majority congregations and denominations, the turn of the twentieth century found most blacks as members of one the seven independent African American denominations. These institutions worked to define African American emancipation in the broadest possible terms. For example, African American congregations throughout the South embraced a "Gospel of Freedom" that asserted that exercising political and social independence was inextricably tied to controlling institutional expressions of their spirituality.

African American Education

Education was an extremely high priority for African Americans during the postbellum era. This was especially true for African Americans living in Southern cities. Throughout most of the South, African Americans aggressively worked to establish educational facilities—from elementary schools to colleges and universities. Aided in their efforts by Northern missionaries, African Americans eagerly sought to educate themselves and their children. A number of African American colleges were established during these years including: Howard University in Washington, DC; Hampton Institute in Virginia; St. Augustine's College in North Carolina, Benedict College in South Carolina; Spelman College, Morehouse College, and the Atlanta University system in Georgia; Alabama State University and Tuskegee Institute in Alabama; and Jackson State College in Mississippi.

Still, the overwhelming majority of African Americans had very little access to any kind of formal education, though many church congregations used their Sunday school programs to teach members how to read the Bible. Education was funded by the state, and states and local schools boards openly discriminated against African American schools, chiefly by appropriating less money, providing fewer teachers and allowing for a shorter school terms than that enjoyed by whites (i.e., white schools convened for nine months while most African American schools met for four months). The small number of African Americans who managed to obtain some level of formal education worked with countless others to secure a measure of political, economic, and social freedom.

◆ AFRICAN AMERICAN STATUS AFTER RECONSTRUCTION

The Fourteenth and Fifteenth Amendments

On July 23, 1868, the Fourteenth Amendment was ratified, providing definitions of national and state citizenship, effectively overriding the Supreme Court's decision in Dred Scott v. Sandford, and providing for equal privileges of citizenship and protection of the law. On March 30, 1870, the Fifteenth Amendment was ratified to ensure the right to vote. But the amendment proved unsuccessful in its aims, as many state and local governments created voting regulations that ensured African Americans would not vote; these included grandfather clauses, requiring that one's grandfather had voted; literacy tests; poll taxes; and "white primaries," which were held prior to general elections and permitted only whites to vote. In addition, Southern states enacted many laws (known as black codes) that curbed the new rights of the freed slaves: South Carolina made it illegal for African Americans to possess firearms, and other states restricted their right to make and enforce contracts; to marry and intermarry; and even to assemble, "wander," or be "idle."

The Civil Rights Act of 1875

In 1875, Congress attempted to establish a semblance of racial equality by enacting a law that made it illegal to deprive another person of the "full and equal enjoyment of the accommodations, advantages, facilities, and privileges of inns, public conveyance, . . . and other places of public amusement" on account of race. In a number of cases (known as the Civil Rights cases), the Supreme Court ruled that the Fourteenth Amendment did not authorize Congress to legislate against discriminatory state action, while disregarding discrimination by private individuals including the owners of hotels, theaters, and restaurants.

The Removal of Federal Troops from the South

The U. S. Presidential election of 1876 between Samuel J. Tilden and Rutherford B. Hayes was a hotly disputed one. Both Southern Democrats and Northern Republicans claimed the electoral votes of South Carolina, Louisiana, and Florida. So, Congress established an electoral commission to settle the argument. In return for Southerners agreeing to allow Presidential Republican candidate Rutherford B. Hayes to become president, a compromise was reached in which the South was promised that all federal troops, assigned to protect African American freedoms and oversee states' readmission into the Union, would be removed. In 1877, soon after taking office, Hayes withdrew all federal troops from the South. This led to an end of federal efforts to protect African Americans' civil rights until passage of the 1964 Civil Rights Act.

Plessy v. Ferguson

In *Hall v. DeCuir* (1878), the Supreme Court decided that states could not outlaw segregation on common carriers, such as streetcars and railroads, and in 1896 the Court again faced the issue of segregation on public transportation in the case of *Plessy v. Ferguson*. The case concerned Homer Adolph Plessy, an African American who was arrested for refusing to ride in the "colored" railway coach while traveling by train from New Orleans to Covington, Louisiana. The law in Louisiana required that "equal but separate" accommodations for blacks and whites be maintained in public facilities, but Plessy challenged this law. Justice Billings Brown delivered the majority opinion that separate but equal accommodations constituted a reasonable use of state police power, and that the Fourteenth Amendment could not have been an effort to abolish social or racial distinctions or to force a co-mingling of the races. In his dissenting opinion, Justice John Marshall Harlan remarked that, "The judgement this day rendered will, in time, prove to be quite as pernicious as the decision made by this tribunal in the *Dred Scott v. Sandford* case. The thin disguise of equal accommodation for passengers in railroad coaches will not mislead anyone nor atone for the wrong this day has done." The ruling paved the way for the doctrine of separate but equal in all walks of life, and not until the case of *Brown v. Board of Education of Topeka* (1954) would the constitutionality of segregation be seriously challenged.

Racial Nadir

In the wake of almost thirty-five years of hard earned but seemingly steady progress in successful institution-building within the African American community, the turn of the century ushered in a period of fermented political enervation, economic deprivation, and social segregation for African Americans—what has been dubbed a nadir of postbellum race relations. Despite the efforts of African Americans to establish stable family life, independent churches, and educational facilities,

Southern states held conventions in which they rewrote their constitutions to disfranchise African Americans and enforce social segregation. To prevent blacks from voting, whites engaged numerous techniques including poll taxes, literacy tests, and violence in the form of lynching. Perhaps most indicative of the overthrow of African Americans' gains during Reconstruction was the Wilmington race riot of 1898.

Located on the coast of North Carolina, Wilmington has been a prosperous city known for its naval stores since colonial times. While slavery had existed in Wilmington as in other parts of the South, there had always been a sizable free African American population, many of whom had achieved middle-class status. As late as the 1890s, African Americans held several important positions in the town: three of the ten alderman posts; one of three chairs on the school committee; and a coroner, deputy superior court clerk, justice of the peace, and mail clerk. In addition, there were African American policemen, and the health board was entirely composed of African Americans. On November 10, 1898, the most ghastly offense of the Progressive era occurred in Wilmington as whites took to the streets and refused to allow Republicans—many of whom were African Americans—to take their elected offices. Eventually, President William McKinley had to intervene in the conflict before order could be restored. When the conflict was settled, armed white Democrats had overthrown duly elected Republican officeholders. The physical oppression of slavery had now met its twentieth century incarnation—second class citizenship.

Accommodation, Confrontational Activism, and Self-Help Movements

In the face of these grave circumstances, African Americans employed several approaches to continue their efforts toward self-determination and self-expression. Some African Americans, following the beliefs and teachings of Booker T. Washington became accommodationists. They worked to develop industrial skills and to make themselves an essential component of the manual labor force and postponed demanding social and political equality, believing that they needed to prove to whites that African Americans were capable of handling the responsibilities and privileges of citizenship. In 1895 at the Atlanta Exposition, Washington made a speech in which he told white philanthropists that if they would support African Americans in their attempt to secure economic means, there would be no concerted effort to push for political rights, and furthermore that "In all things purely social we [blacks and whites] can be as separate as the fingers, yet one as the hand in all things essential to mutual progress."

W. E. B. Du Bois articulated a more confrontational philosophy and strategy. Du Bois and William Monroe Trotter, editor of a Boston newspaper *The Guardian*, argued that as American citizens, African Americans should not have to earn nor prove themselves worthy of rights guaranteed in the Declaration of Independence and U. S. Constitution. Du Bois expressed his fear of the accommodationist approach arguing "if we make technical skill the object of education, we may possess artisans but not, in nature men." Du Bois and his proponents therefore argued that, led by an elite "talented tenth" of the African American race, African Americans should demand immediate political, social, and economic equality.

The third strategy employed was the self-help movement. Proponents of this movement include white philanthropists, such as John D. Rockefeller and George Peabody, both of whom established education funds that helped to bankroll African American education. Most of the effort in the self-help movement came, however, from such women's organizations as The Colored Women's Federated Clubs, the National Association of Colored Women, and missionary societies of various African American churches. Such Women as Ida Wells-Barnett, Susie A. Stone, Henrietta Gibbs, Nannie Helen Burroughs, and Mary Church Terrell were involved in a panoply of activities that included: agitating for women's suffrage, raising money to build schools and hospitals, holding parenting classes, helping to sustain the livelihood of African American churches, and assisting in creating strong, financially solvent state, local, and national church conventions—thereby giving African Americans a national voice. As Mary Church Terrell aptly described this effort, African Americans became involved in the self-help movement with the goal of "Lifting as We Climb."

Historians today debate which of the numerous strategies African Americans employed was most effective, but African Americans living during the time period employed all strategies—often in combination. They engaged accommodation, confrontational activism, and self-help in their effort to secure for themselves and their posterity, the benefits of opportunity, self-expression, and self-determination.

◆ FIGURES OF THE PAST

(To locate biographical profiles more readily, please consult the index at the back of the book.)

Crispus Attucks (1723?–1770)
Revolutionary Patriot

A runaway slave who lived in Boston, he was the first of five men killed on March 5, 1770, when British troops fired on a crowd of colonial protesters in the Boston Massacre. The most widely accepted account of the incident is that of John Adams, who said at the subsequent trial of the British soldiers that Attucks undertook "to be the hero of the night; and to lead this army with banners, to form them in the first place in Dock Square, and march them up to King Street with their clubs." When the crowd reached the soldiers, it was Attucks who "had hardiness enough to fall in upon them, and with one hand took hold of a bayonet, and with the other knocked the man down." At that point the panicked soldiers fired, and in the echoes of their volley, five men lay dying; the seeds of the Revolution were sown. Attucks is remembered as "the first to defy, the first to die."

Joseph Cinque (1811–1879)
Insurrectionist

Born in Sierra Leone in 1811 and purchased by Spaniards in Havana, Cuba, in 1838, Cinque was placed aboard the *Amistad* bound for Puerto Principe. When the crew became exhausted from battling a storm, Cinque led the slaves in seizing the ship and killing all but two of the crew, who were kept alive to navigate a course back to Africa. The captive pilots headed north, against the slaves' knowledge, and when the ship was sighted off the coast of Long Island, the slaves were taken to Connecticut and placed in prison. Abolitionists took up the cause of the men and enabled Cinque to raise funds for judicial appeals by speaking on their lecture circuit; his words were translated from Mendi, and he became known as an excellent speaker. In 1841, John Quincy Adams won the slaves' case, and they were released and returned to Africa.

Frederick Douglass (1817–1895)
Lecturer, Abolitionist, Editor, Diplomat, Federal Government Official, Federal Legislator, Municipal Government Official, Marshall

Born in Talbot County, Maryland, on February 14, 1817, Frederick Douglass was sent to Baltimore as a house servant at the age of eight, where his mistress taught him to read and write. Upon the death of his master, he was sent to the country to work as a field hand. During his time in the South, he was severely flogged for his resistance to slavery. In his early teens he began to teach in a Sunday school that was later forcibly shut down by hostile whites. After an unsuccessful attempt to escape from slavery, he succeeded in making his way to New York disguised as a sailor in 1838. He found work as a day laborer in New Bedford, Massachusetts, and after an extemporaneous speech before the Massachusetts Anti-Slavery Society, he became one of its agents.

Joseph Cinque (The Library of Congress)

Douglass quickly became a nationally recognized figure among abolitionists. In 1845 he bravely published his *Narrative of the Life of Frederick Douglass*, which related his experiences as a slave, revealed his fugitive status, and further exposed him to the danger of reenslavement. In the same year, he went to England and Ireland, where he remained until 1847, speaking on slavery and women's rights, and ultimately raising sufficient funds to purchase his freedom. Upon returning to the United States, he founded the *North Star*. In the tense years before the Civil War he was forced to flee to Canada when the governor of Virginia swore out a warrant for his arrest.

Douglass returned to the United States before the beginning of the Civil War and, after meeting with President Abraham Lincoln, he assisted in the formation of the 54th and 55th Negro regiments of Massachusetts. During Reconstruction, he became deeply involved in the Civil Rights movement, and, in 1871, he was appointed to the territorial legislature of the District of Columbia. He served as one of the presidential electors-at-large for New York in 1872 and, shortly thereafter, became the secretary of the Santo Domingo Commission. After serving for a short time as the police commissioner of the District of Columbia, he was appointed marshall in 1871, and held the post until he was appointed the recorder of deeds in 1881. In 1890, his support of the presidential campaign of Benjamin Harrison won him his most important federal post: he became minister resident and consul general to the Republic of Haiti and, later, the charge d'affaires of Santo Domingo. In 1891, he resigned the position in protest of the unscrupulous business practices of U.S. businessmen. Douglass died at his home in Washington, DC, on February 20, 1895.

Lemuel Haynes (1753–1833)
Religious Leader

The son of a black father and white mother and born in 1753, he was deserted and brought up by Deacon David Rose of Granville, Massachusetts. He was a precocious child and began writing mature sermons while still a boy. His preparation for the ministry was interrupted by the American Revolution. On April 19, 1775 he fought in the first battle of the war at Lexington, Massachusetts; he then joined the regular forces and served with Ethan Allen's Green Mountain Boys at the capture of Fort Ticonderoga.

Josiah Henson (1789–1883)
Educational Administrator, Abolitionist, Religious Leader

Born a slave in a log cabin in Charles County (near Rockville), Maryland on June 15, 1789, Josiah Henson grew up with the experience of his family being cruelly treated by his master. By the time he was 18 years of age, Henson was supervising the master's farm. In 1825 he and his wife and children were moved to Kentucky, where conditions were greatly improved, and in 1828 he became a preacher in a Methodist Episcopal Church. Under the threat of being sold, he and his family escaped to Ohio in 1830, and in the following year entered Canada by way of Buffalo, New York. In Canada he learned to read and write from one of his sons, and he soon began preaching in Dresden, Ontario.

While in Canada he became active in the Underground Railroad, helping nearly two hundred slaves to escape to freedom. In 1842 he and several others attempted to start the British-American Manual Labor Institute, but the industrial school proved unsuccessful. Henson related his story to Harriet Beecher Stowe (the author of *Uncle Tom's Cabin*), and it has been disputed whether or not her story is based in part on aspects of his life. He traveled to England three times, where he met distinguished people, was honored for his abolitionist activities and personal escape from slavery, and was offered a number of positions that he turned down in order to return to Canada. He published his autobiogra-

James Armistead Lafayette

phy in 1849 and rewrote and reissued it in 1858 and 1879. Henson died in Ontario in 1883.

James Armistead Lafayette (17??–?)
Spy

Born a slave, he risked his life behind enemy lines collecting information for the Continental Army. He furnished valuable information to the Marquis de Lafayette and enabled the French commander to check the troop advances of British General Cornwallis; this set the stage for General George Washington's victory at Yorktown in 1781 and for the end of the Revolutionary War. In recognition of his services, he was granted his freedom by the Virginia legislature in 1786, although it was not until 1819 that Virginia awarded him a pension of $40 a year and a grant of $100. He adopted the surname "Lafayette" in honor of his former commander, who visited him during a trip to the United States in 1824.

Toussaint L'Ouverture (1743–1803)
Insurrectionist

Born Francois Dominique Toussaint L'Ouverture, a slave on the island of Hispaniola (now Haiti and the

Dominican Republic) in 1743, he learned to read and write under a benevolent master. When he was fifty years of age, a violent revolt erupted on the island. White French planters, African slaves, and free mulattoes (some of whom owned slaves) clashed over issues of rights, land, and labor, as the forces of France, Britain, and Spain manipulated the conflict. At first the slaves and mulattoes shared the goals of the French revolution in opposition to the royalist French planters, but with time a coalition of planters and mulattoes arose in opposition to the slaves.

L'Ouverture became the leader of the revolutionary slave forces, which by mid-1790s consisted of a disciplined group of four thousand mostly ex-slaves. He successfully waged a campaign against the British. At the height of L'Ouverture's power and influence in 1796, General Rigaud, who led the mulatto forces, sought to re-impose slavery on the black islanders. L'Ouverture quickly achieved victory, captured Santo Domingo, and by 1801 had virtual control of the Spanish part of the island. In 1802, a French expeditionary force was sent to re-establish French control of the island. Following a hard-fought resistance to French colonial ambitions in the Western Hemisphere, Toussaint L'Ouverture struck a peace treaty with Napoleon. However, L'Ouverture was tricked, captured, and sent to France where he died on April 7, 1803, under inhumane conditions.

Toussaint L'Ouverture

Gabriel Prosser (1775–1800)
Insurrectionist

Gabriel Prosser was born around 1775. He became the coachman of Thomas Prosser of Henrico County, Virginia, and planned a large, highly organized revolt to take place on the last night of August of 1800 around Richmond, Virginia. About 32,000 slaves and only eight thousand whites were in the area, and it was his intention to kill all of the whites except for the French, Quakers, elderly women, and children. The ultimate goal was that the remaining 300,000 slaves in the state would follow his lead and seize the entire state. The revolt was set to coincide with the harvest so that his followers would be spared any shortage of food, and it was decided that the conspirators would meet at the Old Brook Swamp outside of Richmond and marshal forces to attack the city.

The insurrection fell apart when a severe rainstorm made it impossible for many of the slaves to assemble and a pair of house slaves who did not wish their master killed revealed the plot. Panic swept through the city, martial law was declared, and those suspected of involvement were rounded up and hanged; when it became clear that the slave population would be decimat-

ed if all of those implicated were dealt with in similar fashion, the courts began to mete out less severe sentences. Prosser was apprehended in the hold of a schooner that docked in Norfolk, Virginia. Brought back in chains, he was interrogated by the governor. When he refused to divulge details of the conspiracy, he was hung.

Dred Scott (1795–1858)
Negotiator

Born in Southhampton, Virginia, in 1795, his first name was simply "Sam." He worked as a farmhand, handyman, and stevedore, and moved with his master to Huntsville, Alabama, and later to St. Louis, Missouri. In 1831 his owner, Peter Blow, died, and he was bought by John Emerson, a surgeon in the U.S. Army. Sam accompanied his new master to Illinois (a free state) and Wisconsin (a territory). Sometime after 1836 he received permission to marry, and by 1848 he had changed his name to Dred Scott. At various times he attempted to buy his freedom or escape but was unsuccessful. In 1843, Emerson died and left his estate to his widow Irene Emerson, who also refused Scott his freedom. He then obtained the assistance of two attorneys who helped him to sue for his freedom in county court.

Scott lost this case, but the verdict was set aside, and in 1847 he won a second trial on the grounds that his slave status had been nullified upon entering into a free state. Scott received financial backing and legal representation through the sons of Peter Blow, Irene Emerson's brother John Sanford, and her second husband, Dr. C. C. Chaffee, all of whom apparently saw the case as an important challenge to slavery. In 1857, the U.S. Supreme Court ruled against Scott, stating that slaves were not legally citizens of the United States and, therefore, had no standing in the courts. Shortly after the decision was handed down, Mrs. Emerson freed Scott. The case led to the nullification of the Missouri Compromise of 1820, allowing the expansion of slavery into formerly free territories and strengthening the abolition movement.

Sojourner Truth (1797–1883)
Lecturer, Abolitionist

Born Isabella Baumfree in Ulster County, New York, around 1797, she was freed by the New York State Emancipation Act of 1827 and lived in New York City for a time. After taking the name Sojourner Truth, which she felt God had given her, she assumed the "mission" of spreading "the Truth" across the country. She became famous as an itinerant preacher, drawing huge crowds with her oratory—and some said "mystical gifts"— wherever she appeared. She became one of an active group of African American women abolitionists, lectured before numerous abolitionist audiences, and was friends with such leading white abolitionists as James and Lucretia Mott and Harriet Beecher Stowe. With the outbreak of the Civil War she raised money to purchase gifts for the soldiers, distributing them herself in the camps. She also helped African Americans who had escaped to the North to find habitation and shelter. Age and ill health caused her to retire from the lecture circuit, and she spent her last days in a sanatorium in Battle Creek, Michigan.

Harriet (Ross) Tubman (1826–1913)
Lecturer, Abolitionist, Nurse

Born in 1826 in Dorchester County, Maryland, she had the hard childhood of a slave: much work, little schooling, and severe punishment. In 1848 she escaped, leaving behind her husband John Tubman, who threatened to report her to their master. As a free woman, she began to devise practical ways of helping other slaves escape. Over the following ten years she made about twenty trips from the North into the South and rescued more than three hundred slaves. Her reputation spread rapidly, and she won the admiration of leading abolitionists—some of whom sheltered her passengers. Eventually a reward of $40,000 was posted for her capture.

Tubman met and aided John Brown in recruiting soldiers for his raid on Harpers Ferry—Brown referred to her as "General Tubman." One of her major disappointments was the failure of the raid, and she is said to have regarded Brown as the true emancipator of her people, not Lincoln. In 1860 she began to canvass the nation, appearing at anti-slavery meetings and speaking on women's rights. Shortly before the outbreak of the Civil War, she was forced to leave for Canada, but she returned to the United States and served the Union as a nurse, soldier, and spy. She was particularly valuable to the army as a scout because of the knowledge of the terrain that she had gained as a conductor on the Underground Railroad.

Tubman's biography, from which she received the proceeds, was written by Sarah Bradford in 1868. Tubman's husband, John, died two years after the end of the war, and in 1869 she married the war veteran Nelson Davis. Despite receiving many honors and tributes, including a medal from Queen Victoria, she spent her last days in poverty, not receiving a pension until thirty years after the Civil War. With the $20 dollars a month that she finally received, she helped to found a home for the aged and needy, which was later renamed the Harriet Tubman Home. She died in Auburn, New York.

Nat Turner (1800–1831)
Insurrectionist

Born a slave in Southampton County, Virginia, on October 2, 1800, he was an avid reader of the Bible who prayed, fasted, and experienced "voices," ultimately becoming a visionary mystic with a belief that God had given him the special destiny of conquering Southampton County. After recruiting a handful of conspirators, he struck at isolated homes in his immediate area, and within 48 hours the band of insurrectionists had reached sixty armed men. They killed 55 whites before deciding to attack the county seat in Jerusalem, but while en route they were overtaken by a posse and dispersed. Turner took refuge in the Dismal Swamp and remained there for six weeks before he was captured, brought to trial, and hanged along with 16 other African American slaves.

Gustavus Vassa (1745?–1801?)
Narrative Writer

Gustavus Vassa was born around 1745 in southern Nigeria. At the age of eleven, he was kidnapped and shipped to the New World as a slave. His masters

Olaudah Equiano (also known as Gustavus Vassa) (The Library of Congress)

included a Virginia plantation owner, a British officer, and a Philadelphia merchant from whom he eventually purchased his freedom. Vassa then settled in England where he worked diligently for the elimination of slavery. He even went so far as to present a petition to Parliament calling for its abolition.

Vassa's autobiography *The Interesting Narrative of the Life of Olaudah Equiano, or Gustavus Vassa* was published in London in 1789 and went through five editions in the next five years. It is regarded as a highly informative account of the evils of slavery as it affected both master and slave, as well as the precursor to other important slave narratives, such as the *Narrative of the Life of Frederick Douglass.* It is believed that Vassa died around 1801.

Denmark Vesey (1767–1822)
Religious Leader

Born in 1767, Vesey was sold by his master at an early age and later bought back because of epilepsy. He sailed with his master, Captain Vesey, to the Virgin Islands and Haiti for twenty years. He enjoyed a considerable degree of mobility in his home port of Charleston, South Carolina, and eventually purchased his freedom from his master for $600—he had won $1500 in a lottery. He became a Methodist minister and used his church as a base to recruit supporters to take over Charleston. The revolt was planned for the second Sunday in July of 1822.

Vesey's plans were betrayed when a slave alerted the white authorities of the city. Hundreds of African Americans were rounded up, though some of Vesey's collaborators most likely escaped to the Carolinas where they fought as maroons. After a twenty-two day search, Vesey was apprehended and stood trial. During the trial he adeptly cross-examined witnesses, but ultimately could not deny his intention to overthrow the city, and he was hung along with several collaborators.

David Walker (1785?–1830)
Abolitionist, Civil Rights Activist, Writer

The offspring of a white mother and a black slave father, Walker was born free as stipulated by North Carolina law. Though not known how, Walker acquired an education before moving to Boston in the late 1820s. Besides starting a used clothes business, he became an active member of the Massachusetts General Colored Association and an agent for the first African American newspaper *Freedom's Journal.* In 1829, Walker published*Walker's Appeal to the Colored Citizens of the World*, which advocated the violent overthrow of slavery, the formation of African American civil rights and self-help organizations, and racial equality in the United States and independence for the peoples of Africa.

Walker's pamphlet alarmed Southerners who responded by enacting stricter laws against such "seditious" literature and educating free African Americans. In the North, he also experienced sharp criticism, including from such prominent abolitionists as William Lloyd Garrison and Benjamin Lundy. Nine months after publishing his pamphlet, Walker mysteriously died, leaving behind his wife, Eliza. Though never verified, rumor suggests that he was poisoned.

7

Civil Rights

◆ Early Rights Movements ◆ Civil Rights during the Reconstruction Period
◆ Civil Rights in the Early Twentieth Century
◆ Civil Rights during the Mid– to Late Twentieth Century ◆ Civil Rights Activists
◆ Federal and State Civil Rights Agencies ◆ Civil Rights Statistics
by Linda T. Wynn

Throughout the history of the United States, African Americans have struggled to obtain basic civil rights. It is a struggle that has spanned several centuries—from the mutinies by Africans during the Atlantic crossing to the insurrections organized by slaves in the New World, from the founding of such organizations as the Free African Society and the abolition movement to the civil rights marches and demonstrations of the twentieth century.

◆ EARLY RIGHTS MOVEMENTS

The Free African Society

In 1787, as a result of segregation and discriminatory practices within the Methodist church, the Reverends Richard Allen and Absalom Jones formed the Free African Society in Philadelphia. (Seven years later, Allen founded the Bethel African Methodist Church, the first African Methodist Episcopal (A.M.E.) Church in America; Jones became the rector of a Protestant Episcopal Church.) The society was an important model for political consciousness and economic organization for African Americans throughout the country. It provided spiritual guidance and religious instruction; economic aid, burial assistance, relief to widows; and medical and financial assistance to orphans. The society also advocated abolition and maintained channels of communication with African Americans in the South. Similar to the many other African American organizations that followed, the society was rooted in religious principles. Throughout the nineteenth century, a number of mutual aid societies sprang up in African American communities in eastern cities, such as New York, Newport, and Boston, providing loans, insurance, and various other economic and social services to their members and the larger community. The society also helped to facilitate communications between free African Americans throughout the country.

The Abolition Movement

The press and the pulpit served as important tools in the anti-slavery movement. In 1827 Samuel Cornish and John Russwurm founded *Freedom's Journal* in New York, the first African American-owned and operated newspaper in the United States. *Freedom's Journal,* which ceased publication after only three years, was concerned not only with eradicating slavery but also with the growing discrimination and cruelty against free African Americans in both the South and North.

In 1847, abolitionist Frederick Douglass published the first edition of the *North Star*, which eventually became one of the most successful African American newspapers in America prior to the outbreak of the Civil War. Douglass, an escaped slave from Maryland, became one of the best known African American abolitionists in the country. He lectured extensively throughout the United States and England. In 1845, he published his autobiography *Narrative of the Life of Frederick Douglass.*

Although the abolition movement was dominated by whites, numerous African American leaders played a major role in the movement including such figures as Henry Highland Garnet, Harriet Tubman, and Sojourner Truth.

Richard Allen (New York Public Library)

◆ CIVIL RIGHTS DURING THE RECONSTRUCTION PERIOD

Following the Civil War, Republicans, who controlled the U.S. Congress, took up the cause of the newly freed African Americans. Between 1865 and 1875, Congress passed three amendments to the Constitution and a string of civil rights and Reconstructionist legislation. The Thirteenth Amendment, ratified December 18, 1865, abolished slavery and involuntary servitude. The Fourteenth Amendment, ratified July 28, 1868, guaranteed citizenship and provided equal protection under the laws. Ratified on March 30, 1870, the Fifteenth Amendment protected the right of all citizens to vote. In 1866, 1870, 1871, and 1875, Congress passed civil rights legislation outlining and protecting basic rights including the right to purchase and sell property and access to public accommodations. The Reconstruction Acts, passed between 1867 and 1869, called for new state constitutional conventions in those states that had seceded from the Union prior to the Civil War.

Reconstruction eventually produced a wave of anti-African American sentiment, though. White organizations such as the Ku Klux Klan, which aimed at intimidating African Americans and preventing them from taking their place in society, sprang up throughout the North and the South. In 1871, Congress enacted the Ku Klux Klan Act as an effort to end intimidation and violence directed at African Americans. However, the act failed to exterminate the Klan and other terrorist organizations.

The civil rights and Reconstructionist legislation were difficult for many whites to accept and did little to change racist attitudes. The last of the civil rights acts, passed by Congress in 1875, prohibited discrimination in public accommodations. However, by the 1880s the debate as to the constitutionality of such legislation had reached the U.S. Supreme Court. Ruling in a group of five cases in 1883, which became known as the *Civil Rights Cases*, the U.S. Supreme Court concluded that the 1875 Civil Rights Act was unconstitutional on the grounds that the Fourteenth Amendment authorized Congress to legislate only against discriminatory state action and not discrimination by private individuals. The Court's ruling brought about an end to federal efforts to protect the civil rights of African Americans until the mid-twentieth century.

Anti-lynching Efforts

By the late nineteenth and early twentieth century, lynching had become a weapon used by whites against African Americans throughout the country. Between 1882 and 1990, approximately 1,750 African Americans were lynched in the United States. Victims included women who had been accused of a variety of "offenses" ranging from testifying in court against a white man to failing to use the word "mister" when addressing a white person. Ida B. Wells-Barnett, a journalist and social activist, became one of the leading voices in the anti-lynching crusade by writing and lecturing throughout the United States and England against its practice.

Institutionalized Segregation

Prior to the case of *Plessy v. Ferguson*, the court had started to build a platform upon which the doctrine of "separate but equal" would be based. In 1878, ruling in the case *Hall v. DeCuir*, the court declared that states could not prohibit segregation on common carriers, such as streetcars and railroads. Thereafter, segregation laws sprang up throughout the South.

In 1896, the U.S. Supreme Court faced the issue of segregation on public transportation. At the time, as was the case in many parts of the South, a Louisiana state law was enacted requiring that "separate but equal" accommodations for blacks and whites be maintained in all public facilities. When Homer Adolph Plessy, an African American man traveling by train from New Orleans to Covington, Louisiana, refused to ride in the "colored" railway coach, he was arrested.

With Justice Billings Brown delivering the majority opinion in the *Plessy* case, the Court declared that "separate but equal" accommodations constituted a reasonable use of state police power and that the Fourteenth Amendment of the Constitution could not be used to abolish social or racial distinctions or to force a co-mingling of the two races. The Supreme Court effectively reduced the significance of the Fourteenth Amendment, which was designed to give African Americans specific rights and protections. The ruling in the *Plessy* case, which was termed the "separate but equal" doctrine, paved the way for the segregation of African Americans in all walks of life.

◆ CIVIL RIGHTS DURING THE EARLY TWENTIETH CENTURY

Booker T. Washington and W. E. B. Du Bois

During the late nineteenth and early twentieth centuries, two figures—Booker T. Washington and William Edward Burghardt Du Bois—emerged as leaders in the struggle for African American political and civil rights. Washington, an educator and founder of the Tuskegee Normal and Industrial Institute, was a strong advocate of practical, utilitarian education and manual training as a means for developing African Americans. (Founded in 1881, Tuskegee Normal and Industrial Institute was based on a program at Hampton Institute that provided vocational training and prepared its students to survive economically in a segregated society.) In Washington's opinion, education should provide African Americans with the means to become economically self-supporting. Speaking at the Cotton States International Exposition in Atlanta in 1895, Washington outlined his philosophy of self-help and cooperation between African Americans and whites:

> "To those of my race who depend on bettering their condition in a foreign land, or who underestimate the importance of cultivating friendly relations with the Southern white man, who is their next door neighbor, I would say: 'Cast down your bucket where you are'—cast it down in making friends in every manly way of the people of all races by whom we are surrounded."

W. E. B. Du Bois, a young historian and Harvard graduate, challenged Washington's passive policies in a series of stinging essays and speeches. Du Bois advocated the uplifting of African Americans through an educated African American elite, which he referred to as the "Talented Tenth," or roughly a tenth of the African American population. He believed that these African Americans must become proficient in education and culture, which would eventually benefit all. In 1905, Du Bois, along with a group of other African American

W.E.B. Du Bois (Corbis Corporation [Bellevue])

intellectuals, formed the Niagara Movement. The group drew up a platform that called for full citizenship rights for African Americans and public recognition of their contributions to America's stability and progress. The movement eventually evolved into what became known as the National Association for the Advancement of Colored People (NAACP).

A. Philip Randolph

In 1941, A. Philip Randolph, organizer of an employment bureau for untrained African Americans and founder of the Brotherhood of Sleeping Car Porters, came up with the idea of leading a march of African Americans in Washington, DC, to protest discrimination. On July 25, less than a week before the scheduled demonstration, President Franklin D. Roosevelt issued Executive Order No. 8802, which banned discrimination in the defense industry and led to the creation of the Fair Employment Practices Committee.

◆ CIVIL RIGHTS DURING THE MID- TO LATE TWENTIETH CENTURY

The Civil Rights movement suffered many defeats in the first half of the twentieth century. Repeated efforts

A. Philip Randolph (AP/Wide World Photos, Inc.)

to obtain passage of federal anti-lynching bills failed. The all-white primary system, which effectively disenfranchised Southern citizens of African descent, resisted numerous court challenges. The Depression worsened conditions in rural and in urban areas. On the positive side, the growing political power of African Americans in Northern cities and an increasing liberal trend in the Supreme Court portended the legal and legislative victories of the 1950s and 1960s.

Brown v. Board of Education of Topeka, Kansas

A great deal of the civil rights struggle throughout this period was carried on by the NAACP, which began chipping away at the roots of legalized segregation in a series of successful lawsuits. A major breakthrough for the NAACP came in 1954, when the U.S. Supreme Court ruled in *Brown v. Board of Education of Topeka, Kansas* that discrimination in education was unconstitutional. The *Brown* case involved the practice of denying African American children equal access to state public schools, due to state laws requiring or permitting racial segregation. The U.S. Supreme Court unanimously held that segregation deprived the children of equal protection under the Fourteenth Amendment to the U.S. Constitution, overturning the "separate but equal" doctrine established in *Plessy*.

Civil Rights in the 1960s

Rosa Parks was one of the major catalysts for the 1960s Civil Rights movement. On December 1, 1955, when Parks refused to give up her seat on a Montgomery bus to a white man—as the law required—she was arrested and sent to jail. As a result of Parks' arrest, African Americans throughout Montgomery refused to ride city buses. The Montgomery Bus Boycott led by Martin Luther King, Jr. was highly successful and ultimately led to the integration of all Montgomery city buses, when on November 13, 1956, the U.S. Supreme Court in *Gayle et al. v. Browder* ruled that bus segregation in Montgomery was unconstitutional.

The eventual success of the Montgomery Bus Boycott encouraged a wave of massive demonstrations that swept across the South. On February 1, 1960, four students denied service at a Greensboro, North Carolina, lunch counter started the sit-in movement. While the North Carolina students received the attention of the national media, a small cadre of Nashville students and adult leaders had tested the city's exclusionary racial policies in the final months of the preceding year. Twelve days after the sit-ins began in North Carolina, African American students in Nashville launched their first full-scale sit-ins. In response to white harassment, Nashville students formulated ten rules of conduct for demonstrators that later became the code of behavior for protest movements in the South. The Nashville student movement was described by Dr. Martin Luther King, Jr., as the "best organized and most disciplined movements in the South." On May 10, 1960, Nashville became the first major city to begin desegregating its public facilities. That same year, the Student Non-Violent Coordinating Committee (SNCC) was created and included among its members Julian Bond, H. Rap Brown, Stokely Carmichael, and John Lewis.

The Civil Rights movement of the 1960s galvanized African Americans and sympathetic whites as nothing had ever done before, but was not without cost. Thousands of people were jailed because they defied Jim Crow laws. Others were murdered, and homes and churches were bombed. People lost their jobs and their homes because they supported the movement.

On August 28, 1963, nearly 250,000 people marched in Washington, DC, to awaken the nation's conscience regarding civil rights and to encourage the passage of civil rights legislation pending in Congress. The march was a cooperative effort of several civil rights organizations including the Southern Christian Leadership Conference (SCLC), the Congress of Racial Equality (CORE), the NAACP, the Negro American Labor Council, and the

Martin Luther King, Jr. delivering his famous "I Have a Dream" speech in 1963 (Corbis Corporation [Bellevue]).

National Urban League. It was during this demonstration that Dr. Martin Luther King, Jr., in the shadow of the Lincoln Memorial, gave his "I Have a Dream" speech. More than a oration about a dream that America would put into practice its tenet that all were "created equal," King told the nation that as far as African Americans were concerned, it had failed to make payment on its promissory note—one that guaranteed the "unalienable rights of life, liberty and the pursuit of happiness," to all. He stated, ". . .We have come to cash this check—a check that will give us upon demand the riches of freedom and the security of justice."

At its zenith, the Civil Rights movement was the most important event taking place in America. Through demonstrations, "sit-ins," marches, economic boycotts, and soaring discourse, the movement aroused widespread public indignation, thus creating an atmosphere in which it was possible to make positive changes in American society.

Civil Rights Legislation in the 1990s

The Civil Rights movement of the 1950s and 1960s produced significant gains for African Americans. However, historic patterns of hiring and promotion left minorities vulnerable, especially during downward spirals in the national economy. In June 1989, the U.S. Supreme Court delivered opinions in several cases dealing with seniority systems and racial discrimination in employment. Ruling in the cases *Lorance v. AT&T Technologies Inc.*, *Martin v. Wilks*, *Patterson v. McLean Credit Union*, and *Wards Cove Packing Co. v. Antonio*, the Court appeared to reverse earlier civil rights rulings.

Prior to the Court's ruling in *Wards Cove*, the burden of proof in job discrimination suits had been placed on employers, requiring businesses to prove that there was a legitimate business reason for alleged discriminatory practices. With the *Wards Cove* decision, the Court made it more difficult for groups to win such suits by requiring workers to prove that no clear business reason existed for an employer's use of practices that result in discrimination. Civil rights organizations were quick to protest the rulings; opponents of the ruling, including the NAACP Legal Defense and Educational Fund and the Leadership Conference on Civil Rights, argued that the Court had undermined the protection granted by federal civil rights and equal employment legislation.

On October 16 and 17, 1990, both houses of Congress approved a bill designed to reverse the Court's ruling.

Firefighters using high pressure hoses to disrupt a 1963 civil rights demonstration in Birmingham, Alabama (AP/Wide World Photos, Inc.).

The proposed legislation not only reversed the Court's ruling in *Wards Cove*, but it also strengthened provisions of the 1964 Civil Rights Act. On October 22, President George Bush vetoed the bill, claiming that its provisions would encourage employers to establish hiring quotas.

This was not the first time that Congress moved to reverse a Court action in the area of civil rights; Congress passed the Civil Rights Restoration Act of 1988 that reversed the Court's ruling in *Grove City College v. Bell* (1984). In the *Grove City College* case, the U.S. Supreme Court ruled that not all programs and activities of an institution were covered by Title IX of the Education Amendments of 1972 (Public Law 89–10, 79 Stat. 27), prohibiting discrimination in educational programs receiving federal financial assistance.

After vetoing Congress' 1990 civil rights legislation, the Bush administration joined both houses of Congress in working on alternative bills. Following months of negotiation, the Senate passed a bill designed to provide additional remedies for deterring harassment and intentional discrimination in the workplace, to provide guidelines for the adjudication of cases arising under Title VII

of the Civil Rights Act of 1964, and to expand the scope of civil rights legislation weakened by Supreme Court decisions. The House of Representatives passed the bill on November 7, and on November 21, and President George Bush signed the Civil Rights Act of 1991.

The Continuation of Police Brutality in the 1990s

In the late 1960s, incidents of police abuse sparked civil unrest, costly and violent uprisings, and a lingering distrust between minority communities and the police. In an effort to understand the causes of these incidents, President Johnson created the National Advisory Commission on Civil Disorders, also known as the Kerner Commission. On July 27, 1968, the commission released its findings which stated, among other things, that 12 "deeply held grievances" had been found in the communities that it studied—the most intense being police practices. Unfortunately, as the examples below confirm, major problems in police treatment of minority communities still exists several decades later.

In late 1989, a pregnant white woman, Carol Stuart, was murdered in the racially-divided city of Boston. Her husband told the police that her killer was an African

American male. His allegations led police to conduct a manhunt in the predominantly African American neighborhood of Roxbury. African Americans in the community were outraged once it was revealed that Charles Stuart had murdered his wife (Stuart, who was having an extramarital affair and financial problems, subsequently committed suicide), and they charged the police department with applying a "double standard of justice." In response, then-Boston Mayor Raymond Flynn appointed the St. Clair Commission to examine allegations of abuse of power by the police department.

In 1991, following a high speed chase, African American motorist Rodney King was subdued with extreme force and arrested by officers of the Los Angeles Police Department (LAPD). The broadcast of a videotape of the King beating galvanized international attention on police brutality in Los Angeles. In a subsequent court trial, however, a predominantly white jury found the four officers not guilty of charges filed against them. The verdict ignited one of the worst race riots in the history of the United States. Later, the federal government indicted the officers on violating King's civil rights, and three of the officers were convicted and incarcerated.

In response to these chain of events, Mayor Tom Bradley created an independent commission to investigate the LAPD. In July 1991, the Christopher Commission released its findings. Documenting the systematic use of excessive force and racial harassment in the LAPD, the report called for structural reforms and the resignation of Los Angeles Police Chief Daryl Gates. "Within minority communities of Los Angeles, there is a widely-held view that police misconduct is commonplace," stated the Christopher Report. "...Long standing complaints [are held] by African-Americans, Latinos and Asians that LAPD officers frequently treat minorities differently from whites. . .employing unnecessarily intrusive practices such as the 'prone-out,' and engaging in use of excessive force when dealing with minorities."

Well into the 1990s, scores of other police brutality incidents against blacks surfaced in numerous cities across the nation. These reports included: the 1995 videotaped beating of Corey West in Providence, Rhode Island; the killing of motorist Jonny Gammage in Pittsburgh, Pennsylvania; the 1996 killing of TyRon Lewis in St. Petersburg, Florida; the fatal shooting of unarmed Nathaniel Gaines, Jr. in New York City; the 1997 alleged beating of Jeremiah Mearday in Chicago; the 1997 New York police assault of Haitian immigrant Abner Louima, which resulted in the admission of guilt by one of the assailants in 1999; the 1998 fatal shooting of Tyisha Miller in Riverside, California; and the 1999 fatal shooting of unarmed Guinean immigrant Amadou Diallo in Bronx, New York.

Many of these incidents, which occurred under questionable circumstances, produced protests and investigations by the U.S. Civil Rights Commission and prompted a national debate on police, race, and the use of deadly force. Civil rights organizations asserted that these incidents mirrored a discriminatory use of deadly force and critical problems ranging from racially-motivated police brutality to unprovoked stops and interrogation of minorities based on racial profiling.

Number of Hate Crimes Against African Americans Increases

Just as police brutality became a national focal point, so, too, did the proliferation of hate crimes against African Americans. (By definition, hate crimes are "crimes against persons or property motivated in whole or in part by racial, ethnic, religious, gender, sexual orientation and other prejudices.") Based on the data collected under the Hate Crime Statistics Acts of 1990 and 1996, the number of hate crimes perpetrated against African Americans and reported to the Federal Bureau of Investigation (FBI) increased from 2,988 in 1995 to 3,838 in 1997. These malicious acts of violence, similar to lynchings of the past, were intended not only to be injurious to individuals but to intimidate and dispirit an entire group of people. An example of such crimes included the destruction of African American churches in the South.

Between 1995 and mid-1996, hundreds of African American churches were set ablaze in the South. These incidents of church arson invoked grievous memories of racist violence during the 1960s, particularly the bombing of Birmingham's Sixth Street Baptist Church in which four small girls were killed on September 15, 1963. In response, President Clinton declared the "investigation and prevention of church arsons to be a national priority."

In June 1996, President Clinton established the National Church Arson Task Force and proposed a three-pronged strategy that called for prosecution of the arsonists, the rebuilding of church edifices, and the prevention of additional fires. In addition, on July 3, he signed the Church Arson Prevention Act of 1996, which passed both chambers of the Congress unanimously. On June 6, 1997, the National Church Arson Task Force released its report: Of the 429 incidents of church burnings, bombings, and attempted bombings investigated, 162 involved African American churches, 75 percent of which were located in the South. The majority of those convicted of destroying African American churches were white males.

Hate crimes were not restricted to the destruction of African American church buildings, though. Three of the more high profile incidents included: the 1995 murder of two African Americans residents of Fayetteville, North Carolina, by three Army soldiers who identified themselves as "neo-Nazi skin heads"; the 1996 racial harassment of Bridget Ward and her two daughters who moved into a rented home in the virtually all-white Bridesburg neighborhood in Philadelphia; and the 1998 brutal murder of James Byrd, Jr. in Jasper, Texas, by three white males who chained him to the back of their pick-up truck and dragged him to his death. One of Byrd's assailants, self-proclaimed white supremacist John William King, was convicted of capital murder, and the jury recommended the death sentence in February 1999.

Modern technology by means of the Internet has also provided an opportunity for hate groups to spread their racist beliefs and increase their membership. Data recently compiled by the Southern Poverty Law Center indicated that Internet hate sites grew from 163 in 1997 to 254 in 1998.

On June 13, 1997, President Clinton established the seven-member President's Advisory Board to the President's Initiative on Race. Headed by historian John Hope Franklin, the advisory board was given the responsibilities of promoting national dialogue on race issues, increasing the nation's understanding of the history and future of race relations, identifying and creating plans to calm racial tension and promote increased opportunity for all Americans, and addressing crime and the administration of justice. On September 18, 1998, the advisory board concluded its work and presented its recommendations to President Clinton. Its report *One America in the 21st Century: Forging a New Future* recommended that the President institute a standing advisory board to build upon its foundation and for a public education program to underscore the "common values" of a diverse multiracial nation. The report, however, was criticized by civil rights groups and others for not imploring the President or Congress to take definitive action to challenge institutionalized racism and economic disparity. Ironically, on the same day, the President's Council of Economic Advisers released its report revealing the vast disparities in education, economic status, and health between Americans of color and members of the majority.

◆ CIVIL RIGHTS ACTIVISTS

(To locate biographical profiles more readily, please consult the index at the back of the book.)

Ralph D. Abernathy (1926–1990)
Religious Leader, Civil Rights Activist, Organization Executive/Founder

Born March 11, 1926, in Linden, Alabama, the Reverend Ralph David Abernathy was ordained a minister in 1948. He received his bachelor's degree from Alabama State College (now Alabama State University) in 1950 and his master's degree from Atlanta University in 1951. The alliance between Abernathy and Martin Luther King, Jr. stretched back to the mid-1950s. While attending Atlanta University, Abernathy had the opportunity to hear King preach at Ebenezer Baptist Church.

After obtaining his master's degree, Abernathy returned to Alabama to serve as a part-time minister at the Eastern Star Baptist Church in Demopolis. In 1951 Abernathy moved to First Baptist Church in Montgomery. Around this time King accepted a position at Montgomery's Dexter Avenue Baptist Church; Abernathy and King became close friends.

In 1955, the two organized the Montgomery Improvement Association to coordinate a citywide bus boycott. The success of the Montgomery Bus Boycott led to the creation of the Southern Negro Leaders Conference; the organization's name was later changed to the Southern Leadership Conference and finally the Southern Christian Leadership Conference (SCLC). In January of 1957, Dr. King was elected the organization's first president.

From the time of Martin Luther King's death in 1968 until 1977, Abernathy served as president of the Southern Christian Leadership Conference. Abernathy continued as a leading figure in the movement until his resignation in 1977, when he made an unsuccessful bid for a U.S. Congressional seat. In 1989, he published his autobiography *And The Walls Came Tumbling Down*, which was criticized by some African American leaders for Abernathy's inclusion of details regarding King's extramarital affairs. Abernathy died of cardiac arrest on April 17, 1990.

Ella Baker (1903–1986)
Community Activist, Civil Rights Activist, Executive/ General Manager

In 1903, Ella Baker was born in Norfolk, Virginia, to Blake and Georgianna Ross Baker, both educated people who worked hard to educate their children. The family and community in which she grew up instilled in her a sense of sharing and community cooperation. Baker's family imbued her with a sense of racial pride and resistance to any form of oppression. Her grandfather, a minister and community leader, was an ardent proponent of civil rights and universal suffrage, and passed his beliefs on to her.

Ralph D. Abernathy speaking at the Poor People's Campaign in 1968 (Corbis Corporation [Bellevue]).

When she was 15, Baker was sent to the Shaw Boarding School (now Shaw University) in Raleigh, where she graduated with a bachelor's degree as valedictorian in 1927. After graduation, she moved to New York City. Baker quickly became involved in progressive politics and attended as many meetings and discussions as she could find. During the Depression, she was outraged at the poverty she saw in the African American areas of the city. Believing in the power of community and group action, she became one of the founders of the Young Negroes Cooperative League, a buying cooperative that bought food in bulk to distribute at low prices to members; in 1931, she became the national director of the League. When President Franklin Roosevelt's Works Progress Administration started, she became involved with their literacy program. Throughout these years she worked closely with other politically aware and motivated people, discussing and evolving a political philosophy of cooperation, equality, and justice.

In the in the late 1930s, Baker began to work for the NAACP. Between 1940 and 1943, she served as a field secretary, traveling all over the country setting up branch offices and teaching people to fight for their rights.

During her travels, Baker developed a vast network of contacts in the South that she later relied on when working for the Southern Christian Leadership Conference (SCLC) and the Student Non-Violent Coordinating Committee (SNCC). In 1943, she became the director of branches for the NAACP. During the 1950s, she started fund-raising activities in New York for civil rights struggles in the South. In 1958, Baker moved to Atlanta to work with the SCLC.

Working for the SCLC, Baker became disillusioned with the male clergy-dominated organizational structure of the group. In 1960, she quit the SCLC and took a job with the Young Women's Christian Association. When students began leading sit-ins, the civil rights activist shifted her focus to the development of SNCC. She acted as an unofficial advisor for the group, counseling them to set up their own student-run organization rather than be subsumed under the SCLC or the NAACP. Baker helped launch the Mississippi Freedom Democratic Party that challenged the all-white Democratic delegation at the 1964 presidential convention. She also acted as staff consultant for the interracial SCLC educational fund.

Baker returned to New York City in 1965, but kept working with national and international civil rights organizations. Among her other activities, she raised money to send to the freedom fighters in Rhodesia and South Africa. She remained an active organizer and speaker as long as her health allowed. Baker's belief in the power of communal action and reliance on the workers rather than the leaders had an enormous impact. She worked for all of the major civil rights organizations at their time of greatest need. By the time the SCLC and SNCC were formed, Baker had almost thirty years of civil rights and community organizing experience to offer. She continually strove to keep the movement people-oriented, and she succeeded in helping SNCC remain a student group. Through her philosophy and actions, Ella J. Baker motivated hundreds to act and to help themselves and their neighbors, as she learned to do as a child.

Daisy Lee Gatson Bates (c.1914–)
Publisher, Civil Rights Activist, Executive/General Manager

After attending segregated schools where all of the new equipment and up-to-date texts were only reserved for whites, Daisy Bates spent much of her energy as an adult successfully integrating the schools of Little Rock, Arkansas.

Shortly after their marriage in 1942, Daisy and her husband Lucius Christopher Bates, a journalist, published a newspaper, the *Arkansas State Press*. They made it a point in their paper to keep track and report

Daisy Bates leaving the Little Rock police headquarters in 1957 (AP/Wide World Photos, Inc.).

incidents of police brutality and other racially-motivated violence; their paper became known throughout the state for its campaign to improve the social and economic circumstances of African Americans. Because of their work, the city of Little Rock began to hire African American police officers, and the number of racial incidents decreased.

In 1952, Daisy Bates became the Arkansas president of the NAACP; after the 1954 court decision in the *Brown v. Board of Education of Topeka, Kansas* case, she became very active in school desegregation. She began taking African American children to white schools to be registered. If the school refused to register the children, she would report it in her paper. In 1957, the superintendent of schools in Little Rock decided to try to integrate the schools and chose nine students, now called the "Little Rock Nine," to be the first African American children to attend Central High, a white school. Most white citizens of Little Rock objected. Bates organized the Little Rock Nine, accompanied them to Central High, and stood with them against the state troopers that Governor Orval Faubus sent to prevent the integration. For days she escorted the children to school, only

to be turned away by an angry mob. On September 25, 1957, Daisy Bates entered Central High in Little Rock with the nine children, escorted by 1,000 paratroopers that President Dwight Eisenhower sent; the first steps towards integration were successful. For the rest of their years at Central High, Bates kept track of the students and acted as their advocate when problems arose, frequently accompanying them and their parents to meetings with school officials.

In October of 1957, one month after she marched into Central High, Daisy Bates was arrested on charges of failing to provide membership information on the NAACP to city officials. The charges were later overturned. Two years later, the *Arkansas State Press* folded, but Bates kept active in the civil rights fight, touring and speaking, and working with the Student Non-Violent Coordinating Committee to register voters. Her memoir of the Little Rock crisis *The Long Shadow of Little Rock* was published in 1962. In 1985, 26 years after her newspaper ceased production, the *Arkansas State Press* began to publish again, and it has continued to serve the needs of the African American community in Little Rock.

Stokely Carmichael (Kwame Toure) (1941–1998)
Civil Rights Activist, Nationalist/Repatriationist, Executive/General Manager

If one individual stood at the forefront of the Black Power movement during the 1960s, Stokely Carmichael was that person. He soared to fame as popularizer of the dynamic phrase "Black Power" and as one of the most powerful and influential leaders of the Student Non-Violent Coordinating Committee (SNCC).

Carmichael was born in Trinidad on June 29, 1941, and moved to the United States with his family when he was 11 years of age. As a teenager, Carmichael was jolted by ghetto life in which "black" and "impotent" seemed to be synonymous terms. He was not reassured later when he was admitted to the Bronx High School of Science, encountered white liberals, and felt he had been adopted by them as a mascot. Although he was offered scholarships to predominantly white universities, Carmichael opted to attend Howard University. In 1960, during his first year at the university, he joined the Congress of Racial Equality (CORE) in its efforts to desegregate public accommodations in the South. After graduation in 1964, he rejected scholarship opportunities for graduate school and went South to join SNCC. As one of their finest organizers, he worked ceaselessly, registering and educating voters in the South. In 1966, he was elected chairman of SNCC; however, as the organization's youngest chair, some members considered his views too radical.

Kwame Toure (formerly known as Stokely Carmichael) (AP/
Wide World Photos, Inc.).

Carmichael's cry for "black power" thrilled many disenfranchised young African Americans, but troubled others, who thought it sounded too violent. He was labeled as potentially violent by the media and the legal authorities. Disagreement with SNCC members arose over the issues of self-defense versus nonviolence and the participation of whites in African American grass roots organizations. In 1967, he resigned as chairperson, and was later expelled from SNCC.

Carmichael spent much of 1968 traveling around the world, speaking to many organizations including some in communist countries. His travels included Ghana, where he joined the Pan-African movement. After returning to the United States, he went to work for the Black Panther party. He was subject to almost constant harassment from the FBI because of his connection with the Panthers, and because he had visited communist countries while traveling. In 1969, he resigned from the Black Panthers and moved to Guinea, where he had been offered political asylum.

In Guinea, Carmichael turned his efforts to supporting Pan-Africanism; he organized many local chapters throughout the world of the All Afrikan Peoples Revolu-

tionary Party. In 1978, to honor the two men who most influenced his Pan-African philosophical education, SeKou Toure and Kwame Nkrumah, he changed his name to Kwame Toure. Four years after being awarded the LL.D. from Shaw University in recognition of his efforts to free African American people, Kwame Toure died in 1998 from prostate cancer.

Mandy Carter (1948–)
Civil Rights Activist

Carter was born in Albany, New York, in the late 1940s and spent her childhood in orphanages. She attended community college for a time in Troy, New York, but moved to New York City in 1967 with a savings of $100. There she slept in Central Park before taking a job at drug guru Timothy Leary's League for Spiritual Discovery; she moved to San Francisco later that year and soon became active in protests against the war in Vietnam. For several years Carter was involved with the War Resister's League, and it was to her colleagues there that she first admitted her sexual orientation. She worked for the group's San Francisco offices for a number of years, and it was during this time, the late 1970s, that she first became active in gay and lesbian politics.

In 1982, Carter moved to North Carolina, where she continued her work with the War Resister's League, and also became involved on a national level with gay and lesbian organizations; one of her accomplishments was helping coordinate the 1987 lesbian and gay march on the nation's capital, a role she reprised in 1993. In addition to co-producing an annual festival of women's music and art, Carter has also been instrumental (but ultimately unsuccessful) in campaigns to unseat North Carolina's right-wing Republican senator, Jesse Helms. She has also worked to combat the Christian Right's attempts to infiltrate African American churches in efforts to stymie support of gay and lesbian rights among the congregations; she has done this work in her role as liaison of the Human Rights Campaign Fund to the National Black and Gay Lesbian Leadership Forum. Carter has spoken of her political activism in the 1994 volume *Uncommon Heroes: A Celebration of Heroes and Role Models for Gay and Lesbian Americans.*

Angela Y. Davis (1944–)
Women's Rights Activist, Civil Rights Activist, Professor, Lecturer, Author/Poet, Organization Founder

Angela Yvonne Davis was born on January 26, 1944, in Birmingham, Alabama, to middle-class parents, B. Frank and Sallye E. Davis, who stressed academic excellence, political awareness, and activism. Her mother had been politically active since her college days, and Angela participated in demonstrations with her from the time she was in elementary school. To ensure a

Angela Davis (Corbis Corporation [Bellevue])

better education than she would be able to receive in the segregated schools of the South, her parents sent her to Elizabeth Irwin High School, a private progressive school in New York. The school had many radical teachers and students, and Angela soon joined a Marxist study group.

After graduation, Davis continued to seek high quality education. She majored in French at Brandeis College and studied at the Sorbonne in Paris during her junior year. She then pursued graduate studies in philosophy at the Johann Wolfgang von Goethe University in Frankfurt, West Germany. In 1967, she returned to the United States to study at the University of California at San Diego. When she had almost completed her doctorate degree, she took a teaching job at the University of California at Los Angeles.

In 1969, Davis joined the Communist party; the regents of UCLA tried to fire her, but she fought them in court. The following year she became involved with the Black Panther Party. Guns that she had bought for self-defense were used by a member of the Black Panthers in a courtroom shooting. Believing she was involved, the Federal Bureau of Investigation (FBI) sought her arrest. To avoid the federal authorities Davis went underground. She was placed on the FBI's ten most wanted

list and was later arrested. In 1972, she was acquitted of all charges, but was not reinstated by the university. Then-California Governor Ronald Reagan and the state's board of regents decreed that she would never teach in California again.

Following her trial, Davis founded the National Alliance against Racist and Political Repression, a legal group providing defense of minority prisoners. In 1980 and 1984, she ran for vice president of the United States on the Communist party ticket. A writer and philosopher, Davis has written several books including *If They Come in the Morning* (1971), *Women, Race and Class* (1983), *Angela Davis: An Autobiography* (1988), and *Women, Culture and Politics* (1989).

During the 1990s, Davis remained politically active and a popular yet controversial figure. Her 1995 appointment as presidential chair in charge of developing new ethnic studies courses at University of California-Santa Cruz was heavily opposed by state Republican legislators concerned with her Communist party affiliation. Much sought after, though often protested against, Davis has lectured around the country about "envisioning a new movement" set apart from the radicalism of the 1960s. She continues to write and to support such causes as women's rights, workers' rights, health care, and nuclear disarmament.

William Edward Burghardt Du Bois (1868–1963)
Organization Executive/Founder, Civil Rights Activist, Professor, Lecturer, Author/Poet, Editor, Critic, Women's Rights Activist, Sociologist, Executive Director, Political Scientist, Correspondent/Reporter

An outstanding critic, editor, scholar, author, and civil rights leader, W. E. B. Du Bois is certainly among the most influential African Americans of the twentieth century. Born in Great Barrington, Massachusetts, on February 23, 1868, Du Bois received a bachelor's degree from Fisk University. Upon completion of his academic career at Fisk, Du Bois entered Harvard University where he earned a second bachelor's degree in 1890; a master of arts degree in 1891; and a Ph.D. degree in 1895, making him the first African American to earn a doctorate degree from Harvard. For a time, Du Bois held teaching positions at Wilberforce University, University of Pennsylvania, and Atlanta University.

One of the founders of the National Association for the Advancement of Colored People (NAACP) in 1910, Du Bois served as that organization's director of publications and editor of *Crisis* magazine until 1934. In 1944, he returned from Atlanta University to become head of the NAACP's special research department, a post he held until 1948. Du Bois emigrated to Ghana in 1961 and became editor-in-chief of the *Encyclopaedia*

Africana, his enormous Afrocentric publishing venture that was supported by Kwame Nkrumah, since then deposed as president. Du Bois died in Ghana on August 27, 1963, at the age of 95.

Du Bois's numerous books include: *The Suppression of the African Slave Trade to the United States of America, 1638–1870* (1896); *The Philadelphia Negro* (1899); *The Souls of Black Folk: Essays and Sketches* (1903); *John Brown* (1909); *Quest of the Silver Fleece* (1911); *The Negro* (1915); *Darkwater* (1920); *The Gift of Black Folk* (1924); *Dark Princess* (1928); *Black Folk: Then and Now* (1939); *Dusk of Dawn* (1940); *Color and Democracy* (1945); *The World and Africa* (1947); *In Battle for Peace* (1952); and a trilogy *The Black Flame* (1957–1961). It is this enormous literary output on such a wide variety of themes which offers the most convincing testimony to Du Bois's lifetime position that it was vital for African Americans to cultivate their own aesthetic and cultural values even as they made valuable strides toward social emancipation. In this he was opposed by Booker T. Washington, who felt that African Americans should concentrate on developing technical and mechanical skills before all else.

Du Bois was one of the first male civil rights leaders to recognize the problems of gender discrimination. He was among the first men to understand the unique problems of African American women and to value their contributions. He supported the women's suffrage movement and strove to integrate this mostly white struggle. Additionally, Du Bois championed the reproductive freedom of women and women's economic independence from men. He encouraged many African American female writers, artists, poets, and novelists, featuring their works in *Crisis* and sometimes providing personal financial assistance to them. Several of his novels, most notably *The Quest of the Silver Fleece* and *Dark Princess,* feature women as prominently as men, an unusual approach for an author of his day. Du Bois spent his life working not just for the equality of all men, but for the equality of all people.

Medgar Evers (1925–1963)
Civil Rights Activist

Medgar Evers was one of the first martyrs of the Civil Rights movement. He was born in 1925 in Decatur, Mississippi, to James and Jessie Evers. After serving in the U.S. Army during World War II, he enrolled in Alcorn Agricultural & Mechanical College in Mississippi, graduating in 1952. His first job out of college involved traveling around rural Mississippi and selling insurance. He soon grew enraged at the despicable conditions of poor African American families in his state and joined the Mound Bayou Chapter of the NAACP. In 1954, he was appointed Mississippi's first field secretary.

Medgar Evers (AP/Wide World Photos, Inc.)

Evers was outspoken and his demands were radical for his rigidly segregated state. He fought for the enforcement of the 1954 U.S. Supreme Court decision of *Brown v. Board of Education of Topeka, Kansas,* which outlawed school segregation. Evers fought for the right to vote, and he advocated boycotting merchants who discriminated against African Americans. He worked unceasingly despite the threats of violence that his speeches engendered. Evers gave much of himself to this struggle, and in 1963, he gave his life. On June 13, 1963, he drove home from a meeting, stepped out of his car, and was mortally shot in the back.

Immediately after Evers's death, the shotgun that was used to kill him was found in nearby bushes, with the owner's fingerprints still fresh. Byron de la Beckwith, a vocal member of a local white supremacist group, was arrested. Despite the evidence against him, which included an earlier statement that he wanted to kill Evers, two trials with all-white juries ended in deadlock decisions, and de la Beckwith walked free. Twenty years later, in 1989, information surfaced that suggested jury tampering in both trials. The assistant district attorney, with the help of Evers's widow, Myrlie Evers-Williams, began putting together a new case. In 1990,

Beckwith was arrested once again. On February 5, 1995, a multiracial jury found him guilty of Evers's assassination and sentenced him to life imprisonment.

Evers did not die in vain. His death changed the tenor of the civil rights struggle. Anger replaced fear in the South, as hundreds of demonstrators marched in protest. His death prompted President John Kennedy to ask Congress for a comprehensive civil rights bill, which due to the assassination of President Kennedy in November of 1963, President Lyndon Johnson signed into law in July of 1964. Evers's death, as his life had, contributed much to the struggle for equality.

James L. Farmer, Jr. (1920–)
Civil Rights Activist, Educator, Organization Founder

James Leonard Farmer, Jr., the founder of the Congress of Racial Equality (CORE), was born to James L. Farmer, Sr. and Pearl Houston Farmer on January 12, 1920, in Marshall, Texas. He graduated from Wiley College in 1938 and two years later received his masters in Sacred Theology from Howard University's School of Divinity.

Electing not to enter the ministry, Farmer became a warrior in the struggle to dismantle America's all-encompassing system of racial segregation. Committed to direct, nonviolent protest, in 1941 Farmer and others became involved in efforts to desegregate Chicago housing. In June of the following year, he launched a sit-in movement that resulted in the desegregation of a local coffeehouse. Later in June of 1942, he established CORE. During the early 1960s, under Farmer's leadership and using the principles of civil disobedience, CORE conducted freedom rides, voter registration drives, and protest marches to eradicate racial segregation.

In 1963, when President John F. Kennedy proposed legislation to enact a civil rights bill eliminating racial segregation in public accommodations, Farmer, along with Martin Luther King, Jr., Whitney Young, and Roy Wilkins, was one of the "Big Four" in the Civil Rights movement of the 1960s. As President Johnson shepherded the civil rights bill through Congress in 1964, three CORE workers—Andrew Goodman, Michael Schwerner, and James Chaney—disappeared while registering African American voters in Philadelphia, Mississippi. Outrage over their deaths and other atrocities suffered by Southern citizens of African descent who attempted to register and exercise their right to vote led to the Voting Rights Act of 1965.

In 1966, James Farmer left CORE after serving as national director for five years. Three years later he joined the administration of President Richard M. Nixon as assistant secretary for administration in the Department of Health, Education, and Welfare, where he served

until the end of 1970. Farmer, during the 1970s developed the Council on Minority Planning and Strategy (COMPAS) at Howard University and the Fund for an Open Society, a nonprofit organization that granted low-interest mortgage loans to people planning to live in desegregated neighborhoods. His first book *Freedom When* was published in 1976. Farmer entered the arena of higher education as a visiting professor at Mary Washington College in Fredericksburg, Virginia, in 1985, the same year his second book *Lay Bare the Heart: An Autobiography of the Civil Rights Movement* came off the press.

On January 15, 1998, James L. Farmer, Jr., the only surviving civil rights activist of the "Big Four," was awarded the Medal of Freedom by President Bill Clinton.

Fannie Lou Townsend Hamer (1917–1977)
Lecturer, Civil Rights Activist, Organization Executive/Founder

As a poor sharecropper she had only an elementary education, yet Fannie Lou Hamer was one of the most eloquent speakers for the Civil Rights movement in the South. She worked for political, social, and economic equality for herself and all African Americans; Hamer fought to integrate the national Democratic party, and became one of its first African American delegates to a presidential convention.

The youngest of twenty siblings, Hamer was born on October 6, 1917, to Jim and Lou Ella Townsend in Montgomery County, Mississippi. She began picking cotton at the age of six. Because she had to work full-time, Baker dropped out of school in the sixth grade. She began working on the Marlow plantation as a sharecropper. In 1944, when the plantation's owner, W. D. Marlow, learned she was literate, she was given the job as a time and record keeper on the plantation until 1962. In 1962, she lost her job because she tried to exercise her right to vote. Frightened by threats of violent reprisals, Hamer was forced to move away from her home and her family. Angered into action, she went to work for the Student Non-Violent Coordinating Committee (SNCC), helping many African Americans register to vote.

Because the Democratic party refused to send African Americans as delegates to the national presidential convention in 1964, Hamer and others formed the Mississippi Freedom Democratic Party (MFDP). Arguing that the all-white delegation could not adequately represent their state which had a large African American population, Hamer and the MFDP challenged the Democratic delegates from Mississippi for their seats at the convention in Atlantic City, New Jersey. Hamer's speech

Fannie Lou Hamer testifying before the U.S. Senate (AP/Wide World Photos, Inc.).

Jesse L. Jackson, Sr. taking notes in front of the bombed Alfred P. Murrah Federal Building in Oklahoma City in 1995 (AP/Wide World Photos, Inc.).

on their behalf so alarmed the incumbent President Lyndon Johnson that he tried to block the televised coverage of her efforts. The MFDP lost its bid that year, however, their actions did result in a pledge from the national party not to exclude African Americans as delegates in the 1968 convention. In 1968, Fannie Lou Hamer was among the first African American delegates to the Democratic National Convention.

For the next decade, Hamer remained active in the struggle for civil and economic rights. In 1969, she founded the Freedom Farm Cooperative to help needy families raise food and livestock. They also provided basic social services, scholarships and grants for education, and helped fund minority business opportunities. Hamer became a sought after speaker, and in the 1970s, even as her health was failing from cancer, she still toured the country speaking about civil rights for all. Fannie Lou Hamer Hamer died on March 14, 1977.

Jesse L. Jackson, Sr. (1941–)
Religious Leader, Civil Rights Activist, Organization Executive/Founder

Jesse Louis Jackson, Sr. was born October 8, 1941, in Greenville, South Carolina. In 1959 Jackson left South Carolina to attend the University of Illinois. Dissatisfied with his treatment on campus, he decided to transfer to North Carolina Agricultural and Technical College. After receiving his B.A. in sociology, Jackson attended the Chicago Theological Seminary. In 1968, he was ordained a Baptist minister.

Jackson joined the Southern Christian Leadership Conference (SCLC) in 1965. The following year he became involved with the SCLC's Operation Breadbasket. From 1967 to 1971, Jackson served as the program's executive director. Resigning from the SCLC in 1971, he formed his own organization, Operation PUSH (People United to Save Humanity). Through PUSH Jackson continued to pursue the economic objectives of Operation Breadbasket and expanded into areas of social and political development.

Jackson soon became the most visible and sought after civil rights leader in the country. While he described himself as a "country preacher," his magnetic personality had television appeal. Jackson's command of issues and his ability to reach the heart of matters marked him as an individual of intellectual depth. Of all the civil rights leaders, Jackson was the one who could best relate to the young. In a phrase that became his trademark "I am somebody," Jackson was able to bring out the best in them.

From this came Jackson's PUSH-Excel program that sought to motivate young school children to improve academically. In 1981 *Newsweek* magazine credited Jackson with building a struggling community improvement organization into a nationwide campaign to revive pride, discipline, and the work ethic in inner-city schools. With funding from the Carter administration, the PUSH-Excel program was placed in five other cities.

The Jesse Jackson of the 1980s will be best remembered for his two runs for the Democratic nomination for president of the United States. In 1983, many, but not all, African American political leaders endorsed the idea of an African American presidential candidate to create a "people's" platform, increase voter registration, and have a power base from which there could be greater input into the political process. His 1984 campaign was launched under the aegis of the National Rainbow Coalition, Inc., an umbrella organization of minority groups. African American support was divided, however, between Jackson and former Vice President Walter Mondale. During this campaign, Jackson attracted considerable media coverage with controversial remarks and actions, demonstrating a lack of familiarity with national politics.

The 1988 campaign of Jackson showed enormous personal and political growth; his candidacy was no longer a symbolic gesture but was a real and compelling demonstration of his effectiveness as a candidate. By the time the Democratic convention rolled around, media pundits were seriously discussing the likelihood of Jackson's nomination as the Democratic presidential candidate. "What to do about Jesse" became the focus of the entire Democratic leadership. At the end of the primary campaign, Jackson had finished a strong second to Massachusetts Governor Michael Dukakis. He changed forever the notion that an African American president in America was inconceivable. Jackson took his defeat in stride and continued to campaign for the Democratic ticket until the November election.

Since the 1988 election, Jackson has worked less publicly, but no less energetically. In 1989, he moved with his Rainbow Coalition from Chicago to Washington, DC, believing that the coalition could be more effective in the nation's capital. Jackson continued to write, speak, and lead protests for social change. His primary concerns included crime, violence, drug use, and teenage pregnancy in inner-city neighborhoods, voter registration, health care, affirmative action, and baseball hiring practices. In 1993, Jackson was awarded the Martin Luther King, Jr. Nonviolent Peace Prize.

Jackson was active in foreign affairs as well. In 1991, he traveled to Iraq and convinced Saddam Hussein to begin releasing Americans held hostage after Hussein's invasion of Kuwait. In 1994, Jackson met with Fidel Castro in Cuba and, later during the year, President Bill Clinton sent him on a peace mission to Nigeria. Al-

though many expected him to run for presidency again in 1992 or 1996, Jackson decided against it, saying that he was too tired and the strain on his family too severe. However, he did support his son, Jesse Jackson, Jr., who was elected to the House of Representatives (Chicago's 2nd Congressional District) on December 12, 1995. As the decade was coming to a close, Jessie Jackson, Sr., continued to be a civil and human rights activist, as well as a political force in American society. As he had done since the mid-1980s in Syria, Cuba, and Iraq, in May of 1999, the Reverend Jesse Jackson, Sr. successfully secured the release of three captive U.S. soldiers held as prisoners of war during the Kosovo crisis.

Coretta Scott King (1927–)
Organization Executive/Founder, Civil Rights Activist, Women's Rights Activist, Lecturer, National/International Diplomat, Educator, Community Activist

As the wife of civil rights leader Martin Luther King, Jr., Coretta Scott King was ready to continue his work and perpetuate his ideals after his 1968 assassination. While her primary role in the early years of marriage concerned the rearing of their four children, she became increasingly involved in the struggle for civil rights through her husband's activities. After his death, she quickly became a dynamic activist and peace crusader.

Born on April 27, 1927, to Obie Leonard and Bernice McMurray Scott, King is a native of Marion, Alabama. One of three children, during the Depression she was forced to contribute to the family income by hoeing and picking cotton. Early in life she resolved to overcome adversity, seek equal treatment, and achieve a sound education. In 1945, after graduating from the private Lincoln High School, she entered Antioch College in Yellow Springs, Ohio, on a scholarship, majoring in elementary education and music. A teaching career appealed to her; however, she became disillusioned when she was not allowed to practice teaching in the town's public schools. No African American had ever taught there, and Coretta Scott was not destined to be the first to break the tradition.

Musical training in voice and piano absorbed much of her time. After receiving her undergraduate degree from Antioch College, she continued her studies at the New England Conservatory of Music in Boston, where she earned a Mus.B. in voice. In Boston she met Martin Luther King, Jr. and they married on June 18, 1953. An exceptional young minister, King's intense convictions and concern for humanity brought her a measure of rare self-realization early in life. Sensing his incredible dynamism, she suffered no regrets at the prospect of relinquishing her own possible career. The Kings had four children: Yolanda Denise (November 17, 1955);

Coretta Scott King (AP/Wide World Photos, Inc.)

Martin, III (October 23, 1957); Dexter (January 30, 1961); and Bernice (March 28, 1963).

Completing her studies in 1954, King moved back south with her husband, who became pastor of Dexter Avenue Baptist Church in Montgomery, Alabama. Within a year, the Reverend King led the Montgomery bus boycott and brought forth a new era of civil rights agitation. Two years later, he helped to organize and was elected head of the Southern Christian Leadership Conference (SCLC).

Over the years King gradually became more involved in her husband's work. She occasionally performed at his lectures, raising her voice in song as he did in speech. She became involved in separate activities as well. In 1962, she served as a Woman's Strike for Peace delegate to the 17-nation Disarmament Conference in Geneva, Switzerland. In the mid-1960s, she sang in the multi-arts Freedom Concerts that raised money for the SCLC. As demands on Martin became too much, she filled the speaking engagements he could not keep. After his assassination, Coretta King kept many of the commitments his death left empty. Soon, however, she became a much sought after speaker in her own right.

King's speech on Solidarity Day, June 19, 1968, is often identified as a prime example of her emergence from the shadow of her husband's memory. In it, she called upon American women to "unite and form a solid block of women power" to fight the three great evils of racism, poverty, and war. Much of her subsequent activity revolved around building plans for the creation of

a Martin Luther King, Jr. Memorial in Atlanta, which she began to work on in 1969. Located in the Martin Luther King, Jr., Historic District and designated a national historic landmark on May 5, 1977, the Martin Luther King, Jr. historical site became a unit of the National Park Service in 1980. In the same year that she began developing plans for the Martin Luther King, Jr., Center for Nonviolent Social Change, King also penned her autobiography *My Life with Martin Luther King, Jr.*, a book of reminiscences.

After years of lobbying to have Dr. King's birthday celebrated as a national holiday, she and others were rewarded for their efforts when in November of 1983, President Ronald Reagan signed the bill creating the King holiday. The following year, Coretta Scott King was elected chair of the Martin Luther King, Jr., Federal Holiday Commission, established by Congress to formalize plans for the first legal celebration of the King holiday. Beginning on January 20, 1986, the country celebrated the first Martin Luther King, Jr. national holiday.

King's activism has extended beyond the borders of the United States. In the mid-1980s, she and two of her children were arrested for demonstrating against apartheid outside of the South African embassy in Washington, DC. In 1986, she visited South Africa for eight days, meeting with businessmen and anti-apartheid leaders. King has also condemned the human rights violations of the Haitian military regime against Haitian citizens. In 1993, she implored the United Nations to reimpose an embargo against the nation.

The well-respected Martin Luther King, Jr. Center for Nonviolent Social Change became embattled in an ugly scuffle with the National Park Service over the issue of how best to utilize some of the historic Atlanta district in which the King memorial is located. As chief executive officer (CEO), King was forced to mediate between the family's desire for an interactive museum with exhibitions and programs for children and the National Park Service's plan for a visitor's center on the same site. The dispute was not resolved until April of 1995, a few months after King had officially stepped down as CEO, handing the reigns of leadership over to her son Dexter, who was unanimously voted the center's director and CEO.

Controversy continued to brew. In 1964, Martin Luther King, Jr. had given nearly 83,000 documents, including correspondence and other manuscripts, to Boston University. Coretta King had hoped to regain control of that legacy, but in April of 1995, the Massachusetts Supreme Judicial Court ruled in favor of the university.

On a brighter note, Coretta Scott King remains an eloquent and respected spokesperson on behalf of African American and human rights causes and nonviolent philosophy. She is often recognized for keeping her husband's dream alive. In September of 1995, King, along with two other famous civil rights widows—Myrlie Evers-Williams and Betty Shabazz—were honored for their influence by the National Political Congress of Black Women.

Dexter King (1961–)
Civil Rights Activist, Organization Executive

The youngest son of the King family, Dexter Scott King was born in Atlanta, Georgia, on January 30, 1961. Dexter's early days were filled with his parents' involvement in the nonviolent Civil Rights movement. Not only did his father participate in the movement, but by the mid-1960s his mother, Coretta Scott King, was heavily involved as well.

King's early education was a blend of both private and public academies. In 1979, he graduated from Atlanta's Frederick Douglass High School, where he was recognized not only as the son of the Reverend Martin L. King, Jr., but as an individual with a multifaceted identity. His interests included both music and athletics. Offered an athletic scholarship at the nationally recognized University of Southern California, Dexter opted to study at his father's alma mater, Morehouse College.

Dexter did not follow in his father's footsteps by becoming a Morehouse alumnus. Instead, his interest carried him into the world of music video production. In collaboration with Phillip M. Jones, he produced a music video in observance of the first nationally celebrated Martin Luther King, Jr. holiday. That endeavor led to an album in remembrance of Dr. King. Pop icons Prince, Whitney Houston, Run-DMC, and others rendered musical performances. By 1989, Dexter King returned to the civil rights arena when he was named president of the Martin Luther King, Jr. Center for Nonviolent Social Change, while his mother remained as the chief operating officer (CEO). Dexter King only remained as president of the center for four months, concerned that he only served as a titular head. However, with the retirement of Coretta Scott King in 1994, Dexter by a unanimous vote of the board of directors, became president and CEO. He was officially installed in January of the following year.

In March of 1997, Dexter King confronted James Earl Ray, the man convicted of his father's assassination, at the Lois DeBerry Special Needs Facility in Nashville, Tennessee. Dexter King asked Ray if he had assassinated Martin Luther King, Jr. Ray stated that he had not, and Dexter began working towards Ray's release from prison. However, 13 months after their meeting, James Earl Ray died of liver failure.

Wanting to educate people about his father's nonviolent philosophy, Dexter King's task is finding the most effectual method to bring his father's message of constructive change into the twenty-first century.

Martin Luther King, Jr. (1929–1968)
Religious Leader, Civil Rights Activist, Author/Poet, Labor Activist, Organization Executive/Founder, Minister, Anti-war Activist

Any number of historic moments in the civil rights struggle have been used to identify Martin Luther King Jr.—prime mover of the Montgomery bus boycott (1955–1956), keynote speaker at the March on Washington (1963), and the youngest Nobel Peace Prize laureate (1964). However, in retrospect, single events are less important than the fact that King, and his policy of nonviolent protest, was the dominant force in the Civil Rights movement during its decade of greatest achievement, from 1957 to 1968.

King was born Michael Luther King in Atlanta on January 15, 1929—one of the three children of Martin Luther King, Sr., pastor of Ebenezer Baptist Church, and Alberta Williams King, a former schoolteacher. (He did not receive the name "Martin" until he was about six years of age.) After attending grammar and high schools locally, King enrolled in Morehouse College in 1944. At this time he was not inclined to enter the ministry, but while there he came under the influence of Dr. Benjamin Mays, a scholar whose manner and bearing convinced him that a religious career could have its intellectual satisfactions. After receiving his B.A. degree in 1948, King attended Crozer Theological Seminary in Chester, Pennsylvania. Graduating in 1951, King was the recipient of the Plafker Award as the outstanding student of the graduating class and the J. Lewis Crozer Fellowship. In 1951, King entered Boston University to pursue his Ph.D. Two years later, he completed his course work. After completing his dissertation for his doctorate in 1955, King was granted a Ph.D. from Boston University.

Married by then, King returned to the South, accepting the pastorate of the Dexter Avenue Baptist Church in Montgomery, Alabama. It was here that he made his first mark on the Civil Rights movement by mobilizing the African American community during a 382-day boycott of the city's bus lines. Working through the Montgomery Improvement Association, King overcame arrest and other violent harassment including the bombing of his home. In 1956, the U.S. Supreme Court declared the Alabama laws requiring bus segregation unconstitutional, thereby granting African Americans equal access on the buses of Montgomery.

A national hero and a civil rights figure of growing importance, King summoned together 115 African American leaders in 1957 and laid the groundwork for a new

Martin Luther King, Jr. waving to the massive crowd at the 1963 March on Washington while holding notes from his famous speech (AP/Wide World Photos, Inc.).

civil rights organization, now known as the Southern Christian Leadership Conference (SCLC). Elected its president, he soon sought to assist other communities in the organization of protest campaigns against discrimination and to promote voter-registration activities among African Americans.

After the 1958 publication of his first book *Stride Toward Freedom: The Montgomery Story* and a trip to India the following year, where he enhanced his understanding of the non-violent strategies of Gandhi, King returned to the United States and subsequently resigned as pastor of Dexter Avenue Baptist Church. In 1960, he returned to Atlanta where the headquarters of SCLC was located and became co-pastor, with his father of Ebenezer Baptist Church. A sympathizer with the African American Southern student movement, King spoke at the organizational meeting of the Student Non-Violent Coordinating Committee (SNCC) in April of 1960. He soon garnered criticism from the student activists who were intent on maintaining their independence. King was arrested after participating in a student sit-in at Rich's Department Store in Atlanta on October 19, 1960. Similar to the students, he refused to post bail and was

incarcerated with the student protesters. Three years later, in Birmingham, Alabama, where white officials were known for their anti-African American attitudes, King's nonviolent tactics were put to their most severe test. On April 16, King was arrested during a mass protest for fair hiring practices, the establishment of a biracial committee, and the desegregation of department store facilities. Police brutality (i.e., police dogs and fire hoses) used against the marchers dramatized the plight of African Americans to the nation and the world at large with enormous impact. Although arrested, King's voice was not silenced as he issued his classic "Letter from a Birmingham Jail" to refute the criticism of white clergy. In June of 1963, President Kennedy agreed to put sweeping civil rights legislation before the U.S. Congress.

Later that year King was a principal speaker at the historic August 28 March on Washington, where he delivered the "I Have A Dream" speech, one of the most passionate addresses of his career. At the beginning of the next year, *Time* magazine designated him as its Man of the Year for 1963. A few months later he was named recipient of the 1964 Nobel Peace Prize. Upon his return from Oslo, Norway, where he had gone to accept the award, King entered a new battle in Selma, Alabama, where he led a voter registration campaign which culminated in the Selma-to-Montgomery Freedom March. King next brought his crusade to Chicago where he launched a slum rehabilitation and open housing program.

In the North, however, King soon discovered that young and angry African Americans cared little for his pulpit oratory and even less for his solemn pleas for peaceful protest. Their disenchantment was clearly one of the factors influencing his decision to rally behind a new cause and stake out a fresh battleground: the war in Vietnam. Although his aim was to fuse a new coalition of dissent based on equal support for the peace crusade and the Civil Rights movement, King antagonized many civil rights leaders by declaring the United States to be "the greatest purveyor of violence in the world."

The rift was immediate. The National Association for the Advancement of Colored People (NAACP) saw King's shift of emphasis as "a serious tactical mistake"; the Urban League warned that the "limited resources" of the Civil Rights movement would be spread too thin; Bayard Rustin claimed African American support of the peace movement would be negligible; and Ralph Bunche felt King was undertaking an impossible mission in trying to bring the campaign for peace in step with the goals of the Civil Rights movement.

From the vantage point of history, King's timing could only be regarded as superb. In announcing his opposition to the war and in characterizing it as a "tragic adventure" which was playing "havoc with the destiny of the entire world," King again forced the white middle class to concede that no movement could dramatically affect the course of government in the United States unless it involved deliberate and restrained aggressiveness, persistent dissent, and even militant confrontation. These were precisely the ingredients of the civil rights struggle in the South in the early 1960s.

As students, professors, intellectuals, clergymen, and reformers of every stripe rushed into the movement and, in a sense forcing fiery black militants such as Stokely Carmichael and Floyd McKissick to surrender their control over anti-war polemics, King turned his attention to the domestic issue which, in his view, was directly related to the Vietnam struggle: the War on Poverty. At one point, he called for a guaranteed family income, he threatened national boycotts, and spoke of disrupting entire cities by nonviolent "camp-ins." With this in mind, he began to draw up plans for a massive march of the poor on Washington, DC, envisioning a popular demonstration of unsurpassed intensity and magnitude designed to force Congress and the political parties to recognize and deal with the unseen and ignored masses of desperate and downtrodden Americans.

King's decision to interrupt these plans to lend his support to the Memphis sanitation men's strike was based in part on his desire to discourage violence, as well as to focus national attention on the plight of the poor, unorganized workers of the city. The men were bargaining for little else beyond basic union representation and long overdue salary considerations. Though he was unable to eliminate the violence that had resulted in the summoning and subsequent departure of the National Guard, King stayed in Memphis and was in the process of planning for a march that he vowed to carry out in defiance of a federal court injunction, if necessary. On April 3, 1968, the Reverend Dr. Martin Luther King, Jr. rendered his last and most foreboding speech "I See the Promise Land," better known as "I've Been to the Mountaintop." Delivered at (the Bishop Charles H.) Mason Temple, King prophesied his demise.

Death came for King on the balcony of the African American-owned Lorraine Hotel just off Beale Street on the evening of April 4. While standing outside with Jesse Jackson and Ralph Abernathy, a shot rang out. King fell over, struck in the neck by a rifle bullet which left him moribund. At 7:05 P.M. he was pronounced dead at St. Joseph's Hospital. His death caused a wave of violence in more than one hundred major cities across the country. However, King's legacy has lasted much longer than the memories of those post-assassination riots. In 1969, his widow, Coretta Scott King, organized the Martin Luther King, Jr. Center for Non-Violent Social Change. Today, it stands next to his beloved Ebenezer Baptist Church in Atlanta and, with the surrounding buildings, is a national historic landmark under the administration of the National Park Service. Additionally, the Lorraine Hotel, which is listed in the National Register of Historic Places, now serves as the National Civil Rights Museum.

The only twentieth century American accorded a national holiday, Dr. King's birthday is celebrated each year with educational programs, artistic displays, and concerts throughout the United States.

Martin Luther King III (1957–)
Civil Rights Activist, Community Activist, Political Leader, Organization Executive/Founder

Martin Luther King, III, the oldest son and second child of the Reverend and Mrs. Martin L. King, Jr., was born in Montgomery, Alabama, on October 23, 1957. Reared in Atlanta, M. L. King, III received his primary and secondary education in the schools of Atlanta. After completing his secondary studies, King entered Morehouse College majoring in political science and history.

A child of the Civil Rights movement, after graduating from his father's alma mater, King, III devoted his energies to voter registration campaigns, lobbying to make his father's birthday a national holiday, and pursuing political office. King, a civil and human rights advocate, has been involved in meaningful policy strategies to provide just and equal treatment to citizens throughout the world.

During the administration of President Jimmy Carter, King represented the president on two official delegations to promote peace in foreign countries. In 1984, as a member of the board of directors of the Martin Luther King, Jr. Center for Non-Violent Social Change, he went to five poverty- and drought-stricken African nations on a fact-finding mission. This mission produced an initiative to end starvation in Africa. Later, he focused his energy on the injustices of South Africa's system of racial apartheid and joined in the struggle to gain the freedom of Nelson Mandela.

In 1986, King entered the political arena and was elected to office as an at-large representative on the Fulton County Board of Commissioners. Serving until 1993, his tenancy was characterized by enactments regulating minority business participation in public contracting, ethics, purification of the county's natural water resources, and strict hazardous waste disposal provisions. After leaving office, King returned to public speaking, worked with Atlanta youth groups, and continued to be a community and human rights activist. Later, in response to California's Proposition 209, which outlawed policies of affirmative action, he organized Americans United for Affirmative Action (AUAA). A

Martin Luther King III (AP/Wide World Photos, Inc.)

coalition of national groups, the AUAA's purpose is to safeguard affirmative action programs and to maintain the principles of equal opportunity and diversity championed by the Civil Rights movement. A year after founding AUAA, King was appointed president of the Southern Christian Leadership Conference. The Southern Christian Leadership Conference's fourth president and its first lay person, Martin Luther King, III was sworn into office on January 15, 1998.

Raised among those who were ardently committed to inclusive civil and human rights and a nonviolent fellowship of humanity; Martin Luther King, III infuses and applies the belief system into his personal and public life.

Harry T. Moore (1905–1951)
Educator, Civil Rights Activist, Organization Founder

One of the unknown warriors to give his life for the cause of civil rights and racial justice, Harry Tyson Moore was born on November 19, 1905, in Suwannee County, Florida, to Johnny and Rosa Tyson Moore. He received his education in the schools of Daytona Beach and Jacksonville, Florida. In 1925, Moore graduated from the Florida Memorial College with a high school

diploma. After graduation, he taught school in Cocoa for one year. In 1926, Moore served as principal of Titusville Colored School and later as principal of the Mims Elementary School.

A member of the Florida State Teachers' Association, Moore organized the Brevard chapter of the NAACP in 1934. He investigated lynchings and indescribable deeds of mob brutality and launched a campaign against segregated academies of learning and unequal compensation for African American teachers. In 1944, Moore co-founded and became executive secretary of the Progressive Voters' League. Under his leadership, the league successfully inaugurated a state-wide voter registration drive. Because of Moore's activist role in the struggle for civil rights among African Americans in the state of Florida, the Brevard County officials relieved him of his duties as principal in 1946. In May of the same year, he became the first full-time, paid executive secretary of an NAACP state conference.

As the most visible and outspoken African American leader in Florida, Moore received numerous threats. The 1949 alleged rape of a Groveland white woman by four African American men ignited four days of virulent rioting by unrestrained white mobs in African American neighborhoods. A month after the alleged incident, Moore, to no avail, corresponded with President Harry S Truman and Florida's congressional representatives, calling for a review of the Groveland riots and pressing for a special session of Congress to pass laws to protect the civil rights of African Americans. Because Moore sought justice for the accused individuals, he captured the ire of the Ku Klux Klan. His unrelenting campaign for racial equity also placed him at odds with local government officials. When the U.S. Supreme Court reversed the convictions and death sentences of the remaining two defendants in April of 1951, the simmering embers of hostilities over the Groveland case ignited once again.

In the summer of 1951, Moore earned his bachelor's degree from Bethune-Cookman College. Within months of completing his undergraduate studies, the death threats became an absolute reality. Death came to the ever-vigilant warrior for civil rights on December 25, 1951, when a bomb placed beneath his bed exploded. Harry T. Moore, as recorded by Ben Green in his book *Before His Time: The Untold Story of Harry T. Moore, America's First Civil Rights Martyr*, became the first person to lose his life for what became the modern Civil Rights movement. Recognizing his achievements and sacrifices, in 1952 the NAACP posthumously awarded Harry T. Moore the Spingarn Medal, the organization's highest honor.

In 1991, after evidence came to the forefront, then-Florida's Governor Lawton Chiles ordered a re-investigation of the Moore murder. Ironically, this was the same year that Byron de la Beckwith was re-indicted for the 1965 murder of Medgar Evers. By some accounts, Moore's death is as monumentous as those of Evers, Malcolm X, and Martin Luther King, Jr.

Diane J. Nash (1938–)
Civil Rights Activist

In the vanguard of the national civil rights and anti-war movements from 1959 to 1967, Diane Judith Nash was born in Chicago, Illinois on May 15, 1938. Reared in a Catholic middle-class home, she received her primary and secondary education in parochial and public schools of Chicago. Nash began her collegiate career at Howard University. Her transfer to Fisk University in Nashville, Tennessee, projected her into the African American struggle for civil rights.

When Diana Nash arrived in the "Athens of the South," racial segregation permeated Nashville. Her personal encounters with the code of "separate but unequal" led Nash to actively seek rectification. Early in 1959 she attended workshops on nonviolence directed by the Reverend James Lawson, under the agency of the Nashville Christian Leadership Conference, an affiliate of SCLC. Nash became imbued with and an ardent supporter of the direct nonviolent protest philosophy.

In November and December of 1959, Nash was among those who "tested" the racial segregation policy of Nashville's downtown lunch counters. Elected chair of the Student Central Committee, she played a pivotal role in Nashville's student sit-in movement. Before the Nashville students could initiate their first full-scale sit-in, North Carolina A & T students staged a sit-in on February 1, 1960, in Greensboro.

When the Nashville students decided on the "jail—no bail" strategy, Nash stated to the judge, "We feel that if we pay these fines we would be contributing to and supporting the injustice and immoral practices that have been performed in the arrest and convictions of the defendants." Responding to her April 19 query about the immorality of segregation, Mayor Ben West said that lunch counters should be desegregated. On May 10, 1960, Nashville became the first Southern city to begin desegregating its lunch counters.

In April of 1960, Diane Nash was one of the founding students of the Student Non-Violent Coordinating Committee (SNCC). The following February, she participated in the Rock Hill, South Carolina, protests for desegregation. After being arrested, Nash and the other students refused to pay bail. When CORE's original freedom riders were beaten unmercifully in Alabama and aborted the last leg of the ride to New Orleans, John Lewis and Diane Nash determined that permitting the violence

of the white mob to overthrow the nonviolence of the demonstrators conveyed the wrong message to the movement's enemies. Nash accepted the responsibility of coordinating this monumental mission.

In May, Nash coordinated the Freedom Rides from Birmingham, Alabama, to Jackson, Mississippi. Three months later, Nash became the director of the direct-action wing of SNCC. Between 1961 and 1965 she worked for SCLC as a field staff person, organizer, strategist, and workshop instructor. Nash was imprisoned for instructing African American children in the techniques of direct nonviolent protest after moving to Jackson, Mississippi. Holding steadfastly to the principles developed in Nashville, she chose jail rather than pay bail.

Nash's ideas were instrumental in initiating the 1963 March on Washington. She and James Bevel conceptualized and planned the initial strategy for the Selma Right-to-Vote Movement that helped produce the Voting Rights Act of 1965. Nash's civil rights activities led her to the Vietnam peace movement. She continued working for political and social transformation through the 1970s and lectured nationally on the rights of women during the 1980s. Nash continues to lecture across the country. Nonviolence was not a tactic for Diane Nash, an unsung but outstanding woman of the Civil Rights movement of the 1960s. For her it became a way of life.

Rosa L. McCauley Parks (1913–)
Aide, Civil Rights Activist

Rosa Parks has been called "the Patron Saint," the spark that lit the fire, and the "mother of the movement." Her courage to defy custom and law to uphold her personal rights and dignity inspired African Americans in Montgomery, Alabama, to fight for their rights by staging one of the longest boycotts in history.

Born Rosa Louise McCauley on February 4, 1913, in Tuskegee, Alabama, she was one of two children born to James and Leona Edwards McCauley. Her mother, a schoolteacher, taught Parks until age 11, when she entered Montgomery Industrial School for Girls. Later, she attended Booker T. Washington High School. After attending segregated schools, she went to the all-African American Alabama State College. In 1932, she married Raymond Parks. Eleven years later, she and her husband joined the local National Association for the Advancement of Colored People (NAACP) chapter. One of the first women to join the NAACP, Parks served as the chapter's secretary from 1943 to 1956. Also a member of the Montgomery Voters League, during the summer of 1955, Parks attended workshops at Highlander Folk School, in Monteagle, Tennessee, which had been active in the civil rights struggle since the 1930s.

On December 1, 1955, as Parks was riding the Cleveland Avenue bus home from work, she was ordered by the bus driver to give up her seat to a white man. When she refused to move, the bus driver threatened to call law enforcement officials. Arrested and fined, her case was the last straw for Montgomery's African American citizenry. They were as tired of being underclass citizens as Parks. The Women's Political Council protested her arrest by organizing a boycott of the buses. A young, unknown minister named Martin Luther King, Jr., became immediately involved. Realizing the immensity of the opportunity to begin dismantling the code of Southern segregation, he and other members of the community organized the Montgomery Improvement Association. African Americans and a few whites transported boycotters to and from work, and they continued, despite opposition from the city and state governments, for 382 days.

Following her trial, upon the advice of her attorneys, Parks refused to pay the $14 fine and court costs. Parks's case was appealed all the way to the U.S. Supreme Court. On December 20, 1956, the country's highest tribunal ruled Montgomery's segregated seating unconstitutional. When the boycott ended the following day, both Parks and King were national heroes. Lasting over a decade, the mass movement of non-violent social change that started in Montgomery culminated in the Civil Rights Act of 1964, the Voting Rights Act of 1965, and the Fair Housing Act of 1968.

Because of the harassment that Rosa and Raymond Parks received during and after the boycott, in 1957 they and her mother moved to Detroit, Michigan. Working in various capacities, she later became a staff assistant in Congressman John Conyers' Detroit office. Parks continued to be involved in the civil rights struggle, giving speeches and attending marches and demonstrations. She marched on Washington in 1963 and into Montgomery in 1965. Parks has received numerous tributes for her dedication and inspiration: in 1979, she received the NAACP's Spingarn Medal; and in 1980, she became the first woman to receive the Martin Luther King, Jr. Nonviolent Peace Prize. As she approached retirement, Parks became involved in other activities, such as the Rosa and Raymond Parks Institute for Self-Development. In 1988, the same year that she retired from U. S. Representative Conyers' office, Detroit's Museum of African-American History unveiled her portrait. Two years later, her birthday was celebrated in Washington's Kennedy Center. A recipient of the Presidential Medal of Freedom and the International Freedom Conductor Award in April 1999, Congress passed legislation authorizing President Bill Clinton to award the Congressional Gold Medal to Rosa Parks in recognition of her contributions to the nation.

Jo Ann Gibson Robinson (1912–1992)
Civil Rights Activist, Educator, Author

As president of the Montgomery, Alabama, Women's Political Council during the 1950s, Jo Ann Gibson Robinson was one of the several significant originators of the 1955–1956 Montgomery Bus Boycott. The youngest of twelve children, she was born on April 17, 1912, to Owen Boston and Dollie Webb Gibson, near Culloden, Georgia. The first member of her family to obtain a college degree, Robinson graduated from Fort Valley State College and taught for five years in the Macon public schools. Moving to Atlanta, she earned a master's degree in English from Atlanta University.

In 1949, Robinson joined the faculty of Alabama State College as a professor of English. Later, she joined Montgomery's Dexter Avenue Baptist Church and the Women's Political Council (WPC). A young organization, the WPC was founded in the fall of 1946 by Mary Fair Burks, also a member of Alabama State's English Department. Burks was inspired to organize the WPC after a sermon by the Reverend Vernon Johns, then-pastor of the Dexter Avenue Baptist Church, serving as president of the WPC for four years. Organized to protest racial abuse, the WPC developed a program of political action. The programs consisted of four points: voter registration; protest demonstrations of African American abuse on Montgomery city buses; the education of the young about democracy; and literacy programs.

Because she and others came face to face with the degrading effects of racial abuse by drivers of Montgomery city buses, Robinson and the WPC targeted the racial seating practices. On several occasions, the WPC sought a remedy from city officials about African American seating and the imperious conduct of contemptuous city drivers. A year and a half before Rosa Parks refused to give up her seat, in May of 1954—soon after the unanimous Supreme Court decision in the *Brown v. Board of Education of Topeka, Kansas* case—Robinson corresponded with Mayor W. A. Gayle and alluded to the possibility of a boycott by African Americans of the city's public transportation system if the abuses did not stop. Resultant to Parks' arrest on December 1, 1955, she played a prominent role in the Montgomery bus struggle. A member of the executive board of the Montgomery Improvement Association (MIA), Robinson wrote the organization's newsletter.

Martin Luther King, Jr. described Robinson as "apparently indefatigable, she perhaps more than any other person, was active on every level of the protest." Robinson's 1987 memoir *The Montgomery Bus Boycott and the Women Who Started It* took her and other middle-class women from a footnote status to one of centrality within the narrative for open seating on the buses of

Al Sharpton (center) leading a demonstration in New York City (AP/Wide World Photos, Inc.).

Montgomery. Joann Gibson Robinson died five years after the publication of her memoir.

Al Sharpton (1954–)
Religious Leader, Community Activist, Sports Manager, Public Relations Manager, Organization Executive/Founder

While being shunned by many middle-class African Americans, Al Sharpton draws support from the ranks of the youth and the disenfranchised. Sharpton was born in 1954 in Brooklyn, New York. At the early age of four, Sharpton began delivering sermons and at the age of 13 he was ordained a Pentecostal minister. During and after high school, Sharpton preached in neighborhood churches and went on national religious tours, often with prominent entertainers. Soon he was befriended by a number of well known and influential African Americans including Congressman Adam Clayton Powell, Jr., Jesse Jackson, Sr., and singer James Brown.

In 1969, Jackson appointed Sharpton youth director of Operation Breadbasket. Around this same time James Brown made Sharpton one of his bodyguards and soon

he was doing promotions for the singer. In 1985, Sharpton married singer Kathy Jordan and soon became involved with fight promoter Don King. Even though Sharpton promoted boxers and entertainers, he had long before put himself in the public spotlight as a social activist. In 1971, he founded the National Youth Movement (later called the United African Movement) ostensibly to combat drug use. The movement, however, soon became a vehicle for Sharpton to draw attention to himself. He urged children to forsake Christmas in favor of a Kwanzaa celebration and the elderly to protest New York City police tactics.

Sharpton made himself part of the publicity surrounding the Bernard Goetz murder trial (1984), the Howard Beach racial killing (1986), the Twana Brawley debacle (1987), and the Yusef Hawkins-Bensonhurst killing (1989). In 1988, Sharpton was accused of being an FBI informant and passing on information about Don King, reputed organized crime figures, and various African American leaders. In 1989 and 1990, he was acquitted on charges of income tax evasion and embezzling National Youth Movement funds. In 1991, Sharpton was briefly hospitalized after being stabbed by a man wielding a pocket knife.

Rev. Fred Shuttlesworth (center) marching with Rev. Ralph Abernathy (left) and Dr. Martin Luther King, Jr. (right) in 1965 (AP/Wide World Photos, Inc.).

On August 2, 1994, Sharpton announced the formation of a new political party. He aimed to counter the Liberal Party by reaching African American voters that traditional, mainstream parties have ignored. Sharpton unsuccessfully ran for the U.S. Senate as a candidate of his own Freedom Party, even participating in that year's New York Democratic primary.

Fred Lee Shuttlesworth (1922–)
Civil Rights Activist, Clergyman

Born March 18, 1922 in Mugler, Alabama, Fred L. Shuttlesworth was once referred to as "one of the nation's most courageous freedom fighters" by none other than Dr. Martin Luther King, Jr. From his 1956 founding of the Alabama Christian Movement for Human Rights through the historic Birmingham demonstrations of 1963, driven by a sense of divine mission, Shuttlesworth pressured Jim Crow restrictions in Birmingham with radically confrontational acts of bravery. His intensive civil rights campaign pitted him against the staunchly segregationist police commissioner Eugene "Bull" Connor and ultimately brought him to the side of Martin Luther King, Jr., and to the inner chambers of the White House during the Kennedy administration. Throughout these struggles, Shuttlesworth demonstrated incredible courage and persistence in the face of peril.

When Shuttlesworth sustained only a bump on the head in the 1956 bombing of his home, members of his church called it a miracle. Shuttlesworth took it as a sign that he would be protected on the civil rights mission that had made him a target that night. Standing in front of his demolished home, Shuttlesworth vigorously renewed his commitment to integrate Birmingham's public facilities and police department. The incident transformed him, in the eyes of Birmingham blacks, from an up-and-coming young minister to a virtual folk hero and, in the view of white Birmingham residents, from obscurity to agitator extraordinaire.

Shuttlesworth earned an associate's degree from Selma University and a bachelor's degree from Alabama State College in 1955; in 1969, he received a doctorate of laws degree from Birmingham Baptist College. He has also received a multitude of awards including: Rosa Parks Award from the Southern Christian Leadership Conference (SCLC), 1963; Excellence Award from PUSH, 1974; Martin Luther King, Jr. Civil Rights Award from the Progressive National Baptists, 1975; and the Founders Award from the SCLC, 1977. Since 1966, Shuttlesworth has served as pastor of the Greater New Light Baptist Church in Cincinnati, Ohio.

Leon H. Sullivan (1922–)
Civil Rights Activist, Organization Founder

Leon Howard Sullivan was born October 16, 1922, in Charleston, West Virginia. Reared by his grandmother after his parents' divorce, Sullivan attended Charleston's segregated elementary and secondary schools. After being ordained a Baptist minister at the age of 17, Sullivan earned a B.A. from West Virginia State College (1943) and an M.A. from Columbia University (1947). He also attended the Union Theological Seminary (1945) and earned a D.D. from Virginia Union University.

At age 21, during the first March on Washington movement (1941–1942) organized by A. Philip Randolph, Leon Sullivan was elected president of the South Orange Council of Churches. As president, Sullivan worked with civil rights leaders such as Bayard Rustin. From 1950 to 1988 Sullivan was the pastor of the Zion Baptist Church in Philadelphia. While there he entered into a lifelong crusade to provide better job opportunities for African Americans. Using the method of direct nonviolent action taught him by Randolph, Sullivan fought racist hiring practices through protest and economic boycott. A promoter of economic self-determination, he provided job training through the Opportunities Industrialization Center. Opening in 1964 with money from a Ford Foundation grant, the Center offered training in electronics, cooking, power-sewing, and drafting. Sullivan also founded Zion Investment Associates, which makes seed money available for new African American business ventures. Sullivan has also been associated with Progress Aerospace Inc., General Motors, and Mellon Bank.

Author of *Build Brother Build*, Sullivan is a recipient of the Russwurm Award (National Publisher's Association, 1963); the Philadelphia Fellowship Communion Award (1964); the Philadelphia Book Award (1966); the American Exemplar Medal (1969); the NAACP's Spingarn Medal (1971); and the Franklin D. Roosevelt Four Freedom Medal (1987). In 1991, he received the Presidential Medal of Freedom and the Distinguished Service Award, the Ivory Coast's highest honor. Upon retiring from Zion Baptist Church in 1988, Sullivan was made pastor emeritus.

After leaving the pulpit of Zion Baptist Church, Sullivan concentrated his energies on concerns in Africa. Attempting to bring an end to apartheid in South Africa, he called upon American corporations to sell their South African investments and petitioned the U.S. government to bring sanctions against the racially-biased country. Because of Sullivan's efforts, the departure of international businesses, and the sweeping institution of international sanctions, the shackles of South Africa's system of racial segregation were unchained. He founded the International Foundation for Education and Self-Help to combat illiteracy, famine, and joblessness in Africa and to advance the concept of African self-reliance. In April of 1991, Leon Howard Sullivan organized and co-chaired the first African and African American Summit held at Abidjan, Ivory Coast. Six months later, he officiated at the United Nations Day for Africa, a function he inaugurated to bring attention to the issue of debt relief for sub-Saharan African countries. A pathfinder, Sullivan's achievements have made lasting universal contributions to the improvement of humankind throughout the world.

Mary E. Church Terrell (1863–1954)
Organization Executive/Founder, Civil Rights Activist

Mary Eliza Church Terrell, born on September 23, 1863, in Memphis, Tennessee, was the oldest of Robert and Louisa Ayers Church's two children. Because of the racial climate in her native city and its deficient educational facilities for African American children, Church's parents enrolled her in the Antioch College "Model School" in Yellow Springs, Ohio. She attended the public schools in Yellow Springs and in 1879 completed her secondary education in Oberlin, Ohio. Church earned her bachelor's degree from Oberlin College in 1884. The following year she accepted a faculty position at Wilberforce College in Xenia, Ohio. After two years at Wilberforce, Church joined the Colored High School faculty in Washington, DC. She married Robert Heberton Terrell on October 18, 1891. Residing in Washington, the

Terrells became the parents of two children, their daughter Phyllis, and Mary, an adopted daughter.

Terrell became active in the feminist movement and founded the Colored Women's League in 1892. Later, this organization merged with the Federation of Afro-American Women and became the National Association of Colored Women (NACW). Organized in 1896, she was elected its first president. In 1895, Terrell was appointed to the school board in the District of Columbia and served until 1901. Her appointment was the country's first for a woman of color. Reappointed in 1906, she held the position for five years.

By 1901, Terrell operated as a leader outside the sphere of women's organizations. She wrote numerous articles denouncing racial segregation. Writing under the pseudonym Euphemia Kirk, which she soon discarded, Terrell's treatises were covered in the national and international media. Terrell sought redress for the three companies of African American soldiers dismissed after the 1906 outbreak of racial violence in Brownsville, Texas. In 1909, she was one of two African American women who signed the "Call" for the organizational meeting of the National Association for the Advancement of Colored People. During the Women's Suffrage Movement, Terrell worked with other women for the 1920 ratification of the Constitution's Nineteenth Amendment. In 1940, she wrote her autobiography *A Colored Woman in a White World*.

After World War II, Terrell aggressively fought racial discrimination. In 1950, she filed suit against Thompson's Restaurant in Washington, DC, for not adhering to the city's 1872 and 1873 public accommodation laws. As chair of the Coordinating Committee for the Enforcement of the District of Columbia Anti-Discrimination Laws, Terrell focused on other segregated facilities. At age 89, she led the picket lines. On June 8, 1953, the Supreme Court ruled Washington's segregated eating facilities unconstitutional in the *District of Columbia v. John Thompson* case. This ardent activist fought more than 66 years for gender and racial equality. Mary Church Terrell died on July 24, 1954, two months after the Supreme Court case of *Brown v. Board of Education of Topeka, Kansas* ruled segregation unlawful.

William M. Trotter (1872–1934)
Organization Executive/Founder, Civil Rights Activist, Publisher

William Monroe Trotter was born to James Monroe and Virginia Issacs Trotter on April 7, 1872, near Chillicothe, Ohio. Reared in predominantly white suburban Hyde Park near Boston, he attended and excelled academically at Hyde Park Grammar School and Hyde Park High School. In 1891, Trotter entered Harvard, where he became the university's first African American

Phi Beta Kappa. He graduated magna cum laude in 1895 with a B.A. degree. In 1899, after working for various employers, Trotter started his business venture as an insurance agent and mortgage negotiator. Two years later, he, along with William H. Scott and George W. Forbes, founded the *Guardian*. A militant newspaper, it addressed the needs and aspirations of African Americans and served as an organ against racial discrimination. The same year that he co-founded the newspaper, Trotter married Geraldine Louise Pindell who assisted in publishing the *Guardian*.

An ideological opponent of the "Wizard of Tuskegee," in 1903, Trotter deliberately disrupted a meeting in Boston at which Booker T. Washington was advocating support of segregation. Subsequently, in 1905, Trotter joined W. E. B. Du Bois in founding the Niagara Movement. However, he refused to move with Du Bois into the National Association for the Advancement of Colored People because he felt it would be too moderate. Neither could he accept the financial and leadership role assumed by whites. Instead, Trotter formed the Negro Equal Rights League. In protest against the segregation policies of President Woodrow Wilson, Trotter led a delegation to the White House to meet with Wilson in 1914. After a heated debate between Trotter and the president, Wilson ordered the group to leave. The following year, he led demonstrations against the showing of D.W. Griffith's racist film *The Birth of a Nation* that glorified the Ku Klux Klan. In 1919, Trotter appeared at the Paris Peace Conference in an unsuccessful effort to have it outlaw racial discrimination. Although the State Department had denied him a passport to attend the conference, he had reached Paris nonetheless by working as a cook on a ship.

Because of his strident unwillingness to work with established groups, chroniclers of the Civil Rights movement have been slow to recognize Trotter. However, many of his methods were adopted in the struggle for racial equality and justice in the late 1950s and 1960s, notably his use of nonviolent protest. Arrested numerous times, Trotter's purpose for consistent direct protest was to eradicate the virulent malevolence of racial segregation.

Booker T. Washington (1856–1915)
Lecturer, Civil Rights Activist, Educational Administrator, Professor, Organization Executive/Founder, Author/Poet

Booker Taliaferro Washington was born a slave in Hale's Ford, Virginia, on April 5, 1856, to Jane Ferguson, a bonded person. The first nine years of Washington's life was spent in slavery on the farm of James Burroughs, the place of his birth. After emancipation, his family was so poverty stricken that he worked in salt furnaces and

Booker T. Washington (Corbis Corporation [Bellevue])

coal mines from age nine. Attending school sporadically in Malden, West Virginia, Booker added the surname Washington. Always an intelligent and curious child, he yearned for an education and was frustrated when he could not receive one locally. When he was 16 years of age, his parents allowed him to quit work to go to school. They had no money to help him, so he walked two hundred miles to attend the Hampton Institute in Virginia and paid his tuition and board there by working as the janitor.

Dedicating himself to the idea that education would raise his people to equality in this country, Washington became a teacher. He first taught in his hometown, then at the Hampton Institute, and in 1881, he founded the Tuskegee Normal and Industrial Institute in Tuskegee, Alabama. As head of the Institute, he traveled the country constantly to raise funds from both African Americans and whites; soon he became a well-known speaker.

In 1895, Washington was asked to speak at the opening of the Cotton States Exposition, an unprecedented honor for an African American man. His Atlanta Compromise speech explained his major thesis, that African Americans could secure their constitutional rights through their own economic and moral advancement rather than through legal and political changes. Although his conciliatory stand angered some African Americans who feared it would encourage the foes of equal rights, whites approved of his views. Thus his major achievement was to win over diverse elements among Southern whites, without whose support the programs he envisioned and brought into being would have been impossible. Washington penned two autobiographies *The Story of My Life and Work* (1900) and *Up From Slavery* (1901).

In addition to Tuskegee Institute, which still educates many today, Washington instituted a variety of programs for rural extension work and helped to establish the National Negro Business League. Shortly after the election of President William McKinley in 1896, a movement was set in motion to name Washington to a cabinet post, but he withdrew his name from consideration, preferring to work outside the political arena. One of the most significant leaders among African Americans in the early twentieth century, Booker T. Washington died on November 14, 1915.

Ida B. Wells-Barnett (1862–1931)
Journalist, Lecturer, Civil Rights Activist, Anti-lynching Crusader, Feminist

The oldest of James and Elizabeth Warenton Wells's eight children, Wells-Barnett was born a slave in Holly Springs, Mississippi, on July 16, 1862. The yellow fever epidemic of 1878 claimed the lives of her parents and youngest brother. At the age of sixteen, Wells-Barnett assumed responsibility for her siblings. Leaving Shaw University (now Rust College) and passing a teachers' examination, she briefly taught in rural Mississippi to support her brothers and sisters. Wells-Barnett moved to Memphis, Tennessee, and taught in the county and city public school systems.

A train ride from Memphis to Woodstock was the beginning of Wells-Barnett's lifelong public campaign against the injustices faced by African Americans throughout the South. In 1884, after being forcibly removed from the first-class ladies' coach, she filed suit against the Chesapeake, Ohio and Southwestern Railroad. Although she won in the Memphis Circuit Court, the state's Supreme Court reversed the lower court's decision in 1887 because the railroad company had satisfied Tennessee's 1881 statutory requirements to provide "separate but equal" accommodations.

Wells-Barnett published accounts of her experience in the local African American press and wrote for the African American press throughout the country. In 1889, she was elected secretary of the Afro-American Press Association. Wells-Barnett's editorials critical of the Memphis Board of Education led to her dismissal as teacher in 1891. Afterwards, she became a full-time

Lynch Law in Georgia.

BY

IDA B. WELLS-BARNETT

A Six-Weeks' Record in the Center of Southern Civilization, As Faithfully Chronicled by the "Atlanta Journal" and the "Atlanta Constitution."

ALSO THE FULL REPORT OF LOUIS P. LE VIN,

The Chicago Detective Sent to Investigate the Burning of Samuel Hose, the Torture and Hanging of Elijah Strickland, the Colored Preacher, and the Lynching of Nine Men for Alleged Arson.

Lynch Law in Georgia was one of numerous publications released by anti-lynching crusader Ida B. Wells-Barnett (The Library of Congress).

journalist and editor. The March 9, 1892, lynching of three African American male proprietors of the People's Grocery Store caused Wells-Barnett to declare journalistic war on lynching. When her protest writings outraged white men in the South, a mob destroyed her newspaper office on May 27, 1892, and she was banished from the region.

Wells-Barnett moved to New York and continued her struggle against racial injustice and lynching as a columnist for the *New York Age*, edited by T. Thomas Fortune. On June 7, 1892, the *New York Age* published her detailed analysis of lynching, refuting the myth that, by killing African American men, white men intended to shield white women against rape. Her detailed statistics and findings formed the basis of two pamphlets *Southern Horrors* (1892) and *A Red Record* (1895). Lecturing in Great Britain in 1893 and 1894, Wells-Barnett internationalized her anti-lynching campaign.

In 1893, Wells-Barnett focused her attention on the exclusion of African Americans from the World's Columbian Exposition in Chicago. Working with Frederick Douglass, Ferdinand Lee Barnett, and I. Garland Penn,

Wells-Barnett co-wrote an 81-page pamphlet entitled *The Reason Why the Colored American is Not in the World's Columbian Exposition—The Afro-American's Contribution to Columbian Literature.* Later in the year, she moved to Chicago and began working for the *Chicago Conservator,* the first African American newspaper in the city, founded by Barnett.

On June 27, 1895, Ida B. Wells-Barnett married Ferdinand L. Barnett and they became the parents of four children. Domesticity did not detract Wells-Barnett from her crusade. Her militant views and support of Marcus Garvey caused her to be branded a radical by the U.S. Secret Service. Wells-Barnett continued to write articles and participate in local and national affairs. In 1898, she and others met with President William McKinley to seek redress for the lynching of an African American postmaster in South Carolina. They also urged passage of a federal anti-lynching bill.

Wells-Barnett was one of two African American women who signed the "Call" for a conference on the Negro. Convening on May 31, 1909, the conference led to the formation of the National Association for the Advancement of Colored People (NAACP).

A champion of women's rights, Wells-Barnett was one of the founders of the National Association of Colored Women. Believing in the power of the ballot box, she founded the Alpha Suffrage Club of Chicago. As a delegate to the National American Woman Suffrage Association's parade in Washington, DC, Wells-Barnett refused to march in the back of the procession. She desegregated the parade by joining the Illinois delegation. Wells-Barnett actively campaigned for Oscar DePriest, the first African American elected as an alderman in Chicago. In 1930, she made an unsuccessful bid for an Illinois State Senate seat.

With a passion for justice, Ida B. Wells-Barnett fought for civil and human rights. One of the most important persons of the late nineteenth and early twentieth centuries, she actively participated in the struggle from the 1890s until her death on March 25, 1931.

◆ FEDERAL AND STATE CIVIL RIGHTS AGENCIES

Equal Employment Opportunity Commission
1801 L St., NW
Washington, DC 20507
(202)663-4900

United States Commission on Civil Rights
624 Ninth St., NW
Washington, DC 20425
(800)552-6843

Alabama Attorney General's Office
State House
Montgomery, AL 36130
(334)242-5748

Alaska Human Rights Commission
800 A St., Ste. 202
Anchorage, AK 99501-3669
(907)276-7474

Arizona Attorney General's Office
1275 W. Washington St.
Phoenix, AZ 85007
(602)542-5025

Arkansas Attorney General's Office
200 Catlett-Prien Tower
323 Center St.
Little Rock, AR 72201-2610
(501)682-2007

California Attorney General
1300 I St., Ste. 1101
PO Box 944255
Sacramento, CA
(916)445-9555

California Fair Employment and Housing Commission
1390 Market St., Ste. 410
San Francisco, CA 94102-5377
(415)557-0855

Colorado Attorney General's Office
1525 Sherman St., 5th Fl.
Denver, CO 80203
(303)866-3617

Connecticut Attorney General's Office
55 Elm St.
Hartford, CT 06106
(806)808-5318

Delaware Attorney General's Office
Carvel State Office Bldg.
820 N. French St.
Wilmington, DE 19801
(302)577-2610

Florida Attorney General's Office (Legal Affairs Dept.)
The Capitol
Tallahassee, FL 32399-1050
(850)414-3300

Georgia Equal Opportunity Commission
710 International Tower, Peachtree Ctr.
229 Peachtree St. NE
Atlanta, GA 30303-1650
(404)656-1736

Hawaii Attorney General's Office
425 Queen St.
Honolulu, HI 96813
(808)586-1500

Idaho Human Rights Commission
Owyhee Plaza, Ste. 400
1109 Main St.
Boise, ID 83720-0040
(208)334-2873

Illinois Human Rights Department
100 W. Randolph St.
Ste. 10-100
Chicago, IL 60601
(312)814-6200

Indiana Civil Rights Commission
Indiana Government Ctr. North
100 N. Senate Ave., Rm. N-103
Indianapolis, IN 46204
(317)232-2600

Iowa Human Rights Department
Lucas State Office Bldg.
Des Moines, IA 50319
(515)281-7300

Kansas Human Rights Commission
851S Landon State Office Bldg.
900 SW Jackson St.
Topeka, KS 66612-1252
(785)296-3206

Kentucky Human Rights Commission
Heyburn Bldg., 7th Fl.
332 W. Broadway
Louisville, KY 40202
(502)595-4024

Louisiana Attorney General's Office
Justice Dept.
PO Box 94005
(225)342-7013

Maine Human Rights Commission
51 State House Station
Augusta, ME 04333-0051
(207)624-6050

Maryland Human Relations Commission
William Donald Schaefer Tower
Sixth St. Paul St., 9th Fl.
Baltimore, MD 21202-1631
(410)767-8600

Massachusetts Attorney General's Office
One Ashburton Pl., Rm. 2010
Boston, MA 02108
(617)727-2200

Michigan Attorney General's Office
Law Bldg.
PO Box 30212
Lansing, MI 48909
(517)373-1110

Michigan Civil Rights Department
Lansing Executive Office Bldg.
Victor Office Ctr., Ste 700
201 Washington Sq.
Lansing, MI 48913
(517)335-3165

Minnesota Human Rights Department
Army Corps of Engineers Centre
190 E. Fifth St., Ste. 700
St. Paul, MN 55101
(651)296-5663

Mississippi Attorney General's Office
PO Box 220
Jackson, MS 39205
(601)359-3680

Missouri Human Rights Commission
3315 W. Truman Blvd.
PO Box 1129
Jefferson City, MO 65102-1129
(573)751-3325

Montana Attorney General's Office
Justice Bldg.
215 N. Sanders
PO Box 201401
Helena, MT 59620-1404
(406)444-2026

Nebraska Equal Opportunity Commission
301 Centennial Mall South, 5th Fl.
PO Box 94934
Lincoln, NE 68509-4934
(402)471-2024

Nevada Equal Rights Commission
1515 E. Tropicana Ave., Ste. 590
Las Vegas, NV 89119-6522
(702)486-7161

New Hampshire Human Rights Commission
Two Chenell Dr.
Concord, NH 03301-5101
(603)271-2131

New Jersey Attorney General's Office
Justice Complex
PO Box 080
Trenton, NJ 08625
(609)292-4925

New Mexico Labor Department
Human Rights Division
PO Box 1928
Albuquerque, NM 87103
(505)827-5346

New York Human Rights Division
55 W. 125th St.
New York, NY 10027
(212)961-8400

North Carolina Human Relations Commission
217 W. Jones St., 4th Fl.
Raleigh, NC 27603-1336
(919)733-7996

North Dakota Attorney General's Office
State Capitol, 1st Fl.
600 E. Boulevard Ave.
Bismarck, ND 58505-0040
(701)328-2210

Ohio Civil Rights Commission
1111 E. Broad St., Ste. 301
Columbus, OH 43205-1379
(614)466-2785

Oklahoma Human Rights Commission
2101 N. Lincoln Blvd., Rm. 480
Oklahoma City, OK 73105
(405)522-3993

Oregon Attorney General's Office
Justice Department
Justice Bldg., 1162 Court St., NE
Salem, OR 97310
(503)378-4400

Pennsylvania Human Relations Commission
101 Second St., Ste. 300
Box 3145
Harrisburg, PA 17015-3145
(717)787-4410

Rhode Island Human Rights Commission
10 Abbott Park Pl.
Providence, RI 02903-3768
(401)222-2616

South Carolina Human Affairs Commission
PO Box 4490
Columbia, SC 29240
(803)737-7800

South Dakota Attorney General's Office
State Capitol
500 E. Capitol Ave.
Pierre, SD 57501-5070
(605)773-3215

Tennessee Human Rights Commission
400 Cornerstone Square Bldg.
530 Church St.
Nashville, TN 37243-0745
(615)532-3475

Texas Attorney General's Office
Price Daniel, Sr. Bldg.
PO Box 12548
Austin, TX 78711-2548
(512)463-2100

Utah Attorney General's Office
236 State Capitol
Salt Lake City, UT 84114
(801)366-0260

Vermont Attorney General's Office
Pavilion Office Bldg.
109 State St.
Montpelier, VT 05609-1001
(802)828-3171

Virginia Human Rights Council
Washington Bldg., Ste. 901
1101 Bank St.
Richmond, VA 23219
(804)371-7952

Washington Human Rights Commission
711 S. Capitol Way, Ste. 402
PO Box 42490
Olympia, WA 98504-2490
(360)753-6770

West Virginia Human Rights Commission
1321 Plaza East
Charleston, WV 25301
(304)558-2248

Wisconsin Attorney General's Office
PO Box 7857
Madison, WI 53707-7857
(608)266-1221

Wyoming Attorney General's Office
123 State Capitol
Cheyenne, WY 82002
(307)777-7841

◆ CIVIL RIGHTS STATISTICS

Hate Crimes—Number of Incidents, Offenses, Victims, and Offenders, by Bias Motivation: 1996

[The FBI collects statistics on hate crimes from 11,354 law enforcement agencies representing over 223 million inhabitants. Hate crime offenses cover incidents motivated by race, religion, sexual orientation, and ethnicity/national origin]

BIAS MOTIVATION	Incidents	Offenses	Victims	Known offenders
Total bias motivations	**8,759**	**10,706**	**11,039**	**8,935**
Race, total	5,396	6,767	6,994	6,122
Anti-White	1,106	1,384	1,445	1,783
Anti-Black	3,674	4,469	4,600	3,701
Anti-American Indian/Alaskan native	51	69	71	56
Anti-Asian/Pacific Islander	355	527	544	374
Anti-multi-racial group	210	318	334	208
Ethnicity/national origin, total	940	1,163	1,207	1,095
Anti-Hispanic	564	710	728	734
Anti-other ethnicity/national origin	376	453	479	361
Religion, total	1,401	1,500	1,535	523
Anti-Jewish	1,109	1,182	1,209	371
Anti-Catholic	35	37	38	17
Anti-Protestant	75	80	81	44
Anti-Islamic	27	33	33	16
Anti-other religious group	129	139	145	64
Anti-multi-religious group	24	27	27	11
Anti-atheism/agnosticism/etc	2	2	2	-
Sexual orientation, total	1,016	1,256	1,281	1,180
Anti-male homosexual	757	927	940	925
Anti-female homosexual	150	185	192	150
Anti-homosexual	84	94	99	93
Anti-heterosexual	15	38	38	4
Anti-bisexual	10	12	12	8
Multiple bias	6	20	22	15

- Represents zero.

Source: U.S. Federal Bureau of Investigation, <http://WWW.fbi.GOV/ucr/hateinfo.htm>.

⑧

Black Nationalism

◆ The Ideology of Black Nationalism ◆ Early Black Nationalism in the United States
◆ Black Nationalism in the Twentieth Century ◆ Black Nationalists and Pan–African Theorists
by Raymond A. Winbush

◆ THE IDEOLOGY OF BLACK NATIONALISM

Black nationalism is the ideology of creating a nation-state for Africans living in the *Maafa* (A Kiswahili term used to describe the continued suffering of Africans throughout the world). Black nationalism is expressed orally and in writing with its core philosophy being the cultural and political return of African people to a place that would allow for complete self-determination in all aspects of their lives. The earliest protests against American slavery had black nationalistic overtones as evidenced by written narratives that emerged during the last half of the eighteenth century. The nineteenth century would see attempts to establish self-governing homelands for Africans in the *Maafa* that continue today in the United States and Africa. At the core of all black nationalistic philosophy is resistance to either cultural or political assimilation into western culture. The expression of this resistance was seen in revolts of Africans during the Middle Passage within certain countries where displaced Africans resided.

African nationalism is distinguished from Pan-Africanism with the former describing political ideology focusing on Africa, and the latter describing its expression by Africans throughout the *Maafa*. Kwame Nkrumah, Julius Nyerere, and Jomo Kenyatta advocated an "Africa for Africans" when they rebelled against colonialism during the twentieth century. Their ideological ancestors were Paul Cuffe, Martin Delany, Alexander Crummell, and other Pan-Africanists who linked black freedom with Africa.

Since their forced removal from Africa, Africans in the *Maafa* created political and cultural representations of their yearning to return. These creations were often

mythological as in the folklore of captured Africans who felt that they could literally fly back to Africa. Beginning with the horrors of the Middle Passage, Africans created a folklore that emphasized joining forces with their ancestors to defeat their European captors. The oft-repeated but mistaken notion that most of the Africans who jumped from the ships during the Middle Passage were committing suicide ignores the fact that emerging from the folk traditions of many of the captives was the belief that they would reunite with their drowned ancestors and revolt against their enslavers. Similar resistance was seen in the members of the Igbo tribe, who upon being removed from the hull of a slave ship bringing them to the Georgia Sea Islands in 1803 marched slowly but deliberately into the cold Atlantic Ocean and drowned themselves rather than undergo the humiliation of slavery. The resistance aspect of black nationalism is often disconnected from the history of black nationalism but it is fundamental in understanding how Africans responded to slavery and its aftermath. It explains how the Underground Railroad was a sophisticated resistance movement created by blacks to obtain their freedom, and that while whites participated at several levels, the movement was led by the notion of black self-determination—the cornerstone of black nationalism.

Nationalistic revolts on slave ships frequently took place and reached their zenith in 1839 with the *Amistad* incident. Sengbe Pieh (renamed Joseph Cinque by his captors), a Mende farmer from Sierra Leone, mutinied aboard the Spanish ship *Amistad* and told its captain to return the ship and its human cargo back to Africa. The incident, which garnered international attention, illustrated how black nationalism is more than a political ideology. It is a philosophy centered on resistance and self-determination. It is rooted in the desire for liberation and is reflected in movements as diverse as the Universal Negro Improvement Association of Marcus Garvey, the notion of a unified Africa in the writings of George Padmore, and the Haitian revolution in 1789 led by Touissant L'Ouverture. In Europe, black nationalist thought appeared in the writings of several Africans captured during the Middle Passage. In British African Olaudah Equiano's best-selling book of 1789, *The Interesting Narrative of the Life of Olaudah Equiano, or Gustavus Vassa, the African. Written by Himself,* Equiano saw the return of Africans to Africa as critical to their future.

◆ EARLY BLACK NATIONALISM IN THE UNITED STATES

Most historians consider Paul Cuffe the father of black nationalism in the United States. One of the wealthiest men in the American colonies, Cuffe believed that "commerce furnished to industry more ample rewards than agriculture" and turned to shipbuilding as an expression of his belief. Cuffe acquired enormous wealth after the American Revolutionary War. The crews on his ships were always black, demonstrating Cuffe's belief that the best proof of black excellence was to show that they could manage, work exclusively with one another, and turn out quality products. In 1780 at the age of 21, he and his brother refused to pay taxes since blacks and Native Americans were excluded from voting in Massachusetts.

After his first voyage to Africa in 1811, Cuffe became convinced that economic and cultural exchange was possible between the Africans there and in America. James Forten, Absalom Jones, and Richard Allen supported Cuffe's idea of providing African American workers to Sierra Leone to aid in the resettling of African Americans in Africa. Cuffe would increasingly support these efforts with his generous gifts to the American Colonization Society (ACS), a group dominated by whites who wanted free blacks returned to Africa. Several persons criticized Cuffe and accused him of being used by the ACS. This would be the first time black nationalists would confer with white supremacists in support of their philosophy of separatism. Marcus Garvey, over a century later, would receive similar criticism from W. E. B. Du Bois after meeting secretly with the Ku Klux Klan to solicit their aid in financing a resettlement movement.

In the 1791 Haitian revolt, L'Ouverture used Boukman, a Jamaican, as his secretary because L'Ouverture knew of rebellious efforts in Jamaica. Discussion among enslaved Africans throughout the *Maafa* about insurrections were numerous and were influenced by persons

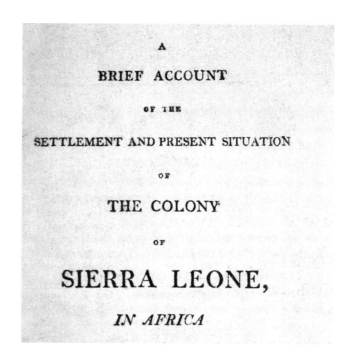

A
BRIEF ACCOUNT
OF THE
SETTLEMENT AND PRESENT SITUATION
OF
THE COLONY
OF
SIERRA LEONE,
IN AFRICA

This pamphlet dictated by Paul Cuffe described his visit to Sierra Leone from 1811–1812 (The Library of Congress).

such as Gabriel Prosser of Virginia. In 1800, he organized six hundred people and nearly consummated what historians believe would have been a successful takeover of the entire state of Virginia by enslaved Africans. Only a last minute thunderstorm and betrayal by nervous conspirators sabotaged the rebellion. Denmark Vesey, though freed in 1800, would later organize nine thousand people in 1822 to lead another nearly successful rebellion. Vesey saw both Prosser and L'Ouverture as inspiration for his quest to free enslaved people in South Carolina.

Maria Stewart of Boston, the first African American woman to record her speeches, spoke about slave rebellions and always referred to herself as an "African." She opposed the white-controlled American Colonization Society—a group that sought to repatriate free African Americans to Liberia—and helped to establish Boston as the seat of early black nationalism. Born in Connecticut in 1803, she remained outspoken about the need for African Americans to "build their own schools and stores." Her essays were published by the abolitionist William Lloyd Garrison. Her book *Meditations from the Pen of Mrs. Maria Stewart* was published in 1879 and outlines her feelings about being an African in America.

The nineteenth century spawned other black nationalists who were vocal in their denunciation of slavery and their advocacy of an African homeland. In 1829, David Walker published *Walker's Appeal in Four Articles: Together with a Preamble, to the Coloured Citi-*

*zens of the World, but in Particular, and Very Express-
ly, to Those of the United States of America.* Widely
known as *Walker's Appeal*, it said that "it is no more
harm for you to kill the man who is trying to kill you than
it is for you take a drink of water." The *Appeal*, published in four articles, saw violence as self-defense in
the war against slavery. Walker felt that peaceful means
of eliminating slavery had failed and that violent retaliation was the only way to succeed. The *Appeal* was
denounced, even by William Lloyd Garrison. The Georgia State Legislature placed a $10,000 reward on Walk-
er's head if he were delivered alive and a $1000 reward if
he was delivered dead. In the South it was illegal to
distribute his missive. Walker died mysteriously nine
months after the *Appeal* was published.

Walker's appeal was well-received by Pan-Africanist
Martin Delany, the highest-ranking African American in
the Union army. His 1852 work *The Condition, Eleva-
tion, Emigration, and Destiny of the Colored People of
the United States* was the first book that described the
conditions of African Americans in the United States
from a black nationalist perspective. Delany was strongly in favor of African Americans voluntarily emigrating
to Africa, although he denounced the actions of the
American Colonization Society as a form of forced
emigration. In 1859, he signed a contract with the Nigerian
government that allowed cotton production by free
West Africans and the eventual repatriation of Africans
in the *Maafa*.

Delany's ally Alexander Crummell shared similar
emigrationist views. In 1861 he published *The Relations
and Duties of Free Colored Men in America to Africa*
and argued that because of white supremacist views,
blacks should be motivated to return to Africa and
support the continent's development. Crummell saw
Christianity as a vehicle for achieving that development.
It is clear that nineteenth century black nationalists
were ambivalent about the role that Christianity played
in their liberation. Crummell adopted a traditional view
of Christianity and molded it to fit his political views
toward black nationalism. Although advocating self-
help, which took the form of establishing the American
Negro Academy while he taught at Howard University,
he was highly critical of Booker T. Washington's obse-
quious nature toward whites. Crummell's Christianity
informed his 1892 book *The Greatness of Christ* which
argued for a social gospel that fused religion and works
into the liberation of Africans from slavery. In 1797,
Richard Allen and Absalom Jones founded the Free
African Society and their subsequent establishment of
the African Methodist Episcopal Church reflected the
"spiritual nationalism" advocated by nineteenth century
black nationalists showing their firm Christianity. Rem-

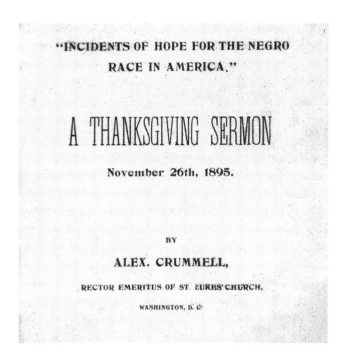

In this 1895 sermon, Reverend Alexander Crummell comments
on the struggles of African Americans to achieve full citizenship
in the United States (The Library of Congress).

nants of African religious rites were already part of this
modified Christianity in the form of music, worship, and
scriptural interpretation. They formed the basis for
what would be known in the twentieth century as Black
Theology. Henry McNeal Turner would expand the membership of Richard Allen's AME Church during the latter
half of the nineteenth century and would advocate
emigration to Haiti as he grew more disgruntled with the
treatment of African Americans after the Civil War. His
views would be echoed by Henry Highland Garnet,
who—like David Walker—called for violence in the
fight against slavery. He ended his 1843 speech in Buffalo by declaring to the persons at the National Negro
Convention:

> Let your motto be Resistance! Resistance! Resist-
> ance! No oppressed people have ever secured
> their Liberty without resistance. What kind of
> resistance you had better make, you must decide
> by the circumstances that surround you, and ac-
> cording to the suggestion of expediency. Brethren,
> adieu. Trust in the living God. Labor for the peace
> of the human race, and remember that you are
> three millions.

In the speech, Garnet cited the rebellions of Vesey,
Turner, and Cinque as examples of the type of resistance that would eventually lead to the freedom of
Africans in America. The use of violence as an alternative was a common thread through many of the writings
of early black nationalists.

The century would end with the writings of one of Pan-Africanist theorist Edward Wilmot Blyden. Born in the Virgin Islands his unwavering devotion to Africa led him to attend school in 1850 in the American Colonization Society's Liberian colony. The publication of *A Vindication of the Negro Race* was one of the earlier treatises that challenged the notion of black intellectual inferiority. Blyden became a Liberian citizen and his devout Christian beliefs resembled that of many nineteenth century black nationalists. Blyden, like Crummell and Walker, saw a love for capitalism, Christianity, and Western education as key to the liberation of Africans in the *Maafa*. The contradictions in this view became the focus of contemporary black scholars such as Wilson Jeremiah Moses and Frances Cress Welsing who saw Christianity as part of the system of white supremacy that had historically oppressed Africans in the *Maafa*.

There was an elitism about nineteenth century black nationalism that would become even more apparent during the colonial struggle against the European powers during the second half of the twentieth century. This elitism would emerge as one of the major deterrents to a "United States of Africa" as advocated by Kwame Nkrumah and Julius Nyerere.

The differences that were emerging among the various factions of Pan-Africanists during the late nineteenth century were set aside in 1884 when German Chancellor Otto von Bismarck convened a meeting in Berlin of 14 European nations regarding the partitioning of Africa. No Africans were invited, and what would become known as the "scramble for Africa" began. The conference gave the European nations the opportunity to expand their political and economic powers without resorting to military conflict in Europe or Africa. From a Pan-African viewpoint, the conference was the most destructive action toward Africa since the advent of slavery. The economic dependency that the Berlin Conference would spawn among African nations is still being felt on the continent.

◆ BLACK NATIONALISM IN THE TWENTIETH CENTURY

Six years after the partitioning summit, Henry Sylvester Williams called the first Pan-African Conference in London as a reaction to what Europeans were doing in Africa. Thirty delegates attended the meeting including a recent graduate of Fisk University named W. E. B. Du Bois who would later be dubbed the "Father of Pan-Africanism." There were discussions about bringing African persons together through better communication but what united the delegation was the anxiety over how the European powers were shaping the destiny of Africans in the *Maafa*. It was in London that Du Bois would first utter his famous phrase that the "problem of the twentieth century was the problem of the color line—the relation of the darker to the lighter races of men in Africa, in America, and the islands of the sea."

Du Bois, along with Marcus Garvey of Jamaica and George Padmore of Trinidad, would dominate the Black Nationalist movement during the first quarter of the twentieth century. Du Bois drew deeply from the influence of Crummell and Delany, but rejected their amalgam of Christianity in his Pan-Africanism. Garvey and Du Bois would clash despite the similarity of their views. The issue of skin color ran through the early writings of Du Bois, who referred to Garvey as a "fat black monkey." They were opposites in personality—Du Bois seeking links with whites and other progressives interested in the future of Africa and Garvey seeing whites as destroying black self-determination and therefore excluding their participation in the United Negro Improvement Association (UNIA). Du Bois's founding of the National Association for the Advancement of Colored People (NAACP) in 1909 was an anathema to Garvey. The First Black Parliament held in New York by Garvey in 1916, would rival in size the 1900 London Pan-African Conference and Du Bois countered these large meetings by convening the First Pan-African Conference in Paris in 1919 and several others in following years. It was clear that Du Bois's meetings were more elitist and drew from the European-educated leaders of Pan-Africanism. No amount of editorializing by Du Bois against Garvey during his editorship of *The Crisis* affected Garvey's influence over the masses of black people throughout the world. What was even more frustrating to Du Bois was the evidence of Garvey's Pan-Africanism. Ships, businesses, and newspapers flourished under his leadership, whereas Du Bois's vision of Pan-Africanism remained primarily theoretical. Even during Garvey's imprisonment, Amy Jacques Garvey ran the UNIA and Henrietta Davis directed the Black Star Line. Du Bois gloated when Garvey was convicted in 1922 by the government and deported in 1926, although their black nationalist goals were nearly identical. Garvey had been successful in mobilizing the largest mass movement ever among African Americans, but the visceral contempt that he and Du Bois had for one another hindered the realization of their dream of an Africa for Africans.

In 1909 Du Bois proposed the publication of an "Encyclopedia Africana," a Pan-African treatise that would examine the world from an African-centered point of view—an important perspective not found in European-centered encyclopedias. Lacking the funds in the United States for its completion, Du Bois would

Marcus Garvey riding in an open carriage in full military uniform. The photograph was taken by famed African American photographer James VanDerZee (Corbis Corporation [Bellevue]).

later revive the project at Nkrumah's invitation during his self-imposed exile in Ghana. However, it remained a goal that Du Bois would never see realized. Since that time though, the project has been resurrected by a publishing team in Accra, Ghana, under the title *Encyclopaedia Africana*. According to Grace Bansa, secretary of the project, three volumes have been published with the remaining volumes scheduled for completion by 2009—the one hundredth anniversary of Du Bois's initial conception of the reference work.

The 1920s would see the emergence of black nationalistic expression throughout the *Maafa*. In the United States it was called the Harlem Renaissance and was led by the poetry and writing of persons such as Claude McKay, Zora Neale Hurston, Countee Cullen, Langston Hughes, Jessie Fauset, and Alain Locke. In Africa Aime Cesaire, Leon Demas, and Leopold Senghor would create a movement known as Negritude. A reaction against colonialism in general and French colonialism specifically, the movement had inherent contradictions. While describing an "African personality" common to all black people in the world, it was heavily influenced by a love for the colonial powers and sought to merge the two together in what was really an "African-European" personality. The effects of nearly a half century of colonialism were evidenced in the psychological attachment that many Africans still had toward their European colonizers, and while Negritude reacted to the colonized mentality, many felt it did not go far enough in its denunciation of European domination and support of the nascent freedom struggles beginning in Africa.

Garvey's influence on black nationalism would last for the remainder of the twentieth century and was dynamically linked to several movements. Jamaicans were attracted to his reference to the rise of kings in Africa. In 1928, when Ras Tafari was crowned Haile Selassie I of Ethiopia, another black nationalist religion, Rastafarianism, was born. Rastafarianism would establish its roots in Jamaica but its influence would be global with musicians such as Bob Marley and Peter Tosh teaching others about the white supremacist world of "Babylon." It would emphasize pride in appearance, and the religion's "dreadlocks" hairstyle would become famous around the world.

Garvey's death in 1940 did not subdue his influence on black nationalism. Elijah Poole, a Georgia farmer who had come under the influence of Islam in 1931, began to carve out an urban religion known as the Nation of Islam that would include a mystical theology that described the white man as the "devil" and characterized African Americans as a "lost people" in a strange land. C. L. R. James would fuse Marxism with black nationalism in England and write *Black Jacobins*, a book that provided a Marxist critique of the Haitian Revolution under Touissant L'Ouverture. With Duse Mohammed Ali and Adelaide Hayford, England became the center of black nationalism in Europe. George Padmore befriended Du Bois and Nkrumah as Ghana began its struggle for independence from the United Kingdom. Padmore rejected Marxism when it took a soft approach to the colonization of Africa, and his vocal opposition to its indifference toward the third world led to his break from the philosophy. His criticism of the Communist Party eventually led to his ouster in 1934 and he spent his final years in England and Ghana.

World War II forced the end of the colonial system. The colonized nations of Africa with their allies in the United States and Great Britain took notice of this and called for a Fifth Pan-African Congress in 1945. This Manchester, England, conference included T. R. Makonnen of Ethiopia, George Padmore of Trinidad, Kwame Nkrumah of Ghana, Jomo Kenyatta of Kenya, and chairman Peter Millard of British Guiana. Its honor-

ary chair was W. E. B. Du Bois. Padmore advised the politically-minded Nkrumah to return to the Gold Coast and become involved with the rapidly evolving anti-colonial waves sweeping the country. Nkrumah's subsequent rise to power in Ghana was heavily influenced by the ideas of Padmore.

Nkrumah made several attempts at uniting Africa's newly independent nations. The Gold Coast attended and was inspired by the final declaration of the 1955 Bandung Conference, where 24 nations called for increased economic, political, and educational cooperation among their countries. The conference also featured a forceful condemnation. In 1958, just one year after becoming Prime Minister of Ghana, Nkrumah called for the first Conference of Independent African States. The eight states in attendance included members above and below the Sahara and discussed the challenges ahead of them as independent states. That same year, Guinea became independent of France under the leadership of Sekou Toure and rejected France's offer to become part of what was referred to as "The New French Community." France's anger led it to order its colonial bureaucrats home, which caused the collapse of the infrastructure of the country. Toure turned to several nations to aid the newly freed Guinea. Nkrumah answered Toure's call and formed a union between the two nations outlined in the Conakry Declaration of 1959. The Central Intelligence Agency added to the chaos of independence by participating in the destabilization of the Congo and the assassination of Patrice Lumumba in 1964. Nkrumah was ousted from Ghana in a coup in 1966.

In the United States, black nationalism took a back seat to integration when the nation began a long period of national introspection over treatment of its African American citizens after the *Brown v. Board of Education* decision in 1954, declared segregated schools unconstitutional. Rosa Parks and Martin Luther King, Jr. became household names as the struggle for liberation in the form of desegregation engulfed the nation. The most significant group espousing black nationalism during this time was the Nation of Islam. Elijah Poole had become Elijah Muhammad and was slowly building a religious group that rejected Christianity as a tool of the white man and encouraged its followers to change their last name to "X."

Before his release from prison in 1952, Malcolm Little discovered the urban prophet's writings and was converted to Islam. The legacy of Marcus Garvey was influential in Malcolm since his father had been an active member of the UNIA in Michigan. Despite his career as a criminal, Malcolm was transformed by the ideology in the teachings of those who told black people in the *Maafa* to look inward for self-determination. Malcolm's attraction to the Nation of Islam and his outspoken critique of white America soon became the subject of newspaper articles and television documentaries. The religion flourished with the attention toward civil rights and through Malcolm's fiery oratory. Television aided the personalization of the Civil Rights movement, and Malcolm provided a counterpoint to Martin Luther King, Jr.'s racial inclusiveness in a way similar to that of Du Bois, who had castigated Booker T. Washington. Malcolm's speech, made shortly after the 1963 March on Washington, criticized the entire civil rights establishment and his story of the "Field Negro" and the "House Negro" captured the black nationalist philosophy of separation. His break with the Nation of Islam and his trips to Africa led him to increase his Pan-African views. He was assassinated in 1965 before these views could be fully articulated in a theory of Pan-Africanism. After the death of Elijah Muhammad in 1975, the Nation of Islam would struggle with internal division but would be revitalized by Louis Farrakhan. His Million Man March in 1995 attracted global attention.

The political assassinations of the 1960s brought a renewed interest in black nationalism due to the cynicism that African Americans felt toward the Civil Rights movement. Stokely Carmichael, H. "Rap" Brown, and others forced integrationists to deal with the issue of black pride and self-determination. The Black Pride movement begun by Malcolm X and exemplified in South Africa by Steven Biko led to the Black Arts movement of the 1960s that saw the most creative expression of black artists since the Harlem Renaissance. Nikki Giovanni, Don Lee, and Gwendolyn Brooks wrote poetry that was uncompromising in its call for black introspection into white supremacy. Plays, books, films, and festivals, celebrated the African roots of the black struggle and created meetings that discussed black self-determination. Maulana Karenga would introduce *Kwanzaa*, an African American holiday that would be celebrated by many African Americans by the end of the century.

A 1972 meeting in Gary, Indiana, established a black political agenda similar to the Negro conventions of the nineteenth century. There were tensions that had always existed between those who wanted a Marxist approach to political empowerment and those who wanted nothing to do with any white philosophy. There had always been a close relationship between blacks and Marxists dating back to the early 1920s. Du Bois, Padmore, Randolph, Baraka, and others had believed that a coalition of labor, progressive whites, and committed blacks could eliminate racial injustice. The most organized though short-lived movement of Black Marx-

ism was the Black Panther Party of the 1960s. Though it is popular to portray it as being all black, the BPP allowed for white membership from its very beginning. Haki Madhubuti, offering a stinging rebuke of Marxism as a viable alternative to black suffering, argued:

Our major problem is not with the white communists, but with their trained Black ones who are trying to co-op Black nationalism and Pan Afrikanism [*sic*] to make these ideologies and movements something they ain't. There in our midst the subtle presence of 'Black Marxists' pushing a European socialist analysis of Black nationalism and Pan Afrikanism [*sic*]. The Marxist position is that white racism—which to us is the only functional system of racism in the world—is a result of the profit motive brought on by the European slave trade and that white racism or anti-Black feelings didn't exist before such time. The left (generally described as Marxist-Leninist) whether white or black has always been anti-Black nationalism and this can be documented. Yet, one of the major facts of history is that white racism preceded and advanced itself thousands of years before European capitalism and imperialism was [*sic*] even systematically conceived. It is important to understand that the ideology of white supremacy precedes the economic structure of capitalism and imperialism, the latter of which are falsely state as the cause of racism.

The conflict between black nationalists and Marxists continues with the formation of the Black Radical Congress which convened in its first annual meeting in June 1998. Formed immediately after the Million Man March, part of its aim is to regain its influence over young black people who are perceived as deserting Marxism with the rise of Afrocentric analysis espoused by John Henrik Clarke, Molefi Asante, Marimba Ani, and Theophile Obenga. The BRC held its first meeting in Chicago and pointedly denounced Louis Farrakhan as being sexist, homophobic, and exclusionary. Attendees included socialists such as Angela Davis, Amiri Baraka, Manning Marable, Cornel West, and Barbara Smith. It was noted by many in attendance that "exclusionary ideologues," such as the Afrocentrists and Nation of Islam, were absent as main program participants. Black nationalists argue that the absence of "spirituality" in Marxist ideology is inimical to religious expression—an ever-present factor in most black nationalist ideology. Most black nationalists see spirituality as necessary in a world replete with white supremacy and struggle with a religious expression that will fit their aims. The rise of "urban religions" among young African Americans, such as Ausar Auset, the Five Percent Nation, and the Nation

Malcolm X addressing a Harlem, New York rally (Corbis Corporation [Bellevue]).

of Islam, reflect the need of a younger generation to embrace faiths that speak to their condition. Contemporary hip hop artists openly mention Louis Farrakhan and the "Mother" (Africa) in their lyrics. Their rhymes reflect the black nationalist tradition of making all things black including religion, viewed by many Marxists as unnecessary.

◆ BLACK NATIONALISTS AND PAN-AFRICAN THEORISTS

(To locate biographical profiles more readily, please consult the index at the back of the book.)

Edward Wilmot Blyden (1832–1912)
Black Nationalist, Repatriationist

Although he was not American, Edward Blyden had a great influence on American Pan-African philosophy. He wrote about blacks in Africa and America and about Christianity and Islam. Later, he held many different political and diplomatic offices in Liberia.

Blyden was born in 1832 in St. Thomas, Virgin Islands. When he was twelve, a white pastor undertook

his education and encouraged him to become a minister. When he was 18 he went to the United States, but was unable to find a seminary that would accept a black student. Instead, under the sponsorship of the New York Colonization Society, he went to Liberia to study at the new Alexander High School in Monrovia. Seven years later, he became the principal of the school.

As a writer and editor, he constantly defended his race, championed the achievements of other blacks, attacked slavery, and advocated the repatriation of blacks in Africa. As a teacher, he held many prominent posts at Liberia College. He was a professor of classics from 1862 to 1871 and the school's president from 1880 to 1884. At the same time, Blyden was also a politician and diplomat in Liberia, holding many different offices. He was Secretary of State from 1864 to 1866, Minister of the Interior from 1880 to 1882, Minister to Britain from 1877 to 1878 and in 1892, and Minister Plenipotentiary to London and Paris in 1905.

Blyden traveled to the United States eight times. In 1861, he was commissioned by the Liberian government to interest Americans in a Liberian education. He returned the following year to recruit African American immigrants to Africa. His last visit in 1895 was in hope of furthering racial accommodation in the South so that racial problems in America would not travel to Africa with new emigrants.

Because of his own religious training, Blyden was interested in Islam as a religion for Africans. Between 1901 and 1906, he was director of education in Sierra Leone. He studied both Christianity and Islam extensively and summed up his views in an influential book *Christianity, Islam and the Negro Race*.

Elaine Brown (1943–)
Political Activist, Author

When Huey Newton, the founder of the Black Panther Party, fled the United States in 1974 to avoid a murder charge, he appointed Elaine Brown as his successor. In the mid-1960s, Brown became involved with the Black Congress, a group of African American organizations in the Los Angeles area that served African Americans. By 1967, Brown had become acquainted with the Black Panther Party, and in 1968, she joined the Southern California chapter.

The Black Panther program combined revolutionary rhetoric, violent actions in the name of self-defense, and a strong commitment to building and strengthening African American communities. It evolved from a black nationalist neighborhood organization under Newton's leadership. However, after his 1968 imprisonment, Eldridge Cleaver made alliances with Marxist organizations advocating a more integrationist approach to worldwide revolution. Building African American communities appealed to Brown, who saw the party as a unifying force.

By the early 1970s, much of the party leadership had been either killed or jailed in police battles. In 1974, with the expulsion of co-founder Bobby Seale, Brown became chairperson of the Black Panther Party. Later that same year, Huey Newton appointed her the Minister of Defense after he fled to Cuba to escape criminal prosecution.

Brown guided the Black Panther Party's efforts to elect an African American mayor in the city of Oakland, California. The party registered 90,000 African American Democrats and secured the endorsement of California Governor Jerry Brown for Black Panther candidate Lionel Wilson in 1976. Wilson won, becoming the first African American mayor of Oakland.

Shortly after the election, Newton was cleared of any charges and returned to Oakland. His return led to the ouster of Brown and her progressive, feminist agenda. Brown left Oakland and immigrated to France in 1977. She lives outside of Paris. In 1992, she wrote her autobiography *A Taste of Power: A Black Woman's Story*.

Edward Wilmont Blyden (The Library of Congress)

John Henrik Clarke (1915–1998)
Black Nationalist, Educator

John Henrik Clarke was born on New Year's Day, 1915, in Alabama. His family moved to Georgia when he was four and he was raised in the South. Despite an aptitude for reading, he was forced from school after the eighth grade by poverty. In 1933, he left Georgia to go to Harlem and begin a new life.

In Harlem, Clarke discovered new reading materials on African American history. He studied at New York and Columbia Universities, and found a mentor in Arthur Schomburg. After serving in the Army during World War II, he began to teach African American history at community centers in Harlem. From 1956 to 1958, he taught at the New School for Social Research in New York. He then traveled to West Africa and taught at universities in Ghana and Nigeria.

In 1964, Clarke was licensed to teach at People's College on Long Island and began a career in academia. Clarke was a leading exponent of Afrocentric scholarship and the Black Power movement. In 1969, he began teaching at Hunter College, City University of New York, and in 1970 was appointed a professor in the department of Black and Puerto Rican studies. Clarke retired in 1985.

Alexander Crummell (1819–1898)
Black Nationalist, Repatriationist, Minister

Alexander Crummell was born in New York City on March 3, 1819. Crummell began his education at the Mulberry Street School in New York City. In 1831 he began attending high school but transferred in 1835 to a school founded by abolitionists in Canaan, New Hampshire. The school was destroyed by a mob of angry townspeople and Crummell began attending the Oneida Institute in Whitesboro, New York. He later studied in Boston and was ordained into the Episcopal Church in 1844. In 1847 he went to England and studied at Queens College, Cambridge, from 1851 to 1853, and was awarded an A.B. degree.

Crummell then spent several years in Liberia as professor of mental and moral science at the College of Liberia and in Sierra Leone. In 1873 he returned to St. Mary's Mission in Washington, DC, and founded the St. Luke's Protestant Episcopal Church. In 1897 he was instrumental in the founding of the American Negro Academy.

Crummell published three collections of his essays and sermons titled *Future of Africa* (1862), *Greatness of Christ* (1882), and *Africa and America* (1892). Crummell died on September 10, 1898, at Point Pleasant, New York.

Paul Cuffe (1759–1817)
Black Nationalist, Repatriationist, Entrepreneur

Cuffe was born January 17, 1759 on Cuttyhunk Island near New Bedford, Massachusetts. He was the son of Cuffe Slocum and Ruth Moses, a Wampanoag Indian.

When Cuffe was 16 he was a sailor on a whaling vessel. After making numerous voyages, he was captured by the British and later released. He then studied arithmetic and navigation, but soon returned to the sea. In 1795 he had his own ship *Ranger* and in 11 years he had become a landholder and owner of numerous other sailing vessels. He employed only African Americans on all of his ships because he believed in creating wealth within African American communities and showing whites that blacks were competent in the business of merchant seamanship.

Besides being a merchant seaman, Cuffe was also a black nationalist activist. He discarded his father's slave surname and took his father's Christian first name in its place. He filed suffrage complaints in Massachusetts court; and, although unsuccessful, his legal action laid the groundwork for later civil rights legislation.

Cuffe was also a believer in free blacks repatriating to Africa. In 1811, he sailed to Sierra Leone where he founded the Friendly Society which helped African Americans return to Africa. In 1815, he sailed with 38 colonists for Africa. It was to be his last voyage as he died on September 9, 1817.

Martin Robinson Delany (1812–1885)
Black Nationalist, Repatriationist

Born in Charles Town, Virginia, in 1812, Martin Delany received his first education from a book peddler who also served as an itinerant teacher. Since African Americans were forbidden in the South to learn to read, his family was forced to flee north to Pennsylvania so that their children could continue to study. At the age of 19, he left home to seek further education. He then studied with a divinity student and a white doctor for a time.

As an adult, he became involved in anti-slavery reform, and the literacy movement. He began to publish *The Mystery*, a weekly newspaper devoted to news of the anti-slavery movement. When it folded after only a year of publication, Delany became co-editor of the *North Star*, a newspaper started by Frederick Douglass.

In 1848, Delany quit the *North Star* to pursue his medical studies. After being rejected because of his race by several prominent Pennsylvania medical schools, he was able to attend Harvard Medical School. However, after a year he was again expelled due to his race. While he did not receive his degree, he did learn enough to practice medicine the rest of his life. In the 1850s, he saved many lives during a fierce cholera epidemic in Pittsburgh.

Delany became an ardent black nationalist and recommended emigration to establish an independent colony for African Americans in South America or Africa. He wrote on the subject, held several national conventions, and set out on an exploratory expedition to Africa.

After the Emancipation Proclamation of 1863, Delany met with President Abraham Lincoln to discuss the establishment of African American regiments in the army. Lincoln commissioned him as the first African American major and highest ranking person of color in the United States Army.

After the Civil War, Delany worked with reconstructionists trying to get fair treatment for newly freed slaves and advocated emigration to Africa. He also continued to pursue his scholarship and published *Principal of Ethnology: The Origin of Races and Color* in 1879, in which he discussed the role of black people in the world's civilization. He died in 1885, before he was able to move to Africa.

Martin R. Delany (Archive Photos, Inc.)

Louis Farrakhan (1933–)
Black Nationalist, Nation of Islam National Minister

Born in New York City in 1933, Louis Farrakhan (then known as Louis Eugene Walcott) was an honor student at Boston English High School and then attended Winston-Salem Teacher's College. Farrakhan was a musician who played the violin and was a calypso singer. While a singer in the 1950s, Farrakhan converted to Elijah Muhammad's Nation of Islam. He quickly worked his way up to a leadership position, becoming the minister of the Boston mosque. He denounced Malcolm X after Malcolm split with Elijah Muhammad in 1963, and assumed leadership of Malcolm's Harlem mosque. After Elijah Muhammad's death in 1975, he briefly supported Muhammad's son and designated successor, Warith Muhammad, as leader of the Nation of Islam. Shortly after Warith Muhammad began accepting whites as members of the Nation of Islam, now renamed the World Community of Al-Islam in the West, Farrakhan split from the group and established a rival organization with about ten thousand members.

Farrakhan's vigorous support for Jesse Jackson's presidential candidacy in 1984 quickly became an issue after Farrakhan made several controversial statements,

most notably, calling Judaism a "gutter religion." Overshadowed in the controversy was the involvement of Nation of Islam leaders in American electoral politics for the first time. Previously, Muslims had generally followed Elijah Muhammad's counsel not to vote or to take part in political campaigns.

In January of 1995 Qubilah Bahiyah Shabazz, the daughter of Malcolm X, was arrested and charged with trying to hire FBI informant, Michael Fitzpatrick, to kill Farrakhan whom some believe was involved in the 1965 assassination of her father. Farrakhan publicly defended Shabazz and claimed that the charges were an FBI attempt to entrap her.

On October 16, 1995, African American men from across the United States convened in Washington, DC, for the Million Man March. The march was organized by Farrakhan. Marchers were urged to make a commitment to improve themselves, their families, and their communities. The U.S. Park Service and organizers of the march have conflicted as to how many people actually attended the rally in which Farrakhan challenged the marchers to return home and work to make their communities "safe and decent places to live."

Farrakhan embarked on an 18-nation tour of Africa and the Middle East in early 1996. During the tour, he visited Iran and Libya, nations that the United States believes support international terrorism. Farrakhan, always a lightning rod for criticism, was attacked for the trip.

In 1999, Farrakhan became gravely ill with prostate cancer and sought medical treatment in Phoenix, Arizona.

James Forten (1766–1842)
Black Nationalist, Entrepreneur

Forten was born to free African American parents in Philadelphia in September of 1766. He studied at a Quaker school but at the age of 15 quit to serve as a powder boy aboard the privateer *Royal Louis* during the American Revolution. He was captured by the British and held prisoner for seven months. He eventually spent a year in England where he was introduced to abolitionist philosophy.

Upon his return to America he apprenticed to a sailmaker. In 1786, he became foreman and by 1798 was owner of the company. The business prospered and in 1832 employed forty workers.

By the 1830s, Forten had become active in the abolitionist movement and was a strong opponent of African colonization. He became a noted pamphleteer, a nineteenth century form of social activism and was an early fund-raiser for William Lloyd Garrison's *The Liberator*.

Louis Farrakhan delivering his speech at the 1995 Million Man March (Archive Photos, Inc.)

Forten was president and founder of the American Moral Reform Society and was active in the American Anti-Slavery Society. He was a vigorous opponent of northern implementation of the Fugitive Slave Act of 1793. Forten died in Philadelphia on March 4, 1842.

Henry Highland Garnet (1815–1882)
Black Nationalist, Religious Leader

Henry Highland Garnet was born a slave in Maryland on December 23, 1815. His family escaped to Pennsylvania and then arrived in New York. In 1826, Garnet attended the African Free School and was first exposed to abolitionism. In 1829, he made several voyages on schooners, working as a steward. When he returned he found his family was in hiding from slave catchers and all their possessions had been taken.

In 1835, Garnet and his friend Alexander Crummell attended the Noyes Academy in Canaan, New Hampshire, until hostile residents destroyed the school. They then attended the Oneida Institute in Whitesboro, New York. Garnet graduated with honors in 1840 from Oneida.

Garnet worked as a Presbyterian minister and abolitionist after his graduation. He also was active in the temperance movement. He became dissatisfied with the moral suasion abolitionists used and urged direct action by slaves against the institution of slavery. He also became active in the American Colonization Society.

Garnet supported the employment of African American soldiers by the Union during the U.S. Civil War, and in 1865, became the first African American to deliver a sermon in the chamber of the House of Representatives in the U.S. Capital. In 1881, he was appointed minister to Liberia. He died there the following year.

Marcus Garvey (1887–1940)
Black Nationalist, Pan-African Theorist

Marcus Garvey was born in St. Ann's Bay, Jamaica, on August 17, 1887. Garvey moved to Kingston at the age of 14, found work in a printshop, and became acquainted with the living conditions of the laboring class. He quickly involved himself in social reform, participating in the first Printers's Union strike in Jamaica in 1907 and in setting up the newspaper *The Watchman*. He left Jamaica to earn money and found similar living conditions for blacks in Central and South America.

Garvey returned to Jamaica in 1911 and began to lay the groundwork of the Universal Negro Improvement

Association. Garvey left for England in 1912 to find additional financial backing. While there, he met a Sudanese-Egyptian journalist, Duse Mohammed Ali. While working for Ali's publication *African Times and Oriental Review*, Garvey began to study the history of Africa particularly. He read Booker T. Washington's *Up From Slavery*, which advocated black self-help.

In 1914 Garvey organized the Universal Negro Improvement Association and its coordinating body, the African Communities League. In 1920, the organization held its first convention in New York. The convention opened with a parade down Harlem's Lenox Avenue. That evening, before a crowd of 25,000, Garvey outlined his plan to build an African nation-state. In New York City, his ideas attracted support, and thousands enrolled in the UNIA. He began publishing the newspaper *The Negro World* and toured the United States preaching black nationalism. In a matter of months, he had founded over thirty UNIA branches and launched various business ventures including the Black Star Shipping Line.

In the years following the organization's first convention, the UNIA began to decline in popularity. With the Black Star Line in serious financial difficulties, Garvey promoted two new business organizations, the African Communities League and the Negro Factories Corporation. He also tried to salvage his colonization scheme by sending a delegation to appeal to the League of Nations to transfer the African colonies taken from Germany during World War I to the UNIA.

Mail fraud charges led to Garvey's imprisonment in the Atlanta Federal Penitentiary for a five-year term. In 1927, his sentence was commuted and he was deported to Jamaica by order of President Calvin Coolidge. Garvey then became involved in Jamaican politics. However, defeats in elections ended his career and he died in 1940 in England.

Charshee McIntyre (1942–1999)
Educator, Black Nationalist

Charshee McIntyre was born in Andover, Massachusetts, on May 14, 1942, and was raised in Roxbury, Massachusetts. She married jazz instrumentalist Makenda Ken McIntyre and helped George Wein, founder of the Newport Jazz Festival, to bring key jazz figures to the event. In her early thirties, she entered Central State University in Ohio to pursue her education. She transferred to Wesleyan University in Connecticut, majored in African history, and was inducted into Phi Beta Kappa after graduating summa cum laude in 1971. She earned a M.A. in philosophy, a M.A. in African history and a Ph.D. in history from the State University of New York at Stony Brook. She taught at various universities in New York including SUNY Old Westbury, Rutgers, and City College.

McIntyre was the first woman president of the African Heritage Studies Association. She also was active in the National Council for Black Studies and the Association for the Study of Classical African Civilizations (whose membership included John Henrik Clarke), First World, and the African American Heritage of Long Island.

In 1994, McIntyre published her work on the impact of African, Native American, and European worldviews on people of African descent. She believed that the struggle of Africans in the *Maafa* was primarily based on the ancient and sacred relationship between African men and women—a critical bond that had been severely damaged during the period of slavery and its aftermath. Her belief in the male-female bond in Africa influenced many black nationalists to reconsider and in most cases abandon their belief in the primacy of males at the expense of women. When the 1999 African-African American conference convened in Ghana in May, 1999, it paused when the news of her death reach the delegates.

Audley Moore (1898–1997)
Black Nationalist, Pan-African Theorist

Audley Moore was born in New Iberia, Louisiana, on July 27, 1898. Her parents were both dead by the time she was 14, and she became the primary support for her two sisters. She worked as a nurse during World War I, and after moving to Anniston, Alabama, organized the first USO for African American soldiers who had been denied entrance by the official USO organization. She also assisted them in receiving medical care and food.

Moving with her sisters and husband to New York City in the 1920s, she became an active member of the Communist Party and help organize support for the 1932 Scottsboro Boys case in Alabama. She was considered the best African American community organizer in the country and helped local groups protest racist policies in housing discrimination, political prosecutions, and unfair employment practices. She created the model for organizing legal redress for political prisoners in the United States.

She became increasingly disenchanted with the Communist Party and resigned her membership in the 1950s. Her roots in Marcus Garvey's teachings could be heard in speeches that encouraged "denegroization" and a demand for reparations for Africans living in the *Maafa*. During the last twenty years of her life she traveled internationally and continued to exhort others to pay attention to the "little people" that needed help against racism in the community. She traveled to Ghana where she was officially installed in an Ashanti ceremony as a "Queen Mother." Nelson Mandela met with her during his visit to New York in 1990. She, Rosa Parks, and Dorothy Height were featured prominently by Louis Farrakhan at the Million Man March.

Many believe that Queen Mother Moore, Marcus Garvey, and Elijah Muhammad are the greatest organizers of black nationalism of the twentieth century. She died on May 2, 1997.

Elijah Muhammad (1897–1975)
Black Nationalist, Nation of Islam Spiritual Leader

Elijah Muhammad was born Elijah Poole in Sandersville, Georgia, on October 10, 1897. His father, was a Baptist preacher and former slave. As a boy, Elijah worked as a manual laborer. At the age of 26, he moved with his wife and two children to Detroit. In 1930, he met Fard Muhammad, also known as W. D. Fard, who had founded the Lost-Found Nation of Islam. Poole soon became Fard's chief assistant and in 1932 went to Chicago where he established the Nation of Islam's Temple, Number Two. In 1934, he returned to Detroit. When Fard disappeared later that year, political and theological rivals accused Poole of foul play. He returned to Chicago where he organized his own movement's followers. In the resultant organization, which came to be known as the "Black Muslims," Fard was deified as Allah, and Elijah (Poole) Muhammad became known as Allah's Messenger.

During World War II, Elijah Muhammad expressed support for Japan, on the basis of its being a non-white country, and was jailed for sedition. The time Muhammad served in prison was significant in his later, successful attempts to convert large numbers of black prison inmates, including Malcolm X, to the Nation of Islam. During the 1950s and 1960s, the Nation grew under Muhammad's leadership. Internal differences between Muhammad and Malcolm X, followed by the break between the two men and Malcolm's assassination, provided a great deal of unfavorable media coverage that did not slow the growth of the movement. In the late 1960s and early 1970s, Elijah Muhammad moderated the Nation's criticism of whites. When Muhammad died on February 25, 1975, the Nation was an important religious, political, and economic force among African Americans, especially in this country's major cities.

Elijah Muhammad was not original in his rejection of Christianity as the religion of the oppressor. Noble Drew Ali and the black Jews had arrived at this conclusion well before him. However, Muhammad was the most successful salesman for this brand of African American religion. He was able to build the first strong, African American religious group in the United States that appealed primarily to the unemployed and under-employed city dweller. In addition, his message on the virtues of being black was explicit and uncompromising. He also sought to bolster the economic independence of African Americans by establishing schools and businesses under the auspices of the Nation of Islam.

Khallid Abdul Muhammad (1948?–)
Black Nationalist Nation of Islam Lecturer

Muhammad was born Harold Moore, Jr. in January of 1948 in Houston, Texas. He excelled in academics and athletics as a youth and graduated from high school in 1966. He spent then four years at Dillard University, where his attendance at a speech given by Nation of Islam figure Louis Farrakhan in 1967 changed his life. He became one of Farrakhan's original security personnel and soon changed his name to Khallid Abdul Muhammad.

After the death of longtime Nation of Islam leader Elijah Muhammad, Khallid Muhammad relocated to Uganda to work with black nationalist leader Idi Amin. He returned to the United States upon learning that Farrakhan was reviving the Nation of Islam, and by the late 1970s was a minister of the group's Los Angeles mosque. Farrakhan depended heavily on Muhammad to resurrect the Nation of Islam after the death of Elijah Muhammad in 1975. Beginning in 1978, he and Farrakhan traveled by car throughout the United States establishing study groups and making speeches that eventually led in 1981 to Farrakhan announcing the rebirth of the Nation. Muhammad led the Nation's fund-raising, spoke on Farrakhan's behalf, and organized mosques that had deteriorated since the death of Elijah Muhammad. He later headed congregations in New York City and Atlanta. He continued to play a role in the Fruit of Islam, the security team assigned to protect the outspoken Farrakhan. In 1988 Muhammad was charged with the fraudulent use of a Social Security number to obtain a mortgage and spent nine months in prison.

After his release, Muhammad became supreme captain of the Fruits of Islam and in 1991 became Farrakhan's national assistant, a position once held by Farrakhan and Malcolm X. Muhammad's speeches soon attracted renewed interest in the Nation of Islam, especially from among prominent figures in rap music. His discourses often promote an independent nation for people of African descent. A 1993 oration in Union, New Jersey, that invoked fiery pronouncements on black-white relations and anti-Semitic remarks caused controversy. Muhammad was soon demoted by Farrakhan, but continues his work as a lecturer and activist.

He organized the Million Youth March in New York in October of 1998. Muhammad continues to be popular on

Khallid Abdul Muhammad (AP/Wide World Photos, Inc.)

the lecture circuit and maintains ties with the Nation despite his demotion by Farrakhan.

Henry McNeal Turner (1834–1915)
Black Nationalist, Repatriationist, Minister

Henry McNeal Turner was born on February 1, 1834, near Abbeville, South Carolina. He was ordained a minister in the African Methodist Episcopal Church in 1853 and as a bishop in 1880. In 1863 Turner became the first African American Army chaplain. He was also president of Morris Brown College for 12 years.

Turner was a leading advocate of repatriation. In 1876 he was elected vice president of the American Colonization Society. He made several trips to Africa and lectured throughout world. Turner was convinced that African Americans had no future in America. Instead, he felt that God had brought African Americans to the New World as a means of spreading Christianity and preparing them to redeem Africa. Turner edited and published several papers including *Voice of Missions* and *Voice of the People*, in which he advocated African American repatriation to Africa. Turner died on May 8, 1915.

Henry McNeal Turner

Robert F. Williams (1925–)
Civil Rights Activist

Robert Williams was born in Monroe, North Carolina. In 1956, he was elected president of the Monroe NAACP. The organization's membership had dwindled to six. Williams went out and recruited working class people and the unemployed to become members, as opposed to the NAACP's practice of appealing to middle and upper-class professionals.

Williams then targeted institutions in Monroe for desegregation. He tried the county library. It was desegregated without protest. Williams then tried to desegregate Monroe's municipal swimming pool, which failed. In response, Williams led groups of African American youths on sit-ins and other organized protests.

In 1959, responding to the acquittal in Monroe of a white man for the attempted rape of a pregnant African American woman, Williams pronounced: "Since the federal government will not bring a halt to lynching in the South, and since the so-called courts lynch our people legally, if it's necessary to stop lynching with lynching, then we must be willing to resort to that method. We must meet violence with violence." The next day the national office of the NAACP suspended Williams from office for six months. Later in 1959, he was indicted for kidnapping. He became a fugitive and fled to Cuba.

He was reelected president of Monroe's NAACP chapter in 1960. From Cuba, Williams produced a revolutionary radio program "Radio Free Dixie" and produced a

Malcolm X (center) attending a Nation of Islam convention (Archive Photos, Inc.).

Cuba edition of the *Crusader*. In 1966, Williams sought refuge in the People's Republic of China. In 1968, Williams published a pamphlet "Listen Brother!," hoping to dissuade African American servicemen to stop fighting in Vietnam.

In 1968, a group of African Americans, dedicated to establishing a separate African American nation within the United States, formed the revolutionary Marxist-Leninist Republic of New Africa. The RNA elected Williams as its president-in-exile. In 1969, the U.S. embassy granted Williams a passport to return to the United States. Disillusioned with the RNA's internal struggles, he resigned as its president in December of 1969.

Williams was awarded by a Michigan branch of the NAACP the chapter's Black Image Award. He battled Hodgkin's disease and wrote his autobiography *While God Lay Sleeping: The Autobiography of Robert F. Williams*. He died in 1996.

Malcolm X (El-Hajj Malik El-Shabazz) (1925–1965)
Black Nationalist

Born Malcolm Little in Omaha, Nebraska, on May 19, 1925, Malcolm was the son of a Baptist minister, who was a supporter of Marcus Garvey's Universal Negro Improvement Association. In 1929, the family moved to Lansing, Michigan. While in Michigan, Malcolm's father was killed. In his autobiography, written with Alex Haley, Malcolm asserted that his father might have been killed by members of the Ku Klux Klan. His mother, stricken by the death of her husband and the demands of providing for the family, was committed to a mental institution.

Malcolm left school after the eighth grade and made his way to New York. He worked as a waiter at Smalls Paradise in Harlem. Malcolm began selling and using drugs. He then turned to burglary and was sentenced to a ten-year prison term on burglary charges in 1946.

While in prison Malcolm converted to the Nation of Islam, headed by Elijah Muhammad. Following his parole in 1952, he soon became an outspoken defender of Muslim doctrines, accepting the basic argument that evil was an inherent characteristic of the "white man's Christian world."

Unlike Muhammad, Malcolm sought publicity by making provocative statements on white supremacy to both black and white audiences. Based on the theology taught by Elijah Muhammad, he branded white people "devils," and spoke of a philosophy of self-defense and "an eye for an eye" when white supremacists attacked African Americans. When, in 1963, he characterized the Kennedy assassination as a case of "chickens coming home to roost," he was suspended from the Nation of Islam by Elijah Muhammad.

Disillusioned with Elijah Muhammad's teachings, Malcolm formed his own organizations, the Organization of Afro-American Unity and the Muslim Mosque Inc. In 1964 he made a pilgrimage to Islam's holy city, Mecca, and adopted the name El-Hajj Malik El-Shabazz. The pilgrimage gave birth to the views that not all whites were evil and that African Americans could make gains by working through established channels.

His new view brought him death threats. On February 14, 1965, his home was firebombed. A week later, Malcolm was shot and killed at the Audubon Ballroom in Harlem. Although three men were arrested for the crime, there remains a controversy to the present day over who conspired to kill Malcolm.

Malcolm X had a profound influence on both blacks and whites. Many African Americans responded to a feeling that he was a man of the people, experienced in the ways of the street rather than the pulpit or the college campus, which traditionally had provided the preponderance of African American leaders. His emphasis on black pride and doing for self was in the tradition of black nationalism and similar to that of Steven Biko of South Africa. He provided a contrast to Martin Luther King, Jr.'s idea of integration.

9

National Organizations

◆ A Brief History ◆ National Organization Leaders ◆ National Organizations
by Jessie Carney Smith

In a dispute between the National Association for the Advancement of Colored People and the State of Alabama, Justice John Marshall Harlan of the United States Supreme Court pointed out the significance of association membership, claiming that it is through associations that individuals have sought "to make more effective the expression of their own views." Associations are one of the largest and most influential forces in the United States and have played an important part in the economic, social, and educational development of African Americans. Organizations also have been crucial in developing and disseminating information, ensuring representation for private interests, and promoting social and policy objectives.

◆ A BRIEF HISTORY

Early African American Organizations

Due to restrictive ordinances and limited tolerance by whites, prior to the eighteenth century only the most informal and limited assembling of African Americans was permitted. Often meeting as religious assemblies, African Americans were forced to meet secretly, in small numbers. Thus, the very first African American organizations to exist in the United States cannot definitively be identified.

The Free African Society, organized in Philadelphia in 1787, has been generally accepted as the first African American organization in the United States. Founded by Methodist ministers Richard Allen and Absalom Jones, the Free African Society served as an important source of political consciousness and welfare for African Americans throughout the country by combining economic and medical aid for poor African Americans with support of abolition and sub rosa communication with African Americans in the South.

The abolitionist movement of the nineteenth century produced numerous organizations concerned with issues of importance to African Americans including the American Colonization Society (founded in 1816), the New England Anti-Slavery Society (founded in 1832), and the American Anti-Slavery Society (founded in 1833). Although most of these organizations were dominated by whites, African American leaders, including Paul Cuffe and Frederick Douglass, played an active role in the movement and in anti-slavery organizations of the time.

During the late nineteenth and early twentieth centuries, many African American organizations came into existence. The primary concern of most of these groups was education, improvement of the race as a whole, and religious training. In 1895, the National Medical Association was founded to further the interests of African American physicians, pharmacists, and nurses. African American women also sought a national network to bring about reform for women and for the race. In 1896, the National Federation of Afro-American Women and the Colored Women's League fused to create the National Association of Colored Women and elected Mary Church Terrell as the first president. In 1900 Booker T. Washington organized the National Negro Business League to promote commercial development. The success of these organizations stimulated an increase in new African American organizations, such as the National Negro Banker's Association, the National Negro Press Association, and the National Negro Funeral Directors' Association.

The Niagara Movement

The Niagara Movement of 1905 marked a turning point in African American history. This new organization was founded by a group of African American intellectuals from across the nation—headed by W. E. B. Du Bois—and approved a "Declaration of Principles," or resolutions calling for full equality for African Americans in American life.

However, the Niagara Movement suffered from weak finances and a policy that restricted membership to African American intellectuals. In 1909, the Niagara Movement was succeeded by a new organization—later known as the National Association for the Advancement of Colored People.

National Association for the Advancement of Colored People

The new organization was largely the brainchild of three people: William English Walling, a white Southerner who feared that racists would soon carry "the race war to the North"; Mary White Ovington, a wealthy young white woman who had attended the 1905 meeting of the Niagara group as a reporter for the *New York Evening Post* and had experience with conditions in the African American ghettos of New York City; and Henry Moskowitz, a New York social worker. The trio proposed that a conference be called "for the discussion of present evils, the voicing of protests, and the renewal of the struggle for civil and political liberty." The three-day conference was followed by four meetings, the results of which were an increase in membership and the selection of an official name—the National Negro Committee. In 1910, the organization adopted its present name and was incorporated in New York state, and by 1914 the association had established some fifty branches throughout the country.

Over the years, the organization has attempted to improve the condition of African Americans through litigation, legislation, and education. *Crisis* magazine, edited by W. E. B. Du Bois, became its chief vehicle for the dissemination of information. Perhaps its most significant legal victory was won in 1954 when the historic *Brown v. Board of Education of Topeka* case threw out the "separate but equal" doctrine established by the Supreme Court in *Plessy v. Ferguson* in 1896 and eliminated legal segregation in public education.

NAACP Legal Defense and Educational Fund, Inc.

Established in 1939 by the National Association for the Advancement of Colored People, the NAACP Legal Defense and Educational Fund maintained its own board, program, staff, office, and budget for some twenty years. It has served in the forefront of legal assaults against discrimination and segregation and has an outstanding record of victories. In addition to its litigation, the Legal Defense Fund provides scholarships and training for young lawyers, advises lawyers on legal trends and decisions, and monitors federal programs.

Originally for tax purposes, the NAACP Legal Defense Fund had been maintained as a separate arm of the NAACP, until it officially was divorced from its parent organization in 1959. Following the separation of the organizations, a dispute over identity and the use of the parent organization's name erupted. The National Association for the Advancement of Colored People sued the NAACP Legal Defense Fund for name infringement. However, after several months of legal wrangling, a federal court ruled that the LDF could keep NAACP in its name since the NAACP was its parent organization.

Organizations Concerned with Urban Problems

During the early part of the twentieth century, several organizations concerned with the plight of urban African Americans emerged. In 1906, at the urging of Long Island Railroad President William H. Baldwin, a group of African Americans and whites met for the purpose of studying the employment needs of African Americans. This group, known as the Committee for the Improvement of Industrial Conditions among Negroes in New York, studied the racial aspects of the labor market (particularly the attitudes and policies of employers and unions) and sought to find openings for qualified African Americans.

At the same time, the League for the Protection of Colored Women was established to provide similar services for African American women in New York and Philadelphia arriving from various parts of the South. These women, who often had no friends or relatives in the North, often fell prey to unscrupulous employment agencies, which led them into low wage jobs.

A third organization, the Committee on Urban Conditions among Negroes, appeared in 1910. It was organized by Ruth Standish Baldwin, the widow of the former Long Island Railroad president, and George Edmund Haynes, one of only three trained African American social workers in the country and the first African American to receive a doctorate from Columbia University. Haynes was named as the first executive secretary of the new agency. A year later the organization merged with the Committee for the Improvement of Industrial Conditions among Negroes in New York and the National League for the Protection of Colored Women to form the National League on Urban Conditions among Negroes. That name was later shortened to the National Urban League.

From the outset, the organization focused on the social and economic needs of African Americans, seeking training, improved housing, health, recreation, and job assistance for African Americans. The organizational model that the league had established in New York City attracted attention and affiliates were formed in various cities across the United States.

A major goal of the National Urban League was to broaden economic opportunities for African Americans. It was not until the 1960s when Whitney M. Young Jr. became its new leader that the league began to emerge as a force in the civil rights struggle.

Leadership Conference on Civil Rights

The Leadership Conference on Civil Rights was organized in 1950 by A. Philip Randolph, Roy Wilkins, and Arnold Aronson to implement the historic report of President Harry S. Truman's Committee on Civil Rights *To Secure These Rights*. Beginning with only thirty organizations, the conference has grown in numbers, scope, and effectiveness, and has been responsible for coordinating the campaigns that have resulted in the passage of the civil rights legislation of the 1950s and 1960s including the Civil Rights Act of 1957, the Civil Rights Act of 1960, the Civil Rights Act of 1964, the Voting Rights Act of 1965, and the Fair Housing Act of 1968 (also known as the Civil Rights Act of 1968).

The Leadership Conference on Civil Rights currently consists of approximately 157 national organizations representing minorities, women, major religious groups, the handicapped, the aged, labor, and minority businesses and professions. These organizations speak for a substantial portion of the population and together comprise one of the most broad based coalitions in the nation.

Southern Christian Leadership Conference and the Arrest of Rosa Parks

Following the arrest of Rosa Parks who had refused to give up her seat on a public bus in Montgomery, Alabama, on December 1, 1955, Martin Luther King, Jr. and Ralph Abernathy organized the Montgomery Improvement Association that year to coordinate a city wide bus boycott. The success of the boycott led to the creation of a new organization.

This new organization, consisting mainly of African American ministers, met at the Ebenezer Baptist Church in January 1957 and elected King as its first president. Initially called the Southern Negro Leaders Conference and later the Southern Leadership Conference, the Southern Christian Leadership Conference grew to become

James Farmer (AP/Wide World Photos, Inc.)

one of the most influential and effective of all the civil rights organizations.

Organizations and the Court

Although public and private associations of all kinds have traditionally flourished in this country, that has not always been true for African American organizations. The freedom of association—the freedom to assemble, immunity from state scrutiny—similar to the First Amendment freedoms of speech and press, has from time to time been questioned and challenged.

Since the founding of the National Association for the Advancement of Colored People and similar organizations, state and local governments have attempted to prevent the operation of such groups. During the late 1950s, the state of Alabama set out to ban the NAACP from conducting activities within the state, claiming that the association had failed to comply with statutes governing corporations operating within the state. The dispute of *NAACP v. Alabama* was finally resolved by the United States Supreme Court in 1958 in favor of the association. However, the association was met with other interferences—some of the most notable disputes include *Bates v. Little Rock* (1960), Louisiana ex rel.

Gremillion v. NAACP (1961), and *Gibson v. Florida Legislative Investigating Committee* (1963).

Congress of Racial Equality

The Congress of Racial Equality (CORE), an interracial organization organized to confront racism and discrimination, was founded in 1942 by James Farmer as the result of a campaign protesting discrimination at a Chicago restaurant. From Chicago, the organization spread to other cities and other causes, organizing sit-ins and freedom rides throughout the South.

By the mid-1960s, CORE had changed directions, and Farmer turned leadership of the organization over to a North Carolina lawyer named Floyd McKissick. With McKissick as national director the organization moved toward an exclusively African American membership and staff. In 1967, CORE, at its convention, eliminated the word "multiracial" from its constitution. McKissick left the organization in 1968 and was replaced by the present national director, Roy Innis, the former chairperson of the Harlem chapter.

Student Non-Violent Coordinating Committee

In 1960, a group of African American college students founded the Student Non-Violent Coordinating Committee (SNCC) to coordinate the activities of students engaged in direct action protest. SNCC achieved enormous results in the desegregation of public facilities and earned respect for its determination to act peacefully, no matter how violent or demeaning the provocation.

By 1964 the organization's leader, Stokely Carmichael, had become convinced that the United States could not be turned around without the threat of wholesale violence. In 1967 Carmichael left the organization to join the more militant Black Panther Party. H. Rap Brown, the former minister of justice in the old organization, took over leadership, renaming the organization the Student National Coordinating Committee and promoting violent retaliation in some situations. The organization gradually declined in membership and is now essentially defunct.

Black Panther Party

From its founding by Huey P. Newton and Bobby Seale in 1966, the Black Panther Party was a departure from the platform and tactics of other civil rights organizations. It rejected the institutional structure that, in its view, made American society corrupt, rejected established channels of authority that oppressed the African American community, and middle class values, which it felt contributed to indifference toward, and contempt for, African American urban youth.

Elmer "Geronimo" Pratt (AP/Wide World Photos, Inc.)

The party imposed strict discipline on its members, denouncing the use of intoxicants, drugs, and artificial stimulants "while doing party work." The intellectual fare of every party member is the ten-point program (supplemented by daily reading of political developments), which every member is obliged to know and understand.

By 1970, most of the organization's leadership was either jailed, in exile, or dead—Newton was jailed in 1968 on manslaughter changes; Seale had been jailed on charges stemming from the 1968 Chicago convention riot; Minister of Information Eldridge Cleaver fled to Algeria in 1969 to avoid a prison sentence; and Mark Clark and Fred Hampton were killed during a police raid in 1970.

In June of 1997, former Black Panther leader Geronimo Pratt made headlines when he was released from prison after wrongfully being accused of the 1968 murder of a woman in Santa Monica, California. Throughout his 27 years in prison, Pratt (also known as geronimo ji Jaga) maintained his innocence. In his decision, Superior Court Judge Everett W. Dickey held that the prosecution denied Pratt a fair trial in violation of his constitutional rights. The prosecution suppressed material evidence relating to the question of guilt and to the credibility of a material witness, in violation of the 1966 U.S. Supreme Court ruling in *Brady v. Maryland.*

Organizations Providing Community Support

In 1967, the National Urban Coalition was founded to improve the quality of life for the disadvantaged in urban areas through the combined efforts of business, labor, government, and community leaders. Another organization, the National Black United Fund, which provides financial and technical support to projects serving the critical needs of African American communities nationwide, was founded in 1972.

The Reverend Jesse Jackson organized Operation PUSH (People United to Save Humanity, later changed to People United to Serve Humanity) in 1971. The organization has pursued its economic objectives through its Operation Breadbasket Program. It also has worked to motivate young people through its PUSH-EXCEL program which is designed to instill pride and build confidence in young people. Jackson left Operation PUSH to organize another group, the National Rainbow Coalition, Inc., in 1984.

Organizations Responding to Africa and the Caribbean

During the nineteenth and early part of the twentieth centuries, a number of individuals and organizations arose to unite Africans throughout the world. Most notable was the Universal Negro Improvement, founded in 1914 by black nationalist Marcus Garvey. The organization's goals were to instill pride in African American by gaining economic and political power for African Americans in the United States, establishing an independent black colony in Africa, and promoting African nationalism. On February 19, 1918, under the leadership of W. E. B. Du Bois, the first Pan-African Congress was held in Paris. The meeting was attended by blacks from around the world and focused on the problems facing blacks worldwide.

Recently, new organizations have formed to address the concerns of blacks around the world. TransAfrica, founded in 1977 by Randall Robinson, has worked to influence U.S. foreign policy regarding political and human rights in Africa and the Caribbean by informing the public of violations of social, political, and civil rights. Other organizations have also taken a stand on policies affecting blacks around the world.

Greek Letter Organizations

The first Greek letter fraternity established in the United States was Phi Beta Kappa, organized on December 5, 1776, at William and Mary College in Williamsburg, Virginia. At first a secret social club with scholas-

Randall Robinson meets with ANC President Nelson Mandela in 1991 (AP/Wide World Photos, Inc.).

tic, inspirational, and fraternal aims, it abandoned its secrecy in 1826 and became an honorary fraternity based on scholarship. It was not until 1877, however, that Phi Beta Kappa accepted its first African American into membership—George Washington Henderson at the University of Vermont. The undergraduate fraternity movement began to spread throughout colleges in New England and the Middle States. Women's sororities also emerged in the mid-nineteenth century. Although many colleges were racially integrated during this period, their fraternities and sororities were not.

The first decade of the twentieth century was a period of great organizational activity for African Americans, in which organizations dealing with business, education, social, and economic conditions, and other issues were founded. African American colleges and schools of this period also enjoyed the spirit of brotherhood, and their students found social outlet in clubs, literary societies, and other groups. But both on and outside campus, African Americans were confronted by the pressures of racism and sexism and sought relief in a number of ways. African Americans explored ways to form strong social bonds through the founding of their own Greek letter organizations. In time these organizations became a dominant force in undergraduate college life, as well as in the African American community.

Historical African American Fraternities

Sigma Pi Phi Fraternity, also known as the Boulé, was founded by six African American men in Philadelphia in

1904. It serves as the forerunner of the Greek letter organizations existing in the African American community today. It focuses on the post-college years and historically has been comprised of an elite group of college graduates who have "like attributes, education, skills, and attainments," or who "ha[ve] made places for themselves in their communities through useful service."

Two other well-established Greek letter fraternities were actually founded on white college campuses. Initially organized as a social study club, Alpha Phi Alpha, was founded on December 4, 1906, by a small group of men at Cornell University. The other fraternity, Kappa Alpha Psi, was founded in 1911 at the University of Indiana. Most of the African American Greek letter fraternities and sororities, however, were founded at Howard University in Washington, DC. Other historically prominent African American fraternities include Omega Psi Phi, founded in 1911, and Phi Beta Sigma, established in 1914.

Historical African American Sororities

African American Greek letter sororities date back to 1910, when nine students founded Alpha Kappa Alpha Sorority. Those organizations that followed included Delta Sigma Theta in 1913, organized by 22 young women, and Zeta Phi Beta, established in 1920. Sigma Gamma Rho was founded in 1924 at Butler University in Indianapolis, the only African American sorority founded on a white college campus. The mutual interests of both sororities and fraternities have been promoted by the National Pan-Hellenic Council, established in 1930.

In addition to these organizations, other African American Greek letter organizations were founded as early as 1906 with specialized professional interests in mind. Examples of such groups are Phi Delta Kappa Sorority (education) and Alpha Pi Chi Sorority (business and other professions).

Present-Day African American Fraternities and Sororities

Present-day chapters of Greek letter fraternities and sororities for African Americans have been founded on many traditional white college campuses. Chapters also extend beyond campus grounds into the community, where graduate chapters—sometimes more than one in a city—have been established. Members of both undergraduate and graduate chapters include many well-known individuals who have left their mark on Greek letter organizations as well. For example, in 1914 Mary Church Terrell wrote the "Delta Oath" for Delta Sigma Theta Sorority—an oath that is still recited at formal meetings. Poet and journalist Alice Dunbar-Nelson wrote the lyrics and internationally-known singer Florence Cole Talbert wrote the music for the official Delta

Hymn. Historian Charles Wesley wrote the history of Sigma Pi Phi, as well as the history of Alpha Phi Alpha Fraternity.

African American Greek letter organizations continue to focus on various areas of need in the African American community, such as health, education, literacy, housing, juvenile delinquency, teenage pregnancy, family issues, and generally improving the human condition for African Americans. Some have even established non-profit educational foundations to provide for scholarships, research, and foreign travel.

◆ NATIONAL ORGANIZATION LEADERS

(To locate biographical profiles more readily, please consult the index at the back of the book.)

H(ubert) Rap Brown(Jamil Abdullah Al-Amin) (1943–)
Former SNCC Chairperson

H. Rap Brown was born on October 4, 1943, in Baton Rouge, Louisiana. In 1967 he took over leadership of the Student Non-Violent Coordinating Committee, renaming the organization the Student National Coordinating Committee. During his leadership of the committee, Brown was an advocate of violence against the white establishment and used fiery rhetoric in many of his speeches, often saying that "violence is as American as cherry pie." Since the late 1960s, the organization has gradually declined in membership and is now essentially defunct.

In 1968, Brown was charged with inciting a riot in Cambridge, Maryland, and was convicted in New Orleans on a federal charge of carrying a gun between states. In 1969, Brown published the book *Die Nigger Die*. He disappeared in 1970 after being slated for trial in Maryland, and in 1972 he was shot, arrested, and eventually convicted for a bar holdup in New York City.

While in prison, Brown converted to the Islamic faith and took the name of Jamil Abdullah Al-Amin. After his release he founded a community grocery store in Atlanta and is currently leader of the Community Mosque in Atlanta.

In August 1994, Al-Amin was arraigned on weapons possession and assault charges stemming from a shooting in an Atlanta city park. Al-Amin claimed that the charges were the result of harassment by federal agents who targeted him because of his radical past and Muslim beliefs.

Benjamin F. Chavis (Muhammad), Jr. (1948–)
Former NAACP Executive Director

Benjamin Franklin Chavis was born on January 22, 1948, in Oxford, North Carolina. He received a B.A. from

Jamil Abdullah Al-Amin (formerly known as H. Rap Brown) (AP/Wide World Photos, Inc.).

Benjamin Chavis Jr. (AP/Wide World Photos, Inc.)

the University of North Carolina in 1969, a M.A. from the Duke University Divinity School, and a Ph.D. in theology from Howard University in Washington, DC.

He came to national attention in 1971 when, as a civil rights organizer for the United Church of Christ, he was indicted along with nine other people for the fire bombing of a grocery store in Wilmington, North Carolina, during a period of racial unrest. In the controversial trial that followed all of the "Wilmington 10" were found guilty. Chavis was sentenced to a prison term of 29 to 34 years. Chavis was later granted parole and, in 1980, his conviction was reversed amidst conflicting testimony by various witnesses.

Prior to becoming active in the Civil Rights movement, Chavis taught chemistry at the high school level. He also worked as an AFSCME labor organizer (1969), a civil rights organizer for the Southern Christian Leadership Council (1967–1969), as a minister for the United Church of Christ, and as director of their Commission for Racial Justice in Washington, DC (1972). In 1985, he was appointed executive director of the Commission for Racial Justice. Chavis has also served as co-chairperson of the National Alliance Against Racism and Politi-

cal Repression (1977) and as co-chairperson of the Organizing Committee for Economic and Social Justice.

In 1977, Chavis wrote *Let My People Go: Psalms From Prison.* He received the George Collins Service Award (1977) given by the Congressional Black Caucus, the William L. Patterson Award given by the Patterson Foundation, and the Shalom Award presented by the Eden Theological Seminary. He is also a recipient of the Gertrude E. Rush Distinguished Service Award, J. E. Walker Humanitarian Award, and the Martin Luther King, Jr. Freedom Award. Chavis was also active in the South African civil rights struggle.

On April 9, 1993, the National Association for the Advancement of Colored People's board of directors elected Chavis to succeed retiring executive director Benjamin Hooks. Chavis assumed leadership of the NAACP with an agenda designed to increase the membership of young African Americans and revitalize an organization that some people viewed as stagnant. However, Chavis's early initiatives, which included defending "gangsta rap" music, meetings with street gang leaders, and seeking closer ties with controversial Nation of Islam leader Louis Farrakhan, angered many of the NAACP's more traditional members. By the time the NAACP met for its 85th annual convention in July 1994, the NAACP had been split into two factions, one supporting Chavis and the other that believed the organization was being overrun by radical and extremist elements.

In August 1994, it was disclosed that Chavis committed hundreds of thousands of dollars of NAACP money during the preceding autumn to settle a sexual harassment suit against him. On the weekend of August 20, 1994, the NAACP board of directors met and voted to oust Chavis as executive director. Chavis sued the NAACP, claiming that he had been wrongfully terminated. The NAACP settled out of court with Chavis, but he was not reinstated as executive director.

Following his dismissal from the NAACP, Chavis formed a new civil rights organization, the National African American Leadership Summit. He continued his close association with Rev. Louis Farrakhan and together they organized the Million Man March, which convened on October 16, 1995, in Washington, DC. Chavis also serves as a talk show host on Washington, DC's WOL- AM. In 1997 he converted to Islam, took the name Benjamin Chavis Muhammad, and joined the Nation of Islam headed by Rev. Farrakhan.

Ramona Hoage Edelin (1945–)
National Urban Coalition President and Chief Executive

Born in Los Angeles, California, on September 4, 1945, Ramona Hoage Edelin received her B.A. (magna cum laude) from Fisk University, her M.A. from the University of East Anglia in Norwich, England, and her Ph.D. from Boston University. She has been a lecturer at the University of Maryland, a visiting professor at Brandeis University, and has served as chair of Afro-American studies at Emerson College.

In 1977, Edelin joined the National Urban Coalition as an executive assistant to the president. The National Urban Coalition, an organization to improve the quality of life for the disadvantaged in urban areas, has been active in advocating initiatives designed to encourage youth and promote leadership. Between 1979 and 1982, she moved from director of operations to vice president of operations, then moved to senior vice president of program and policy directing programs in housing, health, education, and advocacy. In 1982, Edelin became the organization's chief executive.

Marian Wright Edelman (1939–)
Children's Defense Fund President

Born in Bennettsville, South Carolina, on June 6, 1939, Marian Wright Edelman received her undergraduate degree from Spelman College in 1960, where she was class valedictorian. That fall she entered Yale University Law School as a John Hay Whitney Fellow and received her law degree in 1963. Later that year she joined the NAACP Legal Defense and Education Fund as staff attorney. One year later she organized the Jackson, Mississippi, branch of the NAACP Legal Defense and Education Fund, serving as its director until 1968 when she founded the Washington Research Project of the

Marian Wright Edelman (AP/Wide World Photos, Inc.)

Southern Center for Public Policy, which later developed into the Children's Defense Fund.

Wright has served as director of the Harvard University Center for Law and Education, chairperson of the Spelman College board of trustees, a member of the Yale University Corporation, the National Commission on Children, and on the boards of the Center on Budget and Policy Priorities, the U. S. Committee for UNICEF, and the Joint Center for Political and Economic Studies.

As president of the Children's Defense Fund, Edelman has become the nation's most effective lobbyist on behalf of children. Even while social spending was being cut she has managed to score some victories. In 1986, nine federal programs known as "the Children's Initiative" received a $500 million increase in their $36 billion budget for families and children's health care, nutrition, and early education.

The most visible focus of CDF is its teen pregnancy prevention program. Through Edelman's efforts, Medicaid coverage for expectant mothers and children was boosted in 1984. In 1985, Edelman began holding an annual Pregnancy Prevention Conference, bringing thousands of religious leaders, social and health workers, and community organizations to Washington to discuss ways of dealing with the problem.

In her 1987 book *Families in Peril: An Agenda for Social Change*, Edelman wrote, "As adults, we are responsible for meeting the needs of children. It is our moral obligation. We brought about their births and their lives, and they cannot fend for themselves." Her other books include *Children Out of School in America, School Suspensions: Are They Helping Children?, Portrait of Inequality: Black and White Children in America, Families in Peril: An Agenda for Social Change, The Measure of Our Success: A Letter to My Children,* and *Guide My Feet: Prayers and Meditations on Loving and Working for Children.*

Myrlie Evers-Williams (1933–)
Former NAACP Chair, Civil Rights Activist, Civic Worker

Known for many years as the widow of civil rights worker Medgar Evers, Myrlie Evers-Williams has become prominent in her own right as a civil rights activist, speaker, and the second African American woman to chair the National Association for the Advancement of Colored People's board of directors. As board chair, she rekindled the spirit of the organization, led it to greater fiscal integrity, and increased national membership.

Myrlie Louise Beasley Evers-Williams was born on March 17, 1933, in Vicksburg, Mississippi. In 1950, Evers-Williams enrolled in Alcorn Agricultural and Mechanical College (now University) in Lorman, Mississippi, where she met Medgar Evers on her first day. They married on Christmas Eve of the following year.

The couple lived in the historic, all-African American town of Mound Bayou, Mississippi. During the 1950s and early 1960s, Medgar Evers became active with the NAACP as field secretary. The racially charged atmosphere in Mississippi, as well as the death threats that they received, led the family to take extreme precautions. Their home was firebombed in the spring of 1963. On June 12 of that same year, the death threats became a reality when Medgar Evers was shot in the driveway of his home and died soon afterwards at the University of Mississippi Hospital. Eventually, the home was donated to Tougaloo College. After thirty years of Evers-Williams's dogged determination for justice, on February 5, 1994, Byron De La Beckwith was convicted for the murder of her husband and sentenced to life in prison.

Evers-Williams and her three children moved to Claremont, California, in July 1964. She became highly visible in the NAACP and lectured to branches around the country about her life and the work of her husband. She also continued her education and graduated from

Myrlie Evers-Williams (AP/Wide World Photos, Inc.)

Pomona College in 1968 with a B.A. degree in sociology. Later she received a certificate from the Simmons College of Management in Boston, then became director of planning at Claremont College's Center for Educational Opportunity.

From 1973 to 1975 she was vice president for advertising and publicity with the New York-based firm of Seligman and Lapz. In 1975, Evers-Williams moved to Los Angeles and became national director for community affairs with ARCO. She unsuccessfully ran for a seat in California's 24th Congressional District, as well as a seat on the Los Angeles City Council. She married Walter Edward Williams during that same year.

A long-time member of the NAACP, Evers-Williams's work with the organization was acknowledged among its leadership. In 1995, she was elected chairperson of the NAACP's board of directors—the third woman to hold the post. Immediately upon taking office, Evers-Williams faced unpaid organization debts and a cloud of uncertainty among the national membership over the organization's future. Evers-Williams led a successful campaign to restore the NAACP's posture as a viable civil rights organization, strengthen its financial base, and increase membership. After turning around the

NAACP, Evers-Williams resigned from the office in 1998 and was succeeded by Julian Bond.

Evers-Williams has been active in other arenas as well. In 1967, she recounted Evers's family life in Mississippi in her book *For Us, the Living.* She was also a contributing editor to the *Ladies' Home Journal.* Among the many honors that have been bestowed on her is the Spingarn Medal, which the NAACP awarded her in 1998. She continues to lecture widely and appear on radio and television programs.

James Farmer (1920–1999)
CORE Founder and Former National Director

Born in Marshall, Texas, on January 12, 1920, Farmer attended public schools throughout the South. He earned his B.S. in chemistry from Wiley College in 1938 and his B.D. from Howard University in 1941. Active in the Christian Youth movement and once vice-chairperson of the National Council of Methodist Youth and the Christian Youth Council of America, Farmer refused ordination when confronted with the realization that he would have to practice in a segregated ministry.

In 1941, Farmer accepted a post as race relations secretary for the Fellowship of Reconciliation. The following year he and a group of University of Chicago students organized the Congress of Racial Equality (CORE), the first protest organization in the United States to utilize the techniques of nonviolence and passive resistance advocated by the Indian nationalist Mohandas Karamchand Gandhi.

In June 1943, CORE staged the first successful sit-in demonstration at a restaurant in the Chicago Loop. The organization soon supplemented this maneuver with what came to be known as the standing-line, which involved the persistent waiting in line by CORE members at places of public accommodation where African Americans had been denied admission.

In 1961, CORE introduced the freedom ride into the vocabulary and methodology of civil rights protest, dispatching bus riders throughout the South for the purpose of testing the desegregation of terminal facilities. Attacked in Alabama and later arrested in Mississippi, the Freedom Riders eventually succeeded in securing the court ordered desegregation of bus terminals in 1960 when the United States Supreme Court outlawed segregation in interstate transportation.

Farmer left the organization in 1966, and in 1969 President Richard M. Nixon appointed Farmer to the post of assistant secretary of Health, Education, and Welfare. The appointment created a furor in some African American circles, where it was felt that it was inappropriate for a former civil rights leader to serve in the Nixon administration; in other circles, the appoint-

ment was praised by those who thought it necessary for African Americans to be represented in all areas. However, Farmer found that there was little substance to the position and resigned.

Farmer began to give lectures and briefly headed a think tank at Howard University. In 1976, he broke all ties with CORE, criticizing its leader, Roy Innis, for such actions as attempting to recruit African American Vietnam veterans as mercenaries in Angola's civil war. Farmer, along with Floyd McKissick, attempted to meet with Innis to reach an agreement on the future of the organization, but these discussions failed. Disturbed over the course that the organization had taken, Farmer and a score of former CORE members attempted to create a new racially mixed civil rights organization in 1980.

Since 1985 Farmer had been a visiting professor at Mary Washington College in Fredericksburg, Virginia. He had also written several books including *Freedom When?* (1976) and his autobiography *Lay Bare the Heart* (1985). Farmer was honored for his civil rights achievements and was awarded nearly twenty honorary degrees. In January 1998, President Bill Clinton presented him with the highest civilian honor, the Presidential Medal of Freedom.

Farmer, who had been in ill health, died at Mary Washington Hospital in Fredericksburg, Virginia on July 9, 1999.

Prince Hall (1735?–1807)
Founder of Black Freemasonry in the United States

Prince Hall is believed to have been born in Bridge Town, Barbados, around 1735. Historians contend that he migrated to the United States in 1765, while others claim that during the late 1740s he had been a slave to William Hall of Boston, Massachusetts, and was freed on April 9, 1770.

In March 1775 Hall, along with 15 other African Americans, were initiated into a lodge of British army freemasons stationed in Boston. The group of African American masons was issued a permit to meet at a lodge on March 17, 1775, and on July 3, 1775, they organized the African Lodge No. 1, with Hall as master of the lodge. The lodge received official recognition from England as a regular Lodge of Free and Accepted Masons in 1784 and was designated the African Lodge 459.

Hall, in addition to leading the organization of African American Freemasonry, was active as an abolitionist. In January 1777, he was the prime force behind an African American petition sent to the Massachusetts state legislature requesting the abolition of slavery in

A

CHARGE,

DELIVERED TO THE

AFRICAN LODGE,

JUNE 24, 1797,

In this 1797 address, Prince Hall charges his brother Masons to respect and help each other, work to end slavery, and show love to all of humanity (The Library of Congress).

the state. Another important petition, drawn up under his leadership in 1788, called for an end to the kidnapping and sale of free African Americans into slavery. He also actively lobbied for the organization of schools for African American children in Boston. Prince Hall died on December 4, 1807, in Boston.

George E. Haynes (1880–1960)
NUL Co-founder, Sociologist, Educator

A pioneer in the area of social work and an advocate for the urban African American worker, George Edmund Haynes helped to found the National Urban League in 1910 and became its first executive director. He also led NUL into its role as advocate for the needs of the African American urban poor.

Born in Pine Bluff, Arkansas, on May 11, 1880, Haynes moved to Hot Springs in search of better educational, social, and vocational opportunities. He was encouraged during a visit to Chicago where he saw a close-knit African American community engaged in discussions about contemporary issues involving their status. After one year of study at the Agricultural and Mechanical College in Normal, Alabama, and a college preparatory course at Fisk University in Nashville, he enrolled in the latter institution in 1899 and received his B.S. in 1903. Haynes received a master's degree in sociology from Yale University in 1904 and then entered the Yale Divinity School. He also enrolled in summer courses at the

University of Chicago in 1906 and 1907. In 1912 he became the first African American to received a doctorate from Columbia University. The research for his dissertation was on the working life of African Americans in New York City, culminating in the dissertation topic "The Negro At Work in New York City."

After college Haynes worked with the Colored Department of the International Committee of the YMCA, but left in 1908 to continue graduate study. In 1911, Haynes founded the Association of Colleges and Secondary Schools and was its first secretary. He was a member of the Fisk University faculty from 1910 to 1921, although he was on leave between 1918 and 1921. At Fisk he chaired the social science department, developed a pioneer program in social work education, and led the university to become a preeminent institution for social work education. He also established affiliate programs in social work education with other African American colleges. In turn, the National Urban League gave fellowships to promising students in the field to pursue advanced degrees in social work.

Haynes had been active in several organizations including three that were the precursors of the National Urban League: the National League for the Protection of Colored Women; the Committee on Urban Conditions among Negroes; and the Committee for Improving Industrial Conditions of Negroes. These organizations merged in 1910 and became the National Urban League. He was the NUL's executive director until 1918.

Haynes became director of Negro economics for the U.S. Department of Labor between 1918 and 1921. From 1921 to 1947 he was executive secretary of the Department of Race Relations of the Federal Council of Churches. Under his leadership, the department established Race Relations Sunday, which is observed nationwide on the second Sunday of each February. From 1942 to 1955, he was a YMCA regional consultant in South Africa, where he collected and disseminated data on the organization's work in these countries. From 1950 to 1959, he was lecturer at the City College of New York.

Throughout his life, Haynes was active in numerous organizations and held membership on boards of trustees at Fisk and Dillard Universities and the State University of New York. His publications included: *Africa: Continent of the Future* (1950); *The Negro at Work during the World War* (1921); *The Trend of the Races* (1929); articles for the *Social Work Yearbook*; and entries on African Americans in the *Encyclopedia Britannica*.

Due to Haynes's efforts, the NUL continues its focus on social work initiatives at local and national levels. After a brief illness, Haynes died in King County Hospital in Brooklyn on January 8, 1960.

Dorothy Height (Corbis Corporation [Bellevue])

Dorothy I. Height (1912–)
National Council of Negro Women Former President

Born in 1912 in Richmond, Virginia, Dorothy Irene Height holds a master's degree from New York University and has studied at the New York School of Social Work. In the fall of 1952, she served as a visiting professor at the Delhi School of Social Work in New Delhi, India. Six years later, she was appointed to the Social Welfare Board of New York by Gov. Averell Harriman and was reappointed by Gov. Nelson Rockefeller in 1961. In 1957, she was named president of the National Council of Negro Women, an organization founded by Mary McLeod Bethune in 1935.

Before becoming the fourth president of the National Council of Negro Women, Height had served on the organization's board of directors. She has also served as associate director for leadership training services for the Young Women's Christian Association, as a member of the Defense Advisory Committee on Women in the Services, as president of Delta Sigma Theta Sorority, as vice president of the National Council of Women, as president of Women in Community Services, Inc., as well as in numerous other organizations. Height is also the founder of the Black Family Reunion, which she

created in the 1980s to combat negative media stereotypes of African Americans.

In 1994, President Bill Clinton presented Height and nine other distinguished Americans with the Medal of Freedom, America's highest civilian honor. She was also awarded the Salute to Greatness Award. Height retired from the presidency of NCNW in February 1998 and was named chair and president emeritus of the organization. Jane E. Smith then became NCNW's president and chief executive officer.

Benjamin L. Hooks (1925–)
Former NAACP Executive Director, Minister

Benjamin L. Hooks was born in Memphis, Tennessee, on January 31, 1925, and attended LeMoyne College and Howard University. He received his J.D. from DePaul University in 1948. During World War II, he served in the 92nd Infantry Division in Italy.

From 1949 to 1965, and again from 1968 to 1972, Hooks worked as a lawyer in Memphis. In 1965, Hooks became the first African American judge to serve in the Shelby County (Tennessee) criminal court. As an ordained minister, he preached at Middle Baptist Church in Memphis and the Greater New Mount Moriah Baptist Church in Detroit. As a prominent local businessman, he was the co-founder and vice president of the Mutual Federal Savings and Loan Association in Memphis.

On January 10, 1977, Hooks was unanimously elected executive director of the National Association for the Advancement of Colored People by the board of directors, succeeding the retiring Roy Wilkins.

Under his progressive leadership, the association took an aggressive posture on U.S. policy toward African nations. Among his many battles on Capitol Hill, Hooks led the historical prayer vigil in Washington, DC, in 1979 against the Mott busing amendment, which was eventually defeated in Congress; led in the fight for passage of the District of Columbia Home Rule Bill; and was instrumental in gathering important Senate and House votes on the Humphrey-Hawkins Full Employment Bill.

At the NAACP's national convention in 1986, Hooks was awarded the association's highest honor, the Spingarn Medal. In March 1993, Hooks retired as executive director of the NAACP and was replaced by Benjamin F. Chavis.

Following his retirement, Hooks became senior vice president of Chapman Co., a minority brokerage firm, and returned to the pulpit as minister of Greater Middle Baptist Church in Memphis. He was also installed as professor of social justice at Fisk University with a distinguished chair named in his honor.

Roy Innis speaking at a press conference in 1976 (AP/Wide World Photos, Inc.).

Roy E. Innis (1934–)
CORE Chairperson

Born June 6, 1934, in St. Croix, Virgin Islands, Roy Emile Alfredo Innis has lived in the United States since the age of twelve. He attended Stuyvesant High School in New York City and majored in chemistry at City College of New York.

In 1963, Innis joined the Congress of Racial Equality (CORE). In 1965, Innis was elected chairperson of the Harlem branch and went on to become associate national director three years later. In 1968, Innis became national director of the organization. Innis founded the Harlem Commonwealth Council, an agency designed to promote the development of African American owned businesses and economic institutions in Harlem. He also worked in journalism, serving with William Haddad as co-editor of the *Manhattan Tribune*, a weekly featuring news from Harlem and the upper West Side.

Innis's leadership of CORE, however, has been marked with controversy. Numerous members have left the organization, charging that Innis has run the organization as a one-man show. CORE was also the target of a three-year investigation by the New York state attorney general's office into allegations that it had misused charitable contributions. (An agreement was reached in 1981 that relieved CORE from admitting to any wrongdoing in its handling of funds, but stipulated that Innis would have to contribute $35,000 to the organization over the next three years.) Innis was challenged by a group of former CORE members, headed by James Farmer, the founder and former chairperson of organization, but the effort was unsuccessful and Innis continued as head of the organization. In 1981, Innis became national chairperson of the organization.

While remaining president of the largely inactive CORE, Innis has sought to build a political base in Brooklyn and run for public office on several occasions. In 1986, Innis was a Republican candidate for Brooklyn's 12th Congressional District, but lost the election. He also ran unsuccessfully for the Democratic mayoral nomination in New York City in 1993 against David Dinkins. In 1994, Innis unsuccessfully challenged Mario Cuomo for the governorship of New York.

John E. Jacob (1934–)
NUL President

Born in Trout, Louisiana, on December 16, 1934, John Edward Jacob grew up in Houston, Texas. He received his B.S. and M.S. in social work from Howard University. During the early 1960s Jacob worked for the Baltimore Department of Public Welfare, first as a caseworker, then later as a child welfare supervisor. In 1965, he joined the Washington Urban League as director of education and youth incentives.

During his early career with the organization he held a number of increasingly important positions, serving as director of its Northern Virginia Branch in 1966, associate director for administration of the affiliate in 1967, and as its acting executive director from 1968 until 1970. He also spent several months as director of community organization training in the eastern regional office of NUL.

Jacob left the Washington Urban League in 1970 to serve as executive director for the San Diego Urban League, a post he held until his return to the Washington Urban League in 1975. In 1982, Jacob replaced Vernon E. Jordan, Jr. as the organization's president, when Jordan retired after ten years as Urban League president.

Jacob has also served on the Howard University board of trustees, the board of the Local Initiatives Support Corporation, the board of A Better Chance, Inc., the Community Advisory Board of New York Hospital, and the National Advertising Review Board, among others.

In 1994, Jacob retired as president of the National Urban League and was succeeded by Hugh B. Price.

John Jacob (AP/Wide World Photos, Inc.)

Jacob is currently an executive vice president for Anheuser-Busch Inc.

Vernon E. Jordan, Jr. (1935–)
Former NUL President, Presidential Advisor

Vernon Eulion Jordan Jr. was born in Atlanta on August 15, 1935. After graduating from DePauw University in 1957 and from Howard Law School in 1960, he returned to Georgia.

From 1962 to 1964, Jordan served as field secretary for the Georgia branch of the National Association for the Advancement of Colored People. Between 1964 and 1968, Jordan served as director of the Voter Education Project of the Southern Regional Council and led successful drives that registered nearly two million African Americans in the South. In 1970, Jordan moved to New York to become executive director of the United Negro College Fund (now the College Fund/UNCF), helping to raise record sums for its member colleges, until he was selected by the Urban League to become the successor to Whitney M. Young Jr.

Taking over as National Urban League executive director in January 1972, Jordan moved the organization into new areas, including voter registration in Northern and Western cities, while continuing and strengthening the league's traditional social service programs. An outspoken advocate of the cause of African Americans and the poor, Jordan took strong stands in favor of busing, an income maintenance system that ends poverty, scatter-site housing, and a federally financed and administered national health system. Maintaining that the "issues have changed," since the 1960s, Jordan called for "equal access and employment up to and including top policy-making jobs."

The nation was stunned on May 29, 1980, when Jordan, who had just delivered an address to the Fort Wayne Urban League, was shot by a sniper as he returned to his motel. Jordan was confined to the hospital, first in Fort Wayne and later in New York City, for ninety days.

On September 9, 1981, Jordan announced his retirement, after ten years as head of the National Urban League. During Jordan's tenure, the League increased its number of affiliates from 99 to 118, its staff from 2,100 to 4,200, and its overall budget from $40 million annually to $150 million.

In January 1993, Jordan served as a member of President Bill Clinton's transition team. President Clin-

Vernon Jordan (AP/Wide World Photos, Inc.)

ton appointed Jordan to his Foreign Intelligence Advisory Board in April 1993. He is also senior partner at the Washington, DC law firm of Akin, Gump, Strauss, Hauer & Feld and serves on several boards of directors.

Joseph E. Lowery (1924–)
Former SCLC President, Minister

Joseph E. Lowery was born in Huntsville, Alabama, on October 6, 1924. He holds a Ph.D in divinity and has attended numerous educational institutions including Clark College, the Chicago Ecumenical Institute, Garrett Theological Seminary, Payne College and Theological Seminary, and Morehouse College. Lowery's ministry began in 1952 at the Warren Street Church in Birmingham, where he served until 1961. From there he moved on to become pastor of St. Paul Church from 1964 to 1968.

Lowery was one of the co-founders of the Southern Negro Leaders Conference (which later became the Southern Christian Leadership Conference), serving as vice president.

In 1977, Lowery succeeded Ralph David Abernathy as president of the SCLC. Under his leadership, the SCLC broadened its activities to include: the reinstitution of its Operation Breadbasket; encouraging businesses that earn substantial profits in the African American community to reinvest equitably and employ African Americans in equitable numbers; involvement in the plight of Haitian refugees jailed by the U.S. government; and a march from Selma to Washington, DC, in coordi-

nation with the renewal of the Voting Rights Act of 1982. From 1986 until he retired in 1992, Lowery served as pastor of Cascades United Methodist Church in Atlanta, Georgia. Lowery stepped down from the SCLC post in 1997 and was succeeded by Martin Luther King III.

Jewell Jackson McCabe (1945–)
Former President of the National Coalition of 100 Black Women

Jewell Jackson was born in Washington, DC, on August 2, 1945. McCabe studied at New York City's High School for the Performing Arts as a teen and studied dance at Bard College from 1963 to 1966. She married Frederick Ward, who worked in advertising, while at Bard, whom she later divorced. Her marriage to Eugene McCabe, president of North General Hospital in New York City, also ended in divorce, but McCabe chose to keep his name.

Several years after studying at Bard, McCabe took a job as director of public affairs for the New York Urban Coalition in 1970 and, concurrently, joined an organization called the New York Coalition of 100 Black Women, founded by her mother, businessperson Julia Jackson. At that time, the group was about 75 women shy of the 100 mark; the group reached this goal by the mid-1970s. She left the Urban Coalition in 1973 to become the public relations officer for Special Services for Children in New York City. In 1975, she took a post as associate director of public information in the Women's Division of the Office of the Governor in New York City and then became director of government and community affairs at WNET-TV in 1977.

From 1975 to 1977, she published *Women in New York* and also donated her time to the United Way, the National Association for the Advancement of Colored People, the United Hospital Fund, and the Association for the Betterment of New York. In 1977, because of her good work, she was named president of the National Coalition of 100 Black Women, a post she held until 1991, when she became chair of the board of directors. By 1981, McCabe had established the organization nationally with chapters in 22 states, attracting some of the most well-known African American women in the United States.

Within two years, McCabe received several prestigious awards including an Eastern Region Urban League Guild Award in 1979, a Seagrams Civic Award, a Links Civic Award, and an outstanding community leadership award from Malcolm/King College, all in 1980. In that same year, she served as deputy grand marshal of the annual Martin Luther King Jr. Parade in New York City. In addition to her chair duties for the coalition, McCabe is president of her own Jewell Jackson McCabe Associ-

Reverend Joseph Lowery (AP/Wide World Photos, Inc.)

ates, a firm that does consulting work on government relations, marketing, and events dealing with minority issues.

Floyd B. McKissick (1922–1981)
Former CORE National Director

Born in Asheville, North Carolina, on March 9, 1922, Floyd Bixler McKissick did his undergraduate work at Morehouse and North Carolina Colleges. Having determined that he wanted to become a lawyer, McKissick applied to the University of North Carolina at Chapel Hill Law School. Since the school was racially segregated at that time, he was denied admission. With the help of NAACP lawyer Thurgood Marshall, McKissick sued the university and became the first African American to earn an LL.B. degree at that institution.

While still in school, McKissick had become an active member of the Congress of Racial Equality (CORE). When McKissick replaced James Farmer as head of CORE on January 3, 1966, he quickly made a name for himself. Under McKissick's direction, the organization moved more firmly into the Black Power movement, refusing to support Martin Luther King's call for massive nonviolent civil disobedience in northern cities, concen-

trating instead on programs aimed at increasing the political power and improving the economic position of African Americans. In 1967, the organization moved to eliminate the word "multiracial" from its constitution.

McKissick resigned as national director of CORE in 1968. After leaving CORE, he launched a plan to establish a new community, Soul City, in Warren County, North Carolina. McKissick saw Soul City as a community with sufficient industry to support a population of 50,000. For his venture, he received a $14 million bond issue guarantee from the Department of Housing and Urban Development and a loan of $500,000 from the First Pennsylvania Bank.

Soul City, however, ran into difficulties and despite the best efforts of McKissick the project never developed as planned. In June 1980, the Soul City Corporation and the federal government reached an agreement that would allow the government to assume control of the project. Under the agreement, the company retained 88 acres of the project including the site of a mobile home park and a 60,000 square foot building that had served as the project's headquarters.

McKissick died on April 28, 1981, of lung cancer and was buried at Soul City.

Floyd B. McKissick (AP/Wide World Photos, Inc.)

Huey P. Newton (1942–1989)
Black Panther Party Co-Founder

The youngest of seven children, Huey P. Newton was born in Monroe, Louisiana, on February 17, 1942. He attended Oakland City College, where he founded the Afro-American Society, and later studied at San Francisco Law School. In 1966, Newton joined forces with Bobby Seale and established the Black Panther Party for Self-Defense.

Newton and his partner almost immediately became targets of police resentment and uneasiness. The hostility came to a climax in 1967, when Newton allegedly killed an Oakland police officer. His eight-week trial was a cause celebre in which more than 2,500 demonstrators surrounded the courthouse chanting Panther slogans and demanding his release. Newton was convicted of voluntary manslaughter and sent to the California Men's Colony. His conviction was later overturned by the California court of appeals.

By the 1970s, the Black Panther Party became a potent political force in California. Co-leader Bobby Seale made an almost successful bid for the mayorship of Oakland in 1973. In 1977, the Panthers helped to elect the city's first African American mayor, Lionel Wilson.

Meanwhile, Newton continued to have problems with the law. He was charged with shooting a prostitute, but after two hung juries, the charges were dropped. He was retried and convicted for the 1969 death of the police officer and again the conviction was reversed.

In 1980, he earned his Ph.D. in philosophy from the University of California; his doctoral thesis was "War Against the Panthers: Study of Repression in America." However, this achievement was followed by further problems. He was charged with embezzling state and federal funds from an educational and nutritional program that he headed in 1985. In 1987, he was convicted of illegal possession of guns. In 1989, he was fatally shot by a small-time drug dealer.

Frederick D. Patterson (1901–1988)
UNCF Founder, Former College President

Frederick D. Patterson was the force behind the first collective fund-raising efforts among African American colleges—the United Negro College Fund. He was also influential in the development of African American higher education through his presidency of Tuskegee Institute. It was during his administration that the internationally known Tuskegee Airmen was formed.

Frederick Douglass Patterson was born in the Anacostia neighborhood of Washington, DC, on October 10, 1901. His parents died before young Patterson was two years old, forcing him to live with various family members while attending school. He worked his way through veterinary school in Iowa, receiving a B.S. and later a M.S. in veterinary medicine. Before and after receiving his master's degree, Patterson taught at Virginia State College (now University) in Petersburg, then moved to Tuskegee Normal and Industrial Institute (now University) in Alabama, where he was teacher and head of the Veterinary Department. He obtained a Ph.D. in bacteriology from Cornell University in the early 1930s and returned to Tuskegee as head of the Agriculture Department. A year later he was named president of Tuskegee.

Among Patterson's accomplishments at Tuskegee was the establishment of an accredited school of veterinary medicine. It remains the only such school ever established on an African American college campus. Patterson began a program in commercial aviation in 1939 to train Tuskegee's students as pilots. He was lobbied successfully to have a training program for military pilots at Tuskegee and train commercial aviators as well. His military trainees became the celebrated Tuskegee Airmen, an African American pilots group that fought in World War II. In 1940, Patterson founded the George Washington Carver Foundation to encourage and financially support scientific research by African Americans. In 1948, he started the School of Engineering at Tuskegee.

In 1943 Patterson proposed the creation of an African American college consortium to raise money for their mutual benefit. In 1944, 27 schools came together to form the United Negro College Fund. Some view Patterson's efforts as the most important act during his lifetime. He also was UNCF president from 1964 to 1966. UNCF, now called The College Fund/UNCF, continues as an important national fund-raising effort for the member colleges. Its annual telethons, with singer Lou Rawls as host, raises millions of dollars and promotes financial support for the member colleges locally as well as nationally.

In 1953, Patterson retired from Tuskegee and became president of the Phelps Stokes Fund, an organization established in 1901 to support the education of African, African American, and Native American students in the United States. He left the fund in 1970 to head the Robert R. Moton Institute, another effort to boost the endowments of African American colleges.

President Ronald Reagan honored Patterson in 1987 with the Presidential Medal of Freedom. Patterson's autobiography *Chronicles of Faith* was completed after his death on April 26, 1988. In recognition of his work, he received the Spingarn Medal from the NAACP posthumously in 1988. Since then, the College Fund/UNCF named its new institute the Frederick D. Patterson Research Institute.

Hugh B. Price (1941–)
NUL President and CEO

When Hugh Price was named president and CEO of the National Urban League in 1994, he inherited an organization with financial problems and a lack of visibility. He proved to be the person to address and eradicate those problems. Price graduated from Amherst in 1963, then received his J.D. from Yale in 1966. Immediately going to work in the inner city, Price worked as an attorney for the New Haven Legal Assistance Association and later as executive director of the Black Coalition of New Haven.

In 1970 Price continued to focus on inner city issues by joining the urban affairs consulting firm of Cogen, Holt & Associates in New Haven, specializing in the analysis of municipal government. After serving as human resources administration director for the city of New Haven, Price was offered the opportunity to express his opinions to a much larger audience on the editorial board of the *New York Times*. Price primarily concentrated on writing about domestic policy issues.

After spending six years at WNET-TV, New York City's public television station, Price became vice presi-

dent of the Rockefeller Foundation, helping minorities to obtain more opportunities from groups served by the organization. With his extensive background, Price caught the attention NUL board of directors and was named president in 1994.

Price continued to focus on poorly funded schools, inner city youth, and unemployment. He vowed that the Urban League would not be race-specific in its help—it would be need-specific. During his tenure, the Urban League has changed its focus by helping entire urban neighborhoods, instead of singling out a particular race in that neighborhood. This approach has gained Hugh Price much deserved attention in the media.

A. Philip Randolph (1889–1979)
Brotherhood of Sleeping Car Porters and A. Philip Randolph Institute Founder

Asa Philip Randolph was born in Crescent City, Florida, on April 15, 1889. He attended Cookman Institute in Jacksonville, Florida, before moving to New York City.

In New York, Randolph worked as a porter, railroad waiter, and an elevator operator. While attending the College of the City of New York, he was exposed to the socialist movement, and in 1917 he organized *The Messenger*, a socialist newspaper. In 1925 Randolph founded the Brotherhood of Sleeping Car Porters to help African American railway car attendants working for the Pullman Palace Car Company. After a ten year struggle, Randolph and the union negotiated a contract with Pullman in 1935.

Randolph served as a member of New York City's Commission on Race and as president of the National Negro Congress. In 1941, Randolph organized a march on Washington, DC, to bring attention to discrimination in employment. In 1942, he was appointed to the New York Housing Authority and was appointed to the AFL-CIO executive council in 1955.

In 1960, Randolph organized the Negro American Labor Council. He was also one of the organizers of the 1963 March on Washington. In 1964, he founded the A. Philip Randolph Institute in New York City to eradicate discrimination and to defend human and civil rights. He died on May 16, 1979.

Randall S. Robinson (1942–)
TransAfrica Founder and Director

Randall Robinson, brother to the late news anchor Max Robinson, was born in Richmond, Virginia, and is a

Bayard Rustin (The Library of Congress)

graduate of Virginia Union University and Harvard Law School. In 1977, Robinson founded TransAfrica to lobby Congress and the White House on foreign policy matters involving Africa and the Caribbean. Since its creation, the organization has grown from two to over 15,000 members.

In 1984 and 1985, in protest to the policy of apartheid in South Africa, TransAfrica organized demonstrations in front of the South African embassy in Washington, DC; Robinson, along with other protesters including singer Stevie Wonder, were arrested. In addition, the organization has advocated for the cessation of aid to countries with human rights problems. In 1981 TransAfrica Forum, an educational and research arm of TransAfrica, was organized to collect and disseminate information on foreign policy affecting Africa and the Caribbean and to encourage public participation in policy debates.

In 1994, the United States was besieged by scores of refugees seeking to escape Haiti's brutal military dictatorship. Many of these refugees, upon reaching the United States or the U.S. military base in Guantanamo, Cuba, were often sent back to Haiti without receiving

asylum hearings. On April 12, 1994, Robinson began a liquid-fast diet in an attempt to increase awareness of the plight of Haitian refugees and to pressure the Clinton administration to change its refugee policy. On May 8, Robinson ended his fast after the Clinton administration announced that it would grant Haitian refugees asylum hearings.

On March 16, 1995, Robinson announced that TransAfrica would lead a group of prominent African Americans to pressure Nigeria's brutal military leaders to step down from power. Along with other demonstrators, Robinson was arrested during protests in front of the Nigerian Embassy in Washington, DC. On November 10, 1995, Robinson, along with notable South African Archbishop Desmond Tutu, announced that they would seek economic sanctions or an oil embargo against Nigeria after its military regime executed a prominent Nigerian writer and eight other minority rights activists.

Bayard Rustin (1910–1987)
Former A. Philip Randolph Institute Executive Director, Civil Rights Organizer

Bayard Rustin was born in West Chester, Pennsylvania, on March 17, 1910. While in school, he was an honor student and star athlete, experiencing his first act of discrimination when he was refused restaurant service in Pennsylvania while on tour with the football team. He attended Wilberforce University, Cheyney State Normal School (now Cheyney University of Pennsylvania), and the City College of New York.

Rustin was active in various peace organizations, efforts to restrict nuclear armaments, and movements toward African independence. Between 1936 and 1941, Rustin worked as an organizer of the Young Communist League. In 1941, he joined the Fellowship of Reconciliation, a nonviolent antiwar group, and later served as its director of race relations. In 1942, Rustin, along with James Farmer, became active in the Chicago Committee of Racial Equality, out of which the Congress of Racial Equality was formed.

Rustin was one of the founding members of the Southern Christian Leadership Conference (SCLC). In 1963, he was named chief logistics expert and organizational coordinator of the March on Washington. From 1964 to 1979, Rustin served as executive director of the A. Philip Randolph Institute in New York City. In 1975, he founded the Organization for Black Americans to Support Israel.

Throughout the 1960s, Rustin maintained support for the nonviolent philosophy to which he had dedicated

Black Panther founders Bobby Seale (left) and Huey Newton (right) in 1969 (AP/Wide World Photos, Inc.).

his life. Nonviolence, he argued, was not outdated; it was a necessary and inexorable plan called for by the African American's condition in the United States. Rustin continued to be active in the Civil Rights movement until his death on August 24, 1987, at the age of 77.

Bobby Seale (1936–)
Black Panther Party Co-Founder

Born Robert George Seale in Dallas, Texas, on October 20, 1936, Bobby Seale, along with Huey P. Newton

and Bobby Hutton, was one of the founding members of the Black Panther Party for Self-Defense. His family moved from Dallas to Port Arthur, Texas, before settling in Oakland, California.

After leaving high school, Seale joined the United States Air Force and trained as a sheet-metal mechanic. However, he was discharged for disobeying an officer. Returning home, he found sporadic work as a sheet metal mechanic. In 1959, Seale enrolled at Merritt College and studied engineering drafting. While attending

Merritt, Seale joined the Afro-American Association, a campus organization that stressed African American separatism and self-improvement. It was through this organization that Seale met Panther co-founder Huey Newton.

Seale and Newton soon became disenchanted with the association. In 1966, Seale and Newton formed the Black Panther Party for Self-Defense. One of their objectives was to form armed patrols to protect citizens from what they considered racist police abuse.

In March of 1971, Seale was charged with kidnapping and killing Panther Alex Rackley, a suspected police informant. However, a mistrial was declared, and the charges dismissed. Seale began to steer the Panthers away from its revolutionary agenda and toward one of creating community action programs. In 1974, Seale left the party to form Advocates Scene, an organization aimed at helping the underprivileged from grass root political coalitions.

More recently, Seale has served as a community liaison for Temple University's African American Studies Department. He has lectured throughout the country and has written several books including: *Seize the Time: The Story of the Black Panther Party* (1970), *A Lonely Rage: The Autobiography of Bobby Seale* (1978), and *Barbeque'n with Bobby Seale* (1987).

Mabel K. Staupers (1890–1988)
Former National Association of Colored Graduate Nurses President; Nurse, Civil Rights Advocate

As president of the National Association of Colored Graduate Nurses, Mabel Keaton Staupers led a successful drive to integrate the mainstream nursing profession and to end segregation in the U.S. Armed Forces Nurse Corps in World War II.

Staupers was born in Barbados, West Indies, on February 27, 1890, and migrated to the United States in 1903, settling in Harlem. She began her nursing education in 1914 at Freedmen's Hospital School of Nursing (now known as Howard University College of Nursing) in Washington, DC, and in 1917 graduated with class honors. After graduation, she began private-duty nursing until, with the assistance of physicians Louis T. Wright and James Wilson, she helped to found the Booker T. Washington Sanitarium in Harlem in 1922. This served as Harlem's first inpatient center for African American patients with tuberculosis.

With a working fellowship, Staupers spent time at Jefferson Hospital Medical College in Philadelphia, then conducted a survey of health needs in Harlem for the New York Tuberculosis Association. She identified the health care problems of minorities, leading to the establishment of the Harlem Committee of the New York Tuberculosis and Health Association. Ultimately, she served twelve years as executive secretary.

During the 1930s and 1940s, Staupers worked closely with association president Estelle Massey Riddle in a fight to integrate African American nurses into the mainstream of nursing. On January 20, 1945, the surgeon general of the U.S. Army announced that race would no longer be a factor in accepting nurses into the Army Nurse Corps. The U.S. Navy followed five days later by integrating the Navy Nurse Corps.

Later Staupers fought to end the racial barriers of the American Nurses' Association (ANA); in 1948, its House of Delegates opened the organization to African American members. By 1949, however, Staupers persuaded the NACGN's members that the organization had realized its goals and was now obsolete. The organization's convention in that year voted to dissolve the organization, and Staupers presided over the formal dissolution.

In recognition of her leadership and efforts to remove racial barriers for African American women in the military and the ANA, Staupers was widely honored. Among her honors was the Spingarn Medal, which she received from the National Association for the Advancement of Colored People in 1951. She recorded the plight of African American nurses in her book *No Time for Prejudice: A Story of the Integration of Negroes in the United States*. Staupers died on November 29, 1989.

Faye Wattleton (1943–)
Former Planned Parenthood Executive Director, Women's Rights Activist

One of the most influential African American women in the area of reproductive rights, Faye Wattleton propelled Planned Parenthood Association into a high profile, aggressive, and vocal public health organization.

Born Alyce Faye Wattleton on July 8, 1943, in St. Louis, Missouri, her family, though poor, stressed the importance of helping others who were less fortunate. She graduated from Ohio State University Nursing School in 1964, and then spent two years as a maternity nursing instructor for the Miami Valley Hospital School of Nursing in Dayton. Wattleton received an M.S. degree in maternal and infant health care from Columbia University, as well as certification as a nurse-midwife, after studying on a full scholarship 1967. While at Columbia, she interned at Harlem Hospital and saw firsthand the risks involved in induced abortions by the untrained. The death of a young woman stressed to her the importance of safe abortions.

Faye Wattleton (AP/Wide World Photos, Inc.)

Wattleton returned to Dayton in 1967 as assistant director of Public Health Nursing Services. She also joined the local Planned Parenthood board and became its executive director two years later. In 1975, she chaired a council representing executive directors of Planned Parenthood affiliates around the country, increasing her visibility nationally. Three years later, she was elected president of Planned Parenthood, becoming the first African American woman and the youngest person to head the organization.

Immediately after her appointment, Wattleton insisted that the organization become a strong advocate for women's rights and reproductive freedom. She worked to unite the organization's mostly white, middle, and upper class women who belonged to the organization and the mostly poor women who were clients in the parenthood clinics. Wattleton also argued for equal access to the full range of health services by the rich and poor.

She has an impressive list of awards and honors in recognition of her work including the American Humanist Award (1986), Women's Honors in Public Service from the American Nursing Association (1986), Con-

gressional Black Caucus Humanitarian Award (1989), and the American Public Health Association's Award of Excellence (1989).

In January 1992, Wattleton retired from her position with Planned Parenthood and became host of a syndicated talk show that originated in Chicago.

Walter White (1893–1955)
Former NAACP Executive Secretary

Walter Francis White was born on July 1, 1893, into a middle class family that lived on the boundary between an African American and a white neighborhood in Atlanta. His family was modestly successful, allowing him to attend Atlanta University. He eventually came to the attention of the NAACP and began to work for the organization in 1918.

White's light completion and hair color allowed him to conduct several undercover investigations of lynching in the South during the 1920s. This later provided him with material for his novel *The Fire in the Flint*, a brutal depiction of the lynching of an innocent African American doctor. Along with his national efforts to end lynching, the book aroused controversy and brought White greater recognition.

In 1931 White became executive secretary of the NAACP, helping to lift the organization from obscurity to a position of influence in which its support was sought even by U.S. presidents. Under his leadership, the NAACP fought for the right to vote, the right of African Americans to be admitted to professional and graduate schools in state universities, and for equal pay for African American teachers in public schools.

Walter White did not live to see the flowering of the Civil Rights movement in the second half of the 1950s. He died of a heart attack on March 21, 1955. However, more than 3,000 people attended his funeral, and President Eisenhower praised him as "a vigorous champion of justice and equality."

Roy Wilkins (1901–1981)
Former NAACP Executive Director

Born in St. Louis, Missouri, on August 30, 1901, Roy Wilkins was reared in St. Paul, Minnesota. He attended the University of Minnesota, where he majored in sociology and minored in journalism. He served as night editor of the *Minnesota Daily* (the school paper) and edited an African American weekly, the *St. Paul Appeal*. After receiving his B.A. in 1923, he joined the staff of the *Kansas City Call*, a leading African American weekly.

Roy Wilkins (Encore)

In 1931, Wilkins left the *Call* to serve under Walter White as assistant executive secretary of the National Association for the Advancement of Colored People. In 1934, he succeeded W. E. B. Du Bois as editor of *Crisis* magazine. Wilkins was named acting executive secretary of the NAACP in 1949, when White took a year's leave of absence from the organization. Wilkins assumed the position as executive secretary of the NAACP in 1955. He quickly established himself as one of the most articulate spokesmen in the Civil Rights movement. He testified before innumerable Congressional hearings, conferred with United States presidents, and wrote extensively.

For several years, Wilkins served as chairperson of the Leadership Conference on Civil Rights, an organization of more than 100 national civic, labor, fraternal, and religious organizations. He was a trustee of the Eleanor Roosevelt Foundation, the Kennedy Memorial Library Foundation, and the Estes Kefauver Memorial Foundation. He was also a member of the board of directors of the Riverdale Children's Association, the John LaFarge Institute, and the Stockbridge School, as well as the international organization, Peace with Freedom. Wilkins died on September 8, 1981.

Carter G. Woodson (1875–1950)
Association for the Study of Afro-American Life and History Cofounder, Historian, Writer, Publisher, Black History Month Founder

Often called "The Father of Black History," Carter Godwin Woodson was a tireless advocate of African American history in school curriculum, the promotion of African American achievements through the work of the Association for the Study of Negro Life and History that he co-founded, and the promotion of the African American heritage through Negro History Week (now Black History Month).

Woodson was born to former slaves in 1875, in New Canton, Virginia. In 1898, he studied at Berea College in Kentucky, then taught school in Fayette County, West Virginia. In 1900, he was appointed principal of his alma mater, Douglass High School, then returned to Berea until the school, racially integrated at first, was forced to close its doors to African American students because of the state's segregation laws. Woodson then studied at the University of Chicago and returned to Berea, after it readmitted African Americans.

Woodson then taught school and later served as school supervisor in the Philippines. He spent a semester at the Sorbonne, where he improved his French-speaking skills. He returned to the University of Chicago, where he received a B.A. in 1907 and M.A. degrees in history, romance languages, and literature in 1908. Woodson began studying for his doctorate at Harvard University in 1908 and later taught at a several schools in the District of Columbia; his longest tenure was at the M Street High School where he remained from 1911 to 1917. He completed his dissertation and received his Ph.D. from Harvard in 1912, becoming the second African American man to receive such a degree from that institution (i.e., the first was W. E. B. Du Bois).

Deeply devoted to the study and promotion of African American history and to the preservation of the culture of his race, Woodson joined several other men in founding the Association for the Study of African-American Life and History in 1912 (ASALH). Woodson's obsession with the history of African Americans remained foremost throughout his life's work. In 1916, the association began publishing the widely recognized *Journal of Negro History*.

Woodson held several positions in academia in the District of Columbia: principal of Armstrong Manual Training School (1918–1919); faculty member, dean, and head of the graduate faculty at Howard University (1919–1920); and dean at West Virginia Collegiate Institute (1920–1922). After that, he concentrated on the work of the ASALH. In 1921, he organized Associated Publishers, the publishing arm of ASALH. Among his own works issued by the press were *The History of the Negro Church* (1921) and *The Mis-Education of the Negro* (1933).

Woodson remained concerned that young people, teachers, laymen, and others should know about African American history. As a partial solution, beginning February 1926, he promoted a special commemoration, or Negro History Week, to incorporate the birthdays of Booker T. Washington, Abraham Lincoln, and Frederick Douglass. The celebration had national appeal and, during 1976, Negro History Week became Black History Month. In that same year, ASALH changed its name to the Association for the Study of Afro-American Life and History. To further promote African American history among the schools, Woodson founded the Negro History Bulletin in 1937. On April 3, 1950, Woodson died in Washington, DC.

Whitney M. Young, Jr. (1922–1971)
Former NUL Director

Whitney Moore Young Jr. was born in Lincoln Ridge, Kentucky, on July 31, 1922. He received his B.A. degree from Kentucky State College (now University) in 1941. He went on to attend the Massachusetts Institute of Technology, and in 1947, he earned an M.A. degree in social work from the University of Minnesota.

In 1947, Young was made director of industrial relations and vocational guidance for the St. Paul, Minnesota, Urban League. In 1950, he moved on to become executive secretary of the St. Paul chapter. Between 1954 and 1961, Young was dean of the Atlanta University School of Social Work. He also was a visiting scholar at Harvard University through a Rockefeller Foundation grant.

In 1961, the National Urban League's board of directors elected Young as president of the organization. Young instituted new programs such as the National Skills Bank, the Broadcast Skills Bank, the Secretarial Training Project, and an on-the-job training program with the U.S. Department of Labor. Between 1961 and 1971, the organization grew from 63 to 98 affiliates.

In addition to his work with the National Urban League, Young served as president of the National Association of Social Workers and the National Conference on Social Welfare, served on the boards and advisory committees of the Rockefeller Foundation, Urban Coa-

Whitney Young, Jr. (National Urban League, Inc.)

lition, and Urban Institute, as well as on seven presidential commissions. In 1969, Young was selected by President Lyndon B. Johnson to receive the Presidential Medal of Freedom, the nation's highest civilian award. Young wrote two books *To Be Equal* (1964) and *Beyond Racism: Building an Open Society* (1969). He was also coauthor of *A Second Look* (1958). Young died on March 11, 1971, while attending a conference in Africa.

◆ NATIONAL ORGANIZATIONS

A Better Chance (ABC)
419 Boylston St.
Boston, MA 02116
(617) 421-0950
www.abetterchance.org
Founded 1963.

A Better Chance identifies, recruits, and places talented minority students into leading secondary and public schools. Member schools provide financial assistance for those students who are need of assistance. The group also conducts research and technical assistance on expanded opportunities for minority students in secondary and higher education.

A. Philip Randolph Educational Fund

1444 I St., NW, No. 300
Washington, DC 20005
(202) 289-2774
www.aprihq.org
Founded 1964.

The Fund seeks to: eliminate prejudice and discrimination from all areas of life; educate individuals and groups on their rights and responsibilities; defend human and civil rights; assist in the employment and education of the underprivileged; and combat community deterioration, delinquency, and crime.

A. Philip Randolph Institute

1444 I St., NW, No. 300
Washington, DC 20005
(202) 289-2774
www.aprihq.org
Founded 1964.

The Institute promotes cooperation between the African American community and the labor force. The Institute's primary interest is political action through coalition building and the organization of affiliate groups. It also conducts research, runs specialized education programs, and maintains a speakers's bureau.

Africa Faith and Justice Network

401 Michigan Ave.
PO Box 29378
Washington, DC 20017
(202) 832-3412
www.acad.cua.edu/afjn
Founded 1983.

The purpose of the Network is to examine the role that Europe, America, and other northern countries play in causing injustices in Africa. It challenges national policies found to be detrimental to the interest of African peoples. In addition, the Network gathers information on issues and policies that adversely affect Africa, analyzes the data, and makes recommendations for advocacy or action. It also consults with churches of Africa, field missionaries, and other African individuals and groups.

The Africa Fund

50 Broad St., Ste. 711
New York, NY 10004
(212) 785-1024
www.prairienet.org/acas/afund.html
Founded 1966.

Established by the American Committee on Africa to do the following: defend human and civil rights of needy Africans by providing or financing legal assistance; provide medical relief to Africans, particularly refugees; render aid to indigent Africans in the United States, Africa, or elsewhere who are suffering economic, legal, or social injustices; provide educational aid or grants to Africans, particularly refugees; inform the American public about the needs of Africans; and engage in study, research, and analysis of questions relating to Africa.

Africa News Service

PO Box 3851
Durham, NC 27702
(919) 286-0747
www.africanews.org
Founded 1973.

A news agency whose purpose is to supply material on Africa for broadcast and print media. Covers African politics, economy and culture, and U.S. policy and international issues affecting Africa. Obtains news by monitoring African radio stations on short-wave equipment, by subscribing to African publications, and through a network of reporters based in Africa. Also produces investigative stories on U.S. policy and its implications. Provides audio news and programming for radio, articles and graphics for newspapers and magazines, and prints for libraries and institutions. Carries out research for feature articles, news programs, and individuals.

Africa Travel Association

347 Fifth Ave., Ste. 610
New York, NY 10016
(212) 447-1926
Founded 1975.

The Association conducts regional seminars and trade show exhibitions and sponsors the Africa Guild to help develop a general interest in Africa.

Africa Watch

Human Rights Watch
485 Fifth Ave.
New York, NY 10017-6104
(212) 972-8400
www.hrwnyc@hrw.org
Founded 1988.

The Watch monitors and promotes internationally recognized human rights in Africa.

Africa World Press

PO Box 1892
Trenton, NJ 08607
(609) 771-1666
www.africanworld.com
Founded 1979.

Founded by scholar activists and members of the African intellectual community. The Press promotes and maintains the development of an independent, democratic, and critical thinking African intellectual community. It also utilizes the scientific knowledge and skills of the community to give service to African peoples and social movements. It further conducts seminars on various subjects, such as the energy crisis, human rights, political repression, and food.

African-American Institute

380 Lexington Ave., Ste. 4200
New York, NY 10168
(212) 949-5666
Founded 1953.

The Institute works to further development in Africa, improve African American understanding, and inform Americans about Africa. In addition, it engages in training, development assistance, and informational activities. It sponsors African American conferences, media and congressional workshops, and regional seminars.

African-American Labor Center

1925 K St., NW, Ste. 300
Washington, DC 20006
(202) 778-4600
Founded 1964.

The Center assists, strengthens, and encourages free and democratic trade unions in Africa. It has undertaken projects in 43 countries in partnership with African trade unions. Programs are developed upon request and advice of African unions with knowledge of host government. Projects are geared to eventual assumption of complete managerial and financial responsibility by African labor movements. The objective is to help build sound national labor organizations that will be of lasting value to workers and the community, institutions that contribute to the economic and social development of their countries and to Africa's total political and economic independence. Major areas of activity are workers's education and leadership training, vocational training, cooperatives and credit unions, union medical and social service programs, administrative support for unions, and communication and information. The Center sponsors study tours and visitor programs to permit African and American trade unionists to become familiar with each other's politics, economies, and trade union movements; Africans are exposed to technical training not available in their homeland.

African American Museums Association

PO Box 548
Wilberforce, OH 45394-0548
(937) 376-4611
Founded 1978.

The Association represents museums, scholars, and museum professionals who are concerned with preserving, restoring, displaying, researching, and collecting African American culture and history. The group also provides technical assistance to African American museums.

Africare

440 R St., NW
Washington, DC 20001
(202) 462-3614
www.africare.org
Founded 1971.

Africare seeks to improve the quality of life in rural Africa. It provides health and environmental protection services in rural areas of Africa, works to improve African water and agricultural resources, and conducts public education programs in the United States on African development.

Alcoholism in the Black Community

ABC Addiction Services
East Orange General Hospital
East Orange, NJ 07019
(973) 678-8300

All-African People's Revolutionary Party

1738 A St., SE
Washington, DC 20003
Founded 1971.

Founded by Africans and persons of African descent who support Pan-Africanism, "the total liberation and unification of Africa under an all-African socialist government."

Alpha Kappa Alpha

5656 S. Stony Island Ave.
Chicago, IL 60637
(773) 684-1282
Founded 1908.

A service sorority founded in 1908.

Alpha Phi Alpha

2313 St. Paul St.
Baltimore, MD 21218
(410) 554-0040
Founded 1906.

A service fraternity founded in 1906.

Alpha Pi Chi

PO Box 255
Kensington, MD 20895
(301) 559-4330
Founded 1963.

A service sorority founded in 1963.

American Association of Blacks in Energy

927 15th St., NW, Ste. 200
Washington, DC 20005
(202) 371-9530
www.aabe.org
Founded 1977.

Founded by African Americans in energy-related professions including: engineers, scientists, consultants, academicians, and entrepreneurs; government officials and public policymakers; interested students. The Association represents African Americans and other minorities in matters involving energy use and research, the formulation of energy policy, the ownership of energy resources, and the development of energy technologies. It seeks to increase the knowledge, understanding, and awareness of the minority community in energy issues by serving as an energy information source for policymakers, recommending African Americans and other minorities to appropriate energy officials and executives, encouraging students to pursue professional careers in the energy industry, and advocating the participation of African Americans and other minorities in energy programs and policymaking activities. It also updates members on key legislation and regulations being developed by the Department of Energy, the Department of Interior, the Department of Commerce, the Small Business Administration, and other federal and state agencies.

American Baptist Black Caucus

Beth Eden Baptist Church
Tenth and Adeline Sts.
Oakland, CA 94607
(510) 444-1625
Founded 1968.

The Caucus is concerned with reforming the American Baptist Convention in terms of bridging the gap between whites and minority members. It seeks to: develop convention support of scholarship aid for disadvantaged students; resources for business and religious projects in the inner city; adequate representation of minorities in the convention structure; support for African American colleges and universities; and open hiring policies on local, state, and national levels.

American Black Book Writers Association

PO Box 10548
Marina Del Rey, CA 90295
(323) 822-5195
Founded 1980.

The Association represents African Americans in the United States publishing industry. It encourages development of African American authors and works to preserve and advance African American literature. The Association promotes and gives market support to members's works; holds mutual promotions and tours; sponsors cooperative advertising in African American-oriented media; and conducts research on problems affecting African American authors and their works in the United States.

American Committee on Africa

50 Broad St., Ste. 711
New York, NY 10004
(212) 785-1024
www.prairienet.org/acas/afund.html
Founded 1953.

Devoted to supporting African people in their struggle for freedom and independence, the Committee focuses on southern Africa and the Western Sahara and support for African liberation movements. It works with legislators, churches, trade unions, and interested students; arranges speaking tours for African leaders; publicizes conditions and developments in Africa; and sponsors research, rallies, and demonstrations.

American Tennis Association

8100 Cleary Blvd.
Plantation, FL 33324-1370
Founded 1916.

Founded by persons interested in tennis, the Association promotes and develops tennis among African Americans. It supports training programs for coaches, sponsors tournaments, and training programs for young players.

Anti-Repression Resource Team

PO Box 8040
State College, PA 16803-8040
(814) 237-3095
Founded 1979.

The team combats all forms of political repression including police violence and misconduct, Ku Klux Klan and Nazi terrorism, and spying and covert action by secret police and intelligence agencies. It focuses on research, writing, lecturing, organizing, and publishing and conducts training workshops for church, labor, and community organizations.

Association of African American People's Legal Council

c/o William Bert Johnson
13902 Robson St.
Detroit, MI 48227
(313) 231-6320
Founded 1959.

The Council seeks to achieve equal justice under the law for African Americans and to provide free legal counsel to people of African American descent. It compiles statistics and reports on cases of international inequality and obtains research from public systems on education and its effect on discrimination.

Association of Black Admissions and Financial Aid Officers of the Ivy League and Sister Schools

Admissions Office
PO Box 208234
Yale University
New Haven, CT 06520-8234
(203) 432-9316
www.yale.edu
Founded 1970.

The Association was founded by present and former minority admissions and financial aid officers employed at Ivy League or sister schools. These schools include: Brown, Columbia, Cornell, Dartmouth, Harvard/Radcliffe, Massachusetts Institute of Technology, University of Pennsylvania, Princeton, Yale, Barnard, Bryn Mawr, Mount Holyoke, Smith, and Wellesley. The Association aids minority students who wish to pursue a college education and seeks to improve methods of recruitment, admittance, and financial services that support the growth and maintenance of the minority student population at these institutions. It encourages Ivy League and sister schools to respond to the needs of minority students and admissions and financial aid officers.

Association of Black Anthropologists

4350 N. Fairfax Dr., Ste. 640
Arlington, VA 22203
(703) 528-1902
www.ameranthassn.org
Founded 1970.

The Association works to: formulate conceptual and methodological frameworks to advance understanding of all forms of human diversity and commonality; advance theoretical efforts to explain the conditions that produce social inequalities based on race, ethnicity, class, or gender; develop research methods that involve the peoples studied and local scholars in all stages of investigation and dissemination of findings.

Association of Black Cardiologists

Peachtree Center
South Tower 225, Ste. 1420
Peachtree St. NE
Atlanta, GA 30303
(404) 582-8777
www.abcardio.org
Founded 1974.

The Association seeks to improve prevention and treatment of cardiovascular diseases.

Association of Black Foundation Executives

1828 L St., NW
Washington, DC 20036
(202) 466-6512
www.cof.org.
Founded 1971.

The Association encourages increased recognition of economic, educational, and social issues facing African Americans in the grant making field. It seeks to: promote support of African Americans and their status as grant making professionals, increase the number of African Americans entering the grant making field, and helps members improve their job effectiveness. Though involved with grant making organizations, the ABFE itself does not award grants.

Association of Black Nursing Faculty

c/o Dr. Bess Stewart
7219 Saddle Creek
San Antonio, TX 78238
(210) 680-2064
Founded 1987.

The Association works to promote health-related issues and educational concerns of interest to the African American community and ABNF. It serves as a forum for communication and the exchange of information among members, as well as develops strategies for expressing concerns to other individuals, institutions, and communities. It aims to do the following: assists members in professional development; develops and sponsors continuing education activities; fosters networking and guidance in employment and recruitment activities; and promotes health-related issues of legislation, government programs, and community activities.

Association of Black Psychologists

PO Box 55999
Washington, DC 20040-5999
(202) 722-0808
www.adpsi.org
Founded 1968.

The Association aims to do the following: enhance the psychological well-being of African American people; define mental health in consonance with newly established psychological concepts and standards; develop policies for local, state, and national decision-making, which have impact on the mental health of the African American community; support established African American sister organizations and aid in the development of new, independent African American institutions to enhance the psychological, educational, cultural, and economic situation.

Association of Black Sociologists

Dept. of Sociology
Central Michigan University
Mt. Pleasant, MI 48859
(517) 774-3160
www.chsbs.cmich.edu/Soc/index2.html
Founded 1968.

Purposes are to: promote the professional interests of African American sociologists; promote an increase in the number of professionally trained sociologists; help stimulate and improve the quality of research and the teaching of sociology; provide perspectives regarding African American experiences, as well as expertise for understanding and dealing with problems confronting African American people; protect professional rights and safeguard the civil rights stemming from executing the above objectives.

Association of Concerned African Scholars

c/o Steven Rubert
Department of History
306 Milan Hall
Oregon State University
Corvallis, OR 97331-5104
(541) 737-3661
www.prairienet.org/acas
Founded 1977.

The Association facilitates scholarly analysis and opinion in order to impact U.S. policy toward Africa; formulates alternative government policy toward Africa and disseminates it to the public; works to develop a communication and action network among African scholars. It mobilizes support on current issues; participates in local public education programs; stimulates research on policy-oriented issues and disseminates findings; and informs and updates members on international policy developments.

Black Americans for Life

419 Seventh St., NW, Ste. 500
Washington, DC 20004
(202) 626-8800
www.nrlc.org

The group promotes alternatives to abortion for women with crisis pregnancies and strives to be a visible presence defending the rights of the unborn in the African American community. It asserts that African American women are twice as likely as white women to have abortions and believes that abortions are counter-productive to advances made through civil rights efforts.

Black and Indian Mission Office

2021 H St., NW
Washington, DC 20006
(202) 331-8542
Founded 1884.

The Office coordinates the distribution of funds from the annual Black and Indian Mission Collection in Catholic churches across the United States. These funds go to support priests, nuns, and other religious workers at African American and Native American missions and schools.

Black Caucus of the American Library Association

Newark Public Library
5 Washington St.
Newark, NJ 07101
(973) 773-7784
www.bcala.org
Founded 1970.

The Association promotes librarianship and encourages active participation of African Americans in library associations and boards and all levels of the profession. It monitors activities of the American Library Association with regard to its policies and programs and how they affect African American librarians and library users. In addition, it reviews, analyzes, evaluates, and recommends to the ALA actions that influence the recruitment, development, advancement, and general working conditions of African American librarians. It facilitates library services that meet the informational needs of African American people, including increased availability of materials related to social and economic concerns, and encourages development of authoritative information resources concerning African American people and dissemination of this information to the public.

Black Coaches Association
PO Box
Stone Mountain, GA 30086
(877) 789-1222
www.bca-org.com
Founded 1986.

The Association promotes the creation of a positive environment in which issues such as stereotyping, lack of significant media coverage, and discrimination can be exposed, discussed, and resolved. It provides member services and petitions the NCAA legislative bodies to design, enact, and enforce diligent guidelines and policies to improve professional mobility for minorities.

Black Data Processing Associates
PO Box 7466
Philadelphia, PA 19101
(215) 844-3235
Founded 1975.

This organization seeks to accumulate and share information processing knowledge and business expertise in order to increase the career and business potential of minorities in the information processing field.

Black Entertainment and Sports Lawyers Association
1502 Fairlakes Pl.
Mitchellville, MD 20721
(301) 333-0003
www.besla.org
Founded 1979.

The purpose of the Association is to provide more efficient and effective legal representation to African American entertainers and athletes. It offers a referral system for legal representation and a resource bank for providing information to students, groups, and nonprofit and civic organizations involved in the entertainment industry; and serves as an industry watchdog in protecting the rights of African Americans within the entertainment community.

Black Filmmaker Foundation
670 Broadway, Ste. 304
New York, NY 10012
(212) 253-1690
Founded 1978.

This group fosters audience development by programming local, national, and international film festivals. The Foundation maintains a video library and conducts seminars and workshops.

Black Filmmakers Hall of Fame, Inc.
405 14th St., Ste. 515
Oakland, CA 94612
(510) 465-0804
www.blackfilmmakershall.org
Founded 1973.

The Foundation seeks to study, teach, and preserve the contributions of African American filmmakers to American cinema. It fosters cultural awareness through educational, research, and public service programs in the film arts. It also holds film-lecture series, the Black Filmworks Festival, and the annual International Film Competition.

Black Methodists for Church Renewal
601 W. Riverview Ave.
Dayton, OH 45406
(937) 227-9460
Founded 1968.

The group serves as platform from which African Americans can express concerns to the general church on issues such as: revival and survival of the African American church; involvement of African Americans within the structure of the church; the conduct of the church as it relates to investment policies and social issues; economic support in the African American community; and the support of the 12 African American colleges. It encourages African American Methodists to work for economic and social justice and works to expose racism in agencies and institutions of the United Methodist Church. The group also seeks improvement of educational opportunities for African Americans, the strengthening of African American churches, and an increase in the number of African American persons in Christian-related vocations. It advocates liberation, peace, justice, and freedom for all people and supports programs that alleviate suffering in developing countries.

Black Psychiatrists of America
c/o Dr. Ramona Davis
1305 Franklin, Ste. 210
Oakland, CA 94612
(510) 834-7103
Founded 1968.

African American psychiatrists, either in practice or training, united to promote African American behavioral science and foster high quality psychiatric care for African Americans and minority group members. The group sponsors public information service.

Black Revolutionary War Patriots Foundation
1612 K St., NW, Ste. 1104
Washington, DC 20006
(202) 452-1776
Founded 1985.

The Foundation raises private funds for the establishment of a memorial in Washington, DC, to commemorate African American patriots of the American Revolutionary War.

Black Rock Coalition
PO Box 1054, Cooper Sta.
New York, NY 10276
(212) 713-5097
www.brcny@aol.com
Founded 1985.

The Coalition promotes, produces, and distributes alternative/African American music and provides information, technical expertise, and performance and recording opportunities for "musically and politically progressive musicians." It also works to increase the visibility of African American rock artists in music media and on college radio stations.

Black Veterans for Social Justice
686 Fulton St.
Brooklyn, NY 11217
(718) 935-1116
Founded 1979.

The group seeks to aid African American veterans in obtaining information concerning their rights, ways to upgrade a less-than-honorable discharge, and Veterans Administration benefits due them and their families. It seeks to prohibit discrimination against African American veterans; provides educational programs; and facilitates veterans's sharing of skills acquired while in service. The group's services include counseling and community workshops on veteran issues and a program to provide services to veterans in local prisons. It also assists veterans who have suffered from the effects of Agent Orange, an herbicide containing dioxin and used as a defoliant in Vietnam until 1969.

Black Women in Church and Society
700 Martin Luther King, Jr. Dr.
Atlanta, GA 30314
(404) 527-7740
Founded 1982.

Founded to provide: structured activities and support systems for African American women whose goals include participating in leadership roles in church and society; a platform for communication between laywomen and clergywomen. It conducts research into questions and issues pivotal to African American women in church and society and maintains a research/resource center and a library with subject matter pertaining to liberation and African American theology, feminism, and feminist movements.

Black Women in Publishing
PO Box 6275
FDR Station
New York, NY 10150
www.bwip.org
Founded 1979.

A networking and support group whose purpose is to encourage minorities interested in all sectors of the print industry including book, newspaper, and magazine publishing. It promotes the image of minorities working in all phases of the book, newspaper, and magazine industries; and recognizes achievements of minorities in the media. It works for a free and responsible press and facilitates the exchange of ideas and information among members, especially regarding career planning and job security. Members are kept informed about the publishing industry and their impact on it. The group encourages and works to maintain high professional standards in publishing and collaborates with other organizations in striving to improve the status of women and minorities.

Black Women Organized for Educational Development
449 15th St., Ste. 310
Oakland, CA 94612
(510) 763-9501
Founded 1984.

The Organization fosters self-sufficiency in and encourages empowerment of low-income and socially disadvantaged women by establishing and maintaining programs that improve their social and economic well-being. The group sponsors mentor program for junior high-aged young women in low-income urban areas; and offers support groups, workshops, and seminars. In addition, it maintains the Black Women's Resource Center, an information and referral service for African American women and youth.

Black Women's Network
www.blackwomensnetwork.org
Founded 1979.

African American professional women organized to improve the political, economic, and educational conditions of minority women. The Network offers support services and networking opportunities to address issues affecting African American women.

Black Women's Roundtable on Voter Participation

1629 K St., NW, Ste. 801
Washington, DC 20006
(202) 659-4929
www.bigvote.org
Founded 1983.

A program of the National Coalition on Black Voter Participation. The Roundtable consists of African American women's organizations committed to social justice and economic equity through increased participation in the political process. The Roundtable organizes voter registration, education, and empowerment programs in the African American community; and emphasizes the importance of the women's vote. It seeks to: develop women's leadership skills through nonpartisan political participation; and encourage African American women's involvement in discussions concerning the influence of the women's vote in elections. It supports volunteer coalitions that work on voter registration, voter education, and get-out-the-vote efforts.

Black World Foundation

PO Box 2869
Oakland, CA 94609
(510) 547-6633
www.theblackscholar.org
Founded 1969.

Composed of African Americans united to develop and distribute African American educational materials and to develop African American cultural and political thought. It offers books in the areas of African American literature, history, fiction, essays, political analysis, social science, poetry, and art. In addition, it maintains a library.

Blacks in Government

1820 Eleventh St., NW
Washington, DC 20001-5015
(202) 667-3280
www.bignet.org
Founded 1975.

Founded by federal, state, or local government employees or retirees concerned with the present and future status of African Americans in government. It develops training and other programs to enhance the liberty and sense of well-being of African Americans in government.

Blacks in Law Enforcement

256 E. McLemore Ave.
Memphis, TN 38106
(901) 774-1118
Founded 1986.

The group seeks to educate the public concerning the contributions made by African Americans in the field of law enforcement. It documents the lives and achievements of the first African Americans to participate in law enforcement in the United States. It also develops programs to improve the public image of law enforcement officers; and has established a short-term training program for law enforcement officers.

Catholic Interracial Council of New York

c/o John Jay College
899 Tenth Ave.
New York, NY 10019
(212) 237-8255
Founded 1934.

The Council works in cooperation with local parishes and governmental and voluntary groups to combat bigotry and discrimination and to promote social justice for all racial, religious, and ethnic groups. It sponsors research, educational forums, workshops, and community action programs. It presents the annual John LaFarge Memorial Award for Interracial Justice to community leaders and the annual Hoey Award to community leaders who have worked to promote objectives of the Council.

Center for Constitutional Rights

666 Broadway, Seventh Fl.
New York, NY 10012
(212) 614-6464
Founded 1966.

The Center works in such areas as abuse of the grand jury process, women's rights, civil rights, freedom of the press, racism, electronic surveillance, criminal trials, and affirmative action. It conducts the Ella Baker Student Program, the Movement Support Network, and in Mississippi, The Voting Rights Project.

Center for Third World Organizing

1218 E. 21st St.
Oakland, CA 94606-3132
(510) 533-7583
www.ctwo.org
Founded 1980.

The Center provides training, issue analyses, and research to low-income minority organizations including welfare, immigrant, and Native American rights groups. It monitors and reports on incidents of discrimination against people of color. It also sponsors the

Minority Activist Apprenticeship Program, which works to develop minority organizers and leaders for minority communities.

Center for Urban Black Studies

Graduate Theological Union
2465 LeConte Ave.
Berkeley, CA 94709
(510) 649-2400
Founded 1969.

The Center provides seminarians and laypersons with resources "to respond to life in the urban community and to represent its oppressed minority people." It develops and offers courses, seminars, and other training programs dealing with issues of race, social justice, urban life, and the African American religious experience. It initiates new ministries; develops and implements community service programs; counsels and assists African American seminarians in placement and in obtaining and developing employment. It also conducts workshops and seminars addressing racial justice, church and race, and urban ministry.

Chi Eta Phi

3029 13th St., NW
Washington, DC 20009
(202) 232-3858
www.ncat.edu/~nursing/chietaphi.html
Founded 1932.

Founded by registered and student nurses. Its objectives are to: encourage continuing education; stimulate friendship among members; and develop working relationships with other professional groups for the improvement and delivery of health care services. It sponsors leadership training seminars and offers educational programs for entrance into nursing and allied health fields. It presents scholarships and other financial awards to assist students; sponsors recruitment and retention programs for minority students; and operates speakers's bureau on health education and biographical archives on African American nurses.

Citizens for a Better America

PO Box 7647
Van Nuys, CA 91409-7647
(818) 757-1776
home.earthlink.net/~colaco/
Founded 1975.

Churches and individuals united to create a better America by strengthening individual rights in the United States. The group serves as a public advocacy organization that lobbies for civil rights and environmental legislation. It conducts legal research in civil rights cases and provides research services to communities

investigating such issues as fair housing and toxic waste disposal.

Coalition of Black Investors

PO Box 30553
Winston-Salem, NC 27130-0553
(336) 922-6240
Fax: (336) 924-0071
Founded 1997.

A national organization that promotes financial literacy among African Americans by addressing issues ranging from savings plans, economic and investment education, and the formation of investment clubs to raising capital for new businesses. It also serves as a link to connect African American investors and investment clubs to communicate ideas and investment strategies.

Coalition of Black Trade Unionists

PO Box 66268
Washington, DC 20035
(202) 429-1203
Founded 1972.

Members of 76 labor unions united to maximize the strength and influence of African American and minority workers in organized labor. Activities include: voter registration and education; improvement of economic development; employment opportunities for minority and poor workers; and sponsoring regional seminars.

College Language Association

c/o Dr. Cason Hill
Morehouse College
830 Westu Dr. SW
Atlanta, GA 30314
(404) 681-2800
Founded 1937.

Founded by teachers of English and several foreign languages at historically African American universities. The Association maintains placement services and a speakers's bureau.

Community Access Producers and Viewers Association

PO Box 68002
Jackson, MS 39286-8002
(601) 362-3431
Founded 1965.

The Association researches the activities of workers, African Americans, and grass roots organizations through the FIS Deep South People's History Project. It maintains extensive Mississippi-centered library and archives; distributes press releases on current southern news; and reprints items on women's liberation and political education.

Conference of Minority Public Administrators

1120 G St., NW, Ste. 700
Washington, DC 20005
(202) 393-7878
www.aspanet.org
Founded 1971.

Composed of members of the American Society of Public Administration who belong to a minority group or are interested in the promotion of minorities within public administration.

Congress of National Black Churches

1225 I St., NW, Ste. 750
Washington, DC 20005-3914
(202) 371-1091
www.cnbc.org
Founded 1978.

Founded to find answers to problems that confront blacks in the United States and Africa including economic development, family and social support, housing, unemployment, education, and foreign relations. The focus is on religious education and evangelism.

Congress of Racial Equality

817 Broadway, Third Fl.
New York, NY 10003
(212)598-4000
www.core-online.org/index.htm
Founded 1942.

CORE is the third oldest civil rights groups in the United States and champions equality for all people regardless of race, creed, sex, age, disability, religious, or ethnic background. CORE seeks to establish, in practice, the inalienable right for all people to determine their own destiny, to decide for themselves what social and political organizations can operate in their best interest, and to do so without gratuitous and inhibiting influence from those whose interest is diametrically opposed. CORE administers several major programs including: Project Independence, which is designed to address the lack of skills among inner-city young adults by providing intensive training in office skills and helping them to find meaningful employment; Project Internet Watch; Civil Rights Boot Camp; a legal defense fund; and an immigration program.

Congressional Black Caucus

2244 Rayburn
Washington, DC 20515
(202) 225-3121
Founded 1971.

Founded by African American members of the U.S. House of Representatives. The Caucus seeks to address the legislative concerns of African American and other underrepresented citizens and to formalize and strengthen the efforts of its members. It establishes a yearly legislative agenda setting forth the key issues that it supports: full employment, national health care, education, minority business assistance, urban revitalization, rural development, welfare reform, and international affairs. It works to implement these objectives through personal contact with other House members, through the dissemination of information to individual African American constituents, and by working closely with African American elected officials in other levels of government. Operates the Congressional Black Caucus Foundation.

Delta Sigma Theta

1707 New Hampshire Ave., NW
Washington, DC 20009
(202) 986-2400
www.dst1913.org
Founded 1913.

A service sorority founded in 1913.

Educational Equity Concepts

114 E. 32nd St., Ste. 701
New York, NY 10016
(212) 725-1803
www.edequity.org
Founded 1982.

Organized to create educational programs and materials that are free of sex, race, and disability bias. It offers training programs for parents, teachers, and students; conducts seminars, symposia, and workshops. It also provides conference planning, consulting, and materials development services. Conducts Women and Disability Awareness Project, which discusses and writes on matters concerning disabled women, feminism, and the links between the disability rights and women's movements.

Episcopal Commission for Black Ministries

815 Second Ave.
New York, NY 10017
(212) 867-8400
Founded 1973.

The Commission works to strengthen the witness of African American Episcopalians in the church through programs that include parish and clergy development, scholarships and grants, and international relations. It provides financial assistance and consultations to parishes and church organizations.

Eta Phi Beta
16815 James Couzens
Detroit, MI 48235
(313) 862-0600
Founded 1942.

A professional business sorority founded in 1942.

Frontiers International
6301 Crittenden St.
Philadelphia, PA 19138
(215) 549-4550
Founded 1936.

A multinational group interested in social justice. The group works through member services to assist individual communities focus on constructive action by members in their community.

Institute for the Advanced Study of Black Family Life and Culture
175 Filbert St., Ste. 202
Oakland, CA 94607
(510) 836-3245

The Institute seeks to reunify African American families and to revitalize the African American community. It advocates the reclamation of what the group considers traditional African American culture. In addition, it conducts research on issues impacting the African American Community, such as teenage pregnancy, child-rearing practices, mental health support systems, and the effects of alcohol and drugs. It also maintains HAWK Federation (High Achievement, Wisdom, and Knowledge Federation), a training program employed in school systems to aid in the character development of young African American males. It sponsors in-service training for agencies, school systems, and the juvenile justice system; and develops training curricula for teen parents.

International Association of Black Professional Fire Fighters
8700 Central Ave., Ste. 206
Landover, MD 20785
(301) 808-0804
www.iabpff.org
Founded 1970.

The Association strives to: promote interracial communication and understanding; recruit African Americans for the fire services; improve working conditions for African Americans in the fire services; assist African Americans in career advancement; promote professionalism; and represent African American fire fighters before the community.

International Black Women's Congress
1081 Bergen St.
Newark, NJ 07112
(973) 926-0570
Founded 1983.

The objective is to unite members for mutual support and socioeconomic development through: annual networking tours to Africa; establishing support groups; assisting women in starting their own businesses; assisting members in developing resumes and other educational needs; offering to answer or discuss individual questions and concerns.

International Black Writers and Artists
PO Box 43576
Los Angeles, CA 90043
(213) 964-3721
Founded 1974.

Founded by African American writers and artists in the United States and West Indies. It provides encouragement and support to members.

Jack and Jill of America
2802 Gulfstream Ct.
Orlando, FL 32805-5811
(407) 843-6132
Founded 1938.

A parental group designed to help parents learn more about their children. The group seeks to increase community awareness and to ensure equal opportunity and advancement for all children.

Kappa Alpha Psi
2322-24 N. Broad St.
Philadelphia, PA 19132
(215) 228-7184
www.kapsi.org
Founded 1911.

A social fraternity founded in 1911.

Leadership Conference on Civil Rights
1629 K St., NW, Ste. 1010
Washington, DC 20006
(202) 466-3311
www.civilrights.org
Founded 1950.

A coalition of national organizations working to promote passage of civil rights, social and economic legislation, and enforcement of laws already on the books. It has released studies examining former President Ronald Reagan's tax and budget programs in such areas as housing, elementary and secondary education, social welfare, Indian affairs, and tax cuts. It has also evaluated the enforcement of activities in civil rights by the U.S. Department of Justice and reviewed civil rights activities of the U.S. Department of Education.

Minority Business Enterprise Legal Defense and Education Fund

900 Second St., Ste. 8
Washington, DC 20002
(202) 289-1700
www.mbeldef.org
Founded 1980.

The Fund serves as an advocate and legal representative for the minority business community.

NAACP Legal Defense and Educational Fund

99 Hudson St., 16th Floor
New York, NY 10013
(212) 219-1900
Founded 1940.

The legal arm of the Civil Rights movement, functioning independently of the National Association for the Advancement of Colored People since the mid-1950s. It works to provide and support litigation on behalf of African Americans, other racial minorities, and women defending their legal and constitutional rights against discrimination in employment, education, housing, and other areas. Also, it represents civil rights groups as well as individual citizens who have bona fide civil rights claims. Contributed funds are used to finance court actions for equality in schools, jobs, voting, housing, municipal services, land use, and delivery of health care services. Has organized litigation campaign for prison reform and the abolition of capital punishment and hosts an annual institute to develop public awareness of new problems being faced by minorities. It also maintains Herbert Lehman Education Fund, through which scholarships are awarded to African American students attending state universities, and sponsors Earl Warren Legal Training Program, which provides scholarships to African American law students.

National Action Council for Minorities in Engineering

350 Fifth Ave., Ste. 2212
New York, NY 10118-2299
(212) 279-2626
www.nacme.org
Founded 1980.

The Council seeks to increase the number of minority students enrolled in and graduating from engineering schools. Works with support organizations to motivate and encourage pre-college students to engage in engineering careers. Operates project to assist engineering schools in improving the retention and graduation rates of minority students.

National Alliance of Black Interpreters

PO Box 70322
New Orleans, LA 70172-0322
(504) 943-6597

National Alliance of Black School Educators

2816 Georgia Ave., NW
Washington, DC 20001
(202) 483-1549
www.nabse.org
Founded 1970.

The purpose is to promote awareness, professional expertise, and commitment among African American educators. Its goals are to: eliminate and rectify the results of racism in education; work with state, local, and national leaders to raise the academic achievement level of all African American students; increase members's involvement in legislative activities; facilitate the introduction of a curriculum that more completely embraces African America; improve the ability of African American educators to promote problem resolution; create a meaningful and effective network of strength, talent, and professional support. It plans to establish a National Black Educators Data Bank and offer placement service.

National Alumni Council of the United Negro College Fund

8260 Willow Oaks Corporate Dr.
PO Box 10444
Fairfax, VA 22031
(703) 205-3463
www.uncf.org
Founded 1946.

The Fund provides a structure for cooperation among African American college alumni groups and friends of African American colleges and works to acquaint the public with the value of African American colleges and higher education. It informs students and the public about contributions of African American college alumni to civic betterment and community progress and recruits students for United Negro College Fund member colleges.

National Association for Equal Opportunity in Higher Education

8701 Georgia Ave.
Silver Spring, MD 20910
(301) 650-2440
www.nafeo.org
Founded 1969.

The Association represents historically African American colleges and universities in their attempt to continue as a viable force in the education community. It seeks to increase funding for member schools through federal and private sources. In addition, it compiles biographical data on schools and individuals, provides placement services, and collects statistics.

National Association for the Advancement of Colored People

4805 Mt. Hope Dr.
Baltimore, MD 21215
(410) 358-8900
www.naacp.org
Founded 1909.

Founded by persons "of all races and religions" who believe in the objectives and methods of the NAACP, which are to achieve equal rights through the democratic process and eliminate racial prejudice by removing racial discrimination in housing, employment, voting, schools, the courts, transportation, recreation, prisons, and business enterprises. It offers referral services, tutorials, job referrals, and day care; sponsors seminars; maintains a law library; and awards the Spingarn Medal annually to an African American for distinguished achievement. It also sponsors the NAACP National Housing Corporation to assist in the development of low and moderate income housing for families.

National Association of Black Accountants

7249A Hanover Pkwy.
Greenbelt, MD 20770
(301) 474-6222
www.nabainc.org
Founded 1969.

Founded to unite accountants and accounting students who have similar interests and ideals, who are committed to professional and academic excellence, who possess a sense of professional and civic responsibility, and who are concerned with enhancing opportunities for minorities in the accounting profession.

National Association of Black and White Men Together

1747 Connecticut Ave., NW
Washington, DC 20009-1108
(800) NA4-BWMT
(202) 462-3599
Fax: (202) 462-3690

National Association of Black Catholic Administrators

1531 W. Ninth St.
Los Angeles, CA 90015-1194
(213) 251-3435
Founded 1976.

Founded to assist the church in its role of evangelization and in defining its mission to the African American community and to provide an inner resource for the social and spiritual needs and concerns of Catholics of African ancestry.

National Association of Black Consulting Engineers

c/o Melle Company
1979 Beaumont Dr.
Baton Rouge, LA 70806
(504) 927-7240
Founded 1975.

The purpose is to gain recognition and increase professional opportunities for African American consulting engineers by lobbying the federal government.

National Association of Black Geologists and Geophysicists

c/o U.S. Geological Survey
2255 N. Gemini Dr.
Flagstaff, AZ 86001-1698
(520) 556-7220
www.nabgg.org
Founded 1981.

Founded to assist minority geologists and geophysicists in establishing professional and business relationships. It informs minority students of career opportunities in geology and geophysics and seeks to motivate minority students to utilize existing programs, grants, and loans. The Association provides scholarships and oversees the educational careers of scholarship recipients.

National Association of Black Hospitality
Professionals
PO Box 195
Smith, AL 36877
(334) 298-4121
www.blackhospitality.com
Founded 1985.

Founded to develop global educational and economic opportunities for the hospitality industry through the expansion and diversification of minority involvement in the industry. It encourages professional development and opportunity in the industry through the design and implementation of workshops and seminars and seeks to increase the number, size, and capability of minority-owned businesses within the hospitality and tourism industries.

National Association of Black Journalists
8701-A Adelphi Rd.
Adelphi, MD 20783
(301) 445-7100
www.nabj.org
Founded 1975.

The Association's aims are to: strengthen the ties between African Americans in the African American media and African Americans in the white media; sensitize the white media to the "institutional racism in its coverage"; expand the white media's coverage and "balanced reporting" of the African American community; and become an exemplary group of professionals that honors excellence and outstanding achievement among African American journalists. It works with high schools to identify potential journalists and awards scholarships to journalism programs that especially support minorities.

National Association of Black Owned
Broadcasters
1333 New Hampshire Ave., NW, Ste. 1000
Washington, DC 20036
(202) 463-8970
www.babob.org
Founded 1976.

The Association represents the interests of existing and potential African American radio and television stations. It is currently working with the Office of Federal Procurement Policy to determine which government contracting major advertisers and advertising agencies are complying with government initiatives to increase the amount of advertising dollars received by minority-owned firms. It conducts lobbying activities

and provides legal representation for the protection of minority ownership policies.

National Association of Black Professors
PO Box 526
Crisfield, MD 21817
(410) 968-2393
Founded 1974.

The Association's goals are to: provide a forum for the exchange of information among college professors; enhance education for African American people and enrich the educational process in general; and support and promote intellectual interests of African American students.

National Association of Black Social Workers
1969 Madison Ave.
New York, NY 10027
(212) 348-0035
Founded 1968.

Founded to support, develop, and sponsor community welfare projects and programs that will serve the interest of the African American community and aid it in controlling its social institutions. It also assists with adoption referrals.

National Association of Black Storytellers
PO Box 33361
Charlotte, NC 28333
(704) 568-3153
Founded 1984.

The Association seeks to establish a forum to promote the African American oral tradition and to attract an audience and works for the reissue of out-of-print story collections.

National Association of Black Women Attorneys
1110 Hamlin St.
Washington, DC 20017
(202) 526-5200
Founded 1972.

Founded to: Advance jurisprudence and the administration of justice by increasing the opportunities of African American and non-African American women at all levels; aid in protecting the civil and human rights of all citizens and residents of the United States; expand opportunities for women lawyers through education; and promote fellowship among women lawyers.

National Association of Blacks in Criminal Justice

c/o North Carolina Central University
PO Box 19788
Durham, NC 27707
(919) 683-1801
www.nabcj.org

Founded by criminal justice professionals concerned with the impact of criminal justice policies and practices on the minority community. It advocates with local, state, and federal criminal justice agencies for the improvement of minority recruitment practices and for the advancement of minority career mobility within those agencies. It also sponsors regional conferences, career development seminars, and annual training institutes; maintains speakers's bureau; and provides financial and in-kind services to community groups.

National Association of Colored Women's Clubs

5808 16th St., NW
Washington, DC 20011
(202) 726-2044
Founded 1896.

A federation of African American women's clubs. It carries on civic service, education, social service, and philanthropy programs.

National Association of Investment Companies

733 15th St., NW, Ste. 700
Washington, DC 20005
(202) 289-4336
Founded 1971.

The Association represents the minority small business investment company industry by monitoring regulatory action and collecting and disseminating trade and business information.

National Association of Minority Contractors

666 11th St., NW, Ste. 520
Washington, DC 20004
(202) 347-8259
samcname@aol.com
Founded 1969.

Founded by minority construction contractors and companies interested in doing business with minority contractors. It identifies procurement opportunities. It provides specialized training and serves as a national advocate for minority construction contractors.

National Association of Minority Political Women

6120 Oregon Ave., NW
Washington, DC 20015
(202) 686-1216
Founded 1983.

Founded by professional women interested in the American political process. The Association conducts research and educational programs.

National Association of Minority Women in Business

906 Grand Ave., Ste. 200
Kansas City, MO 64106
(816) 421-3335
Founded 1972.

Founded to serve as a network for the exchange of ideas and information on business opportunities for minority women.

National Association of Negro Business and Professional Women's Clubs

1806 New Hampshire Ave., NW
Washington, DC 20009
(202) 483-4206
www.nanbpwc.org
Founded 1935.

Founded by women actively engaged in a business or a profession and who are committed to rendering service through club programs and activities.

National Association of Negro Musicians

11551 S. Laflin St.
Chicago, IL 60643
(312) 568-3818
www.edtec.morehouse.edu/cgrines/
Founded 1919.

Founded to promote the advancement of all types of music, especially among young African American musicians. It sponsors annual competitions in which winners compete for scholarships.

National Association of Urban Bankers

1801 K St., NW, Ste. 200-A
Washington DC, 20036
(202) 861-0000
www.naub.org
Founded 1975.

Founded by minority professionals in the financial services industry.

National Bankers Association
1802 T St., NW
Washington, DC 20009
(202) 588-5432
Founded 1927.

Founded by minority banking institutions. The Association serves as an advocate for the minority banking industry.

National Bar Association
1225 Eleventh St., NW
Washington, DC 20001
(202) 842-3900
www.nationalbar.org
Founded 1925.

Founded by minority attorneys, members of the judiciary, law students, and law faculty. It sponsors educational and research programs.

National Black Alcoholism Council
1101 14th St., NW, Ste. 630
Washington DC 20005-5601
(202) 296-2696
www.borg.com/~nbac
Founded 1978.

The Council works to support and initiate activities that will improve alcoholism treatment services and lead to the prevention of alcoholism in the African American community. It provides training on how to treat African American alcoholics from a cultural perspective and compiles statistics concerning alcoholism among African Americans.

National Black Catholic Clergy Caucus
343 N. Walnut St.
PO Box 1088
Opelousas, LA 70571
(318) 942-2392
Founded 1968.

Founded by African American priests, brothers, seminarians, and deacons. Its purpose is to support the spiritual, theological, educational, and ministerial growth of the African American Catholic community within the Catholic Church and serves as a vehicle to bring contributions of the African American community to the Catholic Church. It also advances the fight against racism within the Catholic Church and society.

National Black Caucus of Local Elected Officials
1301 Pennsylvania Ave., NW, Ste. 600
Washington, DC 20004
(202) 626-3000
www.nlc.org
Founded 1970.

Founded by elected African American municipal and county officials united to recognize and deal with problems of members. The Caucus attempts to provide the organizational structure required to better present and respond to issues affecting constituents. It seeks to influence the National League of Cities in the development of policies affecting African Americans; and promotes legislative and economic development initiatives directed toward the needs of the African American community.

National Black Caucus of State Legislators
Hall of States
444 N. Capitol St., NW, Ste. 622
Washington, DC 20001
(202) 624-5457
www.nbcsl.com
Founded 1977.

Organized to provide more political networking to African American legislators from the federal and state levels. Its goals are to: provide a network through which state legislators can exchange information and ideas on state and national legislation; provide a unified front or platform; serve as a focal point for involvement of African American legislators in the "new federalism." Its activities include arranging meetings between all governmental groups representing African American elected officials and analyzing and forming a position on the "new federalism," conducting seminars, maintaining speakers's bureau and biographical archives, and compiling statistics.

National Black Chamber of Commerce
1350 Connecticut Ave., NW, Ste. 825
Washington, DC 20036
(202) 466-6888
www.nationalbcc.org
Founded 1983.

Founded by African American chambers of commerce organized to create a strategy for members of local chambers to share in the collective buying power of African American minority communities. Its primary focus is on the tourism industry because, according to the association, African Americans spend approximately $25 billion in the tourism market each year, but African American-owned businesses net very little from this industry. It conducts training sessions to acquaint

African American businesspeople with the tourism market and marketing strategies.

National Black Child Development Institute
1023 15th St., NW, Ste. 600
Washington, DC 20005
(202) 387-1281
www.nbcdi.org
Founded 1970.

The Institute conducts direct services and advocacy campaigns aimed at both national and local public policies focusing on issues of health, child welfare, education, and child care. It organizes and trains network of members in a volunteer grassroots affiliate system to voice concerns regarding policies that affect African American children and their families. It stimulates communication between African American community groups, through conferences and seminars, to discuss and make recommendations that will be advantageous to the development of African American children. In addition, it analyzes selected policy decisions and legislative and administrative regulations to determine their impact on African American children and youth. Finally, it informs national policymakers of issues critical to African American children.

National Black Coalition of Federal Aviation Employees
Washington Headquarters
PO Box 44392
Washington, DC 20026-4392
(202) 267-9941
www.faa.gov/acr/cae.htm
Founded 1976.

The Coalition's purposes are to: promote professionalism and equal opportunity in the workplace; locate and train qualified minorities for FAA positions; help the FAA meet its affirmative action goals; monitor African American, female, and minority trainees; educate members and the public about their rights and FAA personnel and promotion qualifications; and develop a voice for African American, female, and minority FAA employees.

National Black Deaf Advocates
c/o Arkansas Rehabilitation Services
PO Box 3781
1616 Brookwood
Little Rock, AR 72203
(501) 296-1635
TDD: (501) 296-1670
Fax: (501) 296-1675

National Black Gay and Lesbian Leadership Forum (BGLLF)
1219 S. La Brea Ave.
Los Angeles, CA 90019
(323) 964-7820
Fax: (323) 964-7830
www.nblglf.org

The nation's leading organization addressing the leadership and skill development needs of the African American lesbian and gay communities relative to social, legal, economic, and health issues. The BGLLF maintains the AIDS Prevention Team, an innovative national AIDS education and prevention model. Other major BGLLF programming includes the Women's Caucus and sponsorship of the "Black Lesbian and Gay Leadership Summit: Our Families, Our Communities, Our Lives."

National Black Law Student Association
1225 Eleventh St., NW
Washington, DC 20001
www.nblsa.org
Founded 1967.

Founded by African American law students united to meet the needs of African American people within the legal profession and to work for the benefit of the African American community. The Association's objectives are to: articulate and promote professional competence, needs, and goals of African American law students; focus on the relationship between African American students and attorneys and the American legal system; instill in African American law students and attorneys a greater commitment to the African American community; and encourage the legal community to bring about change to meet the needs of the African American community.

National Black Leadership Roundtable
1025 Connecticut Ave., NW, Ste. 2615
Washington, DC 20036
(202) 296-2543
www.nblr.org
Founded 1983.

The Roundtable's goals are to: provide a forum for leaders of national African American organizations to discuss and exchange ideas on issues critical to African Americans; aid in the development of political, economic, and networking strategies that are advantageous to the needs of the African American community; and ensure that elected and appointed officials represent and are accountable to the African American community.

National Black MBA Association
180 N. Michigan Ave., Ste. 1515
Chicago, IL 60601
(312) 236-2622
www.nbmbaa.org
Founded 1971.

Founded by business professionals, lawyers, accountants, and engineers concerned with the role of African Americans who hold Master of Business Administration degrees. It encourages African Americans to pursue continuing business education; assists students preparing to enter the business world; provides programs for minority youths, students, and professionals including workshops, panel discussions, and Destination MBA seminar; works with graduate schools; and grants scholarships to graduate business students.

National Black McDonald's Operators Association
6363 W. Sunset Blvd., Ste. 80
PO Box 8204
Los Angeles, CA 90008
(213) 296-5495
www.nbmla.org
Founded 1972.

Founded to provide a forum for the exchange of ideas on the improvement of community relations and on the operation and management of restaurants. The Foundation seeks to build and improve the McDonald's restaurant image throughout the community and sponsors training seminars on marketing, better sales practices, labor relations, and profit sharing.

National Black Media Coalition
1738 Elton Rd., Ste. 314
Silver Spring, MD 20903
(301) 445-2600
www.nbmc.org
Founded 1973.

Founded by African American media advocacy groups seeking to maximize media access for African Americans and other minorities in the communications industry through employment, ownership, and programming. It has been recognized by the FCC, Congress, and trade organizations concerned with African Americans and other minorities in the media. Past activities include participating in FCC rule-making proceedings, speaking before university and professional audiences, conduct-

ing classes, and negotiating affirmative action plans with large media corporations.

National Black Music Caucus of the Music Educators National Conference
c/o Dr. Ted McDaniel
School of Music, Ohio State University
Columbus, OH 43210
(614) 292-4657
Founded 1972.

The Caucus's purpose is to foster the creation, study, and promotion of African American-derived music in education. It seeks to heighten public awareness of the problems faced by African American music educators and students and to increase public understanding of those problems. In addition, it provides a forum for the discussion of concerns, coordinates and disseminates materials concerning African American-derived music in order to assist music teachers in teaching African American music and students, and encourages African Americans to aspire to leadership positions and to demand inclusion in the development and presentation of Music Educators National Conference activities including participation in MENC's regional conferences.

National Black Nurses Association
8630 Fenton St., Ste. 330
Silver Spring, MD 20910
(301) 589-3200
Founded 1971.

Founded to function as a professional support group and as an advocacy group for the African American community and their health care. It recruits and assists African Americans interested in pursuing nursing as a career.

National Black on Black Love Campaign
1024 E. 87th St.
Chicago, IL 60619
(773) 978-0868
Founded 1983.

Founded by individuals and businesses united to promote the motto "Replace Black on Black crime with Black on Black love" and foster love and respect in all communities where people are, the group believes, inordinately affected by crime. It organizes "No Crime Day" in various communities and "Adopt A Building Program" for businesses. It also sponsors youth organizations and seminars in schools and communities to educate the public in ways of dealing with crime.

National Black Police Association

3251 Mt. Pleasant St., NW
Washington, DC 20010-2103
(202) 986-2070
www.nbpa.org
Founded 1972.

The Association seeks to: improve relationships between police departments and the African American community; recruit minority police officers on a national scale; and eliminate police corruption, brutality, and racial discrimination.

National Black Sisters' Conference

3027 Fourth St., NE
Washington, DC 20017
(202) 529-9250
Founded in 1968

The Conference seeks to develop the personal resources of African American women; challenges society, especially the church, to address issues of racism in the U.S. Its activities include: retreats; consulting, leadership, and cultural understanding; and formation workshops for personnel. It maintains educational programs for facilitating change and community involvement in inner-city parochial schools and parishes and operates Sojourner House to provide spiritual affirmation for African American religious and laywomen.

National Black Survival Fund

PO Box 3885
Lafayette, LA 70502-3885
(318) 232-7672
Founded 1982.

A project of the Southern Development Foundation. Its objective is to improve the ability of African American and other minority poor to achieve economic progress through their own effort and initiative. It believes that the economic, cultural, and physical survival of the nation's African American community is endangered due to the recession, discrimination, and government cutbacks in social assistance programs. It seeks to maintain and increase support for programs that can avert the economic and human catastrophe the fund says will result if the opportunities offered to African Americans are undermined by current assistance cutbacks. The Fund also maintains: Food for Survival Program, in which landowners and sharecroppers in Mississippi volunteer land, equipment, and labor to provide food and employment for needy families; Health Care for Survival Program, a cooperative low-cost health center in Mississippi; and Jobs for Survival Program, which has assisted in providing jobs for African American workers in Alabama in construction, farming, and community service.

National Black United Front

12817 S. Ashland
Calumet Park, IL 60827
(708) 389-9929
www.nbufront.org
Founded 1980.

The Front's purpose is to unite African American people of diverse political ideologies, age groups, socioeconomic backgrounds, and religious beliefs in order to build "a viable force for social transformation." Its goals are: the elimination of racism, sexism, bigotry, and racial violence; redistribution of the resources and wealth of the nation to provide abundantly for all citizens; and elimination of the "genocidal mis-education system," police brutality, and denial of human rights nationally and internationally. It believes that current conditions in the United States threaten the survival of African American people as a whole, and urges African Americans to overlook individual differences by working together for common goals. It also addresses such issues as unemployment, police brutality, budget cuts harmful to African American communities, and the resurgence of the Ku Klux Klan. The Front conducts seminars and forums; maintains speakers's bureau; offers charitable program; and sponsors competitions and plans to organize boycotts, hold demonstrations, engage in electoral politics, and seek new vehicles for change.

National Black United Fund

40 Clinton, Fifth Fl.
Newark, NJ 07102
(973) 643-5122
www.nbuf.com
Founded 1972.

The Fund provides financial and technical support to projects serving the critical needs of African American communities nationwide. Local affiliates solicit funds through payroll deduction to support projects in the areas of education, health and human services, economic development, social justice, arts and culture, and emergency needs. Programs supported by NBUF emphasize self-help, volunteerism, and mutual aid. The Fund maintains the Walter Bremond Memorial Fund Campaign.

National Black Women's Health Project

600 Pennsylvania Ave., SE, Ste. 310
Washington DC 20003
(202) 543-9311
Founded 1981.

The Project encourages mutual and self-help advocacy among women to bring about a reduction in health care problems prevalent among African American women. It urges women to communicate with health care providers, seek out available health care resources, become aware of self-help approaches, and communicate with other African American women to minimize feelings of powerlessness and isolation, and, thus realize, they have some control over their physical and mental health. It points out that higher incidence of high blood pressure, obesity, breast and cervical cancers, diabetes, kidney disease, arteriosclerosis, and teenage pregnancy occur among African American women than among other racial or socioeconomic groups. It also notes that African American infant mortality is twice that of whites and that African American women are often victims of family violence. The Project offers seminars outlining demographic information, chronic conditions, the need for health information and access to services, possible methods of improving the health status of African American women, and sponsors the Center for Black Women's Wellness.

National Black Youth Leadership Council

250 W. 54th St., Ste. 800
New York, NY 10019
(212) 541-7600
Founded 1983.

The Council conducts workshops for groups involved with African American youth and minority student academic and leadership development; and works to reduce the number of minority students that do not finish high school. It provides resources, information, skills, and strategies for fostering such development; advises educators and parents on their role and responsibility to display leadership and success skills to youths they come in contact with; and makes available to educational institutions training and expertise on cultural diversity, multiculturalism, and problems of bigotry and racism. It also sponsors drug abuse awareness programs.

National Business League

2218 Brainard St.
New Orleans, LA 70113
(504) 523-4443
www.thenbl.com
Founded 1900.

Founded to encourage minority ownership and management of small businesses and support full minority participation in the free enterprise system.

National Catholic Conference for Interracial Justice

1200 Varnum St.
Washington, DC 20017-1102
(202) 529-6480
Founded 1959.

A Catholic organization working for interracial justice and social concerns in the United States, it initiates programs within and outside the Catholic church to end discrimination in community development, education, and employment.

National Caucus and Center on Black Aged

1424 K St., NW, Ste. 500
Washington, DC 20005
(202) 637-8400
www.ncba-aged.org
Founded 1970.

Founded to seek to improve living conditions for low-income elderly Americans, particularly African Americans. It advocates changes in federal and state laws in improving the economic, health, and social status of low-income senior citizens. It also does the following: promotes community awareness of problems and issues effecting low-income aging population; operates an employment program involving 2,000 older persons in 14 states; sponsors, owns, and manages rental housing for the elderly; and conducts training and intern programs in nursing home administration, long-term care, housing management, and commercial property maintenance.

National Coalition of Black Meeting Planners

8630 Fenton St., Ste. 328
Silver Spring, MD 20910
(202) 628-3952
www.ncbmp.org
Founded 1983.

The Planners's purposes are to: act as liaison with hotels, airlines, convention centers, and bureaus in an effort to assess the impact of minorities in these fields;

assess the needs of the convention industry and how best to meet these needs; enhance members's sophistication in planning meetings; and maximize employment of minorities in the convention industry.

National Conference of Black Lawyers

Two W. 125th St.
New York, NY 10027
(212) 864-4000
Founded 1968.

The Conference maintains projects in legal services to community organizations, voting rights, and international affairs; provides public education on legal issues affecting African Americans and poor people; researches racism in law schools and bar admissions; conducts programs of continuing legal education for member attorneys; maintains general law library; compiles statistics; and maintains lawyer referral and placement services.

National Conference of Black Mayors

1422 W. Peachtree St., NW, Ste. 800
Atlanta, GA 30309
(404) 892-0127
Founded 1974.

Founded to: Improve the executive management capacity and efficiency of member municipalities in the delivery of municipal services; create viable communities within which normal government functions can be performed efficiently; provide the basis upon which new social overhead investments in the infrastructure of municipalities can utilize federal, state, local, and private resources to encourage new industry and increase employment; and assist municipalities in stabilizing their population through improvements of the quality of life for residents and, concurrently, create alternatives to outward migration. The Conference facilitates small town growth and development through energy conservation.

National Conference of Black Political Scientists

c/o Dr. Lois Hollis
Albany State University
504 College Dr.
Albany, GA 31705
(912) 430-4870
Founded 1969.

Founded by political and social science faculty, lawyers, and related professionals interested in African American politics and related fields. The Conference seeks to encourage research, publication, and scholarship by African Americans in political science; and to improve the political life of African Americans.

National Coalition for Quality Integrated Education

1201 16th St., NW
Washington, DC 20036
(202) 822-7708
www.nfie.org
Founded 1975.

Founded by national organizations committed to desegregating and improving the quality of elementary and secondary schools in the United States. It serves as a forum for issues and developments pertaining to quality integrated education; and encourages and coordinates citizen involvement in legislative developments.

National Coalition of 100 Black Women

38 W. 32nd St., Ste. 1610
New York, NY 10001-3816
(212) 947-2196
orgs.womenconnect.com/ncbw/
Founded 1981.

Founded by African American women actively involved with issues such as economic development, health, employment, education, voting, housing, criminal justice, the status of African American families, and the arts. It seeks to provide networking and career opportunities for African American women in the process of establishing links between the organization and the corporate and political arenas. It encourages leadership development. It also sponsors role-model and mentor programs to provide guidance to teenage mothers and young women in high school or who have graduated from college and are striving for career advancement.

National Coalition on Black Voter Participation

1629 K St., NW, Ste. 801
Washington, DC 20006
(202) 659-4929
www.bigvote.org
Founded 1976.

Founded to: Increase African American voter registration and participation in electoral voting; develop and fund local independent coalitions that will conduct campaigns to increase nonpartisan voter participation and citizenship empowerment programs. It conducts training programs; collects and analyzes data; disseminates information on voter education including data on the African American voting age population; and sponsors Operation Big Vote and Black Women's Roundtable on Voter Participation.

National Consortium of Arts and Letters for Historically Black Colleges and Universities
c/o Dr. Walter Anderson
The Westbridge, Ste. 818
2555 Pennsylvania Ave., NW
Washington, DC 20037
(202) 833-1327
Founded 1984.

Founded to encourage academic excellence with an emphasis on cultural growth. The Consortium promotes the study of African American history and culture in the context of the scholarly study of world cultures. It offers no grants, but helps sponsor programs through fundraising efforts.

National Council of Negro Women
633 Pennsylvania Ave., NW
Washington, DC 20003
www.usbol.com/ncnw/
Founded 1935.

Founded by Mary McLeod Bethune to assist in the development and utilization of the leadership of women in community, national, and international life. The Council maintains the Women's Center for Education and Career Advancement, which offers programs designed to aid minority women in pursuing nontraditional careers; also maintains the Bethune Museum and Archives for Black Women's History.

National Dental Association
3517 16th St., NW
Washington, DC 20010
(202) 588-1697
www.howard.edu/collegealliedhealth.ndamain
Founded 1913.

The Association was formed by minority health professionals who had been denied access to national associations formed by whites. The Association champions the interests and concerns of poor and minority patients and their doctors. The group has several auxiliary chapters and sponsors symposia and student organizations.

National Forum for Black Public Administrators
777 N. Capitol St., NE, Ste. 807
Washington, DC 20002
(202) 408-9300
www.nfbpa.org
Founded 1983.

Founded to promote, strengthen, and expand the role of African Americans in public administration. The Forum seeks to focus the influence of African American administrators toward building and maintaining viable communities; develop specialized training programs for managers and executives; provide national public administrative leadership resource and skills bank; work to further communication among African American public, private, and academic institutions; and address issues that affect the administrative capacity of African American managers. The Forum maintains an Executive Leadership Institute, which grooms mid-level executives for higher positions in Government; the Mentor Program, which matches aspiring African American managers with seasoned executives over an eight-month period; and the Leadership Institute for Small Municipalities, which provides intensive training for elected and appointed officials from small communities. It offers training programs for black South Africans intent on achieving public administrative positions in the post-apartheid era. It also sponsors the National Minority Business Development Forum to increase the participation of small and minority businesses in local government procurement and contracting programs.

National Funeral Directors and Morticians Association
3951 Snapfinger Dr., Suite 570
Omega World Center
Decatur, GA 30035
(404) 286-6680
www.nfdma.com
Founded 1924.

An association of state and local embalmers and funeral directors seeking to promote ethical standards and laws for the profession.

National Medical Association
1012 10th St., NW
Washington DC 20001
(202) 347-1895
www.nmanet.org
Founded 1895.

A professional society formed by African American physicians. The Association maintains 24 separate scientific sections representing major specialties of medicine. It also hosts a symposium and conducts workshops.

National Minority Health Association
PO Box 11876
Harrisburg, PA 17108
(717) 260-0409
Founded 1987.

Founded by health care providers and associations, consumers, executives and administrators, educators, pharmaceutical and health insurance companies, and other organizations with an interest in health. Seeks to focus attention on the health needs of minorities.

National Organization for the Professional Advancement of Black Chemists and Chemical Engineers

525 College St.
PO Box 5
Washington, DC 20059
(800) 776-1419
www.nobcche.org
Founded 1972.

Founded to aid African American scientists and chemists in reaching their full professional potential; encourages African American students to pursue scientific studies and employment; promotes participation of African Americans in scientific research. The group provides volunteers to teach science courses in selected elementary schools; sponsors scientific field trips for students; maintains speakers's bureau for schools; provides summer school for students of the U.S. Naval Academy. It also conducts technical seminars in Africa.

National Organization of Black County Officials

440 First St., NW, Ste. 500
Washington, DC 20001
(202) 347-6953
www.nobco.org
Founded 1982.

Founded by African American county officials to provide program planning and management assistance to selected counties in the United States. The group acts as a technical information exchange to develop resolutions to problems on the local and national levels; promotes the sharing of knowledge and methods of improving resource utilization and government operations; conducts seminars and training sessions; and plans to maintain resource file on the achievements and history of African American county officials.

National Organization of Black Law Enforcement Executives

4609 Pinecrest Office Park Dr., Ste. 2-F
Alexandria, VA 22312
(703) 658-1529
www.noblenatl.org
Founded 1976.

Founded to provide a platform from which the concerns and opinions of minority law enforcement executives and command-level officers can be expressed; to facilitate the exchange of programmatic information among minority law enforcement executives; to increase minority participation at all levels of law enforcement; to eliminate racism in the field of criminal justice; to secure increased cooperation from criminal justice agencies; and to reduce urban crime and violence. It

seeks to develop and maintain channels of communication between law enforcement agencies and the community; and encourages coordinated community efforts to prevent and abate crime and its causes.

National Rainbow Coalition, Inc.

1002 Wisconsin Ave., NW
Washington, DC 20006
(202) 333-5270
www.rainbowpush.org
Founded 1984.

Founded by the Reverend Jesse L. Jackson, Sr. to build a consensus in the area of civil rights, government, politics, labor, education, and business. The Coalition provides a platform for debate and encourages the development of a new political leadership committed to progressive domestic and international policies and programs.

National Society of Black Engineers

1454 Duke St.
Alexandria, VA 22313-5588
(703) 549-2207
www.nsbe.org
Founded 1975.

Founded to increase the number of minority graduates in engineering and technology.

National Society of Black Physicists

c/o International Business and Management Center
University of Kentucky
Lexington, KY 40506-0034
(606) 257-4067
www.nsbp.org

The Society addresses the needs of African American physicists, works to create opportunities for minorities in the field, and sponsors mentor program and lectures on research findings.

National Urban Coalition

8601 Georgia Ave., Ste. 500
Silver Spring, MD 20910
(301) 495-4999
www.nucnet.org
Founded 1967.

The National Urban Coalition seeks to improve the quality of life for the disadvantaged in urban areas through the combined efforts of business, labor, government, and community leaders. It operates programs that work to increase the participation by minority students in science, math, and computer education; and operates the Say Yes to a Younger's Future program.

442 • National Organizations

Reference Library of Black America

National Urban League
120 Wall St.
New York, NY 10065
(212) 558-5300
www.nul.org
Founded 1910.

Founded to eliminate racial segregation and discrimination in the United States and to achieve parity for African Americans and other minorities in every phase of American life. The League works to eliminate institutional racism and to provide direct service to minorities in the areas of employment, housing, education, social welfare, health, family planning, mental retardation, law and consumer affairs, youth and student affairs, labor affairs, veterans's affairs, and community and minority business development.

Office for Advancement of Public Black Colleges, National Association of State Universities and Land Grant Colleges
New York Ave., NW, Ste. 400
Washington, DC 20005
(202) 478-6040
www.nasulgc.org
Founded 1968.

Founded to collect, organize, interpret, and disseminate data on thirty-five predominantly African American public colleges. The colleges, located in 18 states, enroll over 135,000 students.

Omega Psi Phi
2714 Georgia Ave., NW
Washington, DC 20001
(202) 667-7158
Founded 1911.

A social fraternity founded in 1911.

100 Black Men of America, Inc.
www.100blackmen.org
Founded 1963.

The 100 Black Men of America, Inc. is a national alliance of leading African American men of business, industry, public affairs and government, devoting their combined skills and resources to confronting the challenges facing African America youth. Its mission is to "improve the quality of life of our citizens and enhance educational opportunities for African American youth, in all communities with special emphasis on young African American males." A total of 82 national chapters and 2 international chapters are responsible for mentoring, educational, anti-violence, and economic development programs. These programs nurture crea-

tivity, emphasize academic achievement, and reinforce social responsibility.

Operation Crossroads Africa
475 Riverside Dr., Ste. 1366
New York, NY 10115
(212) 870-2106
www.igc.org/ocu
Founded 1958.

Founded by students and professionals, mostly from the United States, who live and work with African counterparts during July and August on self-help community development projects in Africa. Opportunities are provided for interaction with village elders, educators, and political and other community leaders. The group emphasizes community growth from within a "Third World" structure. Before departure, participants make an intensive study of Africa; after their return, they give speeches about their experiences. Participants pay part of the cost of the project. It organizes workcamp projects for U.S. high school students in the Caribbean and handles the visits of African and Caribbean leaders to the United States. It also sponsors training and exchange programs.

Operation PUSH (People United to Serve Humanity)
930 E. 50th St.
Chicago, IL 60615
(773) 373-3366
Founded 1971.

Founded by the Reverend Jesse L. Jackson, Sr. as a national and international human rights organization directed toward education and economic equity and parity for all, particularly African American, Hispanic Americans, and poor people. PUSH seeks to create an ethical atmosphere and encourages self and community motivation and social responsibility. It also sponsors PUSH for Education Program to aid the nation's public schools and restore academic excellence and discipline.

Organization of Black Airline Pilots
2740 Greenbriar Park, Ste. A-3128
Atlanta, GA 30331
(800) JET-OBAP
www.obap.org
Founded 1976.

Founded to enhance minority participation in the aerospace industry. Maintains liaison with airline presidents and minority and pilot associations; conducts lobbying efforts including congressional examinations into airline recruitment practices; provides scholarships; and cosponsors the Summer Flight Academy for Youth at Tuskegee Institute in Alabama.

Phi Beta Sigma
145 Kennedy St., NW
Washington, DC 20011-5294
(202) 726-5424
www.pbs1914.org
Founded 1914.

A service fraternity that sponsors the Sigma Beta Club for high school-aged males.

Phi Delta Kappa
408 N. Union St.
PO Box 789
Bloomington, IN 47402-0789
(800) 766-1156
www.pdkintl.org

An international organization for professional educators.

Phylaxis Society
c/o Col. Joseph A. Walker, Jr.
PO Box 3151
Ft. Leavenworth, KS 66207
Founded 1973.

Founded by Prince Hall Masonic writers and editors of Masonic publications.

Project Equality
6301 Rock Hill Rd.
Kansas City, MO 64131
(816) 361-9222
www.projectequality.org
Founded 1965.

A nationwide interfaith program enabling religious organizations, institutions, and others to support equal opportunity employers with their purchasing power. Services include: validation of hotels for conventions and meetings of organizations; validations of suppliers to member organizations and institutions; and consultant and educational services to assist employers in affirmative action and equal employment opportunity programs.

Quality Education for Minorities Network
1818 N St., NW, Ste. 350
Washington, DC 20036
(202) 659-1818
www.qemnetwork.qem.org
Founded 1987.

Founded to implement the plan developed by the Quality Education for Minorities Project. The Network believes that minorities are under served by the educational system and thus disproportionately lack the skill needed to participate effectively in a society increasingly based on high technology. It plans to work with school systems, communities, universities, and public and private sector institutions to ensure that minority students have equal access to educational opportunities.

Sigma Pi Phi
920 Broadway, Ste. 703
New York, NY 10010
(212) 477-5550
www.sigma-pi-phi.net
Founded 1904.

Founded as a social fraternity. It maintains the Boulé Foundation. Sigma Pi Phi is the oldest African American Greek letter society in the United States.

Southern Christian Leadership Conference
334 Auburn Ave., NE
Atlanta, GA 30303
(404) 522-1420
www.sclcnational.com
Founded 1957.

A nonsectarian coordinating and service agency for local organizations seeking full citizenship rights, equality, and the integration of African Americans in all aspects of life in the United States and subscribing to the Gandhian philosophy of nonviolence. It works primarily in 16 southern and border states to improve civic, religious, economic, and cultural conditions. It also fosters nonviolent resistance to all forms of racial injustice including state and local laws and practices; conducts leadership training program embracing such subjects as registration and voting, social protest, use of the boycott, picketing, nature of prejudice, and understanding politics; sponsors citizenship education schools to teach reading and writing; helps persons pass literacy tests for voting; provides information about income tax forms, tax-supported resources, aid to handicapped children, public health facilities, how government is run, and social security; and conducts Crusade for the Ballot, which aims to double the African American vote in the South through increased voter registrations.

Southern Coalition for Educational Equity
PO Box 22904
Jackson, MS 39225-2904
(601) 362-6774
Founded 1978.

Founded by a coalition of parents, students, teachers, and administrators that operates in Alabama, Georgia, Louisiana, Mississippi, and North Carolina, with plans to include eight additional states. The Coalition works toward developing more efficient educational programs and eliminating racism and sexism within southern schools. It has organized projects including: Arkansas Career Resources Project, which provides minorities and single heads of households with marketable skills and jobs; New Orleans Effective Schools Project, which attempts to increase school effectiveness through high expectations, stressing academic achievement, and quality instruction; Project MiCRO, which seeks to provide computer access for, and sharpen analytical skills of, minority students; and Summer Program, which focuses on students's reading comprehension skills.

Southern Poverty Law Center
400 Washington Ave.
Montgomery, AL 36104
www.splcenter.org
Founded 1971.

Founded to protect and advance the legal and civil rights of poor people, regardless of race, through education and litigation. The Center does not accept fees from clients. It is currently involved in several lawsuits representing individuals injured or threatened by activities of the Ku Klux Klan and related groups and attempts to develop techniques and strategies that can be used by private attorneys. It also operates Klanwatch.

Southern Regional Council
1900 Rhodes Haverty Bldg.
133 Carnegie Way, NW, Ste. 5900
Atlanta, GA 30303
(404) 522-8764
www.src.wl.com
Founded 1944.

Founded by leaders in education, religion, business, labor, the community, and the professions interested in improving race relations and combatting poverty in the South. The Council comprises an interracial research and technical assistance center that addresses issues of social justice and political and economic democracy. It seeks to engage public policy as well as personal conscience in pursuit of equality. It develops educational programs; provides community relations consultation and field services when requested by official and private agencies; distributes pamphlets pertaining to desegregation of various public facilities and fosters elimination of barriers to African American voting registration; and

acts as official sponsor of overseas government officials, leaders, and other visitors who wish to view race relations in the South.

369th Veteran's Association
369th Regiment Armory
One 369th Plaza
New York, NY 10037
(212) 281-3308
Founded 1953.

Founded to support all patriotic endeavors of the United States and to assist members and their families through charitable programs and community activities. The Association donates funds, equipment, and other supplies to children's camps, needy families, religious institutions, Veterans Administration hospitals, and community and senior citizen centers. It conducts seminar and counseling sessions to assist unemployed veterans and offers study classes to adults for preparation in civil service examinations.

TransAfrica
1744 R St., NW
Washington, DC 20009
(202) 797-2301
www.igc.org/transafrica
Founded 1977.

The group is concerned with the political and human rights of people in Africa and the Caribbean, as well as those of African descent throughout the world. It attempts to influence U.S. foreign policy in these areas by informing the public of violations of social, political, and civil rights and by advocating a more progressive attitude in the U.S. policy stance. It supports the work of the United Nations in Africa and sponsors TransAfrica Action Alert to mobilize African American opinion nationally on foreign policy issues by contacting influential policymakers.

TransAfrica Forum
1744 R St., NW
Washington, DC 20009
(202) 797-2301
www.igc.org/transafrica
Founded 1981.

TransAfrica Forum is the research and education arm of its parent organization, TransAfrica. The Forum seeks to provide an independent review of differing perspectives on political, economic, and cultural issues affecting African American communities globally through its publications. It also conducts seminars with scholars and government officials.

Try Us Resources
2105 Central Ave., NE
Minneapolis, MN 55418
(612) 781-6819
www.tryusdir.com
Founded 1968.

The group compiles and publishes minority business directories and sponsors minority purchasing seminars.

Union of Black Episcopalians
6105 S. Michigan Ave.
Chicago, IL 60637
(312) 288-0038
www.afroanglican.org
Founded 1968.

The Union is dedicated to involving Christians in every facet of church life. It encourages mission, stewardship, education, evangelism, and involvement in church governance and politics.

Unitarian Universalist Association Black Concerns Working Group
25 Beacon St.
Boston, MA 02108
(617) 742-2100
Founded 1985.

Founded to raise denominational public awareness of racism as a current justice issue. It works to implement recommendations regarding racial justice that were adopted by the Unitarian Universalist General Assembly in 1985 and conducts local and regional workshops in an effort to coordinate racial justice work among Unitarian Universalist congregations.

United Black Church Appeal
c/o Christ Church
860 Forest Ave.
Bronx, NY 10456
(718) 665-6688
Founded 1980.

Founded to awaken the power of the African American clergy and the African American church in order to provide leadership for the liberation of the African American community. The Appeal is concerned with African American economic development and political power and the strengthening of African American families and churches. It believes pastors in African American churches should reestablish legitimate leadership roles within the African American community. It works with troubled African American youths in the community and rallies against drugs in urban areas. It also supports community betterment projects including surplus food programs and distribution of food to needy families.

United Church of Christ Commission for Racial Justice
c/o United Church of Christ
700 Prospect Ave., E.
Cleveland, OH 44115-1110
(216) 736-2161
Founded 1965.

Founded to ensure racial justice and social equality for ethnic and racial minorities worldwide. It maintains higher education program to provide scholarships to minority college students.

United Negro College Fund
8260 Willow Oak Corporation Dr.
Fairfax, VA 22031
(703) 205-3432
www.unf.org
Founded 1944.

Founded as a fund-raising agency for historically African American colleges and universities that are private and fully accredited. It provides information on educational programs, sponsors college fairs for high school and community college students, and administers scholarship awards and corporate and foundation programs.

Washington Office on Africa
110 Maryland Ave., NE, Ste. 112
Washington, DC 20002
(202) 546-7961
www.africapolicy.org
Founded 1972.

Founded to monitor and analyze developments in U.S. policy toward southern Africa and work with national and local groups that support the attainment of majority rule. It lobbies on congressional legislation affecting southern Africa.

Young Black Programmers Coalition
PO Box 2661
Mobile, AL 36652-2261
(334) 456-9175
www.nbpcine.ore
Founded 1976.

Founded to provide professional training and offer technical assistance to African American entrepreneurs in the broadcast and music industries. The Coalition conducts lobbying activities pertaining to legislation affecting the music industry and provides scholarships to attend African American colleges and universities.

Zeta Phi Beta
1734 New Hampshire Ave., NW
Washington, DC 20009
(202) 387-3103
www.zpb1920.org
Founded 1920.

Founded as a service and social sorority in 1920. It maintains the Zeta Phi Beta Sorority Educational Foundation.

⑩

Law

◆ The Legal Status of African Americans: 1787–1883
◆ African Americans and the Criminal Justice System ◆ African Americans in the Federal Courts
◆ African Americans on the U.S. Supreme Court ◆ Major Federal Legislation
◆ Major U.S. Court Decisions ◆ Attorneys, Judges, and Legal Scholars
◆ Criminal Justice Statistics
by DeWitt S. Dykes, Jr.

◆ THE LEGAL STATUS OF AFRICAN AMERICANS: 1787–1883

The attitude toward the legal treatment of African Americans before 1883 was one of ambivalence. An understanding of the treatment of African Americans during the period must begin in 1787 with the adoption of the U.S. Constitution. In addition, the Supreme Court's treatment of African Americans during this period in the nation's history must be viewed in the context of the history and of the events that gave shape to the period.

The United States began in 1776 with a declaration of universal equality. But that promise did not include people of color. The ringing testimony to equality in the Declaration of Independence had its limits. In short, America began with a contradiction that centered on race. The constitutional debates of the 1780s highlight the nation's contradictory, confusing positions on race questions. The United States was founded on the principle of individual liberty, but that liberty did not extend to the African slaves and their progeny. The leading questions of the era were: Should the slaves be counted for purposes of representation? Should Congress be empowered to prohibit slavery and the slave trade? Should an escaped slave be "free" to live among the rest of us?

From its beginning, the United States was mired in a debate over the question of slavery. Southerners wanted slaves counted towards representation in the U.S. House of Representatives, while still insisting that slaves were property. This contradiction led to a compromise in which slaves counted as three/fifths of a person for representational purposes. However, this compromise indicated that the problem of slavery would be one that would not easily recede.

Even though the institution of human slavery vexed members of the Constitutional Convention, not once was the word itself used in the document submitted to the convention for ratification. The contradiction between the equality the Constitution espoused and the reality of slavery that the Constitution tolerated would tear the country apart.

The original Constitution also forbade the new federal government from abolishing the slave trade or otherwise affecting matters of race before the year 1808. Runaway slaves were referred to as "person[s] held to service or labour in one state. . . escaping into another. . . ." This fugitive-slave clause sought to ensure that the slaveowners's "escaped" property, when found, would be returned. The purpose of these provisions was to ensure the political superiority of white Americans over the African slaves and their progeny. At the time of the Constitution's framing, African slaves and their descendants were politically inferior to white people.

Even though the framers of the Constitution recognized the peculiar dilemma of racial discrimination, they decided that they could postpone a decision on the "race question." The idea that matters of racial justice and racial equality could be put off was established. With conflicting constitutional antecedents, the Supreme Court has been enormously conflicted on matters of race. The Court takes its cases as it finds them, and cases on race have never been easily or calmly settled in this country.

The Early Days: *Prigg v. Pennsylvania*

Before the 1800s the Court had very few opportunities to render a decision directly on the question of slavery as it was an accepted institution as a feature of American life. The law clearly recognized slaves as property and therefore subject to regulation as other real property might be. This regulation was often justified by citing the fugitive-slave clause of the Constitution (Art. 4, section 2). One of the few pre-Civil War cases to address the slavery question and state regulatory powers was *Prigg v. Pennsylvania* (41 US [16 Peters] 539, 1842).

Pennsylvania had enacted a statute prohibiting any person from removing blacks from the state by force or violence with the intention of detaining them as slaves. The Court explained that the fugitive-slave clause "contemplates the existence of a positive, unqualified right on the part of the owner of the slave, which no state law or regulation can in any way qualify, regulate, control, or restrain." The statute was declared invalid with respect to an escaped slave because, in the words of the Court, "any state law which interrupts, limits, delays, or postpones the right of the owner to the immediate possession of the slave, and the immediate command of his service and labor, operates pro tanto, a discharge of the slave therefrom." The Court further held that the clause implicitly vested Congress with the power to assist owners in securing the return of escaped slaves, that Congress had exercised that power by enacting the Fugitive Slave Act of 1793, that this national power was exclusive, and that any state laws regulating the means by which slaves were to be delivered up were unconstitutional.

Prigg announced no landmark policy. It simply affirmed the social and political realities of its time. However, during the period 1790 to 1883, two major cases involving African Americans and the issues of race did reach the Supreme Court. These two cases—*Dred Scott v. Sandford* (60 US [19 Howard] 393, 1856) and *The Civil Rights Cases* (109 US 18, 1883)—and the relatively minor case *Strauder v. West Virginia* (100 US 303, 1880) reveal the abiding ambivalence that consistently has characterized American race relations.

Dred Scott v. Sandford

The 1800s were consumed with sectional strife, primarily strife about race. In 1856 *Dred Scott* was decided. The case would be an impetus toward civil war. Few cases in judicial American history have achieved as much notoriety as *Dred Scott*. The case continues to

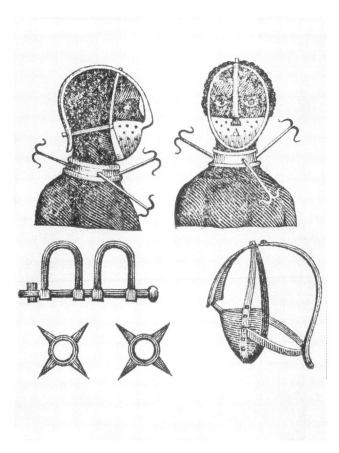

Illustration depicting various slave trading and catching apparatuses (The Library of Congress).

symbolize the marginal status that African Americans have often held in the nation's social and political order.

Dred Scott was the slave of a U.S. Army surgeon, John Emerson of Missouri. In 1834, Scott traveled with Emerson to live in Illinois, where slavery was prohibited. They later lived in the Wisconsin Territory, where slavery was prohibited by the Missouri Compromise. In 1838, Scott returned to Missouri with Emerson. Emerson later died there in 1843, and three years later Scott sued Emerson's widow for his freedom.

Scott's claim was based on the argument that his former residence in a free state and a free territory, made him a free man. A Missouri state circuit court ruled in Scott's favor, but the Missouri Supreme Court later reversed that decision. Meanwhile, Scott had become legally regarded as the property of John F. A. Sandford of New York. Because Sandford did not live in Missouri, Scott's lawyers were able to transfer the case to a federal court. The lower federal court ruled against Scott, and his lawyers appealed to the Supreme Court of the United States. By a vote of seven to two, the Supreme Court ruled that Scott could not bring a suit in federal court. The decision was announced on March 6,

1857, two days after the inauguration of President James Buchanan.

Dred Scott declared that no African American, whether free or slave, could claim U.S. citizenship. It also held that Congress could not prohibit slavery in the U.S. territories. In his opinion, Chief Justice Roger Brooke Taney wrote that African Americans had "no rights which any white man was bound to respect."

This decision—only the second in the nation's history in which the Supreme Court declared an act of Congress unconstitutional—was a clear victory for the political interests that supported slavery. Southerners long had argued that neither Congress nor the territorial legislature had the power to exclude slavery from a territory. Only a state could exclude slavery, they maintained.

The ruling in *Dred Scott* aroused angry resentment in the North and other parts of the country and launched the nation further along the course to civil war. It also influenced the introduction and the adoption of the Fourteenth Amendment to the Constitution after the Civil War. The 1868 amendment, which explicitly overruled *Dred Scott*, extended citizenship to former slaves and sought to give them full civil rights.

Each justice in the majority wrote a separate opinion. However, Chief Justice Taney's opinion is most often cited because of its far-reaching implications for sectional crisis and for the view of the rights of African Americans that it announced. Speaking for the majority, Chief Justice Taney declared that Scott was not entitled to rights such as the right to vote or to sue in a federal court, because, as an African American, he was not a citizen of the United States. The Court did not dismiss the case after ruling on Scott's citizenship. Because there was a growing national desire for a ruling on the constitutionality of such laws as the Missouri Compromise of 1820, the Taney Court seized the opportunity to express its views on both congressional power and the legal status of African Americans

The Missouri Compromise had forbidden slavery in that part of the Louisiana Territory north of the latitude 36 ° 30', except for Missouri. Instead of dismissing the suit, the Court discussed this issue as a part of its decision in *Dred Scott*. By the same seven to two margin, it ruled that the Missouri Compromise, which had been repealed in 1854, was unconstitutional. Taney argued that because slaves were property, Congress could not forbid slavery in territories without violating a slaveowner's right to own property under the Fifth Amendment. As for Scott's temporary residence in the free state of Illinois, the majority ruled that Scott then had still been subject to Missouri law. Dred Scott was

sold shortly afterward, and his new owner gave him his freedom two months after the decision.

The *Dred Scott* decision energized the newly created Republican Party, which had been formed to curb the expansion of slavery into the Western territories. The decision forced Democrat Stephen A. Douglas, an advocate of popular sovereignty to devise a system that would enable settlers to ban slavery in their jurisdictions. President Buchanan, the South, and a majority of the Supreme Court had hoped that the decision would end the anti-slavery agitation that consumed the country. Instead, the decision increased antislavery sentiment in the North, strengthened the Republican Party, and fed the sectional antagonisms that finally exploded into war in 1861.

Strauder v. West Virginia and the *Civil Rights Cases*

Between the time of the Civil War and the *Civil Rights Cases*, the only case to protect the rights of African Americans was *Stauder v. West Virginia* (100 US 303, 1880). The State of West Virginia permitted only "white male persons who are 21 years of age" to serve on juries in the state. This, of course, meant that it was impossible for African Americans to serve on a jury. The Supreme Court invalidated this provision as a violation of the Fourteenth Amendment's guarantee of equal protection.

Ironically, the Civil War, caused in part by Justice Taney's decision in *Dred Scott* that Congress could not bar slavery in the territories, actually resulted in the destruction of slavery. Moreover, the war also resulted in a completely new balance of power between the national and the state governments. Federalism, unlike it had been understood prior to the Civil War, now would function with a totally new calculus in which the federal government was the dominant power.

The years following the war produced the Thirteenth Amendment, the Fourteenth Amendment, and the Fifteenth Amendment to the Constitution. The purpose of the amendments was to emancipate and empower the former slaves. These three amendments are compelling evidence of the relationship between the federal and state governments. The text of the Fourteenth Amendment, overturning *Dred Scott*, emphasized the significance of this new relationship and the new power realignments.

Citizenship in the United States was now defined and protected by the national constitution. State citizenship was subordinate to national citizenship. Augmented by Congress's enforcement powers, these amendments were the constitutional foundations that supported Reconstruction. A principal legislative result of this period was the passage of the Civil Rights Act of 1875. According to the statute, its purpose was "to protect all citizens in their civil and legal rights." Even though couched in general terms, the statute was designed to aid recently emancipated slaves.

The 1870s became unique years for testing race relations in the United States. During this period there were no state laws requiring the separation of the races in places of public accommodation. Practices in particular establishments or particular jurisdictions were matters of local custom, individual choice, or personal preference. An earlier statute, the Civil Rights Act of 1866, and the ratification of the Fourteenth Amendment in 1868 had spawned cases throughout the country including suits for denying sleeper accommodations to African Americans on a Washington-to-New York train, for refusing to sell theater tickets to African Americans in Boston, for restricting African Americans to front platforms in Baltimore streetcars, and for barring African American women from the waiting rooms and parlor cars of railroads in Virginia, Illinois, and California. There also had been massive resistance on the part of whites to the social integration of the races.

Faced with these challenges, Congress, controlled by the Republicans, enacted the Civil Rights Act in 1875. The 1875 statute invalidated all racially motivated interference with individuals's use of "the accommodations, advantages, facilities, and privileges of inns, public conveyances and theatres. . . " (109 US 9–10). In short, the statute sought to provide legislative specificity to the constitutional norms embodied in the Fourteenth Amendment.

The *Civil Rights Cases* were actually six different cases: *United States v. Singleton, United States v. Stanley, United States v. Nichols, United States v. Ryan, United States v. Hamilton,* and *Robinson v. Memphis & Charleston Railroad.* Five of these cases were criminal prosecutions which directly challenged the constitutionality of the 1875 statute. The first of these cases, *United States v. Singleton,* involved the refusal of Samuel Singleton, doorkeeper of New York's Grand Opera House, to honor the tickets of William R. Davis, Jr. and his fiancé.

On November 22, 1879, the pair had attempted to see a matinee performance of Victor Hugo's *Ruy Blas.* Davis, the business agent of the African American newspaper *The Progressive-American,* was obviously African American. However, his fiancée was light complected and had purchased the tickets earlier that day. When the couple returned for the performance, they were denied entrance.

Stanley involved the refusal of hotelier, Murray Stanley, to serve a meal to Bird Gee, an African American in his Kansas hotel. *Nichols* involved the refusal of the Nichols House in Jefferson City, Missouri, to accept an African American as a guest. In *Ryan,* the doorkeeper at Maguire's Theater in San Francisco denied an African American man entry to the dress circle at the theater. In *Hamilton,* the conductor of the Nashville, Chattanooga & St. Louis Railroad denied an African American access to the ladies's car. Instead, she was relegated to a smoking car.

The sixth case *Robinson v. Memphis & Charleston Railroad* was not a criminal case. The case involved travel on the Memphis & Charleston Railroad by a young African American woman, Mrs. Sallie Robinson, and her nephew, Joseph C. Robinson. Mr. Robinson was described as a young African American "of light complexion, light hair, and light blue eyes." The train's conductor attempted forcibly to refuse the two passengers entry to the first-class parlor car for which they had purchased tickets. The conductor mistook the pair for a white man and his paramour. The railroad conceded the constitutionality of the 1875 statute, but argued that it did not apply to the conductor's actions. The trial judge ruled that motive was dispositive under the act. Thus, if the conductor believed Mrs. Robinson to be a prostitute, whether reasonable or not in that assumption, the exclusion was not based on race and the railroad was not liable. The jury found for the railroad and the Robinsons appealed.

The United States, represented before the Supreme Court by Solicitor General Samuel F. Phillips, argued that the act should be upheld in every case. In addition, the government's brief discussed the history of the American race relations and the genesis of the Civil War amendments and their statutory descendants. The government stressed particularly the importance of equal access to public accommodations. The Solicitor General emphasized that this act was one of several enacted by "a Congress led by men who had fought in the Civil War and had framed the war amendments." Implicit in the Solicitor General's position was the idea that Congress understood, as clearly as anyone could, that it was not sufficient to outlaw slavery and to declare equal protection to be the law of the land. Specific statutory protection was necessary to ensure that every vestige of slavery and every reminder of its stigma were eliminated from public life.

The government's arguments, however, did not persuade the Court. It announced its decision on October 15, 1883. The Court ruled against the United States. The vote in the *Civil Rights Cases* was eight to one. Justice Bradley wrote the opinion of the Court, which asserted two conclusions—the Fourteenth Amendment is prohibitory upon the states only, and the Thirteenth Amendment relates only to slavery and involuntary servitude.

Bradley maintained that the Fourteenth Amendment operated only as a prohibition and restriction against the states. Because the Civil Rights Act of 1875 sought to outlaw acts of private individuals, shopkeepers, and other businesses, it violated the constitution. This "state action" doctrine holds that because the government was not the actor in these cases, the Fourteenth Amendment did not empower Congress to outlaw these practices. Also, Bradley's opinion held that, while Congress was empowered by the Thirteenth Amendment to eliminate slavery and all its vestiges, the denial of access to accommodations in commercial establishments, public conveyances, and public amusements was not a "badge or incident of slavery." The opinion halted the progress of civil rights and limited the ability of the federal government, acting through Congress, to eliminate and eradicate racial discrimination for almost ninety years.

Justice John Marshall Harlan dissented. At the time, Harlan was the Court's only Southerner and a former slaveholder. Ironically, he had also been a bitter critic of the Civil War Amendments during the 1860s. However, Harlan had undergone a transformation.

Justice Harlan's dissent was not announced on the day of the majority's decision. The dissent may not have been written until November. It attacks what he believed the central failing of the majority's assertions: that the grounds for the decision were "too narrow and artificial." According to Harlan, the majority refused to embrace both "the substance and the spirit" of the Civil Rights Act. "It is not the words of the law but the internal sense of it that makes the law. The letter of the law is the body; the sense and reason of the law is the soul." And, in Justice Harlan's view, the purpose of the act "was to prevent *race* [emphasis in original] discrimination." The majority, as Harlan develops the dissent, betrayed this purpose "by a subtle and ingenious verbal criticism."

Neither the majority of the Supreme Court nor the nation it represented cared to do much else to promote the civil rights of its new African American citizens. Harlan's dissent in the *Civil Rights Cases* forecasted his more famous one in *Plessy v. Ferguson*, as the decision in the *Civil Rights Cases* led to the black codes, Jim Crow laws, and other examples of *de jure* (by law) segregation that came to define race relations in the United States.

The *Civil Rights Cases* revealed the nation's ambivalence on the questions of race. On one hand, Congress had sought to guarantee the rights of the recently freed slaves by proposing constitutional amendments that were ultimately ratified. Congress went further and augmented the constitutional guarantees with addition-

al legislative protections and safeguards. The Supreme Court, however, frustrated these constitutional and legislative initiatives with a constricted reading of the Thirteenth and the Fourteenth Amendments.

◆ AFRICAN AMERICANS AND THE CRIMINAL JUSTICE SYSTEM

Criminal justice in the United States consists of three major components, law enforcement, judicial and legal services, and corrections. In the past 25 years, African Americans have assumed significant leadership roles in both law enforcement and correctional services as evidenced by the rising number of African American judges, prosecutors, and defense attorneys. However, since 1970, the employment of African Americans as judges and prosecutors has not increased at the rate that gives African Americans working in the system a formidable presence.

Law Enforcement

As the largest arm of the criminal justice system, police are the most visible criminal justice servants. As the first point of contact for persons entering the system, officers make discretionary, often quasi-judicial decisions as to whether an arrest should be made when an offense is alleged to have occurred. Law enforcers have been organized and empowered to support the interest of those with means to shape law, a factor that had significant bearing on the prior relationship African Americans have had with the police.

Just as any other community, African Americans look to law enforcement for protection from an criminal elements present in their midst. However, until the recent integration of many urban police departments, law enforcement officers were used as agents of segregation and fear in many areas. This legacy still causes problems in African Americans relationship with the police.

Judicial and Legal Services and the Correctional System

Recently, a debate on the merits of sentencing and capital punishment has arisen. Statistics show that African Americans are likely to receive stiffer penalties for killing whites than whites would receive for killing African Americans. This is true in the administration of the death penalty, which disproportionately is used against African Americans who kill whites. In 1987, the Supreme Court took up the issue in *McKleskey v. Kemp*, and ruled that statistics could not be used to prove the death penalty was being administered in a discriminatory manner. The Court required more evidence and evinced a fear that if they had ruled the other way, that all African Americans on death row would come forward with claims. The issue has not died, as in 1999, Illinois announced a moratorium on executions to study the issue.

The "Trial of the Century"

On June 12, 1994, a brutal, double-murder led to one of the most sensational criminal trials of the twentieth century. Nicole Brown Simpson, former wife of African American football legend O. J. Simpson, was brutally slain outside of her house with her friend Ron Goldman. Almost immediately, evidence pointed to O. J. Simpson as the primary suspect. The subsequent, year-long trial was aired on television, allowing viewers to witness the entire spectacle almost as if it were a soap opera.

Prosecutors Marcia Clark and Christopher Darden, an African American, portrayed Simpson as a jealous husband who had for years been locked in a pattern of domestic abuse. The murder of a spouse by a habitual abuser is common, and the prosecutors used this as the motive. Simpson's "Dream Team" of defense attorneys focused on an alleged police conspiracy theory based on race. Simpson was found not guilty trial in October of 1995. Ultimately, the case had little to do with the actual murders. *Broadcasting & Cable* reported that "the verdict . . . broke all previous TV viewing records, with over 150 million people tuning in to watch the jury's decision."

Rather than addressing the crime, the proceedings brought the ugly underbelly of the country's prejudices, fears, and values to light. Polls showed that most whites thought Simpson was guilty, while blacks were divided on the verdict. Many African Americans viewed Simpson as another African American man caught trapped in a judicial system enforced by the bigoted Los Angeles Police Department. The trial was the first in which overwhelming DNA evidence was not persuasive to a jury, as the defense attorney's alleged it had been rendered useless by police errors. The impression that Simpson had purchased his freedom with his high-priced lawyers grew in the years following the trial. Following the verdict, the Brown and Goldman families won a wrongful death civil suit against Simpson, forcing him to sell most of his assets. Simpson became a recluse, innocent in the eyes of the court, but guilty in the eyes of many.

The Case of Mumia Abu-Jamal

Though not as big a newsmaker as "The Trial of the Century," the case of outspoken journalist and former Black Panther Mumia Abu-Jamal caused quite a ripple in the legal system during the mid-1990s. During an altercation between a Philadelphia police officer and Jamal's brother, Jamal claims to have entered the fracas in order to keep his brother from being beaten. Though details are sketchy and contested, the aftermath of the fray left Jamal wounded by a gunshot from the officer's gun and the officer dead. Arrested and convicted, Jamal received the death sentence in 1982 for that death.

Since then, a group of national and international supporters have advocated for Jamal's release, alleging that aspects of Jamal's case were improperly handled in regards to the U.S. Constitution and correct legal procedure. Many believe Jamal was framed by the Philadelphia police who wanted to keep the blunt and forthright reporter from exposing evidence of corruption within the law enforcement agency.

On August 7, 1995, ten days before his execution was scheduled, Jamal was granted a one-year stay of execution in order to complete his state court appeals. As of June 1999, that issue was still pending. Meanwhile, Jamal filed a suit against National Public Radio (NPR), who had hired him in 1994 as a news commentator. Jamal's commentaries about life on death row did not bode well in the conservative sector, however. In Jamal's suit, he claims that NPR gave in to pressure from the Fraternal Order of Police and refused to air his segments. Jamal hoped the court would force NPR to broadcast his prison recordings and then return them to him.

◆ AFRICAN AMERICANS IN THE FEDERAL COURTS

Less than four percent of all judges are African American. Nonetheless, the amazing fact is that despite African Americans's complete lack of legal rights as slaves, they made the first in-roads into the courts. In separate incidents, escaped slave Elizabeth Freeman, New England slave Lucy Prince, and Southern slave Dred Scott, all battled racial barriers with courage and dignity.

African Americans did not enter the courts just as parties to actions, they also participated in the system in professional capacities. In 1844, Macon Allen became the first African American admitted to a state bar. Charlotte Ray later became the first African American woman to gain the same distinction. Other pioneering woman followed, including Ellen Craft, Francis Watkins Harper, Laetitia Rowley, Maria Stewart, Mary Church Terrell, and Ida B. Wells-Barnett. John S. Rock became the first African American lawyer to argue a case before the Supreme Court in 1865. In 1873, Mifflin Gibbs became the first African American municipal judge. Though

O.J. Simpson conferring with his team of lawyers (left to right: Carl Douglas, Johnnie L. Cochran, Jr., and Robert Shapiro) during the "trial of the century" (AP/Wide World Photos, Inc.).

he only served a single term, his reputation for fairness was legendary, and he was named U.S. consul to Madagascar in 1897. Jonathan Jasper White was elected to the South Carolina State Supreme Court in 1870. In 1937, President Franklin D. Roosevelt appointed William H. Hastie to the Territorial Court of the Virgin Islands, making him the first African American federal trial court judge. Hastie was succeeded in 1939 by an African American man, Herman E. Moore, and Jane Matilda Bolin became the first African American female judge. In 1945, President Harry S. Truman appointed Irwin C. Mollison to the U.S. Customs Court (now the U.S. Court of International Trade), thus making him the first African American lifetime appointee to a federal court.

Nominated by the U.S. president and confirmed through Senate hearings, federal judgeships are lifetime appointments. Of the less than 1,000 active federal judges, by 1999, just under one hundred were African American. Still, African Americans have received appointments since the early 1960s, beginning with James B. Parsons, who was nominated by President John F. Kennedy to sit on the bench of the U.S. District Court for the Northern District of Illinois in 1961. At that time, the

lack of federal African American judges was noticeable. Kennedy appointed Wade Hampton McCree, Jr., to the U.S. District Court for the Eastern Districts of Michigan in 1961, and Thurgood Marshall to the Second Circuit Court of Appeals in 1962. In five years, Marshall would go on to become the first African American appointed to the Supreme Court of the United States.

President Lyndon B. Johnson followed Kennedy's lead, nominating 11 African Americans to federal benches. Among them were A. Leon Higginbotham, Jr.— Johnson's first appointee—and Constance Baker Motley. As a member of the U.S. District Court for the Southern District of New York, she became the first African American woman to hold a federal judgeship in 1966. The next female appointee did not come for 12 years, when Mary Johnson Lowe was appointed in 1978 by President Jimmy Carter in the same district court venue. Carter also chose Amalya Lyle Kearse, in 1979, to become the first African American woman on the U.S. Court of Appeals. She was seated in the same venue in which Thurgood Marshall began his judicial career.

Republican presidents have had the poorest record of nominating African Americans to the federal courts.

Mumia Abu-Jamal (AP/Wide World Photos, Inc.)

Presidents Richard Nixon and Gerald R. Ford only nominated 11 African American judges, four of which were nominated in Ford's two-year term, over an eight-year period. Lyndon Johnson nominated the same number in half the time. Of note is Nixon's ground breaking appointment of Robert M. Duncan to the U.S. Court of Military Appeals in 1971. Republicans Ronald Reagan and George Bush in 12 years nominated fewer African American judges than their successor, Democrat Bill Clinton. By 1999, Clinton had appointed 45 African American federal judges.

◆ AFRICAN AMERICANS ON THE U.S. SUPREME COURT

Thurgood Marshall, a graduate of Lincoln University and Howard University Law School, was admitted to the Maryland Bar in 1933. He joined the National Association for the Advancement of Colored People staff as assistant to special counsel Charles Hamilton Houston. In 1938 Marshall succeeded Houston as special council, and in 1950, he became director of the NAACP Legal Defense and Education Fund. While working the NAACP

and the NAACP Legal Defense and Education Fund, Marshall played a major role in some of the Supreme Court history's most important cases including *Smith v. Allwright* (1944), *Morgan v. Virginia* (1946), *Shelley v. Kraemer* (1948), *Sweatt v. Painter* (1950), and *Brown v. Board of Education of Topeka*. Between 1938 and 1961, Marshall argued 32 cases before the U.S. Supreme Court, winning 29.

In 1961, Marshall became the second African American to serve on the U.S. Circuit Court of Appeal, when President John F. Kennedy named Marshall to fill a vacancy. In 1965, President Lyndon B. Johnson appointed Marshall to the post of U.S. Solicitor General. With the retirement of Associate Justice Tom Campbell Clark in 1967, Marshall was nominated to fill the vacancy. Marshall's nomination was met with objections from Southern Senators. Nevertheless, he was confirmed, becoming the first African American justice in U.S. history. While on the Court, Marshall served as a supporter of affirmative action, free speech, and the rights of workers. He wrote few famous decisions, but his dissenting opinions in such cases as *Milliken v. Bradley* (1974), and *Regents of the University v. Bakke* (1978), are famous.

On June 27, 1991, Justice Marshall announced his plan to retire after 24 years on the U.S. Supreme Court. On July 1, President George Bush announced that he had chosen Clarence Thomas, an African American, conservative, appeals court judge, as his choice to fill the vacancy created by Marshall. In 1981, President Ronald Reagan appointed Clarence Thomas, a graduate of a Holy Cross College and Yale University Law School, to head the civil rights division of the Department of Education. A year later, Thomas was appointed to head the Equal Employment Opportunity Commission. In 1990 Thomas was appointed by President Bush to fill a vacancy on the U.S. Court of Appeals for the District of Columbia.

In a flurry of controversy, Clarence Thomas was appointed an associate justice of the U.S. Supreme Court in 1991, after being nominated by President George Bush. Besides Thomas's relative youth and judicial inexperience, his nomination hearings were marred by the accusations from Anita Hill that she had suffered from sexual harassment while under his employ at the Equal Employment Opportunity Commission (EEOC).

The nation, as well as the Senate, seemed divided by Hill's shocking testimony. Thomas denied the allegations and had many of his former co-workers testify for him. After the confirmation votes were counted, Thomas was nominated by the narrow margin of 52 to 48.

Clarence Thomas testifying before the U.S. Senate Judiciary Committee in 1991 (AP/Wide World Photos, Inc.).

◆ MAJOR FEDERAL LEGISLATION

Emancipation Act (April 1862)
ch.54, 12 state. 376

This law, abolishing slavery in the District of Columbia, was enacted April 16, 1862.

Emancipation Act (June 1862)
ch. 111, 12 Stat. 432

This act, abolishing slavery in all other territories of the United States, was enacted June 19, 1862.

Amendment Thirteen to the U.S. Constitution (1865)

This Amendment, abolishing slavery and involuntary servitude in all of the United States, was ratified December 16, 1865.

Civil Rights Act (1866)
ch. 31, 14 Stat. 27

This act was enacted April 9, 1866, to provide all citizens, especially recently freed slaves, with basic civil rights including the right to make and enforce contracts, to bring suits in court, to purchase and sell real and personal property, and to enjoy security of person and property.

Amendment Fourteen to the United States Constitution (1868)

This Amendment defined United States and state citizenship, and provided all citizens with the privileges and immunities of citizenship, the right to life, liberty and property, and equal protection under the law. It was ratified July 20, 1868.

Amendment Fifteen to the United States Constitution (1870)

This Amendment was designed to protect the right of all citizens to vote. It was ratified March 30, 1870.

Civil Rights Act (1870)
ch. 114, 16 Stat. 140

This act was enacted May 31, 1870, to carry out the provisions of the Fifteenth Amendment. It established penalties for violations of the provisions of the Amendment.

Civil Rights Act (1871)
ch. 99, 16 Stat. 433

This law was enacted February 28, 1871, to further define the protections established in the Fifteenth Amendment.

Civil Rights Act (April 1871)
ch. 22, 17 Stat. 13

This law was enacted April 20, 1871, to further outline the protections provided for by the Fourteenth Amendment. It provides for the vindication of crimes committed under the act in federal court.

Civil Rights Act (1875)
ch. 114, 18 Stat. 335

This act was designed to provide all citizens with equal access to public places. Ruling in 1883 in a set of cases, known as the *Civil Rights Cases*, the U.S. Supreme Court invalidated the act.

Civil Rights Act of 1957
Pub.L. No. 85–315, 71 Stat. 634

This act created the Commission on Civil Rights and empowered it to investigate allegations of deprivation of a U.S. citizen's right to vote, to appraise laws and policies of the federal government with respect to equal protection of the law, and to submit a report to the President and to the Congress within two years.

The Fifteenth Amendment guaranteed that all African American adult males were entitled to vote (The Library of Congress).

Civil Rights Act of 1960
Pub.L. No. 86–449, 74 Stat. 86

This law guaranteed the provision of criminal penalties in the event a suspect crosses state lines to avoid legal process for the actual or attempted bombing or burning of any vehicle or building, and provided penalties for persons who obstructed or interfered with any order of a federal court.

Civil Rights Act of 1964
Pub.L. No. 88–352, 78 Stat. 241

This act prohibited discrimination in the use of public accommodations whose operations involve interstate commerce and provided enforcement measures to ensure equal access to public facilities. Also the Civil Rights Act of 1964 prohibited racial discrimination in any program receiving federal aid and prohibited discrimination in most areas of employment.

Voting Rights Act of 1965
Pub.L. No. 89–110, 79 Stat. 437

The Voting Rights Act of 1965 struck down requirements such as literacy and knowledge tests and poll tax payments which had been used to restrict African American participation in voting, and provided for federal registrars to register voters should state registrars refuse to do so. It further stipulated that registered voters cannot be prohibited from voting.

Civil Rights Act of 1968
Pub.L. No. 90–284, 82 Stat. 73

This act provided for open housing by prohibiting discrimination based on race, color, religion, or national origin.

Equal Employment Opportunity Act of 1972
Pub.L. No. 92–261, 86 Stat. 103

This act provided the Equal Employment Opportunity Commission (established by the Civil Rights Act of 1964) with the authority to issue judicially enforceable cease and desist orders in cases involving discriminatory employment practices.

Public Works Employment Act of 1977
Pub.L. No. 95–28, 91 Stat. 116, Title I

The Public Works Employment Act of 1977 provided that ten percent of funds expended as a result of federal grants be earmarked to minority business enterprises.

Voting Rights Act of 1965 Amendment
Pub.L. No. 97–205, 96 Stat. 131 (1982)

This Amendment was a congressional response to the Supreme Court's ruling in *City of Mobile v. Bolden* that required proof of discriminatory intent in voting rights cases. Section 2 of the Voting Rights Act prohibits any voting practice or procedure "imposed or applied by any state or political subdivision in a manner which results in a denial or abridgement of the right of any citizen of the United States to vote on account of race or color."

Civil Rights Commission Act of 1983
Pub.L. No. 98–183, 87 Stat. 1301

This act created an eight-member bipartisan commission with four members appointed by the president, and two by the Senate and House respectively. The Commissioners are appointed to four or six year terms and can be fired only for neglect of duty or malfeasance in office. The statute was enacted after President Reagan attempted to fire Commissioners who did not express his views on civil rights. The act extended the life of the Civil Rights Commission Authorization Act of 1978, which was scheduled to expire in 1983.

Civil Rights Restoration Act of 1988
Pub.L. No. 100–259, 102 Stat. 31

The U.S. Supreme Court ruled in 1984 in the case *Grove City College v. Bell* that not all programs and activities of an institution were covered by Title IX of the Education amendments of 1972 (Public Law 89–10, 79 Stat. 27) and that discrimination can be barred only in programs that directly receive federal funds. The act

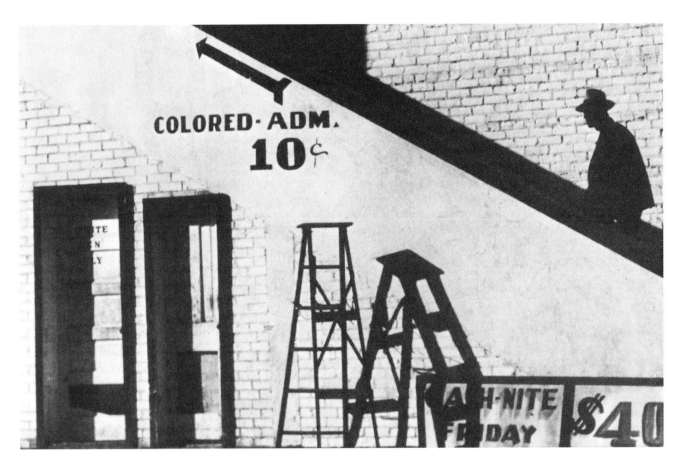

Prior to the Civil Rights Act of 1964, blacks were continually denied access to the same public accommodations as whites (The Library of Congress).

amended portions of the Civil Rights Act of 1964, refined the definition of programs and activities which are covered by the Civil Rights Act and other legislation. Specifically the amendment addressed Title IX of the Education Amendments of 1972, which prohibits discrimination in educational programs receiving federal financial assistance.

Fair Housing Amendments Act of 1988
Pub.L. No. 100–430, 102 Stat 1619

The Fair Housing Amendments Act of 1988 strengthens laws that resulted from passage of the Fair Housing Act of 1968. The act of 1988 gives the Department of Housing and Urban Development (HUD) the authority to issue discrimination charges, allows administrative law justices the ability to review housing discrimination cases, and removed the $1000 limit on punitive damages that a victim of discrimination may receive.

Civil Rights Act of 1991
Pub.L. 102–166, 105 Stat. 1071

This act is designed to provide additional remedies to deter harassment and intentional discrimination in the workplace, to provide guidelines for the adjudication of cases arising under Title VII of the Civil Rights Act of 1964, and to expand the scope of civil rights legislation weakened by Supreme Court decisions, particularly the Court's ruling in *Wards Cove Packing Co. v. Antonio*, 490 US 642 (1989).

Glass Ceiling Act of 1991
Pub.L. 102–166, 105 Stat. 1081

This law was designed to establish a means for studying and addressing the underrepresentation of women and minorities at management and decision making levels in the workforce.

◆ MAJOR U.S. SUPREME COURT DECISIONS

Access to the Polls

United States v. Reese
92 U.S. 214 (1876)

Prior to the Fifteenth Amendment, states regulated all details of state and local elections—they prescribed the qualifications of voters and the manner in which those desiring to vote at an election should make their qualifications known to the election officers. Thus, the Fifteenth Amendment changed the past practice and provides rules not prescribed by state law. However, the Court restricted the scope of the Fifteenth Amendment and the ability of Congress to enforce it by not punishing election officials who unlawfully interfered with and prevented the free exercise of the elective franchise.

The federal government indicted two Kentucky election inspectors for refusing to receive and count the vote of an African American citizen. The Supreme Court held that Congress had not yet provided "appropriate legislation'" for the punishment of the offense charged under any sections of the Fifteenth Amendment.

Guinn v. United States
238 U.S. 347 (1915)

In 1910, an amendment to the constitution of Oklahoma restricted voting rights according to a "grandfather clause" that provided that no illiterate person could be registered. The clause, however, granted an exemption for persons who resided in a foreign country prior to January 1, 1866, and had been eligible to register prior to that date or had a lineal ancestor who was eligible to vote at that time. Since no African Americans were eligible to vote in Oklahoma prior to 1866, the law disenfranchised all African Americans.

The U.S. Supreme Court ruled that the grandfather clause was invalid in Oklahoma or in any other state.

Nixon v. Herndon
273 U.S. 536 (1927)

Dr. L. A. Nixon, an African American, was refused the right to vote in a primary election because of a state statute that prohibited African Americans from participating in Democratic Party primaries in Texas. Nixon filed suit against the election officials and his case ultimately reached the U.S. Supreme Court. Justice Oliver Wendell Holmes wrote, "[i]t is too clear for extended argument that color cannot be made the basis of a statutory classification affecting the right set up in this case." As a result, the Texas statute was declared unconstitutional.

Nixon v. Condon
286 U.S. 73 (1932)

As a result of the U.S. Supreme Court ruling in *Nixon v. Herndon*, the Texas legislature passed a new statute. This statute empowered the state Democratic executive committee to set up its own rules regarding primary elections. The party promptly adopted a resolution stipulating that only white Democrats be allowed to partici-

pate in primaries. Dr. Nixon again filed suit, and his right to vote was again upheld by the U.S. Supreme Court.

Lane v. Wilson
307 U.S. 268 (1939)

In an attempt to restrict voter registration, the Oklahoma legislature stated that all Oklahomans who were already registered would remain qualified voters and that all others would have to register within 12 days (from April 30 to May 11, 1916) or be forever barred from the polls. In 1934, I. W. Lane, an African American, was refused registration on the basis of this statute. The U.S. Supreme Court declared that the statute was in conflict with the Fifteenth Amendment to the U.S. Constitution and was unconstitutional.

Smith v. Allwright
321 U.S. 649 (1944)

The Texas State Democratic Party, during its convention in 1932, limited the right of membership to white electors. As a result, nonwhites were unable to participate in a Democratic Party primary. In *Grovey v. Townsend* (295 US 45), the Supreme Court had upheld this limitation because it was made by the party in convention, not by a party executive committee. In *Smith v. Allwright*, the Court overruled *Grovey*, stating, "[T]he United States is a constitutional democracy. Its organic law grants to all citizens a right to participate in the choice of elected officials without restriction by any state because of race." The Court noted that a political party makes its selection of candidates as an agency of the state. Therefore, it cannot exclude participation based on race and remain consistent with the Fifteenth Amendment.

Gomillion v. Lightfoot
364 U.S. 339 (1960)

African American citizens challenged an Alabama statute that redefined the boundaries of the City of Tuskegee. The statute altered the shape of Tuskegee and placed all but four of Tuskegee's 400 African American voters outside of the city limits, while not displacing a single white voter. The Court struck down the statute as a violation of the Fifteenth Amendment.

Baker v. Carr
369 U.S. 186 (1962)

Baker v. Carr was brought to the Supreme Court by electors in several counties of Tennessee, who asserted that the 1901 legislative reapportionment statute was unconstitutional because the numbers of voters in the various districts had changed substantially since 1901.

The plaintiffs requested that the Supreme Court either direct a reapportionment by mathematical application of the same formula to the 1960 Census, or instruct the state to hold direct at-large elections. The state district court had dismissed the case on the grounds that it was a political question and did not fall within the protection of the Fourteenth Amendment. The U.S. Supreme Court ruled that the case involved a basic constitutional right and thereby was within court jurisdiction.

South Carolina v. Katzenbach
383 U.S. 301 (1966)

The Voting Rights Act of 1965 was designed to eliminate racial discrimination in voting, which had influenced the electoral process for nearly a century. The act abolished literacy tests, waived accumulated poll taxes, and allotted the U.S. attorney general vast discretionary powers over regions suspected of discriminatory legislation and practices against African American voters.

The Supreme Court dismissed South Carolina's petition asserting that the act violated the U.S. Constitution because it encroached on state sovereignty. The Constitution holds true under Section 1 of the Fifteenth Amendment, ". . . [t]he right of citizens of the United States to vote shall not be denied or abridged by the United States or by any state on account of race, color, or previous condition of servitude."

Allen v. State Board of Elections
393 U.S. 110 (1969)

The Supreme Court emphasized that subtle as well as obvious state regulations, "which have the effect of denying citizens their right to vote because of their race," are prohibited. The Court confirmed that Section 5 of the Voting Rights Act covered a variety of practices other than voter registration.

Georgia v. United States
411 U.S. 526 (1973)

This case confirmed the propriety of the Voting Rights Act of 1965, which forbids states with a history of racial discrimination (Alabama, Georgia, Louisiana, Mississippi, North Carolina, South Carolina and Virginia) from implementing any change in voting practices and procedures without first submitting the proposed plan to the U.S. attorney general for approval.

White v. Regester
412 U.S. 755 (1973)

The Supreme Court struck down a Texas multimember districting scheme that was used to prevent African Americans from being elected to public office. The Court upheld a finding that even though there was no evidence that African Americans faced official obstacles to registration, voting, or running for office, they had been excluded from effective participation in the political process in violation of the Equal Protection Clause of the Constitution.

City of Mobile, Alabama v. Wiley L. Bolden
446 U.S. 55 (1980)

A class action suit was filed in the U.S. District Court for the Southern District of Alabama on behalf of African American citizens in Mobile. The suit alleged that the city's practice of electing commissioners at large by a majority vote unfairly diluted the voting strength of African Americans in violation of the Fourteenth Amendment and the Fifteenth Amendment. The district court ruled that the constitutional rights of Mobile's African American citizens had been violated and entered a judgment in their favor. The court also ruled that Mobile's city commissioners be replaced by a municipal government consisting of a mayor and a city council composed of persons selected from single member districts. The lower court decision was upheld.

Thornburg v. Gingles
478 U.S. 30 (1986)

Thornburg v. Gingles was the Supreme Court's first decision interpreting the provisions of the 1982 amendments to Section Two of the Voting Rights Act. The amendments prohibited voting schemes that result in a denial or abridgement of the right to vote due to race or color. In this decision, the Court ruled that the redistricting plan adopted by the North Carolina legislature, which unintentionally led to racially polarized voting by whites and diluted African Americans voting strength was in violation of the Voting Rights Act. The Voting Rights Act prohibits neutral voting requirements that have a discriminatory effect, as well as those that are intentionally discriminatory.

Shaw v. Reno
509 U.S. 630 (1993)

The Court ruled that using race as a principle of drawing the boundaries of a voting district solely to increase the number of minority voters is a violation of the Equal Protection Clause.

Miller v. Johnson
115 S.Ct. 2475 (1995)

The Court ruled that a congressional district purposely drawn to contain a majority of African American voters is a violation of the Equal Protection Clause.

Education

Missouri ex rel. Lloyd Gaines v. Canada
305 U.S. 339 (1938)

Gaines v. Canada was brought before the Supreme Court by Lloyd Lionel Gaines, an African American who had been refused admission to the School of Law of the State University of Missouri. Gaines contended that the University of Missouri's actions were a violation of his rights under the Fourteenth Amendment of the U.S. Constitution.

The University of Missouri defended its action by maintaining that Lincoln University, a predominantly African American institution, would eventually establish its own law school. The Supreme Court of Missouri dismissed Gaines's petition and upheld the university's decision to reject his application. The U.S. Supreme Court, however, reversed this decision, maintaining that the State of Missouri was obliged to provide equal facilities for African Americans or, in the absence of such facilities, to admit them to the existing facility.

Sipuel v. Board of Regents of the University of Oklahoma
332 U.S. 631 (1948)

Ada Lois Sipuel, an African American, was denied admission to the law school of the University of Oklahoma in 1948. Sipuel and the NAACP filed a petition in Oklahoma requesting an order directing her admission. The petition was denied on the grounds that the *Gaines* decision did not require a state with segregation laws to admit an African American student to its white schools. In addition, the Oklahoma court maintained that the state itself was not obligated to set up a separate school unless first requested to do so by African Americans desiring a legal education. The court's decision was affirmed by the Supreme Court of Oklahoma. The Supreme Court, however, reversed this decision, and held that the state was required to provide African Americans with equal educational opportunities.

Sweatt v. Painter
339 U.S. 629 (1950)

Heman Marion Sweatt was refused admission to the University of Texas Law School on the grounds that substantially equivalent facilities were already available in another Texas State law school open only to African American students. The U.S. Supreme Court ruled that Sweatt be admitted to the University of Texas Law School. Chief Justice Fred M. Vinson wrote that "in terms of number of the faculty, variety of courses and opportunity for specialization, size of the student body, scope of the library, availability of law review and similar activities, the University of Texas Law School is

Lloyd Gaines (NAACP)

superior" to those in the state law school for African Americans. Therefore, the refusal to admit Sweatt to the University of Texas Law School was unconstitutional.

McLaurin v. Oklahoma State Regents for Higher Education
339 U.S. 637 (1950)

After having been admitted to the University of Oklahoma, G. W. McLaurin, an African American, was required by school officials to occupy a special seat in each classroom and a segregated table in both the library and the cafeteria because of his race. The U.S. Supreme Court declared unanimously that African American students must receive the same treatment at the hands of the state as other students and could not be segregated.

Gray v. University of Tennessee
342 U.S. 517 (1952)

This case resulted from the refusal of a U.S. district court to force the University of Tennessee to admit African American students. The lone judge to whom the matter was then referred ruled that the African American students were entitled to admission, but did not order the university to enforce this ruling. The Supreme Court was asked to refer the case back to the district court for further proceedings. Pending this appeal, however, one of the students seeking admission was enrolled at the University of Tennessee. Since the Court found no suggestion that persons "similarly situated would not be afforded similar treatment," the case was dismissed as moot.

Brown v. Board of Education of Topeka
347 U.S. 483 (1954)

This case involved the practice of denying African American children equal access to state public schools due to state laws requiring or permitting racial segregation. The U.S. Supreme Court unanimously held that segregation deprived the children of equal protection under the Fourteenth Amendment to the U.S. Constitution. The "separate but equal" doctrine of *Plessy v. Ferguson* was overturned. After reargument a year later, the case was remanded (along with its four companion cases) to the district court, which was instructed to enter necessary orders to ensure the admission of all parties to public schools on a racially nondiscriminatory basis.

Hawkins v. Board of Control
347 U.S. 971 (1954)

This case resulted from a ruling of the Florida Supreme Court which denied an African American the right to enter the University of Florida Law School on the grounds that he had failed to show that a separate law school for African Americans was not substantively equal to the University of Florida Law School. The U.S. Supreme Court vacated the judgment and remanded the case to the Florida Supreme Court for a decision in light of the ruling in *Brown* which overruled the separate but equal doctrine.

After two years, the Florida Supreme Court continued to deny Hawkins the right to enter the University of Florida. Also, it had appointed a commissioner to determine if there was a time in the future that Hawkins could be admitted "without causing public mischief." However, the Supreme Court ruled that Hawkins should be admitted to the school promptly, since there was no palpable reason for further delay.

Turead v. Board of Supervisors
347 U.S. 971 (1954)

This case was the result of a provisional injunction requiring the admittance of African Americans to Louisiana State University. The state court of appeals reversed this action, declaring that it required the decision of a district court of three judges. The U.S. Supreme Court vacated this judgment and remanded the case for consideration, in light of *Brown v. Board of Education of Topeka*.

Frazier v. University of North Carolina
350 U.S. 979 (1956)

The U.S. Supreme Court affirmed a district court judgment that African Americans may not be excluded from institutions of higher learning because of their race or color.

Cooper v. Aaron
358 U.S. 1 (1958)

The impact of *Brown v. Board of Education of Topeka* was very slight until the Justice Department began to initiate its own desegregation lawsuits. Arkansas state officials passed state laws contrary to the Fourteenth Amendment holdings in *Brown I* and *Brown II* that forbid states to use their governmental powers to bar children on racial grounds from attending schools where there is state participation through any arrangement, management, funds, or property. The cases also ordered the states to immediately cease and desist from desegregation practices immediately.

In *Cooper*, the attorney general of the United States filed a petition on behalf of the U.S. government to enjoin the governor of Arkansas and officers of the National Guard from preventing the admittance of nine African American children into Central High School in September of 1957 in Little Rock. A law was passed relieving school children from compulsory attendance at racially mixed schools. The Supreme Court declared that the Fourteenth Amendment outlined in the *Brown* case is the supreme law of the land and cannot be nullified by state legislators, executive or judicial officers, or evasive schemes for segregation.

Lee v. Macon County Board of Education
389 U.S. 25 (1967)

The U.S. Supreme Court affirmed a lower court decision ordering the desegregation of Alabama's school districts and declared state school grants to white students attending segregated private schools unconstitutional.

Alexander v. Holmes County Board of Education
396 US 19 (1969)

The U.S. Supreme Court ordered all 33 school districts in Mississippi to desegregate. The Department of Health, Education and Welfare (HEW) had asked that the districts be granted more time to desegregate. This was the first time HEW had sought a delay in integration, but the Court ordered that integration proceed immediately.

A segregated schoolroom of African American students in Missouri, c. 1930 (Corbis Corporation [Bellevue]).

North Carolina State Board of Education v. Swann
402 U.S. 43 (1971)

&

Swann v. Charlotte Mecklenburg Board of Education
402 U.S. 1 (1971)

In these two cases the U.S. Supreme Court affirmed the use of busing and faculty transfers to overcome the effects of dual school systems—segregated school systems resulting from residential patterns. Writing the decision, Chief Justice Warren E. Burger noted that "bus transportation has long been a part of all public educational systems and it is unlikely that a truly effective remedy could be devised without continued reliance upon it." The Court declared that segregation resulted from past misconduct and affirmed the lower court's order that the school board bus students to achieve a racial mix at each school. The ruling, however, left local district judges the authority to decide whether a desegregation plan was constitutionally adequate.

The school system of Detroit had become heavily African American due to white flight to the suburbs. Fearing that *Brown* would be crippled, the district court ordered busing between the districts of Detroit and its white suburbs.

However, the Court overturned this decision as there was no evidence that the suburbs had contributed to the segregation. Integrationists attacked this decision as the end of *Brown*.

Runyon v. McCrary
427 U.S. 160 (1976)

In a unanimous decision, the Court held that the Constitution places no value on discrimination, and while invidious, private discrimination may be characterized as a form of exercising the freedom of association protected by the First Amendment. The Civil Rights Act of 1866 prohibited racial discrimination in the making and enforcing of contracts. The case arose when two African American children were denied admission to private schools in Virginia.. The children's parents sought to enter into a contractual relationship with the private schools on an equal basis to white and nonwhite students.

Regents of University of California v. Allan Bakke
438 U.S. 265 (1978)

Allan Bakke, a white male who had been denied admission to the University of California Medical School at Davis for two consecutive years, charged that the university's minority quota system—under which only disadvantaged members of certain minority races were considered for 16 of the 100 places in each year's class—denied him equal protection.

The trial court declared that the school could not take race into account in making the admissions decision and held that the challenged admissions program violated the federal and state constitutions and Title VI of the 1964 Civil Rights Act. The university appealed. The Supreme Court ruled that Bakke had been illegally discriminated against and that numerical quotas based on race were unconstitutional.

Bob Jones University v. IRS
461 U.S. 574 (1983)

Contrary to long-standing IRS policy, the Reagan administration sought to extend tax-exempt status to schools that discriminate on the basis of race. The U.S. Supreme Court recognized the inability of the Justice Department to argue the case fairly, and requested that former Secretary of Transportation William T. Coleman present the argument. The Supreme Court rebuffed the Justice Department's arguments and unanimously agreed

Black students being bused to schools during desegregation efforts of the 1970s (Corbis Corporation [Bellevue]).

Wright v. City of Emporia
402 U.S. 43 (1971)

&

Cotton v. Scotland Neck Board of Education
407 U.S. 485 (1972)

The Supreme Court held that two towns with heavy concentrations of white students could not secede from a largely African American county school system and form its own school district in an attempt to frustrate integration.

Richmond, Virginia School Board v. State Board of Education
412 U.S. 92 (1973)

In a four to four vote, the Supreme Court declined to reinstate an order to integrate the predominantly African American schools in Richmond with those of two white suburbs. The Court did not come reach a decision and integrationists expressed concern that permitting *de facto* segregation to stand in this manner would hinder corrective action in other metropolitan areas, perpetuate "neighborhood" one-race schools, and lessen the extent of integration in unitary school systems.

Milliken v. Bradley
418 U.S. 717 (1974)

After failing to reach a decision in *Richmond School Board*, the full Court reached a decision outlawing inter-district remedies to end segregation in schools.

with Coleman's position that the IRS could deny tax-exempt status to racially discriminatory schools.

Allen v. Wright
488 U.S. 737 (1984)

Parents of African American children instituted a nationwide lawsuit claiming that the Internal Revenue Service's failure to deny tax-exempt status to racially discriminatory private schools constituted federal financial aid to racially segregated institutions and diminished the ability of their children to receive a racially an adequate education. The U.S. Supreme Court refused to hear the case on the grounds that the plaintiffs did not have "standing" because they failed to show that the injury suffered was "fairly traceable" or caused by the conduct of the IRS. In addition the Court maintained that the remedy was "speculative" since there was no evidence that the withdrawal of tax-exempt status would cause schools to end their racially discriminatory practices.

Oklahoma City Board of Education
498 U.S. 237 (1991)

The Court ruled that when a school district petitioned to end a desegregation order, the petition could be approved if the district has been in good faith compliance with the order from the beginning and if remnants of past discrimination have been eliminated to the degree possible in the situation.

United States v. Fordice
505 U.S. 717 (1992)

The Court ruled that when a state higher education system continues to use educational practices which were started to keep the races segregated and which perpetuate segregation, the practices violate the equal protection guarantee if they can be ended without significantly changing the quality of the education offered.

Jenkins v. Missouri
115 S.Ct. 2038 (1995)

The Court ruled that a federal district court erred in ordering increased salaries for school system employees as part of a program to motivate attendance by non-minority students living outside the district in an effort to increase desegregation.

Employment

Griggs v. Duke Power Co.
401 U.S. 424 (1971)

African American employees challenged their employer's requirement of a high school diploma or pass-ing of intelligence tests as a condition of employment. African Americans were employed only in the labor department where the highest paying jobs paid less than the lowest jobs in the other departments. When the company abandoned its policy restricting blacks to labor in 1965, completion of high school and median scores on two aptitude tests were required to transfer from labor to another department.

The Supreme Court found the objective of Congress in Title III was to achieve equality of employment opportunities and remove barriers that have operated in the past. Under the Act, practices, procedures, or tests neutral on their face and even neutral in their intent cannot be maintained if they operate to "freeze" the status quo of prior discrimination. The employment practice must be related to job performance.

It was determined that neither the high school diploma nor the intelligence tests were shown to bear a demonstrable relationship to successful job performance. Good intent or absence of discriminatory intent does not redeem employment procedures and practices. The employment policies had a discriminatory effect toward African American employees and were struck down.

Albemarle Paper Co. v. Moody
422 U.S. 405 (1975)

African American employees of a paper mill in Roanoke Rapids, North Carolina successfully challenged the company's use of written tests which allegedly measured numerical and verbal intelligence. Based upon the standards enunciated in *Griggs v. Duke Power Co.*, the U.S. Supreme Court determined that the tests were discriminatory because they were not job-related and did not predict success on the job. The Court held that the plaintiffs were entitled to "complete justice" and necessary relief that would "make them whole." The Court awarded the African American employees back pay and made it clear that back pay should rarely be denied once there has been a showing of discrimination. The Court also stated that back pay cannot be denied simply because the employer acted in good faith or did not intend to discriminate.

Hazelwood School District v. United States
433 U.S. 299 (1977)

Several African American teachers seeking jobs in suburban St. Louis, Missouri offered statistical data indicating they had been denied employment opportunities. The plaintiffs attempted to prove their case by showing that the percentage of African American students was greater than the percentage of African American teachers in the school district.

Although the U.S. Supreme Court affirmed that "statistics can be an important source of proof in employment discrimination cases," it rejected the plaintiffs's statistical evidence and called it irrelevant. The Court concluded that relevant statistical data would be the percentage of qualified African American teachers in the relevant geographical area compared with the percentage of African Americans in Hazelwood's teaching staff.

Teamsters v. United States
431 U.S. 324 (1977)

In enforcing the Civil Rights Act of 1964, the Supreme Court held that victims of past union discrimination were entitled to retroactive seniority benefits. However, the Supreme Court required proof of "intent to discriminate," in order to establish that a given seniority system is illegal. Subsequent cases in lower federal courts during the late 1970s entitled discrimination victims to retroactive back pay in addition to retroactive seniority benefits.

Louis Swint and Willie Johnson v. Pullman Standard and the United Steelworkers of America
72 L.Ed. 66 (1982)

African American employees of Pullman Standard brought a lawsuit against Pullman Standard and the United Steelworkers of America. The lawsuit alleged that Title VII of the Civil Rights Act of 1964 was violated by a seniority system. In its decision, the district court ruled "that the difference in terms, conditions or privileges of employment resulting from the seniority system are not the result of an intention to discriminate because of race or color" and held that the system satisfied the requirements of Section 703(h) of the Civil Rights Act. This decision was later reversed by the court of appeals for the fifth circuit which stated that, "because we find the differences in the terms, conditions and standards of employment for black workers and white workers at Pullman Standard resulted from an intent to discriminate because of race, we hold that the system is not legally valid under Section 703(h) of Title VII U.S.C. 2000e–2(h)."

Meritor Savings Bank, FSB v. Vinson
106 S.Ct. 2399 (1985)

Michelle Vinson, an African American woman employed as a teller at a bank in Washington, D.C., claimed that she had been sexually harassed for more than two months by her supervisor. Vinson alleged that employment benefits were granted or denied based upon her performance of sexual favors.

In this first Supreme Court ruling on sexual harassment, the Court firmly condemned sexual harassment that creates an intimidating, hostile, and offensive working environment even when the harassment does not have economic ramifications. The unanimous ruling made it clear that Title VII of the Civil Rights Act prohibits sexual harassment that involves economic reprisals or harassment that creates a hostile, sexually charged atmosphere in the workplace.

Watson v. Fort Worth Bank and Trust
108 U.S. 2777 (1987)

Clara Watson, an African American woman, alleged that she was repeatedly denied promotion to supervisory positions which were awarded to white employees with equivalent or lesser experience. The bank contended that its promotion decisions were based on various subjective criteria including experience, previous supervisory experience, and the ability to get along with others.

The U.S. Supreme Court held that Watson did not have to prove intentional discrimination. The Court concluded that subjective facially neutral selection devices which disadvantage African Americans in much the same way as objective criteria written tests are unlawful.

Patterson v. McLean Credit Union
491 U.S. 164 (1989)

An African American female was employed as a teller and file coordinator for ten years until she was laid-off. She alleged that she had been harassed, denied promotion to accounting clerk, and later discharged because of her race. She filed suit asserting violations of Section 1981 of the Civil Rights Act.

Racial harassment relating to conditions of employment are not actionable under Section 1981 which provides, ". . . [a]ll persons . . . shall have the same right to make and enforce contracts . . . as any white citizen," because that provision does not apply to conduct which occurs after the formation of a contract including the breach of the contracts terms and enforcement thereof. Rather, the harassment asserted by the petitioner is past formation conduct of the employer which is actionable only under Title VII of the Civil Rights Act of 1964.

Wards Cove Packing Co. Inc. v. Antonio
490 U.S. 642 (1989)

This case was brought by a class of non-white salmon cannery workers who allege that the employer's hiring and promotion practices were responsible for the workforces racial stratification. There were two types of jobs: unskilled cannery jobs, which were filled predominately by non-whites; and non-cannery jobs, mostly classified as skilled positions which paid more and were held by whites. Statistics were used to show a high percentage of non-whites in cannery jobs and a low percentage in non-cannery positions.

The Supreme Court found that the cannery workforce did not reflect the pool of qualified job applicants or the qualified labor force population. An employer's selection methods or employment practices cannot be said to have a disparate impact on non-whites if the absence of minorities holding such skilled jobs reflects a dearth of qualified non-white applicants. A mere showing that non-whites are underrepresented in the non-cannery jobs will not suffice for a Title VII violation.

Martin v. Wilks
490 U.S. 755 (1989)

In an attempt to remedy past racial discrimination in hiring and promotion practices, the City of Birmingham and its fire department consented to hiring African Americans as firefighters as part of a settlement. White firefighters subsequently challenged the city, alleging that because of their race they were denied promotions in favor of less qualified African Americans in violation of Title VII. Promotion decisions were made on the basis of race in reliance on the consent decree. The Court held that a voluntary settlement between one group of employees and their employer cannot possibly settle the conflicting claims of another group of employees who do not join in the agreement. This settlement would result in a person being deprived of their legal rights in a proceeding to which he is not a party.

Jury Selection and Service

Neal v. Delaware
103 U.S. 370 (1880)

The jury commissioner's conduct was found in violation of the U.S. Constitution when an African American criminal defendant proved that African Americans were excluded from the jury based on their race. Every citizen is afforded the right to equal protection of the laws including that the selection of jurors to pass upon his life, liberty, or property, shall not be hindered by the exclusion of members of his race.

Strauder v. West Virginia
100 U.S. 303 (1880)

The Supreme Court overturned the conviction of an African American criminal defendant due to racial discrimination in the selection of jurors. West Virginia passed a state law that prohibited African American men from eligibility to serve as a member of a grand jury

African Americans are now represented on most city fire and police forces (Corbis Corporation [Bellevue]).

or a petit jury in the state. The law denied equal protection of the laws to a citizen.

Virginia v. Rives
100 U.S. 313 (1880)

The petitioners asserted that African Americans had never been allowed to serve as jurors in their county in any case where a African American man was involved. Virginia had no formalized or specific statute restricting African American jurors from certain trials. It was held that a mixed jury in a particular case is not essential to the equal protection of the laws and that the right is not given by any state or federal statute.

Hollins v. Oklahoma
295 U.S. 394 (1935)

Hollins, an African American, was charged with rape and convicted at a trial held in the basement of the jail. Three days before the scheduled execution, the NAACP secured a stay of execution. Later the Supreme Court of Oklahoma reversed his conviction.

The U.S. Supreme Court—in a memorandum opinion—affirmed the principle that the conviction of an

African American by a jury from which all African Americans had been excluded was a denial of the equal protection clause of the Fourteenth Amendment to the U.S. Constitution.

Hale v. Commonwealth of Kentucky
303 U.S. 613 (1938)

In 1936, Joe Hale, an African American, was charged with murder in McCracken County, Kentucky. Hale moved to set aside the indictment on the grounds that the jury commissioners had systematically excluded African Americans from jury lists. Hale established that one out of every six residents of the county was African American, and that at least 70 African Americans out of a total of 6,700 persons qualified for jury duty. Still, there had not been an African American on jury duty between 1906 and 1936. Hale's conviction and death sentence were upheld by the Court of Appeals of Kentucky, but both were struck down by the Supreme Court on the grounds that he had been denied equal protection of the law.

Patton v. Mississippi
332 U.S. 463 (1947)

This case involved Eddie Patton, an African American who was convicted of the murder of a white man in Mississippi. At his trial and as part of his appeal, Patton alleged that all qualified African Americans had been systematically excluded from jury service solely because of race. The state maintained that since jury service was limited by statute to qualified voters and since few African Americans were qualified to vote, such a procedure was valid in the eyes of the law. The Supreme Court, however, reversed Patton's conviction on the grounds that such a jury plan, resulting in the almost automatic elimination of African Americans from jury service, constituted an infringement on Patton's rights under the Fourteenth Amendment.

Shepherd v. Florida
341 U.S. 50 (1951)

The Supreme Court reversed the convictions of a Florida state court involving African American defendants solely on the grounds that the method of selecting the grand jury discriminated against African Americans.

Turner v. Fouche
396 U.S. 346 (1970)

The Court affirmed the right of defendants to bring an action in federal court to end discrimination in jury selection.

Castanda v. Partida
430 U.S. 482 (1977)

The Supreme Court upheld the use of statistical evidence demonstrating that Mexican Americans had been systematically excluded from jury selection, and that such discrimination on the basis of race or color violated the Equal Protection Clause of the Fourteenth Amendment. The principle established in this case, that statistical evidence can be used to prove intentional discrimination, has been used in later cases involving employment, housing, voting and education.

Batson v. Kentucky
476 U.S. 79 (1986)

Justice Lewis F. Powell, writing for the majority, held that the prosecution in a criminal case may not use its "preemptory challenge," those challenges to an individual juror for which no cause need be stated, to exclude African American jurors in a case involving an African American defendant.

Turner v. Murray
106 US 1683 (1986)

The Supreme Court expanded the right of African American defendants in capital cases to question potential white jurors to uncover their racial prejudices and biases.

Public Accommodations

Hall v. DeCuir
95 U.S. 485 (1878)

This case involved an unsuccessful attempt of the Louisiana legislature to prohibit segregation in any form of transportation in the state. The statute was attacked as an interference with interstate commerce because it imposed a direct burden and control over common carriers when entering the state. The statute was declared unconstitutional because it required common carriers to transport African American passengers in Louisiana in the same cabin with white passengers.

Plessy v. Ferguson
163 U.S. 537 (1896)

Homer Plessy, an African American, was assigned to the wrong coach on a train traveling within Louisiana. Plessy was arrested and challenged an 1890 state statute that provided for "separate but equal" railway carriages for whites and blacks.

In the majority opinion of the Supreme Court, "separate but equal" accommodations for African Americans constituted a "reasonable" use of state police power. Furthermore, the Court said that the Fourteenth Amendment "could not have been intended to abolish distinctions based on color, or to enforce social . . . equality or a co-mingling of the two races upon terms unsatisfactory to either."

Civil Rights Cases
332 U.S. 46, 332 U.S. 784, 333 U.S. 831, 334 U.S. 834, 378 U.S. 226 (1883)

This group of civil rights cases was heard before the Supreme Court in an effort to determine the constitutionality of the Civil Rights Act of 1875, the first piece of national legislation which attempted to guarantee people of all races "full and equal enjoyment" of all public accommodations including inns, public conveyances, theaters, and other places of amusement. The Court ruled, however, that the act was unconstitutional inasmuch as it did not spring directly from the Thirteenth and Fourteenth Amendments to the Constitution. In the view of the Court, the Thirteenth Amendment was concerned exclusively with the narrow confines of slavery and involuntary servitude. The Fourteenth Amendment did not empower Congress to enact direct legislation to counteract the effect of state laws or policies. The effect of this ruling was to deprive African Americans of the very protections which the three postwar "freedom" amendments were designed to provide.

Morgan v. Commonwealth of Virginia
328 U.S. 373 (1946)

Irene Morgan, an African American, refused to move to the rear seat of a Greyhound bus which was traveling from Virginia to Washington, DC. She was convicted in Virginia for violating a state statute requiring segregation of the races on all public vehicles.

NAACP attorneys then carried the case through the Virginia courts and on to the U.S. Supreme Court, where it was decided that the Virginia statute could not apply to interstate passengers or motor vehicles engaged in such traffic.

Bob-Lo v. Michigan
333 U.S. 28 (1948)

The operator of a line of passenger ships used to transport patrons from Detroit to an island amusement park was convicted of violating the Michigan Civil Rights Act for refusing passage to an African American. The Supreme Court upheld the application of the Michigan Civil Rights Act.

Rice v. Arnold
340 U.S. 848 (1950)

This case involved the successful attempt to abolish segregation on a Miami, Florida, golf course owned and operated by the city. The U.S. Supreme Court granted a writ of certiorari and overturned the judgment of the Florida Supreme Court which authorized the segregated use of the course.

District of Columbia v. John R. Thompson
346 U.S. 100 (1952)

The Supreme Court unanimously held that a restaurant owner had violated federal law by discriminating against and refusing service to patrons on the basis of race.

Muir v. Louisville Park Theatrical Association
347 U.S. 971 (1954)

In 1954, several African Americans were refused admission to an amphitheater located in a Louisville city park. The park was leased and operated by a privately owned group not affiliated in any way with the city. The Kentucky Court of Appeals found no evidence of unlawful discrimination, but the U.S. Supreme Court overturned this judgment and remanded the case for consideration in the light of the prevailing legal climate as articulated in *Brown*.

Mayor and City Council of Baltimore v. Dawson
350 U.S. 377 (1955)

The Supreme Court affirmed a judgment that the enforcement of racial segregation in public beaches and bathhouses maintained by public authorities is unconstitutional.

Holmes v. Atlanta
350 U.S. 859 (1955)

This case involved a suit brought by African Americans to integrate a city-owned and operated golf course in Atlanta, Georgia. The segregated arrangements were ordered sustained by a lower court, but that order was overturned by the U.S. Supreme Court and the case was remanded to the district court with directions to enter a decree for the plaintiffs in conformity with *Mayor and City Council of Baltimore v. Dawson*.

Flemming v. South Carolina Electric
351 U.S. 901 (1956)

This case involved a suit brought by an African American passenger against a bus company for damages due to the bus driver's having required her to change seats in accordance with South Carolina's segregation law. The trial judge dismissed the case on the grounds that the statute in question was valid, but the court of appeals reversed this decision, holding that the "separate but equal" doctrine was no longer valid. The Supreme Court upheld the court of appeals decision.

Gayle v. Browder
352 U.S. 114 (1956)

This case challenged the constitutionality of state statutes and ordinances in the city of Montgomery, Alabama, which required the segregation of whites and blacks on public buses. These statutes were declared unconstitutional by the decision of a three-judge federal district court. The Supreme Court then affirmed this judgment.

Katzenbach v. McClung
379 U.S. 802 (1964)

&

Heart of Atlanta v. United States
379 U.S. 803 (1964)

The attorney general of the United States sued Ollie's Barbecue Restaurant in Birmingham, Alabama, for its refusal to serve African Americans in its dining accommodations, a direct violation of the anti-discriminatory public accommodations clause of the 1964 Civil Rights Act. The U.S. District Court, Northern District of Alabama, held that the Civil Rights Act could not be applied under the Fourteenth Amendment to the U.S. Constitution, as there was no "demonstrable connection" between food purchased in interstate commerce and sold in a restaurant that would affect commerce. The U.S. Supreme Court, however, held that "the Civil Rights Act of 1964, as here applied, [is] plainly appropriate in the resolution of what [Congress has] found to be a national commercial problem of the first magnitude."

The *Heart of Atlanta* case dealt with a Georgia motel which solicited patronage in national advertising and had several out-of-state residents as guests from time to time. The motel had already instituted the practice of refusing to rent rooms to African Americans prior to the passage of the 1964 Civil Rights Act and continued this practice afterward. The motel owner filed suit, maintaining that the 1964 Civil Rights Act violated both the Fifth Amendment and the Thirteenth Amendment. The United States countered with the argument that the refusal to accept African Americans interfered with interstate travel, and that Congress in voting to apply nondiscriminatory standards to interstate commerce was not violating either amendment. The Supreme Court upheld the right of congressional regulation, stating that the power of Congress was not confined to the regulation of commerce among the states. "It extends to those

activities intrastate which so affect interstate commerce, or the exercise of the power of Congress over it, as to make regulation of them appropriate means to the attainment of a legitimate end."

Bell v. Maryland
378 U.S. 226 (1964)

The Supreme Court ordered a Maryland district court to reconsider its affirmation of a state court conviction of twelve African Americans for trespassing when they refused to leave a restaurant that refused to serve them entirely on the basis of their color.

Evans v. Newton
382 U.S. 296 (1966)

The Supreme Court ruled that transfer of a city park from municipal ownership to a board of private trustees does not remove its obligations under the Fourteenth Amendment.

Shuttlesworth v. Birmingham
394 U.S. 147 (1969)

The U.S. Supreme Court invalidated Birmingham's Parade-Permit Law which had been used in 1963 to harass participants in an Easter March organized by Dr. Martin Luther King, Jr.

New York State Club Association v. City of New York
108 S.Ct. 2225 (1988)

In a unanimous decision, the Supreme Court upheld the constitutionality of a New York City ordinance that forbids private clubs from discriminating against women and minorities.

Interracial Marriage

Loving v. Virginia
388 U.S. 1 (1967)

This case nullified anti-miscegenation laws. It concerned a white man and an African American woman, residents of Virginia, who married in Washington, DC. The State of Virginia indicted and convicted them of violating its laws against racial intermarriage when the couple returned to Virginia and attempted to reside there, but released them when the couple agreed not to reside in the state for 25 years. The Lovings, however, decided to challenge the agreement and the law. Their appeal was rejected by the Virginia courts but upheld by the U.S. Supreme Court, which ruled the Virginia law

Plaintiffs Woodrow Lewis, Albert Dunn, and George Willis meeting with attorneys William Alexander and D.L. Hollowell during a suit against an Atlanta restauranteur in 1965 (AP/Wide World Photos, Inc.).

unconstitutional. Soon thereafter, federal district courts in other states which forbade intermarriage ordered local officials to issue marriage licenses to interracial couples applying for them.

Requirements for Legislative Membership

Powell v. McCormack
395 U.S. 486 (1969)

According to the Constitution, only three basic factors govern eligibility to serve as a legislator in the U.S. House of Representatives: a minimum age requirement, the possession of U.S. citizenship, and the fulfillment of the state's residency requirement. When U.S. Representative Adam Clayton Powell, Jr. was excluded from the 90th Congress on the grounds that he had misused public funds and defied the courts of his home state, he filed suit in federal court in an attempt to force the House of Representatives to review only the necessary credentials for membership.

The district court dismissed the first petition on the grounds that it lacked jurisdiction. By the time the case was finally heard before the U.S. Supreme Court, the

90th Congress had adjourned. Powell, however, was reelected and finally seated in the 91st Congress, a gesture which in the view of the Court did not settle the case. The legal point on which the case hinged involved the distinction between "expulsion" and "exclusion." Despite the more than two-thirds majority required for expulsion, the Court ruled that the intent of the House was to "exclude," not to "expel." The Court summation stated flatly that "the House was without power to exclude him from its membership."

Right of Sale and Restrictive Covenants

Buchanan v. Warley
245 U.S. 60 (1917)

The plaintiff brought an action for the performance of a sale of real estate in Louisville, Kentucky. The purchaser, Warley, an African American, maintained that he would be unable to occupy the land since it was located within what was defined by a Louisville ordinance as a white block. (The ordinance prohibited whites from living in black districts, and vice versa.) Buchanan alleged that the ordinance was in conflict with the Fourteenth Amendment to the U.S. Constitu-

Adam Clayton Powell, Jr. leaves the U.S. Capitol after the House voted to take away his Education and Labor Committee chairmanship (AP/Wide World Photos, Inc.).

tion. The U.S. Supreme Court maintained that the ordinance was unconstitutional.

Shelley v. Kraemer
334 U.S. 1 (1948)

&

Hurd v. Hodge
334 U.S. 26 (1948)

In 1945 an African American family, the Shelleys, received a warranty deed to a parcel of land which was subject to a restrictive covenant barring its sale to African Americans. A lawsuit was subsequently brought in the Circuit Court of St. Louis seeking to divest the Shelleys of the title to the land. The Supreme Court of Missouri directed the trial court to strip the petitioners of their warranty deed.

The U.S. Supreme Court reversed this decision, maintaining that restrictive covenants, though valid contracts, could not be enforced by state courts. In *Hurd v. Hodge,* involving a similar set of circumstances, federal courts were similarly prohibited from enforcing such restrictive covenants.

Reitman v. Mulkey
387 U.S. 369 (1967)

In 1964, California voters passed a referendum granting "absolute discretion" to real estate owners in the sale and rental of real property. Lincoln Mulkey filed suit against property owners in Orange County to challenge the validity of the referendum. Mulkey's complaint failed in the lower courts but was granted by the California Supreme Court on the grounds that the California referendum violated the Fourteenth Amendment of the U.S. Constitution. The U.S. Supreme Court upheld the decision.

Jones v. Alfred H. Mayer, Co.
392 U.S. 409 (1968)

Joseph Lee Jones alleged that the sole reason a real estate agent refused to sell him a home was because he was African American. The Supreme Court held that 42 U.S.C. 1982, a federal statute created during the Reconstruction era to eliminate the vestiges of slavery, prohibits all racial discrimination, public and private, in the sale or rental of property.

Trafficante v. Metropolitan Life Insurance
409 U.S. 205 (1972)

The U.S. Supreme Court ruled that a complaint of racial discrimination in housing may be brought by parties who have not themselves been refused accommodation but who, as members of the same housing unit, allege injury by discriminatory housing practices. The suit had been filed by a black and a white resident of a housing development in San Francisco who contended that the owner of the development was depriving plaintiffs of the right to live in a racially integrated community.

Sentencing and Incarceration

McKleskey v. Kemp
481 U.S. 279 (1987)

Warren McKleskey, a 38-year-old African American man accused of killing a police officer while robbing a furniture store, was sentenced to death by the State of Georgia. In support of his claim that the sentence violated his constitutional rights, McKleskey introduced a sophisticated statistical study that analyzed more than 2,000 murder cases in Georgia. The study demonstrated that there was a disparity in the imposition of the capital sentence based on the race of the victim, as well as the race of the defendant.

Defendants charged with killing white persons received the death penalty in 11 percent of the cases, but defendants charged with killing African Americans received the death penalty in only 1 percent of the cases. The study further showed that prosecutors asked for the death penalty in 70 percent of the cases involving black defendants and white victims, and only 19 percent of the cases involving white defendants and African American victims. In sum, the analysis revealed that African Americans who kill whites are 4.3 times more likely to receive the death sentence.

The Supreme Court acknowledged that it had accepted statistics as proof of intent to discriminate in employment, housing, and voting cases. However, the Court rejected McKleskey's claim that the death penalty in Georgia was applied in a racially discriminatory manner. The Court's reasoning was that although McKleskey showed the existence of racial discrimination in sentencing, he failed to prove that "racial considerations played a part in his sentence." Finally, Justice Powell expressed concern that acceptance of McKleskey's argument would open the floodgates of litigation by African American defendants seeking to introduce statistical evidence to demonstrate that race affected the outcome of their case.

Slavery

Prigg v. Pennsylvania
16 Peters 539 (1842)

In violation of a 1826 Pennsylvania anti-kidnapping statute, Edward Prigg, a professional slave catcher, took captive Margaret Morgan, a fugitive slave residing in Pennsylvania, and was tried and convicted for kidnaping. Hearing the case, the Supreme Court ruled that the Pennsylvania law was unconstitutional, on the grounds that the statute was an interference with Congress's power under Art. IV, sec. 2 of the Constitution.

Strader v. Graham
10 Howard 82 (1850)

In 1841, three slaves owned by Christopher Graham of Kentucky, boarded a steamboat owned by Jacob Strader and traveled to Cincinnati, from where they ultimately escaped to freedom in Canada. Graham sued Strader for the value of the slaves and the expenses incurred while trying to recover them. Graham won the case. However, Strader appealed, claiming that the slaves had become free under Ohio law and provisions of the Northwest Ordinance. The Supreme Court ruled unanimously that each state had the right to determine the status of slaves within its jurisdiction, that the status of these slaves was to be determined by the State of Kentucky, and that the Northwest Ordinance was no longer in force, since those territories had become states.

Dred Scott v. Sandford
19 Howard 393 (1857)

In 1835, Dred Scott became the property of John Emerson, a U.S. Army doctor, in the slave state of Missouri. From there, he was taken into the free state of Illinois and later to the free territory of Wisconsin.

In 1847, Scott initiated suit in the circuit court of St. Louis County, arguing that he should be given his freedom by virtue of his having resided on free soil. After nine years, his case came before the U.S. Supreme Court.

In delivering his opinion, Chief Justice Roger Brooke Taney declared that, by virtue of both the Declaration of Independence and the Constitution, African Americans could not be regarded as citizens of the United States. Moreover, the Court could not deprive slaveholders of their right to take slaves into any part of the Union. In effect, therefore, the Missouri Compromise, as well as other antislavery legislation, was declared to be unconstitutional.

Ableman v. Booth
21 Howard 506 (1859)

The U.S. Supreme Court upheld Congress's fugitive slave law and all its provisions. Booth was held in a state jail for violating the federal fugitive slave laws. Booth secured a writ of habeas corpus from a state judge who declared the federal laws unconstitutional and the Wisconsin Supreme Court affirmed. The state court had stepped beyond its sphere of authority. The federal court held Booth guilty, although the State of Wisconsin was deemed a sovereign within its territorial limits and was regarded as limited and restricted by the U.S. Constitution.

State and Local Affirmative Action Requirements

United States Steelworkers of America v. Brian Weber
433 U.S. 193 (1979)

The United Steelworkers of America and Kaiser Aluminum Company entered into a collective bargaining agreement including a voluntary affirmative action plan designed to eliminate conspicuous racial imbalances in Kaiser's almost exclusively white skilled workforce. The plant in Gramercy, Louisiana, agreed to reserve 50 percent of the openings in the skilled job training programs for blacks until the percentage of black skilled workers was equal to the percentage of blacks in the local labor force. Brian Weber, a white production worker, who was turned down for the training program although he had more seniority than many accepted

Handbill advertising a public hearing to discuss the *Dred Scott v. Sanford* case.

blacks, sued the United Steelworkers of America, claiming that the affirmative action program discriminated against whites.

The Supreme Court limited the issue to the narrow question of whether Title VII prohibited private employers and unions from establishing voluntary affirmative action plans. In a five to two decision, the Court upheld the affirmative action plan and established three factors to determine the validity of racial preference. The Court approved the plan because it was designed to break down Kaiser's historic patterns of racial segregation, it did not unnecessarily diminish the rights of white employees since it did not require the firing of white employees, and it was a temporary measure not intended to maintain racial balance but simply to eliminate an imbalance.

Fullilove v. Klutznik
448 U.S. 448 (1980)

The Supreme Court upheld a provision of the Public Works Employment Act of 1977 that required a 10 percent set-aside of federal funds for minority business enterprises on local public work projects. The provision

had been challenged as violation of the Equal Protection Clause of the Fourteenth Amendment.

Firefighters Local Union No. 1784 v. Stotts
467 U.S. 561 (1984)

In May of 1981, for the first time in its history, the City of Memphis announced layoffs of city employees, due to a projected budget deficit. The layoffs, which also affected the fire department, were to be made based on a citywide seniority system that had been adopted in 1973. Carl Stotts, an African American firefighter, sued to stop the layoffs, claiming that since blacks had been hired pursuant to the affirmative action provisions of a 1980 court decree, they would be laid off in far greater numbers than their white coworkers. In a six to three decision the Supreme Court held that since the 1980 court decree did not say that African Americans had special protection during a layoff, the layoffs had to be made according to the 1973 seniority system.

Wygant v. Jackson Board of Education
476 U.S. 267 (1986)

The U.S. Supreme Court dealt a blow to affirmative action in this case involving a public school system's

An1837 newspaper depiction of a fugitive slave.

affirmative action plan. The record reflected that the first African American school teacher was not hired in Jackson, Michigan, until 1953. By 1969, only 3.9 percent of the teachers were African American although 15.2 percent of the students were African American. In response, the school board developed an affirmative action plan that protected African American faculty members during layoffs.

Although the U.S. Supreme Court had approved affirmative action plans in prior cases, it rejected the Jackson plan. The Court found that the goal of the plan, to remedy societal discrimination and afford positive role models to African American students, was nebulous and not sufficiently compelling.

Local No. 93, International Association of Firefighters v. City of Cleveland
106 S.Ct. 3063 (1986)

The city of Cleveland, which had a long history of racial discrimination, negotiated a consent decree with black firefighters who had filed a lawsuit alleging that they had been unlawfully denied jobs and promotions. The decree included an affirmative action plan with numerical goals for promotion of blacks to the position of supervisor.

In response to the union's challenge on behalf of white firefighters, the Supreme Court ruled that the lower courts had broad discretion to approve decrees in which employers settle discrimination suits by agreeing to preferential promotions of blacks, in spite of the objections of white employees.

Local 28, Sheet Metal Workers International Association v. EEOC
106 S.Ct. 3019 (1986)

After finding that the all-white union had discriminated against blacks and Hispanics seeking to enter the sheet metal trades for more than a decade, the trial court ordered the union to establish a 29 percent non-white membership goal. The court also ruled that the union would have to pay substantial fines if the union failed to meet the goals. After the union failed to reach the goal, the court found the union in contempt and established a new goal of 29.3 percent. The union challenged the court's order.

The Supreme Court upheld the affirmative action goal in light of the union's "persistent or egregious discrimination" and to eliminate "lingering effects of pervasive discrimination." This was the first time the Court expressly approved the use of race conscious relief to African Americans and Hispanics who were not identified victims of discrimination.

United States v. Paradise
480 U.S. 149 (1987)

This case originated in 1972 when the NAACP sued the Alabama Department of Highways because of its long-standing history of racially discriminating employment practices. More than 11 years later, after the department had failed to hire or promote African Americans, the trial court ordered the promotion of one black trooper for every white. The U.S. attorney general challenged the constitutionality of the plan. The U.S. Supreme Court upheld the use of strict racial quotas and found that the plan was "narrowly tailored to serve the compelling government interest" of remedying "egregious" past discrimination against African Americans.

Johnson v. Transportation Agency, Santa Clara County, California
480 U.S. 616 (1987)

The U.S. Supreme Court held that the state transportation agency's voluntary affirmative action plan, under which a female had been promoted to the position of road dispatcher over a male was consistent with Title VII of the Civil Rights Act of 1964. The Court held that an employer does not have to admit or prove that it has discriminated in order to justify efforts designed to achieve a more racially balanced workforce. The employer only needs to demonstrate that there is a "conspicuous . . . imbalance in traditionally segregated job categories."

City of Richmond v. J. A. Croson Co.
109 S.Ct. 706 (1989)

The Court upheld a court of appeals decision that Richmond's Minority Business Utilization Plan was not sufficiently narrowly tailored to remedy past discrimination in the construction industry. The Plan allowed minorities a fixed thirty percent quota of the public contracts based solely on their race.

Adarand Constructors v. Pena
115 S.Ct. 2097 (1995)

The Court ruled that affirmative action programs of the federal government can only be acceptable if they show a "compelling" interest for the program and the program is narrowly tailored to accomplish this interest.

◆ ATTORNEYS, JUDGES, AND LEGAL SCHOLARS

(To locate biographical profiles more readily, please consult the index at the back of the book.)

Clifford L. Alexander, Jr. (1933–)
Attorney, Federal Government Official

Clifford Alexander was born in New York City on September 21, 1933. Alexander went to Harvard and earned his B.A. in 1955, graduating *cum laude*. He then attended Yale Law School, and in 1958 earned his LL.B. He then became the assistant district attorney of New York County from 1959 to 1961. He was the executive director of the Hamilton Grange Neighborhood Conservation district in Manhattanville from 1961 to 1962. In 1963, he became a staff member of the National Security Council.

Alexander was hired by President Lyndon B. Johnson as his deputy special assistant in 1964, and quickly rose to become the president's deputy special counsel. He became chairman of the Equal Employment Opportunity Commission in 1967, where he was accused of bullying reluctant employers into complying with federal guidelines for minority employment. In 1969, he left the position.

From 1969 to 1976, Alexander worked for several different law firms. He also became a Harvard overseer. At Harvard, he was involved in working with craft unions to improve minority employment opportunities.

President Jimmy Carter appointed Alexander secretary of the Department of the Army, the first African American to serve in that position. Alexander won the Outstanding Civilian Service Award from the Department of the Army in 1980. Since 1981, Alexander has been president of Alexander Associates, Inc., and served as a consultant on minority hiring practices to Major League Baseball. In the early 1990s, Alexander served as Washington, DC's chief negotiator in hammering out a deal to build a new stadium for the National Football League's Washington Redskins.

In addition, Alexander has had his own television program "Black on White," has been director of several Dreyfus money funds, has served on the board of directors for the Mexican-American Legal Defense and Education Fund, and has taught at Howard University.

Joyce London Alexander (1949–)
Judge

Joyce London Alexander was born in Cambridge, Massachusetts. She graduated in 1969 from Howard University after studying there on a scholarship from the NAACP. She worked for congressman Tip O'Neill and then graduated in 1972 from the New England School of Law.

She practiced law for several public foundations and worked as an assistant professor at Tufts University before being appointed to a U.S. district court as a magistrate. In 1996, she was named chief judge.

Alexander is known for her activities in the legal community. She has held various positions for the National Bar Association and has founded several educational programs for her peers.

Violette Anderson (1882–1937)
Judge, Attorney

Violette Anderson was born on July 16, 1882, in London, England. Her family moved to the United States, where she attended North Division High School in Chicago, Illinois, from 1895 to 1899. She then attended the Chicago Athenaeum in 1903, the Chicago Seminar of Sciences from 1912 to 1915, and Chicago Law School from 1917 to 1920, where she earned her LL.B. in 1920. She then wed Albert E. Johnson.

Anderson worked as a court reporter from 1905 to 1920, which sparked her interest in law. She began a private practice in 1920, becoming the first African American woman to practice law in the U.S. District Court, Eastern Division. From 1922 to 1923, she served as the first female city prosecutor in Chicago.

After five years of practice before the high court of Illinois, Anderson was admitted to practice for the Supreme Court of the United States, becoming the first

African American woman to obtain this post. Her admission became a precedent for other African American women.

Anderson also belonged to the Federal Colored Women's Clubs, was the first vice president of the Cook County Bar Association, president of Friendly Big Sisters League of Chicago, and secretary of the Idlewild Lot Owners Association. In addition, she was a member of the executive board of the Chicago Council of Social Agencies.

Deborah A. Batts (1947–)
Judge

The first openly lesbian federal judge, Batts was confirmed in 1994 to the U.S. District Court. A graduate of Radcliffe and the Harvard Law School, Batts clerked for a federal judge before joining Cravath, Swaine & Moore, where she worked as a litigator for six years. Next she served as assistant U.S. attorney in New York for five years before accepting a teaching post at Fordham University in 1994.

A supporter of equal rights for gays and lesbians, Batts is known to be a an independent thinker unafraid to speak her mind. She was drawn to the legal field after experiencing the political turmoil of the 1960s. She was initially recommended for a federal judgeship during the Bush administration but did not receive a nomination. U.S. Senator Daniel Moynihan recommended her a second time when President Bill Clinton assumed office. Clinton's nomination of Batts was confirmed by the Senate with no challenges.

Derrick Albert Bell, Jr. (1930–)
Attorney, Educator

Derrick Albert Bell, Jr. was born in Pittsburgh, Pennsylvania, on November 6, 1930. He attended Duquesne University and received his LL.B. from the University of Pittsburgh Law School. He married Jewel A. Hairston and the couple has three children. Bell is a member of the bar in Washington, DC, Pennsylvania, New York, California; the U.S. Supreme Court; the U.S. Courts of Appeals for Fourth, Fifth, Sixth, Eighth, and Tenth Circuits; and several federal district courts. In 1969 he began teaching law at Harvard Law School. Bell has written several important books on the law including *Race, Racism and American Law*, second edition, 1980, and *And We Are Not Saved, The Elusive Quest for Racial Justice*, 1987. Bell also served as editor of *Desegregation Dialogue, Searching for Remedies Under Brown*.

After graduating from law school, Bell worked for the U.S. Department of Justice from 1957 to 1959, the Pittsburgh Branch of the NAACP as executive secretary from 1959 to 1960, and for the NAACP Legal Defense and Education Fund as staff attorney from 1960 to 1966. In 1966 he was made deputy assistant to the secretary for civil rights for the Department of Health, Education and Welfare. He also served for a year as the director of the Western Center on Law and Poverty.

Bell began as a lecturer on law at Harvard Law School in 1969, became a professor in 1971, and left in 1980 to be dean of the University of Oregon Law School for five years. After spending one year teaching at Stanford University, he returned to Harvard Law School in 1986. Four years later, Bell took an unpaid extended leave from his teaching duties at Harvard in protest over the institution's lack of a tenured black woman professor. Bell was formally removed from his position in 1992. Bell wrote in 1992 *Faces at the Bottom of the Well: The Permanence of Racism*, and in 1994 *Confronting Authority: Reflections of an Ardent Protester*.

Jane Matilda Bolin (1908–)
Judge, Attorney

At the age of 31, Jane Matilda Bolin was honored by being chosen to be the first African American female judge in the United States. She presided over the Domestic Relations Court of the City of New York (subsequently called the Family Court of the State of New York) for forty years. Her first ten-year appointment came from Mayor Fiorello La Guardia in 1939. She was appointed to three more successive ten-year terms by mayors William O'Dwyer, Robert F. Wagner, Jr., and John Lindsay. After forty years of service, Bolin reached the mandatory retirement age.

Bolin was born on April 11, 1908, in Poughkeepsie, New York, her father was the first African American graduate of Williams College. Bolin attended Wellesley College and Yale University School of Law, where she received her LL.B. in 1931. She worked with her father until she passed the New York State Bar examination and then practiced in Poughkeepsie before moving to New York City to practice law with her husband, Ralph E. Mizelle.

In 1937, Bolin was appointed assistant corporation counsel for New York City, a post which she held until she received her appointment to the Domestic Relations Court. Outside of her career, Bolin has taken an active role in the Wiltwyck School for Boys, the Child Welfare League of America, the Neighborhood Children's Center, and the local and national NAACP. She has also traveled extensively and met several heads of state in Africa. Her friends included Eleanor Roosevelt, educator Mary McLeod Bethune, and Judge Waties Waring, who ruled in the first public school desegregation case. Bolin has received honorary degrees from Morgan State

University, Western College for Women, Tuskegee Institute, Hampton University, and Williams College.

After her retirement, Bolin became a volunteer reading teacher for the New York City public schools. She received an appointment to the Regents Review Committee of the New York State Board of Regents, which holds hearings involving professional discipline of more than 32 professions. Bolin was honored for her distinguished service by the corporation counsel's office on May 17, 1993.

Johnnie L. Cochran, Jr. (1937–)
Attorney

Born in Shreveport, Louisiana on October 2, 1937, Johnnie L. Cochran Jr. grew up in Los Angeles. He received a B.A. in 1959 from the University of California. After finishing his law studies at the Loyola Marymount University School of Law in 1963, he passed the California bar exam. Cochran began his law career as prosecutor in the criminal division of the deputy city attorney's office in Los Angeles. In 1965, he left that post to join criminal lawyer Gerald Lenoir in private practice. He then created the firm of Cochran, Atkins & Evans.

During his first stint in private practice, Cochran established himself by defending high-profile African American clients, such as the family of Leonard Deadwyler, a young man shot to death by police while driving his pregnant wife to the hospital, and Geronimo Pratt, a former Black Panther charged with murder. Cochran lost both cases, but he demonstrated how such cases could garner media attention and foment the African American community into action.

Cochran returned to the Los Angeles County district attorney's office in 1978. After two years as a prosecutor, he returned to private practice in 1980. Shortly thereafter, Cochran won a settlement for the family of Ron Settles, who had been strangled by police officers, though his death was originally identified as a suicide.

Cochran's victories increased, and he began representing celebrities such as pop singer Michael Jackson and actor Todd Bridges. Beginning in the summer of 1994, Cochran served as one of the team of defense lawyers for O. J. Simpson, accused of murdering his ex-wife Nicole Brown Simpson and her friend Ronald Goldman. Cochran wore down the prosecution by challenging evidence and concentrating on racially prejudiced officers. Cochran's racially charged closing arguments alleged the police framed O. J. Simpson for murder. In response, the jury acquitted Simpson on all counts.

Following the Simpson case—described in the media as "The Trial of the Century," Cochran became one of the best known lawyers in the country and was offered a

Johnnie L. Cochran, Jr. (Archive Photos, Inc.)

million-dollar advance for his memoirs. Cochran has served as an adjunct professor at both the Los Angeles School of Law and the Loyola University School of Law. He served as chairman of the Rules Committee of the Democratic National Convention in 1984. In 1995, he was awarded the Trumpet Award by the Turner Broadcasting System.

William T. Coleman (1920–)
Civil Rights Activist, Cabinet Officer

William T. Coleman was born in Philadelphia, Pennsylvania. Coleman graduated *summa cum laude* in 1941 from the University of Pennsylvania. His law studies at Harvard University were interrupted by World War II; however, Coleman returned to the school after the war, and in 1946, received his LL.B., graduating first in his class. He was also the first African American to serve on the editorial board of the *Harvard Law Review*.

In 1948, Coleman became the first African American to clerk for a Supreme Court Justice, when he clerked for Mr. Justice Felix Frankfurter. In the mid 1950s, Coleman joined the Philadelphia firm of Dilworth, Paxon, Kalish, Levy & Green. By the mid 1960s, he had become a partner in the firm. In 1959, Coleman served on an employment commission for President Dwight D. Eisenhower, and served Presidents John F. Kennedy, Lyndon B. Johnson, and Richard M. Nixon.

In 1975, President Gerald Ford appointed Coleman as the secretary of transportation. Coleman reorganized the department, and issued a statement of the department's goals. President Ford's defeat in the 1976 election ended his reign at the department. Coleman returned to private practice in Los Angeles. In 1995, President Bill Clinton presented him with the Presidential Medal of Freedom.

George Crockett, Jr. (1909–1997)
Attorney, Judge, Legislator, Civil Rights Activist

Born in Jacksonville, Florida, on August 10, 1909, Crockett began working when he was 12 and graduated from Morehouse College. Traveling north to Michigan to pursue a law degree, Crockett returned to his hometown and opened a law practice. In 1939, his accomplishments as a lawyer and community activist led him to be chosen as the first African American attorney in the U.S. Department of Justice.

While in Washington, DC, Crockett distinguished himself as counsel for cases concerning the Fair Labor Standards Act, and in 1943, his work led to his appointment by President Franklin D. Roosevelt as an examiner with the Fair Employment Practices Committee. That same year, he was hired by the United Auto Workers in Detroit, to serve as director of their Fair Employment Practices Office during a time of increased racial tensions in the city. In 1946, he went into private practice in Detroit in a firm that took on significant civil rights cases. Crockett once argued a case on behalf of accused Communists in a courtroom battle landed him in prison for four months for a contempt of court violation.

Crockett became intensely involved in the civil rights struggle in the South during the 1960s, leaving Michigan for a time to direct the National Lawyers Guild civil rights efforts through an effort known as Project Mississippi. In 1966, he was elected to Detroit Recorder's Court, a bench that handled the city's criminal docket. In 1969, members of a leftist group who were meeting at an African American church were brought en masse into police custody after a shooting outside the church, Crockett went down to the station in the middle of the night and set up his own impromptu court, releasing most of the charged on the basis of constitutional law. He was vilified by Detroit's white establishment for his application of the Bill of Rights.

In 1980, two years after he had left the Recorder's Court bench, Crockett was elected as a Democratic Congressional representative for a Michigan district that included part of Detroit. He served in Washington for the next decade, continuing to distinguish himself by speaking out on civil rights issues and even serving another stint in jail for participating in a demonstration against apartheid in South Africa. The legislator was also a vocal opponent of President Ronald Reagan's administration's policies in Central America, especially during his tenure as chair of the Foreign Affairs Subcommittee on the Western Hemisphere. After his retirement from politics in 1990, Crockett, founder of the National Bar Association Judicial Council, died in 1997.

Drew S. Days III (1941–)
Attorney, Educator

Days was born in Atlanta, Georgia on August 29, 1941. He received his B.A. from Hamilton College in 1963 and continued his studies at the Yale Law School. During his free summer months, Days returned to Georgia to champion civil rights causes and represent the poor as an intern. After graduating in 1966 from law school near the top of his class, Days moved to Chicago to represent minorities in cases of housing discrimination in the city. Later Days quit practicing law to work in Honduras for the U.S. Peace Corps.

Upon his return to the United States, Days worked in the Legal Defense and Educational Fund for the NAACP. While working for them, he served as an associate professor at Temple University in Philadelphia. In 1977, Days accepted a post as the first African American as the head of the Civil Rights Division of the U.S. Department of Justice. In 1980, Days left the government to teach at Yale University.

In 1992, President Bill Clinton nominated Days to the position of solicitor general of the United States, the second leading position at the Justice Department. In this position, Days criticized poorly conceived or poorly managed minority assistance programs. In 1995, he argued before the Supreme Court to keep in place minority voting districts in the Deep South. Early in 1996, Days resigned his position at the Justice Department to return to teaching law at Yale University.

Jerome Farris (1930–)
Attorney, Judge

Jerome Farris was appointed circuit judge of the U.S. Court of Appeals Ninth Circuit in 1979. Judge Farris was born on March 4, 1930, in Birmingham, Alabama. He earned his B.S. degree from Morehouse College in 1951. In 1952, he joined the U.S. Army Signal Corps. He received a M.S.W. from Atlanta University in 1955 and received his J.D. from the University of Washington in 1958. Farris is married to Jean Shy and has two children.

Farris started out in 1958 with Weyer, Schroeter, and Sterne and in 1959 became a partner. He stayed in private practice until, in 1969, he became a Washington State Court of Appeals judge. He was the chairman of the State Federal Judicial Council of Washington from 1983 to 1987. In addition, he has served as president on the Washington State Jr. Chamber of Commerce from 1965 to 1966; a trustee with the Pacific Northwest Ballet from 1978 to 1983; and has been since 1985, a regent of the University of Washington.

Farris has been honored with the Clayton Frost Award from the Jaycees in 1966, received an honorary LL.D. from Morehouse College in 1978, and the Order of the Coif from the University of Washington Law School.

Archibald H. Grimké (1849–1930)
Attorney, Writer, Activist, Diplomat

Archibald Grimké was born on a plantation near Charleston, South Carolina, in 1849. His father was a successful lawyer who had given up his profession to become a planter. His mother had been a family slave and served as the nurse for Henry Grimké's first wife, Selena. Archibald was considered a slave at the time. He, along with his mother and siblings, were passed on to relatives after his father's death. Grimké attended a special school during his youth. Grimké enrolled in a school directed by Frances Pillsbury and impressed the instructors there with his superior academic abilities. He completed undergraduate studies in only three years and obtained his master's degree in 1872 from Lincoln University.

Grimké moved to Boston and practiced law there from 1875 to 1883. Beginning in 1885, he presided over the Women's Suffrage Association of Massachusetts. In the early 1890's, Grimké wrote for Boston-area publications, before being appointed the American consul for Santo Domingo (now the Dominican Republic) for four years. He then assumed the presidential role for the Washington chapter of the NAACP while writing, lecturing, and presiding over the American Negro Academy. Grimké wrote several books including biographies of William Lloyd Garrison in 1891 and Charles Sumner in 1892, numerous essays, and speeches.

William H. Hastie (1904–1976)
Attorney, Judge, State Government Official

From 1949 to 1971, William H. Hastie served as a U.S. Court of Appeals Judge of the Third Circuit, the first African American man to hold a federal appeals judicial position. Hastie was born in Knoxville, Tennessee, November 17, 1904. He was the son of William Henry and Roberta Child Hastie. He received his A.B. from Amherst College in 1925, an LL.B.in 1930, and a S.J.D. in 1933 from Harvard University. He received honorary LL.D.s from many institutions including Rutgers University, Howard University, and Temple University. In 1943, he married Beryl Lockhart. The couple had three children.

Hastie was admitted to the bar in 1930 and was in private practice from 1930 to 1933. In 1933, he became assistant solicitor of the Department of the Interior, where he served until 1937. In 1937, he became a judge of the District Court of the Virgin Islands, leaving in 1939 to become dean of the Howard University School of Law. In 1942, he was the first civilian aide to the secretary of war. He was governor of the Virgin Islands between 1946 and 1949, before his subsequent position as U.S. Circuit Court of Appeals judge. Hastie was also a Trustee of the Amherst College and a Fellow of the American Academy of Arts and Sciences. Hastie died on April 14, 1976, in Philadelphia, Pennsylvania.

Joseph W. Hatchett (1932–)
Attorney, Judge, Author

Judge Joseph W. Hatchett was appointed a circuit judge of the U.S. Court of Appeals on October 1, 1981, and he currently retains that position. Judge Hatchett was the first African American to be appointed to the highest court of a state since Reconstruction, the first African American to be elected to public office in a statewide election in the South, and first African American to serve on a federal appellate court in the South.

Born in Clearwater, Florida, on September 17, 1932, Hatchett received his A.B. from Florida A&M University in 1954 and his J.D. from Howard University in 1959. He also has certification in his specialties—a Naval Justice School Certificate in 1973, an Appellate Judge Course in 1977, and an American Academy of Judicial Education Appellate Judge Course in 1978.

Hatchett was in private practice in Florida from 1959 to 1966, and served as the contract consultant for the City of Daytona Beach for three years. He became an assistant U.S. attorney in Jacksonville, Florida, in 1966, then served as the first assistant of the U.S. Attorney for the Middle District of Florida. In 1971, he became the U.S. magistrate for the Middle District of Florida, and was a justice for the Florida State Supreme Court from 1975 to 1979. He was a circuit judge for the U.S. Court of Appeals, Fifth Circuit, from 1979 to 1981, before transferring to the Eleventh Circuit in and in 1996 becoming chief judge.

Hatchett was honored with a Howard University Post Graduation Achievement Award in 1977, named Most Outstanding Citizen from the Broward County National Bar Association in 1976, received a Medallion for Human Relations from Bethune-Cookman in 1975, and has been awarded several honorary doctorates. He is the author of several publications in the field of law.

A. Leon Higginbotham, Jr. (1928–1998)
Judge, Author

Leon Higginbotham, Jr. was appointed in 1977 by President Jimmy Carter as a judge of the U.S. Court of Appeals and became the circuit's chief judge before his retirement in 1993. He had served on the Federal Trade Commission—the first African American and the youngest person ever to hold the post of commissioner. Born in Trenton, New Jersey, on February 25, 1928, Higginbotham began as an engineering student at Purdue University, but later went to Antioch College to study liberal arts. He received his LL.B. in 1952 from Yale School of Law.

After graduation, he became an assistant district attorney in Philadelphia and later moved into private practice. He was sought out by Pennsylvania Governor David Lawrence to become a member of the Pennsylvania Human Rights Commission. Elected president of the Philadelphia chapter of the NAACP, Higginbotham later earned the honor of "One of the 10 Outstanding Young Men in America" by the U.S. Junior Chamber of Commerce. He was appointed a federal district judge in 1964, where he served until his appointment as a federal appellate judge in 1977. Higginbotham was also a lecturer at Harvard Law School and an adjunct professor at the University of Pennsylvania. In 1993, he was nominated for a position on the New York Times Co. board of directors.

In 1995, a retired Higginbotham levied criticism at Supreme Court Justice Clarence Thomas, whose judicial philosophy differs greatly from his own. While Higginbotham advocated social engineering through legislation, Thomas vigorously held that law should be colorblind. Higginbotham was criticized for what some saw as an unprovoked attack on a colleague.

Higginbotham was known for his writing. He authored more than 100 articles as well as an acclaimed book *In the Matter of Color: Race and the American Legal Process: The Colonial Period*. He was also praised for his logic and language. In his esteemed career, he won more than 40 honorary degrees. Higginbotham was awarded the nation's highest medal in 1995, when the Presidential Medal of Freedom was bestowed upon him by President Bill Clinton.

Anita Hill (1956–)
Educator, Author, Lecturer

Born on July 30, 1956, in Morns, Oklahoma, Anita Hill was a relatively unknown law professor at the Universi-

A. Leon Higginbotham, Jr. (foreground) (Corbis Corporation [Bellevue])

ty of Oklahoma until 1991. It was during the Senate confirmation hearings for U.S. Supreme Court Justice Clarence Thomas that Hill became famous. She came forward with sexual harassment charges against Judge Thomas that shocked the nation, and many watched as she poured out details of Thomas's alleged sexual harassment, purportedly committed when both had worked for the Equal Employment Opportunities Commission. Hill claimed that Thomas repeatedly pressured her to date him, told her plots of pornographic movies, and bragged about his sexual exploits. When asked why she didn't quit her job or report Thomas when the incidents occurred during the early 1980s, Hill answered that she feared she would not be able to get another job. Thomas told a conflicting story, and without corroborative evidence for either side, was confirmed by the Senate.

Following the hearings, Hill continued to be hounded by the press. Several books were written and a 76-minute documentary composed of testimony clips entitled *Sex and Justice: The Highlights of the Anita Hill/ Clarence Thomas Hearings* was released. Her experience with the hearings had changed her life. She decided to take a year-long sabbatical in order to look at the possibility of founding an institute with the purpose of researching racism and sexism. Hill also made many speeches around the country about her experience.

Controversy did not escape her on campus. Several lawmakers made news when they requested that Hill be fired. However, the University of Oklahoma dean and other members of the faculty supported her. In 1993, a

Anita Hill (AP/Wide World Photos, Inc.)

Charles Hamilton Houston (Corbis Corporation [Bellevue])

university professorship to be established in Hill's name was proposed. Though the suggestion met much opposition, the endowed chair was approved two years later. The Anita Faye Hill Professorship provides a salary and money for research and travel expenses incurred in the study of women's rights in the workplace.

On March 9, 1995, Hill announced her resignation from the university, but after taking an unpaid leave during which she presumably intended to write, she resumed her teaching post in September of the same year. *Race, Gender, and Power in America,* co-edited by Hill and Emma Coleman Jordan, in 1995 was published. In 1997, *Speaking the Truth*, Hill's second book, was published.

Charles Hamilton Houston (1895–1950)
Attorney, Educational Administrator

Charles Hamilton Houston was born in Washington, DC, on September 3, 1895. After he finished high school at the age of 15, he attended Amherst College and earned his A.B. in 1915 as one of six valedictorians. He briefly taught English, then enlisted in the U.S. Army in 1917, and served in France and Germany. He attended Harvard Law School and became the first African Ameri-

can editor of the *Harvard Law Review.* He received his LL.B. in 1922, and was in the top five percent of his class. He also became the first African American to receive a S.J.D. in 1923 from Harvard University. Later that year he received a Sheldon Fellowship and studied civil law at the University of Madrid. In 1924, he was admitted to the Washington, DC, bar in 1924.

Houston was in private practice with his father from 1924 to 1950. Between 1929 and 1935, he was vice dean of the school of law at Howard University. He was special counsel to the NAACP from 1935 to 1940 and a member of the national legal aid committee from 1940 to 1950. He served as the vice president for the American Council on Race Relations from 1944 to 1950, and was a member of the President's Commission on Fair Employment Practice in 1944.

While with the NAACP, Houston teamed with the American Fund for Public Service to direct a program of legal action and education aimed at the elimination of segregation. Former student Thurgood Marshall served under Houston for several years. While in this position, Houston argued several cases before the U.S. Supreme Court including *Missouri ex rel. Gaines v. Canada.* The court ruled that Missouri could not keep an African

American from attending the white state law school because no such school existed for African Americans.

Historically, Houston's major impact was in his strengthening of Howard University's Law School, as well as his work in civil rights litigation. Many of the cases he argued were instrumental in setting precedents that were to be used in the historic *Brown v. Board of Education* and *Bolling v. Sharpe* cases that were to outlaw racial segregation. In addition, he was a columnist for *The Afro-American.*

Houston died April 22, 1950, of a heart ailment and was buried in Lincoln Memorial Cemetery. Five Supreme Court justices attended his funeral. He received a great deal of recognition after his death including the Springarn Medal awarded by the NAACP.

Norma Holloway Johnson (1932–)
Judge

Norma Holloway Johnson was born in Louisiana but left to attend high school in Baltimore, Maryland. She was the valedictorian in 1955 at Miner Teacher's College and graduated in 1962 from the Georgetown Law Center while working as a teacher.

Johnson worked in the Justice Department until 1967, when she became chief of the juvenile division for the District of Columbia. In 1970, President Richard M. Nixon appointed her associate judge for the district's superior court.

In 1980, President Jimmy Carter named her to the United States Circuit Court. In 1997, she became the chief judge of this circuit. She has rendered many high-profile decisions involving corruption and civil rights.

Elaine R. Jones (1944–)
Attorney, Organization Executive, Civil Rights Activist

Jones was born on March 2, 1944, in Norfolk, Virginia. She earned a B.A. with honors in 1965 from Howard University, and she became the first African American female law student admitted to the University of Virginia School of Law.

Jones received her law degree in 1970 and was offered a job with a prestigious Wall Street firm. She eventually turned down the job on Wall Street and went to work instead for the NAACP Legal Defense and Educational Fund (LDF). The LDF had argued more cases before the Supreme Court than any other organization except the U.S. Department of Justice.

In 1973, Jones became the managing attorney in the LDF's New York City office. In the late 1970s, she helped set up and run the LDF's new Washington, D.C., office. In 1988, Jones was promoted to deputy director-counsel of the LDF, making her second-in-command to the director, Julius Chambers. Jones used this higher profile position to challenge the administrations of Ronald Reagan and George Bush on their federal judicial appointments. She was an outspoken opponent of both Robert Bork in 1987 and Clarence Thomas in 1991.

Julius Chambers resigned from the LDF directorship in 1993, and the organization's board unanimously chose Jones to succeed Chambers. As director, Jones has broadened the organization's agenda to include more cases of environmental and health care discrimination. In addition to litigation, she is concerned with the group's fund-raising efforts.

Nathaniel R. Jones (1926–)
Judge, Civil Rights Activist

Born in 1926, Nathaniel R. Jones is a judge, attorney, and administrator. President Jimmy Carter appointed him to the Sixth Circuit Court of Appeals in Cincinnati, Ohio, on October 15, 1979, where he served until 1995, when he retired. Prior to that, he was general counsel for the NAACP from 1969 to 1979, executive director of the Fair Employment Practices Commission of the City of Youngstown, Ohio, from 1966 to 1969, in private practice, and a U.S. Attorney for the Northern District of Ohio.

While with the NAACP, Judge Jones organized the attack against northern school segregation and also argued in the Supreme Court case *Bradley v. Milliken.* The Dayton and Columbus, Ohio, school desegregation cases heard before the Supreme Court were also organized by Jones. He has headed a three-man team that investigated grievances of African American servicemen in Germany and responded to the attacks against affirmative action. He was made deputy general counsel to the President's Commission on Civil Disorders in 1967 and co-chairman of the Civilian Military Task Force on Military Justice in 1972.

Jones received a B.A. degree from Youngstown University in 1951, and his LL.B. in 1956. He has honorary degrees from Youngstown University and Syracuse University.

Star Jones (1962–)
Attorney

Star Jones was born Starlet Marie Jones in 1962 and grew up in Trenton, New Jersey. She shortened her name in 1979 upon entering American University. Jones took an active role in college and even served as a national officer of Alpha Kappa Alpha. After earning a law degree from the University of Houston, Jones went to work for the Kings County District Attorney's office, whose jurisdiction included the crime-plagued New York City borough of Brooklyn. She served as a member of its prosecuting staff from 1986 until her promotion to senior assistant district attorney in 1991.

The year 1991 also landed Jones an invitation to appear on Court TV, a cable television network that broadcasts high-profile trials interjected with commentary from experts on the judicial system. The channel soon hired her to appear regularly in conjunction with the William Kennedy Smith rape trial in Florida, and Jones's performance earned her network attention.

NBC lured her away from her tough job at the Brooklyn D.A.'s office by offering her its legal correspondent slot. During the two years she appeared on the network, several notable trials attracted the attention of the American viewing public, and Jones was there to provide commentary as well as explanation of some of the more complex legal points involved on both the *Today* show and *NBC Nightly News*. Those cases included the criminal trial of the Los Angeles police officers charged with beating motorist Rodney King and the rape trial of boxer Mike Tyson.

In 1994, Group W Communications offered Jones her own syndicated television show. Debuting that fall, *Jones & Jury* gave plaintiffs and defendants who had lawsuits pending in California's equivalent of small claims court a chance to resolve their disputes on television before a studio audience, who would then render the verdict. The show was cancelled in 1995.

Amalya Lyle Kearse (1937–)
Judge

Judge Amalya Lyle Kearse was born June 11, 1937, in Vauxhall, New Jersey. She received her B.A. in 1959 from Wellesley College, and her J.D. in 1962 from the University of Michigan. Kearse was in private practice from 1962 to 1969 and worked as an adjunct lecturer for the New York University Law School from 1968 to 1969. In 1979, President Jimmy Carter appointed her a U.S. Court of Appeals circuit judge.

Kearse has won the Jason L. Honigman Award for Outstanding Contribution to the Law Review Editorial Board. She has also served on the board of directors for the NAACP Legal Defense and Education Fund, as well as the National Urban League. She was appointed to the President's Commission for the Selection of Judges and served between 1977 and 1978. She served on the executive committee for Civil Rights Under Law for nine years, has been a member of the American Law Institute since 1977, and has been a fellow in the American College of Trial Lawyers since 1979.

Damon Keith (AP/Wide World Photos, Inc.)

Damon J. Keith (1922–)
Judge, Attorney

Damon J. Keith was appointed to the U.S. district court by President Lyndon B. Johnson and served from 1967 to 1977. From 1977 to 1995, he served as a judge for the U.S. Court of Appeals, Sixth Circuit Court in Cincinnati, Ohio. Born on July 4, 1922 in Detroit, Keith attended West Virginia State College and in 1943 received his A.B. Following graduation, he served in the army for three years. He returned to school to earn his LL.B. in 1949 from Howard University. In 1951 Keith took a job as an attorney for the Office of the Friend of the Court in Detroit and held that position from 1951 to 1955. He received an LL.M. from Wayne State University in 1956.

Keith worked for the Wayne County Board of Supervisors from 1958 to 1963 and went into private practice from 1964 to 1967 before being appointed a judge. He has been active in the Michigan Civil Rights Commission, a trustee in the Medical Corporation of Detroit, a member of the Citizen's Advisory Committee on Equal Educational Opportunity, first vice president emeritus of the Detroit Chapter of the NAACP, a member of the management committee of the Detroit YMCA, a member of the Detroit Council of the Boy Scouts of America, a member of the Detroit Arts Commission, and vice president of the United Negro College Fund of Detroit. Keith is also a trustee of the Interlochen Arts Academy and the Cranbrook School.

Judge Keith has been honored with many accolades including being named among 100 Most Influential Black Americans by *Ebony* magazine, in 1971 and 1977. He received a citizen award from Michigan State University and was named a Springarn Medalist in 1974. He has received honorary degrees from the University of Michigan, Howard University, Wayne State University, Michigan State University, and New York Law School.

Wade Hampton McCree, Jr. (1920–1987)
Judge, Attorney

Wade Hampton McCree, Jr. was solicitor general under President Jimmy Carter from 1977 to 1981. McCree had already led a distinguished career as a judge and lawyer by the time he reached that position. He died on August 30, 1987. McCree was born in Des Moines, Iowa, on July 3, 1920. He graduated in 1941 from Fisk University, earning his A.B. In 1944 he received his LL.B. from Harvard University. In 1948, he was admitted to the bar in Michigan.

McCree had a private law practice from 1948 to 1952. From 1952 to 1954 he was commissioner of the Michigan Workmen's Compensation Commission. He was a circuit judge for Wayne County, Michigan, from 1954 until 1961. Then he was a judge for the U.S. District Court, Eastern District, in Michigan from 1961 to 1966. McCree had the honor of being the first African American federal judge in the state of Michigan. From 1966 to 1977 he served as a U.S. Court of Appeals, Sixth Circuit Judge. From 1981 until his death in 1987, he was a member of the faculty at the University of Michigan Law School. Three years later, the Wade H. McCree, Jr. Professorship was established at the University of Michigan Law School, making it the first endowed chair at a major American law school to be named after an African American. McCree was honored with more than 30 honorary degrees in his lifetime including LL.D. degrees from Howard University, Harvard University, Boston University, Brandeis University, and Tuskegee Institute.

Gabrielle Kirk McDonald (1942–)
Judge

McDonald was born in St. Paul, Minnesota. She attended Hunter College and then, in 1966, graduated *cum laude* from the Howard University School of Law. McDonald worked for the NAACP until 1969 when she went into private practice in Houston, Texas, with her husband.

Wade McCree, Jr. (AP/Wide World Photos, Inc.)

She earned a reputation as one of the top litigators in the state and won several large settlements for her clients in civil rights cases. Her record attracted national attention and in 1979 President Jimmy Carter appointed her a federal district court judge. In 1988, she resigned from her position and went back into private practice. She also taught at several law schools.

In 1993, McDonald was the only U.S. citizen elected to the United Nations International War Crimes Tribunal at the Hague, Netherlands. She was reelected in 1997 and is the presiding judge of the tribunal.

Theodore McMillian (1919–)
Judge, Educator

Born on January 28, 1919, in St. Louis, Missouri, Theodore McMillian received his B.S. degree in 1941 from Lincoln University and in 1949, earned his LL.B. degree from St. Louis University Law School. He served in the Signal Corps from 1942 to 1946.

McMillian has been a lecturer at St. Louis University Law School as well as a faculty member of Webster College. He became a circuit judge for the State of Missouri and served as an assistant circuit attorney for the City of St. Louis from 1953 to 1956. From 1972 to

Gabrielle Kirk McDonald (Archive Photos, Inc.).

1978, he was a Judge with the Missouri Court of Appeals. He became a U.S. Circuit Court of Appeals Judge for the Eighth Circuit in 1978.

Judge McMillian has been a member of the board of trustees for Blue Cross, and a member of the Danforth Foundation Advisory Council. He served on the Presidential Council of St. Louis University, and as a board chairman for Human Development Corporation between 1964 and 1977. He has also been a member of the National Legal Aid Advisory Board. He has been honored with an Alumni Merit Award from St. Louis University, an Award of Honor from the Lawyers Association in 1970, and a Man of the Year Award in 1970.

Carmel Carrington Marr (1921–)
Attorney, Diplomat, State Government Official

Carmel Carrington Marr was born in Brooklyn in 1921 and received her B.A. in 1945 from Hunter College. She earned her J.D. from Columbia University Law School in 1948. As an experienced lawyer in international law, she was appointed by President Harry Truman to the position of legal advisor to the U.S. mission to the United Nations in 1953. She served that position until 1967, keeping in constant contact with missions from

other parts of the world and serving on a number of key committees of the United Nations General Assembly.

Marr began her career in private practice from 1949 to 1953. After her position as legal advisor to the United Nations, she became the senior legal officer of the United Nations Secretariat from 1967 to 1968, and then left to become a member of the New York State Human Rights Appeal Board from 1968 to 1971. Between 1971 and 1986 she served as commissioner of the New York State Public Service Commission. She retired from that position, becoming an energy consultant from 1987 until 1990.

Marr was also the chairperson of the advisory council of the Gas Research Institute between 1979 and 1986, the chairperson of the U.S. Department of Transportation Technology Pipeline Safety Standards Commission from 1979 to 1985, and the chairperson of the National Association of Regulatory Utility Commissioners Gas Commission from 1984 to 1986. She became president of NARUC's Great Lakes Conference of Public Utility Commission and was on the board of the National Arts Stabilization Fund.

Marr has been honored as an Outstanding Community Service by the Brooklyn Urban League and has been honored by Gas Research Institute, New York State Public Service Commission, American Red Cross, National Council of Churches, and *Mademoiselle* magazine.

Thurgood Marshall (1908–1993)
Judge, Federal Government Official, Attorney, Civil Rights Activist

Thurgood Marshall's long and illustrious career was capped by his 1967 nomination to the U.S. Supreme Court, where he became the first African American to hold the position of Supreme Court Justice. He retired on June 27, 1991. Marshall died at the age of 84 in 1993. He was laid in state in the Great Hall of the Supreme Court of the United States on the same bier where Abraham Lincoln once rested. More than 20,000 mourners paid their respects to Justice Marshall.

Born in Baltimore, Maryland, on July 2, 1908, Marshall earned a B.A. degree from Lincoln University and hoped to become a dentist. He changed his mind, and instead went to Howard University Law School where he graduated in 1933 at the top of his class. He immediately went into private practice in Baltimore for five years. In 1936, Marshall entered into what was going to be a long and career with the NAACP, starting as an assistant special counsel, and eventually becoming director-counsel of the Legal Defense and Educational fund until 1961. In 1938, as a national special counsel, he handled all cases involving the constitutional rights of African Americans. Then, in 1950, he was named director-counsel of the organization's 11-year-old Legal Defense and Education Fund.

In 1954, Marshall was the lead lawyer for the NAACP in Supreme Court case *Brown v. Board of Education.* He also figured prominently in such important cases as *Sweatt v. Painter* and *Smith v. Allwright.* Of the 32 cases that he argued before the Supreme Court, Marshall won 29.

Marshall was also known for his lifelong support of rights for women. Constance Baker Motley commented that Marshall hired her for a NAACP counsel position when virtually every other employer had turned her down. He also encouraged her when he argued cases before the Supreme Court, and made certain he pointed out other African American women role models.

In 1961, Marshall became a federal circuit judge for the second circuit. In 1946, he was awarded the prestigious Springarn Medal for his many achievements. He had over twenty honorary degrees to his credit including LL.D. honors in 1960 from the University of Liberia, in 1964 from the University of Michigan, and in 1968 from the University of Otago, in Dunedin, New Zealand. Marshall was also the representative for the White House Conference on Youth and Children, and a member of the National Bar Association. He was sent by President John F. Kennedy to be a personal representative to the independence ceremonies of Sierra Leone.

Constance Baker Motley (1921–)
Federal Government Official, Judge, Civil Rights Activist, Attorney

Born on September 14, 1921, in New Haven, Connecticut, Constance Baker Motley became the first African American woman to become a federal judge. She was appointed in 1966 by President Lyndon B. Johnson to the U.S. District Court for Southern New York.

While still a law student at Columbia University, Motley began working with the NAACP Legal Defense and Educational Fund. In 1946, she was awarded her LL.B. and began to work full-time with the NAACP, eventually becoming an associate counsel. During her twenty-year career with the organization, Motley had argued nine successful NAACP cases before the U.S. Supreme Court, and had participated in almost every important civil rights case that had passed through the courts since.

In 1964, Motley made a successful run for the New York State Senate. She became the first African American woman elected to that position. After only a year in the Senate, Motley ran for the position of Manhattan Borough President, emerging the victor by the unanimous final vote of the city council. She thus became the first woman to serve as a city borough president, and, therefore, also the first woman on the Board of Estimate.

Motley was appointed to the U.S. District Court in 1966. In 1982, she was named chief judge of the federal district court that covers Manhattan, the Bronx, and six counties north of New York City. In 1986 she was named senior U.S. district judge.

During her career, Motley has received several awards for her contributions to the legal profession and for her role in the advancement of civil rights. She holds more than 20 honorary degrees from prestigious universities including Princeton and Howard Universities. In 1993, Motley was inducted into the National Women's Hall of Fame.

James Ogletree (1952–)
Lawyer

James Ogletree was born in Merced, California, and attended Stanford University. In 1974, he received his B.A. and followed it the next year with his M.A. While at Stanford he became involved with the Black Power Movement. He edited a Black Panther newspaper and traveled to Africa and Cuba. His attendance at Angela Davis's trial first attracted him to a career in the law.

Ogletree graduated in 1978 from Harvard Law School and went to work as a public defender in Washington DC. He established a reputation as a top trial lawyer and taught at American University and Antioch Law School. In 1985, while in private practice, Ogletree became a visiting professor at Harvard Law School and helped the school develop its trial advocacy workshops.

Ogletree served as Anita Hill's attorney during her testimony before the U.S. Senate concerning the nomination of Clarence Thomas to the Supreme Court. In 1989, he became a full professor at Harvard.

Bernard Parks (1943–)
Police Chief

Bernard Parks was born in Texas but raised in Los Angeles. After bouncing between jobs, Parks became a police officer in Los Angeles in 1965. Parks received his B.A. in 1973 from Pepperdine University and his M.A. in public administration in 1976 from the University of Southern California.

Parks steadily moved up the ladder at the Los Angeles Police Department. By 1988 he was the assistant police chief. The Los Angeles riots of 1992 forced incumbent police chief Darryl Gates from his position. Gates was accused by many of racism during his reign as police chief. An African American chief was picked to replace Gates.

Bernard Parks

The new chief, Willie Williams, clashed frequently with Parks. He demoted Parks in 1994. However, the City Council restored Parks's salary. In 1996, Williams was removed as chief and the next year Parks became the head of the LAPD. He has instituted changes at the department to increase flexibility and bring captains closer to their officers.

James B. Parsons (1911–1993)
Judge

James B Parsons was born in Kansas City, Missouri. He graduated in 1934 from the James Milliken University and Conservatory of Music and began to teach at Lincoln University. He later taught in Greensboro, North Carolina, until he joined the U.S. Navy in 1942. After World War II, he received a M.A. in political science and a J.D. from the University of Chicago.

Parsons went into private practice and taught constitutional law at the John Marshall Law School. He served as assistant U.S. district attorney for nine years until he became a judge of the Cook County Superior Court. He was appointed a U.S. district court judge in 1961 by President John F. Kennedy. He became the first African American to sit as a federal judge in the continental

United States. In 1975, Parsons was named chief judge of the court.

He retired in 1992 after many tributes from other African American judges. Parsons died in 1993.

Spottswood Robinson (1916–1998)
Attorney, Judge

Spottswood Robinson was born in Richmond, Virginia. He received his B.A. in 1936 from Virginia Union University and his L.LB. in 1939 from Howard University Law School. He graduated *magna cum laude* from Howard.

Robinson has had a long career in private and public practice. He was an attorney in Richmond until 1960. However, during that time he also taught at the Howard University Law School from 1945 until 1964. He was dean of the school of law from 1960 to 1964. Robinson gained notoriety during the period for his work with the NAACP. He worked for the Legal Defense and Education Fund from 1948 to 1950, working with Thurgood Marshall. From 1951 to 1960 he was the regional council for the NAACP in the southeast.

In 1964, President Johnson appointed Robinson as a federal circuit court judge in the state of Washington. In 1966, Robinson was promoted to the Ninth Circuit Court of Appeals. He also served on the United States Civil Rights Commission from 1961 to 1963.

Robinson died in 1998 in Virginia.

George Ruffin (1834–1886)
Judge, Attorney, Civil Rights Activist

George Ruffin was born in Richmond, Virginia, in 1834, the first son of free African Americans. In 1853, the family moved to Boston and Ruffin graduated from Chapman Hall school and joined with the Republican Party. He moved for a short while to Liverpool, England, after becoming disillusioned by the *Dred Scott* decision. Returning to Boston, Ruffin worked as a barber. He wrote a review for the *Anglo-African* in 1863 and attended the National Negro Convention in 1864.

Ruffin also began to read law with a local law firm. He graduated in 1869 from the Harvard Law School. He became the first African American to earn an LL.B. from Harvard, and perhaps the first to graduate from a university law school in the United States. He joined the firm of Harvey Jewell, and then won a seat on the Massachusetts legislature in 1869, becoming the second African American to serve in that body.

Ruffin became known as an exceptional speaker and debater as he focused his attention to the problems in the South. In 1876 and 1877, he won election to the Boston Common Council. He presided over the Negro

Convention of New Orleans in 1872. Frederick Douglass was a friend of Ruffin's, and Ruffin was asked to contribute to the introduction to the 1881 revision of *The Life and Times of Frederick Douglass*. Ruffin was appointed in November of 1883 as judge of a municipal court in Charlestown. He became the first African American judge in Massachusetts. In 1883, he was made consul resident for the Dominican Republic in Boston. Ruffin's other activities included being named president of the Wendell Phillips Club of Boston, member and president of the Banneker Literary Club of Boston, and superintendent and officer of the Twelfth Baptist Church of Boston. Ruffin died of Bright's disease on November 20, 1886.

Robert H. Terrell (1857–1925)
Educator, Judge, Attorney

Robert H. Terrell was born in Charlottesville, Virginia, on November 27, 1857. He worked in a dining hall to pay for his classes at Harvard, where he graduated *magna cum laude*, in 1884. He went to work in the Washington, DC, public schools, and also attended Howard University Law School, earning his LL.B. in 1889 and his LL.M. in 1893. In 1889, he went to work as the chief clerk in the office of the auditor of the U.S. Treasury Department.

Terrell was involved in the private practice of law from 1892 to 1898, until he become a teacher, and later became principal at the M Street High School. He was also elected to the Board of Trade in the 1890s. In 1901, he was appointed as a justice of the peace in Washington, DC. Similar to many African Americans of his day, Terrell was torn between his strongly held civil rights beliefs and Booker T. Washington's conservative ideas. Through Washington's influence, Terrell was nominated by President William H. Taft for the position of judge of the Municipal Court of the District of Columbia in 1910. Despite racial protests in the Senate, Terrell signed the appointment and held the position until his death on December 20, 1915. Terrell suffered two strokes and battled asthma while on the court.

Terrell taught at the Howard University Law School from 1910 to 1925. He was grand master of the Grand United Order of Odd Fellows of the District of Columbia.

Clarence Thomas (1948–)
Attorney, Judge/Magistrate

Thomas was born June 23, 1948, in Pin Point, Georgia. As a youth, Thomas lived with his maternal grandparents in Savannah. While his grandfather had little education, he was determined that Thomas would go to school and make something of himself. He attended various all-African American and mixed-race Catholic schools. He intended to enter the priesthood, but left when he encountered a racist seminarian.

Thomas earned his B.A. from Holy Cross College. He was accepted into Yale Law School in 1971 after Yale had adopted an affirmative action program. In 1974, he earned his J.D. After graduating, Thomas became an assistant attorney general for the State of Missouri from 1974 to 1977. Thomas then worked briefly at Monsanto Company in St. Louis, specializing in pesticide, fungicide, and rodenticide law. He also worked as a legal assistant for Senator John C. Danforth.

From 1981 to 1982, Thomas was an assistant secretary for civil rights with the Department of Education, then moved on to chair for the Equal Employment Opportunity Commission (EEOC) until 1990. His time there was controversial, as he was not allied with either liberals or civil rights leaders, and he did not feel comfortable with the white conservative hierarchy.

After Robert H. Bork resigned his Circuit Court position because he had been rejected for a place on the U.S. Supreme Court, Thomas was appointed to the post. He served there until he was made a justice on the Supreme Court in 1991. Thomas's nomination hearings were marred by accusations of sexual harassment levied against him by former EEOC employee Anita Hill.

Hill became a household name when she came forward with her allegations. The Senate was divided by Hill's testimony. Though Thomas denied the charges and many of his former coworkers testified for him, the case became highly politicized. Thomas was nominated by a vote of 52 to 48, one of the closest margins in Supreme Court history.

Thomas has gone on to carve out a prominent role as one of the most conservative justices on the Court. Together with conservative Justice Scalia, Thomas forms the right-wing backbone of the Court. In his tenure Thomas has presented strong opinions against affirmative action and desegregation. He also supports limiting the fundamental powers of the federal government. In 1992, Thomas was one of ten people to receive the Horatio Alger Award. However, he has consistently been criticized by African American lawyers and judges for his conservative stances. In 1998, he attacked his critics at a speech before the National Bar Association.

Evelyn Williams (1922–)
Attorney

Williams grew up in Queens, New York, in a close-knit family. After graduating from Brooklyn College, she became a social worker for New York City. Shaken by the poverty she encountered and hoping to take a more active role in helping her community, Williams became a juvenile probation officer, but that too offered little satisfaction.

In the late 1950s, Williams graduated from law school as one of two African Americans in her class. By 1960, she was active in defending those accused of crimes who had little means for expensive legal representation. She also helped raise her niece, who when grown became involved with the Black Liberation Army in the early 1970s.

For several years Williams—then working with the New York University Urban Affairs and Poverty Law Program—served as the attorney for her niece, Assata Shakur and her co-defendants against a series of legal charges involving a shootout with police. The case, which included the mysterious death of one of Williams's fellow attorneys, was chronicled in her 1993 autobiography *Inadmissable Evidence: The Story of the African-American Trial Lawyer Who Defended the Black Liberation Army.*

Williams's high-profile defense of Shakur would cost her in more ways than she had imagined. During the 1980s, Williams again entered private practice, but became the target of an unsuccessful FBI sting operation. By 1989, she had joined the firm of Stevens, Hind, and White in New York City.

◆ CRIMINAL JUSTICE STATISTICS

Jail Inmates, by Race and Detention Status: 1986 to 1996

[Data are for midyear. Excludes federal and state prisons or other correctional institutions; institutions exclusively for juveniles; state-operated jails in Alaska, Connecticut, Delaware, Hawaii, Rhode Island, and Vermont; and other facilities which retain persons for less than 48 hours. As of **June 30.** Data for 1993 based on National Jail Census; for other years, based on sample survey and subject to sampling variability]

CHARACTERISTIC	1986	1990	1991	1992	1993	1994	1995	1996
Total inmates [1]	274,444	405,320	426,479	444,584	459,804	486,474	507,044	518,492
Percent of rated capacity	96	104	101	99	97	96	93	92
Male	251,235	368,002	386,865	403,768	415,576	437,600	455,400	462,400
Female	21,501	37,318	39,614	40,816	44,228	48,800	51,600	56,100
White [2]	159,178	186,989	190,333	191,362	180,914	253,500	266,200	288,900
Black [2]	112,522	174,335	187,618	195,156	203,463	224,900	232,000	221,000
Other races [2]	2,744	5,321	5,391	5,831	6,178	8,100	8,800	8,600
Hispanic [3]	38,422	57,449	60,129	62,961	69,200	74,900	74,400	81,000
Non-Hispanic	236,022	347,871	366,350	381,623	390,600	411,600	432,600	437,500
Adult [4]	272,736	403,019	424,129	441,781	455,500	479,800	499,300	510,400
Juvenile [5]	1,708	2,301	2,350	2,804	4,300	6,700	7,800	8,100

[1] 1990 to 1993, includes 31,356, 38,675, 43,138, and 52,235 persons, respectively, of unknown race not shown separately. [2] Beginning 1993, data represent White, non-Hispanic and Black, non-Hispanic and rounded to nearest 100. [3] Hispanic persons may be of any race. Data for 1993 to 1996 are estimated and rounded to nearest 100. [4] Includes inmates not classified by conviction status. [5] Juveniles are persons defined by state statute as being under a certain age, usually 18, and subject initially to juvenile court authority even if tried as adults in criminal court. In 1994 the definition was changed to include all persons under age 18.

Source: U.S. Bureau of Justice Statistics, through 1994, *Jail Inmates,* annual; beginning 1995, *Prison and Jail Inmates at Midyear,* annual.

Prisoners Under Sentence of Death: 1980 to 1996

[As of **December 31.** Excludes prisoners under sentence of death who remained within local correctional systems pending exhaustion of appellate process or who had not been committed to prison]

CHARACTERISTIC	1980	1985	1987	1988	1989	1990	1991	1992	1993	1994	1995	1996
Total [1]	688	1,575	1,967	2,117	2,243	2,346	2,466	2,575	2,727	2,905	3,064	3,219
White	418	896	1,128	1,235	1,308	1,368	1,450	1,508	1,575	1,653	1,732	1,820
Black and other	270	679	839	882	935	978	1,016	1,067	1,152	1,252	1,332	1,399
Under 20 years	11	13	10	11	6	8	14	12	13	19	20	16
20 to 24 years	173	212	222	195	191	168	179	188	211	231	264	281
25 to 34 years	334	804	969	1,048	1,080	1,110	1,087	1,078	1,066	1,088	1,068	1,076
35 to 54 years	186	531	744	823	917	1,006	1,129	1,212	1,330	1,449	1,583	1,707
55 years and over	10	31	39	47	56	64	73	85	96	103	119	139
Years of school completed:												
7 years or less	68	147	181	180	183	178	173	181	185	186	191	196
8 years	74	159	183	184	178	186	181	180	183	198	195	199
9 to 11 years	204	483	650	692	739	775	810	836	885	930	979	1,026
12 years	162	440	591	657	695	729	783	831	887	939	995	1,034
More than 12 years	43	127	168	180	192	209	222	232	244	255	272	280
Unknown	163	235	211	231	263	279	313	315	332	382	422	484
Marital status:												
Never married	268	655	856	898	956	998	1,071	1,132	1,222	1,320	1,412	1,498
Married	229	487	571	594	610	632	663	663	671	707	718	731
Divorced [2]	217	449	557	632	684	726	746	780	823	863	924	990
Time elapsed since sentencing:												
Less than 12 months	185	273	295	293	231	231	252	265	262	280	287	285
12 to 47 months	389	739	804	812	809	753	718	720	716	755	784	815
48 to 71 months	102	303	412	409	408	438	441	444	422	379	423	447
72 months and over	38	276	473	610	802	934	1,071	1,146	1,316	1,476	1,560	1,672
Legal status at arrest:												
Not under sentence	384	861	1,123	1,207	1,301	1,345	1,415	1,476	1,562	1,662	1,764	1,863
Parole or probation [3]	115	350	480	545	585	578	615	702	754	800	866	892
Prison or escaped	45	81	91	93	94	128	102	101	102	103	110	111
Unknown	170	299	290	279	270	305	321	296	298	325	314	353

[1] Revisions to the total number of prisoners were not carried to the characteristics except for race. [2] Includes persons married but separated, widows, widowers, and unknown. [3] Includes prisoners on mandatory conditional release, work release, leave, AWOL, or bail. Covers 24 prisoners in 1989, 28 in 1990, 29 in 1991 and 1992, 33 in 1993 and 1995, and 31 in 1994 and 1996.

Source: U.S. Bureau of Justice Statistics, *Capital Punishment,* annual.

Appendix

◆African American Recipients of Selected Awards
◆African American Federal Judges
◆African American Olympic Medalists

◆ AFRICAN AMERICAN RECIPIENTS OF SELECTED AWARDS

ACADEMY AWARD OF MERIT (OSCAR)— ACADEMY OF MOTION PICTURE ARTS AND SCIENCES

Best Performance by an Actor in a Leading Role

1963 Sidney Poitier, in *Lilies of the Field*

Best Performance by an Actor in a Supporting Role

1982 Louis Gossett, Jr., in *An Officer and a Gentleman*

1989 Denzel Washington, in *Glory*

1996 Cuba Gooding, Jr., in *Jerry Maquire*

Best Performance by an Actress in a Supporting Role

1939 Hattie McDaniel, in *Gone with the Wind*

1990 Whoopi Goldberg, in *Ghost*

Best Original Score

1984 Prince, for *Purple Rain*

1986 Herbie Hancock, for *'Round Midnight*

AMERICAN ACADEMY AND INSTITUTE OF ARTS AND LETTERS AWARD

Art

1946 Richmond Barthé

1966 Romare Bearden

1971 Norman Lewis

Literature

1946 Gwendolyn Brooks; Langston Hughes

1956 James Baldwin

1961 John A. Williams

1970 James A. McPherson

1971 Charles Gordone

1972 Michael S. Harper

1974 Henry Van Dyke

1978 Lerone Bennett, Jr.; Toni Morrison

1985 John Williams

1987 Ernest J. Gaines

1992 August Wilson

Music

1974 Olly Wilson

1981 George Walker

1988 Hale Smith

1991 Tania J. Leon

AUSTRALIAN OPEN

Men's Singles

1970 Arthur Ashe

Men's Doubles

1977 Arthur Ashe

Women's Doubles

1957 Althea Gibson, with Darlene Hard

CONGRESSIONAL GOLD MEDAL

1978 Marian Anderson

1990 Jesse Owens

1994 Colin L. Powell, Jr.

1998 Little Rock Nine: Jean Brown Trickey, Carlotta Walls LaNier, Melba Patillo Beals, Terrence Roberts, Gloria Ray Karlmark, Thelma Mothershed Wair, Ernest Green, Elizabeth Eckford, and Jefferson Thomas

1999 Rosa Louise McCauley Parks

EMMY AWARD—ACADEMY OF TELEVISION ARTS AND SCIENCES

Primetime Awards

Outstanding Lead Actor in a Drama Series

1966 Bill Cosby, in "I Spy" (NBC)

1967 Bill Cosby, in "I Spy" (NBC)

1968 Bill Cosby, in "I Spy" (NBC)

1991 James Earl Jones, in "Gabriel's Fire" (ABC)

1998 Andre Braugher, in "Homicide: Life on the Street" (NBC)

Outstanding Lead Actor in a Comedy, Variety, or Music Series

1959 Harry Belafonte, in "Tonight with Belafonte"

1985 Robert Guillaume, in "Benson" (ABC)

Outstanding Lead Actress in a Comedy, Variety, or Music Series

1981 Isabel Sanford, in "The Jeffersons" (CBS)

Outstanding Lead Actress in a Comedy or Drama Special

1974 Cicely Tyson, in "The Autobiography of Miss Jane Pittman" (CBS)

Outstanding Lead Actress in a Miniseries or Special

1991 Lynn Whitfield, in "The Josephine Baker Story" (HBO)

1997 Alfre Woodard, in "Miss Evers' Boys" (HBO)

Outstanding Supporting Actor in a Comedy, Variety, or Music Series

1979 Robert Guillaume, in "Soap" (ABC)

Outstanding Supporting Actor in a Miniseries or Special

1991 James Earl Jones, in "Heatwave" (TNT)

Outstanding Supporting Actress in a Drama Series

1984 Alfre Woodard, in "Doris in Wonderland" episode of "Hill Street Blues" (NBC)

1991 Madge Sinclair, in "Gabriel's Fire" (ABC)

1992 Mary Alice, in "I'll Fly Away" (NBC)

Outstanding Supporting Actress in a Comedy, Variety, or Music Series

1987 Jackee Harry, in "227"

Outstanding Supporting Actress in a Miniseries or Special

1991 Ruby Dee, in "Decoration Day," *Hallmark Hall of Fame* (NBC)

Outstanding Directing in a Drama Series

1986 Georg Stanford Brown, in "Parting Shots" episode of "Cagney & Lacey" (ABC)

1990 Thomas Carter, in "Promises to Keep" episode of "Equal Justice" (ABC)

1991 Thomas Carter, in "In Confidence" episode of "Equal Justice" (ABC)

1992 Eric Laneuville, in "All God's Children" episode of "I'll Fly Away" (NBC)

Outstanding Producing in a Miniseries or Special

1989 Suzanne de Passe, in "Lonesome Dove"

Outstanding Producing in a Variety, Music, or Comedy Special

1984 Suzanne de Passe, in "Motown 25: Yesterday, Today and Forever"

1985 Suzanne de Passe, in "Motown at the Apollo"

Outstanding Variety, Music, or Comedy Special

1997 "Chris Rock: Bring on the Pain" (HBO)

Outstanding Achievement in Music Composition

1971 Ray Charles, in "The First Nine Months Are the Hardest" (NBC)

1972 Ray Charles, in "The Funny Side of Marriage" (NBC)

Outstanding Achievement in Music Composition for a Series

1977 Quincy Jones and Gerald Fried, in "Roots" (ABC)

Outstanding Choreography

1981 Debbie Allen, for "Come One, Come All" episode of "Fame"

1982 Debbie Allen, for "Class Act" episode of "Fame"

1989 Debbie Allen, for "Motown 30: What's Goin' On!"

Daytime Awards

Outstanding Talk Show

1987 "The Oprah Winfrey Show"

1988 "The Oprah Winfrey Show"

1989 "The Oprah Winfrey Show"

1991 "The Oprah Winfrey Show"

1992 "The Oprah Winfrey Show"

1994 "The Oprah Winfrey Show"

1995 "The Oprah Winfrey Show"

1996 "The Oprah Winfrey Show"

1997 "The Oprah Winfrey Show"

Outstanding Talk Show Host

1987 Oprah Winfrey, "The Oprah Winfrey Show"

1991 Oprah Winfrey, "The Oprah Winfrey Show"

1992 Oprah Winfrey, "The Oprah Winfrey Show"

1993 Oprah Winfrey, "The Oprah Winfrey Show"

1994 Oprah Winfrey, "The Oprah Winfrey Show"

1995 Oprah Winfrey, "The Oprah Winfrey Show"

1996 Montel Williams, "The Montel Williams Show"

Sports Awards

Outstanding Sports Personality/Studio Host

1998 James Brown (Fox Sports Network)

Outstanding Sports Event Analyst

1997 Joe Morgan (ESPN/NBC)

Outstanding Sports Journalism

1995 "Broken Promises" and "Pros and Cons" episodes of "Real Sports with Bryant Gumbel"

1998 "Diamond Buck$" and "Winning at All Costs" episodes of "Real Sports with Bryant Gumbel"

Hall of Fame Award

1992 Bill Cosby

1994 Oprah Winfrey

FRENCH OPEN

Men's Doubles

1971 Arthur Ashe

Women's Singles

1956 Althea Gibson

Women's Doubles

1956 Althea Gibson

1999 Venus and Serena Williams

GRAMMY AWARDS—NATIONAL ACADEMY OF RECORDING ARTS AND SCIENCES

Record of the Year

1963 *I Can't Stop Loving You*, by Count Basie

1967 *Up, Up and Away*, by 5th Dimension

1969 *Aquarius/Let the Sun Shine In*, by 5th Dimension

1972 *The First Time Ever I Saw Your Face*, by Roberta Flack

1973 *Killing Me Softly with His Song*, by Roberta Flack

1976 *This Masquerade*, by George Benson

1983 *Beat It*, by Michael Jackson

1984 *What's Love Got To Do with It?*, by Tina Turner

1985 *We Are the World*, by USA For Africa; produced by Quincy Jones

1988 *Don't Worry, Be Happy*, by Bobby McFerrin

1991 *Unforgettable*, by Natalie Cole with Nat "King" Cole

1993 *I Will Always Love You*, by Whitney Houston

1995 *Kiss From a Rose* by Seal

Album of the Year

1973 *Innervisions*, by Stevie Wonder; produced by Stevie Wonder

1974 *Fulfillingness' First Finale*, by Stevie Wonder; produced by Stevie Wonder

1976 *Songs in the Key of Life*, by Stevie Wonder; produced by Stevie Wonder

1983 *Thriller*, by Michael Jackson; produced by Quincy Jones

1984 *Can't Slow Down*, by Lionel Richie; produced by Lionel Richie and James Anthony Carmichael

1990 *Back on the Block*, by Quincy Jones; produced by Quincy Jones

1991 *Unforgettable*, by Natalie Cole

1999 *The Miseducation of Lauryn Hill*, by Lauryn Hill; produced by Lauryn Hill

HEISMAN MEMORIAL TROPHY—DOWNTOWN ATHLETIC CLUB OF NEW YORK CITY, INC.

1961 Ernie Davis, Syracuse University, TB

1965 Michael Garrett, University of Southern California, TB

1968 O. J. Simpson, University of Southern California, TB

1972 Johnny Rodgers, University of Nebraska, FL

1974 Archie Griffin, University of Ohio State, HB

1975 Archie Griffin, University of Ohio State, HB

1976 Anthony (Tony) Dorsett, University of Pittsburgh, HB

1977 Earl Campbell, University of Texas, FB

1978 Billy Sims, University of Oklahoma, HB

1979 Charles White, University of Southern California, TB

1980 George Rogers, University of South Carolina, HB

1981 Marcus Allen, University of Southern California, TB

1982 Herschel Walker, University of Georgia, HB

1983 Mike Rozier, University of Nebraska, TB

1985 Bo Jackson, Auburn University, TB

1987 Tim Brown, University of Notre Dame, FL

1988 Barry Sanders, Oklahoma State University, HB

1989 Andre Ware, University of Houston, QB

1991 Desmond Howard, University of Michigan, WR

1993 Charlie Ward, Florida State University, QB

1994 Rashaan Salaam, Colorado, RB

1995 Eddie George, Ohio State, RB

1997 Charles Woodson, University of Michigan, DB/R

1998 Ricky Williams, University of Texas at Austin, TB

CLARENCE L. HOLTE LITERARY PRIZE (BIANNUAL)—CO-SPONSORED BY THE PHELPS-STOKES FUND AND THE SCHOMBURG CENTER FOR RESEARCH IN BLACK CULTURE OF THE NEW YORK PUBLIC LIBRARY

1979 Chancellor Williams, for *The Destruction of Black Civilization: Great Issues of a Race from 4500 B.C. to 2000 A.D.*

1981 Ivan Van Sertima, for *They Came Before Columbus*

1983 Vincent Harding, for *There Is a River: The Black Struggle for Freedom in America*

1985 No award

1986 John Hope Franklin, for *George Washington Williams: A Biography*

1988 Arnold Rampersad, for *The Life of Langston Hughes, Volume 1 (1902-1941): I, Too, Sing America*

KENNEDY CENTER HONORS—JOHN F. KENNEDY CENTER FOR THE PERFORMING ARTS

1978 Marian Anderson

1979 Ella Fitzgerald

1980 Leontyne Price

1981 William "Count" Basie

1983 Katherine Dunham

1984 Lena Horne

1986 Ray Charles

1987 Sammy Davis, Jr.

1988 Alvin Ailey

1989 Harry Belafonte

1990 Dizzy Gillespie

1991 Fayard and Harold Nicholas

1992 Lionel Hampton

1993 Arthur Mitchell; Marion Williams

1994 Aretha Franklin

1995 B. B. King; Sidney Poitier

1996 Benny Carter

1997 Jessye Norman

1998 Bill Cosby

MARTIN LUTHER KING, JR. NONVIOLENT PEACE PRIZE—MARTIN LUTHER KING, JR. CENTER FOR NONVIOLENT SOCIAL CHANGE, INC.

1973 Andrew Young

1974 Cesar Chavez

1975 John Lewis

1976 Randolph Blackwell

1977 Benjamin E. Mays

1978 Kenneth D. Kaunda; Stanley Levison

1979 Jimmy Carter

1980 Rosa Parks

1981 Ivan Allen, Jr.

1982 Harry Belafonte

1983 Sir Richard Attenborough; Martin Luther King, Sr.

1984 No award

1985 No award

1986 Bishop Desmond Tutu

1987 Corazon Aquino

1988 No award

1989 No award

1990 Mikhail Gorbachev

1991 No award

1992 No award

1993 Jesse Jackson

MISS AMERICA—MISS AMERICA ORGANIZATION

1984 Vanessa Williams (New York); Suzette Charles (New Jersey)

1990 Debbye Turner (Missouri)

MISS BLACK AMERICA—J. MORRIS ANDERSON PRODUCTION COMPANY

1968 Sandy Willliams (Pennsylvania)

1969 G. O. Smith (New York)

1970 Stephanie Clark (District of Columbia)

1971 Joyce Warner (Florida)

1972 Linda Barney (New Jersey)

1973 Arnice Russell (New York)

1974 Von Gretchen Sheppard (California)

1975 Helen Ford (Mississippi)

1976 Twanna Kilgore (District of Columbia)

1977 Claire Ford (Tennessee)

1978 Lydia Jackson (New Jersey)

1979 Veretta Shankle (Mississippi)

1980 Sharon Wright (Illinois)

1981 Pamela Jenks (Massachusetts)

1982 Phyllis Tucker (Florida)

1983 Sonia Robinson (Wisconsin)

1984 Lydia Garrett (South Carolina)

1985 Amina Fakir (Michigan)

1986 Rachel Oliver (Massachusetts)

1987 Leila McBride (Colorado)

1989 Paula Swynn (District of Columbia)

1990 Rosie Jones (Connecticut)

1991 Sharmelle Sullivan (Indiana)

1992 Marilyn DeShields

1993 Pilar Ginger Fort

1994 Karen Wallace

1995 Asheera Ahmad

MISS USA—MADISON SQUARE GARDEN TELEVISION PRODUCTIONS

1990 Carole Gist (Michigan)

1992 Shannon Marketic

1993 Kenya Moore (Michigan)

1994 Frances Louise "Lu" Parker

1995 Chelsi Smith (Texas)

1996 Ali Landry

MS. OLYMPIA WINNERS— INTERNATIONAL FEDERATION OF BODYBUILDERS, WOMEN'S BODYBUILDING CHAMPIONS

1983 Carla Dunlap

1990 Lenda Murray

1991 Lenda Murray

1992 Lenda Murray

1993 Lenda Murray

1994 Lenda Murray

1995 Lenda Murray

MR. OLYMPIA WINNERS— INTERNATIONAL FEDERATION OF BODYBUILDERS, MEN'S BODYBUILDING CHAMPIONS

1967 Sergio Oliva

1968 Sergio Oliva

1982 Chris Dickerson

1984 Lee Haney

1985 Lee Haney

1986 Lee Haney

1987 Lee Haney

1988 Lee Haney

1989 Lee Haney

1990 Lee Haney

1991 Lee Haney

1998 Ronnie Coleman

NATIONAL BASEBALL HALL OF FAME

1962 Jackie Robinson

1969 Roy Campanella

1971 Leroy R. "Satchel" Paige

1972 Josh Gibson; Walter "Buck" Leonard

1973 Roberto W. Clemente; Monte Irvin

1974 James T. "Cool Papa" Bell

1975 William "Judy" Johnson

1976 Oscar M. Charleston

1977 Ernest Banks; Martin Dihigo; John H. Lloyd

1979 Willie Mays

1981 Andrew "Rube" Foster; Robert T. Gibson

1982 Hank Aaron; Frank Robinson

1983 Juan A. Marichal

1985 Lou Brock

1986 Willie L. "Stretch" McCovey

1987 Ray Dandridge; Billy Williams

1988 Willie Stargell

1990 Joe Morgan

1991 Rod Carew; Ferguson Jenkins

1993 Reggie Jackson

1995 Leon Day

1996 Bill Foster

1997 Willie Wells

1998 Larry Doby

1999 Orlando Cepeda; Joe Williams

NATIONAL BASKETBALL HALL OF FAME

1972 Robert Douglass

1974 Bill Russell

1976 Elgin "The Big E" Baylor; Charles Cooper

1978 Wilt Chamberlain

1979 Oscar Robertson

1981 Clarence Gaines; Willis Reed

1983 Sam Jones

1984 Nate Thurmond

1986 Walt "Clyde" Frazier

1987 Wes Unseld

1988 William "Pop" Gates; K.C. Jones; Lenny Wilkins (player)

1989 Dave Bing; Elvin Hayes; Earl "The Pearl" Monroe

1990 Nate "Tiny" Archibald

1991 Lusia Harris-Stewart; Connie Hawkins; Bob Lanier

1992 Walt Bellamy; Julius "Dr. J" Erving; Calvin Murphy

1994 Kareem Abdul-Jabbar; Cheryl Miller

1995 George Gervin; David Thompson

1996 Alex English

1998 Marques Haynes, Lenny Wilkins (coach)

1999 Wayne Embry, John Thompson

NATIONAL BOOK AWARD—NATIONAL BOOK FOUNDATION

1953 Ralph Ellison, for *Invisible Man*, Fiction

1969 Winthrop D. Jordan, for *White over Black: American Attitudes toward the Negro, 1550-1812*, History and Biography

1983 Gloria Naylor, for *The Women of Brewster Place*, First Novel; Joyce Carol Thomas, for *Marked By Fire*, Children's Literature; Alice Walker, for *The Color Purple*, Fiction

1990 Charles Johnson, for *Middle Passage*, Fiction

1991 Melissa Fay Green, for *Praying for Sheetrock*, Nonfiction

1992 Edward P. Jones, for *Lost in the City*, Fiction

NATIONAL MEDAL OF ARTS—NATIONAL ENDOWMENT FOR THE ARTS

1985 Ralph Ellison (writer); Leontyne Price (singer)

1986 Marian Anderson (singer)

1987 Romare Bearden (artist); Ella Fitzgerald (singer)

1988 Gordon Parks (photographer and film director)

1989 Katherine Dunham (choreographer); Dizzy Gillespie (musician)

1990 Riley "B. B." King (musician)

1991 James Earl Jones (actor); Billy Taylor (musician)

1994 Harry Belafonte (singer)

1995 Gwendolyn Brooks (poet); Ossie Davis (actor); Ruby Dee (actress)

1996 The Harlem Boys Choir (chorale); Lionel Hampton (musician)

1997 Betty Carter (singer)

1998 Fats Domino (singer)

NATIONAL SOCIETY OF ARTS AND LETTERS GOLD MEDAL OF MERIT AWARD

1982 Andre Watts (music)

NATIONAL TRACK AND FIELD HALL OF FAME—THE ATHLETICS CONGRESS OF THE USA

1974 Ralph Boston; Lee Calhoun; Harrison Dillard; Rafer Johnson; Jesse Owens; Wilma Rudolph; Malvin Whitfield

1975 Ralph Metcalfe

1976 Robert Hayes; Hayes Jones

1977 Robert Beamon; Andrew W. Stanfield

1978 Tommie Smith; John Woodruff

1979 Jim Hines; William DeHart Hubbard

1980 Wyomia Tyus

1981 Willye White

1982 Willie Davenport; Eddie Tolan

1983 Lee Evans

1984 Madeline Manning Mims

1986 Henry Barney Ewell

1988 Gregory Bell

1989 Milt Campbell; Edward Temple

1990 Charles Dumas

1994 Cornelius Johnson; Edwin Moses

1995 Valerie Brisco; Florence Griffith Joyner

1997 Evelyn Ashford; Henry Carr; Renaldo Nehemiah

NEW YORK DRAMA CRITICS' CIRCLE AWARD

Best American Play

1959 *A Raisin in the Sun*, by Lorraine Hansberry

1975 *The Taking of Miss Janie*, by Ed Bullins

1982 *A Soldier's Play*, by Charles Fuller

1996 *Seven Guitars*, by August Wilson

Best New Play

1985 *Ma Rainey's Black Bottom*, by August Wilson

1987 *Fences*, by August Wilson

1988 *Joe Turner's Come and Gone*, by August Wilson

1990 *The Piano Lesson*, by August Wilson

NOBEL PEACE PRIZE—NOBEL FOUNDATION

1950 Ralph J. Bunche

1964 Martin Luther King, Jr.

NOBEL PRIZE IN LITERATURE—NOBEL FOUNDATION

1993 Toni Morrison

PRESIDENTIAL MEDAL OF FREEDOM—UNITED STATES EXECUTIVE OFFICE OF THE PRESIDENT

1963 Marian Anderson; Ralph J. Bunche

1964 John L. Lewis; Leontyne Price; A. Philip Randolph

1969 Edward Kennedy "Duke" Ellington; Ralph Ellison; Roy Wilkins; Whitney M. Young, Jr.

1976 Jesse Owens

1977 Martin Luther King, Jr. (posthumously)

1980 Clarence Mitchell

1981 James H. "Eubie" Blake; Andrew Young

1983 James Cheek; Mabel Mercer

1984 Jack Roosevelt "Jackie" Robinson (posthumously)

1985 William "Count" Basie (posthumously); Jerome "Brud" Holland (posthumously)

1987 Frederick Douglass Patterson

1988 Pearl Bailey

1991 Colin L. Powell

1992 Ella Fitzgerald

1993 Arthur Ashe, Jr. (posthumously); Thurgood Marshall (posthumously); Colin L. Powell

1994 Dorothy Height; Barbara Jordan

1995 William Thaddeus Coleman, Jr.; John Hope Franklin; A. Leon Higginbotham, Jr.

1996 John H. Johnson; Rosa Parks

1998 James Farmer

PROFESSIONAL FOOTBALL HALL OF FAME

1967 Emlen Tunnell

1968 Marion Motley

1969 Fletcher "Joe" Perry

1971 Jim Brown

1972 Ollie Matson

1973 Jim Parker

1974 Richard "Night Train" Lane

1975 Roosevelt Brown; Leonard "Lenny" Moore

1976 Leonard "Len" Ford

1977 Gale Sayers; Bill Willis

1980 Herb Adderley; David "Deacon" Jones

1981 Willie Davis

1983 Bobby Bell; Bobby Mitchell; Paul Warfield

1984 Willie Brown; Charley Taylor

1985 O. J. Simpson

1986 Ken Houston; Willie Lanier

1987 Joe Greene; John Henry Johnson; Gene Upshaw

1988 Alan Page

1989 Mel Blount; Art Shell; Willie Wood

1990 Junious "Buck" Buchanan; Franco Harris

1991 Earl Campbell

1992 Lem Barney; John Mackey

1993 Larry Little; Walter Payton

1994 Tony Dorsett; Leroy Kelly

1995 Lee Roy Selmon

1996 Charlie Joiner; Mel Renfro

1997 Mike Haynes

1998 Mike Singletary; Dwight Stephenson

1999 Eric Dickerson; Lawrence Taylor

PULITZER PRIZE—COLUMBIA UNIVERSITY GRADUATE SCHOOL OF JOURNALISM

Biography or Autobiography

1994 *W. E. B. Du Bois: Biography of a Race, 1968–1919*, by David Levering Lewis

Journalism: Commentary

1996 E. R. Shipp

Journalism: Feature Writing

1999 Angelo B. Henderson

Letters: Drama

1970 *No Place To Be Somebody*, by Charles Gordone

1982 *A Soldier's Play*, by Charles Fuller

1987 *Fences*, by August Wilson

1990 *The Piano Lesson*, by August Wilson

Letters: Fiction

1978 *Elbow Room*, by James Alan McPherson

1983 *The Color Purple*, by Alice Walker

1988 *Beloved*, by Toni Morrison

Letters: Poetry

1950 *Annie Allen*, by Gwendolyn Brooks

1987 *Thomas and Beulah*, by Rita Dove

Letters: Special Awards and Citations

1977 Alexander Palmer Haley, for *Roots*

Music: Special Awards and Citations

1976 Scott Joplin

1996 George Walker

1997 Wynton Marsalis

1999 Edward Kennedy "Duke" Ellington (posthmously)

ROCK AND ROLL HALL OF FAME

1986 Chuck Berry; James Brown; Ray Charles; Sam Cooks; Fats Domino; Little Richard; Robert Johnson; Jimmy Yancey

1987 The Coasters; Bo Diddley; Aretha Franklin; Marvin Gaye; Louis Jordan; B.B. King; Clyde McPhalter; Smokey Robinson; Big Joe Turner; T-Bone Walker; Muddy Waters; Jackie Wilson

1988 The Drifters; Barry Gordy, Jr.; The Supremes

1989 The Ink Spots; Otis Redding; Bessie Smith; The Soul Stirrers; The Temptations; Stevie Wonder

1990 Louis Armstrong; Hank Ballard; Charlie Christian; The Four Tops; Holland, Dozier, and Holland; The Platters; Ma Rainey

1991 La Vern Baker; John Lee Hooker; Howlin' Wolf; The Impressions; Wilson Pickett; Jimmy Reed; Ike and Tina Turner

1992 Blue Brand, Booker T. and the M.G.'s; Jimi Hendrix; Isley Brothers; Elmore James; Doc Pomus; Professor Longhair; Sam and Dave

1993 Ruth Brown; Etta James; Frankie Lymon and the Teenagers; Sly and the Family Stone; Dinah Washington

1994 Willie Dixon; Bob Marley; Johnny Otis

1995 Al Green; Martha and the Vandellas; The Orioles

1996 Little Willie John; Gladys Knight and the Pips; The Shirelles

1997 Mahalia Jackson; The Jackson Five; Parliament

1998 Jelly Roll Morton; Lloyd Price

1999 Charles Brown; Curtis Mayfield; The Staple Singers

SPRINGARN MEDAL—NATIONAL ASSOCIATION FOR THE ADVANCEMENT OF COLORED PEOPLE

1915 Ernest E. Just—head of the department of physiology at Howard University Medical School.

1916 Charles Young—major in the United States Army.

1917 Harry T. Burleigh—composer, pianist, singer.

1918 William Stanley Braithwaite—poet, literary critic, editor.

1919 Archibald H. Grimké—former U.S. Consul in Santo Domingo, president of the American Negro Academy, author, president of the District of Columbia branch of the NAACP.

1920 William Edward Burghardt DuBois—author, editor, organizer of the first Pan-African Congress.

1921 Charles S. Gilpin—actor.

1922 Mary B. Talbert—former president of the National Association of Colored Women.

1923 George Washington Carver—head of research and director of the experiment station at Tuskegee Institute.

1924 Roland Hayes—singer.

1925 James Weldon Johnson—former United States Consul in Venezuela and Nicaragua, author, editor, poet; secretary of the NAACP.

1926 Carter G. Woodson—editor, historian; founder of the Association for the Study of Negro Life and History.

1927 Anthony Overton—businessman; president of the Victory Life Insurance Company (the first African American organization permitted to do business under the rigid requirements of the State of New York).

1928 Charles W. Chesnutt—author.

1929 Mordecai Wyatt Johnson—the first African American president of Howard University.

1930 Henry A. Hunt—principal of Fort Valley High and Industrial School, Fort Valley, Georgia.

1931 Richard Berry Harrison—actor.

1932 Robert Russa Moton—principal of Tuskegee Institute.

1933 Max Yergan—secretary of the YMCA in South Africa.

1934 William Taylor Burwell Williams—dean of Tuskegee Institute.

1935 Mary McLeod Bethune—founder and president of Bethune Cookman College.

1936 John Hope—president of Atlanta University.

1937 Walter White—executive secretary of the NAACP.

1939 Marian Anderson—singer.

1940 Louis T. Wright—surgeon.

1941 Richard Wright—author.

1942 A. Philip Randolph—labor leader, international president of the Brotherhood of Sleeping Car Porters.

1943 William H. Hastie—jurist, educator.

1944 Charles Drew—scientist.

1945 Paul Robeson—singer, actor.

1946 Thurgood Marshall—special counsel of the NAACP

1947 Percy Julian—research chemist.

1948 Channing H. Tobias—minister, educator.

1949 Ralph J. Bunche—international civil servant, acting United Nations mediator in Palestine.

1950 Charles Hamilton Houston—chairman of the NAACP Legal Committee.

1951 Mabel Keaton Staupers—leader of the National Association of Colored Graduate Nurses.

1952 Harry T. Moore—state leader of the Florida NAACP.

1953 Paul R. Williams—architect.

1954 Theodore K. Lawless—physician, educator, philanthropist.

1955 Carl Murphy—editor, publisher, civic leader.

1956 Jack Roosevelt Robinson—athlete.

1957 Martin Luther King, Jr.—minister, civil rights leader

1958 Daisy Bates and the Little Rock Nine—for their pioneer role in upholding the basic ideals of American democracy in the face of continuing harassment and constant threats of bodily injury.

1959 Edward Kennedy "Duke" Ellington—composer, musician, orchestra leader.

1960 Langston Hughes—poet, author, playwright.

1961 Kenneth B. Clark—professor of psychology at the City College of the City University of New York, founder and director of the Northside Center for Child Development, prime mobilizer of the resources of modern psychology in the attack upon racial segregation.

1962 Robert C. Weaver—administrator of the Housing and Home Finance Agency.

1963 Medgar Wiley Evers—NAACP field secretary for Mississippi, World War II veteran.

1964 Roy Wilkins—executive director of the NAACP.

1965 Leontyne Price—singer.

1966 John H. Johnson—founder and president of the Johnson Publishing Company.

1967 Edward W. Brooke III—the first African American to win popular election to the United States Senate.

1968 Sammy Davis, Jr.—performer, civil rights activist.

1969 Clarence M. Mitchell, Jr.—director of the Washington Bureau of the NAACP, civil rights activist.

1970 Jacob Lawrence—artist, teacher, humanitarian.

1971 Leon H. Sullivan—minister.

1972 Gordon Alexander Buchanan Parks—writer, photographer, filmmaker.

1973 Wilson C. Riles—educator.

1974 Damon Keith—jurist.

1975 Hank Aaron—athlete.

1976 Alvin Ailey—dancer, choreographer, artistic director.

1977 Alexander Palmer Haley—author, biographer, lecturer.

1978 Andrew Young—United States Ambassador to the United Nations, diplomat, cabinet member, civil rights activist, minister.

1979 Rosa Parks—community activist.

1980 Rayford W. Logan—educator, historian, author.

1981 Coleman A. Young—mayor of the City of Detroit, public servant, labor leader, civil rights activist.

1982 Benjamin E. Mays—educator, theologian, humanitarian).

1983 Lena Horne—performer, humanitarian.

1984 Tom Bradley—government executive, public servant, humanitarian.

1985 William H. "Bill" Cosby—comedian, actor, educator, humanitarian.

1986 Benjamin Lawson Hooks—executive director of the NAACP.

1987 Percy Ellis Sutton—public servant, businessman, community leader.

1988 Frederick Douglass Patterson—doctor of veterinary medicine, educator, humanitarian, founder of the United Negro College Fund.

1989 Jesse Jackson—minister, political leader, civil rights activist.

1990 L. Douglas Wilder—governor of Virginia.

1991 Colin L. Powell—general in the United States Army, chairman of the Joint Chiefs of Staff.

1992 Barbara C. Jordan—educator, former congresswoman.

1993 Dorothy L. Height—president of the National Council of Negro Women.

1994 Maya Angelou—poet, author, performing artist.

1995 John Hope Franklin—historian.

1996 A. Leon Higginbotham, Jr.—jurist, judge

1997 Carl T. Rowan—journalist.

1998 Myrlie Evers-Williams—former chair, board of directors, NAACP

1999 Earl G. Graves, publisher and media executive

SULLIVAN AWARD—AMATEUR ATHLETIC UNION

1961 Wilma Rudolph

1981 Carl Lewis

1983 Edwin Moses

1986 Jackie Joyner-Kersee

1988 Florence Griffith-Joyner

1991 Mike Powell

1993 Charlie Ward

1996 Michael Johnson

1998 Chamique Holdsclaw

TONY (ANTOINETTE PERRY) AWARD— LEAGUE OF AMERICAN THEATERS AND PRODUCERS

Actor (Dramatic)

1969 James Earl Jones, for *The Great White Hope*

1975 John Kani, for *Sizwe Banzi*; Winston Ntshona, for *The Island*

1987 James Earl Jones, for *Fences*

Supporting or Featured Actor (Dramatic)

1982 Zakes Mokae, for *Master Harold. . . and the Boys*

1992 Larry Fishburne, for *Two Trains Running*

1994 Jeffrey Wright, for *Angels in America*

1996 Ruben Santiago-Hudson, for *Seven Guitars*

Actor (Musical)

1970 Cleavon Little, for *Purlie*

1973 Ben Vereen, for *Pippin*

1982 Ben Harvey, for *Dreamgirls*

1992 Gregory Hines, for *Jelly's Last Jam*

Supporting or Featured Actor (Musical)

1954 Harry Belafonte, for *John Murray Anderson's Almanac*

1975 Ted Rose, for *The Wiz*

1981 Hinton Battle, for *Sophisticated Ladies*

1982 Cleavant Derricks, for *Dreamgirls*

1983 Charles "Honi" Coles, for *My One and Only*

1984 Hinton Battle, for *The Tap Dance Kid*

1991 Hinton Battle, for *Miss Saigon*

1997 Chuck Cooper, for *The Life*

Supporting or Featured Actress (Dramatic)

1977 Trazana Beverley, for *For Colored Girls Who Have Considered Suicide/When the Rainbow Is Enuf*

1987 Mary Alice, for *Fences*

1988 L. Scott Caldwell, for *Joe Turner's Come and Gone*

1997 Lynne Thigpen, for *An American Daughter*

Actress (Musical)

1962 Diahann Carroll, for *No Strings*

1968 Leslie Uggams, for *Hallelujah, Baby*

1974 Virginia Capers, for *Raisin*

1982 Jennifer Holliday, for *Dreamgirls*

1989 Ruth Brown, for *Black and Blue*

1996 Audra McDonald, for *Master Class*

Supporting or Featured Actress (Musical)

1950 Juanita Hall, for *South Pacific*

1968 Lillian Hayman, for *Halleluja, Baby*

1970 Melba Moore, for *Purlie*

1975 Dee Dee Bridgewater, for *The Wiz*

1977 Delores Hall, for *Your Arms's Too Short To Box with God*

1978 Nell Carter, for *Ain't Misbehavin*

1992 Tonya Pinkins, for *Jelly's Last Jam*

1994 Audra McDonald, for *Carousel*

1996 Ann Duquesnay, for *Bring in 'Da Noise, Bring in 'Da Funk*

1997 Lillias White, for *The Life*

Play

1974 *The River Niger*, by Joseph A. Walker

1987 *Fences*, by August Wilson

UNITED STATES MEDAL OF HONOR

Civil War

Army

William H. Barnes, Private, Company C, 38th United States Colored Troops.

Powhatan Beaty, First Sergeant, Company G, 5th United States Colored Troops.

James H. Bronson, First Sergeant, Company D, 5th United States Colored Troops.

William H. Carney, Sergeant, Company C, 54th Massachusetts Infantry, United States Colored Troops.

Decatur Dorsey, Sergeant, Company B, 39th United States Colored Troops.

Christian A. Fleetwood, Sergeant Major, 4th United States Colored Troops.

James Gardiner, Private, Company 1, 36th United States Colored Troops.

James H. Harris, Sergeant, Company B, 38th United States Colored Troops.

Thomas R. Hawkins, Sergeant Major, 6th United States Colored Troops.

Alfred B. Hilton, Sergeant, Company H, 4th United States Colored Troops.

Milton M. Holland, Sergeant, 5th United States Colored Troops.

Alexander Kelly, First Sergeant, Company F, 6th United States Colored Troops.

Robert Pinn, First Sergeant, Company I, 5th United States Colored Troops.

Edward Radcliff, First Sergeant, Company C, 38th United States Colored Troops.

Charles Veal, Private, Company D, 4th United States Colored Troops.

Navy

Aaron Anderson, Landsman, *USS Wyandank*.

Robert Blake, Powder Boy, *USS Marblehead*.

William H. Brown, Landsman, *USS Brooklyn*.

Wilson Brown, *USS Hartford*.

John Lawson, Landsman, *USS Hartford*.

James Mifflin, Engineer's Cook, *USS Brooklyn*.

Joachim Pease, Seaman, *USS Kearsarge*.

Interim Period

Navy

Daniel Atkins, Ship's Cook, First Class, *USS Cushing*.

John Davis, Seaman, *USS Trenton*.

Alphonse Girandy, Seaman, *USS Tetrel*.

John Johnson, Seaman, *USS Kansas*.

William Johnson, Cooper, *USS Adams*.

Joseph B. Noil, Seaman, *USS Powhatan*.

John Smith, Seaman, *USS Shenandoah*.

Robert Sweeney, Seaman, *USS Kearsage*, *USS Jamestown*.

Western Campaigns

Army

Thomas Boyne, Sergeant, Troop C, 9th United States Cavalry.

Benjamin Brown, Sergeant, Company C, 24th United States Infantry.

John Denny, Sergeant, Troop C, 9th United States Cavalry.

Pompey Factor, Seminole Negro Indian Scouts.

Clinton Greaves, Corporal, Troop C, 9th United States Cavalry.

Henry Johnson, Sergeant, Troop D, 9th United States Cavalry.

George Jordan, Sergeant, Troop K, 9th United States Cavalry.

William McBreyar, Sergeant, Troop K, 10th United States Cavalry.

Isaiah Mays, Corporal, Company B, 24th United States Infantry.

Issac Payne, Private (Trumpeteer) Seminole Negro Indian Scouts.

Thomas Shaw, Sergeant, Troop K, 9th United States Cavalry.

Emanuel Stance, Sergeant, Troop F, 9th United States Cavalry.

Augustus Walley, Private, Troop 1, 9th United States Cavalry.

John Ward, Sergeant, Seminole Negro Indian Scouts.

Moses Williams, First Sergeant, Troop 1, 9th United States Cavalry.

William O. Wilson, Corporal, Troop 1, 9th United States Cavalry.

Brent Woods, Sergeant, Troop B, 9th United States Cavalry.

Spanish-American War

Army

Edward L. Baker, Jr., Sergeant Major, 10th United States Cavalry.

Dennis Bell, Private, Troop H, 10th United States Cavalry.

Fitz Lee, Private, Troop M, 10th United States Cavalry.

William H. Thompkins, Private, Troop G, 10th United States Cavalry.

George H. Wanton, Sergeant, Troop M, 10th United States Cavalry.

Navy

Joseph B. Noil, Non-combatant Service, *USS Powhatan.*

Robert Penn, Fireman, First Class, *USS Iowa.*

World War I

Army

Freddie Stowers, Corporal, Company C, 371st Infantry Regiment, 93rd Infantry Division.

World War II

Army

Vernon Baker, First Lieutenant.

Edward A. Carter, Jr., Staff Sergeant.

John R. Fox, First Lieutenant.

Willy F. James, Jr., Private First Class.

Ruben Rivers, Staff Sergeant.

Charles L. Thomas, First Lieutenant.

George Watson, Private.

Korean War

Army

Cornelius H. Charlton, Sergeant, 24th Infantry Regiment, 25th Division.

William Thompson, Private, 24th Infantry Regiment, 25th Division.

Vietnam War

Army

Webster Anderson, Sergeant, Battery A, 2nd Battalion, 320th Artillery, 101st Airborne Division.

Eugene Ashley, Jr., Sergeant, Company C, 5th Special Forces Group (Airborne), 1st Special Forces.

William M. Bryant, Sergeant First Class, Company A, 5th Special Forces Group, 1st Special Forces.

Lawrence Joel, Specialist Sixth Class, Headquarters and Headquarters Company, 1st Battalion, 173d Airborne Brigade.

Dwight H. Johnson, Specialist Fifth Class, Company B, 1st Battalion, 69th Armor, 4th Infantry Division.

Garfield M. Langhorn, Private First Class, Troop C, 7th Squadron, 17th Cavalry, 1st Aviation Brigade.

Matthew Leonard, Platoon Sergeant, Company B, 1st Battalion, 16th Infantry, 1st Infantry Division.

Donald R. Long, Sergeant, Troop C, 1st Squadron, 4th Cavalry, 1st Infantry Division.

Milton L. Olive III, Private First Class, Company B, 2nd Battalion 503d Infantry, 173d Airborne Brigade.

Riley L. Pitts, Captain, Company C, 2nd Battalion, 27th Infantry, 25th Infantry Division.

Charles C. Rogers, Lieutenant Colonel, 1st Battalion, 5th Infantry, 1st Infantry Division.

Rupert L. Sargent, First Lieutenant, Company B, 4th Battalion, 9th Infantry, 25th Infantry Division.

Clarence E. Sasser, Specialist 5th Class, Headquarters Company, 3rd Battalion, 60th Infantry, 90th Infantry Division.

Clifford C. Sims, Staff Sergeant, Company D, 2nd Battalion, 501st Infantry, 101st Airborne Division.

John E. Warren, Jr., First Lieutenant, Company C, 2nd Battalion, 22d Infantry, 25th Infantry Division.

Marines

James A. Anderson, Jr. Private First Class, 2nd Platoon, Company F, 2nd Battalion, 3rd Marine Division.

Oscar P. Austin, Private First Class, Company E, 7th Marines, 1st Marine Division.

Rodney M. Davis, Company B, First Battalion, 5th Marines, 1st Marine Division.

Robert H. Jenkins, Jr., Private First Class, 3rd Reconnaissance Battalion, 3rd Marine Division.

Ralph H. Johnson, Private First Class, Company A, 1st Reconnaissance Battalion, 1st Marine Division.

UNITED STATES OPEN

Men's Singles

1968 Arthur Ashe

Women's Singles

1957 Althea Gibson

1958 Althea Gibson

Mixed Doubles

1957 Althea Gibson

UNITED STATES POET LAUREATE

1993 Rita Dove (served until 1995)

UNITED STATES POSTAL SERVICE STAMPS ON AFRICAN AMERICAN HISTORY

Louis Armstrong

Benjamin Banneker

William "Count" Basie

James Pierson Beckwourth

Mary McLeod Bethune

James Hubert "Eubie" Blake

Ralph Johnson Bunche

George Washington Carver

Nat "King" Cole

Bessie Coleman

John Coltrane

Allison Davis

Benjamin O. Davis, Sr.

Frederick Douglass

Charles Richard Drew

(W)illiam (E)dward (B)urghardt Du Bois

Jean Baptiste Pointe Du Sable

Paul Laurence Dunbar

Edward Kennedy "Duke" Ellington

Erroll Garner

(W)illiam (C)hristopher Handy

Coleman Hawkins

Matthew Alexander Henson

Billie Holiday

Mahalia Jackson

James Price Johnson

James Weldon Johnson

Robert Johnson

Scott Joplin

Percy Lavon Julian

Ernest Everett Just

Martin Luther King, Jr.

Joe Louis

Hudson William Ledbetter, "Leadbelly"

Roberta Martin

Jan E. Matzeliger

Clyde McPhatter

Charles Mingus

Thelonious Sphere Monk

Ferdinand "Jelly Roll" Morton

James Cleveland "Jesse" Owens

Charlie "Bird" Parker

Bill Pickett

Salem Poor

Gertrude "Ma" Rainey

(A)sa Philip Randolph

Otis Redding

John Roosevelt "Jackie" Robinson

James Andrew "Jimmy" Rushing

Bessie Smith

Henry Ossawa Tanner

Sonny Terry

Sister Rosetta Tharpe

Sojourner Truth

Harriet Tubman

Madame C. J. Walker

Clara Ward

Booker Taliaferro Washington

Dinah Washington

Ethel Waters

Muddy Waters

Ida Bell Wells-Barnett

Josh White

Howlin' Wolf

Carter Godwin Woodson

Whitney Moore Young

WIMBLEDON—ALL ENGLAND LAWN TENNIS AND CROQUET CLUB

Men's Singles

1975 Arthur Ashe

Ladies' Singles

1957 Althea Gibson

1958 Althea Gibson

Ladies' Doubles

1957 Althea Gibson, with Darlene Hard

1958 Althea Gibson, with Maria Bueno

◆ AFRICAN AMERICAN FEDERAL JUDGES

PRESIDENT FRANKLIN D. ROOSEVELT

| 1937 | William H. Hastie* | District Court, Virgin Islands |
| 1939 | Harnian E. Moore* | District Court, Virgin Islands |

PRESIDENT HARRY S TRUMAN

1945	Irvin C. Mollison*	United States Customs Court
1949	William H. Hastie*	Court of Appeals, Third Circuit
1949	Harnian E. Moore (a)*	District Court, Virgin Islands

PRESIDENT DWIGHT D. EISENHOWER

| 1957 | Scovel Richardson* | United States Customs Court |
| 1958 | Walter Gordon* | District Court, Virgin Islands |

PRESIDENT JOHN F. KENNEDY

1961	James B. Parsons**	Senior Judge, District Court, Illinois
1961	Wade M. McCree**	District Court, Michigan
1961	Thurgood Marshall**	Court of Appeals, Second Circuit

PRESIDENT LYNDON B. JOHNSON

1964	Spottswood Robinson**	District Court, District of Columbia
1964	A. Leon Higginbotham**	District Court, Pennsylvania
1965	William B. Bryant	Senior Judge, District Court, District of Columbia
1966	Wade H. McCree*	Court of Appeals, Sixth Court
1966	James L. Watson	United States Customs Court
1966	Constance B. Motley	Senior Judge, District Court, New York
1966	Spottswood Robinson	Senior Judge, Court of Appeals for the Federal Circuit
1966	Aubrey E. Robinson	Chief Judge, District Court, District of Columbia
1967	Damon Keith**	District Court, Michigan
1967	Thurgood Marshall*	Associate Justice, Supreme Court
1967	Joseph C. Waddy**	District Court, District of Columbia

PRESIDENT RICHARD M. NIXON

1969	Almeric Christian**	District Court, Virgin Islands
1969	David W. Williams	Senior Judge, District Court, California
1969	Barrington D. Parker	Senior Judge, District Court, District of Columbia
1971	Lawrence W. Pierce**	District Court, New York
1971	Clifford Scott Green	District Court, Pennsylvania
1972	Robert L. Carter	Senior Judge, District Court, New York
1972	Robert M. Duncan**	Military Court of Appeals
1974	Robert M. Duncan**	District Court, Ohio

PRESIDENT GERALD R. FORD

1974	Henry Bramwell**	Senior Judge, District Court, New York
1976	George N. Leighton**	Senior Judge, District Court, Illinois
1976	Matthew Perry**	Military Court of Appeals
1976	Cecil F. Poole**	District Court, California

PRESIDENT JIMMY CARTER

1978	Almeric Christian (a)**	Chief Judge, District Court, Virgin Islands
1978	U.W. Clemon	District Court, Alabama
1978	Robert F. Collins**	District Court, Louisiana

1978	Julian A. Cook, Jr.	District Court, Michigan
1978	Damon J. Keith	Court of Appeals, Sixth Circuit
1978	A. Leon Higginbotham*	Court of Appeals, Third Circuit
1978	Mary Johnson Lowe	District Court, New York
1978	Theodore McMillian	Court of Appeals, Eighth Circuit
1978	David S. Nelson	District Court, Massachusetts
1978	Paul A. Simmons**	District Court, Pennsylvania
1978	Jack E. Tanner	District Court, Washington
1979	Harry T. Edwards	Court of Appeals for the Federal Circuit
1979	J. Jerome Farris	Court of Appeals, Ninth Circuit
1979	Joseph W. Hatchett	Court of Appeals, Eleventh Circuit
1979	Terry J. Hatter	District Court, California
1979	Joseph C. Howard	District Court, Maryland
1979	Benjamin T. Gibson	District Court, Michigan
1979	James T. Giles	District Court, Pennsylvania
1979	Nathaniel R. Jones	Court of Appeals, Sixth Circuit
1979	Amalya L. Kearse	Court of Appeals, Second Circuit
1979	Gabrielle Kirk McDonald**	District Court, Texas
1979	John Garrett Penn**	District Court, District of Columbia
1979	Cecil F. Poole	Court of Appeals, Ninth Circuit
1979	Matthew J. Perry	District Court, South Carolina
1979	Myron H. Thompson	District Court, Alabama
1979	Anne E. Thompson	District Court, New Jersey
1979	Odell Horton	District Court, Tennessee
1979	Anna Diggs Taylor	District Court, Michigan
1979	Horace T. Ward	District Court, Georgia
1979	Alcee L. Hastings***	District Court, Florida
1980	Clyde S. Cahill, Jr.**	District Court, Missouri
1980	Richard C. Erwin	District Court, North Carolina
1980	Thelton E. Henderson	District Court, California
1980	George Howard, Jr.	District Court, Arkansas
1980	Earl B. Gilliam	District Court, California
1980	Norma Holloway Johnson	District Court, District of Columbia
1980	Consuela B. Marshall	District Court, California
1980	George White	District Court, Ohio

PRESIDENT RONALD REAGAN

1981	Lawrence W. Pierce	Court of Appeals, Second Circuit
1982	Reginald Gibson	United States Court of Claims
1984	John R. Hargrove	District Court, Maryland
1984	Henry Wingate	District Court, Mississippi
1985	Ann Williams	District Court, Illinois
1986	James Spencer	District Court, Virginia
1987	Kenneth Hoyt	District Court, Texas
1988	Herbert Hutton	District Court, Pennsylvania

PRESIDENT GEORGE BUSH

1990	Clarence Thomas**	Court of Appeals for the Federal Circuit
1990	James Ware	District Court, California
1991	Saundra Brown Armstrong	District Court, California
1991	Fernando J. Giatan	District Court, Missouri
1991	Donald L. Graham	District Court, Florida
1991	Sterling Johnson	District Court, New York
1991	J. Curtis Joyner	District Court, Pennsylvania
1991	Timothy K. Lewis	District Court, Pennsylvania

1991	Joe B. McDade	District Court, Illinois
1991	Clarence Thomas	Associate Justice, Supreme Court
1992	Garland E. Burrell, Jr.	District Court, California
1992	Carol Jackson	District Court, Missouri
1992	Timothy K. Lewis	Court of Appeals, Third Circuit

PRESIDENT BILL CLINTON

1993	Henry Lee Adams	District Court, Florida
1993	Wilkie Ferguson	District Court, Florida
1993	Raymond Jackson	District Court, Virginia
1993	Gary Lancaster	District Court, Pennsylvania
1993	Reginald Lindsay	District Court, Massachusetts
1993	Charles Shaw	District Court, Missouri
1994	Deborah Batts	District Court, New York
1994	Franklin Burgess	District Court, Washington
1994	James Beaty, Jr.	District Court, North Carolina
1994	David Coar	District Court, Illinois
1994	Audrey Collins	District Court, California
1994	Clarence Cooper	District Court, Georgia
1994	Michael Davis	District Court, Minnesota
1994	Raymond Finch	District Court, Virgin Islands
1994	Vanessa Gilmore	District Court, Texas
1994	A. Haggerty	District Court, Oregon
1994	Denise Page Hood	District Court, Michigan
1994	Napoleon Jones	District Court, California
1994	Blance Manning	District Court, Illinois
1994	Theodore McKee	Circuit Court, Third Circuit
1994	Vicki Miles‐LaGrange	District Court, Oklahoma
1994	Solomon Oliver, Jr.	District Court, Ohio
1994	Barrington Parker, Jr.	District Court, New York
1994	Judith Rogers	Circuit Court, District of Columbia
1994	W. Louis Sands	District Court, Georgia
1994	Carl Stewart	Circuit Court, Fifth Circuit
1994	Emmet Sullivan	Circuit Court, District of Columbia
1994	William Walls	District Court, New Jersey
1994	Alexander Williams	District Court, Maryland
1995	R. Guy Cole	Circuit Court, Sixth Circuit
1995	Curtis Collier	District Court, Tennessee
1995	Wiley Daniel	District Court, Colorado
1995	Andre Davis	District Court, Maryland
1995	Bernice B. Donald	District Court, Tennessee
1996	Charles N. Clevert, Jr.	District Court, Wisconsin
1996	Joseph A. Greenaway, Jr.	District Court, New Jersey
1997	Eric L. Clay	Circuit Court, Sixth Circuit
1997	Algenon L. Marbley	District Court, Ohio
1997	Martin J. Jenkins	District Court, California
1997	Henry H. Kennedy, Jr.	District Court, District of Columbia
1998	Gregory Sleet	District Court, Delaware
1998	Ivan L.R. Lemelle	District Court, Louisiana
1998	Sam A. Lindsay	District Court, Texas
1998	Johnnie B. Rawlinson	District Court, Nevada
1998	Margaret Seymour	District Court, South Carolina
1998	Richard Roberts	District Court, District of Columbia
1998	Gerald Bruce Lee	District Court, Virginia
1998	Lynn Bush	Court of Federal Claims

1998	Stephan P. Mickle	District Court, Florida
1998	Victoria Roberts	District Court, Michigan
1998	Raner Collins	District Court, Arizona
1998	Ralph Tyson	District Court, Louisiana
1999	William Hibbler	District Court, Illinois

(a) Reappointment

* Deceased

** No longer serving

*** Impeached and removed from the court

◆ AFRICAN AMERICAN OLYMPIC MEDALISTS

Place/Year	Athlete	Event	Place	Time/Distance
St. Louis, 1904	George C. Poag	200 M Hurdles	3rd	
	George C. Poag	400 M Hurdles	3rd	
London, 1908	J.B. Taylor	1600 M Relay	1st	3:29.4
Paris, 1924	Dehart Hubbard	Long Jump	1st	24′ 5.125″
	Edward Gourdin	Long Jump	2nd	23′ 10″
Los Angeles, 1932	Eddie Tolan	100 M Dash	1st	10.3
	Ralph Metcalfe	100 M Dash	2nd	10.3
	Eddie Tolan	200 M Dash	1st	21.2
	Ralph Metcalfe	200 M Dash	3rd	21.5
	Edward Gordon	Long Jump	1st	25′ .75″
Berlin, 1936	Jesse Owens	100 M Dash	1st	10.3
	Ralph Metcalfe	100 M Dash	2nd	10.4
	Jesse Owens	200 M Dash	1st	20.7
	Matthew Robinson	200 M Dash	2nd	21.1
	Archie Williams	400 M Run	1st	46.5
	James DuValle	400 M Run	2nd	46.8
	John Woodruff	800 M Run	1st	1:52.9
	Fritz Pollard, Jr.	110 M Hurdles	3rd	14.4
	Cornelius Johnson	High Jump	1st	6′8″
	Jesse Owens	Long Jump	1st	26′ 5.75″
	Jesse Owens	400 M Relay	1st	39.8
	Ralph Metcalfe	400 M Relay	1st	39.8
London, 1948	Harrison Dillard	100 M Dash	1st	10.3
	Norwood Ewell	100 M Dash	2nd	10.4
	Norwood Ewell	200 M Dash	1st	21.1
	Mal Whitfield	400 M Run	3rd	46.9
	Willie Steele	Long Jump	1st	25′ 8″
	Herbert Douglass	Long Jump	3rd	25′ 3″
	Lorenzo Wright	400 M Relay	1st	40.6
	Harrison Dillard	1600 M Relay	1st	3:10.4
	Norwood Ewell	1600 M Relay	1st	3:10.4
	Mal Whitfield	1600 M Relay	1st	3:10.4
	Audrey Patterson	200 M Dash	3rd	25.2
	Alice Coachman	High Jump	1st	5′ 6.125″
Helsinki, 1952	Andrew Stanfield	200 M Dash	1st	20.7
	Ollie Matson	400 M Run	3rd	46.8
	Mal Whitfield	800 M Run	1st	1:49.2
	Harrison Dillard	110 M Hurdles	1st	13.7
	Jerome Biffle	Long Jump	1st	24′ 10″
	Meredith Gourdine	Long Jump	2nd	24′ 8.125″
	Harrison Dillard	400 M Relay	1st	40.1
	Andrew Stanfield	400 M Relay	1st	40.1
	Ollie Matson	400 M Relay	1st	40.1
	Bill Miller	Javelin	2nd	237
	Milton Campbell	Decathlon	2nd	6,975 pts.
	Floyd Patterson	Boxing: Middleweight	1st	
	Norvel Lee	Boxing: Light Heavyweight	1st	
	Nathan Brooks	Boxing: Flyweight	1st	
	Charles Adkins	Boxing: Light Welterweight	1st	
	Barbara Jones	400 M Relay	1st	45.9
Melbourne, 1956	Andrew Stanfield	200 M Dash	2nd	20.7
	Charles Jenkins	400 M Run	1st	46.7
	Lee Calhoun	110 M Hurdles	1st	13.5
	Charles Dumas	High Jump	1st	6′ 11.25″
	Gregory Bell	Long Jump	1st	25′ 8.25″
	Willye White	Long Jump	2nd	19′ 11.75″
	Ira Murchison	400 M Relay	1st	39.5
	Leamon King	400 M Relay	1st	39.5
	Charles Jenkins	400 M Relay	1st	39.5
	Lou Jones	1600 M Relay	1st	3:04.8

Place/Year	Athlete	Event	Place	Time/Distance
	Milton Campbell	Decathlon	1st	7,937 pts.
	Rafer Johnson	Decathlon	2nd	7,587 pts.
	K.C. Jones	Men's Basketball	1st	
	Bill Russell	Men's Basketball	1st	
	James Boyd	Boxing: Light Heavyweight	1st	
	Mildred McDaniel	High Jump	1st	5′ 9.25″
	Margaret Matthews	400 M Relay	3rd	44.9
	Isabelle Daniels	400 M Relay	3rd	44.9
	Mae Faggs	400 M Relay	3rd	44.9
	Wilma Rudolph	400 M Relay	3rd	44.9
Rome, 1960	Les Carney	200 M Dash	2nd	20.6
	Lee Calhoun	110 M Hurdles	1st	13.8
	Willie May	110 M Hurdles	2nd	13.8
	Hayes Jones	110 M Hurdles	3rd	14
	Otis Davis	400 M Run	1st	44.9
	John Thomas	High Jump	3rd	7′ .25″
	Ralph Boston	Long Jump	1st	26′ 7.75″
	Irvin Robertson	Long Jump	2nd	26′ 7.25″
	Otis Davis	1600 M Relay	1st	3:02.2
	Rafer Johnson	Decathlon	1st	8,392 pts.
	Oscar Robertson	Men's Basketball	1st	
	Walt Bellamy	Men's Basketball	1st	
	Bob Boozer	Men's Basketball	1st	
	Wilbert McClure	Boxing: Light Middleweight	1st	
	Cassius Clay	Boxing: Light Heavyweight	1st	
	Edward Crook	Boxing: Middleweight	1st	
	Quincelon Daniels	Boxing: Light Welterweight	3rd	
	Earlene Brown	Shot Put	3rd	53′ 10.25″
	Wilma Rudolph	100 M Dash	1st	11
	Wilma Rudolph	200 M Dash	1st	24
	Martha Judson	400 M Relay	3rd	44.5
	Lucinda Williams	400 M Relay	3rd	44.5
	Barbara Jones	400 M Relay	3rd	44.5
	Wilma Rudolph	400 M Relay	3rd	44.5
Tokyo, 1964	Robert Hayes	100 M Dash	1st	9.9
	Henry Carr	200 M Dash	1st	20.3
	Paul Drayton	200 M Dash	2nd	20.5
	Hayes Jones	110 M Hurdles	1st	13.6
	Robert Hayes	400 M Relay	1st	39
	Paul Drayton	400 M Relay	1st	39
	Richard Stebbins	400 M Relay	1st	39
	John Thomas	High Jump	2nd	7′ 1.75″
	John Rambo	High Jump	3rd	7′ 1″
	Ralph Boston	Long Jump	2nd	26′ 4″
	Walt Hazzard	Men's Basketball	1st	
	Lucius Jackson	Men's Basketball	1st	
	Charles Brown	Boxing: Featherweight	3rd	
	Ronald Harris	Boxing: Lightweight	3rd	
	Joe Frazier	Boxing: Heavyweight	1st	
	Robert Carmody	Boxing: Flyweight	3rd	
	Wyomia Tyus	100 M Dash	1st	11.4
	Edith McGuire	100 M Dash	2nd	11.6
	Edith McGuire	200 M Dash	1st	23
	Wyomia Tyus	400 M Relay	2nd	43.9
	Edith McGuire	400 M Relay	2nd	43.9
	Willye White	400 M Relay	2nd	43.9
	Marilyn White	400 M Relay	2nd	43.9
Mexico City, 1968	Jim Hines	100 M Dash	1st	9.9
	Charles Greene	100 M Dash	3rd	10
	Tommie Smith	200 M Dash	1st	19.8
	John Carlos	200 M Dash	3rd	20
	Lee Evans	400 M Run	1st	43.8

Place/Year	Athlete	Event	Place	Time/Distance
	Larry James	400 M Run	2nd	43.9
	Ron Freeman	400 M Run	3rd	44.4
	Willie Davenport	110 M Hurdles	1st	13.3
	Ervin Hall	110 M Hurdles	2nd	13.4
	Jim Hines	400 M Relay	1st	38.2
	Charles Greene	400 M Relay	1st	38.2
	Mel Pender	400 M Relay	1st	38.2
	Ronnie Ray Smith	400 M Relay	1st	38.2
	Wyomia Tyus	400 M Relay	1st	42.8
	Barbara Ferrell	400 M Relay	1st	42.8
	Margaret Bailes	400 M Relay	1st	42.8
	Mildrette Netter	400 M Relay	1st	42.8
	Lee Evans	1600 M Relay	1st	2:56.1
	Vince Matthews	1600 M Relay	1st	2:56.1
	Ron Freeman	1600 M Relay	1st	2:56.1
	Larry James	1600 M Relay	1st	2:56.1
	Edward Caruthers	High Jump	2nd	7' 3.5"
	Bob Beamon	Long Jump	1st	29' 2.5"
	Ralph Boston	Long Jump	3rd	26' 9.25"
	Spencer Haywood	Men's Basketball	1st	
	Charlie Scott	Men's Basketball	1st	
	Michael Barrett	Men's Basketball	1st	
	James King	Men's Basketball	1st	
	Calvin Fowler	Men's Basketball	1st	
	John Baldwin	Boxing: Light Middleweight	3rd	
	Alfred Jones	Boxing: Middleweight	3rd	
	Albert Robinson	Boxing: Featherweight	2nd	
	Ronald Harris	Boxing: Lightweight	1st	
	James Wallington	Boxing: Light Welterweight	3rd	
	George Foreman	Boxing: Heavyweight	1st	
	Wyomia Tyus	100 M Dash	1st	11
	Barbara Ferrell	100 M Dash	2nd	11.1
	Madeline Manning	800 M Run	1st	2:00.9
Munich, 1972	Robert Taylor	100 M Dash	2nd	10.24
	Larry Black	200 M Dash	2nd	20.19
	Vince Matthews	400 M Run	1st	44.66
	Wayne Collett	400 M Run	2nd	44.80
	Rod Milburn	110 M Hurdles	1st	13.24
	Eddie Hart	400 M Relay	1st	38.19
	Robert Taylor	400 M Relay	1st	38.19
	Larry Black	400 M Relay	1st	38.19
	Gerald Tinker	400 M Relay	1st	38.19
	Randy Williams	Long Jump	1st	27' .25"
	Arnie Robinson	Long Jump	3rd	26' 4"
	Jeff Bennet	Decathlon	3rd	7,974 pts.
	Wayne Collett	400 M Dash	2nd	44.80
	Marvin Johnson	Boxing: Middleweight	3rd	
	Ray Seales	Boxing: Light Welterweight	1st	
	Cheryl Toussain	1600 M Relay	2nd	3:25.2
	Mable Fergerson	1600 M Relay	2nd	3:25.2
	Madeline Manning	1600 M Relay	2nd	3:25.2
Montreal, 1976	Millard Hampton	200 M Dash	2nd	20.29
	Dwayne Evans	200 M Dash	3rd	20.43
	Fred Newhouse	400 M Run	2nd	44.40
	Herman Frazier	400 M Run	3rd	44.95
	Willie Davenport	110 M Hurdles	3rd	13.38
	Edwin Moses	400 M Hurdles	1st	47.64
	Millard Hampton	400 M Relay	1st	38.83
	Steve Riddick	400 M Relay	1st	38.83
	Harvey Glance	400 M Relay	1st	38.83
	John Jones	400 M Relay	1st	38.83
	Herman Frazier	1600 M Relay	1st	2:58.7

Place/Year	Athlete	Event	Place	Time/Distance
	Benny Brown	1600 M Relay	1st	2:58.7
	Maxie Parks	1600 M Relay	1st	2:58.7
	Fred Newhouse	1600 M Relay	1st	2:58.7
	Arnie Robinson	Long Jump	1st	27′ 4.75″
	Randy Williams	Long Jump	2nd	26′ 7.25″
	James Butts	Triple Jump	2nd	56 8.5″
	Phil Ford	Men's Basketball	1st	
	Adrian Dantley	Men's Basketball	1st	
	Walter Davis	Men's Basketball	1st	
	Quinn Buckner	Men's Basketball	1st	
	Kenneth Carr	Men's Basketball	1st	
	Scott May	Men's Basketball	1st	
	Philip Hubbard	Men's Basketball	1st	
	Johnny Tate	Boxing: Heavyweight	3rd	
	Leo Randolph	Boxing: Flyweight	1st	
	Howard David	Boxing: Lightweight	1st	
	Sugar Ray Leonard	Boxing: Light Welterweight	1st	
	Michael Spinks	Boxing: Middleweight	1st	
	Leon Spinks	Boxing: Light Heavyweight	1st	
	Rosalyn Bryant	1600 M Relay	2nd	3:22.8
	Shelia Ingram	1600 M Relay	2nd	3:22.8
	Pamela Jiles	1600 M Relay	2nd	3:22.8
	Debra Sapenter	1600 M Relay	2nd	3:22.8
	Lusia Harris	Women's Basketball	2nd	
	Charlotte Lewis	Women's Basketball	2nd	
Los Angeles, 1984	Carl Lewis	100 M Dash	1st	9.9
	Sam Graddy	100 M Dash	2nd	10.19
	Carl Lewis	200 M Dash	1st	19.80
	Kirk Baptiste	200 M Dash	2nd	19.96
	Alonzo Babers	400 M Run	1st	44.27
	Antonio McKay	400 M Run	3rd	44.71
	Earl Jones	800 M Run	3rd	1:43.83
	Roger Kingdom	110 M Hurdles	1st	13.20
	Greg Foster	110 M Hurdles	2nd	13.23
	Edwin Moses	400 M Hurdles	1st	47.75
	Danny Harris	400 M Hurdles	2nd	48.13
	Sam Graddy	400 M Relay	1st	37.83
	Ron Brown	400 M Relay	1st	37.83
	Calvin Smith	400 M Relay	1st	37.83
	Carl Lewis	400 M Relay	1st	37.83
	Sunder Nix	1600 M Relay	1st	2:57.91
	Roy Armstead	1600 M Relay	1st	2:57.91
	Alonzo Babers	1600 M Relay	1st	2:57.91
	Antonio McKay	1600 M Relay	1st	2:57.91
	Michael Carter	Shot Put	1st	21.09 m
	Carl Lewis	Long Jump	1st	8.54 m
	Al Joyner	Triple Jump	1st	17.26 m
	Mike Conley	Triple Jump	2nd	17.18 m
	Evelyn Ashford	100 M Dash	1st	10.97
	Alice Brown	100 M Dash	2nd	11.13
	Valerie Brisco-Hooks	200 M Dash	1st	21.81
	Florence Griffith	200 M Dash	2nd	22.04
	Valerie Brisco-Hooks	400 M Run	1st	48.83
	Chandra Cheeseborough	400 M Run	2nd	49.05
	Kim Gallagher	800 M Run	2nd	1:58.63
	Benita Fitzgerald-Brown	100 M Hurdles	1st	12.84
	Kim Turner	100 M Hurdles	2nd	12.88
	Judi Brown	400 M Hurdles	2nd	55.20
	Valerie Brisco-Hooks	1600 M Relay	1st	3:18.29
	Chandra Cheeseborough	1600 M Relay	1st	3:18.29
	Lillie Leatherwood	1600 M Relay	1st	3:18.29
	Sherri Howard	1600 M Relay	1st	3:18.29

Place/Year	Athlete	Event	Place	Time/Distance
	Jackie Joyner	Heptathlon	2nd	6,386 pts.
	Tyrell Biggs	Boxing: Super Heavyweight	1st	
	Henry Tillman	Boxing: Heavyweight	1st	
	Frank Tate	Boxing: Light Middleweight	1st	
	Virgil Hill	Boxing: Middleweight	2nd	
	Evander Holyfield	Boxing: Light Heavyweight	3rd	
	Steven McCrory	Boxing: Flyweight	1st	
	Meldrick Taylor	Boxing: Featherweight	1st	
	Pernell Whitaker	Boxing: Lightweight	1st	
	Jerry Page	Boxing: Light Welterweight	1st	
	Mark Breland	Boxing: Welterweight	1st	
	Patrick Ewing	Men's Basketball	1st	
	Vern Fleming	Men's Basketball	1st	
	Michael Jordan	Men's Basketball	1st	
	Sam Perkins	Men's Basketball	1st	
	Alvin Robertson	Men's Basketball	1st	
	Wayman Tisdale	Men's Basketball	1st	
	Leon Wood	Men's Basketball	1st	
	Cathy Boswell	Women's Basketball	1st	
	Teresa Edwards	Women's Basketball	1st	
	Janice Lawrence	Women's Basketball	1st	
	Pamela McGee	Women's Basketball	1st	
	Cheryl Miller	Women's Basketball	1st	
	Lynette Woodard	Women's Basketball	1st	
Seoul, 1988	Carl Lewis	100 M Dash	1st	9.92
	Calvin Smith	100 M Dash	2nd	9.99
	Joe DeLoach	200 M Dash	1st	19.75
	Carl Lewis	200 M Dash	2nd	19.79
	Steve Lewis	400 M Run	1st	43.87
	Butch Reynolds	400 M Run	2nd	43.93
	Danny Everett	400 M Run	3rd	44.09
	Roger Kingdom	110 M Hurdles	1st	12.98
	Tonie Campbell	110 M Hurdles	3rd	13.38
	Andre Phillips	400 M Hurdles	1st	47.19
	Edwin Moses	400 M Hurdles	3rd	47.56
	Butch Reynolds	1600 M Relay	1st	2:56.16
	Steve Lewis	1600 M Relay	1st	2:56.16
	Antonio McKay	1600 M Relay	1st	2:56.16
	Danny Everett	1600 M Relay	1st	2:56.16
	Carl Lewis	Long Jump	1st	8.72 m
	Mike Powell	Long Jump	2nd	8.49 m
	Larry Myricks	Long Jump	3rd	8.27 m
	Florence Griffith-Joyner	100 M Dash	1st	10.54
	Evelyn Ashford	100 M Dash	2nd	10.83
	Florence Griffith-Joyner	200 M Dash	1st	21.34
	Shelia Echols	400 M Relay	1st	41.98
	Florence Griffith-Joyner	400 M Relay	1st	41.98
	Evelyn Ashford	400 M Relay	1st	41.98
	Alice Brown	400 M Relay	1st	41.98
	Jackie Joyner-Kersee	Long Jump	1st	24' 3.5"
	Jackie Joyner-Kersee	Heptathlon	1st	7,291 pts.
	Denean Howard-Hill	1600 M Relay	2nd	3:15.51
	Valerie Brisco	1600 M Relay	2nd	3:15.51
	Diane Dixon	1600 M Relay	2nd	3:15.51
	Florence Griffith-Joyner	1600 M Relay	2nd	3:15.51
	Kim Gallagher	800 M Run	3rd	1:56.91
	Andrew Maynard	Boxing: Light Heavyweight	1st	
	Ray Mercer	Boxing: Heavyweight	1st	
	Kennedy McKinney	Boxing: Bantamweight	1st	
	Riddick Bowe	Boxing: Super Heavyweight	2nd	
	Roy Jones	Boxing: Middleweight	2nd	
	Kenny Monday	Wrestling: Freestyle	1st	

Place/Year	Athlete	Event	Place	Time/Distance
	Nate Carr	Wrestling: Freestyle	3rd	
	Zina Garrison	Tennis: Doubles	1st	
	Zina Garrison	Tennis: Singles	3rd	
	Tom Goodwin	Baseball	1st	
	Ty Griffin	Baseball	1st	
	Cindy Brown	Women's Basketball	1st	
	Vicky Bullett	Women's Basketball	1st	
	Cynthia Cooper	Women's Basketball	1st	
	Teresa Edwards	Women's Basketball	1st	
	Jennifer Gillom	Women's Basketball	1st	
	Bridgette Gordon	Women's Basketball	1st	
	Katrina McClain	Women's Basketball	1st	
	Teresa Weatherspoon	Women's Basketball	1st	
	Willie Anderson	Men's Basketball	3rd	
	Stacey Augmon	Men's Basketball	3rd	
	Bimbo Coles	Men's Basketball	3rd	
	Jeff Grayer	Men's Basketball	3rd	
	Hersey Hawkins	Men's Basketball	3rd	
	Danny Manning	Men's Basketball	3rd	
	J.R. Reid	Men's Basketball	3rd	
	Mitch Richmond	Men's Basketball	3rd	
	David Robinson	Men's Basketball	3rd	
	Charles D. Smith	Men's Basketball	3rd	
	Charles E. Smith	Men's Basketball	3rd	
Barcelona, 1992	Dennis Mitchell	100 M Dash	3rd	10.04
	Gail Devers	100 M Dash	1st	10.82
	Mike Marsh	200 M Dash	1st	20.01
	Michael Bates	200 M Dash	3rd	20.38
	Gwen Torrence	200 M Dash	1st	21.81
	Quincy Watts	400 M Run	1st	43.50
	Steve Lewis	400 M Run	2nd	44.21
	Johnny Gray	800 M Run	3rd	1:43.97
	Mike Marsh	400 M Relay	1st	37.40
	Leroy Burrell	400 M Relay	1st	37.40
	Dennis Mitchell	400 M Relay	1st	37.40
	Carl Lewis	400 M Relay	1st	37.40
	Evelyn Ashford	400 M Relay	1st	42.11
	Esther Jones	400 M Relay	1st	42.11
	Carlette Guidry-White	400 M Relay	1st	42.11
	Gwen Torrence	400 M Relay	1st	42.11
	Tony Dees	110 M Hurdles	2nd	13.24
	Kevin Young	400 M Hurdles	1st	46.78
	Sandra Farmer	400 M Hurdles	2nd	53.69
	Janeene Vickers	400 M Hurdles	3rd	54.31
	Andrew Valmon	800 M Relay	1st	2:55.74
	Quincy Watts	800 M Relay	1st	2:55.74
	Michael Johnson	800 M Relay	1st	2:55.74
	Steve Lewis	800 M Relay	1st	2:55.74
	Natasha Kaiser	800 M Relay	2nd	3:20.92
	Gwen Torrence	800 M Relay	2nd	3:20.92
	Jearl Miles	800 M Relay	2nd	3:20.92
	Rochelle Stevens	800 M Relay	2nd	3:20.92
	Hollis Conway	High Jump	3rd	7' 8"
	Carl Lewis	Long Jump	1st	28' 5.5"
	Mike Powell	Long Jump	2nd	28' 4.25"
	Joe Greene	Long Jump	3rd	27' 4.5"
	Jackie Joyner-Kersee	Long Jump	3rd	23' 2.5"
	Mike Conley	Triple Jump	1st	59' 7.5"
	Charlie Simpkins	Triple Jump	2nd	57' 9"
	Jackie Joyner-Kersee	Heptathlon	1st	7,044 pts.
	Tim Austin	Boxing: Flyweight	3rd	
	Chris Byrd	Boxing: Middleweight	2nd	

Place/Year	Athlete	Event	Place	Time/Distance
	Kevin Jackson	Wrestling: Middleweight	1st	
	Charles Barkley	Men's Basketball	1st	
	Clyde Drexler	Men's Basketball	1st	
	Patrick Ewing	Men's Basketball	1st	
	Magic Johnson	Men's Basketball	1st	
	Michael Jordan	Men's Basketball	1st	
	Karl Malone	Men's Basketball	1st	
	Scottie Pippen	Men's Basketball	1st	
	David Robinson	Men's Basketball	1st	
	Vicky Bullett	Women's Basketball	3rd	
	Daedra Charles	Women's Basketball	3rd	
	Cynthia Cooper	Women's Basketball	3rd	
	Teresa Edwards	Women's Basketball	3rd	
	Carolyn Jones	Women's Basketball	3rd	
	Katrina McClain	Women's Basketball	3rd	
	Vickie Orr	Women's Basketball	3rd	
	Teresa Weatherspoon	Women's Basketball	3rd	
Atlanta, 1996	Dominique Dawes	Gymnastics: Floor Exercise	3rd	
	Dominique Dawes	Gymnastics: Team	1st	
	Michael Johnson	200 M Dash	1st	19.32
	Michael Johnson	400 M Run	1st	43.49
	Allen Johnson	110 M Hurdles	1st	12.95
	Mark Crear	110 M Hurdles	2nd	13.09
	Derrick Adkins	400 M Hurdles	1st	47.54
	Calvin Davis	400 M Hurdles	3rd	47.96
	Tim Harden	400 M Relay	2nd	38.05
	Jon Drummond	400 M Relay	2nd	38.05
	Michael Marsh	400 M Relay	2nd	38.05
	Dennis Mitchell	400 M Relay	2nd	38.05
	LaMont Smith	1600 M Relay	1st	2:55.99
	Alvin Harrison	1600 M Relay	1st	2:55.99
	Derek Mills	1600 M Relay	1st	2:55.99
	Anthuan Maybank	1600 M Relay	1st	2:55.99
	Dan O'Brien	Decathlon	1st	8,824 pts.
	Charles Austin	High Jump	1st	7' 10"
	Carl Lewis	Long Jump	1st	27' 10.75"
	Joe Greene	Long Jump	3rd	27' .50"
	Kenny Harrison	Triple Jump	1st	59' 4"
	Gail Devers	100 M Dash	1st	10.94
	Gwen Torrence	100 M Dash	3rd	10.96
	Kim Batten	400 M Hurdles	2nd	53.08
	Tonja Buford-Bailey	400 M Hurdles	3rd	53.22
	Gail Devers	400 M Relay	1st	41.95
	Chryste Gaines	400 M Relay	1st	41.95
	Gwen Torrence	400 M Relay	1st	41.95
	Inger Miller	400 M Relay	1st	41.95
	Rochelle Stevens	1600 M Relay	1st	3:20.91
	Maicel Malone	1600 M Relay	1st	3:20.91
	Kim Graham	1600 M Relay	1st	3:20.91
	Jearl Miles	1600 M Relay	1st	3:20.91
	Jackie Joyner-Kersee	Long Jump	3rd	22' 11"
	Floyd Mayweather	Boxing: Featherweight	3rd	
	Terrance Cauthen	Boxing: Lightweight	3rd	
	Rhoshii Wells	Boxing: Middleweight	3rd	
	Antonio Tarver	Boxing: Light Heavyweight	3rd	
	Nate Jones	Boxing: Heavyweight	3rd	
	David Reid	Boxing: Light Middleweight	1st	
	Teresa Edwards	Women's Basketball	1st	
	Ruth Bolton	Women's Basketball	1st	
	Lisa Leslie	Women's Basketball	1st	
	Katrina McClain	Women's Basketball	1st	
	Sheryl Swoopes	Women's Basketball	1st	

Place/Year	Athlete	Event	Place	Time/Distance
	Nikki McCray	Women's Basketball	1st	
	Dawn Staley	Women's Basketball	1st	
	Venus Lacey	Women's Basketball	1st	
	Carla McGhee	Women's Basketball	1st	
	Mitch Richmond	Men's Basketball	1st	
	Scottie Pippin	Men's Basketball	1st	
	Gary Payton	Men's Basketball	1st	
	Charles Barkley	Men's Basketball	1st	
	Hakeem Olajuwon	Men's Basketball	1st	
	David Robinson	Men's Basketball	1st	
	Penny Hardaway	Men's Basketball	1st	
	Grant Hill	Men's Basketball	1st	
	Karl Malone	Men's Basketball	1st	
	Reggie Miller	Men's Basketball	1st	
	Jacque Jones	Baseball	3rd	

Index

Personal names, place names, events, organizations, and various subject areas or keywords contained in the *Reference Library of Black America* are listed in this index with corresponding volume and page numbers indicating text references. Page numbers appearing in boldface indicate major treatments of topics, such as biographical profiles and organizational entries. Page numbers appearing in italics refer to photographs, illustrations, and maps found throughout the reference work.

A

A. Philip Randolph Institute, **II:** 412, **419**

A.A. Alexander, Inc., **V:** 1151

AAMES (African American Male Empowerment Summit), **I:** 108

Aaron, Henry "Hank," **I:** 50 **V:** 1170, **1178–1179**

AARP (American Association of Retired Persons), **I:** 106

Abbott, Robert S., **I:** 193 **IV:** 753, **762,** 780

ABC (American Broadcasting Corporation), **IV:** 757

Abdul-Jabbar, Kareem, **V:** 1173, **1179,** *1179*

Abernathy, Billy, **III:** 718

Abernathy, Ralph, **I:** 32, 42, 43, 46 **II: 350,** *351, 367* **V:** 1166

    and Martin Luther King, Jr., **I:** 67, 219 **II:** 362

    and SCLC, **I:** 41 **II:** 397, 409 **III:** 680

Abiel Smith School, **I:** 198

Ableman v. Booth, **I:** 15 **II:** 472

Abolition and abolitionists, **II:** 328–329, 338–339, 341–343 *See also* Civil rights and Civil Rights movements; Slavery and slaves; Underground Railroad

    in all states, **I:** 17 **II:** 321

    attempts to counter, **I:** 10

    in British empire, **I:** 11

    early societies, **II:** 329

    efforts by church leaders, **III:** 673

    first protests, **I:** 3, 7

    first state to abolish slavery, **I:** 6

    gradual acts, **I:** 8

    and Mennonites, **I:** 3, 112

    movements, **II:** 328–329

    murders, **I:** 11

    organizations and associations, **I:** 5 **II:** 395

poets, **III:** 729

publications, **I:** 10, 11, 13

Abram, Morris B., **I:** 58

Abrams, Muhal Richard, **V: 986**

Abu-Jamal, Mumia, **II:** 452, *454*

Abyssinian Baptist Church, **I:** 207 **III:** 693–694, 702

    See also Churches; Religion

    in New York City, **I:** *208*

Academic scholarships, **I:** 68

    African American firsts, **I:** 89, 104, 194 **III:** 746 **IV:** 937

    African American women's firsts, **III:** 735

Academy Awards, *See also* Actors and actresses; Films and filmmakers

    African American firsts, **I:** 90, 97, 100, 105 **IV:** 833, 840, 844, 847, 868, 869

    African American women's firsts, **IV:** 833, 858

    list of African American recipients, A-1

    youngest director nominated, **IV:** 839

Acapulco Black Film Festival, **IV:** 867

Accidents, boating, **I:** 218

Accommodation, racial, **II:** 337

Accounting organizations, **II:** 431, 442

Ace, Johnny, **V:** 1084

Acquired immune deficiency syndrome *See* AIDS (Acquired Immune Deficiency Syndrome)

Act to Amend the Vagrant Laws of the State, **I:** 136–138

Act to Confer Civil Rights on Freedmen and for Other Purposes, **I:** 136–138

Act to Establish a Bureau for the Relief of Freedmen and Refugees *See* Freedmen's Bureau Acts

Act to Prohibit the Importation of Slaves (1807), **I:** 119–120

Act to Regulate the Relation of Master and

Apprentice, as Relates to Freedmen, Free
    Negroes, and Mulattoes, **I**: 136–138
Act to Suppress the Slave Trade in the District of
    Columbia, **I**: 128
Activists, civil rights *See* Civil rights activists
Actors and actresses *See also* Films and filmmakers;
    Television and television shows
    African American firsts, **I**: 90, 93, 97 **IV**: 833, 840,
        844, 847, 855, 861, 868, 869, 896
    African American women's firsts, **I**: 99, 100, 103
        IV: 858, 860, 904
    biographical profiles, **III**: 714–715 **IV**: 786–787,
        856–875, 890–920
    racial stereotypes, **IV**: 831–832
Actor's Equity, **IV**: 911
Adams, Charity, **V**: **1231–1232**
Adams, John, **I**: 199 **II**: 338
Adams, John Quincy, **I**: 11 **II**: 338
Adams, Leslie, **IV**: 926
Adams Memorial Museum, **I**: 217
Adams v. Richardson, **III**: 626
Adams, Yolanda, **IV**: **964**
Adarand Constructors v. Pena, **II**: 475
Addison, Adele, **IV**: **925**
Address to the Negroes of New York, **III**: 728
Address to the Public (Benjamin Franklin), **I**: 118
*Address to the Slaves of the United States of
    America*, **I**: 125
Addresses, keynote *See* Keynote addresses
Adelle v. Beauregard, **I**: 8
Aden, Alonzo, **V**: 1107
Advertising and advertising agencies, **IV**: 759 *See also*
    Businesses and business professionals
    African American firsts, **IV**: 776
Advisors, military *See* Military advisors and attachés
Affirmative action *See* Equal employment opportunity
    and affirmative action
Africa and Africans, **II**: **317–342** *See also* name of
    specific country, e.g., Kenya
    brief history, **II**: 225–229
    country profiles, **II**: 240–283
    cuisine, **II**: 236
    emigration from, **I**: 180
    family, **II**: 235
    film, **II**: 233–234
    first in United States, **I**: 1
    health concerns, **II**: 235–236
    influences on modern Africa, **II**: 225
    languages spoken, **II**: 231–232
    literature, **II**: 232–233
    maps, **II**: *230*
    music, **II**: 234
    nationalist movements, **II**: 227–229
    oldest independent country, **II**: 254
    one of first British colonies, **II**: 273
    organizations and associations, **II**: 419– 421, 423,
        442, 444–445
    participation in slave trade, **I**: 4
    population, **II**: 230–231
    religions, **III**: 671
    repatriation attempts, **I**: 8 **II**: 328, 378, 379
Africa Faith and Justice Network, **II**: **419**
The Africa Fund, **II**: **419**
Africa News Service, **II**: **419**
Africa Travel Association, **II**: **419**
Africa Watch, **II**: **419**
Africa World Press, **II**: **419** **IV**: 751
African American Art, **V**: 1097
African American chronology, **I**: **1–84**
African American Civil War Memorial, **I**: 189
African American Cultural Center, **III**: 658
African American firsts, **I**: **85–110** *See also* Chapter 2
    for firsts organized chronologically by date
African American Historical and Cultural Society,
    V: 1128
African American Male Empowerment Summit
    (AAMES), **I**: 108
African American migrations *See* Migrations of
    African Americans
African American Museum (Cleveland, Ohio), **V**: 1133
African American Museum (Dallas, Texas), **V**: 1135
African American Museums Association, **II**: **420**
African American National Historic Site, **I**: 198, 199
African American studies, **III**: 626
African American Studies Center, **III**: 658
African American Studies Program (University of
    Houston), **III**: 658
African American-owned buildings *See* Real estate
African American-owned businesses *See* Businesses
    and business professionals
African and African American Summit, **II**: 368
African Art Museums of the SMA Fathers, **V**: 1131
African Communities League, **II**: 389
African Cultural Art Forum, **V**: 1134
African diaspora, **II**: **225–315** **V**: 1146–1147 *See also*
    Africa and Africans; Migrations of African
    Americans
African free schools, **III**: 621–622, *622 See also*
    Education and educators
African Grove Theatre, **IV**: 877–878
African Heritage Studies Association, **II**: 389 **III**: 658
African House, **I**: 197
African Lodge 459, **II**: 404
African Meeting House, **I**: 198, 199
African Methodist Episcopal Book Concern, **IV**: 749
African Methodist Episcopal Church, **I**: 8, 182, 214 **II**:
    379 **III**: **685,** 693 *See also* Churches; Religion
    African American firsts, **I**: 85, 183 **II**: 343
    bishops, **III**: 692
    landmarks, **I**: 180, 183, 188, 194, 217

ministers, **III:** 697, 700
reunions, **III:** *681*
African Methodist Episcopal Sunday School Union
    and Publishing House, **IV:** 749
African Methodist Episcopal Zion Book Concern,
    IV: 749
African Methodist Episcopal Zion Church, **III: 686**
    See also Churches; Religion
bishops, **III:** 703, 705
founding, **I:** 9
ministers, **III:** 702
African National Congress (ANC), **II:** 228
African Orthodox Church, **III: 686** *See also*
    Churches; Religion
African Research Center, **III:** 658
African Studies and Research Center, **III:** 658
African Studies and Research Institute, **III:** 658
African Studies Program (University of Wisconsin,
    Madison), **III:** 658
African Theological Archministry, **III:** 686
African Union First Colored Methodist Protestant
    Church, Inc., **III: 687** *See also* Churches;
    Religion
African-American Atelier, **V:** 1133
African-American Cultural and Arts Network, **V:** 1132
African-American Cultural Center of Buffalo, **V:** 1132
African-American Institute, **II: 420**
African-American Institute Museum, **V:** 1132
African-American Labor Center, **II: 420**
African-American Museum of Nassau County, **V:** 1132
African-American Studies and Research Center,
    III: 658
African-American Visual Arts, **V:** 1130
African-New World Studies Program, **III:** 658
Africans *See* Africa and Africans
*Africans in America: America's Journey through
    Slavery*, **IV:** 838
Africare, **II: 420**
Afrikaner Bond, **II:** 227
Afrikaner Nationalist movement, **II:** 227
Afro-American Arts Institute, **III:** 658
Afro-American Council, **IV:** 769
Afro-American Cultural Center, **V:** 1133
Afro-American Genealogical and Historical Society,
    V: 1130
Afro-American Historical and Cultural Museum,
    V: 1134
Afro-American Historical Society of Delaware,
    V: 1129
Afro-American Society, **II:** 411
Afro-American Studies and Research Program
    (University of Illinois), **III:** 659
Afro-American Studies Program (Brown University),
    III: 659
Afrocentrism, **III:** 629–630 **V:** 1094–1096

Aftermath Entertainment, **V:** 1053
A.G. Gaston Construction Company, **III:** 587
Agassiz School, **I:** 200 **III:** 633
Agencies, state, **II:** 371–374
Agricultural science and scientists, **V:** 1139, 1153–
    1154 *See also* Farms and farmers
Agyeman, Jaramogi Abebe, **III:** 678, **692**
AID (Automatic Implantable Defribullator), **V:** 1166
Aid to Families with Dependent Children (AFDC),
    III: 599
AIDS (Acquired Immune Deficiency Syndrome),
    III: 606
in Africa, **II:** 235
biographical profiles of activists, **III:** 613
and churches, **III:** 681
projects to combat, **III:** 693
research, **V:** 1156–1157
statistics, **III:** 606
AIDS Health Care Foundation, **III:** 613
Aiken, Kimberley Clarice, **I:** 104
Aiken, William A. M., Jr., **III:** 664
Ailey, Alvin, **IV:** *888*, **890–891**, 894, 895
dance company, **IV:** 888, 905, 909
Ain't I a Woman: Black Women and Feminism,
    III: 641
Ain't Misbehavin', **IV:** 884
Air Force and Air Force officers, **V:** 1234–1235, 1235–
    1237 *See also* Military
African American firsts, **I:** 51, 94, 99 **V:** 1225, 1229,
    1230, 1235, 1236
African American women's firsts, **I:** 105 **V:** 1235
Airline pilots *See* Aviation and aviators (Civilian)
Airline stewardesses *See* Flight attendants
Airplane acrobatics *See* Precision flight teams
Airports *See also* Aviation and aviators (Civilian);
    Aviation and aviators (Military)
African American firsts, **V:** 1142
Akyeampong, Emmanuel K., **III:** 664
Al Roker Productions, Inc., **IV:** 779
Alabama
admission into Union, **I:** 9
African American firsts, **I:** 72
African American museums and galleries, **V:** 1119
African American newspapers, **IV:** 791
African American radio stations, **IV:** 811–812
landmarks, **I:** 179–180
school desegregation, **I:** 18, 37, 38
state university system, **I:** 71
Alabama A and M University, **III:** 650
Alabama Attorney General's Office, **II:** 371
Alabama State University, **III:** 650
The Alarm Clock, **III:** 724
Alaska
landmarks, **I:** 181
Alaska Human Rights Commission, **II:** 371

Albany State University, **III:** 650
Albee, Edward, **III:** 734
Albemarle Paper Co. v. Moody, **II:** 464
Alberghetti, Anna Maria, **IV:** 894
Alcoholism, **II:** 420, 434 **III:** 608 *See also* Drug abuse
Alcoholism in the Black Community, **II: 420**
Alcorn Agricultural and Mechanical College *See* Alcorn State University
Alcorn College *See* Alcorn State University
Alcorn, George E., **V:** 1143, **1150**
Alcorn State University, **I:** 204 **III:** 624, 650
Alderpersons
     African American firsts, **II:** 371 **III:** 513, 603
al-Amin, Jamil Abdullah, **I:** 40 **II:** 383, 398, **400,** *401*
Aldridge, Delores P., **III:** 664
Aldridge, Ira, **IV:** 877, **891**
Alert songs, **IV:** 958–959
Alexander and Repass, **V:** 1151
Alexander, Archie, **V: 1151**
Alexander, Clifford L. Jr., **I:** 51, 99, *100* **II: 475**
     V: 1225
Alexander, Erika, **V:** 1076
Alexander, John H., **V:** 1210
Alexander, Joyce London, **II: 475**
Alexander, Larry, **V:** 1062
Alexander, Margaret Walker *See* Walker, Margaret A.
Alexander, Texas, **V:** 1008
Alexander, v. Holmes Board of Education, **I:** 45
     II: 461
Alexander, William, **II:** *470*
Alexandria Black History Resource Center, **V:** 1135
Algeria, **II: 240**
Ali, Duse Muhammad, **II:** 382, 389
Ali, Muhammad, **I:** 48 **V:** 1172, **1179–1180,** *1180,*
     1186, 1188, 1224
Ali, Noble Drew, **II:** 390 **III: 692**
Alice Freeman Palmer Institute *See* Palmer Memorial Institute
Alien and Naturalization Act (1790), **II:** 327
All-African People's Revolutionary Party, **II: 420**
All-American honors
     African American firsts, **I:** 89
Allen, Betsy Mou, **IV: 925**
Allen, Debbie, **IV:** 837, 870, 884, *891,* **891–892**
Allen, Ethan, **II:** 339
Allen, Geri, **V:** 985
Allen, Grace M., **III:** 643
Allen, Henry "Red," Jr., **V: 986,** 1143
Allen, Macon B., **I:** 86 **II:** 452
Allen, Marcus, **I:** 106
Allen Memorial Art Museum, **V:** 1133
Allen, Richard, **I:** 7, 217 **II:** *344,* 378 **III: 692,** 700
     and African Methodist Episcopal Church, **I:** 85,
     216 **III:** 672–673, 685–686, 705 **IV:** 958

and Free African Society, **I:** 6 **II:** 328, 343, 379, 395
     III: 699
Allen, Thomas C., **V:** 1142
Allen University, **I:** 217 **III:** 650
Allen v. State Board of Elections, **II:** 459
Allen v. Wright, **II:** 464
Allen, William, **IV:** 958
Allensworth, Allen, **I:** 182
Allensworth, California, **I:** 182
Alliance of African-American Artists, **V:** 1130
Allied Medical Society *See* Detroit Medical Society
Allies, **IV:** 909
The All-Negro Hour, **IV:** 755
All-Stars Talent Show, **III:** 517
Almanack (Benjamin Banneker)
     title page, **V:** *1138*
Almanacs *See also* Book publishing and publishers
     African American firsts, **V:** 1151
Alpha Kappa Alpha (Sorority), **I:** 89 **II:** 400, **420**
Alpha Phi Alpha (Fraternity), **I:** 86 **II:** 400, **420**
Alpha Pi Chi (Sorority), **II:** 421
Alpha Suffrage Club, **I:** 194 **II:** 371
Alston, Charles, **V:** 1094, **1099,** 1128
Alvin Ailey American Dance Theater, **IV:**
     888–889, 890
Alvin Ailey Repertory Ensemble, **IV:** 888
Alzheimer, Alois, **V:** 1156
Alzheimer's disease, **V:** 1156
Ambassadors
     African American women's firsts, **III:** 519
Ambers, Lou, **V:** 1180
AME Church *See* African Methodist Episcopal Church
Amer-I-can, **V:** 1183
American Academy and Institute of Arts and Letters
     Awards, A-1
American Antebellum period, **IV:** 958
American Anti-Slavery Society, **I:** 10, 123–125
American Association of Blacks in Energy, **II: 421**
American Association of Retired Persons (AARP),
     I: 106
American Baptist Black Caucus, **II: 421**
American Baptist Convention, **II: 421**
American Baptist Home Mission Society, **III:** 624
American Beach, Florida, **III:** 547–548
American Black Book Writers Association, **II: 421**
American Broadcasting Corporation (ABC), **IV:** 757
American Civil War, **I:** 15, 16, 86 **II:** 331 *See also*
     Confederate Army; Union Army
     African Americans in, **I:** 16 **II:** 332–333 **V:** 1206–
     1207, *1207*
     anti-draft riots, **I:** 16
     fleeing of slaves, **I:** *17*
     highest ranking African American, **V:** 1208
     landmarks, **I:** 189, 190, 197, 199, 204, 222

Medals of Honor recipients, A-12–A-13
role of women, **V:** 1209
American College of Surgeons, **I:** 194 **V:** 1140
American Colonial period, **V:** 1205
    African American firsts, **I:** 85 **II:** 317
    art, **V:** 1088–1090
    educational opportunities, **III:** 621
    entrepreneurship, **III:** 575
    influence on sacred music, **IV:** 957
    slavery, **II:** 318–321
American Colonization Society, **I:** 8, 9 **II:** 328
American Committee on Africa, **II: 421**
American Dance Asylum, **IV:** 907
American Family Mutual Insurance Co. v. NAACP,
    I: 74
American Federation of Musicians Local 627, **I:** 205
American Freedmen's Aid Commission, **I:** 16 **III:** 623
American Institute of Chemists, **V:** 1158
American League of Colored Laborers, **I:** 13
American Library Association Black Caucus, **II: 423**
American Medical Association, **I:** 105
American Meteorological Society, **V:** 1145
American Missionary Association, **I:** 180, 216, 219,
    222 **III:** 623, 624
American Nazi party, **I:** 58
American Negro Academy, **I:** 189 **II:** 379, 386 **III:** 626
    IV: 751
American Negro Theater, **IV:** 881, 911
American Nurses' Association, **II:** 415
American Osteopathic Association, **I:** 105
American Postbellum period, **II:** 334–335
American Reconstruction, **II:** 336–337, 344
    churches, **III:** 673–675
    and civil rights, **II:** 333–334, 344–345
    institutionalized segregation, **II:** 344–345
    inventors, **V:** 1138
American Revolution, **I:** 5 **II:** 319–321 **V:** 1205–1206
    African American firsts, **II:** 321
    artifacts, **I:** 209
    battalions of former slaves, **I:** 6
    commemorative coins, **I:** 78
    commemorative organizations, **II:** 425
    landmarks, **I:** 184, 199, 216
    memorials, **V:** 1206
    number of African American soldiers, **I:** 6
    slavery during, **I:** 5, 6
    soldiers commended by the French, **I:** 6
American Shakespeare Festival, **IV:** 860
American Singles Tennis Championship, **I:** 98
American Slavery As It Is, **I:** 123–125
American Society of Public Administration
    Conference of Minority Public Administrators,
    II: 428
American South *See also* name of specific state, e.g.,
    Louisiana

African American firsts, **III:** 731
free African Americans, **II:** 327
migrations of African Americans, **I:** 28
    III: 544–546
organizations and associations, **II:** 443–444
voter qualifications, **I:** 27
American Stock Exchange *See also* NASDAQ; New
    York Stock Exchange
    African American firsts, **III:** 588
American Tennis Association, **II: 421**
American West, **I:** 183 *See also* name of specific
    state, e.g., Montana
Americans United for Affirmative Action, **II:** 362
America's Dream, **IV:** 838
Ames, Alexander, **I:** 199
AMEZ Church *See* African Methodist Episcopal
    Zion Church
Amin, Idi Dada, **II:** 280, 390
Amini, Johari, **III:** 737
Amistad (Film), **IV:** 838
Amistad incident, **I:** 11, 184 **II:** 338, 377 **IV:** 891
    execution of Captain Ferrer, **I:** *12*
Amistad Murals, **I:** 180
Amistad Research Center, **III:** 659
Amos n' Andy show, **IV:** 835
Amos, Wally, Jr., **III:** *582*, **582–583**
Amparo system, **II:** 308
Amsterdam News, **I:** 208 **IV:** 754
Anacostia Museum, **V:** 1129
Anchors, television *See* Television hosts and anchors
And the Walls Come Tumbling Down, **I:** 67
Anderson, Charles Alfred, **I:** 89 **V:** 1142
Anderson, Eddie "Rochester," **IV: 892**
Anderson, Elijah, **III:** 664
Anderson, Gloria Long, **III:** 664
Anderson, James H., **I:** 208 **IV:** 754
Anderson, Joe, **V:** 1137
Anderson, Laurie, **IV:** 907
Anderson, Marian, **I:** 99 **IV:** 922, *923,* **925,** 931, 953
    landmarks, **I:** 187
    singing at Lincoln Memorial, **I:** 25, *26*
Anderson, Robert, **IV:** 970
Anderson, Thomas Jefferson "T.J.", **IV: 925–926,** 941
Anderson, Violette, **I:** 89 **II: 475–476**
Anderson, Wes, **V:** *982*
Anderson, William G., **I:** 105
Andersonville Prison, **I:** 190
Andrew Rankin Memorial Chapel (Howard
    University), **I:** 186
Andrews, Benny, **III:** 714 **V: 1099–1100**
Andrews, Ed, **V:** 974
Andrews, Inez, **IV:** 964
Andrews, Raymond, **III: 714**
Anemia, sickle cell *See* Sickle cell anemia

Angelou, Maya, **III:** 664, *714*, **714–715 IV:** *837*, 899
    V: 1046, 1064, 1108
    and inauguration of Bill Clinton, **III:** 714
Anglican Church *See* Episcopal Church
Angola, **II: 240–241**
Anguilla, **II: 283–284**
ANIA Comics, **IV:** 752
Anita Bush Stock Company, **IV:** 894
Anna (Record label), **V:** 1058
Annapolis Naval Academy *See* United States Naval
    Academy (USNA) at Annapolis
*Announcing an Effort to Promote the Study and
    Facilitate the Teaching of the Fundamentals of
    Negro Life and History*, **III:** 641
Annual Convention of the People of Color, **I:** 10
Anson, Cap, **V:** 1169
Anthrax (Music group), **V:** 1076
Anthropology and anthropologists, **II:** 422 **III:** 637,
    649 **V:** 1154
Antigua, **II: 284**
Anti-Repression Resource Team, **II: 421**
Anti-slavery movements *See* Abolition and
    abolitionists
Apartheid, **II:** 228, 233, 276 *See also* South Africa
Apex Museum, **V:** 1129
Apollo 16, **V:** 1152
Apollo Theater, **I:** 208
Apostolic Overcoming Holy Church of God, Inc., **III:**
    687 *See also* Churches; Religion
Appalachee Red, **III:** 714
An Appeal to the Colored People of the World, **I:** 10
Appiah, Kwame, **III:** 641
Appleton Museum of Art, **V:** 1129
Applied arts *See* Visual and applied arts and artists
Arabian Prince (Musician), **V:** 1053
Archbishops *See* Bishops
Archer, Dennis, **I:** 75 **III: 499–500,** *699* **IV:** 764
Architecture and architects, **I:** 203 **V:** 1122, 1127
    African American firsts, **V:** 1127
    African American women's firsts, **V:** 1122
    landmarks designed by, **I:** 179, 186, 188, 189, 193,
        195, 211, 217
Archives *See* name of specific archive, e.g., Bethune
    Museum and Archives
Archives of African American Music and Culture,
    III: 659
Argentina, **II: 284**
Aristide, Jean-Bertrand, **II:** 240
Aristotle, **III:** 629
Arizona
    African American newspapers, **IV:** 791
    African American radio stations, **IV:** 812
    landmarks, **I:** 181–182
    Martin Luther King, Jr. Day controversy, **I:** 63, 68
Arizona Attorney General's Office, **II:** 371

Arkansas, **IV:** 791, 812
Arkansas Attorney General's Office, **II:** 371
Arkansas Baptist College, **III:** 650
Arkansas National Guard, **I:** 182
Arkansas State Press, **II:** 352
Armed Forces *See* Military
Armstrong Agricultural School, **III:** 525
Armstrong, Henry, **V:** 1172, **1180**
Armstrong, Lilian Hardin, **V:** 984, 986
Armstrong, Louis, **IV:** 965 **V:** 977, *977*, 981, 983, 986,
    986–987, 1019
    and Joseph "King" Oliver, **V:** 976, 1020
    landmarks, **I:** 209
    performances with female musicians, **V:** 984
Armstrong, Samuel Chapman, **I:** 18, 222
Army and Army officers, **I:** 26 **V:** 1227 *See also*
    Military
    African American firsts, **I:** 26, 51, 107 **V:** 1211,
        1212, 1225, 1226, 1242
    African American women's firsts, **I:** 93, 106 **V:**
        1228, 1237
    biographical profiles, **V:** 1227–1243
    Medals of Honor recipients, A-12–A-14
    racial integration, **I:** 27, 28 **V:** 1216
Army Appropriation Act (1864), **V:** 1207
Army Corps of Engineers, **I:** 80
Army secretaries
    African American firsts, **II:** 475
Arnett, Benjamin William, **I:** 88
Aronson, Arnold, **II:** 397
Arrington, Richard, Jr., **I:** 99
Arroyo, Martina, **IV: 926**
Art collections and exhibits, **V:** 1097–1099 *See also*
    Visual and applied arts and artists
    African American firsts, **I:** 106 **V:** 1107, 1120
    African American women's firsts, **V:** 1096, 1122
"Art for Art's Sake" movement *See* Harlem
    Renaissance movement
Art history *See also* Visual and applied arts
    and artists
    African American firsts, **V:** 1119
Art Institute of Chicago, **V:** 1130
Arthur, Chester, **V:** 1210
Artist Formerly Known As (Prince) *See* Prince (Artist
    Formerly Known As)
Artists Collective, Inc., **V:** 1129
Arts, visual and applied *See* Visual and applied arts
    and artists
Aruba, **II: 285**
Asante, Molefi K., **III: 632,** *632*
Asbury, Francis, **I:** 184 **III:** 672, 692, 705
Asbury Methodist Episcopal Church (Wilmington,
    Delaware), **I:** 184
Ashby, Dorothy, **V:** 985
Ashe, Arthur, **I:** 98, 222 **V:** 1175, *1176*, **1180–1181**

Ashford and Simpson, **V: 1046**
Ashford, Emmett, **I:** 97
Ashford, Nicholas, **V: 1046**
Ashley, Maurice, **I:** 110
Ashley, William Henry, **I:** 8 **III:** 583
Assassinations *See* Homicide
Associated Publishers, Inc., **III:** 650
Associates of Negro Folk Education, **IV:** 751
Association for the Advancement of Creative Music,
    V: 986
Association for the Study of African American Life
    and History, **I:** 49, 189 **III:** 659
  and Black History Month, **I:** 23, 89
  establishment, **I:** 21 **II:** 417 **III:** 626, 650
Association for the Study of Afro-American History
    and Literature, **IV:** 751
Association in Negro Folk Education, **III:** 646
Association of African American People's Legal
    Council, **II: 422**
Association of Black Admissions and Financial Aid
    Officers of the Ivy League and Sister Schools,
    II: 422
Association of Black Anthropologists, **II: 422**
Association of Black Cardiologists, **II: 422**
Association of Black Foundation Executives, **II: 422**
Association of Black Nursing Faculty, **II: 422**
Association of Black Psychologists, **II: 423**
Association of Black Sociologists, **II: 423**
Association of Colleges and Secondary Schools,
    II: 405
Association of Concerned African Scholars, **II: 423**
Association of Minority Health Professions, **III:** 534
Association of Trial Lawyers of America, **I:** 107
Association of Volleyball Professionals, **I:** 101
Associations and organizations *See* Organizations and
    associations
Astaire, Fred, **IV:** 911
Astronauts *See* Space exploration and explorers
Astronomy and astronomers, **V:** 1151
Astrophysics and astrophysicists, **V:** 1152–1153
Athletic directors
    African American women's firsts, **I:** 108
Athletics *See* Sports
Atlanta Compromise speech, **I:** 20, 146–148 **II:** 369
Atlanta Metropolitan College, **III:** 651
Atlanta University, **I:** 191, 197
Atlanta University Press, **IV:** 750
Atlanta University Publication Series, **IV:** 750
Atlantic Records, **V:** 1040
Attachés, military *See* Military advisors and attachés
Attorneys *See* Law and lawyers
Attucks, Crispus, **I:** 78 **II:** *321*, 337
    and Boston Massacre, **I:** 5, 85 **II:** 320 **V:** 1205
    landmarks, **I:** 199, *199*
Atwater, Lee, **I:** 67

Augin, Charles, **IV:** 884
Augusta, Alexander T., **I:** 86 **V:** 1140
Austin, John, **V:** 1127
Austin, Regina, **III:** 664
Australian Open (Tennis), A-2
Authors, **III:** 714–748 **IV:** 868–869 *See also* Novels
    and Novelists; Plays and playwrights (Written);
    Poetry and poets
    African American firsts, **III:** 589, 602, 709,
        721, 725, 731
    African American women's firsts, **III:** 729, 735, 740
    breaking genre barriers, **III:** 713
    Colonial and Antebellum, **III:** 709
    organizations and associations, **II:** 421, 429, 432
    twentieth century, **III:** 711–712, 713–714
The Autobiography of an Ex-Colored Man, **I:** 21
The Autobiography of Malcolm X, **III:** 727
The Autobiography of Miss Jane Pittman (Television
    movie), **III:** 726 **IV:** 836, 838
Automatic Implantable Defribullator (AID), **V:** 1166
Automobile designers *See* Visual and applied arts
    and artists
Avery, Margaret, **III:** 744
Avery Normal Institute, **I:** 216
Avery Research Center for African American History
    and Culture, **I:** 216 **III:** 659 **V:** 1134
Aviation and aviators (Civilian), **II:** 435, 442 **V:**
    1142–1143
    African American firsts, **I:** 89 **V:** 1142
    African American women's firsts, **V:** 1142
Aviation and aviators (Military), **V:** 1157, 1162, 1227–
    1228, 1235–1237, 1239–1240, 1242–1243
    African American firsts, **I:** 89, 93, 94, 99, 101, 105
        V: 1227, 1239
    African American women's firsts, **I:** 93, 99
Awards, football *See* Football awards and
    championships
Ayers, Roy, **V:** 984
Ayler, Albert, **V:** 981
Azevedo, Mario J., **III:** 664

B

B. Brown Orchestra, **V:** 1071
B. Brown Productions, **V:** 1048
Ba Kkobhio, Basek, **II:** 233
Babbit, Bruce, **I:** 68
Baby Sweets, **III:** 714
Babyface *See* Edmonds, Kenneth "Babyface"
Back to Africa movement, **III:** 675
Bad Boy Entertainment, **V:** 1051
Badu, Erykah, **V:** *1045*
Baer, Max, **V:** 1194
Bahamas, **II: 285–286**
Bailey, DeFord, **V:** 1074

Bailey, Pearl, **IV: 892**
Bailey v. Patterson, **I:** 33
Bain, Myra, **IV:** 783
Baker, Anita, **V: 1046–1047,** *1047*
Baker, David, **IV: 926–927 V:** 981
Baker, Ella, **II: 350–351**
Baker, Gene, **V:** 1181
Baker, George *See* Father Divine
Baker, Harry, **III:** 525
Baker, Houston A., Jr., **III:** 664, **715–716**
Baker, Joseph Vernon, **I:** 79
Baker, Josephine, **IV:** 880, *881,* **892–893,** 917
Baker, Kristin, **V:** *1226*
Baker, Penniniah, **III:** 696
Baker v. Carr, **II:** 458
Baker, Vernon, **I:** 109
Bakke, Allan P., **I:** 52 **II:** 463
Balanchine, George, **IV:** 894, 897, 906, 910, 911
Balboa, Vasco Nuñez de, **I:** 1 **II:** 236
Baldwin, E.J. "Lucky," **I:** 182
Baldwin, James, **III:** 602, 712, **716,** *717*
Baldwin, James Prize, **III:** 714
Baldwin, Maria Louise, **I:** 200 **III: 632–633**
Baldwin, Ruth Standish, **II:** 396
Baldwin, Violet, **I:** 206
Baldwin, William H., **II:** 396
Balkan War (1999), **I:** 83
Ball, James, **I:** *144* **V:** 1090
Ballard, Florence, **V:** 1078, 1084
Ballard, Hank, **V:** 1036
Ballet and ballet dancers *See* Dance and dancers
Ballou, Charles C., **V:** 1214, 1215
Baltimore Afro-American newspaper, **IV:** 777
  headquarters, **IV:** *754*
Baltimore Conference, **I:** 188
Baltimore, Maryland
  African American firsts, **III:** 532 **V:** 1111
Baltimore's Black American Museum, **V:** 1130
Bambaataa, Afrika, **V:** 984, 1044
Bambara, Toni C., **III: 716–717**
Bancroft, Anne, **III:** 715
Band of Gypsys, **V:** 1061
Banda, H. Kamazu, **II:** 261–262
Banda, Hastings, **II:** 227
Bandung Conference, **II:** 382
Banfield, William C., **III:** 664
Bankhead, Dan, **I:** 91
Banks and bankers, **I:** 19, 72 **II:** 434 **III:** 566 *See also* name of specific bank, e.g., Freedom National Bank
  African American firsts, **I:** 209 **III:** 592
  African American women's firsts, **I:** 88, 222 **III:** 593
Banks, blood *See* Blood and blood banks
Banks, Ernie, **V: 1181**

Banks, Tyra, **I:** 106
Banks v. Perks, **I:** 50
Banks, William, **IV: 762–763**
Banneker, Benjamin, **I:** 6, 85, 198 **V:** 1137, **1151**
  landmarks, **I:** 198, 220
Banneker-Douglass Museum, **I:** 198
Banning, James Herman, **V:** 1142
Bannister, Edward Mitchell, **V:** 1090, **1100**
  works by, **V:** *1091*
Baptism (Christian)
  African American firsts, **I:** 85
Baptist Church, **III:** 672, 693 *See also* Churches; Religion
  African American firsts, **I:** 103, 192 **III:** 672, 700
  African American women's firsts, **III:** 695
  biographical profiles of ministers, **III:** 695, 696–697, 698, 700, 704, 705
  landmarks, **I:** 179, 191, 192, 203, 207
  organizations and associations, **II:** 421
Baraka, Imamu Amiri, **III: 717–718,** *718,* 720, 747 **IV:** 882 **V:** 983
  and National Black Convention, **I:** 49, 50
Barbados, **II: 286–287**
Barber, Amzi L., **I:** 187
Barber-Scotia College, **III:** 651
Barbour, William H., **I:** 81
Barbuda, **II: 284**
Barden Cablevision, **IV:** 763
Barden, Donald, **IV:** *763,* **763–764**
Bargonetti, Jill, **V:** 1145
Barker, Lucius, **III:** 664
Barnes, Ernie, **V: 1100**
Barnett, Charlie, **IV:** 904 **V:** 1022
Barnett, Ferdinand Lee, **II:** 370
Barnett, Ross, **I:** 161
Barrett, Delois, **IV:** 968
Barrett, Jacquelyn, **I:** 72, 104
Barristers *See* Law and lawyers
Barry, Marion S., **I:** 72 **III: 500,** *500,* 522, 527, 715
  drug charges, **I:** 67, 68
Bars Fight, **I:** 4 **III:** 742
Barth, Karl, **III:** 695
Barthé, Richmond, **V: 1100,** *1101*
Barthelmy, Sidney John, **III: 500–501,** *501*
Bartholomew, David, **V:** 1052
Baseball and baseball players, **V:** 1169–1170, 1178–1204
  African American firsts, **I:** 27, 88, 91, 94, 109, 210 **V:** 1181, 1187
  African American women's firsts, **I:** 94 **V:** 1178
  breaking of Babe Ruth's record, **I:** 50
  significance of Jackie Robinson, **I:** 79 **V:** 1169, 1170
Baseball awards and championships
  African American firsts, **I:** 93, 104

Baseball Hall of Fame *See* National Baseball
     Hall of Fame
Baseball league presidents
     African American firsts, **I:** 103 **V:** 1170, 1203
Baseball teams and managers, **I:** 63
     African American firsts, **I:** 86, 88, 91, 99 **III:** 586 **V:**
        1170, 1199
Baseball umpires
     African American firsts, **I:** 97, 104
Basie, William "Count," **I:** 96 **V:** 978, **987–988,** *988,*
     1013, 1026, 1033
Basilio, Carmen, **V:** 1200
Basketball and basketball players, **I:** 84 **III:** 584 **V:**
        1173–1174, 1178–1204
     African American firsts, **I:** 93, 107 **V:** 1173,
        1187, 1199
     African American women's firsts, **I:** 83 **V:** 1188
Basketball awards and championships
     African American firsts, **I:** 100
     African American women's firsts, **I:** 110 **V:** 1188
Basketball coaches, **V:** 1202–1203, 1203–1204
     African American firsts, **I:** 96, 97, 100, 105, 106,
        108 **V:** 1174, 1200, 1203
     African American women's firsts, **I:** 110
     most winning in NBA, **I:** 105
Basketball Hall of Fame *See* National Basketball
     Hall of Fame
Basketball leagues and teams
     African American firsts, **I:** 89 **V:** 1173
     and salary caps, **V:** 1175
Basketball managers and referees
     African American firsts, **I:** 99
     African American women's firsts, **I:** 107
Basquiat, Jean-Michel, **V: 1100–1101**
Bassett, Angela, **III:** 736 **IV: 856 V:** 1062
Bassett, Ebenezer Don Carlos, **I:** 87 **III:** 492, *494*
Basutoland *See* Lesotho
Bates, Daisy Lee Gatson, **II: 351–352,** *352*
Bates, Lucius Christopher, **II:** 352
Bates v. Little Rock, **II:** 397
Batson v. Kentucky, **II:** 467
Battle for Fort Wagner, **I:** 199
Battle, Kathleen, **IV: 927,** *927*
Battle of Bunker Hill, **I:** 5 **V:** 1205
Battle of Ocean Pond, **I:** 190
Battle of Yorktown, **I:** 220
Batts, Deborah A., **II: 476**
Baumgarten, David, **IV:** 863
Baxter, Ivy, **IV:** 897
Baylor, Elgin, **V: 1181**
BDP (Music group), **V:** 1070
The Beach Boys, **V:** 1047
Beaches *See* name of specific beach, e.g., American
     Beach, Florida
Beacons, radio, **V:** 1167

Beale Street Historic District, **I:** 218, *219*
Beam, Joseph, **III:** 730
Beamon, Bob, **V:** 1175
Bean, Carl, **III: 693**
Beard, Andrew J., **V: 1151**
Bearden, Romare, **V:** 1094, **1101**
     works by, **V:** *1101*
Beardsley, John, **V:** 1098
The Beatles, **V:** 1082
Beauty contests and contestants
     African American firsts, **I:** 100, 103, 104, 105, 106
        IV: 874 **V:** 1188
Beauty industry and salons, **I:** 195, 211 **III:** 578, 590
Beavers, Louise, **IV:** 831
Bebe Miller Dance Company, **IV:** 909
Bebop music and musicians, **V:** 978–979, 1011 *See*
     also Music and musicians
Bechet, Sydney, **V:** 976, **988**
Beckworth Pass, **I:** 182
Beckwourth, James P., **I:** 8, 182, 184, 206, 217 **III:**
     583, **583–584**
Beckwourth Trail, **I:** 206
Bedford-Stuyvesant Restoration Center for Arts and
     Culture, **V:** 1132
Before the Mayflower: A History of the Negro in
     America, **III:** 633
Belafonte, Harry, **IV:** 833, *834,* **856**
Belcher, Jacquelyn M., **I:** 106
Belize, **II: 287–288**
Bell, Alexander Graham, **V:** 1137, 1161
Bell, Derrick Albert, Jr., **II: 476**
Bell, Haley, **IV:** 776
Bell, Hubert T., Jr., **I:** 106
Bell, Thomas, **I:** 186 **V:** 1200
Bell v. Maryland, **II:** 469
Bell, William, **V:** 1060
Bellson, Louis, **IV:** 892
Beloved (Book), **III:** 738
Beloved (Film), **IV:** 838
Belton, Sharon Sayles, **I:** 104 **III: 501**
Ben & Jerry's Homemade Ice Cream, Inc., **III:** 588
Ben Vereen School of the Performing Arts, **IV:** 916
Benedict College, **III:** 651
Benezet, Anthony, **I:** 5 **III:** 621
Benin, **II: 241–242**
Ben-Israel, Ben Ami, **III:** 688 **IV:** 832
Benitez, Wilfred, **V:** 1193
Bennett College, **III:** 624, 651
Bennett, Lerone, Jr., **III: 633**
Benny, Jack, **IV:** 892
Benson, George, **IV:** 943
Bentsen, Lloyd, **III:** 522
Berea College, **I:** 196
Berea College v. Kentucky, **I:** 21
Bermuda, **II: 288**

Bernac, Pierre, **IV:** 934, 946
Bernadotte, Folke, **III:** 507
Bernstein, Leonard, **IV:** 942, 946, 955
Berry, Chuck, **V:** 1038, *1038*, **1047,** 1067
Berry Gordy, Jr. Enterprises, **V:** 1058
Berry, Halle, **III:** 728 **IV: 857,** *857*
Berry, Mary Frances, **I:** 58, 59, 60 **III: 501,** *502,* 664
Berry, Shawn Allen, **I:** 83
BET *See* Black Entertainment Television (BET)
Bethel Charity School, **I:** 8
Bethune Council House, **I:** 185
Bethune, John, **IV:** 927
Bethune, Mary McLeod, **III:** 591, 624, *633,* **633–634**
    excerpt from last will and testament, **I:** 158
    landmarks, **I:** 185, *185,* 189
    and National Council of Negro Women, **I:** 24
       II: 406, 440
Bethune Museum and Archives, **I:** 185 **V:** 1129
Bethune, Thomas "Blind Tom," **I:** 192 **IV:** 922,
    927, 928
Bethune-Cookman College, **I:** 158, 185, 189 **III:**
    624, 633, 651
A Better Chance, **II: 418**
Between God and Gangsta Rap, **III:** 639
Beulah, **IV:** 835
Beulah M. Douglas Collection, **I:** 198
Bevel, James, **II:** 364
Beverly Hills Cop, **IV:** 838
Bezanson, Philip, **IV:** 925
Bibbs, Charles, **V:** 1096
Bibbs, Henry, **V:** 1090
Bible Way Church of Our Lord Jesus Christ World
    Wide, Inc., **III: 687** *See also* Churches; Religion
Bicyclists *See* Cyclists
Biddle, Nicholas, **I:** 86
Big Daddy Kane, **V:** 1073
Biggers Art Sales Traveling Gallery, **V:** 1133
Biggers, John, **V: 1101–1102**
Biggie Smalls *See* Notorious B.I.G.
Biko, Steven, **II:** 383, 393
Bilbo, Theodore, **IV:** 867
Bill of Rights, **I:** 116
Billingsley, Andrew, **III:** 595, 596
Billington, James H., **I:** 74
Billops, Camille, **V: 1102**
Billy the Kid, **I:** 207
Bing, Dave, **III: 584,** *584*
Bing Steel, Inc., **III:** 584
Bingo Long Traveling All-Stars & Motor Kings,
    IV: 838
Biology and biologists, **V:** 1154, 1161
    African American firsts, **V:** 1139
Birch, St. Adolpho A., Jr., **I:** 106
Bird, **IV:** 838
Birdsong, Cindy, **V:** 1070

Birmingham, Alabama
    African American firsts, **I:** 99
The Birmingham Manifesto, **I:** 162
Birth of a Nation, **IV:** 829
Birth of a Race, **IV:** 830, 839
Birthplaces *See* Chapter 4 for birthplaces by city
    and state
Births, multiple *See* Multiple births
Bisexuality *See* Gay, lesbian, and bisexual issues
Bishop College, **I:** 64, 67
Bishop, Sanford D., Jr., **III:** 496
Bishop State Community College, **III:** 651
Bishops *See also* Ministers; Monsignors; name of
    specific church, e.g., African Methodist
    Episcopal Church; Priests
    African American firsts, **I:** 85, 87, 88, 102, 216 **III:**
      698, 700, 701
    African American women's firsts, **I:** 100, 102
      III: 697, 699
Bismarck, Otto von, **II:** 380
Bispham Medal, **IV:** 956
Blachard, James, **III:** 499
Black Abolitionist Papers Project, **III:** 659
Black Academy of Arts and Letters, **IV:** 943
Black Aesthetic movement, **II:** 383 **III:** 712–713, *713*
    V: 1094–1096 *See also* Authors; Literature
Black, Alfred, **I:** 39
Black American Studies (Western Michigan
    Unversity), **III:** 659
Black American West Museum and Heritage Center,
    I: 183 **V:** 1129
Black Americans for Life, **II: 423**
Black and Indian Mission Office, **II: 423**
Black Archives of Mid-America, **V:** 1131
Black Archives Research Center and Museum,
    V: 1129
Black Art Gallery, **V:** 1135
Black Artists Guild, **V:** 1133
Black Arts movement *See* Black Aesthetic movement
Black Arts Repertory Theater, **III:** 717
Black Arts Research Center, **III:** 659
Black Arts/West, **III:** 720
Black Bob, **V:** 989
Black Books Bulletin, **III:** 737
Black bourgeoisie, **I:** 211
Black Broadway, **IV:** 894
Black Bull Publishing Company, **V:** 1085
Black Caucus of the American Library Association,
    II: 423
Black Christian Nationalism, **III:** 692
Black churches *See* Churches
Black Civil War Veterans' Memorial, **I:** 222
Black Classic Press, **IV:** 751
Black Coaches Association, **II: 424**
Black Codes of Mississippi, **I:** 136–138

Black College Day, **I:** 54

Black Cultural Exchange Center, **V:** 1134

Black Data Processing Associates, **II: 424**

Black diaspora, **II: 225–315 V:** 1146–1147 *See also*
    Africa and Africans

Black English *See* Ebonics

Black Enterprise, **IV:** 755, 770

Black Entertainment and Sports Lawyers Association,
    II: 424

Black Entertainment Television (BET), **I:** 106 **IV:** 761,
    774, 826, 837

Black Environmental Science Trust, **V:** 1145

Black Expo, **I:** 48 **IV:** 968

Black Family Reunion, **II:** 406

Black Filmmaker Foundation, **II: 424 V:** 1132

Black Filmmakers Hall of Fame, Inc., **II: 424**

Black Folk Arts, **V:** 1131

Black Girl, **IV:** 839

Black Heritage Museum, **V:** 1129

Black Heritage Trail, **I:** 198

Black Historical Museum and Cultural Center,
    V: 1135

Black History Month, **I:** 23, 189 **II:** 417, 418 **III:** 650

Black Horizons on the Hill, **III:** 747

Black, Joe, **I:** 94

Black Journal See Tony Brown's Black Journal

The Black Librarian in America, **III:** 643

*Black Lies, White Lies: The Truth According to Tony
    Brown*, **IV:** 766

Black Like Me, **IV:** 839

Black Literary Society, **IV:** 769

Black Marxism, **II:** 383

Black Masons, **IV:** 763

Black Methodists for Church Renewal, **II: 424** *See
    also* Churches; Religion

Black Muslims (Organization), **II:** 390 *See also*
    Nation of Islam

Black national anthem *See Lift Every Voice and Sing*

Black National Political Convention, **I:** 50

Black nationalism and nationalists, **I:** 50 **II: 377–392**
    See also Black Power movement
    biographical profiles, **II:** 384–392
    and Christianity, **II:** 379–380
    early movements, **II:** 378–380
    ideology, **II:** 377
    and Marxism, **II:** 383
    and non-Christian religions, **III:** 676
    twentieth century, **II:** 380–383
    web sites, **V:** 1147

Black Nativity, **IV:** 883

Black Organizational Autonomy (BOA) Model,
    III: 565

Black Panther Legacy Tour, **I:** 80

Black Panther Manifesto, **I:** 169–171

Black Panther party, **I:** 169 **II:** 383, 385, 398, 411 *See
    also* Black Power movement
    convictions of members, **I:** 43, 44
    demonstrations by, **I:** *170*
    excerpt from *Black Panther Manifesto*, **I:** 169–171
    founding, **I:** 36 **II:** 411, 415
    ten-point program, **I:** 169–171

Black Periodical Literature Project (1827-1940),
    III: 659

Black Power movement, **I:** 39 **II:** 352, 353 *See
    also* Black nationalism and nationalists; Black
    Panther party
    salute incident, **V:** 1175

Black Pride movement, **II:** 383 *See also* Black
    nationalism and nationalists; Black Power
    movement

Black Psychiatrists of America, **II: 424**

Black Radical Congress, **II:** 383

Black Rage, **V:** 1154

"Black Rattlers" *See* 369th Infantry Regiment

Black Revolutionary War Patriots Foundation, **II:
    425**

Black Rock Coalition, **II: 425**

Black Rodeo, **IV:** 839

"The Black Slate," **III:** 500

Black Spectrum Theater Co., **V:** 1132

Black Star Shipping Line, **II:** 389

Black Stars, **IV:** 755

Black Swan, **V:** 1005

Black Theology movement, **III:** 677

Black vaudeville, **IV:** 879–880

Black Veterans for Social Justice, **II: 425**

Black Women in Church and Society, **II: 425** *See
    also* Churches; Religion

Black Women in Publishing, **II: 425**

Black Women Organized for Educational
    Development, **II: 425**

Black Women's Network, **II: 425**

Black Women's Roundtable on Voter Participation,
    II: 425

Black World Foundation, **II: 426**

Blackboard Jungle, **IV:** 839

Blackburn, Robert, **V: 1102,** *1103*

Blackface minstrelsy, **IV:** 830, 878

Blackman, Cindy, **V:** 985

The Blacks, **IV:** 882

Blacks in Government, **II: 426**

Blacks in Law Enforcement, **II: 426**

Blackside, Inc., **IV:** 864

Blackstreet, **V:** 1077

Blackwell, Bumps, **V:** 1052, 1071

Blacula, **IV:** 839

Blair, Henry, **I:** 85 **V:** 1137

Blair, Mary, **IV:** 881

Blake, James Hubert "Eubie," **IV:** 883, *893,* **893–894,** 915

Blakey, Art, **V:** 985, **988–989**

Blalock, Alfred, **V:** 1166

Blanchard, Terence, **V:** 984

Bland, James A., **I:** 26, 79, 215

Blanton, Jimmy, **V:** 978, **989**

Bledsoe, Jules, **IV:** 881

Blige, Mary J., **V:** **1047,** *1048*

Blood and blood banks, **I:** 26, 31 **V:** 1155

Blood of Jesus, **IV:** 839

Bloody Sunday, **I:** 180

Blow, Kurtis, **V:** 1044

Blow, Peter, **II:** 340

The Blue Angels, **I:** 101, 105

Blue Chip Broadcasting Ltd., **IV:** 759

Blue Collar, **IV:** 839

The Blue Notes, **V:** 1073

Blue, Thomas F., **I:** 196

The Bluebelles, **V:** 1070

Bluefield State College, **III:** 651

Blues and blues musicians, **V:** **973–1033** *See also* Music and musicians

    biographical profiles, **V:** 986–1033

    Chicago style, **V:** 975

    Delta style, **V:** 1021

    early recordings, **V:** 974, 984

    future, **V:** 985

    history and styles, **V:** 973

    landmarks, **I:** 218

    migration, **V:** 974–975

    Mississippi Delta style, **V:** 973–974

    Piedmont style, **V:** 974

    and ragtime, **V:** 973

    Texas style, **V:** 974

    varied sounds and styles, **V:** 975–976

    web sites, **V:** 1149

    women musicians, **V:** 984–985

Blues City Cultural Center, **V:** 1134

Bluford, Guion, **I:** 52, 100, *101* **V:** 1143, **1151**

Blumenbach, Johann Friedrich, **I:** 5

Blunden, Geraldyne, **IV:** 890

Blunted on Reality, **V:** 1056

Blunton, Dain, **I:** 101

Blyden, Edward Wilmot, **II:** 380, **384–385,** *385*

Boards of directors *See also* Businesses and business professionals

    African American firsts, **I:** 107 **IV:** 945

Boating accidents, **I:** 218

Bob Jones University v. IRS, **I:** 58 **II:** 463

The Bobby Jones Gospel Hour, **IV:** 968

Bob-Lo v. Michigan, **II:** 468

Body and Soul, **IV:** 839

Bodybuilders

    African American firsts, **I:** 98 **V:** 1177

The Bodyguard, **V:** 1062

Boers Nationalist movement, **II:** 227

Bok, Derek, **III:** 631

Bolden, Buddy, **V:** **989**

Bolden, Charles F., Jr., **I:** 104 **V:** 1143, **1152,** *1152*

Boley, Oklahoma, **I:** 214 **III:** 547

Bolin, Jane Matilda, **I:** 25, 90, *90* **II:** 453, **476–477**

Bolivia, **II:** **288–289**

Bolling v. Sharpe, **III:** 627

Bombings, **I:** 46, 210 **II:** 363, 367, 401 *See also* Church bombings and burnings; Racial violence

Bonaire *See* Netherlands Antilles

Bonaparte, Napoleon, **II:** 237, 340

Bond, Julian, **I:** 48, 81 **II:** 403 **III:** **502–503,** *503*

Bonds, Barry, **I:** 109 **V:** **1181**

Bonds, Bobby, **V:** 1181

Bonds, Margaret, **IV:** 924, **928,** *928*

Bonner, T.D., **III:** 584

Bontemps, Arna Wendell, **I:** 197, 219 **III:** *718,* **718–719**

Book of Life, **I:** 128

Book publishing and publishers, **IV:** 749–753, 787–790 *See also* Authors; Media and publishing

    African American firsts, **IV:** 749, 750

    biographical profiles, **IV:** 762–787

    of comic books, **IV:** 752–753

    commercial, **IV:** 751–752

    imprints of organizations and institutions, **IV:** 750–751

    institutional, **IV:** 750

    oldest African American publisher, **IV:** 751

    of religious material, **IV:** 749–750

Booker T. Washington Burial Society, **III:** 587

Booker T. Washington Business College, **III:** 587

Booker T. Washington Sanitarium, **II:** 415

Books *See* Authors; Novels and novelists; Plays and playwrights (Written); Poetry and poets

Booms, sonic *See* Sonic booms

Boone Infantry Brass Band Quick Step sheet music, **IV:** *922*

Boone, John "Blind," **IV:** 922, **928**

Boone, Sarah, **V:** 1138

Boot Hill Cemetery, **I:** 181

Bootee, Duke, **V:** 1044

Booth, Sherman, **I:** 15

Boothe, John Wilkes, **I:** 190

Borde, Percival, **IV:** 887

Borg, Bjorn, **V:** 1180

Bork, Robert H., **II:** 482, 488

Boston Common, **I:** 199

Boston Massacre, **I:** 5, 85, 199 **II:** 338 **V:** 1205

Boston, Ralph, **V:** 1175

Boston Riot, **I:** 201

Boston Suffrage League, **I:** 201

Boto, Nyo, **III:** 715

Botswana, **II: 242–243**
Bouchet, Edward E., **I:** 87 **V:** 1139
Boukouré, Cheik, **II:** 233
Boulanger, Nadia, **IV:** 945, 947, 948, 953, 954
Boulé (Fraternity), **II:** 399, **443**
Bowditch, William I., **I:** 199
Bowe, Riddick, **V:** 1189
Bowen, William G., **III:** 631
Bowers, Sam, **I:** 40, 84
Bowie State University, **III:** 651
Bowling and bowlers, **I:** 101 **V:** 1177
Bowman, Thea, **III: 693**
Boxing and boxers, **V:** 1171–1173, 1178–1204
    African American firsts, **I:** 89, 107 **IV:** 846 **V:**
        1171, 1191
    wealthiest of all time, **V:** 1173
Boxley, George, **I:** 8
Boy Scouts of America, **I:** 220
Boycotts, **I:** 23, 68, 179 *See also* Civil rights
        campaigns and demonstrations; name of
        specific boycott, e.g., Montgomery Bus Boycott
Boyd, Henry, **V:** 1138
Boyd, Richard Henry, **III:** 675, 689 **IV:** 749
Boykin, Otis, **V:** 1143
Boyle, Robert, **III:** 576
Boyz II Men, **V:** 1054
Boyz N the Hood, **IV:** 839, 871
Bozeman, Maggie, **I:** 57
Brackett, David, **V:** 1039
Brackett, Edmund, **V:** 1114
Braddock, Jim, **V:** 1194
Bradford, Alex, **IV:** 884
Bradford, Janie, **V:** 1058
Bradford, Sarah, **II:** 341
Bradford, William, **I:** 199
Bradley, Edward R., **IV:** 759, **764,** *764*
Bradley, Gwendolyn, **IV: 928–929**
Bradley, Ralph, **I:** 100
Bradley, Thomas, **I:** 50, 57, 66, 99 **III:** *504,* **504–505,**
        IV: 783
    and Rodney King beating, **I:** 71 **II:** 349
Brady, Paul L., **IV:** 768
Bragg, Janet Harmon, **V:** 1142
Branham, George, **I:** 101 **V:** 1177
Branson, Lloyd, **V:** 1106
Braugher, Andre, **IV: 857**
Braun, Carol Moseley, **I:** 73, 82, 103, *104* **III:** 496
Brawley, Twana, **II:** 366
Braxton, Joanne, **III:** 664
Brazil, **II: 289–290**
Breast cancer, **III:** 609 *See also* Cancer and cancer
        research
Breed's Hill, **I:** 199
Brewer, Lawrence Russell, **I:** 83
Brewster, W. Herbert, **IV:** 961

Bridges *See* name of specific bridge, e.g., Red Oak
        Creek Covered Bridge
Bridgewater, Dee Dee, **V:** 983
*A Brief Account of the Settlement and Present
        Situation of the Colony of Sierre Leone*
    title page, **II:** *378*
Briggs v. Eliot, **III:** 627
Briggs-Hall, Austin, **IV:** 881
Bring in 'Da Noise, Bring in 'Da Funk, **IV:** 884, 900
Briscoe, Martin, **I:** 98
Briscoe v. Louisiana, **I:** 32
Briseno, Theodore J., **I:** 74
Bristow, Lonnie, **I:** 105
British Honduras *See* Belize
Britt, Mai, **IV:** 859
Britton, Crystal A., **V:** 1097
Broadcasting, radio *See* Radio broadcasting and
        personalities
Broadcasting, television *See* Television and
        television shows
Broadside Poetry Workshop, **IV:** 777
Broadside Poets Theater, **IV:** 777
Broadside Press, **IV:** 777
Brock, Lou, **V: 1182**
Brockman Gallery, **V:** 1128
Brokaw, Tom, **IV:** 771
Brokers, stock *See* Stockbrokers
Bronze Booklets, **IV:** 751
Bronze Stars, **I:** 109
Brooke, Edward W., **I:** *44,* 49, 51, 97 **II:** 334 **III: 505,**
        505
Brookes (Ship), **I:** *3*
Brooklyn Excelsiors (Baseball team), **I:** 86
Brooklyn Museum of Art, **V:** 1132
Brooklyn Women's Hospital Dispensary, **V:** 1140
Brooks, Arthur, **V:** 1072
Brooks, Gwendolyn, **I:** 93, *94* **II:** 383 **III:** 712, **719,**
        719
Brooks, Richard, **V:** 1072
Broonzy, William Lee Conley, **V: 989**
The Brother from Another Planet, **IV:** 839
Brother John, **IV:** 839
Brother to Brother: New Writings by Black Gay Men,
        III: 730
Brotherhood of Sleeping Car Porters, **I:** 22
        II: 345, 412
Brothers and Keepers, **III:** 746
Brown & Williamson Tobacco Company, **I:** 81
Brown, Alonzo, **V:** 1059
Brown, Ann, **IV:** 883
Brown, "Aunt Clara," **I:** 183
Brown Belle Bottling Company, **III:** 587
Brown, Benjamin, **I:** 38
Brown, Billings, **II:** 336, 345
Brown, Bobby, **V: 1048,** 1062

Brown Chapel African Methodist Episcopal Church
    (Selma, Alabama), **I:** 180
Brown, Charles, **V:** 1049
Brown, Charlotte Hawkins, **I:** 212 **III:** 624, **634–635**
Brown, Clarence "Gatemouth," **V: 989**
Brown, Claude, **III: 720**
Brown, Clifford, **V: 990,** 1024
Brown, Corrine, **I:** 72 **III:** 496
Brown, Edward Sumner, **III:** 634
Brown, Elaine, **II: 385**
Brown, Frank, **III:** 664
Brown, George Stanford, **I:** 100
Brown, H. "Rap" *See* al-Amin, Jamil Abdullah
Brown, Henry, **IV:** 877
Brown, J. Anthony, **IV:** 775
Brown, James (Musician), **II:** 366 **V:** *1039,* 1040,
    1048–1049, 1050, 1060, 1083
Brown, James (Television personality), **IV: 764–765**
Brown, James Willie, Jr. *See* Komunyakaa, Yusef
Brown, Jerry, **II:** 385
Brown, Jesse L., **I:** 73, *73,* 93 **III:** 496 **V:** 1223, 1226,
    1227–1228
Brown, Jill, **V:** 1142
Brown, Jim, **V:** 1171, *1182,* **1182–1183,** 1197, 1202
Brown, Jimmy, **V:** 1049
Brown, Joan Myers, **IV:** 890
Brown, John, **I:** 15, 125 **II:** 330, 341 **III:** 491
    landmarks, **I:** 196, 201, 211, 213, 223
Brown, Karen McCarthy, **III:** 682
Brown, Lee P., **I:** 80, 108
Brown, Leonard Douglas, **I:** 50
Brown, Les, **IV: 765**
Brown, Linda, **I:** 196
Brown, Linda Beatrice, **III:** 664
Brown, Marie Dutton, **III: 584–585**
Brown, Morris, **III:** 673
Brown, Raymond Matthews, **V: 990,** 999
Brown, Ronald H., **I:** 65, 73, 77, 102 **III: 505–506,**
    506
Brown, Ruth, **V: 1049**
Brown, Tony, **I:** 54 **IV:** 756, 760, *760,* **765–766**
Brown v. Board of Education of Topeka, Kansas, **I:**
    28–29, 155 **II:** 461 **III:** 626, 627
    celebrating of ruling, **I:** *29*
    excerpt from ruling, **I:** 155–157
    and Kenneth Clarke, **III:** 636
    landmarks, **I:** 196
    and NAACP, **II:** 346, 396
    reopening, **I:** 61
Brown v. Louisiana, **I:** 37
Brown, Wesley A., **I:** 93 **IV:** 765 **V:** 1222
Brown, Willa B., **V:** 1142
Brown, William, III, **I:** 44
Brown, William Wells, **I:** 7, 13, 86 **III: 720,** 730
Brown, Willie L., Jr., **I:** 105

Brown, Wilson, **I:** 204
Browne, Marjorie L., **V: 1152**
Brownlie, Chris, **III:** 613
Bruce, Blanche K., **I:** 185, 214 **II:** 334 **III:** 492, **506–**
    507, *507*
Brustein, Robert, **III:** 747
Brutality, police *See* Police brutality
Bryan, Andrew, **I:** 5, 192 **III:** 672, 700
Bryant, Bear, **V:** 1199
Bryant, Clora, **V:** 984
Bryce, Herrington J., **III:** 664
Bryce-Laporte, Roy S., **III:** 664
Bryson, Peabo, **V:** 1055
Bubbles, John, **IV:** 883, **894,** *894*
Buchanan, James, **I:** 15
Buchanan v. Warley, **I:** 22 **II:** 470
Buck and the Preacher, **IV:** 839
Buckmire, Ron, **IV: 766**
Buckshot LeFonque, **V:** 1016
Budzyn, Walter, **I:** 72, 74
Bufano, Beniamino, **V:** 1111
Buffalo Soldiers, **V:** 1209
Buffalo Soldiers (Film), **IV:** 840
Buildings, African American-owned *See* Real estate
Bullard, Eugene Jacques, **I:** 89
Bullard, Robert L., **V:** 1214
Bulldogging *See* Steer wrestling
Bullins, Ed, **III: 720,** *721,* 741
Bumbry, Grace Ann, **IV: 929,** *929*
Bunche, Ralph J., **I:** 27, *94* **II:** 361 **III:** *507,* **507–508**
    landmarks, **I:** 186, 202, 209
    and Nobel Peace Prizes, **I:** 28, 93
Bunker Hill, **I:** 199
Bunzel, John H., **I:** 58
Bureau of Educational Research, **III:** 659
Bureau of Refugees, Freedmen, and Abandoned
    Lands *See* Freedmen's Bureau
Burger King restaurants, **III:** 588
Burger, Warren E., **I:** 50, 58 **II:** 462
Burial grounds *See* name of specific graveyard, e.g.,
    Elmwood Cemetery
Burke, Selma, **V: 1102–1103**
Burke, Yvonne Braithwaite, **III: 508,** *508*
Burkina Faso, **II: 243–244**
Burks, Mary Fair, **II:** 365
Burleigh, Harry Thacker, **I:** 210, 215 **IV: 929–930**
Burnings of churches *See* Church bombings and
    burnings
Burns, Anthony, **I:** 14, *14*
Burns, Francis, **III:** 674
Burns, Tommy, **V:** 1191
Burr, Seymour, **I:** 199
Burris, Chuck, **III: 508–509**
Burroughs, James, **II:** 369
Burroughs, Nannie Helen, **III:** 624, **635,** *635,* 693

Burrows, Stephen, **V: 1103**
Burruss, K.H., **III:** 689
Burstyn, Ellen, **III:** 715
Burundi, **II: 244**
The Bus, **IV:** 840
Bus segregation *See* Public transportation segregation
Bush, Anita, **IV: 894**
Bush, George, Sr., **I:** 69, 70, 71 **V:** 1163
   and civil rights, **I:** 67, 68, 174
     excerpt from message on Civil Rights Act (1990),
      I: 173
Businesses and business professionals, **III: 575–594**
   in 1980s and 1990s, **III:** 580
   African American firsts, **I:** 96, 98, 108 **III:** 575, 579,
     592 **V:** 1005, 1066, 1158
   biographical profiles, **III:** 582–594 **IV:** 772, 774–775
   Colonial America, **III:** 575
   Durham, North Carolina, **III:** 578–579
   early twentieth century, **III:** 576–579
   equal employment opportunity, **I:** 25
   geographic distribution, **III:** 580
   and information technology, **III:** 581–582
   organizations and associations, **II:** 427, 430, 433–
     434, 436, 438, 445
   post-Civil Rights era, **III:** 579–580
   post-Civil War America, **III:** 576
   pre-Civil War America, **III:** 575–576
   recent economic trends, **III:** 580–582
   underrepresentation, **III:** 581
   web sites, **V:** 1148
Busing, **I:** 46, 47, 49, 56, 69 *See also* Public
   transportation segregation
Busoni, Ferruccio, **IV:** 939
Bussey, Charles M., **V:** 1222
Busts (Monuments)
   African American firsts, **I:** 52
Butler, Benjamin, **V:** 1206, 1207
Butler, Jerry, **V:** 1072
Butler, John S., **III:** 664
Butler, Nicholas Murray, **V:** 1214
Butler, Norman, **I:** 35
Butler, Octavia E., **III: 720–721**
Butler, Richard Girnt, **I:** 63
Butts, Calvin O., **III: 693–694**
Buy Freedom Network, **IV:** 766
Bynoe, Peter C.B., **V:** 1174
Byrd, Donald, **IV: 894–895 V:** 1003
Byrd, Harry, **I:** 29
Byrd, James, Jr., **I:** 83 **II:** 350

C

Cabez de Vaca, Alvar Nuñez, **II:** 317
Cabin in the Sky, **IV:** 840
Cabin songs, **IV:** 958–960

Cabinet members (Federal)
   African American firsts, **I:** 36, 97 **III:** 534, 537
   African American women's firsts, **I:** 99, 107
Cabinet members (State)
   African American firsts, **III:** 537
Cable networks and television, **IV:** 761, 826 *See also*
   Television and television shows
   African American firsts, **I:** 106 **IV:** 837
Cable News Network (CNN), **IV:** 761
Cadoria, Sherian G., **V: 1228**
Caesar, "Big Jim," **IV:** 964
Caesar, Shirley, **IV: 964**
Caicos Islands, **II: 312–313**
Cain, Richard, **III:** 675
The Cairo Illinois Gazette, **I:** 88
Cakewalk dance, **IV:** 880 *See also* Dance and dancers
Caldwell, James, **I:** 199
Calf ropers *See also* Steer wrestling
   African American firsts, **I:** 109
Calhoun, John C., **II:** 329
California, **I:** 13
   African American firsts, **I:** 57
   African American museums and galleries, **V:** 1128
   African American newspapers, **IV:** 791–794
   African American radio stations, **IV:** 812–813
   African American television stations, **IV:** 826
   landmarks, **I:** 182–183
California Afro-American Museum, **V:** 1128
California Attorney General, **II:** 371
California Fair Employment and Housing
   Commission, **II:** 371
"Call" for initial NAACP conference, **II:** 368, 371
Callender, Clive O., **III:** 664
Calloway, Cab, **V: 990–991**
Camara, Mohamed, **II:** 234
Cambridge, Godfrey, **IV:** 886, 895
Cameras, **V:** 1152
Cameroon, **II: 244–245**
Camp meetings, **IV:** 958
Campaigns, civil rights *See* Civil rights campaigns and
   demonstrations
Campanella, Roy, **I:** 74, 91, 93, *93* **V: 1183**
Campanis, Al, **I:** 63
Campbell, Bill, **III: 509**
Campbell, Chris, **I:** 107
Campbell, Clive, **V:** 1044
Campbell, Edward, Jr., **V:** 1098
Campbell, Mary Schmidt, **V:** 1099
Canada, **I:** 11 **II: 290–291**
Cancer and cancer research, **V:** 1145
   breast, **III:** 609
   prostate, **III:** 609 **V:** 1145
Cancer Research Foundation (Harlem Hospital),
   V: 1141

Candidates, Presidential *See* Presidential candidates
  and nominations
Cane, **III:** 743
Canera, Primo, **V:** 1194
Cannon, Katie, **III:** 677, **694,** 695
Cape Verde, **II: 245–246**
Capital Savings Bank, **I:** 19
Captains, ship *See* Ship captains
The Caravans (Music group), **IV:** 964, 970
Cardiac surgery *See* Surgery and surgeons
Cardozo, Francis, **I:** 188, 216
Careton, S.C., **III:** 690
Carey, Archibald T., Jr., **I:** 93 **III:** 676
Caribbean *See* West Indies
Caring Institute, **I:** 186
Carl Van Vechten Gallery of Fine Arts, **V:** 1135
Carlesimo, P.J., **V:** 1174
Carlos, John, **V:** 1175
Carmen Jones, **IV:** 840
Carmichael, Stokely *See* Toure, Kwame
Carnegie, Andrew, **I:** 20, 196 **III:** 626, 642
Carnegie Corporation, **III:** 626
Carney, William H., **I:** 199 **V:** 1209, **1228–1229**
Carousel, **IV:** 908
Carr, Patrick, **I:** 199
Carr, Randolph, **III:** 691
Carrol, Vinette, **IV:** 883
Carroll, Baikida, **III:** 742
Carroll, Diahann, **I:** 97 **IV:** *835*, 836, **857–858,** 874
Carruthers, George E., **V:** 1143, **1152–1153**
Carry Me Back to Ole Virginia, **I:** 26, 79
Carson, Ben, **V: 1153,** *1153*
Carson, Johnny, **IV:** 896
Carson, Julia, **III:** 497
Carswell, G. Harrold, **I:** 46 **III:** 505
Carter, Ben *See* Ben-Israel, Ben Ami
Carter, Benny, **V:** 978, **991,**1005
Carter G. Woodson Institute for Afro-American and
  African Studies, **III:** 659
Carter, Jimmy, **I:** 51, 52, 53 **III:** 541
  appointment of African Americans, **I:** 51 **II:** 475
    III: 495
Carter, Lisle, **I:** 36
Carter, Mandy, **II: 353**
Carter, Nell, **IV:** 884
Carter, Regina, **V:** 985
Carter, Ron, **V:** 984
Carter, Stephen L., **III:** 664
Caruso, Enrico, **IV:** 904
Carver, George Washington, **I:** 91 **V:** 1139, *1139*,
    1153–1154
  landmarks, **I:** 180, 195, 205
Cary, Lott, **III:** 673
Cary, Mary Ann Shadd, **I:** 186
Casey Jones Railroad Museum, **I:** 218

Cash, Fred, **V:** 1072
Cassavetes, John, **IV:** 858
CasSelle, Malcolm, **III:** *585*, **585–586**
Castanda v. Partida, **II:** 467
Castleberry, Edward J., **IV: 766–767**
Castro, Fidel, **II:** 358
Catering industry, **III:** 576
Catholic Church, **III:** 672 *See also* Churches; Religion
  African American firsts, **I:** 87 **III:** 684,
    698, 700, 701
  African American women's firsts, **I:** 103
  bishops, **III:** 698, 700, 701
  efforts in education, **III:** 621
  membership growth, **III:** 682
  nuns, **III:** 693
  only university run by, **III:** 624
  organizations and associations, **II:** 423, 426,
    431, 434, 438
  position on slavery, **I:** 11
  priests, **III:** 700, 703–704
  racial issues, **III:** 673, 682
  schisms, **III:** 684–685
Catholic Interracial Council of New York, **II: 426**
Catlett, Elizabeth, **V:** 1095, **1103–1104**
  works by, **V:** *1104*
Cato, Gavin, **I:** 70
Cattle War, Lincoln County (1877), **I:** 207
Cayman Islands, **II: 291–292**
CBA (Continental Basketball Association), **I:** 84
Cedar Hill, **I:** 186
Cellar, Emanuel, **I:** 22, 39
Cemeteries *See* name of specific cemetery, e.g.,
    Elmwood Cemetery
Census, **I:** 54, 57
Center for African American Studies (Wesleyan
    University), **III:** 660
Center for African and African-American Studies,
    III: 659
Center for African-American History and Culture,
    III: 659
Center for African/American Studies (University of
    Calinia), **III:** 660
Center for Afro American Studies (Ohio University),
    III: 660
Center for Afro-American and African Studies
    (University of Michigan), **III:** 660
Center for Black Music Research, **III:** 660 **IV:** 924
Center for Black Studies (Northern Illinois
    University), **III:** 660
Center for Black Studies (University of Calinia),
    III: 660
Center for Constitutional Rights, **II: 426**
Center for Multi-Cultural Leadership, **III:** 660
Center for Research on Multi-Ethnic Education,
    III: 660

Center for Southern History and Culture, **III:** 660
Center for Studies of Ethnicity and Race in America, **III:** 660
Center for the Study and Stabilization of the Black Family, **III:** 660
Center for the Study of Black Literature and Culture, **III:** 660
Center for the Study of Civil Rights, **III:** 660
Center for the Study of Race and Ethnicity in America, **III:** 661
Center for the Study of Southern Culture, **III:** 661
Center for Third World Organizing, **II: 426**
Center for Urban Black Studies, **II: 427**
Centers for Disease Control, **I:** 79 **V:** 1156
Central African Republic, **II: 246**
Central America *See* name of specific country, e.g., El Salvador
Central cities *See* Inner cities
Central City Opera House, **I:** 183
Central City Opera House Association, **I:** 183
Central High School, **I:** 181
Central Intelligence Agency (CIA), **V:** 1222
Central Park (New York City, New York), **I:** 209
Central State University, **III:** 651
Césaire, Aimé, **II:** 305, 381
Cesaire, Ina, **III:** 742
Chad, **II: 246–247**
Chadwick, George, **IV:** 948, 952
Chaffee, C.C., **II:** 341
Chairpersons (Committee)
    African American firsts, **I:** 27, 93, 102, 109 **V:** 1158
Chairpersons (Endowed), **III:** 663–667 *See also* Chapter 16 for alphabetic listing of African Americans holding various endowed chairs
Chairpersons (Joint Chiefs of Staff), **V:** 1240–1241
    African American firsts, **I:** 103 **V:** 1226, 1240
Chairpersons (Political party)
    African American firsts, **I:** 65, 102, 109
Chairs (Furniture), **I:** 183
Chalifoux, Alice, **IV:** 939
Challenge See New Challenge
Challenger (Space shuttle), **I:** 100, 207 **V:** 1143, 1163 *See also* Space exploration and explorers
Challengers Air Pilots Association (CAPA), **V:** 1142
Chamberlain, Wilt, **V:** *1174*, **1183**
Chambers, Julius, **II:** 482
Championships, football *See* Football awards and championships
Chandler, Chas, **V:** 1061
Chandler, Dana, **V: 1104**
Chaney, James, **I:** 35, *39* **II:** 356
Change of Mind, **IV:** 840
"Change Your Life TV," **IV:** 787
Chapelle Administration Building (Allen University), **I:** 217

Chaplains
    African American firsts, **I:** 86 **II:** 391
    African American women's firsts, **III:** 695
Chapman, Charles P., **I:** 100
Chapman Holdings Inc., **I:** 108
A Charge Delivered to the African Lodge (Prince Hall)
    title page, **II:** *405*
Charles, Ezzard, **V:** 1194
Charles H. Wright Museum of African-American History, **V:** 1131
Charles, Mary Eugenia, **II:** 296
Charles R. Drew University of Medicine and Science, **III:** 651
Charles, Ray, **V:** 1036, 1038–1039, 1040, 1046, **1049,** *1050,* 1067
Charles, Suzette, **I:** 100, *102*
Charlotte Forten's Mission: Experiment in Freedom, **IV:** 840
Charlotte, North Carolina
    African American firsts, **I:** 59
Charlton, Cornelius H., **V:** 1222, 1223
Charter schools, **III:** 631 *See also* Education and educators
Chase-Riboud, Barbara, **V: 1104–1105**
Chattanooga African America Museum, **V:** 1135
Chavis, Benjamin F., Jr., **I:** 74, 75 **II: 400–402,** *401,* 406 **III:** 682
Chavis, John, **I:** 212
Cheadle, Don, **IV:** *852*
Checole, Kassahun, **IV:** 751
Chemistry and chemists, **II:** 441 **V:** 1139, 1158, 1160, 1166
Chenier, Clifton, **V: 991**
Cherry, F.S., **III:** 687
Chesnutt, Charles W., **III: 721**
Chess and chess players
    African American firsts, **I:** 110
Cheyney University of Pennsylvania, **III:** 624, 651
Chi Eta Phi (Professional society), **II: 427**
Chic (Music group), **V:** 1043
Chicago Bee, **I:** 193
Chicago Conservator, **II:** 371
Chicago Defender, **I:** 22
Chicago, Illinois, **I:** 37, 193
    African American firsts, **I:** 57, 100 **II:** 371 **III:** 513, 535
    first settlements, **I:** 6, 193 **III:** 575, 586
"Chicago Plan," **I:** 48
Chicago State University, **III:** 638, 651
Chief justices *See* Judges and justices (State); Judges and justices (United States Supreme Court)
Chiefs of police *See* Law enforcement officers and administrators
Child abuse, **IV:** 787

Children *See also* Family and marriage
advocacy organizations and associations, **II:** 435
child support, **III:** 604–605
health issues, **III:** 606
living arrangements, **III:** 604
of mixed racial parentage, **III:** 604
statistics on child care, **III:** 617
statistics on family groups with children, **III:** 614
Children's Defense Fund, **II:** 402
Children's Initiative, **II:** 402
Childress, Alice, **III: 722 IV:** 881
Childress, Alvin, **IV:** 881
Chile, **II: 292–293**
Chiles, Lawton, **II:** 364
Chisholm, Shirley, **I:** 49, *49,* 57, 98 **III:** 495, **509**
Chison v. Roemer, **I:** 69
Choirs and choruses, **IV:** 962, *963 See also* Sacred
music and musicians
Choreography and choreographers, **IV:** 890–920 *See
also* Dance and dancers
African American firsts, **I:** 96 **IV:** 887
African American women's firsts, **IV:** 896
Christening *See* Baptism (Christian)
Christian, Charlie, **V:** 978, **992**
Christian Methodist Episcopal Church, **III: 688,** 699,
701 *See also* Churches; Religion
Christian Methodist Episcopal Publishing House,
IV: 749
Christian, Spencer, **IV: 767,** *767*
Christian-Green, Donna, **III:** 497
Christianity, **II:** 379–380 *See also* Churches; name of
specific denomination, e.g., African Methodist
Episcopal Church; Religion
The Chronic, **V:** 1053
Chronology of African Americans, **I: 1–84 V:** 1146
Chuck Berry: Hail! Hail! Rock 'n Roll, **IV:** 840
Chuck D., **V:** 1044, 1063, 1075, 1076
Chung, Chou Wen, **IV:** 945
Church Arson Bill, **I:** 77
Church Arson Prevention Act (1996), **II:** 349
Church bombings and burnings, **I:** 34, 53, 80, 179 **II:**
349 **III:** 684, *685*
Church elders *See also* Bishops; Monsignors
African American firsts, **III:** 603
Church of Christ (Holiness) United States of
America, **III: 688** *See also* Churches; Religion
Church of God by Faith, **III: 689** *See also* Churches;
Religion
Church of God in Christ, **III: 689,** 700 *See also*
Churches; Religion
Church of God in Christ Publishing House, **IV:** 749
Church of the Transfiguration (Los Angeles,
California)
parishioners, **III:** *677*

Churches *See also* Chapter 4 for churches by city and
state; Religion
African American firsts, **I:** 199 **III:** 672, 700
during American Reconstruction, **III:** 673–675
burnings, **III:** 684
and Civil Rights movement, **III:** 677
cooperation between, **III:** 678
early congregations, **III:** 672
emancipation efforts, **III:** 673
female leadership, **III:** 673
membership growth, **III:** 682
oldest in United States, **I:** 199
organizations and associations, **II:** 445
postbellum America, **II:** 334–335
prominent denominations, **III:** 684–691
response to segregation, **III:** 675
and rhythm and blues music, **V:** 1036
and social issues, **III:** 678
successes and failures, **III:** 683–684
trends, **III:** 678–680
twentieth century, **III:** 676–677
Churches, mega *See* Megachurches
Churches of God (Holiness), **III: 689,** 702 *See also*
Churches; Religion
Churchill, Winston, **III:** 736
CIA (Central Intelligence Agency), **V:** 1222
Cigarette smoking, **III:** 608
Cimarronaje *See* Fugitive slaves
Cincinnati Art Museum, **V:** 1133
Cincinnati, Ohio, **I:** 10
Cinema *See* Films and filmmakers
Cinque Gallery, **V:** 1132
Cinque, Joseph, **I:** 11 **II: 338,** *338,* 377
Circuses
African American firsts, **I:** 110
Cities *See* name of specific city, e.g., Chicago, Illinois
Citizens for a Better America, **II: 427**
Citizenship rights, **I:** 11, 14, 140 **II:** 449
City clerks
African American firsts, **I:** 86
City councils
African American firsts, **I:** 104 **III:** 504
City of Mobile, Alabama v. Bolden, **I:** 52 **II:** 459
City of Richmond v. Croson, **I:** 64 **II:** 475
III: 579–580
City planners, **I:** 6
Civil Rights Act (1866), **I:** 139 **II:** 333, 455
Civil Rights Act (1870), **II:** 455
Civil Rights Act (1871), **II:** 455
Civil Rights Act (1875), **I:** 19, 143 **II:** 336,
344, 450, 455
excerpt from, **I:** 143
Civil Rights Act (1957), **I:** 158–159 **II:** 456 **III:** 494
Civil Rights Act (1960), **I:** 31, 160 **II:** 456

Civil Rights Act (1964), **I:** 38, 54, 164–165 **II:** 456
    III: 559
   excerpt from, **I:** 165–166
Civil Rights Act (1965), **II:** 456
Civil Rights Act (1968) *See* Fair Housing Act (1968)
Civil Rights Act (1990), **I:** 68, 173
Civil Rights Act (1991), **I:** 71, 174 **II:** 348, 457
Civil rights activists, **I:** 51, 179 **II:** 350–371, 391–
    392 *See also* Civil rights and Civil Rights
    movements; name of specific person, e.g., King,
    Martin Luther, Jr.
   first to recognize gender bias, **II:** 355
Civil rights and Civil Rights movements, **II: 343–374**
    III: 494–495 *See also* Civil rights activists; Hate
    crimes; Racial prejudice; Racial violence
   during American Reconstruction, **II:** 344–345
   court cases and legislation, **II:** 344, 347–348, 449–
    451 **III:** 560
   early movements, **II:** 343
   effect on African American business, **III:** 579
   federal and state agencies, **II:** 371–374
   first martyr, **II:** 363
   late nineteenth century, **II:** 336–337
   literary foundation, **III:** 711
   memorials, **I:** 67
   musical vehicles, **IV:** 962
   organizations and associations, **II:** 426–431,
    437, 441, 443
   religious influences, **III:** 677
   and television, **IV:** 835
   twentieth century, **II:** 345–350, 346–347, 355, 363
   web sites, **V:** 1147
Civil Rights Bill (1964), **I:** 35
Civil Rights Bill (1968), **I:** 41
Civil rights campaigns and demonstrations, **I:** 33, 35,
    69 **II:** 346–347, 404 *See also* Civil rights
    and Civil Rights movements; specific type of
    demonstration, e.g., Sit-ins
   appeasement of demonstrators, **I:** *35* **II:** *348*
   landmarks, **I:** 180
Civil Rights Cases, **II:** 344, 450–451, 468
Civil Rights Commission, **I:** 27
Civil Rights Commission Act (1983), **II:** 456
Civil Rights Memorial, **I:** 179
Civil Rights Project, **III:** 661
Civil Rights Restoration Act (1988), **II:** 348, 456
Civil War, American *See* American Civil War
Claflin College, **III:** 651
Clark, Ansel, **I:** 224
Clark Atlanta University, **I:** 191 **III:** 651
Clark Atlanta University Art Galleries, **V:** 1129
Clark, James G., **I:** 35 **V:** 1158
Clark, Joe, **III: 635–636,** *636*
Clark, Kenneth, **III: 636**
Clark, Marcia, **II:** 452

Clark, Mark, **II:** 398
Clark, Petula, **IV:** 856
Clark, Ramsey, **I:** 41
Clark, Russell G., **I:** 68
Clark, Septima, **III: 636–637**
Clark, T.A., **III:** 581
Clark, Tom Campbell, **II:** 454
Clark, William, **I:** 206
Clarke, Hope, **IV: 895–896**
Clarke, John Henrik, **I:** 81 **II: 385**
Clarke, Kenneth Spearman "Klook," **V:** 978, **992,** 1014
Classical music and musicians, **IV: 921–956** *See also*
    Music and musicians
   African American firsts, **I:** 98 **IV:** 925, 929, 933,
    937, 938, 943, 948, 955
   African American women's firsts, **IV:** 941
   biographical profiles, **IV:** 925–956
   early America, **IV:** 921–922, *922*
   racism, **IV:** 923–924
   research studies, **IV:** 924–925
   twentieth century, **IV:** 923–924
   web sites, **V:** 1149
Claudine, **IV:** 840
Clay, Cassius *See* Ali, Muhammad
Clay, Henry, **II:** 329–330
Clay, William, **III:** 497, **509–510,** *510*
Clayburn, James E., **III:** 497
Clay's Compromise *See* Compromise of 1850
Clayton, Eva M., **III:** 497, **510**
Clayton, Xernona, **I:** 98 **IV: 767–768**
Cleage, Albert, Jr. *See* Agyeman, Jaramogi Abebe
Cleaver, Eldridge, **I:** 75, 81 **II:** 385, 398
Cleo Parker Robinson Dance Ensemble, **IV:** 890
Cleopatra Jones, **IV:** 840
Clerks, city *See* City clerks
Clerks, court *See* Court clerks
Cleveland, James, **IV:** 964, **965,** *965,* 970 **V:** 1055
Cleveland, Ohio
   African American firsts, **I:** 97 **III:** 495
Cleveland Singers, **IV:** 965
Cleveland, Tom, **IV:** 776
Clifton, Nat "Sweetwater," **V:** 1173
Clinton, Bill, **I:** 72, *73,* 74, 79 **II:** *228* **III:** 495–496,
    506, 678, *688,* 739
   Advisory Board for Initiative on Race, **I:** 177
    II: 350
   appointment of African Americans, **I:** 73, 79 **II:**
    408 **III:** 640 **V:** 1145, 1156
   inauguration, **I:** 188 **III:** 714, 715
   tours of Africa, **I:** 81, *82*
   and Tuskegee Syphilis Study, **I:** 79 **III:** 606, *607*
   welfare reform, **III:** 562
Clinton, George, **V:** 1042, *1043,* **1050–1051**
Clinton, Hillary Rodham, **III:** 715
Clinton Junior College, **III:** 651

Clockers, **IV:** 841

Clocks, **V:** 1137

    African American firsts, **I:** 85

Clotel, or the President's Daughter: A Tale of the Southern States, **I:** 13 **III:** 720

CME Publishing House, **IV:** 749

CNN (Cable News Network), **IV:** 761

Coaches (Sports), **II:** 424 *See also* Basketball coaches; Football coaches and officiates

Coachman, Alice, **I:** 93 **V:** 1177, **1183**

Coahoma Community College, **III:** 651

Coalition of Black Investors, **II:** 427

Coalition of Black Revolutionary Artists (COBRA), **V:** 1095

Coalition of Black Trade Unionists, **II: 427**

Coast Guard of the United States, **I:** 84

Coates, Paul, **IV:** 751

Cobb, Jewel Plummer, **V: 1154**

Cobb, Ty, **V:** 1182

Cobb, W. Montague, **V: 1154**

Cobbs, Price M., **V: 1154–1155**

COBRA (Coalition of Black Revolutionary Artists), **V:** 1095

Coburn, Titus, **I:** 199

Cochran, Donnie, **I:** 77, 101, 105

Cochran, Johnnie L., **II:** *453*, **477** *477*

Code noir, **I:** 3

Coffey, Aaron, **I:** 182

Coffey, Cornelius R., **V:** 1142

Coffey School of Aeronautics, **V:** 1142

Coffin, Levi, **I:** 194

Cogswell, James, **I:** 184

Cohen, Leonard, **V:** 1039

Coincoin, Marie Therese, **I:** 197

Coins, **I:** 78

    African American firsts, **I:** 91

Coker, Daniel, **I:** 8 **III:** 674 **V:** 1090

Cokley, Steve, **I:** 64

Cole, Bob, **IV:** 879, 930, 940

Cole, Frances Elaine, **IV: 930**

Cole, Johnetta B., **I:** 102 **III: 637**

Cole, Nat "King," **IV:** 835 **V: 992,** *993*, 1047, 1049, 1051

Cole, Natalie, **V: 1051**

Cole, Rebecca J., **V:** 1140

Coleman, Bessie, **V:** 1142

Coleman, Johnnie, **III:** 683, **694**

Coleman, J.P., **I:** 31

Coleman, Leonard S., **V:** 1170, **1183–1184**

Coleman, Ornette, **V:** 980, 981, **993,** *993*, 1023

Coleman, William T., **I:** 51 **II:** 463, **477–478**

Coleman, William Thaddeus, Jr., **I:** 91

Coleridge-Taylor, Samuel, **IV:** 940, 956

Coles, Isabella J., **V:** 1143

Coles, Kim, **V:** 1076

Colescott, Robert, **V: 1105**

A Collection of Spiritual Songs and Hymns from Various Authors, **IV:** 958

Collections, art *See* Art collections and exhibits

College Fund (UNCF) *See* United Negro College Fund (UNCF)

College Language Association, **II: 427**

College professors *See* Education and educators

Colleges *See* Universities and colleges

Collins, Addie Mae, **I:** 179

Collins, Bootsy, **V:** 1049, 1051

Collins, Cardiss, **I:** *55* **III: 510–511,** *511*

Collins, George, **III:** 511

Collins, Janet, **I:** 93 **IV:** 888

Collins, Marva Delores Nettles, **III:** 628, *629*, **637**

Collins, Tammy Renee, **IV:** 967

Colon, Alan K., **III:** 664

Colonial America *See* American Colonial period

Colonial National Historic Park, **I:** 220

Color Adjustment, **IV:** 841

The Color Purple (Book), **III:** 744

The Color Purple (Film), **IV:** 841

Colorado

    African American firsts, **I:** 183

    African American museums and galleries, **V:** 1129

    African American newspapers, **IV:** 794

    African American radio stations, **IV:** 813

    landmarks, **I:** 183–184

Colorado Attorney General's Office, **II:** 371

Colorado Pioneers Association, **I:** 183

Colored Agricultural and Normal University *See* Langston University

The Colored American, **I:** 86 **III:** 730

"Colored Battery" military camp, **V:** *1208*

Colored Methodist Church *See* Christian Methodist Episcopal Church

Colored National Labor Union, **I:** 18

Colored Troubadors, **III:** 730

Colored Women's League, **II:** 368, 395

Coltrane, John, **V:** 980, *980*, 980–981, 985, **994**

    and other musicians, **V:** 995, 1012, 1029

Coltrane, Turiya Alice, **V:** 985, **994–995**

Columbia, **II: 293–294**

Columbus, Christopher, **I:** 1 **II:** 236, 317

Columbus Colored Cemetery, **I:** 192

Combs, Sean "Puffy," **V:** 1046, **1051,** 1073

Comedy and comedians, **IV:** 890–920

    African American firsts, **IV:** 901

    twentieth century, **IV:** 885–886

    web sites, **V:** 1149

Comer, James P., **III:** 664

Comic books and comic book publishers, **IV:** 752–753

    See also Media and publishing

Command and General Staff College

    African American women's firsts, **V:** 1228

Commercials, television *See* Television commercials

Commission on Civil Rights *See* United States
    Commission on Civil Rights

Commissioners (Federal Trade)
    African American firsts, **II:** 480

Committee chairpersons *See* Chairpersons
    (Committee)

Committee for a Unified Independent Party, **III:** 517

Committee for the Improvement of Industrial
    Conditions Among Negroes in New York,
    II: 396

Committee on African and African-American Studies
    (University of Chicago), **III:** 661

Committee on Urban Conditions Among Negroes,
    II: 396

Committees, Federal *See* Federal committees

The Commodores, **V:** 1077

Communications industry *See* Media and publishing

Communist party, **III:** 493

Community Access Producers and Viewers
    Association, **II: 427**

Comoros, **II: 247–248**

Complete Poems (Paul L. Dunbar), **III:** 723

Composers (Music), **IV:** 925–956 *See also* Classical
    music and musicians; Conductors (Music)
    African American firsts, **I:** 106 **IV:** 931, 952, 954
    V: 991
    African American women's firsts, **IV:** 924
    in early America, **IV:** 921

Compromise of 1850, **I:** 13 **II:** 329–330

Compton Community College, **III:** 652

Computer science and scientists, **III:** 585 **V:** 1157–
    1158 *See also* Science and technology

Comunity Folk Art Gallery, **V:** 1132

Concerts (Music), **IV:** 959 *See also* Music and
    musicians

Concord Bridge defense, **II:** 320

Concordia College, **III:** 652

Conductors (Music), **IV:** 925–956 *See also* Classical
    music and musicians; Composers (Music)
    African American firsts, **I:** 89, 95 **IV:** 933, 940, 943
    African American women's firsts, **IV:** 940
    in early America, **IV:** 921

Conductors (Streetcar)
    African American firsts, **III:** 714

Cone, James H., **III:** 678, **694–695**

Confederate Army, **I:** 16 **V:** 1208 *See also* American
    Civil War; Union Army

Conference of Independent African States, **II:** 382

Conference of Minority Public Administrators, **II:**
    428

Congo (Brazzville), **II: 248–249**

Congo (Kinshasa), **II: 249–250**

Congress members *See* Members of Congress;

Members of Congress (United States House of
    Representatives)

Congress of National Black Churches, **II: 428**

Congress on Racial Equity (CORE), **II:** 398, 404, 407,
    410, **428**
    demonstrations and campaigns, **I:** 27 **II:** 404
    founding, **I:** 26 **II:** 356, 404

Congressional Black Caucus, **I:** 48, 51, 52, 54 **II: 428**
    III: 495
    members, **I:** *55* **III:** 496–498

Congressional Gold Medals, A-2 **I:** 84
    African American firsts, **I:** 99

Conley, Arthur, **V:** 1076

Connecticut, **I:** 8, 40, 45
    African American museums and galleries, **V:** 1129
    African American radio stations, **IV:** 813
    landmarks, **I:** 184

Connecticut Afro-American Historial Society, **V:** 1129

Connecticut Attorney General's Office, **II:** 371

Connecticut General Assembly, **I:** 184

Connell, Pat, **IV:** 757

Connelly, Marc, **IV:** 881

Connor, Eugene "Bull," **II:** 367

Connors, Jimmy, **V:** 1180

Connors, Norman, **V:** 1062

Consolidated Bank and Trust Company *See* Saint
    Luke Bank and Trust Company

Constitution Hall, **I:** 187

Constitution of the United States of America, **I:** 6,
    115–116 **II:** 321, 447 *See also* name of specific
    amendment, e.g., Thirteenth Amendment to the
    United States Constitution

Constitutional rights organizations, **II:** 426

Construction companies and workers, **I:** 167, 179, 203
    II: 433 **III:** 592
    equal employment, **I:** 45, 46, 48

Conté, Lansana, **II:** 257

*The Content of Our Character: A New Vision of Race
    in America*, **III:** 648

Continental Army, **I:** 184 **V:** 1206 *See also* American
    Revolution

Continental Basketball Association (CBA), **I:** 84

Contractors *See* Construction companies and
    workers

Convention industry organizations, **II:** 438

Convention People's Party, **II:** 228

Conversations with Ed Gordon, **IV:** 770

Converse, Frederick, **IV:** 948

Conversion, religious *See* Missionizing and
    missionaries

Conway, William, **V:** 1152

Conwill, Houston, **V: 1105**

Conyers, James Henry, **I:** 87

Conyers, John, Jr., **III:** 497, **511,** *512*

Cook County Republican Committee, **I:** 193

Cook, Suzan Johnson, **III: 695**
Cook, William Marion, **I:** 209 **IV:** 879, **930,** 940, 956
Cook, William W., **III:** 664
Cooke, Sam, **IV:** 963 **V:** 1036, **1051–1052,** *1052,*
    1060, 1071, 1083
Cookman Institute *See* Bethune-Cookman College
Cookman Institute of Jacksonville, **I:** 185
Cool Herc, **V:** 1044
The Cool World, **IV:** 841
Cooley High, **IV:** 841
Coolidge, Calvin, **I:** 23, 62
Coolio, **V:** 1045
Cooper, Anna Julia, **I:** 188 **III: 637–638,** 673
Cooper, Charles, **I:** 93 **V:** 1173
Cooper, Cynthia, **V: 1184,** *1184*
Cooper, George, **III:** 637 **IV:** 913
Cooper, Jack L., **IV:** 755–756
Cooper, Julia, **I:** 51
Cooper v. Aaron, **II:** 461
Cooper, Wayne, **III:** 736
Copeland, John A., **II:** 331
Coppin, Fanny, **III: 638**
Coppin, Frances Coppin, **III:** 673
Coppin State College, **III:** 652
Copping, Levi J., **III:** 638
Cordero, Roque, **IV: 930**
CORE *See* Congress on Racial Equity (CORE)
Cornbread, Earl, and Me, **IV:** 841
Cornelius, Don, **I:** 75 **IV: 768**
Cornish, Samuel E., **I:** 121 **II:** 329, 343 **IV:** 753, *768,*
    768–769, 780
Cornwallis, General, **II:** 339
Corporate executives *See* Businesses and business
    professionals
Correspondents, news *See* Journalism and journalists
Correspondents, war *See* Journalism and journalists
Cortéz, Hernán, **II:** 236
Cortez, Jayne, **V:** 983
Cortor, Eldzier, **V:** 1094
Cosby, Bill, **I:** 97 **IV:** 870, 886, 896, *896,* **896–**
    897, 919
    and *The Cosby Show,* **IV:** 836
    and *I Spy,* **IV:** 836
The Cosby Show, **IV:** 836
Cosmetics industry *See* Beauty industry and salons
Cosmic Slop, **IV:** 841
Cosmonauts *See* Space exploration and explorers
Costa Rica, **II: 294**
Costello, Marilyn, **IV:** 939
Costner, Kevin, **V:** 1062
Côte d'Ivoire (Ivory Coast), **II: 250**
Cotton Blossom Singers, **III:** 643
The Cotton Club, **IV:** 841
Cotton Comes to Harlem, **IV:** 841
Cotton industry, **I:** 6 **II:** 322

Cotton v. Scotland Neck Board of Education, **II:** 463
Cottrell, Comer, **III: 585–586**
Councils, city *See* City councils
Country music and musicians, **V:** 1074 *See also* Music
    and musicians
    African American firsts, **V:** 1074
    crossovers, **V:** 1038–1039
Country profiles *See* specific country, e.g., Nigeria
County courts *See* Courts (County)
County government officials *See* Government officials
    (County)
County judges *See* Judges (County)
Courlander, Harold, **III:** 728
Court cases *See* name of specific case, e.g., *Brown v.*
    Board of Education of Topeka, Kansas
Court clerks
    African American firsts, **I:** 91
The Court Martial of Jackie Robinson, **IV:** 841
Courthouses *See* name of specific courthouse, e.g.,
    Old Court House (St. Louis, Missouri)
Courts (County)
    African American firsts, **II:** 406
Courts (Federal), **II:** 452–453
    African American firsts, **I:** 87, 90, 91, 93, 97
    African American women's firsts, **I:** 107
Courts (Municipal)
    African American firsts, **I:** 87
    African American women's firsts, **I:** 90 **III:** 532
Courts (State)
    African American firsts, **I:** 88, 99
    African American women's firsts, **I:** 102
Cowboys
    African American firsts, **I:** 109
Cowings, Patricia, **V:** 1143
Cox, Billy, **V:** 1060, 1061
Cox, Elbert F., **V: 1155,** 1155
Cox v. Louisiana, **I:** 35
Cox, W. Harold, **I:** 35
Coyers, John, **I:** 46 **II:** 365
Crandall, Prudence, **I:** 184
Crawford, Tim, **IV:** 964
Cray, Robert, **V:** 976
Creach, Papa John, **V:** 1018
Creatore, Luigi, **V:** 1052
Creed, Linda, **V:** 1062, 1063
Creole (Ship), **I:** 12
Creole Jazz Band, **V:** 1020
The Creole Show, **IV:** 879
The Creolettes, **V:** 1065
Crime, **I:** 72 **II:** 436 *See also* specific type of crime,
    e.g., Homicide
Criminal justice and criminal justice system, **II:** 433,
    451–452 *See also* Law and lawyers
Crisis, **I:** 21 **III:** 724
Crisis at Central High, **IV:** 841

Croce, Arlene, **IV:** 907
Crockett, George, Jr., **II: 478 III:** 499
Croix de Guerre *See* French Croix de Guerre
Cromwell, Oliver, **I:** 5
Crooklyn, **IV:** 841
Cropper, Steve, **V:** 1076
Crosby, Mattie, **I:** 181
Cross, Delores E., **III: 638–639,** 664
Crosse, Rupert, **IV: 858**
Crosson, Wilhelmina Marguerite, **III:** 634
Crosswhite, Adam, **I:** 203
Crosswhite Boulder, **I:** 203
Crouch, Andrae, **IV: 965–966,** 970
Crowdy, William, **III:** 687
Crummell, Alexander, **II:** 377, 379, 380, **386,** 388
    and American Negro Academy, **III:** 626, 647
        IV: 751
    landmarks, **I:** 189
Crumpler, Rebecca Lee, **I:** 86 **V:** 1140
Crunelle, Leonard, **I:** 194
Cruz, Emilio, **V: 1105**
Cuba, **I:** 1 **II: 294–296**
Cuban Giants (Baseball team), **I:** 88
Cuffe, Paul, **I:** 8 **II:** 377, 378, **386**
    landmarks, **I:** 200, 201
Cuisine *See* Food
Cullen, Countee, **III: 722**
Cullen, Frederick, **III:** 722
Culp, Robert, **IV:** 897
Cults (Religious), **III:** 696
Cummings, Elijah E., **III:** 497
Cuomo, Mario, **II:** 407
Curaçoa *See* Netherlands Antilles
Cureton, S.C., **III:** 684
Curry, Charles, **III:** 664
Curtis Mayfield and the Impressions, **V:** 1040
Curtom Publishing Company, **V:** 1072
Cuthbert, Eccles, **III:** 593
Cutters *See* Ships
Cuyahoga Community College, **III:** 652
Cyberspace *See* The Internet
Cyclists, **V:** 1202
    African American firsts, **V:** 1202

D

Dahl-Wolfe, Meyer, **V:** 1107
Dahmer, Vernon, **I:** 84
Dailey, Ulysses G., **V: 1155**
Daily Defender, **IV:** 780
Dakan, **II:** 234
Daley, Phyllis Mae, **I:** 91
Daley, Richard, **I:** 193
Dallapiccola, Luigi, **IV:** 947
Dallas Black Dance Theater, **IV:** 890

Dallas, Texas
    African American firsts, **I:** 105
Daly, Richard J., **III:** 535
Dameron, Tad, **V:** 990
Dana, Charles A., **IV:** 769
Dance and dancers, **IV:** 890–920 *See also*
        Choreography and choreographers; name of
        specific dance theater, e.g., Dance Theater
        of Harlem
    African American firsts, **I:** 93 **IV:** 887, 910
    regional schools, **IV:** 890
    twentieth century, **IV:** 887–890
    web sites, **V:** 1149
Dance Theater of Harlem, **IV:** 889–890, 906, 910
Dandridge, Dorothy, **IV:** *832*, 833, **858,** 911
Dandridge, Ruby, **IV:** 858
The Dandridge Sisters, **IV:** 858
Danforth, John C., **II:** 488
Daniels, Preston, **I:** 107
Danson, Ted, **I:** 75
Darden, Christine, **V:** 1143
Darden, Christopher, **II:** 452
Darity, William, Jr., **III:** 664
Darktown Jubilee, **IV:** 841
Darnell, D.S.B., **III:** 624
Dash, Sarah, **V:** 1070
Data processing organizations, **II:** 424
Daughters of the American Revolution, **I:** 99, 187
Daughters of the Dust, **IV:** 842
David C. Driskell Center for the Study of the African
        Diaspora, **III:** 661
Davidson, Eugene, **V:** 1126
Davies, J.A.V., **V:** 1158
Davies-Hinton test, **V:** 1159
Davis, Angela Y., **I:** 47, 49 **II: 353–354,** *354,* 486
Davis, Anthony Curtis, **IV: 930–931**
Davis, Benjamin O., Jr., **I:** 94 **V:** *1229,* **1229–
        1230,** 1235
Davis, Benjamin O., Sr., **I:** 26, 90, *95* **V:** 1212, *1230,*
        1230–1231
Davis, Billy, **V:** 1058
Davis, Carl, **V:** 1083
Davis Cup, **I:** 98
    African American firsts, **V:** 1180
Davis, Danny, **III:** 497
Davis, Donna P., **I:** 99
Davis, Ernestine "Tiny," **V:** 984
Davis, Ernie, **I:** 96
Davis, Frank, **II:** 353
Davis, Henrietta, **II:** 380
Davis, Jefferson, **I:** 15, 16 **II:** 331 **III:** 492, 530 **V:** 1137
Davis, John, **V:** 1177
Davis, Larry, **III:** 664
Davis, Miles, **IV:** 872 **V:** 980, 981, *995,* **995–996,**
        1003, 1066

and John Coltrane, **V:** 994
Davis, Nelson, **II:** 341
Davis, Ossie, **IV:** 860, *882*, 884
Davis, Sally E., **II:** 353
Davis, Sammy, Jr., **IV: 859,** 884, *884*, 903
Davis, Terrell, **V:** 1171
Davis v. Prince Edward County School Board,
    III: 627
Davis, William R., Jr., **II:** 450
Davis, Willie, **V: 1184–1185**
Davy, Gloria, **I:** 96
Dawes, Dominique, **V:** *1178,* **1185**
Dawson, William L., **I:** 27 **III:** 494 **IV: 931**
Day, Morris, **V:** 1075
Day of Absence *See* Million Man March
Day, Thomas, **I:** 212
Daye, Charles Edward, **III:** 664
Days, Drew S., III, **II: 478**
Daytona Normal and Industrial Institute, **I:** 185, 189
    III: 624
de la Beckwith, Byron, **I:** 69, 75 **II:** 355, 364, 403
De La Soul, **V:** 984, 1044
De Mille, Agnes, **IV:** 905
de Passe, Suzanne, **IV: 859–860**
Deacons *See* name of specific denomination, e.g.,
    Episcopal Church
Deadwyler, Leonard, **II:** 477
Deal, Nathan, **I:** 72
Dearing, George, **I:** 188
Death rates *See* Population
Death row *See* Prisons and prisoners
Death Row Records, **V:** 1053, 1069
Déby, Idriss, **II:** 247
DeCarava, Roy, **V: 1105–1106**
Declaration of Independence, **I:** 5, 115
    signing, **I:** *114*
Dee, Mary, **IV:** 770
Dee, Ruby, **IV:** *851,* 858, 859 **860,** *860, 882*
Def Jam Records, **V:** 1081
Defender, **IV:** 762
Defense of Concord Bridge *See* Concord
    Bridge defense
The Defiant Ones, **IV:** 842
Delaney, Beauford, **V: 1106**
Delany, Martin R., **II:** 377, 379, 380, **386,** *387* **III:** 491
    V: 1209
Delany, Samuel R., **III:** 602, **722**
Delaware, **I:** 8
    African American museums and galleries, **V:** 1129
    African American newspapers, **IV:** 794
    landmarks, **I:** 184
Delaware Attorney General's Office, **II:** 371
Delaware State University, **III:** 652
Delegates (Political party)
    African American firsts, **I:** 87 **II:** 356

Delegates (United Nations), **I:** 27, 28, 52
    African American firsts, **I:** 94
    African American women's firsts, **III:** 531
Dellums, Ronald V., **III:** *512,* **512–513**
Delta Sigma Theta (Sorority), **II:** 400, **428**
Demand and the Supply of Increased Efficiency in
    the Negro Ministry, **III:** 646
Demas, Leone, **II:** 381
Democratic National Committee (DNC)
    African American firsts, **III:** 506
Democratic party, **I:** 24
    African American firsts, **I:** 65, 98, 102 **II:** 356 **III:**
        503, 506, 521
    African American women's firsts, **I:** 76
    nominations, **I:** 70, 71
Democratic Select Committee *See* Congressional
    Black Caucus
Demonstrations, civil rights *See* Civil rights
    campaigns and demonstrations
Denmark Technical College, **III:** 652
Denmark Vesey conspiracy, **I:** 9 **II:** 325, 342
Dennison, Jack, **IV:** 858
Denny, Reginald, **I:** 75
Denny's restaurants, **I:** 75
Dentistry and dentists, **II:** 440
    African American firsts, **I:** 87 **III:** 537
Denton, Sandy, **V:** 1079
Department of Defense, **V:** 1222
DePriest, James Anderson, **IV: 931,** *932*
DePriest, Oscar, **I:** 23, *24* **II:** 371 **III:** 493, **513,** 525
    landmarks, **I:** 193
Derham, James, **I:** 85
Des Moines, Iowa
    African American firsts, **I:** 107
Desegregation of schools *See* School desegregation
Deslands, Charles, **I:** 8
Destro, Robert A., **I:** 58
Detroit Institute of Arts, **V:** 1131
Detroit Medical Society, **I:** 202
Detroit, Michigan, **I:** 39 **IV:** 778 **V:** 1109–1110
    African American firsts, **I:** 99 **IV:** 776
Dett, Robert Nathaniel, **IV: 933,** 944, 959
Devers, Gail, **V:** 1177
Devil in a Blue Dress, **IV:** 842
Devine, Loretta, **III:** 736 **V:** 1062
Devrouax, Paul S., **I:** 189
Dew Thomas, **I:** 10
Dewey, Thomas E., **V:** 1222
DeWindt, Hal, **I:** 96
Dexter Avenue King Memorial Baptist Church and
    Pastorium (Montgomery, Alabama), **I:** 179
DeYoung Museum, **V:** 1128
Diabetes, **III:** 607–608
Dialects
    African American firsts, **III:** 723

Diamond, Billy, **V:** 1052

Diana Ross and the Supremes *See* The Supremes

Dick, Marcel, **IV:** 952

Dickerson, Chris, **I:** 98 **V:** 1177

Dickerson, Dennis C., **III:** 664

Dickey, Everett W., **II:** 398

Dickinson, Edwin, **V:** 1105

Dictionaries, **I:** 81

Diddley, Bo, **V:** 1057

Digable Planets, **V:** 984

Diggs Art Gallery, **V:** 1133

Diggs, Charles C., Jr., **III:** 495

Diggs, Charles C., Sr., **I:** 202

Diggs, George, **I:** 7

Digital Underground, **V:** 1044, 1080

Dillard, James H., **I:** 197

Dillard University, **I:** 197 **III:** 652

Dime Saving Bank of New York, **III:** 592

Dingell, John, Jr., **III:** 511

Dingle, Derek T., **IV:** 752

Dinkins, David, **III:** *513*, **513–514,** 705
   as mayor, **I:** 67, 75, 103 **II:** 407

Diplomats (Federal)
   African American firsts, **I:** 87 **III:** 492
   African American women's firsts, **III:** 519

Directors, athletic *See* Athletic directors

Directors, film *See* Films and filmmakers

Directors, musical *See* Musical directors

Directors, television *See* Television directors and
      producers

The Disciples (Music group), **IV:** 965

Disco music and musicians, **V:** 1043, 1081 *See also*
      Popular music and musicians

Discovery (Space shuttle), **I:** 104 *See also* Space
      exploration and explorers

District of Columbia, **I:** 6, 128, 198
   African American museums and galleries, **V:** 1129
   African American newspapers, **IV:** 794–795
   African American radio stations, **IV:** 813
   African American television stations, **IV:** 826
   African American women's firsts, **I:** 103 **III:** 522
   homicide rates, **I:** 66
   landmarks, **I:** 185–189
   race riots, **I:** 44
   school desegregation, **I:** 39, 60, 68

District of Columbia Teachers College, **I:** 188

District of Columbia v. John R. Thompson, **II:** 468

Diton, Carl Rossini, **IV:** **933**

Divas Live concert, **V:** 1056

Divine, Bishop St. John the *See* Hickerson, John

Divine, Father *See* Father Divine

Divine, Mother *See* Mother Divine

The "Divine" movement, **III:** 696

Division of Negro Affairs, **I:** 189

Dixie Hummingbirds, **III:** 676

Dixon, Alan, **III:** 496

Dixon, Dean, **IV:** **933–934,** *934*

Dixon, George "Little Chocolate," **V:** 1171

Dixon, Julian C., **III:** 497, **514,** *515*

Dixon, Lucille, **IV:** **934**

Dixon, Margaret A., **I:** 106

Dixon, Richard N., **I:** 106

Dixon, Sharon Pratt, **I:** 103

Dixon, Willie, **V:** **996,** 1009

D.J. Jazzy Jeff and the Fresh Prince, **I:** 102 **V:** 1045

Djibouti, **II:** **250–251**

Do the Right Thing, **IV:** 842

Dobbs, Mattiwalda, **IV:** **934–935**

Doby, Larry, **I:** 91 **V:** 1170

Doctoral degrees *See also* Education and educators;
      Professional degrees; Universities and colleges
   African American firsts, **I:** 87, 88, 94 **II:** 396, 405
      III: 636 **V:** 1139
   African American women's firsts, **III:** 637 **IV:** 949
      V: 1144

Doctorow, E.L., **IV:** 908

Doctors, medical *See* Medicine and medical doctors

Documents, historic *See* Historic documents

Dodson, Howard, Jr., **III:** **639** **V:** 1099

Dodson, Owen, **V:** 1102

Dog sled racing *See* Sled dog racing

Dogg, Snoop Doggy *See* Snoop Doggy Dogg

Dogie Club, **I:** 220

Dolphy, Eric, **V:** **996**

Domingo, Placido, **IV:** 936

Dominica, **II:** **296**

Dominican Republic, **I:** 6 **II:** **296–297**

Domino, Fats, **V:** 1037, 1038, **1052**

The Dominoes, **V:** 1036, 1083

Donald Byrd/The Group, **IV:** 895

Donegan, Dorothy, **V:** 984

Donovan, Raymond, **I:** 55

Don't Bother Me, I Can't Cope, **IV:** 884

Doo wop music and musicians, **V:** 1036 *See also*
      Music and musicians

Dorrington, Arthur, **I:** 93

Dorsey, Thomas A., **III:** 676 **IV:** 944, 960–961,
      961,**966,** 969, 970
   discovering gospel musicians, **IV:** 961, 962

Dorticus, Claytonia, **V:** 1138

Douglas, Aaron, **V:** 1093, **1106,** 1115

Douglas, Bob, **V:** 1173

Douglas, Carl, **II:** *453*

Douglas, Freddie, **I:** 72

Douglas, James "Buster," **V:** 1173, 1189

Douglas, Stephen A., **I:** 194 **II:** 449

Douglass Association, **I:** 186

Douglass, Frederick, **I:** 11, 14, 19, *144*, 189 **II:** **338–
      339** **III:** 492
   excerpts from select speeches, **I:** 129–131, 144

landmarks, **I:** 186, *187,* 198, 201, 211, *212*
and *The North Star,* **I:** 13, 126 **II:** 343, 386 **IV:** 753
Seneca Falls convention, **I:** 143
Douglass, Joseph, **IV:** 956
Douglass, Sarah Mapps, **III: 639**
Dove, Rita, **III:** 664, 714, **722–723,** *723*
Down in the Delta, **IV:** 842
Down in the Lonesome Valley
sheet music, **IV:** *959*
Downing, Will, **V:** 983
Dozier, Lamont, **V:** 1041
Dr. Dre *See* Dre, Dr.
Dr. Jekyll and Mr. Hyde (Music group), **V:** 1059
Draft Riots (1863), **II:** 332
Drafting and draftspersons, **V:** 1161
Drake, Dave, **V:** 1089
Drama *See* Theater and theater performers; Theater
and theater performers (Musical)
Draper, Elizabeth, **III:** 593
Drayton, William *See* Flavor Flav
Dre, Dr., **V:** 1045, 1051, **1053,** *1053,* 1063, 1069
A Dream for Christmas, **IV:** 842
Dream Girls, **IV:** 884
Dred Scott v. Sanford, **I:** 14, 131, 140 **II:** 330,
448–449, 472
excerpt from ruling, **I:** 131–133
handbills advertising public hearing, **II:** *473*
landmarks, **I:** 205
Drew, Bonnie Bell, **IV:** 908
Drew, Charles R., **I:** 26 **V:** 1141, *1141,* **1155,** 1157
landmarks, **I:** 220
Drew, Timothy *See* Ali, Noble Drew
Driskell, David, **V: 1106–1107**
Driver, David E., **IV: 769**
Driving Miss Daisy, **IV:** 842
Driving, race car *See* Race car driving and drivers
Drug abuse, **III:** 608 *See also* Alcoholism
Dry Tortugas, **I:** 190
Du Bois, W.E.B., **I:** *21,* 88, 91 **II:** *345,* **354–355,** 380
III: 642, 711
on accomodationism, **II:** 337
biographical works on, **III:** 645
and Booker T. Washington, **I:** 20, 21
as civil rights activist, **II:** 345
and *Crisis,* **I:** 21 **II:** 396, 407, 417
famous dictum, **I:** 20
landmarks, **I:** 201, 219
and Marcus Garvey, **II:** 378, 380
and Niagara movement, **II:** 369, 396 **III:** 492
on *Nigger Heaven,* **I:** 23
and *The Souls of Black Folks: Essays and
Sketches,* **I:** 157
and *Suppression of the African Slave Trade,* **I:** 20
and visual artists, **V:** 1091
Du Sable, Jean Baptiste, **I:** 193 **III:** 575, **586**

Du, Soon Da, **I:** 71
Du Toit, Stephen Jacobus, **II:** 227
Dudley, S.H., **IV:** 879
Dukakis, Michael, **II:** 358
Duke, Bill, **IV: 860–861**
The Duke is Tops, **IV:** 842
Duke University Museum of Art, **V:** 1133
Dukes, Hazel, **I:** 71
Dumas, Charles, **I:** 95
Dumore, Lord, **I:** 5
Dunbar High School, **I:** 188
Dunbar Hospital, **I:** 202
Dunbar, Paul Lawrence, **I:** 187, 213 **III: 723**
IV: 879, 930
Dunbar-Nelson, Alice, **II:** 400
Duncan, Robert M., **II:** 454
Duncan, Robert Todd, **IV: 935**
Duncan, Todd, **IV:** 883
Duncanson, Robert, **V:** 1090, **1107**
DunCombe, Trudy, **III:** 499
Dunham Dance Company, **IV:** 897
Dunham, Katherine, **I:** 96 **IV:** 887, *887,* **897,** 941
Dunmore, Lord, **II:** 321 **V:** 1206
Dunn, Albert, **II:** *470*
Dunn, Duck, **V:** 1060
Dunn, Kaye *See* Dunham, Katherine
Dunn, Oscar, **I:** 18
Dunner, Leslie, **IV:** *935,* **935–936**
Dunsmore, John Ward, **I:** 209
Dunson, Edward D., **I:** 189
Duran, Roberto, **V:** 1193
Durham, North Carolina, **III:** 578–579
African America firsts, **I:** 67
Dushak, Alice, **IV:** 946
Dutch West Indies Company, **I:** 1
Dutchman, **III:** 717 **IV:** 842, 882
Dutton, Charles S., **IV:** 913
Dvorak, Antonin, **I:** 215 **IV:** 929, 930, 959
Dwight, Edward, **V:** 1142
Dyer Anti-Lynching Bill, **I:** 22
Dylan, Bob, **IV:** 909 **V:** 1061, 1078
Dynamic Voices: Black Poets of the 1960s, **III:** 737
Dyson, Michael Eric, **III: 639–640,** 665

E

Earl Graves Associates, **IV:** 770
Earley, Charity Adams, **V: 1231–1232**
Earls, Julian, **V:** 1143
Earthquake science and scientists *See* Seismology
and seismologists
East Cavalry Methodist Episcopal Church
(Philadelphia, Pennsylvania), **IV:** 960
East Ferry Historic District, **I:** 202
Eastman, Max, **III:** 736

Easton, Sheena, **V:** 1075
Eaton, Hosea, **I:** 11
Eatonville, Florida, **III:** 547
Eazy E., **V:** 1045, **1053**, *1054*, 1063
Ebenezer Baptist Church (Atlanta, Georgia), **I:** 191, *191* **II:** 397
Ebenezer Baptist Church (Chicago, Illinois), **IV:** 966
Ebola, **II:** 235
Ebonics, **I:** 79 **III:** 630
Ebony, **IV:** 755, 774
Ebony Fashion Fair, **IV:** 773
Ebony Museum of Art, **V:** 1128
Echebe, Chinua, **II:** 233
Eckstine, Billy, **V:** 983, 1001, 1019, 1029
Ector, Moses, **I:** 106
Ecuador, **II:** **297–299**
Eddie Murphy Productions, **IV:** 886
Edelin, Ramona Hoage, **II:** **402**
Edelman, Marian Wright, **II:** *402*, **402–403**, **III:** 603
Edison Pioneers, **V:** 1137
Edison, Thomas, **V:** 1137
Editors (Magazines and newspapers), **III:** 724–725 **IV:** 768–769, 784–785 **V:** 1154 *See also* Magazines and magazine publishers; Newspapers and newspaper publishers
    African American firsts, **I:** 86, 109, 121 **II:** 481
    African American women's firsts, **I:** 186
Edmonds, Kenneth "Babyface," **IV:** 861 **V:** 1046, **1054**, *1054*
Edmonds, Tracey, **IV:** **861**
Edmondson, William, **V:** 1094, **1107**
Edmonson v. Leesville Concrete Co., **I:** 69
Edmund Pettis Bridge, **I:** 57, 180
Education and educators, **III:** 632–650 *See also* Doctoral degrees; Professional degrees; specific type of school, e.g., Universities and colleges
    African American firsts, **I:** 67, 89, 100, 105 **V:** 1139, 1154, 1159, 1166
    African American women's firsts, **I:** 80, 109 **III:** 729
    in Colonial America, **III:** 621
    efforts of Christian missionaries, **III:** 621
    equal opportunity and pay, **I:** 24, 26, 28
    inferior facilities for African Americans, **I:** *155*
    needs of African American males, **III:** 628
    nineteenth century, **III:** 621–624
    organizations and associations, **II:** 418–419, 422, 428, 430, 432, 436, 440, 442–443, 445
    philanthropic efforts, **III:** 625–626
    in postbellum America, **II:** 335
    proficiency test scores, **III:** 669
    prohibition of education, **I:** 10, 11
    statistics, **III:** 668
    status reports, **I:** 67
    Supreme Court decisions, **II:** 460–464

    trends, **III:** 629–632
    twentieth century, **III:** 626
    web sites, **V:** 1148
Educational Equity Concepts, **II:** **428**
Edutainer Records, **V:** 1070
Edward Waters College, **III:** 652
Edwards, Bernice, **III:** 684
Edwards, Edwin W., **I:** 50
Edwards, Renard, **I:** 98
Edwards, Stoney, **V:** 1039
Edwards, Theodore "Teddy" M., **V:** **997**
Edwin Hawkins Singers, **IV:** 962, 964, 967
Efuntola, King, **III:** 686
Egypt, **II:** 225, **251–252**
Ehrlich, Paul, **V:** 1156
Eight Trey Gangster: The Making of a Crip, **IV:** 842
Eisenhower, Dwight D., **I:** 28, 30, 182 **V:** 1151, 1158
    civil rights legislation, **I:** 30, 31, 158, 160
Eisenhower, Milton, **I:** 48
El Mina fortress, **I:** *2*
El Pueblo Museum, **I:** 184
El Salvador, **II:** **299**
Elam, Harry J., Jr., **III:** 665
Elaw, Zilpha, **III:** 673
Elder, Lee, **V:** 1176, **1185**, *1185*
Elders, church *See* Church elders
Elders, Joycelyn, **I:** 73, 74, *75*, 76, 104 **III:** 496 **V:** **1155–1156**
Elders, Oliver B., **V:** 1156
Eldridge, David Roy "Little Jazz," **V:** **997**, *1000*
Elections, **I:** 37, 62
Elementary and high schools, **III:** 622, 632–633 *See also* Education and educators; name of specific school, e.g., Central High School
    drop-out rates, **I:** 72 **III:** 668
Eliot, T.S., **III:** 723
Elise, Sister, **IV:** 924
Elizabeth (Former slave), **III:** 673
Elizabeth City State University, **III:** 652
Ellington, E. David, **III:** 585, **586**
Ellington, Edward Kennedy "Duke," **IV:** 941, 953 **V:** 977, *978*, 979, **997–998**, 1031
    influence on other artists, **V:** 1027–1028
    landmarks, **I:** 186, 209
    and Pulitzer Prizes, **I:** 83
    and William Strayhorn, **V:** 1026
Elliott, William, **III:** 534
Ellison, Ralph, **I:** 94 **III:** 712, **723–724**, *724*, 732, 736
Ellison, Willie, **V:** 1202
Elmwood Cemetery, **I:** 202, 222
el-Shabbaz, el-Hazz Malik *See* X, Malcolm
Elwell, Herbert, **IV:** 953
Emancipation Act (1862), **II:** 455
Emancipation of slavery *See* Abolition and abolitionists

Emancipation of women *See* Women's rights and
    women's rights activists
Emancipation Proclamation (1863), **I:** 16, 133, 206,
    207 **II:** 332
    excerpt from, **I:** 134
    first reading, **I:** *134*
    watch night gatherings before, **II:** *335*
Emancipation Statue, **I:** 186, *188*
Emerson, Irene, **II:** 340
Emerson, John, **I:** 131 **II:** 340, 448, 472
Emery, Lynne Fauley, **IV:** 887
Emmy Awards
    African American firsts, **I:** 97, 98, 100
    African American women's firsts, **I:** 99, 100, 103
    list of African American recipients, A-2–A-3
Emory, Wayne, **I:** 99
Emperor Jones, **IV:** 842
Employment, **III: 557–566** *See also* Equal
    employment opportunity and affirmative action
    factors in levels, **III:** 557–558
    major Supreme Court decisions, **II:** 464–466
    nonracial changes, **III:** 558–559
    statistics, **I:** 51, 73 **III:** 557–558, 567–569, 570
    trends, **III:** 557
*Empowering the People: A 7-Step Plan to Overthrow
    the Conspiracy That is Stealing Your Money
    and Freedom*, **IV:** 766
Encyclopedia Africana, **II:** 380–381
Endeavor (Space shuttle), **I:** 103, 105 **V:** 1159 *See
    also* Space exploration and explorers
Endowed university chairs *See* Chairpersons
    (Endowed)
Energy Innovations, **V:** 1145
Engineering and engineers, **V:** 1144, 1151, 1165, 1167,
    1232–1233
    African American firsts, **V:** 1137, 1232
    organizations and associations, **II:** 430–431, 441
Engler, John, **III:** 499
Entrepreneurship and entrepreneurs *See* Businesses
    and business professionals
Environmental organizations and associations,
    II: 421, 427
Epidemiology and epidemiologists, **V:** 1156–1157
Episcopal Church *See also* Churches; Religion
    African American firsts, **I:** 7 **III:** 699
    African American women's firsts, **I:** 88
        III: 673, 697
    deacons, **III:** 697, 699
    landmarks, **I:** 189, 210
    membership growth, **III:** 682
    organizations and associations, **II:** 428, 445
    priests, **III:** 697, 699
Episcopal Commission for Black Ministers, **II: 428**
Episteme, **IV:** 931
Epps, William, **III:** 694

Epsy, Michael, **III:** 496, **514–515,** *516*
Epsy, Mike, **I:** 75, 82
Epton, Bernard, **I:** 57, 64
Equal Employment Opportunity Act (1972), **I:** 55
    II: 456
Equal employment opportunity and affirmative
    action, **I:** 61 **II:** 472–475 **III:** 559, 560, 562–563
    See also Employment; Workplace discrimination
    and "Chicago Plan," **I:** 48
    and Civil Rights Act (1964), **I:** 166
    constitutionality issues, **I:** 66
    for construction workers, **I:** 45, 46, 55
    in education, **I:** 26, 52, 76 **III:** 631
    and Executive Order (No. 11246), **I:** 167
    failure to investigate cases, **I:** 64
    and Fair Employment Practices Commission, **I:** 27
    for farmers, **III:** 560
    in the FBI, **I:** 66
    for firefighters, **I:** 59, 67
    for merchants, **I:** 25
    organizations and associations, **II:** 443
    and "Philadelphia Plan," **I:** 45, 46, 54
    in public service jobs, **I:** 49
    racial quotas, **I:** 53, 55, 59, 60, 64
    for sheet metal and steel workers, **I:** 52, 61
    in television broadcasting, **IV:** 759
Equal Employment Opportunity Commission, **I:** 164
    II: 371
Equatorial Guinea, **II: 252–253**
Equiano, Olaudah, **II: 342,** *342,* 378 **III:** 709
Eritrea, **II: 252**
Ervin, Richard, **I:** 28
Erving, Julius "Dr. J.", **I:** 107 **V:** 1053, 1173, 1177,
    1185
Espionage *See* Spies
Espy, Mike, **I:** 73
Essence (Magazine), **IV:** 755, 784–785
Essence Communications, Inc., **IV:** 785
Estes, Simon Lamont, **IV: 936**
Estevanico, **I:** 1, 207 **II:** 236, 317
Eta Phi Beta (Sorority), **II: 429**
Ethiopia, **II: 254–255**
Ethiopian Overcoming Holy Church
    See Apostolic Overcoming Holy Church of
    God, Inc.
Ethnotherapy, **V:** 1155
Europe, James Reese, **V: 998,** *998*
Evans, Ahmed, **I:** 43
Evans, Bill, **V:** 980
Evans, Faith, **V:** 1051
Evans, Gil, **V:** 995
Evans, James C., **V:** 1222, 1224
Evans, Mari, **III: 724**
Evans, Nate, **V:** 1072
Evans, Slayton A., Jr., **III:** 665

Evans v. Newton, **II**: 469
Evans-Tibbs Collection, **V**: 1129
Evers, Medgar, **II**: *355*, **355–356**, 403
 assassination, **I**: 33 **II**: 403 **III**: 495
 murder trial, **I**: 69, 75 **II**: 364
Evers-Williams, Myrlie, **II**: 355, 360, *403*, **403–404**
 and NAACP, **I**: 81
Eve's Bayou, **IV**: 842
Ewing, Patrick, **V**: 1174
Ex parte Virginia case, **I**: 220
Excelsiors, Brooklyn (Baseball team), **I**: 86
Executive Order (No. 8802), **I**: 26, 154
Executive Order (No. 9981), **I**: 27, 154
Executive Order (No. 10730), **I**: 159
Executive Order (No. 11053), **I**: 161
Executive Order (No. 11246), **I**: 167
Executives, business *See* Businesses and business
 professionals
Exhibits, art *See* Art collections and exhibits
The Exile, **IV**: 830
Exodusters, **I**: 195
Exploration and explorers, **I**: 1, 8 **II**: 317 *See also*
 Space exploration and explorers
 African American firsts, **I**: 198, 210
 to North Pole, **I**: 20, 21, 198 **V**: 1158
Explorers Club of America, **V**: 1158
Eyes on the Prize, **IV**: 843
Eyes on the Prize II: America at the Racial
 Crossroads (1965-1985), **IV**: 843

F

FAA (Federal Aviation Administration), **II**: 435
Fagan, Garth, **IV**: 885, 890, **897–898**
Fair Employment Practices Commission, **I**: 27 **II**: 345
Fair housing, **I**: 47, 64 *See also* Public accomodations
 and housing
Fair Housing Act (1968), **I**: 74, 171 **II**: 456
Fair Housing Amendments Acts (1988), **II**: 457
Fair Practices Board of the Civil Service
 Commission, **I**: 27
Falconer, Etta, **III**: 665
Fall, A.B., **V**: 1232
Family and marriage, **III**: **595–613** *See also* Children;
 Interracial marriage; Population; Teenage
 pregnancy
 and accidental death, **III**: 610
 African, **II**: 235
 biographical profiles of activists, **III**: 611–613
 and children, **III**: 604–605
 fertility and births, **III**: 603–604
 health concerns, **III**: 605–609
 and homicide, **III**: 610
 income, **III**: 560–561
 infant mortality rates, **III**: 610

 life expectancy, **III**: 609–610
 miscellaneous statistics, **III**: 596, 600, 601
 organizations and associations, **II**: 429
 in Postbellum America, **II**: 334
 poverty, **III**: 600
 rural underclass, **III**: 600
 socio-political and economic factors, **III**: 597–
  599, 610–611
 statistics on births to teens and unwed mothers,
  III: 616
 statistics on families in poverty, **III**: 571
 statistics on families with children, **III**: 614
 statistics on leisure activities, **III**: 619
 statistics on marriage, **III**: 600–601, 614, 615
 structure and stability, **III**: 595–600
 suicide rates, **III**: 610
 type by economic breakdown, **III**: 599–600
 and unavailability of men, **III**: 601–602
 web sites, **V**: 1148
A Family Thing, **IV**: 843
Famous Amos Chocolate Chip Cookies, **III**: 583
Famous documents *See* Historic documents
Fard, W.D. *See* Muhammad, Fard
Farish Street Neighborhood Historic District, **I**: 203
Farmer, Jackie, **IV**: 760
Farmer, James, **I**: 44 **II**: **356**, *397*, 404
 and Congress on Racial Equity (CORE), **II**: 398,
  407, 410, 413
Farmer, Karen, **I**: 99
Farms and farmers, **I**: 83 **III**: 560 *See also*
 Agricultural science and scientists; name of
 specific farm, e.g., Paul Cuffe Farm
 African American firsts, **I**: 194
 sharecropping after emancipation, **III**: *545*
Farrakhan, Louis, **II**: 384, **387**, 401 **III**: 524, 676, 684
 awards, **I**: 77
 and Khalid Abdul Muhammad, **I**: 75 **II**: 390
 and Million Man March, **I**: 76 **II**: *388*, 389, 402
  III: 611, 678
 and Nation of Islam, **II**: 383 **III**: 682, 689
 plots to kill, **I**: 76 **II**: 387
Farris, Jerome, **II**: **478–479**
Fashion design *See* Visual and applied arts and artists
Fashion Fair Cosmetics, **IV**: 773
Father Divine, **III**: 676, **696**, *696*
Fattah, Chaka, **III**: 497, **515**
Fattah, Falaka, **III**: 515
Faubus, Orval, **I**: 30, 30, *31*, 182 **II**: 352
Fauntroy, Walter E., **I**: 55, *63* **III**: **515–516**
Fauset, Crystal Bird, **I**: 25, 90
Fausset, Jessie Redmon, **III**: 711, **724–725**
Fax, Elton Clay, **V**: **1107**, *1108*
Fayetteville State University, **III**: 652
Fayomi, Ogundipe, **I**: 207
FBI *See* Federal Bureau of Investigation (FBI)

FCC *See* Federal Communications Commission (FCC)
Fear of a Black Hat, **IV:** 843
Fear of a Black Planet, **V:** 1044
Feather, Leonard, **V:** 1030
Federal agencies, **II:** 371–374
Federal Arts Project (FAP), **V:** 1093–1094
Federal Aviation Administration (FAA), **II:** 435
Federal Bureau of Investigation (FBI), **I:** 50, 52, 66, 68
    African American women's firsts, **I:** 105
Federal bureaus
    African American firsts, **III:** 645
Federal cabinet members *See* Cabinet members (Federal)
Federal committees
    African American firsts, **III:** 513, 514, 530, 534
Federal Communications Commission (FCC), **I:** 107, 108
Federal courts *See* Courts (Federal)
Federal diplomats *See* Diplomats (Federal)
Federal government officials *See* Government officials (Federal)
Federal Theater Project, **IV:** 881
Federal Voting Rights Act, **I:** 57
Feelings, Tom, **V: 1107–1109**
Feinstein, Diane, **III:** 526
Fellows, White House *See* White House fellows
Fellowships *See* Academic scholarships
Female circumcision, **II:** 235
Feminism and feminists, **III:** 641 **V:** 1096 *See also* Women's rights and women's rights activists
Fences, **III:** 747
Ferguson, Samuel David, **I:** 88
Ferris, William, **V:** 1098
Fertility rates *See* Population
Fetchit, Stepin, **IV: 861**
Fields, Kim, **V:** 1076
Fiennes, Ralph, **IV:** 856
Fifteenth Amendment to the United States Constitution, **I:** 27, 140 **II:** 336, 344, 449, 455
    excerpt from, **I:** 140
    ratification, **I:** 18, 79
Fifteenth Street Presbyterian Church (District of Columbia), **I:** 188
54th Massachusetts Regiment, **I:** 190, 215 **V:** 1207
    landmarks, **I:** 200, *200*
Figure skating and skaters, **V:** 1202
    African American firsts, **V:** 1177, 1202
    African American women's firsts, **I:** 101, 108
Figure skating championships
    African American women's firsts, **I:** 101, 108
Film awards *See* name of specific award, e.g., Academy Awards
Film directors *See* Films and filmmakers

Film producers *See* Films and filmmakers
Film studios
    African American firsts, **IV:** 830
Filmographies, **IV:** 838–855
Films and filmmakers, **IV: 829–875** *See also* Actors and actresses; Television and television shows; Television directors and producers
    in 1980s and 1990s, **IV:** 834
    African, **II:** 233–234
    African American firsts, **I:** 88 **II:** 234 **IV:** 829, 830, 834, 844, 847, 861, 913
    African American women's firsts, **III:** 715
    biographical profiles, **IV:** 860–861, 861, 867, 868– 869, 870–871, 871, 872–873
    blaxploitation films, **IV:** 833
    breaking into sound, **IV:** 830–831
    establishment of musicals, **IV:** 830
    first use of rock and roll music, **IV:** 839
    future, **IV:** 834
    organizations and associations, **II:** 424
    pioneers, **IV:** 829–830
    post-World War II, **IV:** 833
    propaganda films of World War II, **IV:** 832
    racial stereotyping, **IV:** 831–832
    redefining of images, **IV:** 829–830
    silent film era, **IV:** 829
    transitions, **IV:** 834
    web sites, **V:** 1149
Fire, **III:** 743
Fire Baptized Holiness Church, **III: 689** *See also* Churches; Religion
Firefighters Local Union No. 1784 v. Stotts, **II:** 473
Firefighting and firefighters, **I:** 59, 61 **II:** 429, *466*
First African Baptist Church (Savannah, Georgia), **I:** 192 **III:** *673*
First African Church of St. Thomas (Philadelphia, Pennsylvania), **I:** 7
First African Methodist Episcopal Church (Los Angeles, California)
    parishioners, **III:** *686*
First Black School, **I:** 220
First Bryan Baptist Church (Savannah, Georgia), **I:** 192
First Church of Christ, **I:** 184
1st Kansas Colored Volunteers, **V:** 1207
First National Black Historial Society of Kansas, **V:** 1130
First Rhode Island Regiment, **I:** 216
Firsts, African American *See* African American firsts
Fischer, Ada Lois *See* Sipuel, Ada Lois
Fischer, Rudolph, **III: 725**
Fishburne, Laurence, **IV:** 856, **861**, *862*, 874
Fisher, Elijah John, **III: 696–697**
Fisher, Gail, **I:** 98
Fisher, John, **I:** 182

Fisk Jubilee Singers, **I:** 219
Fisk University, **I:** 219 **II:** 405 **III:** 652
Fisk University Press, **IV:** 750
Fiske, Pomp, **I:** 199
Fitzgerald, Ella, **V:** 990, **999,** *1000*
Fitzgerald, Peter, **I:** 82
Fitzpatrick, John, **III:** 698
Five Civilized Nations, **III:** 546
The Five Heartbeats, **IV:** 843
Flack, Roberta, **V: 1055,** 1056
Flake, Floyd, **III:** 676, **697,** *697*
The Flames, **V:** 1048
Flanagan, Tommy, **V: 999**
Flavor Flav, **V:** 1075
Fleetwood, Christian A., **V:** *1210*
Flemming v. South Carolina Electric, **I:** 29 **II:** 468
Fletcher, Arthur, **I:** 44
Flight attendants
　　African American firsts, **I:** 96
Flint, Michigan
　　African American firsts, **I:** 59
Flint-Goodrich Hospital, **I:** 197
The Flip Wilson Show, **IV:** 836
Flipper, Henry O., **I:** 83, 87 **V:** 1210, *1211,* **1232–**
　　1233
Flood, Curt, **V:** 1170
Florida
　　African American firsts, **I:** 72
　　African American museums and galleries, **V:** 1129
　　African American newspapers, **IV:** 795–796
　　African American radio stations, **IV:** 813–814
　　landmarks, **I:** 189–190
　　race riots, **I:** 43, 53, 55, 64
　　school desegregation, **I:** 28
Florida A and M University, **III:** 652
Florida Attorney General's Office, **II:** 371
Florida East Coast Railroad, **I:** 185
Florida Memorial College, **III:** 652
Floyd, Eddie, **V:** 1060
Floyd, Samuel A., Jr., **IV:** 924
Flynn, Raymond, **II:** 349
Fokker, Anthony H.G., **V:** 1142
Folios, **I:** 200
Folklorists, **III:** 732
Food, **II:** 236
Food manufacturing industry, **V:** 1158
Football and football players, **V:** 1170–1171,
　　1178–1204
　　African American firsts, **I:** 89, 98, 99, 102, 105, 106,
　　　107 **V:** 1171, 1183
Football awards and championships
　　African American firsts, **I:** 89, 96, 99, 102, 107
Football coaches and officiates, **V:** 1198–1199
　　African American firsts, **I:** 99
Football games

African American firsts, **I:** 88
Football Hall of Fame *See* Professional Football
　　Hall of Fame
Foote, Julia A. J., **III:** 673
Footlights Across Tennessee, **IV:** 901
Footwear industry, **I:** 201
For Love of Ivy, **IV:** 843
For Us, the Living, **IV:** 843
Forbes, George W., **II:** 369 **III:** 538
Forbes, James, **III:** 678
Ford, Barney, **I:** 183
Ford, Gerald R., **I:** 51 **II:** 454, 478 **III:** 592
Ford, Harold E., Jr., **I:** 50 **III:** 497
Ford, James, **III:** 493
Ford, Justina, **I:** 183 **V:** 1141
Forde, Kenneth, **III:** 665
Foreman, George, **V:** 1180, **1186,** *1186*
Forman, James, **I:** 44
Forrest, Nathan Bedford, **V:** 1208
Forster, Janee, **III:** 576
Forsythe, Albert Ernest, **I:** 89 **V:** 1142
Fort Blount, **I:** 8
Fort Des Moines Provisional Army Officer Training
　　School, **I:** 195 **V:** 1213
Fort Gadsen, **I:** 190
Fort Manuel, **I:** 206
Fort Pillow Massacre, **V:** 1208
Fort Snelling, **I:** 203
Fort Snelling State Park, **I:** 203
Fort Sumter, **I:** 15
Fort Valley State Unviersity, **III:** 652
Fort Wayne, **I:** 203
Fort William Henry, **I:** 184
Forten, James, **I:** 216 **II:** 378, **387–388, V:** 1138
Forts *See* name of specific fort, e.g., Fort Gadsen
Fortune, Amos, **I:** 206
Fortune, T. Thomas, **I:** 19, 206 **II:** 370 **III:** 492 **IV:**
　　753, **769**
Foster, Frances Smith, **III:** 665
Foster, Henry, **I:** 76
Foster, Rube, **V:** 1169
Foster, William, **IV:** 830
Founder's Library (Howard University), **I:** 186
Founder's Marker (Tuskegee University), **I:** 180
Fountain Hall (Clark Atlanta University), **I:** 191
Fourteenth Amendment to the United States
　　Constitution, **I:** 140 **II:** 336, 344, 345, 449, 455
　　architects, **I:** 215
　　court cases, **I:** 19, 24
　　excerpt from, **I:** 140
　　passage and ratification, **I:** 17, 18
Fourth Ward *See* Freedmen's Town Historic District
48 Hrs., **IV:** 843
Foxx, Redd, **IV:** 886, *886,* 892, **898–899**
Frankfurter, Felix, **II:** 477

Franklin and Armfield Office, **I:** 220
Franklin, Aretha, **IV:** 965 **V:** 984, 1041, **1055,** *1056,*
    1064, 1082
Franklin, Benjamin, **I:** 118, *118*
Franklin, Carl, **III:** 739
Franklin, Charles L., **V:** 1055
Franklin, John Hope, **I:** 79, *178* **II:** 350 **III: 640**
Franklin, Kirk, **IV:** 964, **966–967,** *967*
Franks, Gary A., **III:** 496, **516–517**
Fraser, Don, **III:** 501
Fraternities, **II:** 399–400 *See also* Honor societies;
    Professional societies; Sororities
    African American firsts, **I:** 86, 89 **II:** 368, 399
    historic, **II:** 399–400
    oldest in United States, **II:** 443
    present-day, **II:** 400
    service, **II:** 420, 443
    social, **II:** 429, 442, 443
Fraunces, Samuel, **I:** 209
Fraunces Tavern, **I:** 209
Frazier, E. Franklin, **III: 640**
Frazier, Joe, **V:** 1172, 1180, 1186
Frazier v. University of North Carolina, **II:** 461
Frederick D. Patterson Research Institute, **III:** 661
Frederick Douglass Institute of African and
    African-American Studies, **III:** 661
Free African Society, **I:** 6 **II:** 328, 343, 379, 395
Free Haven, New Jersey, **I:** 206
Free Labor movement, **II:** 329
Free schools *See* African free schools
Free Soil movement, **I:** 13 **II:** 329
"Free South Africa" movement, **III:** 516
Freed, Alan, **V:** 1036
Freed slaves, **II:** 327 **III:** 623–624 *See also* Slavery
    and slaves
    laws, **I:** 3, 7, 8, 10, 13
    seeking employment, **I:** *18*
Freedman's Hospital, **I:** 186 **V:** 1140, 1167
Freedmen's Bureau, **I:** 17, 186, 214, 222 **III:** 624
Freedmen's Bureau Acts, **I:** 135 **III:** 623
Freedmen's Town Historic District, **I:** 220
Freedom Farm Cooperative, **II:** 357
Freedom National Bank, **I:** 209 **III:** 590, *591*
Freedom Rides, **I:** 27, 32, *34* **II:** 404 *See also* Civil
    rights and Civil Rights movements; Civil rights
    campaigns and demonstrations
Freedom's Journal, **I:** 121 **II:** 342, 343 **IV:** 753
    beginning of publication, **I:** 10, 85 **II:** 329
        IV: 768, 780
    excerpt from editorial of first edition, **I:** 121–123
Freeman, Al, Jr., **IV: 899**
Freeman, Al, Sr., **IV:** 899
Freeman, Elizabeth, **II:** 452
Freeman, Morgan, **III:** 635 **IV: 861–862,**
    862, 864, 891

Freeman, Robert Tanner, **I:** 87 **III:** 537
Freeman v. Pitts, **I:** 71
Freemasonry and freemasons, **II:** 404, 443 **IV:** 763
    addresses delivered to, **II:** *405*
    African American firsts, **I:** 85
French and Indian War, **I:** 184
French Croix de Guerre, **I:** 22 **V:** 1214, 1238
French Guiana, **II: 299–300**
French Legion of Honor, **I:** 22
French Open (Tennis), A-3
Frescos, **I:** 180
Fresh, **IV:** 843
Friedman, Paul L., **I:** 83
Friendly Society, **II:** 386
Frissell, Hollis B., **III:** 625
Frontiers International, **II: 429**
Frost, Robert, **III:** 747
Frye, Theodore, **IV:** 966, 969
Fudge, Ann Marie, **III: 586–587**
The Fugees, **V:** 1055, **1056**
Fugitive Slave Act (1793), **I:** 7, 12, 13, 117 **II:** 326
    excerpt from, **I:** 117
    petitioners, **I:** 216
Fugitive Slave Act (1850), **I:** 15, 127, 203
Fugitive slaves, **I:** 1, 2, 11 *See also* Slavery and slaves
    court cases, **I:** 12, 15
    handbills regarding, **II:** *327*
    laws, **I:** 1, 2 **II:** 326
    maroon communities, **I:** 3 **II:** 311, 319
    newspaper depictions, **II:** *474*
    return to owners, **I:** *127*
Fulani, Lenora, **III: 517**
Full Gospel Tabernacle (Memphis, Tennessee),
    V: 1059
Fuller, "Blind Boy," **V: 999**
Fuller, Charles, **III: 725–726**
Fuller, Meta Warrick, **V:** 1092, **1109**
Fuller, Solomon C., **V: 1156**
Fuller, Vivian, **I:** 108
Fullilove v. Klutznick, **I:** 53 **II:** 473
Fullmer, Gene, **V:** 1200
Fulton, Alvenia, **IV:** 901
Fund for Rudimentary Schools for Southern Negroes
    See Southern Education Foundation
Fundi: The Story of Ella Baker, **IV:** 843
Fundraising
    African American firsts, **II:** 411
Funeral directors organizations, **II:** 440
Funk music and musicians, **V:** 1042–1043, 1050–1051
        See also Popular music and musicians
Funkadelic, **V:** 1042, 1050, 1051
Fuqua, Harvey, **V:** 1057
Fur trade and fur traders, **III:** 583–584
Furious Five, **V:** 1044
Future Entertainment Group, Ltd., **V:** 1077

Future Records Recording Studio, **V:** 1077

G

Gabin, Jean, **IV:** 893
Gabon, **II: 255**
"Gag rule," **I:** 11, 12
Gage, Frances D., **I:** 128
Gain, Charlie, **V:** 1067
Gaines, Ernest J., **III:** 726
Gaines, Lloyd Lionel, **II:** 460, *460* **III:** 627
Gaines v. Canada, **III:** 627
Gaither, Barry, **V:** 1111
Galleries *See* Museums and galleries
Gallery Antiqua, **V:** 1129
Gambia, **I:** 1 **II: 255–256**
Gandhi, Mohandas Karamchand, **II:** 361, 404
Gandy, Oscar H., Jr., **III:** 665
Gang Starr, **V:** 984
Gangsta rap *See* Rap music and musicians
Gant-Britton, Lisbeth, **III:** 665
Gantt, Harvey, **I:** 59
Gantt-Blackwell Fort, **I:** 184
Gardiner, Andrea, **I:** 108
Garfield, James A., **III:** 507
Garner, Darlene, **III:** 603
Garner, Erroll, **V: 999–1001**
Garner v. Louisiana, **I:** 32
Garnet, Henry Highland, **I:** 11, 12, 125, *125* **II:** 379,
    388, III: 673
    excerpt from *Address to the Slaves of the United
    States of America*, **I:** 125
Garnett, Stephen, **III:** 597
Garrison, Lucy McKim, **IV:** 958
Garrison, William Lloyd, **I:** *11*, 216 **II:** *330*, 379
    and *The Liberator*, **I:** 10, 123 **II:** 329
Garrison-Jackson, Zina, **V:** 1177
Garth Fagan Dance, **IV:** 897–898
Garvey, Amy Jacques, **II:** 380
Garvey, Marcus, **II:** 371, *381*, 382, **388–389,** 389–390
    III: 686, 691 **V:** *1092*
    deportation, **I:** 23
    excerpt from *Speech at Liberty Hall*, **I:** 151–154
    influence on black nationalism, **II:** 382
    jail term, **I:** 22
    and mail fraud, **I:** 62
    portraits, **V:** 1092
    and UNIA, **I:** 21, 151 **II:** 378, 399
    and W.E.B. Du Bois, **II:** 378, 380
Gary, Indiana
    African American firsts, **III:** 495
Gary, Lawrence E., **III:** 665
Gas masks, **V:** 1164
Gaston, Arthur G., **III: 587**
Gaston-Johansson, Fannie, **III:** 665

Gates, Daryl, **II:** 349, 486 **III:** 504
Gates, Henry Louis, Jr., **III:** 565, **640–641,** 665
Gates, Horatio, **II:** 320
Gates, J.M., **IV:** 960
Gatling, Timmy, **V:** 1077
Gay, lesbian, and bisexual issues
    African American firsts, **II:** 234 **III:** 602, 603
    information on the Internet, **IV:** 766
    organizations and associations, **II:** 435
Gay rights activists, **III:** 613, 730
Gaye, Marvin, **V:** 1042, 1046, **1056–1058,** *1057*, 1082
Gayle, Addison, **V:** 1094
Gayle, Helene D., **V: 1156–1157**
Gayle v. Browder, **II:** 346, 469
Gayle, W.A., **II:** 365
Gebhart v. Belton, **III:** 627
Gee, Bird, **II:** 450
Geechees, **III:** 547
General Education Board, **III:** 626
Genet, Jean, **IV:** 882
Genhart, Cecile, **IV:** 941
Genital mutilation, **II:** 235
Geography, **II:** 229–230
Geology organizations, **II:** 431
Geophysics and geophysicists, **II:** 431 **V:** 1164
    African American firsts, **V:** 1164
George, David, **III:** 672
George, Langston, **V:** 1068
George, Nelson, **V:** 1036
George, R.S., **III:** 579
George, U.M., **III:** 579
George Washington Carver Museum, **V:** 1128
George Washington Carver Foundation, **II:** 411
    V: 1154
George Washington Park, **I:** 223
Georgia
    African American firsts, **I:** 5
    African American museums and galleries, **V:**
        1129–1130
    African American newspapers, **IV:** 796
    African American radio stations, **IV:** 814–815
    African American television stations, **IV:** 826
    African American women's firsts, **I:** 72
    election primary system, **I:** 68
    landmarks, **I:** 190–193
    race riots, **I:** 20, 47, 48
    school desegregation, **I:** 45
    slave laws, **I:** 4
Georgia Bureau of Investigation
    African American firsts, **I:** 106
Georgia Equal Opportunity Commission, **II:** 372
Georgia v. United States, **II:** 459
Germantown Mennonite Resolution Against Slavery,
    I: 112
Gershwin, George, **I:** 217 **IV:** 883, 935

Get On the Bus, **IV:** 843
Ghana, **II:** 228, **256**
Ghettos *See* Inner cities
The Ghetto's Tryin' to Kill Me, **V:** 1071
Ghosts of Mississippi, **IV:** 843
Giannini, Vittorio, **IV:** 947
Giants, Cuban (Baseball team), **I:** 88
Gibbs, Jewelle Taylor, **III:** 665
Gibbs, Mifflin W., **I:** 87 **II:** 452
Gibbs v. Montgomery County, **I:** 24
Gibson, Althea, **I:** 95 **V:** 1175, 1177, *1177*, 1180,
 1186–1187
Gibson, Bob, **V:** **1187**
Gibson, Josh, **V:** **1187**, *1187*
Gibson, Truman K., Jr., **V:** 1222
*Gibson v. Florida Legislative Investigating
 Committee*, **II:** 397
Gibson, William, **III:** 503
Giddings Paula, **III:** **611–612**
Gilder Lehrman Center for the Study of Slavery,
 Resistance, and Abolition, **III:** 661
Giles v. Harris, **I:** 20
Gillam, Isaac IV, **V:** 1143
Gillem, Alvan C., **V:** 1222
Gillem Board, **V:** 1222
Gillespie, Dizzy, **V:** 978–979, *979*, 985, **1001**,
 1011, 1066
 and Charles "Bird" Parker, **V:** 1021
 and John Coltrane, **V:** 994
 and John Lewis, **V:** 996
 and Mary Lou Williams, **V:** 1032
 and Melba Liston, **V:** 1015
 and Sarah Vaughan, **V:** 1029
Gilliam, Joe, Jr., **I:** 99
Gilliam, Sam, **V:** **1109**
Gilmore, Horace W., **I:** 54
Gilpin, Charles, **IV:** 880, **899**
Gingrich, Newt, **III:** 524, 527
Giovanni, Nikki, **II:** 383 **III:** 713, *713*, **726–727**
Gist, Carol, **I:** 103
Giuliani, Rudolph, **I:** 75 **III:** 592
Gladys Knight and the Pips, **V:** 1068–1069, *1069*
Glanville, Max, **IV:** 881
Glass Ceiling Act (1991), **II:** 457
Gleaves, Richard H., **II:** 334
Glen, Beverly, **V:** 1046
Glenn, John, **V:** 1143
Glickman, Dan, **III:** 560
Globetrotters, Harlem (Basketball team), **V:** 1173
Glory, **IV:** 844
Glover, Danny, **IV:** **862–863**, *963*
Glover, Rebecca, **III:** 673
Glover, Savion, **IV:** 884, *885*, **899–900**
Go, Man, Go!, **IV:** 844
Go Tell It on the Mountain, **IV:** 844

Goetz, Bernard, **II:** 366
Going to the Races, **IV:** 904
Gold Coast colony *See* Ghana
Gold Medal of Merit Awards, A-7
Gold Mining Camp, **I:** 182
Goldberg, Whoopi, **I:** 75, 105 **III:** 744 **IV:** **900**, *900*
Golden Boy, **IV:** 884
Golden Gate Strait, **I:** 183
Golden, Thelma, **V:** 1099
Goldman, Ron, **I:** 75, 76 **II:** 452, 477
Goldsby, Richard A., **III:** 665
Golf and golfers, **V:** 1175–1177
 African American firsts, **I:** 79, 105, 106 **V:** 1176,
 1177, 1185, 1201, 1204
 African American women's firsts, **V:** 1176
 biographical profiles, **V:** 1185, 1197, 1201, 1204
Golf championships
 African American firsts, **I:** 105, 106
Gomes, Peter J., **III:** 665
Gomillion v. Lightfoot, **I:** 31 **II:** 458
Gone Are the Days, **IV:** 844
Gone with the Wind (Film), **IV:** 844
Gonzales, Steven, **I:** 83
Goode, Malvin R., **I:** 96 **IV:** 757, *757*, **769–770**
Goode, Sarah, **V:** 1138
Goode, W. Wilson, **I:** 59, 100 **III:** **517–518**, *518*
 IV: 784
Gooding, Cuba, Jr., **IV:** *840*
Gooding, Henry, **I:** 190
Goodman, Andrew, **I:** 35, *39* **II:** 356
Goodman, Benny, **V:** 978, 979, 985, 1002
Goodman, Sam, **V:** 1072
Goodnight, Charles, **I:** 220
Goodwin, John, **I:** 193
Goodwin, Prince, **I:** 184
Gordimer, Nadine, **II:** 233
Gordon, Dexter Keith, **V:** *1000*, **1001**
Gordon, Ed, **IV:** **770**
Gordon, Robert A., **V:** 1143
Gordon, Simon, **V:** 1118
Gordy, Berry, Jr., **I:** 203 **IV:** 834, 859, 874 **V:** *1041*,
 1058, 1084
 and Jackie Wilson, **V:** 1083
 and Motown Records, **V:** 1041
 and Smokey Robinson, **V:** 1078
 and the Supremes, **V:** 1078
 and the Temptations, **V:** 1068
Gordy, Gwen, **V:** 1058
Gore, Al, **III:** 527, *607* **IV:** 776
Gore, Altovise, **IV:** 859
Gospel music and musicians, **IV:** 964–970–971 *See
 also* Sacred music and musicians
 documentaries, **IV:** 852
 first million-selling record, **IV:** 968
 first publishing company, **IV:** 961

golden age, **IV:** 962
   influence on church liturgies, **III:** 676
   influence on rhythm and blues music, **V:** 1036
   quartets and choirs, **IV:** 961, 962, 966
   rise in twentieth century, **IV:** 960–964
   "sermonette and song," **IV:** 961, 969
   web sites, **V:** 1149
Gospel Pearls, **IV:** 960
Gospel Workshop of America, **IV:** 965
Gossett, Louis, Jr., **I:** 100 **IV: 863,** *863*
Gottschalk, Louis Moreau, **IV:** 922, *922,* **936**
Gould, Glenn, **IV:** 955
Gould, William B., IV, **III:** 665
Gouled, Hassan Aptidon, **II:** 251
Gourdine, Meredith, **V:** 1145
Gourdine Systems, **V:** 1145
Government officials (County), **II:** 441 *See also*
   Politics and politicians
   African American women's firsts, **III:** 508
Government officials (Federal), **III:** 507–508 *See also*
   Politics and politicians
   African American firsts, **I:** 80, 96, 105, 106, 107
   III: 506, 514
Government officials (Municipal) *See also* Politics
   and politicians
   African American firsts, **I:** 97
   African American women's firsts, **I:** 106
Government officials (State) *See also* Politics and
   politicians
   African American firsts, **I:** 109 **III:** 546
Governors, **I:** 65 **V:** 1151 *See also* Politics and
   politicians
   African American firsts, **I:** 57, 67, 70, 87, 93, 103
   III: 492, 538
Governors, Lieutenant *See* Lieutenant Governors
G.R. N'namdi Gallery, **V:** 1131
Grace, "Sweet Daddy," **III:** 676, **697**
Graduates, university and college *See* University and
   college graduates and students
Graf, Herbert, **IV:** 937
Grafly, Charles, **V:** 1109
Graham, Billy, **III:** 678
Graham, Christopher, **II:** 472
Graham, Robert, **I:** 209
Grambling State Unviersity, **III:** 652
The Grammer Patrol, **IV:** 752
Grammy Awards, A-4 *See also* Music and musicians
   African American firsts, **I:** 96, 98, 102
Granary Burying Ground, **I:** 199
Grand Ole Opry, **V:** 1074
Grandfather clauses, **I:** 20, 21
Grandmaster Flash, **V:** 1044, 1053
Grandmasters (Chess) *See* Chess and chess players
Grant, Jacquellyn, **III:** 677
Grant, Micki, **IV:** 884

Grant, Ulysses S., **I:** 19 **V:** 1124
Grants organizations, **II:** 422
Granville, Evelyn Boyd, **V: 1157**
Graphic artists *See* Visual and applied arts and artists
Gravely, Samuel L., Jr., **I:** 96, 98 **V: 1233–1234**
Graves and graveyards *See* name of specific
   graveyard, e.g., Elmwood Cemetery
Graves, Denyce, **IV: 936,** *937*
Graves, Earl G., **IV:** 755, **770,** *771*
Gray, Fred, **III:** 606
Gray, Samuel, **I:** 199
Gray v. University of Tennessee, **II:** 460
Gray, William H., III, **I:** *55, 63* **III:** 515, *518,* **518–519**
Greased Lightning, **IV:** 844
Great Blacks in Wax Museum, **V:** 1131
Great Migration (1910-1970), **III:** 545–546
Great Plains Black Museum, **V:** 1131
"Great Society" programs, **III:** 562, 599
The Great White Hope (Film), **IV:** 844
The Great White Hope (Play), **IV:** 865
The Greatest, **IV:** 844
Gree, Shields, **II:** 331
Greek letter organizations *See* Fraternities; Honor
   societies; Sororities
Greeley, Horace, **I:** 16 **II:** 332
Green, A.C., **I:** 107
Green, Al, **V:** 1043, **1058–1059**
Green, Ben, **II:** 363
Green, Darlene, **I:** 106
Green, Grant, **V:** 984
Green, James, **I:** 106
Green, John E., **V:** 1212
Green, Linda, **III:** 611
Green, Malice, **I:** 72, 74
Green Pastures, **IV:** 844
Green, Paul, **IV:** 881
Greenberg, Jack, **I:** 58
Greene, J. Lee, **III:** 665
Greener, Richard, **I:** 87
Greenfield, Elizabeth Taylor, **IV:** 922
Greenfield, Eloise, **III: 727**
Greensboro, North Carolina, **II:** 346
Gregory, Dick, **IV:** 886, **900–901**
Gregory, Frederick D., **I:** 52, *101,* 102 **V:** 1143, **1157**
Grenada, **II: 300**
Grenadines, **II: 310–311**
Grier, David Alan, **IV:** 918
Grier, Pam, **IV: 863–864**
Grier, William H., **V:** 1154
Griff, Professor *See* Professor Griff
Griffen, Gene, **V:** 1077
Griffen, Michael, **V:** 1232
Griffey, Ken, Jr., **V: 1187–1188,** *1188*
Griffin, Eric, **IV:** 752
Griffin, John Arnold "Johnny," III, **V: 1001**

Griffin, Lauree, **I:** 106
Griffin, Richard *See* Professor Griff
Griffith, D.W., **II:** 369 **IV:** 829
Griffith, Michael, **I:** 62
Griggs v. Duke Power Co., **II:** 464
Grimké, Archibald H., **II: 479 III: 587**
Grimké, Charlotte Fortren, **I:** 186
Grimké, Selena, **III:** 587
Grinnell Gallery, **V:** 1132
Grist, Reri, **IV: 936–937,** *937*
Grosz, George, **V:** 1101, 1105
The Ground on Which I Stand, **III:** 747
Grove City College v. Bell, **II:** 348
Grovey v. Townsend, **I:** 24
Guadeloupe, **II: 300–301**
The Guardian, **II:** 369
Guards, tomb *See* Tomb guards
Guatemala, **II: 301**
Guess Who's Coming to Dinner, **IV:** 844
Guest, Eleanor, **V:** 1068
A Guest of Honor, **IV:** 941
Guggenheim Fellowships, **III:** 735
Guiliani, Rudolph, **III:** 513, 514
Guillaume, Robert, **IV:** 884
Guinea, **II: 256–257**
Guinea-Bissau, **II: 257–258**
Guinier, Lani, **I:** 74, 80, 109
Guinn v. United States, **I:** 21 **II:** 458
Guitar Slim, **V:** 1049
Gulf War (1991), **I:** 69
Gullahs, **III:** 547
Gumbel, Bryant C., **I:** 79, 100 **IV:** 759, **770–771,** *771*
Gumbel, Greg, **IV: 771–772**
Gunn, Moses, **IV: 901**
Gunter, Pamela, **III:** 665
Gurdjieff, **III:** 743
Gurewich, Marinka, **IV:** 926
Gutman, Herbert, **III:** 595
Guy (Music group), **V:** 1077
Guy, Beverly, **III:** 665
Guy, Buddy, **V:** 975, **1002**
Guy, Edna, **IV:** 887
Guyana, **II: 301–302**
Guyton, Tyree, **V: 1109–1110,** *1110*
Guzman, Jessie Parkhurst, **IV:** 750
Gymnastics and gymnasts, **V:** 1185
    African American women's firsts, **V:** 1178, 1185

H

Hacker, Marilyn, **III:** 722
Hackford, Taylor, **V:** 1047
Hackley, Emma Azalia, **IV: 937**
Haddad, William, **II:** 407
Hafer v. Melo, **I:** 71

Hagan, Helen Eugenia, **IV:** 922, **937–938**
Hagerty, James, **IV:** 757
Hagler, "Marvelous" Marvin, **V:** 1193
Hailey, Richard D., **I:** 107
Haines Normal and Industrial Institute, **III:** 624, 645
Hair care industry *See* Beauty industry and salons
Hairston, Jewel A., **II:** 476
Haiti, **I:** 6, 16 **II: 302–303**
    refugees fleeing from, **III:** *544*
Haitian voodoo *See* Voodooism
Halasz, Laszlo, **IV:** 942
Hale House, **III:** 612
Hale, Joe, **II:** 467
Hale, Lorraine, **III: 612**
Hale v. Commonwealth of Kentucky, **II:** 467
Haley, Alex, **I:** 51 **II:** 392 **III:** 713, *713*, 715, **727–728, IV:** 836
    death, **I:** 71
    landmarks, **I:** 218
    ship honoring, **I:** 84
Haley, Bill, **V:** 1071
Haley, Harold, **I:** 47
Hall, Aaron, **V:** 1077
Hall, Arsenio, **IV:** 886, **901–902**
Hall, Chuck, **I:** 43
Hall, Juanita, **I:** 93 **IV:** 902
Hall, Lloyd A., **V: 1158**
Hall of Fame (Baseball) *See* National Baseball
    Hall of Fame
Hall of Fame (Basketball) *See* National Basketball
    Hall of Fame
Hall of Fame (Football) *See* Professional Football
    Hall of Fame
Hall of Fame (New York University), **I:** 211
Hall of Fame (Rock and Roll), A-9
Hall of Fame (Track and Field) *See* National Track
    and Field Hall of Fame
Hall, Prince, **I:** 85, 199 **II: 404**
Hall, Raymond L., **III:** 665
Hall v. DeCuir, **I:** 19 **II:** 336, 344, 467 **III:** 576
Hall, William E., **II:** 404 **V:** 1221
Hallelujah!, **IV:** 844
Hallelujah Baby, **IV:** 884
Hamer, Fannie Lou Townsend, **II: 356–357,** *357*
Hamilton, Alexander, **I:** 6
Hamilton, Charles V., **III:** 665
Hamilton, Ed, **I:** 189
Hamilton, Virginia, **III: 728**
Hammer, M.C. *See* M.C. Hammer
Hammon, Jupiter, **I:** 5 **III: 728**
Hammond, John, **IV:** 969 **V:** 1055
Hammonds House Galleries, **V:** 1130
Hampton, Fred, **I:** 50 **II:** 398
Hampton, Henry, **IV:** 760, **864**
Hampton Institute, **I:** 18

Hampton Institute Press, **IV:** 750

Hampton, Lionel, **V:** 978, 984, **1002**, *1003*, 1009, 1066

Hampton University, **I:** 221, *221* **III:** 653

Hampton University Museum, **V:** 1135

Hampton, Vandy, **V:** 1072

Hancock, Barbara, **I:** 99

Hancock, Herbie, **IV:** 943 **V:** 984, **1003,** *1004*, 1043

Hancock, John, **I:** 199

Hand, Daniel Fund, **III:** 625

Handy, D. Antoinette, **IV:** 923, **938**

Handy, William Christopher "W.C.", **V:** 973, *974*,
    1003–1004
    landmarks, **I:** 179, 218

Hangin' with the Homeboys, **IV:** 844

Hank Aaron: Chasing the Dream, **IV:** 845

Hank Ballard and the Midnighters, **V:** 1036

Hannah, John, **III:** 522

Hannah, Marc R., **V:** 1144, **1157–1158**

Hannibal, Chauncey, **V:** 1077

Hannibal Guards *See* 9th Battalion United States V.I.

Hansberry, Lorraine, **I:** 96, *96* **III:** **728–729** **IV:** 881

Hansberry, William L., **III:** **641**

Hanson, Howard, **IV:** 942, 952

Hanson, Latoya, **V:** 1079

Hard, Darlene, **V:** 1187

Harding, Ebby, **V:** 1047

Hare, Maud Cuney, **IV:** 924

Harlan, John Marshall, **I:** 149–151 **II:** 336, 451

Harlem Artists Guild, **V:** 1094

Harlem Commonwealth Council, **II:** 407

Harlem Globetrotters, **V:** 1173, 1177

Harlem Hell Fighters *See* 369th Infantry Regiment

Harlem Historic District, **I:** 209

Harlem Institute of Fashion, **V:** 1132

Harlem, New York, **I:** 209 **V:** 1092

Harlem Nights, **IV:** 845

Harlem Renaissance movement, **I:** 21 **II:** 381 **III:** 711
    V: 1092–1093 *See also* Authors; Literature
    authors, **III:** 742–743
    father of movement, **I:** 210
    landmarks, **I:** 190, 197, 210, 222
    last surviving member, **III:** 745
    leading composers, **IV:** 953
    and Works Progress Administration, **V:** 1093–1094

Harlem School of the Arts, **IV:** 945 **V:** 1132

Harlins, Latasha, **I:** 71

Harmon Foundation, **V:** 1093

Harmon, Leonard Roy, **I:** 91

Harold Melvin and the Blue Notes, **V:** 1073

Harold Washington Party, **I:** 68

Harper, Frances E.W., **I:** 215 **III:** **729**

Harper, Michael S., **III:** 665

Harper, Nettie, **IV:** 960

Harper v. Virginia State Board of Elections, **I:** 37

Harper's Ferry National Historic Park, **I:** 223, *223*

Harper's Ferry Raid *See* John Brown's Raid on
        Harper's Ferry

Harpo, Inc., **IV:** 786

Harpoons, **V:** 1165

Harrell, Andre, **V:** 1047 **1059–1060**

Harriet Tubman Home, **II:** 341

Harriman, Averell, **II:** 406 **III:** 537

Harris, Barbara, **I:** 102 **III:** **697,** *698*

Harris, Bernard A., Jr., **I:** 105 **V:** 1144

Harris, E. Lynn, **III:** 602

Harris, Eddie, **V:** 984

Harris, Lusia, **V:** 1177, **1188**

Harris, Marcelite J., **I:** 105 **V:** *1234*, **1234–1235**

Harris, Margaret, **IV:** 924, **938**

Harris, Maurice Anthony, **V:** 1235

Harris, Patricia Roberts, **I:** 51, 99 **III:** 495, **519**

Harris, Robin, **IV:** **902**

Harris, Rupert H., **V:** 1052

Harris, Sarah, **I:** 184

Harris, Trudier, **III:** 665

Harrison, Benjamin, **II:** 339 **III:** 507

Harrison, Hazel, **IV:** 922, **938–939**, **V:** 1055

Harrison Museum of African American Culture,
    V: 1135

Harrison, Rex, **IV:** 903

Harrison, Richard B., **IV:** 881, **902**

Harris-Stowe State College, **III:** 653

Harshaw, Margaret, **IV:** 928

Harvard Law Review, **II:** 477

Harvey and the Moonglows, **V:** 1057

Harvey, Ben, **IV:** 880

Hastie, William H., **I:** 90, 93 **II:** 453, **479, III:** 649

Hastings, Alcee L., **I:** 72 **III:** 497

Hatch-Billops Collection, Inc, **V:** 1132

Hatcher, Richard G., **I:** 49, 50, 59, 66, 97 **III:** 495

Hatchett, Joseph W., **II:** **479**

Hate crimes, **II:** 349–350, 375 *See also* Racial violence

Hathaway, Donny, **V:** 1055

*Having Our Say: The Delany Sisters' First 100
        Years*, **IV:** 845

Hawaii Attorney General's Office, **II:** 372

Hawkins, Coleman, **V:** 977, **1004–1005,** 1031, 1033

Hawkins, Edwin, **IV:** 962

Hawkins, John, **I:** 1

Hawkins, Le-Van, **III:** **587–588,** *588*

Hawkins, Tramaine, **IV:** **967–968**

Hawkins v. Board of Control, **II:** 461

Hawkins, Walter, **IV:** 967

Hawkins, Yusuf K., **I:** 67

Hawkins-Bensonhurst, Yusef, **II:** 366

Hawthorne, Charles, **V:** 1112

Hayden, Lewis, **I:** 198

Hayden, Robert E., **I:** 219 **III:** **729–730**

Hayer, Talmadge, **I:** 35

Hayes, George, **I:** *29*

Hayes, Isaac, **V:** 1040, 1042, **1060**
Hayes, Marcella, **I:** 99
Hayes, Roland, **IV: 939**
Hayes, Rutherford B., **II:** 336
Hayford, Adelaide, **II:** 382
Haynes, George E., **II:** 396, **405**
Haynes, J.K., **III:** 665
Haynes, Lemuel, **I:** 85, 212 **II: 339**
Haynes, Ron Owen, **V: 1005**
Haynsworth, Clement, **III:** 505
Hayward, Dubose, **I:** 217
Hayward, William, **V:** 1213
Hazelwood School District v. United States,
   II: 464–465
H-D-H, **V:** 1041–1042, 1078
HEAL (Human Education Against Lies), **V:** 1070
Health and health care, **II:** 235–236, 440 **III:** 605–609
   See also name of specific condition, e.g.,
     AIDS (Acquired Immune Deficiency Syndrome);
     Women's health
Health Enterprises, **IV:** 901
Healy, James Augustine, **I:** 87, *88* **III: 698**
Healy, Patrick F., **I:** 19 **III:** 698
Hearing impairment organizations, **II:** 435
Hearns, Tommy, **V:** *1172*, 1193
Heart of Atlanta v. United States, **II:** 469
Heart surgery *See* Surgery and surgeons
Heaven (Music record), **IV:** 970–971
Heels, Tar, **V:** 1191
Heidelberg Project, **V:** 1109–1110, *1110*
Height, Dorothy I., **I:** 54, 81 **II:** 389, **406,** *406*
Heinze, Victor, **IV:** 938
Heisman Memorial Trophies, A-4 **I:** 76
   African American firsts, **I:** 96, 107
Helms, Jesse, **I:** 58 **II:** 353
Hemings, Sally, **I:** 82 **II:** 323
Hemphill, Essex, **III: 730**
Henderson, Fletcher, **V:** 984, **1005**
   orchestra, **V:** 976, 978, 987, 1005, *1006*, 1023
Henderson, George Washington, **I:** 87 **II:** 399
Henderson, Joe, **V:** 985, **1005–1006**
Henderson, Nonah, **V:** 1070
Henderson, Rickey, **V:** 1170
Henderson, Thelton, **I:** 96
Henderson v. United States, **I:** 28
Hendricks, Barbara, **IV: 939**
Hendricks, Jon, **IV:** 943 **V:** 983
Hendrix, Jimi, **IV:** 909 **V:** 1042, *1042* **1060–1061,**
   1070, 1071, 1075
The Hendrix Project, **IV:** 909
Henny, Herbert, **IV:** 881
Henry, Andrew, **I:** 206
Henry, Ragan A., **IV:** 759, **772**
Henson, Josiah, **I:** 10, 198 **II:** 329, **339**
Henson, Matthew A., **I:** 20, 21 **V: 1158,** *1158*

landmarks, **I:** 198, 210
Herman, Alexis M., **I:** 79, 107
Herndon Home, **V:** 1130
A Hero Ain't Nothing but a Sandwich, **IV:** 845
Herring, James V., **V:** 1126
Hersey, John, **V:** 1113
Hertzog, J.M.B., **II:** 227
Hervig, Richard, **IV:** 925
Hewlet, James, **IV:** 877
Heyton, Lennie, **IV:** 904
H.G. Parks, Inc., **III:** 591
Hickerson, John, **III:** 696
Hickey, James, **III:** 684
Higginbotham, A. Leon, Jr., **I:** 98 **II:** 453, **480,** *480*
High jumpers *See* Track and field athletes
High Museum of Art, **V:** 1130
High School of the Performing Arts (New York City,
   New York), **IV:** 910
High schools *See* Elementary and high schools;
   name of specific high school, e.g., Central
   High School
Higher education *See* Doctoral degrees; Professional
   degrees; Universities and colleges
Higher Learning, **IV:** 845
Hill, Abram, **IV:** 881
Hill, Anita, **I:** 73 **II:** 454, **480–481,** *481*, 486
   and Clarence Thomas, **II:** 454, 488
Hill, Lauryn, **V:** 1056, *1057*
Hill, Napoleon, **III:** 589
Hill, Robert B., **I:** 62 **III:** 598
Hill, Teddy, **V:** 1001
Hilliard, Asa Grant, III, **III:** 665
Hilliard, David, **I:** 80
Hilliard, Earl F., **I:** 72 **III:** 497
Hilliard, Wendy, **V:** 1178
Himes, Chester, **III: 730,** *731*
Hindemith, Paul, **IV:** 942
Hinderas, Natalie, **IV:** 922
Hinds Community College, **III:** 653
Hine, Darlene Clark, **III:** 665
Hines, Earl, **V:** 978, 985, **1006,** 1027, 1029
Hines, Gregory, **III:** 736 **IV:** 859, 884, 899, **902–903,**
   903, 911
Hines, Hines, and Dad, **IV:** 902
Hines Kids, **IV:** 902
Hines, Tommy Lee, **I:** 64
Hingis, Martina, **I:** 84 **V:** 1177
Hinton, Milton J. "Milt," **V: 1007**
Hinton test, **V:** 1158
Hinton, William A., **V: 1158–1159**
Hip hop music and musicians, **V:** 1043–1045, 1047,
   1051, 1056, 1073 *See also* Popular music and
   musicians
Hispaniola *See* Dominican Republic; Haiti
Historic districts *See* Chapter 4 for historic districts

by city and state; name of specific district, e.g., Freedmen's Town Historic District

Historic documents, **I: 112–177 V:** 1146 *See also* name of specific document, e.g., Constitution of the United States

History and historians, **III:** 633, 639, 641, 645, 650
   African American firsts, **V:** 1119
   organizations and associations, **II:** 420, 427

Hite, Les, **V:** 1029

Hitler, Adolph, **I:** 24

Hitsville U.S.A., **V:** 1058

HIV *See* AIDS (Acquired Immune Deficiency Syndrome)

Hobson, Charles, **IV:** 758

Hobson-Pilot, Ann Stevens, **IV: 939**

Hockey and hockey players
   African American firsts, **I:** 93, 96

Hodam, Helen, **IV:** 936

Hogan, Ernest, **IV:** 879, 883

Holden, Matthew, Jr., **III:** 665

Holder, Eric, **I:** 107

Holder, Geoffrey, **IV:** 889, **903–904**

Holdsclaw, Chamique, **V: 1188**

Holiday, Billie, **V:** 984, **1007,** *1008*, 1016, 1033, 1049

Holiday, Jennifer, **IV:** 884

Holidays, **II:** 359 **III:** 644
   African American firsts, **I:** 100

Holiness and Sanctified Church, **IV:** 960

Holland, Brian, **V:** 1041

Holland, Eddie, **V:** 1041

Holland, Robert, Jr., **III: 588**

Hollins v. Oklahoma, **II:** 466

Hollister, Dave, **V:** 1077

Hollowell, D.L., **II:** *470*

Holly, James T., **III:** 674

Hollywood Shuffle, **IV:** 845, 871

Holma, Kwame, **IV:** 760

Holmes, Larry, **V:** 1180, **1188–1189**

Holmes, Oliver Wendell, **II:** 458

Holmes v. Atlanta, **II:** 468

Holsey, Lucius, **III:** 675

Holt, Ben, **IV: 939–940**

Holt, Thomas, **III:** 665

Holte, Clarence L. Literary Prizes, A-4–A-5

Holtzman, Red, **V:** 1198

The Holy Ghost Boys, **V:** 1059

Holyfield, Evander, **I:** 80 **V:** 1173, **1189**

Home of the Brave, **IV:** 845

Homecoming queens *See* Beauty contests and contestants

Homer G. Phillips Hospital, **I:** 206

Homesteads *See* Chapter 4 for homesteads by city and state

Homicide, **I:** 41, 50 *See also* Racial violence
   Benjamin Brown, **I:** 38

civil rights volunteers, **I:** 35
   Emmett Till, **I:** 29
   George Jackson, **I:** 48
   Malcolm X, **I:** 35
   Martin Luther King, Jr., **I:** 41, 219
   Medgar Evers, **I:** 33
   rates, **I:** 59, 66
   Robert Kennedy, **I:** 42
   Viola Gregg Liuzzo, **I:** 35

Homosexuality *See* Gay, lesbian, and bisexual issues

Honduras, **II: 303**

Honeywood, Varnetta, **V:** 1096

Honor societies *See also* Fraternities; Professional societies; Sororities
   African American firsts, **I:** 87

Honors, civilian *See* Medals of Honor (Civilian)

Honors, military *See* Medals of Honor (Military)

Hoodlum, **IV:** 845

Hooker, John Lee, **V: 1007,** 1022

Hooks, bell, **III: 641**

Hooks, Benjamin L., **I:** 54, *56* **II: 406 IV:** 760
   and NAACP, **I:** 58, 71 **II:** 401

Hooks, Matthew Bones, **I:** 220

Hooks, Robert, **IV:** 882, 884

Hoop Dreams, **IV:** 845

Hoover, Herbert, **III:** 634

Hoover, J. Edgar, **I:** 46, 48, 52

Hope, John, **III: 642**

Hopkins, Pauline E., **III: 730–731**

Hopkins, Sam "Lightnin,'" **V: 1007–1008**

Hopwood v. Texas, **III:** 631

Horne, Lena, **IV:** 830–831, *831*, **904,** 916

Hornsby, Alton, Jr., **III:** 665

Horowitz, Vladimir, **V:** 984

Horse jockeys
   African American firsts, **I:** 19

Horton, Austin Asadata Dafore, **IV:** 887

Horton, George Moses, **III: 731**

Horton, Lester, **IV:** 890

Hosier, Harry "Black Harry," **I:** 184

Hospitality industry organizations, **II:** 432

Hospitals, **I:** 28, 33 *See also* Chapter 4 for landmark hospitals by city and state; name of specific hospital, e.g., Flint-Goodrich Hospital
   African American firsts, **I:** 202 **V:** 1140

Hostage situations, **I:** 83

Hoster, Brenda, **V:** 1227

Hoston v. Louisiana, **I:** 32

Hosts, television *See* Television hosts and anchors

Hotel Albert, **I:** 35

Hotel Theresa, **I:** 210

Hotels, **I:** 79 *See* Chapter 4 for landmark hotels by city and state; name of specific hotel, e.g., Lorraine Hotel

House Armed Services Committee, **III:** 513

House, Eddie James, Jr., **V: 1008–1009**
House of Umoja, **III:** 515
House Party, **IV:** 845
Houston Center for the Study of the Black
    Experience Affecting Higher Education, **III:** 661
Houston, Charles Hamilton, **II:** 454, *481,* **481–482,**
    III: 642
Houston, Cissy, **V:** 1045, 1061
Houston Lawyers v. Texas, **I:** 69
Houston, Texas
    African American firsts, **I:** 80, 108
Houston, Whitney, **II:** 360 **III:** 736 **V:** 1045, 1048,
    1061, **1061–1062**
Hoving, Thomas, **V:** 1125
How Stella Got Her Groove Back, **IV:** 845
How U Like Me Now?, **IV:** 845
Howard Beach incident, **I:** 62 **II:** 366
Howard, Oliver Otis, **I:** 186 **III:** 624
Howard University, **I:** 214 **III:** 642–643, 649, 653
    V: 1140
    landmarks, **I:** 186, 200
    sit-ins, **I:** 67
Howard University Gallery of Art, **V:** 1129
Howard University Press, **IV:** 750
Howard University School of Communications,
    IV: 766
Howard University School of Law, **III:** 653
Howe, Cato, **I:** 199
Howlin' Wolf, **V: 1009,** 1022
Hoxby, Caroline M., **III:** 665
Hubbard, William DeHart, **I:** 89
Hudgins, Johnny, **IV:** 880
Hudson, Cheryl Willis, **IV:** 751, **772**
Hudson, Wade, **IV:** 751, **772**
Huff's Art Studio, **V:** 1133
Hughes, Cathy, **IV:** 756
Hughes, Langston, **III:** 711, *711,* **731–732 IV:** 881,
    928 **V:** 1105
    films, **III:** 730
    spoken word styles, **V:** 983
    and Wallace H. Thurman, **III:** 743
    on writing, **I:** 23
Hughes, Sara Ann, **III:** 673
Human Education Against Lies (HEAL), **V:** 1070
Human immunodeficiency viruses *See* AIDS
    (Acquired Immune Deficiency Syndrome)
Human population *See* Population
Human rights, **II:** 371–374, 442
Human settlements and towns, **I:** 2, 6 **II:** 317 **III:**
    546–548, 575, 586 *See also* name of specific
    settlement or town, e.g., Jamestown, Virginia
Human sexuality, **III:** 681
Hunt, Jim, **III:** 510
Hunt, Richard, **V: 1110–1111**
Hunter, Alberta, **V:** 984, **1009**

Hunter, Billy, **V:** 1174
Hunter, Clementine, **I:** 197
Hunter, Eddie, **IV: 904**
Hunter-Gault, Charlayne, **IV:** 760, **772–773**
Hurd v. Hodge, **II:** 471
Hurston, John, **I:** 190
Hurston, Zora Neale, **III:** 547, **732,** *732*
    landmarks, **I:** 189, 190
Hurt, John, **V:** 975
Hurt, William, **IV:** 895
Hussein, Saddam, **II:** 358
Huston-Tillotson College, **III:** 653
Hutton, Bobby, **II:** 415
Hyman, Earle, **IV:** 881, **904–905,** *905*
Hyman, Phyllis, **V:** *1062,* **1062–1063**

I

I Got a Woman (Song), **V:** 1049
I Have a Dream speech, **I:** 33, 81, 162 **II:** 347 *See*
    also King, Martin Luther, Jr.
    excerpt from, **I:** 163
    landmarks, **I:** 187
I Know Why the Caged Bird Sings, **III:** 715 **IV:** 845
I See the Promised Land speech, **II:** 362
I Spy show, **IV:** 836
Ice Cube, **V:** 1045, 1053, **1063,** *1063*
Ice-T, **V:** 1045
Idaho Human Rights Commission, **II:** 372
Iditarod Sled Dog Race, **I:** 100
If Beale Street Could Talk, **III:** 716
Ike and Tina Turner Revue, **V:** 1081
I'll Make Me a World: A Century of African
    American Arts, **IV:** 846
Illinois
    African American museums and galleries, **V:** 1130
    African American newspapers, **IV:** 797–798
    African American radio stations, **IV:** 815–816
    African American television stations, **IV:** 826
    landmarks, **I:** 193–194
    race riots, **I:** 21
    school desegregation, **I:** 57
Illinois Human Rights Department, **II:** 372
Illustrators *See* Visual and applied arts and artists
I'm 'Bout It, **V:** 1071
I'm Gonna Git You Sucka, **IV:** 846
Imani Temple African American Catholic
    Congregation, **I:** 67 **III: 684–685,** 704
Imes, Elmer S., **I:** 219 **V:** 1139
Imitation of Life, **IV:** 846
Immigration Act (1924), **I:** 22
Immigration of African Americans, **I:** 180 *See also*
    Migrations of African Americans
The Impressions, **V:** 1072
In Living Color, **IV:** 914, 918

In re Green, **I:** 19

In the Heat of the Night, **IV:** 846

In the Spirit: The Inspirational Writings of Susan L. Taylor, **IV:** 785

Inaugurations, Presidential *See* Presidential inaugurations

Income, **III: 557–566** *See also* Employment; Population; Poverty

and age of householder, **III:** 561

distribution, **III:** 560

gap between racial groups, **III:** 563–564

and household size, **III:** 560

impact of family structure, **III:** 560

nonracial changes, **III:** 558–559

regional differences, **III:** 561

statistics on household income, **III:** 572, 573

statistics on persons below poverty level, **III:** 570, 571

status of African Americans, **III:** 563

various statistics (1990s), **I:** 68, 72 **III:** 560–562

Indentured servants *See* Slavery and slaves

Independence Day Address (Frederick Douglass), **I:** 129–131

Independent Order of St. Luke, **I:** 222

Independent schools, **III:** 624, 628–629 *See also* Education and educators

Indian Campaigns (1866-1890), **V:** 1209–1210

Indiana

African American museums and galleries, **V:** 1130

African American newspapers, **IV:** 798

African American radio stations, **IV:** 816

African American television stations, **IV:** 826

landmarks, **I:** 194–195

Indiana Civil Rights Commisson, **II:** 372

Indiana Univerity Art Museum, **V:** 1130

Indianapolis 500 race, **V:** 1177

Information industry, **III:** 581–582 *See also* Science and technology; The Internet

Ingram, Rex, **IV: 864,** *865*

Initiative on Race and Reconciliation, **I:** 82

Inmates *See* Prisons and prisoners

Inner cities, **III:** 548 *See also* Suburbanization; Urbanization

African American women's firsts, **III:** 740

Inner City Broadcasting Corporation, **III:** 593 **IV:** 756, 784

Inner City Teachers of Science program, **V:** 1163

Innis, Roy, **II:** 398, 404, **407,** *407*

Inside Bedford-Stuyvesant, **IV:** 757–758

Inskip, John, **III:** 703

Institute for African American Affairs, **III:** 661

Institute for African American Studies (City University of New York), **III:** 661

Institute for African-American Studies (University of Connecticut), **III:** 661

Institute for African-American Studies (University of Georgia), **III:** 661

Institute for Colored Youth *See* Cheyney University of Pennsylvania

Institute for Race and Social Division, **III:** 662

Institute for the Advanced Study of Black Family and Life, **II: 429**

Institute for the Preservation and Study of African-American Writing, **III:** 662

Institute of Afro-American Affairs, **III:** 662

Institute of Jazz Studies, **III:** 662

Insurrections and insurrectionists *See* Slave insurrections and insurrectionists

Interdenominational Theological Center, **III:** 653

Interdenominational Theological Seminary, **I:** 191

The Interesting Narrative of the Life of Olaudah Equiano, or Gustavus Vassa, the African, **II:** 342, 377 **III:** 709

title page, **III:** *710*

Intermarriage *See* Interracial marriage

Internal Revenue Service (IRS), **I:** 58

International Agency for Minority Artists Affairs Inc., **V:** 1132

International Association of Black Professional Fire Fighters, **II: 429**

International Black Women's Congress, **II: 429**

International Black Writers and Artists, **II: 429**

International College of Surgeons, **V:** 1155

International Congress of Women, **I:** 189

International Free and Accepted Masons and Eastern Star, **IV:** 762

International Motorsports Hall of Fame, **I:** 97

International Science and Technology Award, **V:** 1160

International Sweethearts of Rythms, **III:** 643

The Internet *See also* Science and technology

African American-related web sites, **IV:** 761–762

hate groups, **II:** 350

impact on African American business, **III:** 582

statistics on usage, **V:** 1146

Inter-Ocean Hotel, **I:** 183, *183*

Interracial marriage, **II:** 323 *See also* Children; Family and marriage

births of mixed racial parentage, **III:** 604

court cases and laws, **I:** 11, 27 **II:** 469

statistics, **III:** 614

Introducing the Winans, **IV:** 970

Intruder in the Dust, **IV:** 846

Inventions and inventors, **V:** 1150–1167 *See also* Science and technology

early period, **V:** 1137–1138

first free African American inventors, **V:** 1137

modern period, **V:** 1144–1145

slaves as, **V:** 1137

women inventors, **V:** 1138

Investment *See* Businesses and business
professionals; Stock exchanges
Investment brokers *See* Stockbrokers
Invisible Man, **III:** 723
Iola Leroy, or Shadows Uplifted, **III:** 729
Iowa
African American newspapers, **IV:** 798
African American radio stations, **IV:** 816
landmarks, **I:** 195
voting rights, **I:** 18
Iowa Human Rights Department, **II:** 372
I.P. Stanback Museum and Planetarium, **V:** 1134
Ira Aldridge Players, **IV:** 911
Ireland, Roderick, **I:** 107
IRS (Internal Revenue Service), **I:** 58
Irving, Larry, **IV:** 761
Ish, G.W., **I:** 182
Ish, Jefferson, **I:** 182
Ish School, **I:** 182
Ishaw, John W., **IV:** 879
Islam, **II:** 226 **III:** 682 *See also* Nation of Islam
mosques in Ethiopia, **II:** *254*
transcription of the Koran, **II:** *226*
Israel Bethel African Methodist Episcopal Church
(District of Columbia), **I:** 188
Ithaca Journal, **I:** 100
I've Been to the Mountaintop speech, **II:** 362
I've Known Rivers: Lives of Loss and Liberation,
III: 645
Iverson, Jonathan Lee, **I:** 110
Ives-Quinn Bill, **I:** 27
Ivey, Glenn, **I:** 109
Ivory Coast (Côte d'Ivoire), **II:** 250

J

Jack and Jill of America, **II: 429**
Jack, Hulan, **I:** 28
Jack Johnson, **IV:** 846
Jack, Sam, **IV:** 879
The Jackie Robinson Story, **IV:** 846
Jackson, Al, **V:** 1060, 1076
Jackson, Andrew, **I:** 11
Jackson, Augustus, **V:** 1137
Jackson, Eugene D., **IV: 773**
Jackson Five, **V:** 1042, 1064
Jackson, George, **I:** 48
Jackson, George Pullen, **IV:** 958
Jackson, Isaiah, **IV: 940**
Jackson, Janet, **V:** 1046, 1055, **1064,** 1065
Jackson, Jesse L., Jr., **II:** 358 **III:** 497, **519–520**
election of, **I:** 76
Jackson, Jesse L., Sr., **I:** 50, 58 **II:** *357*, **357–358,** 362
III: 495 **IV:** 970
and Al Sharpton, **II:** 366

and "Black Expo," **I:** 48
comments by Bill Clinton, **I:** 72
Kosovo hostage situation, **I:** 83
mayoral elections, **I:** 67
meeting with Jewish leaders, **I:** 64
and minorities on Wall Street, **III:** 565
organizations founded by, **II:** 441–442
presidential nomination and race, **I:** 64–65, *65*, 71
II: 387 **III:** 495, 526, 677
on Silicon Valley, **V:** 1145
Jackson, Joseph Henry, **III:** 677, *678*, **698**
Jackson, Julia, **II:** 409
Jackson, Mahalia, **III:** 676 **IV:** 961–962, *962*, 966,
968, V: 1046
Jackson, Maynard, **III:** 508, 509, **520,** 540
Jackson, Michael, **IV:** 764, 871, 899 **V: 1064–1065,**
1065, 1077
and Janet Jackon, **V:** 1064
and Lisa Marie Presley, **I:** 75, 77
and Quincy Jones, **V:** 1066
Jackson, Milt, **V:** 1049
Jackson, Mississippi
African American firsts, **I:** 106
Jackson, Papa Charlie, **V:** 974
Jackson, Rebecca Cox, **III:** 673
Jackson, Reggie, **V: 1189,** *1190*
Jackson, Samuel L., **IV: 864–865,** *865*
Jackson, Sheila Lee, **III: 521**
Jackson, Shirley Ann, **V:** 1144, **1159**
Jackson State University, **III:** 653
Jackson Ward Historic District, **I:** 222
Jacob, John E., **II: 407,** *408*
Jacques-Garvey, Amy, **IV:** 751
Jacquet, Jean-Baptiste "Illinois," **V: 1009**
Jaffrey Public Library, **I:** 206
Jaffrey Social Library, **I:** 206
Jaga, Geronimo ji *See* Pratt, Elmer "Geronimo"
Jail *See* Prisons and prisoners
Jakes, T.D., **III:** 678, 683, **699**
Jam, Jimmy, **V:** 1064
Jamaica, **II: 303–305**
James, Cheryl, **V:** 1079
James, C.L.R., **II:** 382
James, Daniel "Chappie," Jr., **I:** 51, 99 **V:** 1225, **1235–
1237,** *1236*
James, Elmore, **V: 1010,** 1032
James, Etta, **V:** 984, **1065–1066,** *1066*
James, Maurice *See* Hendrix, Jimi
James, Skip, **V:** 974, **1010**
James Weldon Johnson Collection, **I:** 197
Jamestown, Virginia, **I:** 1, 85, 220 **III:** 543
slaves arriving at, **I:** *9*
Jamison, Judith, **IV:** 888, **905–906,** *906*
Jamison Project, **IV:** 905
Jarvis Christian College, **III:** 653

Jason's Lyric, **IV:** 846
Javits, Jacob, **I:** *43*
Jayhawkers *See* Ku Klux Klan
Jazz and jazz musicians, **V: 973–1033** *See also* Music
    and musicians
    acid style, **V:** 982–983
    African American firsts, **I:** 106 **V:** 988, 991,
        992, 1020
    African American women's firsts, **V:** 984
    and bebop music, **V:** 978–979
    biographical profiles, **V:** 986–1033
    cool jazz style, **V:** 980
    creation of Afro-Cuban style, **V:** 1001
    early recordings, **V:** 976
    first integrated group, **V:** 1002
    first musician to use vibraphones, **V:** 1002
    first significant big band, **V:** 976
    fusion and free funk style, **V:** 981
    future, **V:** 985
    and neoclassicism, **V:** 982
    New Orleans style, **V:** 976
    post-bop and avant-garde style, **V:** 980–981
    return to traditionalism, **V:** 981–982
    soul style, **V:** 981
    spoken word and jazz rap style, **V:** 983–984
    swing era, **V:** 976–978
    vocalists, **V:** 983
    women in, **V:** 984–985
JBs, **V:** 1049
Jean, Wyclef, **V:** 1056
Jeanes, Anna T., **III:** 625
Jeanes Fund *See* Southern Education Foundation
Jeanes teachers, **III:** 625
Jefferson, "Blind" Lemon, **V:** 974, 1007, **1010**
Jefferson in Paris, **IV:** 846
Jefferson, Thomas, **I:** 5, *5*, 6, 10 **V:** 1151
    and Declaration of Independence, **I:** 113, 115
    relationship with Sally Hemings, **I:** 82 **II:** 323
    and slavery, **I:** 115
Jefferson, William J., **III:** 497
Jeffries, Jim, **V:** 1191
Jeffries, Leonard, Jr., **I:** 74
Jemison, Mae C., **I:** 103, *105* **V:** 1143, *1159*, **1159–**
    1160
Jenifer, Franklyn G., **I:** 76
Jenkins, Johnny, **V:** 1076
Jenkins v. Missouri, **II:** 464
Jennings, Peter, **IV:** 782
Jennings, Thomas L., **V:** 1137
"Jenny coupler" invention, **V:** 1151
Jessye, Eva, **IV: 940**
Jet, **IV:** 755
Jewell, K. Sue, **III:** 599
J.F. Drake State Technical College, **III:** 653
Jim Crow laws *See* "Separate but equal" doctrine

Jimi Hendrix Experience, **V:** 1061
Jimi James and the Blue Flames, **V:** 1061
Jimmy Jam, **V:** 1046
Jo Jo Dancer, Your Life is Calling, **IV:** 846
Joachim, Joseph, **I:** 209
Jobete Music Publishing, **V:** 1058
Jockeys (Horse racing)
    African American firsts, **I:** 196
Joe's Bed-Sty Barbershop: We Cut Heads, **IV:** 867
Joey Breaker, **IV:** 846
John Brown Memorial State Park, **I:** 196
John Brown's Raid on Harper's Ferry, **I:** 15, 201, 213
        II: 330, 341
    landmarks, **I:** 223
John Chavis Memorial Park, **I:** 212
John, Elton, **V:** 1069
John, Little Willie, **V:** 1067
Johnny Jenkins and the Pinetoppers, **V:** 1076
Johns, Vernon, **II:** 365
Johnson, Albert E., **II:** 475
Johnson, Alex M., Jr., **III:** 665
Johnson, Andrew, **I:** 17, 18, 183 **II:** 333
Johnson, Anna, **IV:** 751
Johnson, Anthony, **I:** 2 **II:** 317 **III:** 575
Johnson, Ben, **V:** 1193
Johnson, Benjamin G., **V:** 1212
Johnson, Bernett L., Jr., **III:** 665
Johnson C. Smith University, **III:** 653
Johnson, Charles R., **III:** 714, **732**
Johnson, Charles S., **III: 642**, 724 **IV:** 750, 751
Johnson, Earvin "Magic," **I:** 75, 77 **V: 1189–1191,**
    1191
Johnson, Eddie Bernice, **III:** 497
Johnson, Frank, Jr., **I:** 32 **IV:** 921
Johnson, George E., **III:** *588*, **588–589**
Johnson, Georgia Douglas, **III:** 711, **732–733**
Johnson, Harvey, **I:** 106
Johnson, Hazel W., **V: 1237,** *1237*
Johnson, Heather Lynn, **I:** 106
Johnson, Henry, **V:** 1214, **1237–1238**
Johnson, J. Rosamond, **I:** 151, 219 **IV:** 879
Johnson, Jack, **I:** 89, *89* **IV:** 830, 865 **V:** 1171, **1191**
Johnson, James A., **I:** 109
Johnson, James Louis "J.J.," **V: 1011**
Johnson, James Price, **V: 1011**
Johnson, James Weldon, **I:** 21–22, *22* **III: 733 IV:**
        879, 940–941 **V:** 1104
    landmarks, **I:** 197, 210, 219
    and *Lift Every Voice and Sing*, **I:** 151
    on *Nigger Heaven*, **I:** 23
Johnson, Joan B., **III:** 588
Johnson, John H., **IV:** 754, **773–774,** *774*
Johnson, John Rosamond, **IV: 940–941**
Johnson, Katherine, **V:** 1142
Johnson, Larry, **V: 1111**

Johnson, Lester L., **V: 1111**
Johnson, Linda, **IV:** *774*
Johnson, Lonnie, **V: 1011–1012**
Johnson, Louis A., **V:** 1223
Johnson, Lyndon B., **I:** 35, 36, 40, 168 **II:** 348, 356
    appointment of African Americans, **I:** 36 **II:** 454
    and civil rights, **I:** 34, 37, 42, 164, 171 **III:** 495
    and Civil Rights Acts, **I:** *44* **II:** 356
    excerpt from Executive Order (No. 11246), **I:** 167
Johnson, Michael, **V:** 1175, *1175*
Johnson, Mordecai Wyatt, **I:** 89 **III: 642–643**
Johnson, Noble, **IV:** 829, 830
Johnson, Norma Holloway, **I:** 107 **II: 482**
Johnson, Oscar, **V:** 1175
Johnson, Pamela, **I:** 100
Johnson Products, **III:** 588
Johnson, Rafer, **V:** 1175
Johnson, Reginald, **V:** 1127
Johnson, Richard, **II:** 317
Johnson, Robert, **IV:** 837, 968 **V:** 974, **1012,** 1018
Johnson, Robert L., **IV:** 761, *761*, **774–775**
Johnson, R.W., **V:** 1180
Johnson, Sargent, **V: 1111–1112**
Johnson, Thomas 15X, **I:** 35
Johnson v. Transportation Agency, Santa Clara County, California, **II:** 474
Johnson, Virginia, **IV: 906–907**
Johnson, William Henry, **V: 1112**
    works by, **V:** *1113*
Johnston, Joshua, **V:** 1090, **1111**
Joint Center for Political and Economic Studies, **III:** 662
Joint Chiefs of Staff chairpersons *See* Chairpersons (Joint Chiefs of Staff)
Jolson, Al, **IV:** 830
Jones & Jury, **II:** 483
Jones, Absalom, **II:** 378 **III: 699,** *699*
    and Free African Society, **I:** 6 **II:** 328, 343, 379, 395
    landmarks, **I:** 216
Jones, Barbara, **V:** 1177
Jones, Ben, **V: 1112**
Jones, Bill T., **IV: 907**
Jones, Bobby, **IV: 968**
Jones, Booker T., **V:** 1040
Jones, Carl, **V:** 1112
Jones, Casey, **I:** 218
Jones, Charles Price, **III:** 676, 688, 689, 700
Jones, Clarence B., **IV: 775**
Jones, Dorothy Walker, **V:** 1154
Jones, E. Edward, **III:** 678
Jones, Edith Irby, **V:** 1155
Jones, Elaine R., **II: 482**
Jones, Elayne, **IV:** 923, **941**
Jones, Elvin Ray, **V:** 994, **1012**
Jones, Etta, **IV:** 858

Jones, Eugene Kinckle, **I:** 21
Jones, Frederick M., **V: 1160**
Jones, Gayl, **III: 733**
Jones, Henry "Hank," **V: 1012**
Jones, James Earl, **III:** 747 **IV:** 856, **865–866,** *866*, 913, 915
Jones, Johnny, **V:** 1047
Jones, Joseph Lee, **II:** 471
Jones, Lawrence Clifton, **I:** 205 **III: 643**
Jones, Leroi *See* Baraka, Imamu Amiri
Jones, Louis, **IV:** 904
Jones, M. Sissieretta, **IV:** 922
Jones, Mac Charles, **III:** 684
Jones, Nathaniel R., **II: 482**
Jones, Phillip M., **II:** 360
Jones, Quincy, **IV:** 837 **V:** 1064, **1066–1067,** *1067*, 1068, 1077
Jones, Richard, **I:** 61
Jones, Robert Earl, **IV:** 865
Jones, Star, **II: 482–483**
Jones, Stephanie Tubbs, **III:** 497
Jones, Thaddeus Joseph "Thad," **V: 1013**
Jones v. Alfred H. Mayer, Co., **II:** 471
Jones, Vivian Malone, **I:** 97
Joplin, Scott, **I:** 205 **IV:** 880, 923, *923*, **941, V:** 973
Jordan, Ann Dibble, **I:** 108
Jordan, Barbara, **I:** 172 **III:** 521, *521*, **521–522,** 523
Jordan, Barbara Charline, **I:** 49, 76, 98
Jordan, James, **I:** 74
Jordan, June, **III: 733**
Jordan, Kathy, **II:** 366
Jordan, Louis, **IV:** 884 **V:** 1035, 1036, *1037*, **1067**
Jordan, Michael, **I:** 74 **V:** 1174, 1177, 1188, **1191–1192,** *1192*
    retirement, **I:** 75, 82
    return to NBA, **I:** 76
Jordan, Robert, **IV: 941–942,** *942*
Jordan, Vernon E., Jr., **I:** 51, 53, 54, 56 **II:** 407, **408,** *409*
    shooting, **I:** 53 **II:** 408
Joseph, Richard A., **III:** 665
The Josephine Baker Story, **IV:** 846
Josey, E.J., **III: 643**
Jotis, **V:** 1076
Journal of African Civilizations, **III:** 649
Journalism and journalists, **IV:** 762–787 *See also* Editors (Magazines and newspapers); Media and publishing
    African, **II:** 233
    African American firsts, **I:** 91, 96 **IV:** 757, 770
    organizations and associations, **II:** 432
Journalism awards *See also* Journalism and journalists
    African American firsts, **IV:** 781
Joyner, Al, **V:** 1192

Joyner, Florence Griffith "Flo-Jo," **I:** 82, 102 **V:** 1177,
    1192, *1192*
Joyner, Tom, **IV: 775**
Joyner-Kersee, Jackie, **V:** 1177, **1192,** *1193*
Jubilee Hall, **I:** 219
Jubilees (Musical), **IV:** 958–960
Judaism, **III: 687**
Judea Cemetery, **I:** 184
Judges (County)
    African American firsts, **II:** 406
Judges (Federal), **II:** 475–489
    African American firsts, **I:** 90, 91, 93, 96, 97 **II:**
        453, 479, 484, 487
    African American women's firsts, **I:** 36, 52, 107
        II: 453, 486
    listed by Presidential term, A-16–A-19
Judges (Municipal), **II:** 475–489
    African American firsts, **I:** 87 **II:** 452
    African American women's firsts, **I:** 25, 90 **II:** 476
        III: 532
Judges and justices (State), **II:** 475–489
    African American firsts, **I:** 88, 99, 106, 107
        II: 479, 488
    African American women's firsts, **I:** 102
Judges and justices (United States Supreme Court),
        II: 475–489
    African American firsts, **I:** 39, 70, 73, 97 **II:** 453,
        454, 485–486
    African American women's firsts, **II:** 475
Juice, **IV:** 846
Julian Laboratories, **V:** 1160
Julian, Percy L., **V:** 1139, **1160,** *1160*
June Kelly Gallery, **V:** 1132
Jungle Brothers, **V:** 984
Jungle Fever, **IV:** 847, 864
Jury duty, **I:** 22, 37, 69, 220 **II:** 466–467
    African American firsts, **I:** 220
Just, Ernest E., **V:** 1139, **1161**
Just Us Books, Inc., **IV:** 751, 772
Justice, David, **IV:** 857
Justices, state *See* Judges and justices (State)
Justices, United States Supreme Court *See* Judges
        and justices (United States Supreme Court)

K

Kabila, Laurent-Désiré, **II:** 249
Kaboré,Gaston, **II:** 234
Kagen, Sergius, **IV:** 936
Kaleidoscope Studio, **V:** 1119
Kani, Karl, **V: 1112**
Kansas, **I:** 14
    African American museums and galleries, **V:** 1130
    African American newspapers, **IV:** 798
    landmarks, **I:** 195–196

migration of African Americans, **I:** 195
        III: 544, 546
Kansas City, **IV:** 847
Kansas City Jazz Museum, **I:** 205
Kansas Human Rights Commission, **II:** 372
Kansas-Nebraska Act, **I:** 14
Kanter, Dee, **I:** 107
Kappa Alpha Psi (Fraternity), **II:** 400, **429**
Karamu House, **V:** 1134
Karenga, Maulana, **I:** 175–177 **II:** 383 **III: 644**
Karl Kani Infinity, **V:** 1112
Katherine Dunham Center for Arts and Humanities,
        IV: 897
Katzenbach v. McClung, **II:** 469
Kaunda, Kenneth, **II:** 227
Kay, UIysses Simpson, **IV: 942**
Kearse, Amalya L., **I:** 52 **II:** 453, **483**
Keb' Mo', **V: 1018**
Keith, Damon J., **II:** *483,* **483–484**
Kellis, Charles, **IV:** 936
Kelly, Leontine Turpeau Current, **I:** 100 **III: 699**
Kelly, Sharon Pratt, **III: 522**
Kendricks, Eddie, **V: 1067–1068**
Kennard, William E., **I:** 108
Kennedy, Adrienne, **III: 734**
Kennedy Center Honors, A-5
Kennedy, Edward M., **I:** 53, 58, 60 **III:** 506
Kennedy, John F., **III:** *647* **IV:** 962 **V:** 1142,
        1158, 1224
    appointment of African Americans, **II:** 453
    assassination, **I:** 34
    and civil rights, **I:** 164 **II:** 356 **III:** 494
    excerpt from Executive Order (No. 11053), **I:** 161
    secret tapes, **I:** 59
Kennedy, Joseph C., **III:** 734
Kennedy, Robert, **I:** 32, 42, *43* **V:** 1224
Kennedy, Ted, **I:** 65
Kennedy-King College, **III:** 653
Kenny, John, **IV:** 750
Kentucky
    African American newspapers, **IV:** 798–799
    African American radio stations, **IV:** 816
    landmarks, **I:** 196–197
Kentucky Derby, **I:** 19, 87, 196
Kentucky Derby Museum, **I:** 196
Kentucky Human Rights Commission, **II:** 372
Kentucky State University, **III:** 653
Kenya, **II:** 229, 258
Kenya African Union (KAU), **II:** 229
Kenyatta, Jomo, **II:** 229, 377
Kérékou, Mathieu, **II:** 242
Kerner Commission, **II:** 348 **IV:** 758
Kersee, Bob, **V:** 1192
Keyes, Alan L., **III:** 496, *496,* **522**
Keynote addresses

African American women's firsts, **I:** 76

Khan, Chaka, **V: 1068,** *1068*

Kid, Billy the *See* Billy the Kid

Kidney transplants

    African American firsts, **V:** 1161

Kikuyu Central Association (KCA), **II:** 229

Kilpatrick, Carolyn, **III:** 497

Kim, Earl, **IV:** 947

Kimbro, Dennis, **III: 589**

Kincaid, Jamaica, **III: 734**

King, **IV:** 847

King, Alberta Williams, **II:** 360

King, Barbara, **III:** 678

King, B.B., **V:** 975, *1013,* **1013–1014,** 1025, 1084

King, Bernice, **III:** 680

King Charles I, **II:** 236

King Cole Trio, **V:** 992

King, Coretta Scott, **I:** 41, 42, *45,* 61, *63* **II: 358–359,** *359,* 360

    and Martin Luther King, Jr. Memorial Center, **I:** 46 **II:** 362

King, Dexter Scott, **I:** 76 **II:** 359, **360**

King, Don, **II:** 366 **V:** 1173, 1189

King Efuntola, **III:** 686

King George, III, **I:** 115

King, Horace, **I:** 193

King, John William, **I:** 83 **II:** 350

King, Martin Luther, III, **I:** 80 **II: 362–363,** *363,* 409

King, Martin Luther, Jr., **II:** 350, **360–362,** 367 **III:** 502, 539 **IV:** 969 *See also* Civil rights and Civil Rights movements; *I Have a Dream* speech

    arrest, **I:** 35

    assassination, **I:** 41–42, 43, 51, 70, 219 **II:** 362

    biographical works on, **III:** 633, 645

    civil rights demonstrations, **I:** 29, 32, 33, 37 **II:** *361,* 365, *367* **III:** 698 **IV:** 856

    and Civil Rights movement, **II:** 346 **III:** 495, 677

    copyright issues, **I:** 81

    council to, **IV:** 775

    and FBI, **I:** 50, 52

    funeral service, **I:** 41, *45,* 191

    and Hotel Albert, **I:** 35

    and John F. Kennedy tapes, **I:** 59

    landmarks, **I:** 52, 60, 79, 179–180, 189–192, *191,* 219

    at Lincoln Memorial, **I:** 162

    and Mahalia Jackson, **IV:** 962, 968

    national holiday, **I:** 58, 61, 73, 100

    and Nobel Peace Prize, **I:** 35, *37*

    operas in memoriam, **IV:** 948

    pre-national holiday celebrations, **I:** 46

    sainthood, **III:** 685

    and SCLC, **I:** 30 **II:** 397 **III:** 680

    and Social Gospel movement, **III:** 676

    speeches, **I:** 33, 37, 73 **II:** *347*

    stance on Vietnam War, **V:** 1224

    and television, **IV:** 835

    in *And the Walls Come Tumbling Down,* **I:** 67

    wiretaps, **I:** 44

King, Martin Luther, Jr. Nonviolent Peace Prizes, A-5 **II:** 365

King, Martin Luther, Sr., **I:** 60 **II:** 360 **III:** 677

King, Rodney, **I:** 71 **III:** 504, 678

    beating, **I:** 69, *70,* 74 **II:** 349, 483

King Strut, **IV:** 784

King-Hammond, Leslie, **V:** 1099

King-Reeves, Hattie, **IV:** 881

Kingsley Plantation, **I:** 190

Kingsley, Zephaniah, **I:** 190

King-Tisdell Cottage of Black History, **V:** 1130

Kinnard, William E., **I:** 107

Kinship *See* Family and marriage

Kinte, Kunta, **III:** 727

Kirk, Andy, **V:** 985, 1032

Kirk, Claude, **I:** 43

Kirk, Euphemia *See* Terrell, Mary E. Church

Kirk Franklin and the Family, **IV:** 967

Kirk, Ronald, **I:** 105 **III: 522–523**

Kirk, Ronald Theodore "Rahsaan Roland," **V: 1014**

Kirkland, Kenny, **V:** 984

Kirkpatrick Center Museum Complex, **V:** 1134

Kirkpatrick, Jeane, **III:** 522

Kitchen Table: Women of Color Press, **IV:** 783

Kiwanis International, **I:** 108

KKK *See* Ku Klux Klan

Kleindienst, Richard, **I:** 49

Knapp, Martin, **III:** 702

Kneel-ins, **I:** 31

Knight, Brenda, **V:** 1068

Knight, Etheridge, **III:** 741

Knight, Gladys, **V: 1068–1069,** *1069*

Knight, Suge, **V:** 1053, **1069**

Knights of the White Camelia *See* Ku Klux Klan

Knoll, Holley, **I:** 220

Knoxville College, **III:** 653

Koch, Edward I., **III:** 513

Komunyakaa, Yusef, **III: 734–735**

Kool and the Gang, **V:** 1043, 1044

Koon, Stacey C., **I:** 74

Koontz, Elizabeth Duncan, **III: 644–645**

Korean War, **V:** 1222–1224

    African American firsts, **V:** 1223, 1228

    first American victory, **I:** 27 **V:** 1222

    Medals of Honor recipients, A-13–A-14

Kosovo incident, **I:** 83

Kountz, Samuel L., **V: 1161**

Kournikova, Anna, **I:** 84

Koussevitzky, Serge, **IV:** 944

Kraepelin, Emil, **V:** 1156

Kraft General Foods, **III:** 586

Kristol, Irving, **III:** 599
Krone, Gerald, **IV:** 882
KRS-One, **V:** 1044, **1069–1070**
Krupa, Gene, **V:** 997
Ku Klux Klan, **I:** 17, 18, 25, 35, 71 **II:** 344
　　burning crosses, **I:** *142*
　　convictions of members, **I:** 58, 64, 81
Ku Klux Klan Act (1871), **I:** 141–143 **II:** 344
Kunstler, William, **I:** 40
Kwaanzaa (Holiday), **II:** 383 **III:** 644 **V:** 1120

L

La Guardia, Fiorello, **II:** 476
LaBelle, **V:** 1043, 1070
LaBelle, Patti, **V:** 1069, **1070**, *1070*
Labor and labor unions, **I:** 30 **II:** 420, 427
　　　　III: 558–559
　　African American firsts, **IV:** 911
LaChiusa, Michael John, **IV:** 908
Ladner, Joyce, **III:** 603
Lady Sings the Blues, **IV:** 834, 847
LaFace Records, **V:** 1054
Lafayette, James Armistead, **II: 339**, *339*
Lafayette, Marquis de, **I:** 6 **II:** 339
Lafayette Players, **IV:** 894
Lafayette Theater Company, **IV:** 899
LaGuardia Community College, **III:** 653
LaGuardia, Fiorello, **I:** 25
Laird, Melvin R., **V:** 1236
Lambert, Dave, **V:** 983
LaMotta, Jake, **V:** 1173
Land *See* Real estate
Land Grant Act (1890), **III:** 624
Landis, Kenesaw Mountain, **V:** 1169
Landmarks, **I: 179–224 V:** 1146 *See also* Chapter 4
　　for landmarks listed by state and city
Lane College, **III:** 654
Lane, Dick "Night Train," **V: 1192–1193**
Lane, Isaac, **III: 699**
Lane, I.W., **II:** 458
Lane, Jim, **V:** 1207
Lane v. Wilson, **II:** 458
Lane, William Henry "Master Juba," **IV:** 878
Laney, Lucy C., **I:** 192 **III:** 624, **645**
Laney-Walker North Historic District, **I:** 192
Langdon, Andrew, **I:** 187
Langdon, LeDroit, **I:** 187
Lange, John, **IV:** 928
Langford, George M., **III:** 665
Langston, John Mercer, **I:** 86, *86* **III: 523**, 546
　　landmarks, **I:** 214
Langston, Oklahoma, **III:** 546
Langston University, **III:** 546, 654
Language interpreters organizations, **II:** 430

Languages (Spoken), **II:** 231–232, 427 *See
　　also* Ebonics
Lankford, John Anderson, **I:** 217
LaParra, Raoul, **IV:** 956
Laramie, Eve, **IV:** 909
Larkin, Tracy, **IV:** 775
LaRock, Scott, **V:** 1070
Larsen, Nella, **III: 735 V:** 1139
Last Poets, **V:** 1044
Last wills and testaments
　　of George Washington, **I:** 119
　　of Mary McLeod Bethune, **I:** 158
Latifah, Queen *See* Queen Latifah
Latimer, George, **I:** 12
Latimer, Lewis H., **V:** 1137, **1161**
Latin America, **II:** 236–240 *See also* name of specific
　　country, e.g., Argentina
Laubenstein, Paul Fritz, **IV:** 959
Laundries and laundry workers
　　African American firsts, **I:** 183
　　strikes for imrpoved wages, **I:** *183*
Laurel Avenue, **IV:** 847
Laurens, Henry, **I:** 6
Lautier, Louis, **I:** 91
Lavallade, Carmen de, **IV:** 904
Lavizzo, Risa L., **III:** 665
Law and lawyers, **II: 447–489** *See also* Criminal
　　justice and criminal justice system; name of
　　specific court case or legislation, e.g., *Dred
　　Scott v. Sanford*; Prisons and prisoners
　　African American firsts, **I:** 86, 88, 93, 96, 107 **II:**
　　　334, 410, 452, 478
　　African American women's firsts, **I:** 87, 89, 186 **II:**
　　　452, 475, 482
　　biographical profiles, **II:** 475–489
　　major court cases and legislation, **II:** 455–
　　　457, 457–475
　　organizations and associations, **II:** 424, 432,
　　　434–435, 439
　　related web sites, **V:** 1148
　　and slavery, **II:** 447–449
　　status of African Americans (1787-1883),
　　　II: 447–451
Law, Bob, **IV:** 756
Law clerks
　　African American firsts, **II:** 477
Law enforcement officers and administrators, **II:**
　　486–487 *See also* Law and lawyers
　　African American firsts, **I:** 93, 106, 107
　　African American women's firsts, **I:** 104, 105
　　　III: 509
　　equal employment opportunity, **I:** 63
　　organizations and associations, **II:** 426, 437, 441
　　as part of criminal justice system, **II:** 451
Law firms

African American firsts, **III:** 589
Law offices of E. David Ellington, **III:** 586
Law, Oliver, **I:** 25
Lawless, Theodore K., **V: 1161–1162**
Lawrence, David, **II:** 480
Lawrence, Jacob, **V:** 1094, **1112–1113**
　works by, **V:** *1093*
Lawrence, Kansas, **I:** 14
Lawrence, Martin, **IV:** 886, **907–908**
Lawrence, Robert H., Jr., **V:** 1142, **1162,** *1162*
Lawrence-Lightfoot, Sarah, **III: 645**
Lawson, James, **II:** 364 **III:** 681
Lawson, Jennifer, **IV:** 760
Lawson, John, **I:** 204
Lawson State Community College, **III:** 654
Lawsuits *See* name of specific case, e.g., *Brown v.*
　Board of Education of Topeka, Kansas
Le Mat, Paul, **IV:** 860
Leadership Conference on Civil Rights, **II:** 397, **429**
League for Community Service, **I:** 200
League for the Protection of Colored Women, **II:** 396
Lean on Me, **IV:** 847
Lear, Norman, **IV:** 836 **V:** 1064
The Learning Tree, **IV:** 847
Leary, Sheridan, **II:** 331
Leatherwood, Robert, **IV:** 776
LeDroit Park Historic District, **I:** 187
Lee, Bertram, **V:** 1174
Lee, Canada, **IV: 866–867**
Lee, Chong S., **III:** 678
Lee, Don L. *See* Madhubuti, Haki
Lee, Ed, **IV:** 861
Lee, Everett, **I:** 95
Lee, Jarena, **III:** 673, **700**
Lee, John, **I:** 91
Lee, Robert E., **II:** 330
Lee, Shirley Jackson, **III:** 498
Lee, Spike, **IV:** 857, 864, **867,** *867,* 902 **V:** 1063
　impact on cinema, **IV:** 834
　and *Malcolm X,* **I:** 73 **IV:** 856
　music in films, **V:** 984, 1016, 1044, 1076
Lee, Tom, **I:** 218
Lee v. Macon County Board of Education, **II:** 461
Lee-Smith, Hughie, **V:** 1094, **1114**
Lefall, LaSalle D., Jr., **III:** 665
Lefkowitz, Mary, **III:** 630
Lefon, Thomy, **I:** 88
Leftenant-Colon, Nancy, **I:** 93
Legal Defense and Education Fund (NAACP), **II:** 396,
　402, **430**
Legett, Joffree, **I:** 83
Lehrer-MacNeil News Hour, **IV:** 760, 773
Leidesdorff Street, **I:** 183
Leidesdorff, William Alexander, **I:** 183
Leland, John, **III:** 672

Leland, Mickey, **III:** *524*
Lemon, Ralph, **IV:** 909
LeMoyne-Owen College, **III:** 654
L'Enfant, Pierre Charles, **I:** 198 **V:** 1151
Lenoir, Gerald, **II:** 477
León, Tania Justina, **IV: 942–943**
Leonard, Lotte, **IV:** 934
Leonard, Sheldon, **IV:** 836
Leonard, "Sugar" Ray, **V:** *1172,* **1193**
Les Brown, Unlimited, Inc., **IV:** 765
Lesbian issues *See* Gay, lesbian, and bisexual issues
Leslie, Lisa, **V:** *1178*
Lesotho, **II: 258–259**
Lessnau, Robert, **I:** 72
Lester, Julius, **III: 735**
LeTang, Henry, **IV:** 902
Lethal Weapon, **IV:** 847
Letter from Birmingham Jail, **II:** 361
Levine, James, **IV:** 927
Levy, Edward, **I:** 51
Lewis, Abraham Lincoln, **III:** 547
Lewis, Byron, **IV: 867**
Lewis, Carl, **V:** 1175, **1193,** *1194*
Lewis College of Business, **III:** 654
Lewis, David Levering, **III: 645,** 665
Lewis, Delano, **IV: 775–776**
Lewis, Edmonia, **V:** *1098,* **1114–1115**
　works by, **V:** *1114*
Lewis, Furry, **V:** 974
Lewis, Henry J., **I:** 98 **IV: 943**
Lewis, James, **I:** 198
Lewis, John, **I:** 84 **II:** 364 **III:** 498, 503, **523–524,**
　524, 676
Lewis, John Aaron, **V: 1014**
Lewis, Mel, **V:** 1013
Lewis, Norman, **V: 1115**
Lewis, Oliver, **I:** 19, 87 **V:** 1177
Lewis, Reggie, **I:** 74
Lewis, Reginald F., **III: 589**
Lewis, Samella, **V:** 1097
Lewis, Terry, **V:** 1064
Lewis, Woodrow, **II:** *470*
Lhevine, Rosina, **IV:** 941
The Liberation of L.B. Jones, **IV:** 847
Liberation of women *See* Women's rights and
　women's rights activists
The Liberator, **I:** 10, 123
　masthead of, **I:** *124*
Liberia, **I:** 9 **II: 259**
Liberty, Jeff, **I:** 184
　gravemarker for, **I:** *185*
Liberty party, **I:** 11, 14
Libraries and librarians, **II:** 423 **III:** 643 **IV: 777–778**
　See also name of specific library, e.g., Jaffrey
　Public Library

African American firsts, **I:** 196
Libya, **II: 259–260**
Liele, George, **I:** 5, 192 **III:** 672, **700**
Lieutenant Governors
    African American firsts, **I:** 61
Life and Adventures of James P. Beckwourth,
        Mountaineer, Scout and Pioneer, **III:** 584
Life expectancy *See* Population
Lift Every Voice and Sing, **I:** 151 **III:** 733 **IV:** 941
Lightfoot, Elba, **V:** 1094
Lightning Rod, **V:** 1044
Lil Kim, **V:** 1045
Lilies of the Field, **IV:** 847
Lillie, Bea, **IV:** 917
Lin, Maya, **I:** 67, 179
Lincoln, Abbey, **V: 1014,** 1024
Lincoln, Abraham, **I:** 16, *16,* 189, 190 **II:** 339, 386
        V: 1206
    assassination, **I:** 17
    election, **I:** 15
    and Emancipation Proclamation, **I:** 16, 133–134,
        134
    landmarks, **I:** 186, 207
    and slavery, **I:** 16 **II:** 331–332, 332
Lincoln County Cattle War (1877), **I:** 207
Lincoln Hall (Berea College), **I:** 196
Lincoln Institute Complex, **I:** 196
Lincoln Memorial, **I:** 33, 187
Lincoln Motion Picture Company, **IV:** 830
Lincoln Park, **I:** 185, 186
Lincoln University (Missouri), **I:** 205 **III:** 654
    buildings, **I:** *204*
Lincoln University (Pennsylvania), **I:** 14 **III:** 624, 654
Lincoln, Wycliffe, **V:** *982*
"Lining out" technique, **IV:** 957
Linstead market, Jamaica, **II:** *304*
The Lion King (Play), **IV:** 898
Lisa, Manuel, **I:** 206
Listen Chicago, **IV:** 756
Listen Up!: The Lives of Quincy Jones, **IV:** 848
Liston, Melba, **V:** 984, **1015**
Liston, Sonny, **V:** 1180
Liston-Smith, Lonnie, **V:** 984
Literary and drama awards *See* name of specific
        award, i.e., Pulitzer Prizes
Literary movements *See* name of specific movement,
        e.g., Harlem Renaissance movement
Literature, **III: 709–748** *See also* Authors; name of
        specific genre, e.g., Novels and novelists
    African, **II:** 232–233
    African American firsts, **III:** 709
    of Antebellum America, **III:** 709
    breaking genre barriers, **III:** 713
    of Colonial America, **III:** 709
    slave narratives, **III:** 710

    twentieth century, **III:** 711–712, 713–714
    web sites, **V:** 1148–1149
Little Henry, **IV:** 880
Little, Levi, **V:** 1077
Little, Malcolm *See* X, Malcolm
Little Richard, **V:** 1037, 1066, **1070–1071,** 1076
Little Rock, Arkansas, **I:** 30
Little Rock Nine, **I:** *32,* 160 **II:** 352
Little Stevie Wonder *See* Wonder, Stevie
Liuzzo, Viola Gregg, **I:** 35
Livingston, Jane, **V:** 1098
Livingstone College, **III:** 654
L.L. Cool J, **IV:** 892
Llewellyn, James B., **III: 589–590**
Lloyd, Anthony, **I:** 64
Lloyd, Earl, **V:** 1173
Lobbyists
    African American firsts, **III:** 602
Local 28, Sheet Metal Workers International
        Association v. EEOC, **II:** 474
Local No. 93, International Association of
        Firefighters v. City of Cleveland, **II:** 474
Locke, Alain, **I:** 89 **III: 645–646 IV:** 751, 858 **V:** 1124
    authors influenced by, **III:** 732 **V:** 1127
    and Harlem Renaissance movement, **III:** 711
        V: 1092
Lockhart, Beryl, **II:** 479
Lodge of Free and Accepted Masons, **II:** 404
Logan, Rayford, **I:** 188
Logan, Samuel, Jr., **IV: 776**
Loitering, **I:** 48
Lomax-Hannon Junior College, **III:** 654
Long, Earl, **I:** 30, 31
Long, Jefferson F., **I:** 87 **III:** 539
Long jumpers *See* Track and field athletes
Long, Richard A., **III:** 665
Long, Vicki, **III:** 700
The Long Walk Home, **IV:** 848
Longfellow, Henry Wadsworth, **V:** 1115
Longshorepersons
    African American women's firsts, **I:** 99
Look Out Sister, **IV:** 848
LOR Records and Management, **V:** 1077
Lorde, Audre, **III:** 602, **735**
Lorraine Hotel, **I:** 70, 219
Los Angeles, California
    African American firsts, **I:** 99 **III:** 504 **IV:** 783
Los Angeles Chamber Orchestra, **IV:** 943
Los Angeles Open (Golf), **V:** 1201
Losing Isaiah, **IV:** 848
Lost Boundaries, **IV:** 848
Louis, Joe, **III:** 591 **V:** 1169, 1172, **1194,** *1194,* 1200
Louis Jordan and His Tympany Five, **V:** 1036, *1037*
Louis, Murray, **IV:** 908
Louis Swint and Willie Johnson v. Pullman

Standard and the United Steelworkers of America, **II**: 465
Louis, Terry, **V**: 1046
Louisiana
    admission into Union, **I**: 8
    African American newspapers, **IV**: 799
    African American radio stations, **IV**: 816–817
    African American television stations, **IV**: 826
    civil rights issues, **I**: 20, 30, 31
    landmarks, **I**: 197
    racial classification law, **I**: 57
    riots and revolts, **I**: 7, 8, 49
    slavery laws, **I**: 8, 16
Louisiana Attorney General's Office, **II**: 372
Louisiana ex rel. Gremillion v. NAACP, **I**: 32 **II**: 397
Louisiana State Museum, **I**: 197
Louisville Free Public Library, **I**: 196
Louisville, New Orleans and Texas Railway v. Mississippi, **I**: 19
Love Jones, **IV**: 848
Love, Nat, **I**: 217, *218*
Love, Ross, **IV**: 759
Love, Ruth, **I**: 100
Lovejoy, Elijah P., **I**: 11
Loving v. Virginia, **II**: 469
Lowe, Mary Johnson, **II**: 453
Lowe, Sylvia, **V**: 1098
Lowe, Warren, **V**: 1098
Lowery, Joseph E., **II**: **409**, *410* **III**: 680
Lucien, Jon, **V**: 983
Lucy, Autherine, **I**: 29
Lula Washington Dance Theater, **IV**: 890
Lumumba, Patrice, **II**: 382
Lunceford, Jimmie, **V**: 978, **1015**
Lunch counters, **I**: 31 **II**: 364
Lupus, **III**: 607
Lyles, Aubrey, **IV**: 883, 893, 915
Lyman, Frank, **V**: 1084
Lynch, John R., **I**: 19, 88 **V**: 1212
Lynch Law in Georgia (Ida Wells-Barnett)
    title page, **II**: *370*
Lynchings, **I**: 23, 27 **II**: 344
    legislation, **I**: 22, 24
    reports, **I**: 28
    speeches against, **I**: 145
Lyons, Deborah, **III**: 684
Lyons, Henry J., **I**: 83 **III**: 684, 690

M

M Street High School, **I**: 188 **III**: 637
Maafa *See* Black Nationalism and nationalists
Mabley, Jackie "Moms," **IV**: 886, **908**
Macedonia Baptist Church (Bloomville, South
    Carolina), **I**: 81

The Mack, **IV**: 848
Mack, Craig, **V**: 1051
Mackey, Edward W.M., **III**: 534
MacNeil-Lehrer NewsHour, **IV**: 760, 773
Madagascar, **II**: **260–261**
Madame C.J. Walker Building, **I**: 195
Madden, Martin, **III**: 513
Maddox, Lester G., **I**: 45 **III**: 503
Madhubuti, Haki, **II**: 383 **III**: **737** **IV**: 751
Magazine editors *See* Editors (Magazines and
    newspapers)
Magazines and magazine publishers, **IV**: 770, 773–
    774 *See also* Editors (Magazines and
    newspapers); Journalism and journalists; Media
    and publishing
    African American firsts, **II**: 477
    African American magazines, **IV**: 806–810
Mahogany, Kevin, **V**: 983
Mahone, Paula, **I**: 109
Mahoney, Charles H., **I**: 94
Mahoney, Mary E., **I**: 88
Maiden Lane, **I**: 3, 210
Maine, **I**: 14
    admission into Union, **I**: 9
    African American television stations, **IV**: 826
    landmarks, **I**: 197
Maine Human Rights Commission, **II**: 372
Makeba, Miriam, **IV**: 775
Makeup industry *See* Beauty industry and salons
*Making Malcolm: The Myth and Meaning of Malcolm
    X*, **III**: 639
Makonnen, Lij Ras Tafari *See* Selassie, Haile
Malan, Daniel, **II**: 227
Malawi, **II**: **261–262**
Malcolm Brown Gallery, **V**: 1134
Malcolm X *See* X, Malcolm
Malcolm X (Film), **I**: 73 **IV**: 848
Malcolm X Academy (Detroit, Michigan)
    students and principals, **III**: *630*
Mali, **II**: **262–263**
Malice Green murder, **I**: 74
Mallett, Conrad L., Jr., **I**: 107
Mamlok, Ursula, **IV**: 942
The Man, **IV**: 848
Manchild in the Promised Land, **III**: 720
Mandela, Nelson, **II**: 227, 228, *228*, 275–276, 362, *399*
    III: 519 **IV**: 970
Mandela, Winnie, **I**: 60, 61
Manilow, Barry, **V**: 1062
Mann, Paul, **IV**: 874
Manned Orbiting Laboratory, **V**: 1162
Manning, Kenneth R., **III**: 666
Manning, Sarah Mae, **III**: 676
Mannion, Elizabeth, **IV**: 946

Mann-Simmons Cottage Museum of African-American
    Culture, **V:** 1134
Mansfield, Jane, **V:** 1071
MAP (Minority AIDS Project), **III:** 693
Map songs, **IV:** 958–959 *See also* Sacred music and
    musicians
Marable, Fate, **V:** 986
Marbury, Donald L., **IV:** 760
March on Washington (1963), **I:** *36*, 187, 187 **II:** 346,
    361
Marchbanks, Vance, **V:** 1143
Marciano, Rocky, **V:** 1194
Marcus, Sydney, **III:** 540
Marie Brown Associates, **III:** 585
Marie Christine, **IV:** 908
Marine biology *See* Biology and biologists
Marine Corps and Marines, A-14 **V:** 1239–1240, 1242–
    1243 *See also* Military
    African American firsts, **I:** 93, 94 **V:** 1239, 1240
Marino, Eugene A., **I:** 102 **III:** **700**, *701*
Markers (Landmarks) *See* Chapter 4 for markers by
    city and state
Markham, Dewey "Pigmeat," **IV:** 879, 880 **V:** 1044
Marley, Bob, **III:** 691 **V:** 1056
Marlow, W.D., **II:** 356
Maroons *See* Fugitive slaves
The Marquees, **V:** 1057
Marr, Carmel Carrington, **II:** **485**
Marriage *See* Family and marriage; Interracial
    marriage
Marronage *See* Fugitive slaves
Marsalis, Branford, **V:** 984, **1016**
Marsalis, Wynton, **I:** 106 **IV:** 906 **V:** 981–982, *982*,
    1016
Marshall, George C., **V:** 1223
Marshall, John R., **V:** 1212
Marshall, Margaret, **IV:** 893
Marshall, Paule, **III:** **738**
Marshall, Thurgood, **I:** *43, 44*, 48, 74 **II:** 453–454,
    485–486 III: 643
    and *Brown v. Board of Education*, **I:** *29*, 155
    as Cabinet secretary, **I:** 107
    death, **I:** 73
    landmarks, **I:** 198
    on *Milliken v. Bradley*, **I:** 50
    as NAACP lawyer, **II:** 410 **III:** 627
    retirement, **I:** 70
    as Solicitor General, **I:** 36
    as Supreme Court Justice, **I:** 39, 70, 97
Martin, **IV:** 907
Martin, Barbara, **V:** 1078, 1084
Martin, Ionis Bracy, **V:** **1115**
Martin Luther King, Jr. Center for Nonviolent Social
    Change, **I:** 191 **II:** 362 **III:** 662 **V:** 1130
Martin Luther King, Jr. Day, **I:** 58 **II:** 359

Arizona controversy, **I:** 63, 68
    first observance, **I:** 61, 73, 100
    honoring of inauguration, **I:** *62*
    official declaration, **I:** 71
Martin Luther King, Jr. National Historic District, **I:**
    191 **II:** 359 **V:** 1130
Martin, Roberta, **IV:** 965, **968**
Martin, Sallie, **IV:** 961, 966, **969**
Martin v. Wilks, **I:** 67 **II:** 466
Martin-Frye Quartet, **IV:** 969
Martinique, **II:** **305**
Martin-Morris Music Company, **IV:** 969
Marxism, **II:** 383
Mary Homes College, **III:** 654
Maryland
    African American museums and galleries, **V:**
        1130–1131
    African American newspapers, **IV:** 799
    African American radio stations, **IV:** 817
    landmarks, **I:** 198
    slave laws, **I:** 2, 15
Maryland Human Relations Commission, **II:** 372
Maryland Museum of African Art, **V:** 1131
Maryland State House, **I:** 198
Masks, gas, **V:** 1164
Mason, Charles H., **III:** 676, 688, 689, **700 IV:** 960
Mason, Julian D., Jr., **III:** 746
Masons (Secret order) *See* Freemasonry and
    freemasons
Massachusetts
    African American firsts, **II:** 488
    African American museums and galleries, **V:** 1131
    African American newspapers, **IV:** 799
    African American radio stations, **IV:** 817
    intermarriage laws, **I:** 11
    landmarks, **I:** 198–201
    race riots, **I:** 39
    school desegregation, **I:** 14, 51
    slavery issues, **I:** 1, 6, 14
Massachusetts Attorney General's Office, **II:** 372
Massey, Walter E., **V:** 1145, **1163**
"Master Juba" *See* Lane, William Henry
    "Master Juba"
Master P, **V:** **1071–1072**, *1072*
Masters golf tournament, **I:** 106
    African American firsts, **I:** 79 **V:** 1176, 1185, 1204
The Matadors, **V:** 1078
Mathematics and mathematicians, **V:** 1151, 1152, 1155
    African American firsts, **V:** 1139, 1155
    African American women's firsts, **V:** 1152, 1157
Matney, William C., Jr., **IV:** 758
Matory, James L., **III:** 666
Matthew, Rabbi, **III:** 687
Matthews, Benjamin, **IV:** 924
Matzeliger, Jan Ernst, **I:** 201 **V:** 1138, **1163–1164**

Mauritania, **II: 263–264**
Mauritius, **II: 264–265**
Maverick, Samuel, **I:** 199
Mayfield, Curtis, **V:** 1040, 1042, **1072**
Mayflower of Liberia, **I:** 9
Maynor, Dorothy Leigh, **IV: 944–945,** 959
Mayor and City Council of Baltimore v. Dawson,
  II: 468
Mayors, **II:** 439 **III:** 499–541
  African American firsts, **I:** 97 **II:** 386 **III:** 495
  African American firsts (1970s), **I:** 99 **II:** 385, 411
    III: 495
  African American firsts (1980s), **I:** 57, 59, 67, 100,
    102 **III:** 513, 518, 531, 532, 535 **IV:** 783
  African American firsts (1990s), **I:** 80, 103, 105,
    106, 107, 108
  African American women's firsts, **I:** 83, 103, 104
    III: 522
Mayotte, **II: 265**
Mays, Benjamin E., **II:** 360 **III: 646,** *647*
Mays, Willie, **V:** 1181, 1195
Mazrui, Ali, **II:** 225
M'Bala, Roger Gneon, **II:** 233
M.C. Hammer, **V:** 1045, **1059,** *1059*
M.C. Ren, **V:** 1053
McAlpin, Harry, **I:** 91
McBride, Patricia, **IV:** 894
McCabe, Edwin P., **III:** 546
McCabe, Eugene, **II:** 409
McCabe, Jewell Jackson, **II: 409**
McCann, Les, **V:** 1055
McCarthy, Eugene, **I:** 42
McCartney, Paul, **V:** 1070, 1085
McCaughey, Karen Drake, **I:** 109
McClendon, Rose, **IV:** 881
McCloy, John R., **V:** 1222
McCormick, Cyrus, **V:** 1137
McCoy, Elijah, **I:** 202 **V:** 1138, **1162**
McCoy, Seth, **IV:** 928
McCree, Wade Hampton, **II:** 453, **484,** *484*
McCullough, Geraldine, **V: 1115**
McDaniel, Hattie, **I:** 90 **IV:** 831, *831,* 844, **867–868**
McDaniel, Reuben R., Jr., **III:** 666
McDonald, Audra, **IV:** 885, **908**
McDonald, Gabrielle Kirk, **II: 484,** *485*
McDonald, Michael, **V:** 1070
McDonald's restaurants, **III:** 587
McDuffie, Arthur, **I:** 53, 54
McFerrin, Bobby, Jr., **IV: 943–944,** *944* **V:** 983
McFerrin, Robert, **IV: 943**
McGee, Brownie, **V:** 975
McGhee, Howard "Maggie," **V:** 997, **1015–1016**
McGovern, George, **I:** 48, 49
McGuire, George Alexander, **III:** 686
McGwire, Mark, **V:** 1188

McHenry, Donald E., **III:** 666
McIntosh Gallery, **V:** 1130
McIntyre, Charshee, **II: 389**
McIntyre, Makenda Ken, **II:** 389
McKane, Alice Woodby, **V:** 1140
McKay, Claude, **I:** 210 **III: 736**
McKenney, Morris, **IV:** 881
McKenzie, Vashti, **III:** 681
McKinley, William, **II:** 337, 370, 371 **III:** 507
McKinney, Cynthia A., **I:** 72, 78 **III:** 498, 517 **IV:** 775
McKinney, Gene C., **I:** 105 **V:** 1226, 1227
McKinney, Susan, **I:** 87
McKissick, Floyd B., **I:** 52 **II:** 398, 404, **410,** *411*
McKlesky v. Kemp, **II:** 451, 471–472
McKlesky, Warren, **II:** 471–472
McLarty, Thomas F., III, **V:** 1243
McLaurin, G.W., **II:** 460
*McLaurin v. Oklahoma State Regents for Higher
  Education*, **II:** 460
McLean, Jackie, **V:** 985
McLendon, John, **I:** 96 **V:** 1173
McLeod Hospital, **III:** 633
McLin Ensemble, **IV:** 944
McLin, Lena Johnson, **IV: 944**
McLin Singers, **IV:** 944
McMillan, Terry, **III: 736,** *737*
McMillian, Theodore, **II: 484–485**
McNair, Denise, **I:** 179
McNair, Ronald E., **I:** 52, *101,* 207 **V:** 1143, **1163,**
  1163
McNamara, Robert, **I:** 39 **V:** 1224
McNeil, John S., **III:** 666
McPhail, Sharon, **I:** 75 **III:** 499
McPhatter, Clyde, **V:** 1036, 1067, 1083
McPherson, James Alan, **III: 736**
McQueen, Butterfly, **IV: 868,** *868*
McRae, Carmen, **V: 1016**
McRoy, Ruth G., **III:** 666
McShann, Jay, **V:** 1021
M.E. Norman (Boat), **I:** 218
Meany, George, **I:** 46
Meat-packing industry, **V:** 1158
Mecham, Evan, **I:** 63, 68
Mechanics (Automotive), **V:** 1160
Mechanics and Farmers Bank, **I:** 212
Medals of Honor (Civilian)
  African American firsts, **I:** 99
Medals of Honor (Military), **I:** 18, 199, 204 **V:**
  1210, 1215
  African American firsts, **I:** 103, 193 **V:** 1209,
    1228, 1238
  American Civil War, **I:** 16
  list of African American recipients, A-12–A-14
  Vietnam War, **V:** 1224
  World War II, **I:** 79 **V:** 1221

Medgar Evers College of City University of New
    York, **III:** 654
Media and publishing, **IV: 749–827** *See also*
    Journalism and journalists; specific type of
    publishing, e.g., Book publishing and publishers
    African American firsts, **III:** 589
    African American publishing companies, **IV:**
        787–790
    biographical profiles, **II:** 762–288
    organizations and associations, **II:** 419, 421, 425–
        426, 432, 436, 446 **IV:** 754
    web sites, **IV:** 762 **V:** 1149
Medicaid, **III:** 606
Medical schools *See also* Medicine and medical
        doctors; Professional degrees; Universities and
        colleges
    African American women's firsts, **V:** 1155
Medicine and medical doctors, **II:** 422, 424, 440 **V:**
        1140, 1141, 1145 *See also* Nursing and nurses;
        Surgery and surgeons
    African American firsts, **I:** 85, 86, 109 **V:** 1140,
        1141, 1161, 1166
    African American women's firsts, **I:** 86, 87, 99, 183
        V: 1140, 1155
    biographical profiles, **V:** 1150–1167
    contributions of women, **V:** 1140
    only African American in Colorado, **V:** 1141
    organizations and associations, **II:** 422, 440
    shortage of African Americans, **V:** 1144
    signs of slow growth, **V:** 1140
Medico-Chirurgical Society, **V:** 1167
Meek, Carrie P., **I:** 72 **III:** 498
Meeks, Gregory W., **III:** 498
Megachurches, **III:** 678–679, 699 *See also* Churches;
        Religion
Meharry Medical College, **III:** 654 **V:** 1140
Mehirge, Robert, **I:** 49
Mehta, Zubin, **IV:** 928
Melba Liston and Company, **V:** 1015
Melrose Plantation, **I:** 197
Melvin B. Tolson Black Heritage Center, **III:** 662
Members of Congress, **III:** 499–541
    African American firsts, **I:** 23, 49, 72, 204 **III:**
        493, 509, 513
    African American women's firsts, **I:** 57, 98
Members of Congress (United States House of
        Representatives), **III:** 499–541, 519–520, 697
    African American firsts, **I:** 87, 104, 193, 217 **III:**
        511, 513, 529, 534, 536
    African American women's firsts, **I:** 25 **III:** 495,
        508, 509, 521
    organizations and associations, **II:** 428
    requirements for membership, **II:** 470
Memorials *See* Chapter 4 for memorials by city and

state; name of specific memorial, e.g., Civil
    Rights Memorial
Memphis Black Arts Alliance, **V:** 1135
Memphis Blues (Song), **V:** 1003
Memphis Engineers Club, **I:** 218
Memphis Minnie, **V:** 974, **1017**
Memphis, Tennesse, **I:** 17
Menace II Society, **IV:** 848
Mennonites, **I:** 112 **II:** 328
Mental health professionals *See* name of specific
        profession, e.g., Psychology and psychologists
Mercury Records, **V:** 1066
Meredith, James H., **I:** 33, 37, 77, 161
Merion Cemetery, **I:** 215
Meritor Savings Bank, FSB v. Vinson, **II:** 465
Merrick, John, **I:** 212
The Message (Song), **V:** 1044
Meteorology and meteorologists, **IV:** 767, 779 **V:**
        1145, 1164
The Meters, **V:** 1040
Method Man, **V:** 1047
Methodist Church, **I:** 214 **II:** 424 **III:** 672 *See also*
        Churches; Religion
    African American firsts, **I:** 85
    African American women's firsts, **I:** 100
Methodist Episcopal Church, **I:** 7 **III:** 699 *See also*
        Churches; Religion
Metro Broadcasting v. FCC, **I:** 68
Metroplitan Opera Company, **IV:** 925
Metropolitan African Methodist Episcopal Church
        (District of Columbia), **I:** 188
Metropolitan Applied Research Center, **I:** 51
Metropolitan Community Church
    African American firsts, **III:** 603
Metropolitan Opera (New York City, New York), **I:** 93
        IV: 943, 945
    African American firsts, **IV:** 887
Metters Industries, Inc., **III:** 590
Metters, Samuel, **III: 590**
Mexican-American War, **II:** 325
Mexico, **II: 305–306**
Mfume, Kweisi, **I:** 76, 77 **III:** 495, **524–525,** *525*
Michael Griffith incident, **I:** 62
Micheaux, Oscar, **IV:** 829–830, **868–869**
Michel, Prakazrel Pras, **V:** 1056
Michell, Abbie, **IV:** 881
Michel'le, **V:** 1053
Michigan, **I:** 39, 47
    African American firsts, **II:** 484
    African American museums and galleries, **V:** 1131
    African American newspapers, **IV:** 799–800
    African American radio stations, **IV:** 817–818
    African American television stations, **IV:** 826
    landmarks, **I:** 201–203
Michigan Attorney General's Office, **II:** 372

Michigan Chronicle, **IV:** 776
Michigan Civil Rights Department, **II:** 372
Michigan Youth Development Foundation, **V:** 1193
Mickens, Ronald E., **III:** 666
Middle Passage, **II:** 377
Middleton, Mark, **V:** 1077
Midshipmen
    African American firsts, **I:** 87 **V:** 1233
Mighty Mystics, **V:** 1077
Migrations of African Americans, **I:** 195 **III:** 545–546
    from American South, **I:** 19, 28, 193, 195
        III: 544–546
Milanov, Zinka, **IV:** 925
Mile, George L., Jr., **IV:** 760
Miles, Buddy, **V:** 1061
Miles College, **III:** 654
Miles, Leo, **I:** 99
Miles to Go, **III:** 626
Miles, William Henry, **III:** 688, **701**
Milestone Comics, **IV:** 752
Milhaud, Darius, **IV:** 925
Military, **V: 1205–1243** *See also* name of specific
        branch, e.g., Army and Army officers; name of
        specific war, e.g., American Revolution
    1970s and 1980s, **V:** 1225–1226
    African American firsts, **V:** 1230, 1231
    biographical profiles of officers, **V:** 1227–1243
    desegregation, **V:** 1221–1222, 1224
    during interwar years, **V:** 1215
    in new millenium, **V:** 1226–1227
    statistics on ready reserves, **V:** 1244
    web sites, **V:** 1150
Military academies and training schools *See* name of
        specific school, e.g., United States Military
        Academy (USMA) at West Point
Military advisors and attachés
    African American firsts, **I:** 103, 214
Military honors *See* Medals of Honor (Military)
Military regiments *See also* name of specific
        regiment, e.g., 54th Massachusetts Regiment
    African American firsts, **V:** 1114, 1209, 1237
    American Revolution, **I:** 6
    best of World War I, **V:** 1213
    World War II, **I:** 26, 27
Militia Act (1862), **V:** 1207
Millender-McDonald, Juanita, **III:** 498
Miller, Bebe, **IV: 908–909**
Miller, Cheryl, **V:** 1177, 1188, **1195**
Miller, Darrell, **V:** 1195
Miller, Doris "Dorie," **I:** 26 **V:** *1238*, **1238–1239**
Miller, Flournoy, **IV:** 883, 893, 915
Miller, Henry, **V:** 1106
Miller, Marilyn, **IV:** 917
Miller, Reggie, **V:** 1195
Miller v. Johnson, **II:** 459

Milliken v. Bradley, **I:** 50 **II:** 463
Milliken v. Michigan Road Builders Association,
        I: 66
Million Man March, **I:** 76, *78*, 175–177 **II:** 387 **III:**
        611, 678, 682
Million Woman March, **I:** 80 **III:** 611
Million Youth March, **I:** 81 **II:** 390
Millionaires
    African American firsts, **I:** 88
    African American women's firsts, **III:** 578
Mills, Florence, **I:** 210 **IV:** 883, **909**
Milner, Thirman, **I:** 59
Milton House and Museum, **I:** 224
Milton, John, **I:** 200
Milton L. Olive Park, **I:** 193
Minelli, Liza, **IV:** 859
Miner Normal School, **I:** 188
Miner Teachers College, **I:** 188
Mingus, Charles, **V:** 980, 983, 996, *1017*, **1017–1018**
Ministers, **II:** 339 **III:** 646 *See also* Bishops;
        Monsignors; name of specific religion, e.g.,
        African Methodist Episcopal Church; Priests
    African American firsts, **I:** 85, 94, 103, 212 **II:** 388
        III: 700
    criminal investigations, **III:** 684
    gender issues, **III:** 681
    in megachurches, **III:** 699
    in Postbellum America, **II:** 334
    techniques for ministering, **III:** 683
Minneapolis, Minnesota
    African American women's firsts, **I:** 104
Minnesota, **I:** 203
    African American museums and galleries, **V:** 1131
    African American newspapers, **IV:** 800
    African American radio stations, **IV:** 818
    African American television stations, **IV:** 826
Minnesota Human Rights Department, **II:** 372
Minnie, Memphis *See* Memphis Minnie
Minority AIDS Project (MAP), **III:** 693
Minority Arts Resource Council, **V:** 1134
Minority Business Enterprise Legal Defense and
        Education Fund, **II: 430**
Minstrelsy and minstrels, **IV:** 830, 878, *878*
The Miracles, **V:** 1078
Miscegenation *See* Interracial marriage
Miss America pageants, A-5
    African American firsts, **I:** 100, 104 **IV:** 874
Miss Black America pageants, A-5–A-6
Miss Evers' Boys, **IV:** 848
Miss New Jersey pageants, **I:** 100
Miss Teen of America pageants
    African American firsts, **I:** 106
Miss United States pageants
    African American firsts, **I:** 103
Miss Universe pageants

African American firsts, **I:** 105
Miss USA pageants, A-6
Missionizing and missionaries, **II:** 423 **III:** 621,
    671–672, 703
    African American firsts, **I:** 85, 192 **III:** 671
Mississippi, **I:** 9
    admission into Union, **I:** 8
    African American museums and galleries, **V:** 1131
    African American newspapers, **IV:** 800
    African American radio stations, **IV:** 819
    civil rights issues, **I:** 31, 33, 72, 136–138
    landmarks, **I:** 203–205
    race riots, **I:** 31, 33, 47
Mississippi Attorney General's Office, **II:** 372
Mississippi Freedom Democratic Party, **II:** 356
Mississippi Masala, **IV:** 848
Mississippi State Sovereignty Commission, **I:** 81
Mississippi Valley State University, **III:** 654
Missouri, **I:** 54
    admission into Union, **I:** 9
    African American firsts, **III:** 509
    African American museums and galleries, **V:** 1131
    African American newspapers, **IV:** 800–801
    African American radio stations, **IV:** 820
    landmarks, **I:** 205–206
Missouri Compromise, **I:** 9, 14, 131 **II:** 325, 341, 449
    landmarks, **I:** 195
Missouri ex rel. Gaines v. Canada, **I:** 155
        II: 460, 481
Missouri Human Rights Commission, **II:** 372
Missouri v. Jenkins, **I:** 68
Mitchell, Abbie, **IV:** 879, **909–910,** 928
Mitchell, Arthur (Dancer), **IV:** 888, 889, *889,* 906,
        910, 943
Mitchell, Arthur (Politician), **I:** 26 **III:** 513, **525–526**
Mitchell, Brandon, **V:** 1077
Mitchell, Charles L., **I:** 86
Mitchell, John, **IV:** 782
Mitchell, Joni, **V:** 1068
Mitchell, Leona, **IV: 945,** *945*
Mitchell, Loften, **III: 738 IV:** 880
Mitchell, Mitch, **V:** 1061
Mitchell, Nicole, **IV:** 910
Mitchell v. United States, **I:** 26
Mitchell, Willie, **V:** 1059
Mitropolous, Dmitri, **IV:** 930
Mizelle, Ralph E., **II:** 476
Mo' Better Blues, **IV:** 848
Mo', Keb', **V: 1018**
Mobutu, Joseph, **II:** 249
Models (Fashion)
    African American firsts, **I:** 96, 106
    African American women's firsts, **III:** 592
Modern Jazz Quartet, **V:** 1014
Mollison, Irving Charles, **I:** 91

Mollison, Irwin C., **II:** 453
Monagas, Lionel, **IV:** 757
Mondale, Walter, **II:** 358
Monk, Thelonious, **V:** 978, 980, 985, 994, **1018,** *1019*
Monroe Elementary School, **I:** 196
Monroe, James, **II:** 328
Monsignors *See also* Bishops; Ministers; Priests
    African American firsts, **I:** 99
Montana
    landmarks, **I:** 206
Montana Attorney General's Office, **II:** 372
Montana, Joe, **V:** 1198
The Montel Williams Show, **IV:** 785–786
Montero, Felipa, **IV:** 952
Montgomery, Benjamin, **V:** 1137
Montgomery Bus Boycott, **I:** 29 **II:** 346, 350,
        360, 365, 397
    landmarks, **I:** 179
Montgomery, Evangeline, **V: 1115–1116**
Montgomery Improvement Association, **II:** 350,
        365, 397
Montgomery, Isiah Thornton, **I:** 204
Montserrat, **II: 306**
Monuments *See also* Chapter 4 for monuments by
        city and state
    African American firsts, **I:** 52, 189, 192, 198, 205
    African American women's firsts, **I:** 185
Moon, Warren, **I:** 105
Moore, Al, **IV:** 880
Moore, Audley "Queen Mother," **II: 389–390**
Moore, Dorothy Rudd, **IV: 945**
Moore, Emerson, Jr., **I:** 99
Moore, Harold, Jr. *See* Muhammad, Khalid Abdul
Moore, Harry T., **II: 363–364**
Moore, Herman E., **II:** 453
Moore, Kermit, **IV: 945–946**
Moore, Matthew, **III:** 700
Moore, Melba, **IV:** 884
Moore, Sarah Peck, **IV:** 925
Moore, Tim, **IV:** 879
Moore, Undine Smith, **IV: 946**
Moore, William, Jr., **III:** 666
Moorehead, Scipio, **V:** 1089
Moorer, Michael, **V:** 1186, 1189
Moorish Science Temple, **III:** 692
Moorland, Jesse Edward, **III: 646**
Moorland-Spingarn Collection, **I:** 186
Moorland-Spingarn Research Center, **III:** 662
Moraga, Cherríe, **IV:** 783
More Than a Melody, **IV:** 964
Morehouse College, **I:** 191 **III:** 654
Morehouse Research Institute, **III:** 662
Morehouse School of Medicine, **III:** 534, 655
Morgan, Garrett, **V:** 1138, **1164,** *1164*
Morgan, Irene, **II:** 468

Morgan, Margaret, **II:** 472
Morgan, Michael DeVard, **IV: 946**
Morgan, Rose Meta, **III: 590–591**
Morgan State University, **I:** 198 **III:** 655
Morgan v. Virginia, **I:** 27 **II:** 468
Morial, Marc, **III: 526**
Morley, Jefferson, **V:** 1043
Morocco, **II: 265–266**
Moroder, Giorgio, **V:** 1081
Morrill Acts, **III:** 624
Morris Brown College, **I:** 191 **III:** 655
Morris, Carolyn G., **I:** 105
Morris College, **III:** 655
Morris, Kenneth, **IV:** 969
Morris, Sam, **III:** 696
Morrison, Toni, **III:** 611, 666, 714, **738–739,** *739*
    IV: 907
    banning of novels, **I:** 80
    and Nobel Prize for literature, **I:** 104
Morront, John, **I:** 85
Morrow, E. Frederic, **III:** 494
Morrow, John Howard, Jr., **III:** 666
Morse, David, **V:** 1067
Morse, Winslow C., **V:** 1222
Mortgage lending, **III:** 566
Morton, Ferdinand "Jelly Roll," **IV:** 884, 899, 919 **V:**
    986, **1018–1019,** *1019*
Moses, Edwin, **V:** 1175, **1195**
Moskowitz, Henry, **II:** 396
Mosley, Walter, **III: 739**
Mosley-Braun, Carol, **III: 526**
Most Valuable Players (Baseball), **I:** 93
Moten, Bennie, **V:** 987
Mother Bethel African Methodist Episcopal Church
    (Philadelphia, Pennsylvania), **I:** 216
Mother Divine, **III:** 696
Mother Waddles Perpetual Mission, **III:** 613
Motion pictures *See* Films and filmmakers
Motivational speakers, **IV:** 765
Motley, Archibald, **V: 1116,** *1116*
Motley, Constance Baker, **I:** 36, 97, *97* **II:** 453, **486,**
Motley, Marion, **V:** 1171
Moton, Robert R., **I:** 220
Motown Museum, **I:** *202*, 203
Motown Records, **V:** 1041–1042, 1058, 1078
    landmarks, **I:** 203
Mott, James, **II:** 329, 341
Mott, Lucretia, **II:** 329, 341
Mouldileno, Lydie E., **III:** 666
Mound Bayou, **I:** 204
Mount Hope Cemetery, **I:** 211
Mount Kilimanjaro, **II:** *231*
Mourning, Alonzo, **V:** *1174*
Movies *See* Films and filmmakers
Moynihan, Daniel Patrick, **I:** 46 **II:** 476 **III:** 599

Mozambique, **II: 266**
Mr. and Mrs. Loving, **IV:** 849
Mr. Olympia titles, A-6
    African American firsts, **V:** 1177
Mr. Universe titles
    African American firsts, **I:** 98
Ms. Olympia titles, A-6
Mswati, III, King, **II:** 277
Mubarak, Hosni, **II:** 252
Mudd, Samuel A., **I:** 190
Muhammad, Benjamin Chavis *See* Chavis,
    Benjamin F., Jr.
Muhammad, Caliph Emmanuel A., **III:** 689
Muhammad, Clara, **III:** 628
Muhammad, Elijah, **I:** 24 **II:** 382, 387, **390 III:** 689,
    690
    call for African American state, **I:** 31
    and Fard Muhammad, **III:** 696
    and Malcolm X, **II:** 392–393
    wiretaps, **I:** 44
    on World War II, **V:** 1216
Muhammad, Fard, **I:** 24 **II:** 390 **III: 696**
Muhammad, Khalid Abdul, **I:** 75 **II: 390,** *391*
Muhammad, Tariq K., **III:** 581
Muhammad, Warith D., **II:** 387 **III:** 689
Muhammad's Temple No. 2 Publications Department,
    IV: 750
Muir, Clive, **III:** 666
Muir v. Louisville Park Theatrical Association,
    II: 468
Mulkey, Lincoln, **II:** 471
Multiple births
    African American firsts, **I:** 107, 109 **III:** 603
Mulzac, Hugh N., **I:** 89
Municipal courts *See* Courts (Municipal)
Municipal government officials *See* Government
    officials (Municipal)
Murders *See* Homicide
Murphy, Eddie, **IV:** 856, 886, 901, **910,** *910*, 914
    V: 1054
Murphy, Harold L., **I:** 71
Murphy, Isaac, **I:** 196 **V:** 1177
Murphy, John Henry, **IV: 777**
Murphy, Thorpe, & Lewis, **III:** 589
Murray, David, **V:** 983
Murray, Donald, **I:** 24
Murray, Ellen, **I:** 217
Murray, Pauli, **III:** 673
Muse, Clarence, **IV: 869**
Museum of African American Art, **V:** 1128
Museum of African and African-American Art and
    Antiquities, **V:** 1132
Museum of Afro American History (Boston), **I:** 198
Museums and galleries, **II:** 420 **V:** 1128–1135 *See also*
    Chapter 4 for museums by city and state; name

of specific museum, e.g., Black American
    West Museum
Music and musicians, **IV:** 921, 924–925 *See also*
    specific type of music, e.g., Gospel music and
    musicians
    African, **II:** 234
    African American firsts, **I:** 96, 98 **V:** 988, 997, 1066
    African American women's firsts, **IV:** 949
    organizations and associations, **II:** 425,
        433, 436, 446
Music awards *See also* Grammy Awards; Music and
    musicians
    African American firsts, **I:** 96, 98, 102, 106
The Music of Black Americans:A History, **IV:** 924
Music promoters, **IV:** 966, 968 *See also* Music and
    musicians
Musical directors *See also* Music and musicians
    African American firsts, **IV:** 940, 943
Musical theater *See* Theater and theater performers
    (Musical)
Mutual Black Network *See* Sheridan
    Broadcasting Network
Mutual Federal Savings and Loan Association, **II:** 406
Mutual Musicians Association Building, **I:** 205
Myers, Amina Claudine, **V:** 983
Myers, Samuel L., Jr., **III:** 666
Myers, Walter Dean, **III: 739–740**
Myrdal, Gunnar, **III:** 507
Myrtilla Miner's School for Colored Girls *See* Miner
    Normal School

N

NAACP (National Association for the Advancement
    of Colored People), **I:** 24 **II:** 345, 354, 380, **431**
    III: 492
    African American firsts, **I:** 22
    "Call" for conference, **II:** 368, 371
    court cases, **I:** 32, 51 **II:** 397
    forerunner, **I:** 20
    founding and development, **I:** 21, 194 **II:** 396
    headquarters, **I:** 60, 61
    leaders, **II:** 401, 403, 406, 416, 417
    membership figures, **I:** 22
    most significant legal victory, **II:** 396
    one of first women to join, **II:** 364
    publishing program, **IV:** 751
    secretaries, **I:** 211
NAACP Legal Defense and Education Fund, **II:** 396,
    402, **430**
NAACP v. Alabama, **II:** 397
Nabrit, James M., **I:** *29*
Nairobi Day School, **III:** 628
Nakasone, Yasuhiro, **I:** 63
Namibia, **II: 266–268**

mining for diamonds in, **II:** *232*
Nannie Helen Burroughs School, **III:** 624, 635
Naomi Sims Collection, **III:** 592
Narratives, slave *See* Slave narratives
Narváez, Pánfilo de, **II:** 236, 317
NASA (National Aeronautics and Space
    Administration), **V:** 1142, 1150, 1151, 1157, 1159
    African American firsts, **I:** 104
NASCAR teams, **V:** 1177
NASDAQ *See also* American Stock Exchange; New
    York Stock Exchange
    African American firsts, **I:** 98
Nash, Diane J., **II: 364**
Nashville, Tennessee, **II:** 364
The Nat King Cole Show, **IV:** 835
Nat Turner's slave insurrection, **I:** 10, 212 **II:** 329, 341
    III: 673
    and *Confessions of Nat Turner*, **II:** *328*
Natchez National Cemetery, **I:** 204
Nathan, Syd, **V:** 1048
Nation of Islam, **II:** 382 **III:** 682, **689** *See also* Islam;
    name of specific person, e.g., Farrakhan, Louis
    converts, **II:** 402
    founding of Temple of Islam, **I:** 24
    headquarters, **I:** 24
    leaders, **I:** 31 **II:** 387, 390, 392 **III:** 696
    publishing enterprises, **IV:** 750
    and rap music, **V:** 1044
    schools founded by, **III:** 628
Nation of Islam's Temple (Number Two), **II:** 390
National Academy of Design
    African American firsts, **I:** 100
National Academy of Recording Arts and Sciences
    Awards *See* Grammy Awards
National Academy of Sciences, **V:** 1139
National Action Council for Minorities in
    Engineering, **II: 430**
National Advisory Commission on Civil Disorder *See*
    Kerner Commission
National Aeronautics and Space Administration *See*
    NASA (National Aeronautics and Space
    Administration)
National African American Leadership Summit,
    II: 402
National African American Museum, **I:** 69
National Afro-American Museum, **I:** 214 **III:** 662
    V: 1134
National Airmen's Association of America, **V:** 1142
National Alliance of Black Interpreters, **II: 430**
National Alliance of Black School Educators, **II: 430**
National Alliance Party (NAP), **III:** 517
National Alumni Council of the United Negro College
    Fund, **II: 430**
National anthem for African Americans *See Lift*
    Every Voice and Sing

National Archives and Records Administration, **I:** 207

National Association for Equal Opportunity in Higher Education, **II: 431**

National Association for the Advancement of Colored People *See* NAACP (National Association for the Advancement of Colored People)

National Association for the Advancement of Colored People (NAACP) Legal Defense and Education Fund *See* NAACP Legal Defense and Education Fund

National Association for the Advancement of Colored People (NAACP) v. Alabama, **II:** 397

National Association of Black Accountants, **II: 431**

National Association of Black and White Men Together, **II: 431**

National Association of Black Catholic Administrators, **II: 431**

National Association of Black Consulting Engineers, **II: 431**

National Association of Black Geologists and Geophysicists, **II: 431**

National Association of Black Hospitality Professionals, **II: 432**

National Association of Black Journalists, **II: 432**

National Association of Black Professors, **II: 432**

National Association of Black Social Workers, **II: 432**

National Association of Black Storytellers, **II: 432**

National Association of Black Women Attorneys, **II: 432**

National Association of Black-Owned Broadcasters, **II: 432**

National Association of Blacks in Criminal Justice, **II: 433**

National Association of Colored Graduate Nurses, **II:** 415

National Association of Colored Women (NACW), **I:** 20, 189 **II:** 368, 371, 395

National Association of Colored Women's Clubs, **I:** 186 **II: 433**

National Association of Investment Companies, **II: 433**

National Association of Media Women, Atlanta Chapter, **IV:** 768

National Association of Minority Contractors, **II: 433**

National Association of Minority Political Women, **II: 433**

National Association of Minority Women in Business, **II: 433**

National Association of Negro Business and Professional Women's Clubs, **II: 433**

National Association of Negro Musicians, **II: 433** **IV:** 933

National Association of Radio and TV News Directors, **IV:** 770

National Association of Securities Dealers Automated Quotation *See* NASDAQ

National Association of State Universities and Land Grant Colleges Office for the Advancement of Public Black Colleges, **II: 442**

National Association of Urban Bankers, **II: 434**

National Bankers Association, **II: 434**

National Baptist Convention of America, Inc., **III: 689 IV:** 960

National Baptist Convention of the USA, Inc., **III: 689**

National Baptist Publishing Board, **IV:** 749

National Bar Association, **II: 434,** 478

National Baseball Hall of Fame, A-6
    African American firsts, **I:** 96

National Basketball Hall of Fame, A-6–A-7
    African American women's firsts, **V:** 1188

National Black Alcoholism Council, **II: 434**

National Black Arts Festival, **V:** 1130

National Black Catholic Clergy Caucus, **II: 434**

National Black Caucus of Local Elected Officials, **II: 434**

National Black Caucus of State Legislators, **II: 434**

National Black Chamber of Commerce, **II: 434**

National Black Child Development Institute, **II: 435** **III:** 662

National Black Coalition of Federal Aviation Employees, **II: 435**

National Black Deaf Advocates, **II: 435**

National Black Gay and Lesbian Conference and Leadership Forum, **II: 435 III:** 613

National Black Independent party, **I:** 54

National Black Law Student Association, **II: 435**

National Black Leadership Roundtable, **II: 435**

National Black MBA Association, **II: 436**

National Black McDonald's Operators Association, **II: 436**

National Black Media Coalition, **II: 436**

National Black Music Caucus of the Music Educators National Conference, **II: 436**

National Black Network, **IV:** 756

National Black Nurses Association, **II: 436**

National Black on Black Love Campaign, **II: 436**

National Black Police Association, **II: 437**

National Black Political Assembly, **I:** 54

National Black Political Convention, **I:** 49

National Black Sisters' Conference, **II: 437**

National Black Survival Fund, **II: 437**

National Black United Front, **II: 437**

National Black United Fund, **II:** 399, 437

National Black Women's Health Project, **II: 438**

National Black Youth Leadership Council, **II: 438**

National Book Awards, A-7 **III:** 732
    African American firsts, **I:** 94

National Business League, **II: 438**

National Catholic Conference for Interracial Justice, **II: 438**

National Caucus and Center on Black Aged, **II: 438** **III:** 662

National Center of Afro-American Artists, **V:** 1131

National Church Arson Task Force, **II:** 349

National Civil Rights Museum *See* Lorraine Hotel

National Coalition for Quality Integrated Education, **II: 439**

National Coalition of 100 Black Women, **II:** 409, **439**

National Coalition of Black Meeting Planners, **II: 438**

National Coalition of Black Voter Participation, **II: 439**

National College Athletic Association *See* NCAA (National College Athletic Association)

National Conference of Black Lawyers, **II: 439**

National Conference of Black Mayors, **II: 439**

National Conference of Black Political Scientists, **II: 439**

National Consortium of Arts and Letters for Historically Black Colleges and Universities, **II: 440**

National Convention of Gospel Choirs and Choruses, Inc., **IV:** 961, 966, 969

National Council of Black Studies, **III:** 662

National Council of Negro Women, **I:** 24, 81, 106 **II:** 406, **440**

National Dental Association, **II: 440**

National Education Association, **III:** 644

National Endowment of the Arts Awards, A-7

National Federation of Afro-American Women, **II:** 395

National Forum for Black Public Administrators, **II: 440**

National Freedmen's Refief Association, **I:** 16

National Funeral Directors and Morticians Association, **II: 440**

National holidays *See* Holidays

National Institute of Arts and Letters, **I:** 91, 93

National League for the Protection of Colored Women, **II:** 396

National League on Urban Conditions Among Negroes *See* National Urban League

National Medal of Arts, A-7

National Medical Association, **II:** 395, **440 V:** 1167

National Minority Health Association, **II:** 440

National Missionary Baptist Convention, **III: 690**

National Museum of African Art, **I:** 188

National Museum of the Tuskegee Airmen, **I:** 203

National Negro Business League, **I:** 20 **III:** 576 **IV:** 769

National Negro Committee *See* NAACP (National Association for the Advancement of Colored People)

National Negro Convention, **I:** 10, 85 **III:** 491

National Negro Finance Corporation, **III:** 579

National Negro Labor Council, **III:** 541

National Negro Network, **I:** 95

National Newspaper Publishers Association, **I:** 79 **IV:** 754, 780

National Organization for the Professional Advancement of Black Chemists and Chemical Engineers, **II: 441**

National Organization of Black County Officials, **II: 441**

National Organization of Black Law Enforcement Executives, **II: 441**

National organizations and associations *See* Organizations and associations

National Pan-Hellenic Council, **II:** 400

National Park Service, **I:** 80, 107

National Primitive Baptist Convention of America, **III: 690**

National Public Radio (NPR), **II:** 452

National Rainbow Coalition, Inc., **II:** 399, **441**

National Security Act of 1947, **V:** 1222

National Society of Arts and Letters Gold Medal of Merit Awards, A-7

National Society of Black Engineers, **II: 441**

National Society of Black Physicists, **II: 441**

National Study of Black College Students, **III:** 662

National Track and Field Hall of Fame, A-7

National Training School for Women and Girls *See* Nannie Helen Burroughs School

National Urban Coalition, **II:** 399, 402, **441**

National Urban League, **II:** 396, 407, 442 **IV:** 751 establishment and development, **I:** 21 **II:** 396 leaders, **I:** 197 **II:** 405, 408, **412,** 418

National Youth movement, **II:** 366

Native Americans, **III:** *547*

Native Guards, **I:** 197

Native Son, **III:** 748 **IV:** 849

"Native Tongues" school of rap, **V:** 1044

NATO (North Atlantic Treaty Organization), **V:** 1242

Natural rights, **I:** 113

Naughty by Nature, **V:** 1045

Naval academies *See* name of specific school, e.g., United States Naval Academy (USNA) at Annapolis

Naval Academy Prep School African American firsts, **IV:** 785

Navarro, Theodore "Fats," **V: 1019**

Navy and naval officers, A-12–A-13 **I:** 7 **V:** 1215 *See also* Military African American firsts, **I:** 90, 98, 106, 109 **V:** 1222, 1228, 1233, 1234, 1242 African American women's firsts, **I:** 77, 99 biographical profiles, **V:** 1223, 1227–1228, 1233–1234, 1238–1239, 1241–1242

Navy Cross, **I:** 26

Naylor, Gloria, **III: 740,** *740*
Nazi party, American, **I:** 58
NCAA (National College Athletic Association), **I:** 82, 100
NCCU Art Museum, **V:** 1133
NdegeOcello, Me'Shell, **III:** 602
Neal, Audrey, **I:** 99
Neal, Larry, **III:** 718 **V:** 1094
Neal v. Delaware, **II:** 466
Neau, Elias, **I:** 3
Nebraska
   admission into Union, **I:** 14
   African American museums and galleries, **V:** 1131
   African American radio stations, **IV:** 820
Nebraska Equal Opportunity Commission, **II:** 372
Negritude, **II:** 381
Negro Actors Guild of America, **IV:** 917
Negro Digest, **IV:** 773
Negro Ensemble Company, **III:** 725 **IV:** 882
Negro Equal Rights League, **II:** 369
Negro Folk Symphony, **IV:** 931
Negro Fort *See* Fort Gadsen
Negro History Bulletin, **II:** 418 **III:** 650
Negro History Week *See* Black History Month
Negro League (Baseball), **V:** 1169
The Negro Mood and Other Essays, **III:** 633
Negro Newspapers Publishers Association *See* National Newspaper Publishers Association
Negro Renaissance movement *See* New Negro era
Negro Society for Historical Research, **III:** 647
Negro Soldiers Monument, **I:** 216
The Negro Yearbook, **IV:** 750
Negro Yearbook Publishing Company, **IV:** 750
Nell, William C., **I:** 86, 199
Nelson, Janet, **IV:** 769
Neo-HooDooism, **III:** 741
Nequai Cosmetics, **IV:** 785
Netherlands Antilles, **II: 306–307**
NetNoir Inc., **III:** 585, 586
Netterville, G. Leon, **I:** 50
Networks, radio *See* Radio networks and stations
Networks, television *See* Television networks and stations
Neumann, J.D., **V:** 1126
Nevada
   African American newspapers, **IV:** 801
   African American radio stations, **IV:** 820
   landmarks, **I:** 206
Nevada Equal Rights Commission, **II:** 373
Nevers, Larry, **I:** 72, 74
Neville Brothers, **V:** 1040
Nevis, **II: 309**
New Bedford Whaling Museum, **I:** 201
New Challenge, **I:** 24 **III:** 745
New Concept Development Center, **III:** 628

New England Anti-Slavery Society, **I:** 10
New England Emigration Society, **I:** 14
New England's Freedmen's Aid Society, **III:** 623
New Hampshire
   landmarks, **I:** 206
New Hampshire Human Rights Commission, **II:** 373
New Haven, Connecticut
   African America firsts, **I:** 67
New Jack City, **IV:** 849
New Jack Swing music, **V:** 1046, 1077 *See also* Popular music and musicians
New Jersey, **I:** 8, 39
   African American museums and galleries, **V:** 1131
   African American newspapers, **IV:** 801
   landmarks, **I:** 206
New Jersey Attorney General's Office, **II:** 373
New Jill Swing music, **V:** 1047 *See also* Popular music and musicians
New Mexico
   African American radio stations, **IV:** 820
   landmarks, **I:** 207
New Mexico Attorney General's Office, **II:** 373
New Negro era, **III:** 710 **V:** 1091–1092
New Orleans, Louisiana, **I:** 17
New Songs of Paradise, **IV:** 960, 970
New Thought movement, **III:** 694
New York (State), **I:** 8, 9, 10
   African American firsts, **III:** 537
   African American museums and galleries, **V:** 1132–1133
   African American newspapers, **IV:** 801–802
   African American radio stations, **IV:** 820
   African American television stations, **IV:** 827
   African American women's firsts, **II:** 486
   landmarks, **I:** 207–212
   race riots, **I:** 35, 39, 48, 70
New York African American Research Foundation, **III:** 662
New York African Free School, **I:** 6 **III:** *622*
New York Age, **I:** 19 **IV:** 769
New York City, New York, **I:** 3, 210 **II:** 329 **III:** 621
   African American firsts, **I:** 67, 103 **III:** 513
   African American women's firsts, **II:** 486
New York City Opera, **IV:** 935
   African American firsts, **I:** 91
New York City Technical College, **III:** 655
New York Drama Critics' Circle Awards
   African American firsts, **I:** 96
New York Freeman, **III:** 492
New York Human Rights Division, **II:** 373
New York Manumission Society, **I:** 6 **II:** 329
New York Metropolitan Opera *See* Metropolitan Opera (New York City, New York)
New York Philharmonic Orchestra, **IV:** 933
New York Public Library, **I:** 211

New York State Library, **I:** 207

New York Stock Exchange *See also* American Stock Exchange; NASDAQ
    African American firsts, **I:** 98 **IV:** 837

New York Tuberculosis and Health Association, **II:** 415

New York University Hall of Fame, **I:** 211

Newark Museum, **V:** 1131

Newby, Dangerfield, **II:** 331

Newman, David "Fathead," **V:** 1049

Newman, Floyd, **V:** 1060

Newport Jazz Festival, **II:** 389

News correspondents *See* Journalism and journalists

NewsHour with Jim Lehrer, **IV:** 760, 773

Newspaper editors *See* Editors (Magazines and newspapers)

Newspapers and newspaper publishers, **I:** 26 **II:** 329 **IV:** 753–754, 791–806 *See also* Editors (Magazines and newspapers); Journalism and journalists; Media and publishing
    African American firsts, **I:** 10, 85, 86, 88, 121, 197 **II:** 329, 343, 370 **IV:** 753, 780
    African American women's firsts, **I:** 100, 186
    biographical profiles, **IV:** 762–787

Newton, Huey P., **II: 411,** *414*
    and Black Panther party, **I:** 36 **II:** 385, 398, 415
    criminal investigations, **I:** 43 **II:** 398, 411

Newton, Lloyd W. "Fig," **I:** 99

Ngabo, Leonce, **II:** 233

Niagara movement, **I:** 20 **II:** 345, 369, 396 **III:** 492

Nicaragua, **II: 307**

Nicholas Brothers, **IV: 911**

Nicholas, Fayard, **IV: 911**

Nicholas, Harold, **IV:** 858, 859, **911**

Nichols, Herbie, **V: 1020**

Nichols, Mike, **IV:** 900

Nicodemus, Kansas, **I:** 195
    advertisements encouraging migration to, **I:** *15*
    African American firsts, **III:** 546
    early migrants to, **I:** *196*

Niger, **II: 268–269**

Nigeria, **II:** 233, 269

Nigger Heaven, **I:** 23

Nike, **I:** 68

Nikolaidi, Elena, **IV:** 936

Nikolais, Alwin, **IV:** 908

NikTom, Ltd., **III:** 726

Nilsson, Birgit, **IV:** 926

92nd Infantry Division, **V:** 1213, 1214, *1217*

93rd Infantry Division, **V:** 1213

Niño, Pedro Alonzo, **I:** 1 **II:** 236, 317

9th Battalion United StatesV.I., **V:** 1211

9th Cavalry Regiment, **V:** 1209

Nix, Robert N.C., **III:** 518

Nixon, L.A., **II:** 458

Nixon, Richard M., **I:** 46, 48, 49, 50 **III:** 505 **IV:** 859
    appointment of African Americans, **I:** 44 **II:** 404, 454 **III:** 644
    and Barbara Jordan speech, **I:** 76, 172
    memo from Daniel P. Moynihan, **I:** 46
    reelection, **I:** 49

Nixon v. Condon, **II:** 458

Nixon v. Herndon, **I:** 23, 24 **II:** 458

Nkanyit, **IV:** 898

Nkrumah, Kwame, **II:** 228–229, 377, 380, 382 **V:** 1108

No Limits (Record company), **V:** 1071

No Maps on My Taps, **IV:** 849

No Way Out, **IV:** 849

Nobel Prizes (Literature),
    African American firsts, **III:** 739
    African American women's firsts, **I:** 104
    African American recipients, A-

Nobel Prizes (Peace), **I:** 186, 209 **II:** 360
    African American firsts, **I:** 93, 202 **III:** 507
    African American recipients, A-8 **I:** 28, 35

Noble, Gil, **IV:** 757

Noble Press, **IV:** 769

Nominations, Presidential *See* Presidential candidates and nominations

Nominations, Vice Presidential *See* Vice Presidential nominations

NORAD (North American Air Defense Command), **I:** 51

Norfolk State University, **III:** 655

Noriega, Manuel, **V:** 1240

Normal schools *See also* Education and educators
    African American firsts, **I:** 180

Normal Vocal Institute, **IV:** 937

Norman, Is That You?, **IV:** 849

Norman, Jessye, **IV:** 922, **946–947,** *947*

North American Air Defense Command (NORAD), **I:** 51

North Atlantic Treaty Organization (NATO)
    African American firsts, **V:** 1242

North Carolina, **I:** 11, 47
    African American museums and galleries, **V:** 1133
    African American newspapers, **IV:** 802–803
    African American radio stations, **IV:** 820–821
    landmarks, **I:** 212

North Carolina A and T State University, **III:** 655

North Carolina Central University, **III:** 655

North Carolina Human Relations Commission, **II:** 373

North Carolina Mutual Life Insurance Company, **I:** 212 **III:** 578

North Carolina State Board of Education v. Swann, **II:** 462

North Dakota, **I:** 18

North Dakota Attorney General's Office, **II:** 373

North Star, **I:** 13, 126 **II:** 338, 343 **IV:** *753*

Northern California State Choir *See* Edwin
    Hawkins Singers
Northwest Ordinance (1787), **I:** 6, 195 **II:** 325
Norton, Dolores G., **III:** 666
Norton, Eleanor Holmes, **I:** 104 **III:** 498, **526–527**
Norton, Ken, **V:** 1188
Norvell, Aubrey James, **I:** 37
Notes on the State of Virginia, **I:** 6
Nothing but a Man, **IV:** 850
Notorious B.I.G., **V:** 1045, 1051, **1073**, *1073*, 1080
Novels and novelists, **III:** 714–748 *See also* Authors;
    Literature
    African American firsts, **I:** 13, 86, 87, 94 **III:** 720,
        721, 725, 739
NPR (National Public Radio), **II:** 452
NTU Art Association, **V:** 1134
Nubin, Katie Bell, **IV:** 969
Nugent, Bruce, **III:** 602
Nuñez, Alvar *See* Cabez de Vaca, Alvar Nuñez
Nuns (Catholic), **III:** 693
    African American firsts, **I:** 85
Nursing and nurses, **II:** 415 **V:** 1165 *See also* Medicine
    and medical doctors
    African American firsts, **I:** 20, 88, 91, 93, 193
        V: 1140
    organizations and associations, **II:** 422, 427, 436
Nw York State Club Association v. City of New York,
    II: 469
N.W.A. (Niggaz with Attitude), **V:** 1045, 1053, 1063
Nyerere, Julius, **II:** 377, 380
Nyumburu Cultural Center, **III:** 663
Nzekwu, Oruora, **II:** 233

O

Oak Hill Cemetery, **I:** 182, 201
Oakland, California
    African American firsts, **I:** 99 **II:** 385, 411
Oakland Chapel (Alcorn University), **I:** 204
Oakland College *See* Alcorn State University
Oakwood College, **III:** 655
Oberlin College, **I:** 214
Oblate Sisters of Providence, **I:** 85
O'Connor, Sandra Day, **I:** 64
Odet, Clifford, **IV:** 884
Office for Advancement of Public Black Colleges
    Colleges, **II:** **442**
Office of Assistant Secretary of Defense for
    Manpower and Reserves, **V:** 1223
Officer Training School (Fort Des Moines, Iowa), **I:**
    195 **V:** 1213
Officers, bank *See* Banks and bankers
Officers, police *See* Law enforcement officers and
    administrators

Officiates, football *See* Football coaches and
    officiates
Ogletree, Charles J., Jr., **III:** 666
Ogletree, James, **II:** **486**
Ohio, **I:** 8, 48, 77
    African American firsts, **III:** 534
    African American museums and galleries, **V:**
        1133–1134
    African American newspapers, **IV:** 803
    African American radio stations, **IV:** 821–822
    landmarks, **I:** 213–214
    race riots, **I:** 37, 43
Ohio Civil Rights Commision, **II:** 373
O.J. Simpson murder trial *See* Simpson, O.J.
The O'Jays, **V:** 1042
Oklahoma, **I:** 22
    African American firsts, **III:** 536
    African American museums and galleries, **V:** 1134
    African American newspapers, **IV:** 803
    African American radio stations, **IV:** 822
    landmarks, **I:** 214
    migration of African Americans, **III:** 546–547
Oklahoma City Board of Education, **II:** 464
Oklahoma City v. Dowell, **I:** 69
Oklahoma Human Rights Commission, **II:** 373
Olano, Nulfo de, **II:** 236
Old Court House (St. Louis, Missouri), **I:** 205, *206*
Old Courthouse (Lincoln, New Mexico), **I:** 207
Old Slave Mart, **I:** 217
Olden, George, **I:** 97
O'Leary, Hazel R., **I:** 73 **III:** 496, **527**
Olive, Milton L., **I:** 193 **V:** 1224
Oliver, Joe "King," **IV:** 942, 966 **V:** 976, 987, **1020**
Olsen, Carl, **V:** 1200
Olustee Battlefield Historic Memorial, **I:** 190
Olympic Games and medals, **I:** 24 **V:** 1175
    African American firsts, **I:** 89, 90 **V:** 1175
    African American women's firsts, **I:** 82, 93, 96, 102
        V: 1177, 1183
    list of African American medalists by place and
        year, A-20–A-26
O'Meally, Robert G., **III:** 666
Omega 7, Inc., **IV:** 752
Omega Psi Phi (Fraternity), **I:** 89 **II:** 400, **442**
Onassis, Jacqueline Kennedy, **III:** 746
Once Upon a Time. . . When We Were Colored,
    IV: 850
*One America in the Twenty-First Century: Forging
    a New Future*, **II:** 350
One False Move, **IV:** 850
101 Ranch, **I:** 214
102nd United States Colored Regiment, **I:** 202
100 Black Men of America, Inc., **II:** **442**
One Potato, Two Potato, **IV:** 850
O'Neal, Frederick, **IV:** 881, **911**

O'Neal, Shaquille, **V: 1195,** *1196*
O'Neill, Eugene, **IV:** 880, 881, 899
O'Neill, Tip, **II:** 475
Open Hand Publishing Inc., **IV:** 751
Opera Ebony, **IV:** 924, 938
Operas and opera singers *See also* Classical music
    and musicians
   African American firsts, **I:** 91, 96 **IV:** 934, 935, 936,
    939, 943, 949, 952
Opera/South, **IV:** 924
Operation Crossroads Africa, **II: 442**
Operation PUSH (People United to Serve Humanity),
    II: 357, 399, **442 V:** 1145
Opportunity, **III:** 642
"Oprah Bill," **IV:** 787
Oprah Winfrey Show, **I:** 100 **IV:** 786, 787
Orchestras and orchestra directors, **IV:** 924
   African American firsts, **I:** 89, 98 **IV:** 931, 933, 943
   African American women's firsts, **IV:** 924, 941
O'Ree, Willie, **I:** 96
Oregon, **IV:** 803
Oregon Attorney General's Office, **II:** 373
Organ donation, **III:** 605
Organization for Afro-American Unity, **I:** 34 **II:** 393
Organization for Black Americans to Support Israel,
    II: 413
Organization of African Unity, **II:** 229
Organization of Black Airline Pilots, **II: 442**
Organizations and associations, **II: 395–446** *See also*
    Chapter 9 for organizations listed and discussed
    alphabetically
   African American firsts, **I:** 105 **II:** 395, 416 **IV:** 770
    V: 1158
   community support, **II:** 399
   history, **II:** 395–400
   publishing imprints, **IV:** 751
   response to Africa and West Indies, **II:** 399
   significance, **II:** 395
   for urban issues, **II:** 396
   web sites, **V:** 1147–1148
Organizations and associations leaders, **II:** 400–418,
    435 *See also* Chapter 9 for leaders listed
    and discussed alphabetically; Organizations and
    associations
   African American firsts, **I:** 105, 106, 107, 108 **II:**
    416 **III:** 522, 644 **V:** 1154
   African American women's firsts, **I:** 59 **II:** 389
   convictions, **III:** 644
The Orioles (Music group), **V:** 1036
Ormandy, Eugene, **IV:** 954
Orrick, William, **I:** 83
Ory, Edward "Kid," **V: 1020,**
Osborne, Estelle Massey, **I:** 89
Oscar Micheaux, Inc., **IV:** 868
Oscar Robertson and Associates, **V:** 1199

Oscars *See* Academy Awards
Othello (Play), **IV:** 904–905
Otis, Johnny, **V:** 1066
Ottolenghi, Joseph, **III:** 621
Ouédraogo, Idrissa, **II:** 233, 234
Outlaw, Lucius, **III:** 666
Outterbridge, John Wifred, **V: 1116–1117**
L'Ouverture, Toussaint, **I:** 6 **II:** 237, 302, **339–340,**
    340, 378
Ovando, Nicolás de, **II:** 236
Overton, Anthony, **I:** 193
Overton Hygenic Manufacturing Company, **I:** 193
Ovington, Mary White, **II:** 396
Owens, Chandler David, **III:** 689
Owens, Dana *See* Queen Latifah
Owens, Jesse, **I:** 24, 90 **V:** 1175, 1193, **1195–1196,**
    1196
Owens, Major R., **III:** 498
Owens, P. Skylar, **IV:** 753
Oyotunji kingdom, **III:** 686
Ozawa, Seiji, **IV:** 941, 942, 946

P

P. Funk, **V:** 1042, 1050
Pacific Management Systems, **V:** 1155
Padmore, George, **II:** 378, 380, 382
Page, Ruth, **IV:** 887
Pageants, beauty *See* Beauty contests and contestants
Paige, Leroy "Satchel," **I:** 91 **V: 1196–1197**
Paine College, **III:** 655
Painter, Nell I., **III:** 666
Painters, artistic *See* Visual and applied arts
    and artists
Paisley Park, **V:** 1075
Palmer, Alice Freeman, **III:** 634
Palmer, Henry, **I:** 194
Palmer Memorial Institute, **I:** 212 **III:** 624, 634
Palmer, Phoebe, **III:** 703
Palmer, Violet, **I:** 107
Pan-Africanism and Pan-Africanists, **II:** 377, 380, 384–
    392, 420 *See also* Black nationalism and
    nationalists
Pan-Africanist Congress (PAC), **II:** 228
Panama, **II: 307–308**
Pan-American Exposition, **I:** 201
Panetta, Leon, **III:** 505
Pánfilo de Narváez *See* Narváez, Pánfilo de
Panther, **IV:** 850
Papp, Joseph, **IV:** 891
Paraguay, **II: 308**
Parham, Charles, **III:** 702
Paris is Burning, **IV:** 850
Park, Robert E., **IV:** 750

Parker, Charlie "Bird," Jr., **V:** 978, 984, 1001, 1011, **1021,** *1021,* 1029
    and Miles Davis, **V:** 980, 995
Parker, John H, **I:** 24
Parkes Sausage Company, **I:** 98
Parks *See* name of specific park, e.g., Fort Snelling State Park
Parks, Bernard, **II: 486–487,** *487*
Parks, Gordon, **V:** *1117,* **1117–1118**
Parks, Henry G., **III: 591**
Parks, Raymond, **II:** 365
Parks, Rosa, **I:** *30,* 75 **II: 364–365,** 382, 389, 397
    awards, **I:** 84 **IV:** 783
    and bus segregation, **I:** 29 **II:** 346, 365
Parkside Hospital *See* Dunbar Hospital
Parliament, **V:** 1042, 1051
The Parliaments, **V:** 1042, 1050
Parrish, Noel F., **V:** 1221
Parsons, James B., **I:** 96 **II:** 453, **487**
Parsons, Richard Dean, **III: 591–592**
Parton, Dolly, **V:** 1062
Pastime, **IV:** 850
Pastoriums, **I:** 179
Pastors *See* Ministers
A Patch of Blue, **IV:** 850
Pate, Johnny, **V:** 1072
Patents, **V:** 1137
    African American firsts, **I:** 85
Paton, Alan, **II:** 233
Patriot party, **III:** 517
Patten, Edward, **V:** 1068
Patterson, Frederick Douglass, **II: 411–412 III: 646–647**
Patterson, John, **I:** 32
Patterson, Mary, **I:** 86
Patterson, Orlando H.L., **III:** 666
Patterson, Robert P., **V:** 1222
Patterson, Rodney S., **I:** 103
Patterson v. McLean Credit Union, **II:** 465
Patti, Adelina, **IV:** 922
Patti Labelle and the Bluebelles, **V:** 1070
Patton, Charley, **V:** 974, 975, 1008, 1009 **1021–1022**
Patton, Eddie, **II:** 467
Patton, George C., **I:** *95*
Patton, Sharon F., **V:** 1097
Patton v. Mississippi, **II:** 467
Paul, Clarence, **V:** 1085
Paul Quinn College, **III:** 655
Paul Robeson: Tribute to an Artist, **IV:** 850
Payne, Daniel, **I:** 188 **III:** 673, 676
Payne, Donald M., **I:** 76 **III:** 498
Payton, Benjamin F., **III: 647**
Payton, Walter, **V:** 1171, **1197,** *1197*
PBS *See* Public Broadcasting Service (PBS)
P.E. Hopkins and Company, **III:** 731

Peabody Education Fund, **III:** 625
Peabody, Endicott, **III:** 505
Peabody, George, **II:** 337 **III:** 625
Peace officers *See* Law enforcement officers and administrators
Peacetime militias, **I:** 6
The Peaches, **V:** 1066
Peake, Mary S., **III:** 623
Peale, Charles Wilson, **V:** 1111
Pearl Harbor attack, **I:** 26
Pearl Primus, Percival Borde, and Company, **IV:** 911
Pearl Street, **I:** 195
Pearson, Pauletta, **IV:** 873
Peary, Robert E., **I:** 20, 21, 198, 210 **V:** 1158
Peck, Carolyn, **I:** 83, 110
Peck, David John, **I:** 86
Peebles, Melvin Van, **IV:** 833
Peery, Benjamin, **V:** 1139
Peete, Calvin, **V:** 1176, **1197**
Pemberton, Gayle, **III:** 666
PEN / Faulkner Award, **III:** 746
Pendergrass, Teddy, **V: 1073–1074,** *1074*
Pendleton, Austin, **IV:** 915
Pendleton, Clarence, **I:** 57, 59, 60 **III: 527,** *528*
Penn Center Historic District, **I:** 217
Penn Community Services, Inc., **I:** 217
Penn, I. Garland, **II:** 370
Penn School, **I:** 217
Penn, William, **II:** 318
Pennimen, Little Richard *See* Little Richard
Pennsylvania
    African American museums and galleries, **V:** 1134
    African American newspapers, **IV:** 804
    African American radio stations, **IV:** 822
    landmarks, **I:** 215–216
    slavery issues, **I:** 3, 6, 8 **II:** 448
Pennsylvania Abolition Society, **II:** *330*
Pennsylvania Augustine Society, **I:** 8
Pennsylvania Freemen's Relief Association, **I:** 217
Pennsylvania Human Relations Commission, **II:** 373
Pennsylvania Society for Promoting the Abolition of Slavery, **II:** 329
Penny Savings Bank, **I:** 192
Pentacostal Assemblies of the World, Inc., **III: 690**
Pentacostal Church, **III:** 676, 682, 703 *See also* Churches; Religion
People United to Serve Humanity *See* Operation PUSH (People United to Serve Humanity)
Peretti, Hugo, **V:** 1052
Perkins, Edward J., **I:** 61
Perkins, Marion, **V:** *1117,* **1118**
Perkinson, Coleridge-Taylor, **IV: 947**
Perlea, Jonel, **IV:** 947
Perot, Ross, **III:** 694

Perpetual Mission for Saving Souls of All Nations *See* Mother Waddles Perpetual Mission

Perry, Harold Robert, **III: 701**, *701*

Perry, Julia, **IV: 947–948**

Perry, Oliver Hazard, **V:** 1206

Perry, Regina A., **V:** 1099

Perry, Tony Antoinette Awards *See* Tony Awards

Pershing, John J., **V:** 1211, 1213

Persian Gulf War (1991), **I:** 69 **V:** 1226

Persichetti, Vincent, **IV:** 931

Person, Waverly J., **V:** 1145, **1164**

Peru, **II: 308–309**

Peter, Dawn, **I:** 107

Peters, Clarke, **IV:** 884

Petersen, Frank E., Jr., **I:** 94 **V:** *1239*, **1239–1240**

Peterson, Louis, **IV:** 881

Peterson, Oscar, **V:** *1000*

Petry, Ann, **I:** 79 **III:** 712, **740**

Pettiford, Oscar, **V: 1022**, 1066

The Pharcyde, **V:** 1044

Phat Pharm, **V:** 1081

Phelps, J. Alfred, **V:** 1240

Phi Beta Kappa (Fraternity), **I:** 87 **II:** 368, 399

Phi Beta Sigma (Fraternity), **II:** 400, **443**

Phi Delta Kappa (Fraternity), **II: 443**

Philadelphia, Pennsylvania, **II:** 329 **III:** 622

    African American firsts, **I:** 59, 100 **III:** 518

"Philadelphia Plan," **I:** 45

Philander-Smith College, **I:** 182 **III:** 655

Philanthropy and philanthropists, **III:** 625–626

    African American firsts, **III:** 625

Philip, Paul R., **I:** 68

Phillips, Homer G., **I:** 206

Phillips, Samuel F., **II:** 450

Phillis Wheatley Folio, **I:** 200

Phipps, Mamie, **III:** 636

Photography and photographers *See* Visual and applied arts and artists

Phylaxis Society, **II: 443**

Phyllis Hyman and PH Factor, **V:** 1062

Physicians *See* Medicine and medical doctors

Physics and physicists, **V:** 1139, 1145, 1150, 1152–1153, 1159, 1163

    African American firsts, **V:** 1139, 1144

    African American women's firsts, **V:** 1159

    organizations and associations, **II:** 441

Piano and pianists *See* Classical music and musicians

The Piano Lesson, **IV:** 850

Pick, Lewis A., **V:** 1222

Pickens, T. Boone, **III:** 587

Pickett, Bill, **I:** 214

Pickett, Wilson, **V:** 1041

Picon, Molly, **III:** 725

Pieh, Sengbe *See* Cinque, Joseph

Pierce, Samuel R., **I:** 54, *56*

Pierce, William, **I:** 1

Pilgrim Health and Life Insurance Company, **I:** 192

Pillsbury, Frances, **III:** 587

Pillsbury House/Cultural Arts, **V:** 1131

Pilots *See* Aviation and aviators (Civilian); Aviation and aviators (Military)

Pinchback, Pinckney Benton Stewart, **I:** 87, *87* **III:** 492, **528**

Pinckney, William, **I:** 103

Pindell, Geraldine Louise, **II:** 369

Pindell, Howardina, **V: 1118**

Pine, Courtney, **V:** 984

Piney Woods Country Life School, **I:** 205

Pinkney, Jerry, **V: 1118–1119**

Pinky, **IV:** 850

Pippin, Horace, **V:** 1094, **1119**

Pitcairn, John, **V:** 1205

Pittman, Evelyn LaRue, **IV: 948**

Pittsylvania County Courthouse, **I:** 220

Pizarro, Francisco, **II:** 236

Planned Parenthood Association, **II:** 415, 416

Plantation songs, **IV:** 958–960

Plantations *See* name of specific plantation, e.g., Kingsley Plantation

Planter (Ship), **V:** 1209

Play awards *See* name of specific award, e.g., Tony Awards

Plays and playwrights (Written), **III:** 714–748 *See also* Authors; Literature

    African American firsts, **I:** 96 **III:** 720 **IV:** 877

Plessy, Homer Adolph, **I:** 148 **II:** 336, 344, 467

Plessy v. Ferguson, **I:** 20, 148 **II:** 336, 344–345, 396, 467

    excerpt from ruling and dissension, **I:** 148–149–151

Plinton, James, Jr., **I:** 96

Plomer, William, **II:** 233

A Poem by Phillis, A Negro Girl, On the Death of Reverend Whitefield, **I:** 5

Poems on Miscellaneous Subjects (Frances E.W. Harper), **III:** 729

Poetic Justice, **IV:** 850 **V:** 1064

Poetry and poets, **I:** 5 **III:** 712, 714–748 *See also* Authors; Literature

    African American firsts, **I:** 4, 93, 213 **III:** 719, 723, 728, 731, 742, 746

    African American women's firsts, **III:** 732

Poets Laureate of the United States, A-14 **IV:** 778

Pointer, Sam, Jr., **I:** 61

Poitier, Sidney, **I:** 97 **IV:** *832*, 833, 847, *851*, **869–870**, 874, 912

Polar expeditions *See* Exploration and explorers

Polasek, Albin, **V:** 1100

Police brutality, **I:** 33, 180 **II:** 348–349

Police chiefs *See* Law enforcement officers and administrators

Police officers *See* Law enforcement officers and
administrators
Political action organizations, **II:** 419, 421,
426, 434, 441
Political parties, **III:** 542 *See also* name of specific
party, e.g., Democratic party
African American firsts, **I:** 65, 87, 102, 109 **II:** 356
III: 506
Political party chairpersons *See* Chairpersons
(Political party)
Political party conventions and primaries, **I:**
23, 24, 68
African American firsts, **I:** 12, 19 **II:** 356 **III:** 521
African American women's firsts, **I:** 76
Political party delegates *See* Delegates
(Political party)
Political science organizations, **II:** 439
Politics and politicians, **III: 491–541** *See also* name
of specific political office, e.g., Governors
African American firsts, **III:** 492
biographical profiles, **III:** 499–541
harassment of African Americans, **I:** 68
statistics, **I:** 52 **III:** 542
Polk, James, **II:** 326
Poll taxes, **I:** 37
Pollard, Fritz, **I:** 89, *90* **V:** 1170
Ponty, Jean-Luc, **V:** 985
Poole, Elijah *See* Muhammad, Elijah
Pools, public, **I:** 31
Poor, Salem, **I:** 5, 199 **V:** 1205
Pope Gregory XVI, **I:** 11
Popular music and musicians, **V: 1035–1085** *See also*
Music and musicians; specific type of popular
music, e.g., Rap music and musicians
African American firsts, **V:** 1036
biggest selling album, **V:** 1065
biographical profiles, **V:** 1046–1085
most successful tour, **V:** 1065
new trends, **V:** 1045–1046
web sites, **V:** 1149
Population, **I:** 6 **III: 543–550,** 551–552, 553, 556 *See*
also Employment; Family and marriage; Income
African, **II:** 230–231
comparison to other countries and races, **III:**
543, 544, 550
estimates of slaves, **I:** 3, 4 **III:** 543
fertility rates, **III:** 544, 603
growth, **III:** 543–544
largest in Western hemisphere, **II:** 290
median age, **III:** 549
projections, **III:** 549–550, 555
regional distribution, **III:** 544–546, 548
statistics on death rates, **III:** 610, 618
statistics on life expectancy, **I:** 25 **III:**
609–610, 617

statistics on metropolitan areas, **III:** 554
statistics on political party identification, **III:** 542
in suburban areas, **I:** 52 **III:** 548–549
suicide rates, **III:** 610
in urban areas, **III:** 548–549
web sites, **V:** 1148
Porgy and Bess, **IV:** 850, 883
Port Hudson Siege, **I:** 197
Porter, Andrew, **IV:** 931
Porter, Dave, **V:** 1040, 1060
Porter, James A., **V: 1119**
Portsmouth, Rhode Island, **I:** 216
Posse, **IV:** 850
Postage stamps, **V:** 1118
African American firsts, **I:** 90, 97
list of African Americans on, A-14–A-15
Postal clerks
African American firsts, **I:** 86
Postbellum period, **II:** 334–335
Potomac River
baptisms at, **III:** *691*
Poverty, **III:** 560–566
advocacy organizations, **II:** 437, 444
economic gap between racial groups, **III:** 563–564
federal and state programs, **III:** 562–563
statistics, **I:** 72 **III:** 561–562, 563, 570–571
and teenage pregnancy, **III:** 562
welfare reform, **III:** 562
Powell, Adam Clayton, III, **IV:** 760
Powell, Adam Clayton, Jr., **I:** 37, *42* **II:** *471* **III:** 493,
528–529, 530, 676 **IV:** 784
and equal employment opportunity, **I:** 25
House of Representatives controversy, **I:** 44
landmarks, **I:** 207
and Nineteenth Congress, **I:** 37, 38
and requirements for legislative membership,
II: 470
Powell, Adam Clayton, Sr., **I:** 207 **III:** 528, **702,** *702*
Powell, Bud, **V: 1022,** 1024, 1027–1028
Powell, Clilan B., **IV:** 754
Powell, Colin L., **I:** 64, *66,* 75, 76, 103 **V:** 1226, *1226,*
1240–1241
Powell, Isaac, **V:** 1145
Powell, Lawrence M., **I:** 74
Powell, Lewis F., **II:** 467
Powell, Mike, **V:** 1175
Powell, Renee, **V:** 1176
Powell, Richard J., **V:** 1097, 1099
Power, Tyrone, **IV:** 832
Powers, Harriet, **V:** 1089
Pozo, Chano, **V:** 1001
Prairie View A and M University, **III:** 655
Pras, Prakazrel, **V:** 1056
Pratt, Awadagin, **IV: 948**
Pratt, Elmer "Geronimo," **II:** 398, *398,* 477

Preachers *See* Ministers
Preaching (Religious), **III:** 678 **IV:** 960
Precision flight teams
    African American firsts, **I:** 77, 99, 101, 105
Pregnancy Prevention Conference, **II:** 402
Prehistoric humans, **II:** 225
Prejudice, racial *See* Racial prejudice
Preparatory High School for Colored Youth *See* M
    Street High School
Presbyterian Church, **II:** 388 **III:** 682, 694 *See also*
    Churches; Religion
Presidential aides
    African American firsts, **III:** 494
Presidential candidates and nominations, **I:** 64, 70, 71
    II: 358
    African American firsts, **III:** 496, 522
    African American women's firsts, **I:** 49, 98 **III:** 517
Presidential inaugurations
    African American firsts, **I:** 188
    African American women's firsts, **I:** 108
Presidential Medals of Freedom, **II:** 404, 406, 412, 418
    list of African American recipients, A-8
Presidents (Student body)
    African American firsts, **III:** 644
Presidents (Universities and colleges) *See also*
    Education and educators; Universities and
    colleges
    African American firsts, **I:** 89 **III:** 638, 642, 649
    African American women's firsts, **I:** 102, 106
President's Initiative on Race, **I:** 177 **II:** 350
Presley, Elvis, **V:** 1065
Presley, Lisa Marie, **I:** 75, 77 **V:** 1065
Preston, Billy, **IV:** 965
Price, Cecil, **I:** 40
Price, Florence B., **IV:** 924, **948–949**
Price, Hugh P., **II:** 407, **412**
Price, Joseph Charles, **III: 702**
Price, Leontyne, **IV:** 922, 925, **949,** *950,* 954
Price, Thomas, **IV:** 949
Price, Vincent, **V:** 1065
Pride, Charley, **V:** 1039, **1074**
Priest, Maxi, **V:** 1055
Priests *See also* Bishops; Ministers; Monsignors;
    name of specific religion, e.g., Catholic Church
    African American firsts, **I:** 194 **III:** 699
    African American women's firsts, **I:** 103 **III:** 673
Prigg, Edward, **I:** 12 **II:** 327, 472
Prigg v. Pennsylvania, **I:** 12 **II:** 326, 448, 472
Prime Ministers
    Africa American women's firsts, **II:** 296
The Primes, **V:** 1067
The Primettes, **V:** 1084
Primus, Pearl, **IV:** 887, **911–912**
Prince (Artist Formerly Known As), **I:** 74 **II:** 360 **V:**
    1068, 1070, **1074–1075,** *1075*

Prince, Lucy, **II:** 452
Principals, elementary and high school *See* Education
    and educators
Príncipe, **II:** 271
Prisons and prisoners, **I:** 70 **II:** 471–472, 490
    See also name of specific prison, e.g.,
    Andersonville Prison
Private schools, **I:** 58 *See also* Education and
    educators
    African American firsts, **I:** 219, 220
Producers, movie *See* Films and filmmakers
Producers, television *See* Television directors and
    producers
Professional Baseball Hall of Fame *See* National
    Baseball Hall of Fame
Professional Bowlers Association, **I:** 101
Professional degrees *See also* Doctoral degrees;
    Education and educators; Universities and
    colleges
    African American firsts, **I:** 87, 89, 93, 193 **II:** 481
        IV: 937
    African American women's firsts, **I:** 86, 88, 186
        IV: 949
Professional Football Hall of Fame, A-8 **I:** 97
Professional societies, **II:** 427
Professor Griff, **V:** 1075, 1076
Professors *See* Education and educators
Proficiency tests, **I:** 48 **III:** 669
Profitts Inc., **I:** 107
Program for Research on Black Americans, **III:** 663
Program in African-American Studies (Princeton
    University), **III:** 663
Progressive National Baptist Convention, Inc., **III:
    690**
Project Equality, **II: 443**
Project Excellence program, **IV:** 780
Pro-life organizations, **II:** 423
Proline, **III:** 585
Promoters, music *See* Music promoters
Propaganda films, **IV:** 832 *See also* Films and
    filmmakers
Prosser, Gabriel, **I:** 7 **II: 340,** 378
Prosser, Thomas, **II:** 340
Prostate cancer, **III:** 609 *See also* Cancer and cancer
    research
Prout, Mary, **I:** 222
Providence Art Club, **V:** 1100
Provident Hospital, **I:** 20, 193 **V:** 1140
Pryor, Richard, **IV:** 834, 886, *886,* **912**
Psychiatry and psychiatrists, **II:** 424 **V:** 1154–
    1155, 1156
Psychology and psychologists, **II:** 423 **III:** 636
    African American firsts, **III:** 636
Public accomodations and housing, **I:** 27, 33, 60, 171
    African American firsts, **I:** 35

court cases and legislation, **I:** 19, 35, 37, 42, 50
    II: 467–469
  labeling of buildings and facilities, **II:** *457*
Public administrators organizations, **II:** 428, 440
Public Broadcasting Service (PBS)
  African American firsts, **IV:** 952
Public Enemy, **V:** 1044, **1075–1076**
Public libraries *See* Libraries and librarians
Public pools, **I:** 31
Public television, **IV:** 760 *See also* Television and
    television shows
  African American firsts, **IV:** 760
Public transportation segregation, **II:** 344–345, 346,
    365 *See also* Racial segregation; School
    desegregation
  on buses, **I:** 19, 27, 29, 30, 33
  court cases, **I:** 19, 29, 33
  demonstrations, **I:** 27, 29 **II:** 404
  landmarks, **I:** 179
  on trains, **I:** 20, 26
Public Works Employment Act of 1977, **II:** 456
    III: 579
Publishing *See* Media and publishing
Puerto Rico, **II:** **309**
Puff Daddy *See* Combs, Sean "Puffy"
Pulitzer Prizes, **I:** 51, 83, 218 *See also* Authors;
    Literature
  African American firsts, **I:** 93, 98, 106 **III:** 719 **IV:**
    954 **V:** 1123
  first jazz-based work to win, **V:** 1016
  list of African American recipients, A-9
Purlie, **IV:** 884
Purple Rain, **IV:** 851
Purvis, Charles, **V:** 1140
Puryear, Martin, **V:** **1119**
PUSH-Excel program, **II:** 357
Putney Swope, **IV:** 851

Q

Qaddafi, Muammar, **II:** 260
Qawi, Dwight Muhammad, **V:** 1189
Quakers, **I:** 4, 5, 10, 112 **II:** 328 **III:** 621
Quality Education for Minorities Project, **I:** 67 **II:**
    443
Quarles, Norma, **IV:** 758, **777,** *777*
Queen Latifah, **V:** 1044, *1044*, **1076**
Queen's Head Tavern *See* Fraunces Tavern
The Queer Resources Directory (QRD), **IV:** 766
Quicksand, **III:** 735
The Quiet One, **IV:** 851
Quilting *See* Visual and applied arts and artists
Quinn Chapel of the African Methodist Episcopal
    Church (Chicago, Illinois), **I:** 194
Quinn, William Paul, **I:** 194

R

Ra, Sun, **V:** **1022**
Rabbis, **III:** *687*
Raboteau, Albert Jordy, **III:** 666
Race car driving and drivers
  African American firsts, **I:** 97 **IV:** 844 **V:** 1177
Race Relations Institute (Fisk University), **III:** 663
Race Relations Institute (Wayne State Unversity),
    III: 663
Race riots, **I:** 16, 20 *See also* Racial violence
  court cases and legislation, **I:** 39, 55
  federal reports and commissions, **I:** 40, 43
*Race to Freedom: The Story of the Underground
    Railroad*, **IV:** 851
Racial accommodation, **II:** 337
Racial prejudice, **I:** 5, 47, 82 **III:** 566, 672–673
    IV: 923–924
Racial segregation *See also* Civil rights and Civil
    Rights movements; specific type of segregation
    e.g., Public transportation segregation
  African American firsts, **II:** 346, 364
  during American Reconstruction, **II:** 344–345
  church response, **III:** 675
  court cases, **I:** 22
  military, **V:** 1216, 1221–1222, 1224
  organizations to combat, **II:** 442
  rise of statutes, **I:** 11
Racial stereotypes, **IV:** 831–832
Racial unity organizations, **II:** 431
Racial violence, **I:** 32, 63 **II:** 348–349, 349–350 *See
    also* Hate crimes; specific type of violence, e.g.,
    Church bombings and burnings
  addressed by churches, **III:** 678
  at demonstrations, **I:** 35, 180
  statistics, **II:** 375
Racism *See* Racial prejudice
Rackley, Alex, **I:** 45 **II:** 415
Radio beacons, **V:** 1167
Radio broadcasting and personalities, **IV:** 755–
    756, 762–788
  advertising, **IV:** 759–760
  African American firsts, **IV:** 755, 756, 775
  dominant formats, **IV:** 756
  historical development, **IV:** 755
  largest African American-owned company, **IV:** 756
  public radio, **IV:** 760–761
  talk radio, **IV:** 756
Radio Hall of Fame, **IV:** 775
Radio networks and stations, **II:** 432 **IV:** 756, 772,
    810–811, 811–825
  African American firsts, **I:** 95 **IV:** 755
Radio One, Inc., **IV:** 756
A Rage in Harlem, **IV:** 851
Ragtime, **IV:** 851, 908

Ragtime music and musicians, **IV:** 880 **V:** 973 *See also*
    Music and musicians
Raid on Harper's Ferry *See* John Brown's Raid on
    Harper's Ferry
Railroad industry, **I:** 218 **V:** 1138, 1151, 1162
Railway trolleys, **I:** 88
Rainbow Coalition, **V:** 1145
Raines, Franklin D., **I:** 81, 105
Rainey, Gertrude "Ma," **I:** 192 **IV:** 960 **V:** 984, **1023,**
    1023
Rainey, Joseph H., **I:** 87, 217 **III:** **529**
Rainey, William "Pa," **I:** 192 **V:** 1023
Raisin, **IV:** 884
Raisin in the Sun, **III:** 728 **IV:** 851, 881, 912
Ramirez, Andrew, **I:** 83
Ramirez, Blandina Cardenas, **I:** 58, 59, 60
Rampersad, Arnold, **III:** 666
Randall, Dudley, **IV:** **777–778**
Randolph, A. Philip, **I:** 22 **II:** 345, *346,* 397, **412 V:**
    1216, 1222
Randolph, A. Philip Educational Fund, **II:** **419**
Randolph, Virginia E., **I:** 221 **III:** 625
Rangel, Charles B., **I:** *55,* 62 **III:** 498, **530,** 649
    V: 1226
Rangers, Texas (Baseball team), **III:** 586
Rankin, Andrew, **I:** 186
Rankin, John, **I:** 214
Ransier, Alonzo J., **II:** 334
Ransom, **III:** 676
Rap music and musicians, **V:** 1043–1045 *See also*
    Popular music and musicians
    African American firsts, **I:** 102
    biographical profiles, **V:** 1046–1085
    boycotts, **I:** 77
    female rappers, **V:** 1044, 1076, 1079
    first female group to earn platinum, **V:** 1079
    first political rap hit, **V:** 1044
    gangsta style, **V:** 1045
    influence on gospel music, **IV:** 963
    jazz style, **V:** 983–984
Rapture, **V:** 1046
Rashad, Ahmad, **IV:** 870
Rashad, Phylicia, **IV:** **870**
Raspberry, William J., **III:** 666 **IV:** **778,** *778*
Rastafarianism, **II:** 382 **III:** **691**
Rather, Dan, **IV:** 764
The Ravens, **V:** 1036
Rawls, Lou, **II:** 412
Ray, Charles, **I:** 12
Ray, Charlotte, **II:** 452
Ray, James Earl, **I:** 43, 51, 81 **II:** 360
Ray, Marcus H., **V:** 1222
Rayfield, Wallace A., **I:** 179
Razaf, Andy, **IV:** 893

R&B music *See* Rhythm and blues music and
    musicians
Reagan, Ronald, **I:** 58 **II:** 354, 359, 412 **III:** 559
    and civil rights, **I:** 54, 58, 59 **III:** 559
    and Martin Luther King, Jr. Day, **I:** 58
Real estate, **I:** 192
    African American firsts, **I:** 106
Reason, J. Paul, **I:** 77, 106 **V:** *1241,* **1241–1242**
Reason, Patrick H., **V:** 1090
Rebellions, slave *See* Slave insurrections and
    insurrectionists
Rebound: The Legend of Earl "The Goat" Manigault,
    IV: 851
"Rebuild L.A.", **III:** 504
Reconstruction Acts, **II:** 333, 344
Reconstruction, American *See* American
    Reconstruction
Record companies
    African American firsts, **V:** 1005
Red Hot Chili Peppers, **V:** 1051
Red Lantern Prizes, **I:** 100
Red Oak Creek Covered Bridge, **I:** 193
Reddick, Robert L., **III:** 666
Redding, Noel, **V:** 1061
Redding, Otis, **V:** 1040, 1055, 1060, **1076,** *1077*
Redman, Dewey, **V:** 982, **1023**
Redman, Don, **V:** 977, 978, **1023–1024**
Redman, Joshua, **V:** 982
Reed, Cannon & Johnson Communications Co.,
    III: 740
Reed, Ishmael, **III:** 712, **740–741,** *741* **V:** 983
Reed, Jimmy, **V:** **1024**
Reed, Willis, **V:** **1198**
Reeves, Diana, **V:** 983
Reeves, Kenneth, **III:** **530**
Reformed Dutch Church *See also* Churches; Religion
    African American firsts, **I:** 94
Refrigerators, **V:** 1160
Regents of University of California v. Allan Bakke,
    II: 463
Regiments, military *See* name of specific regiment,
    e.g., 54th Massachusetts Regiment
Reid, Antonio "L.A.", **V:** 1045, 1054
Reid, Frank J., **IV:** 837
Reilly, Frank J., **V:** 1105
Reitman v. Mulkey, **II:** 471
Religion, **III:** **671–706** *See also* Churches; name of
    specific denomination, e.g. African Methodist
    Episcopal Church
    influence on music, **IV:** 957, 958
    organizations and associations, **II:** 425, 427–
    428, 437, 445
    origins, **III:** 671
    statistics, **III:** 707
    trends, **III:** 678–680

web sites, **V:** 1148
Religious conversion *See* Missionizing and
    missionaries
Religious cults, **III:** 696
Religious leadership, **III:** 673, 692–706 *See also*
    Chapter 17 for leaders listed and discussed
    alphabetically
Religious publishers, **IV:** 749–750 *See also* Media and
    publishing
Remember to Remember, **V:** 1106
Ren, M.C. *See* M.C. Ren
Rendell, Edward, **III:** 518
Rennaissance (Basketball team), **I:** 89
Renoir, Jean, **IV:** 880
"Rent parties," **V:** 1011
Repatriation to Africa movements, **I:** 8 **II:** 328, 378,
    379 **III:** 675 *See also* Black Nationalism and
    nationalists; Pan-Africanism and Pan-Africanists
Reporters *See* Journalism and journalists
Representatives in Congress *See* Members of
    Congress; Members of Congress (United States
    House of Representatives)
Reproductive rights, **II:** 415–416
Republican party, **I:** 87, 88 **III:** 492
    African American firsts, **I:** 19, 87, 88, 109 **III:**
        496, 522, 536
Research Department (National Urban League),
    III: 663
Residences *See* Chapter 4 for residences by city
    and state
Resident Art and Humanites Consortium, **V:** 1134
Restaurant management and managers organizations,
    II: 436
Restrictive covenants, **II:** 470–471
Reúnion, **II: 269–270**
Revelation Corporation of America, **I:** 76
Revels, Hiram R., **I:** 87, 217 **II:** 334 **III:** 492, *493,*
    530–531, *531,* 675
    landmarks, **I:** 204
Revolts, slave *See* Slave insurrections and
    insurrectionists
Revolutionary War *See* American Revolution
Reyneau, Betsy Graves, **V:** 1125
Reynolds, Emma, **V:** 1140
Reynolds, Gary A., **V:** 1099
Reynolds, Mel, **I:** 76 **III:** 519
Reynolds, Ruthie G., **III:** 666
Reynolds, William Bradford, **I:** 57, 58
Rhein, Eduard Foundation's Cultural Journalistic
    Award, **IV:** 781
Rhode Island
    African American firsts, **II:** 321
    African American museums and galleries, **V:** 1134
    African American newspapers, **IV:** 804
    landmarks, **I:** 216

slavery laws, **I:** 5
voting rights, **I:** 9, 12
Rhode Island Black Heritage Society, **V:** 1134
Rhode Island Human Rights Commission, **II:** 373
Rhode Island School of Design, **V:** 1100
Rhodes scholarships and scholars *See also* Academic
    scholarships
    African American firsts, **I:** 89, 104
Rhodes, Ted, **V:** 1185
Rhythm and blues music and musicians, **IV:** 966–967
    V: 1035–1038 *See also* Popular music and
        musicians
    biographical profiles, **V:** 1046–1085
    and churches, **V:** 1036
    most popular of the 1940s, **V:** 1036
    and rock and roll, **V:** 1036–1038
Rhythm Nation 1814, **V:** 1064
Ribbs, Willie T., **V:** 1177
Riboud, Marc, **V:** 1105
Ricci, Ruggero, **IV:** 946
Rice, Jerry, **V:** 1171, **1198**
Rice, Kym S., **V:** 1098
Rice Museum, **V:** 1134
Rice, Norm, **I:** 102 **III: 531**
Rice v. Arnold, **II:** 468
Richard, Little *See* Little Richard
Richard Pryor: Live on the Sunset Strip, **IV:** 851
Richards, Lloyd, **III:** 747 **IV:** 882, **912–913**
Richardson, Elliot, **III:** 505
Richardson, Franklyn, **III:** 681
Richardson, La Tanya, **IV:** 864
Richardson, Tommy, **IV:** 967
Richie, Lionel, **V: 1077**
Richmond Council of Colored Women, **III:** 594
*Richmond, Virginia School Board v. State Board of
    Education*, **II:** 463
Rickey, Branch, **V:** 1170, 1199
Rickford, John R., **III:** 666
Rickover, Hyman G., **V:** 1241
Riddle, Estelle Massey, **II:** 415
Ridenhour, Carlton *See* Chuck D.
Ridley, Walter Nathaniel, **I:** 94
Rigaud, General, **II:** 340
Riggs, Marlon, **III:** 602, 730 **IV:** 760
Right of sale, **II:** 470–471
Rights of women *See* Women's rights and women's
    rights activists
Riley, Markell, **V:** 1077
Riley, Teddy, **V:** 1046, **1077,** *1078*
Rillieux, Norbert, **I:** 197 **V:** 1137, **1165**
Ringgold, Faith, **V:** 1095, *1095,* **1119–1120**
Ringmasters (Circus)
    African American firsts, **I:** 110
Ritchie, Joe, **III:** 666
Rites and Reason, **III:** 663

The River Nigger, **IV:** 851
Rivers, Sam, **V:** 985
Rizzo, Frank, **IV:** 784
Roach, Max, **IV:** 907 **V:** 990, *1000*, 1014, **1024**
Robert, Thomas A., **V:** 1215
Roberta Martin Singers, **IV:** 969
Roberts, Benjamin, **I:** 13
Roberts, Kay George, **IV: 949–950**
Roberts, Needham, **V:** 1214, 1238
Robertson, Carol, **I:** 179
Robertson, Oscar, **V: 1199**
Robeson, Paul, **I:** 89 **IV:** 830, 831, 881, 917, **950–951,**
    951
    landmarks, **I:** 86, 210
Robey, Don, **V:** 1071
Robinson, Berard W., **I:** 90
Robinson, Bill "Bojangles," **IV:** 879, 883, **913,** *913*
Robinson, Cleo Parker, **IV:** 890
Robinson, Eddie, **I:** 76 **V:** 1171, **1198–1199,** *1199*
Robinson, E.R., **I:** 88
Robinson, Frank, **I:** 99 **V:** 1170, 1189, **1199**
Robinson, Holyard, **I:** 186
Robinson, Jackie, **I:** 93, 96 **IV:** 757 **V:** 1170, *1170,*
    1199
    and Civil Rights movement, **V:** 1169
    integration of baseball, **I:** 27, 79, 91 **V:** 1169, 1170
    landmarks, **I:** 210
Robinson, Jo Ann Gibson, **II: 365**
Robinson, Jonny, **V:** 1142
Robinson, Joseph C., **II:** 450
Robinson, Max, **II:** 412 **IV:** 758, *758,* **778–779**
Robinson, Randall S., **I:** *63,* 75 **II:** 399, **412–413**
    III: 495
Robinson, Roscoe, Jr., **V: 1242**
Robinson, Sallie, **II:** 450
Robinson, Smokey, **V:** 1057, 1058, **1078,** 1082
Robinson, Spottswood, **II: 487**
Robinson, "Sugar Ray," **V:** 1172, **1199–1200**
Robinson v. Memphis & Charleston See Civil Rights
    Cases
Robinson, William H., **III:** 746
Rochon, Lela, **III:** 736 **V:** 1062
Rock and Roll Hall of Fame, A-9
Rock and roll music and musicians, **V:** 1036–1038 *See*
    also Popular music and musicians
    biographical profiles, **V:** 1047, 1052, 1060–1061,
        1070–1071, 1081
    first record, **V:** 1037
    first use in film, **IV:** 839
    organizations and associations, **II:** 425
Rock, Chris, **IV:** 887, **913–914,** *914*
Rock, John S., **I:** 86 **II:** 452
Rockefeller Foundation, **III:** 649
Rockefeller, John D., **II:** 337 **III:** 633, 642
Rockefeller, Nelson, **I:** 31 **II:** 406 **III:** 592

Rocky Mountain Fur Company, **I:** 206
Rodeos
    African American firsts, **I:** 109
Rodgers, Griffin, **V:** 1145
Rodgers, Jonathan, **IV:** 759
Rodgers, Moses, **I:** 182
Rodgers, Norman, **V:** 1075
Rodgers, Richard, **IV:** 857
Rodin, **V:** 1109
Rogers, Carolyn, **III:** 737
Rohker J Inc., **III:** 588
Roker, Al, **IV: 779,** *779*
RokerWare, Inc., **IV:** 779
Rolling Stones, **V:** 1047
Rollins, Howard E., **III:** 725
Rollins, Sonny, **V:** 980, 984, **1024–1025,** *1025*
Roman Catholic Church *See* Catholic Church
Romo-Carmona, Mariana, **IV:** 783
Ronald McNair Park, **I:** 207
Roosevelt, Eleanor, **IV:** 933 **V:** 1165
Roosevelt, Franklin D., **I:** 189 **III:** 634 **V:** 1103,
    1224, 1229
    and African American voters, **III:** 493 **V:** 1231
    criticism by NAACP, **I:** 24, 26
    and Executive Order (No. 8802), **I:** 154 **II:** 345
        V: 1216
Roosevelt, Theodore, **I:** 20, 24, 211 **III:** 547, 725
Roots (Book), **I:** 51 **III:** 713, 727–728
Roots (Television miniseries), **IV:** 836, 852
Roots: The Gift, **III:** 728 **IV:** 852
Roots: The Next Generation, **IV:** 852
Roper, Deidre, **V:** 1079
Ropers, calf *See* Calf ropers
Rose Bowl football championships
    African American firsts, **I:** 89
Rose, David, **II:** 339
Rose, Edward, **I:** 206
Rose Meta Morgan House of Beauty, **III:** 590
Rosenberg, Anna M., **V:** 1224
Rosenwald, Julian Fund, **III:** 626
Rosewood, **IV:** 852
Ross, Annie, **V:** 983
Ross, Barney, **V:** 1180
Ross, Diana, **IV:** 834, 874 **V:** 1046, **1078–1079,** 1083
Roundtree, Richard, **IV: 870,** *870*
Rousseau, Henri, **V:** 1119
Roussell, Norman, **I:** 67
Rowan, Carl Thomas, **IV: 779–780,** *780*
Rowe, Debbie, **V:** 1065
Rowe, William L., **I:** 93
Rowicki, Witolf, **IV:** 946
Roxbury Community College, **III:** 655
Roy, Charlotte E., **I:** 87
Royal African Company, **II:** 318
Royal Ballet, **IV:** 940

Ruben, Rick, **V:** 1081
Rudder, John Earl, **I:** 93
Rudolph, Wilma, **I:** 96 **V:** 1177, **1200**
Ruffin, Ben, **I:** 109
Ruffin, David, **V:** 1068
Ruffin, George, **II: 487**
Ruffner, Violla, **I:** 224
Rufus, **V:** 1068
Runaway slaves *See* Fugitive slaves
Run-DMC, **II:** 360
Runners *See* Track and field athletes
Runyon v. McCrary, **II:** 463
RuPaul, **III:** 602
Rush, Bobby L., **III:** 498
Rush, Christopher, **III:** 673
Rush Communications, **V:** 1081
Rush, Otis, **V: 1025**
Rushen, Patrice, **V:** 1043
Rushing, James Andrew "Jimmy," **V: 1026**
Russell, Bill, **I:** 97 **V:** *1174*, **1200,** 1202
Russell, Harvey Jr., **I:** 96
Russell, Herman J., **III: 592**
Russwurm, John B., **I:** 121 **II:** 329, 343 **IV:** 753, 768,
    780, *781*
    landmarks, **I:** 197
Rust College, **III:** 655
Rustin, Baynard, **I:** 46 **II:** 361, 367, **413,** *413*
Ruth, Babe, **I:** 50 **V:** 1179
Ruthless Records, **V:** 1053
Rutledge, Edward, **II:** 320
Rwanda, **II: 270**
Ryan, Timothy, **I:** 55
Ryder, Winona, **III:** 715

S

Saar, Beyte, **V:** 1095, **1120**
Sable, Jean Baptiste Pointe du, **I:** 6
Sacred music and musicians, **IV: 957–971** *See also*
    Gospel music and musicians
    biographical profiles, **IV:** 964–970–971
    early influences, **IV:** 957–958
    emergence of spirituals, **IV:** 958–960
Saddler, Joseph *See* Grandmaster Flash
Sailmaking and sailmakers, **III:** 576
Saint Augustine's College, **III:** 655
Saint Helena, **II: 270–271**
Saint James, Synthia, **V:** 1096, **1120**
Saint Kitts, **II: 309–310**
Saint Lucia, **II: 310**
Saint Luke Bank and Trust Company, **I:** 222 **III:** 593
Saint Paul's College, **III:** 656
Saint Vincent, **II: 310–311**
Saint-Gaudens, Augustus, **I:** 199
Salaam, Rashaan, **I:** 76

Salem, Peter, **I:** 5, 199
Sallee, Charles, **V:** 1094
Salt-N-Pepa, **V:** *1079*, **1079–1080**
Salvation by Christ with Penitential Cries, **I:** 5
Sam and Dave, **V:** 1040, 1060
Sampson, Edith, **I:** 28 **III: 531–532,** *532*
San Francisco, California
    African American firsts, **I:** 105 **III:** 714
Sanchez, Sonia, **III:** 666, 713, **741**
Sand, Leonard B., **I:** 60
Sanders, Barry, **I:** 106 **V:** 1171, *1171*
Sanders, Deion, **V:** 1171, **1201,** *1201*
Sanders, Louis, **III:** 591
Sanders, Wayne, **IV:** 924
Sandford, John F.A., **II:** 448
Sanford and Son, **IV:** 898
Sanford, Isabel, **I:** 100
Sanford, John, **II:** 341
Santa Anita Race Track, **I:** 182
Santo Domingo (Settlement), **II:** 317
São Tomé, **II:** 271
SAP/Stevie Wonder Vision Awards, **V:** 1085
Sarron, Petey, **V:** 1180
Satcher, David, **I:** 79
Satchmo *See* Armstrong, Louis
Satlzman, Murray, **I:** 58, 59
Saturday Night Live, **IV:** 914
Saughter-Defoe, Diana T., **III:** 666
Saunders, Monroe, **III:** 692
Saunders, Wallace, **I:** 218
Savage, Augusta, **V:** 1115, **1120–1121**
    works by, **V:** *1121*
Savannah State University, **III:** 656
Savery Library (Talladega College), **I:** 180
Savings Bank of the Grand Fountain United Order of
    True Reformers, **I:** 19
Say Amen, Somebody, **IV:** 852, 966, 969
Sayers, Gale, **V:** 1171, **1201**
Scalero, Rosario, **IV:** 954
Schein, David, **IV:** 900
Schippers, Thomas, **IV:** 927
Schlesinger, Arthur, **III:** 630
Schmeling, Max, **V:** 1194
Schmoke, Kurt L., **III:** *532*, **532–533**
Scholarships, academic *See* Academic scholarships
Schomburg, Arthur A., **I:** 211 **III: 647–648,** *648*
    V: 1094
Schomburg Center for Research in Black Culture, **I:**
    54, 211 **III:** 663 **V:** 1133
School administrators *See* Education and educators
School Daze, **IV:** 852
School desegregation, **I:** 45 **III:** 626–627, 631–632 *See
    also* name of specific court case, e.g., *Brown v.
    Board of Education of Topeka, Kansas;* Public
    transportation segregation; Racial segregation

African American firsts, **I:** 182, 196
   campaigns, **I:** 28, 29 **II:** *463*
   efforts of Southern Education Fund, **III:** 626
   and George Wallace, **I:** 34
   and Kenneth Clark, **III:** 636
   organizations and associations, **II:** 439
   and private white academies, **I:** 47
   relationship to housing policies, **I:** 60
   segregated schoolrooms, **II:** *462*
   and Southern Governors Conference, **I:** 28
   status, **I:** 29, 46, 47
   tax relief for white parents, **I:** 47
   test cases, **I:** 57
School teachers *See* Education and educators
Schools *See* specific type of school, e.g., Universities
   and colleges
Schreiner's Cemetery, **I:** 215
Schroeder, Charles, **V:** 1100
Schuller, Gunther, **IV:** 924, 946 **V:** 981
Schultz, George P., **I:** 45
Schuur, Diane, **V:** 983
Schuyler, Philippa, **IV:** *951*, **951–952**
Schwartzenegger, Arnold, **IV:** 874
Schwerner, Michael, **I:** 35, *39* **II:** 356
Schwitters, Kurt, **IV:** 907
Science and technology, **V:** **1137–1167**
   academic representation, **V:** 1144
   African American firsts, **V:** 1137
   early contributions, **V:** 1139
   issues for women, **V:** 1154
   modern contributions, **V:** 1144–1145
   and Silicon Valley, **V:** 1145
   web sites, **V:** 1150
SCLC *See* Southern Christian Leadership
   Conference (SCLC)
The Score, **V:** 1056
Scott, Charlotte, **I:** 186
Scott, Dred, **I:** *15*, 131 **II:** 330, **340–341**, 448–449, 472
   excerpt from *Dred Scott v. Sandford* ruling,
     I: 131–133
   landmarks, **I:** 203, 205
Scott, Emmett J., **IV:** 750, 830
Scott, Hazel, **I:** 91
Scott, Robert C., **III:** 498
Scott, Ronald, **V:** 1141
Scott, Wendell, **I:** 97 **IV:** 844 **V:** 1177
Scott, William H., **II:** 369
Scott, W.S., **I:** 88
Scott-Heron, Gil, **V:** 983
Scottsboro trials, **I:** 24, *25*
Sculptors *See* Visual and applied arts and artists
Sea captains *See* Ship captains
Sea Islands, South Carolina, **III:** 547
Seale, Bobby, **I:** 45 **II:** *414*, **415**
   and Black Panther party, **I:** 36 **II:** 385, 398, 411

Searles, Charles, **V:** **1121**
Searles, Joseph L. III, **I:** 98
Seattle, Washington
   African American firsts, **I:** 67, 102 **III:** 531
Second Baptist Church (Detroit, Michigan), **I:** 203,
   203
2nd Infantry Division, **V:** *1223*
Secretaries (Army)
   African American firsts, **I:** 51
Secretaries of Agriculture
   African American firsts, **III:** 514
Secretaries of Commerce
   African American firsts, **III:** 506
Securities dealers *See* Stockbrokers
Segregation, bus *See* Public transportation
   segregation
Segregation, racial *See* Racial segregation
Segregation, school *See* School desegregation
Seismology and seismologists, **V:** 1145, 1164
   African American firsts, **V:** 1145, 1164
Selassie, Haile, **II:** 254, 382 **III:** 666, 691 **IV:** 951
Self-help, **II:** 337
   African American firsts, **III:** 589
Selig, Bud, **V:** 1170
Sellers, Walter G., **I:** 108
Selma, Alabama, **I:** 67
Selma University, **III:** 656
Selma-Montgomery National Historic Trail, **I:** 79
Semiconductors, **V:** 1150
Semple, Jesse B. "Simple," **III:** 731
Senators (Federal) *See also* Politics and politicians
   African American firsts, **I:** 87, 97, 185, 217 **III:**
     492, 530, 675
   African American women's firsts, **I:** 103
     III: 496, 526
Senators (State) *See also* Politics and politicians
   African American firsts, **I:** 76 **III:** 506, 521, 538
   African American women's firsts, **II:** 486
Senbet, Lemma W., **III:** 666
Senegal, **II:** 271–272
Senghor, Leopold, **II:** 381
Sengstacke, John H., **IV:** 762, **780–781**
Senior citizens advocacy organizations, **II:** 438
Separate But Equal (Film), **IV:** 852
"Separate but equal" doctrine, **I:** 13, 19, 20, 28, 148
   See also Racial prejudice; Racial segregation
Serbian-Albanian crisis (1999), **I:** 83
Sergeant Rutledge, **IV:** 852
Serkin, Rudolph, **IV:** 954
"Sermonette and song" technique, **IV:** 961, 969
Sermons *See also* Churches; Ministers
   African American firsts, **II:** 388
Sertima, Ivan Van, **II:** 317 **III:** **649**
Servitude *See* Slavery and slaves
Sessions, William, **I:** 66

Set It Off, **IV**: 852
Settlements, human *See* Human settlements
    and towns
Settlers Association of Amarillo, **I**: 220
Settles, Ron, **II**: 477
Seven Guitars, **III**: 747
Sextuplets
    African American firsts, **I**: 107, 109 **III**: 603
Sexuality, **III**: 681
Seychelles, **II**: **272**
Seymour, Frank, **IV**: 776
Seymour, Truman, **V**: 1207
Seymour, William Joseph, **III**: 676, 700, **702**
Shabbaz, Betty, **I**: *40*, 80 **II**: 360
Shabbaz, Malcolm, **I**: 80
el-Shabbazz, el-Hazz Malik *See* X, Malcolm
Shabbazz, Qubilah Bahiyah, **I**: 76 **II**: 387
Shadows, **IV**: 852
Shaft, **IV**: 853
Sha-Key, **V**: 983
Shakur, Afeni, **I**: 78
Shakur, Assata, **II**: 489
Shakur, Tupak, **I**: 78 **V**: 1045, 1064, 1069, **1080**, *1080*
Shange, Ntozake, **III**: **742**, *742*
Shapiro, Robert, **II**: *453*
Sharkey, Jack, **V**: 1194
Sharp, Henry, **III**: 700
Sharp, James A., Jr., **I**: 59
Sharpeville Massacre (1960), **II**: 228
Sharpton, Al, **II**: *366*, **366–367**
Shaw, Bernard, **IV**: 761, *781*, **781–782**
Shaw, Herman, **III**: *607*
Shaw, Robert Gould, **I**: 190 **V**: 1114, 1207, 1228
    landmarks, **I**: 199, *200*
Shaw University, **III**: 656
Shaw University Art Center, **V**: 1133
Shaw v. Reno, **II**: 459
Shearer, Tremaine, **IV**: 776
Sheet Metal Workers International v. EEOC, **I**: 61
Sheftall, Willis B., Jr., **III**: 666
Shelley v. Kraemer, **I**: 27 **II**: 471
Shelton, Robert M., Jr., **I**: 35
Shepherd v. Florida, **II**: 467
Sheridan Broadcasting Network, **IV**: 756
Sheriffs *See* Law enforcement officers and
    administrators
Sherman, Joe, **V**: 1047
She's Gotta Have It, **IV**: 853, 867
Shields, Gree, **II**: 330
Shinhoster, Earl T., **I**: 75
Ship captains
    African American firsts, **I**: 89 **V**: 1233
Ships, **I**: 84 *See also* name of specific ship, e.g.,
    Amistad (Ship)

African American firsts, **I**: 91, 96, 183 **V**: 1223,
    1228, 1239
Shirley Caesar Singers, **IV**: 964
Shirley, George, **III**: 666
Shocklee, Hank, **V**: 1075
Shoe industry, **V**: 1138, 1163–1164
Shook, Karel, **IV**: 889
Shootings *See* Homicide
Short, Bobby, **I**: 209
Short stories *See also* Authors; Literature
    African American women's firsts, **III**: 729
Shorter College, **III**: 656
Show Boat, **IV**: 853
Shrine of the Black Madonna, **III**: 692
Shubert, Lee, **IV**: 917
Shuffle Along, **IV**: 883
Shurney, Robert E., **V**: 1143
Shutten, J.T., **I**: 86
Shuttlesworth, Fred Lee, **II**: 367, *367*
Shuttlesworth v. Birmingham, **II**: 469
Shy, Jean, **II**: 478
Sickle cell anemia, **III**: 608–609 **V**: 1141, 1145
Siege of Port Hudson *See* Port Hudson Siege
Sierra Nevada Mountains, **I**: 182
Sierre Leone, **II**: **272–273**
Sifford, Charlie, **V**: 1176, **1201**
Sigma Gamma Rho (Sorority), **II**: 400
Sigma Pi Phi (Fraternity), **II**: 399, **443**
Sigma Pi Psi (Fraternity), **II**: 400
Sign of the Times Cultural Workshop and Gallery,
    Inc., **V**: 1129
Significant documents *See* Historic documents
Silent films, **IV**: 829 *See also* Films and filmmakers
Silent Protest Parade, **I**: 21
Silicon Graphics Incorporated, **V**: 1144, 1158
Silver Bluff Baptist Church (South Carolina), **III**: 672
Silver, Horace, **V**: 981
Silver Lake Cemetery, **I**: 224
Silver Streak, **IV**: 853
Simmons, Alex, **IV**: 753
Simmons, Russell, **V**: 1059, **1080–1081**
Simmons University Bible College, **III**: 656
Simms, Hilda, **IV**: 836, 881
Simon & Garfunkel, **III**: 582
Simpson, Carole, **IV**: 759, *782*, **782–783**
Simpson, Lorna, **V**: 1096, **1121–1122**
Simpson, Nicole Brown, **I**: 75, 76 **II**: 452, 477
Simpson, O.J., **V**: 1171, 1197, **1202**, *1202*
    murder trial, **I**: 75, 76, *77* **II**: 452, *453*, 477 **V**: 1202
Simpson, Valerie, **V**: **1046**
Simpson, William D., **III**: 534
Sims, Naomi R., **III**: *592*, **592–593**
Sims, Ronald R., **III**: 666
Sinatra, Frank, **IV**: 859 **V**: 1057, 1066
Sinbad, **IV**: **914–915**

Single-sex schools, **I:** 69 **III:** 631 *See also* Education
      and educators
Singleton, Benjamin "Pap," **I:** 19, 195 **III:** 546
Singleton, John, **III:** 715 **IV:** 834, **870–871,** *871*
Sipuel, Ada Lois, **I:** 93 **II:** 460
Sipuel v. University of Oklahoma, **I:** 27 **II:** 460
Sissle, Noble, **IV:** 883, 893, **915**
Sister Clara Muhammad Schools, **III:** 628
Sister Soulah, **I:** 72
Sisulu, Walter, **II:** 228
Sith, Patricia, **I:** 81
Sit-ins, **I:** 26, 26, 31, *33,* 67 *See also* Civil rights and
      Civil Rights movements; Civil rights campaigns
      and demonstrations
   beginnings, **I:** 31 **II:** 346
   court cases, **I:** 32
   results, **I:** 32
Sixteenth Street Baptist Church (Birmingham,
      Alabama), **I:** 34, 80, 179 **II:** 349
65th United States Colored Infantry, **I:** 205
62nd United States Colored Infantry, **I:** 205
Skaters, figure *See* Figure skating and skaters
Skin Game, **IV:** 853
Skinner, Eliot P., **III:** 666
Skinner, I., **I:** 48
Sklarek, Norma Merrick, **V: 1122,** *1122*
Skulnik, Menasha, **III:** 725
Slam, **IV:** 853
Slater Fund *See* Southern Education Foundation
Slater, John F., **III:** 625
Slaughter, John, **I:** 181
Slaughter-Defoe, Diana T., **III:** 666
Slave insurrections and insurrectionists, **I:** 6, 7
      II: 337–342, 377 *See also* name of specific
      insurrection, e.g., John Brown's Raid on
      Harper's Ferry; Slavery and slaves
   largest in history, **I:** 10
   led by white men, **I:** 8
Slave Law (1663), **II:** 318
Slave narratives, **III:** 710
Slave ships *See* Ships
Slave songs, **IV:** 958–960
Slave Songs of the United States, **IV:** 958
Slave trade and traders, **I:** 1, 12 **II:** 226, 236–237 *See*
      also Slavery and slaves
   apparatuses used, **II:** *448*
   beginnings, **I:** 1
   fortresses, **I:** *2* **II:** *272*
   and Gambia, **I:** 1
   gatherings to buy, **II:** *319, 320*
   landmarks, **I:** 190, 217, 220
   participation of Africans, **I:** *4*
   reopening, **I:** 8, 15
   Trans-Atlantic, **I:** 5 **II:** 318
Slavery and slaves *See also* Abolition and

      abolitionists; Freed slaves; Fugitive slaves; Slave
      trade and traders; Underground Railroad
   and American Civil War, **I:** 15, *17*
   and American Revolution, **II:** *322*
   cells to hold, **I:** *120*
   code noir, **I:** 3
   in Colonial America, **II:** 318–321
   countries from which slaves came, **II:** 318
   cultivation of rice, **II:** *322*
   early arrival, **I:** 1, *9* **II:** 317
   entrepreneurship, **III:** 575–576, *577* **V:** 1137
   first formal protest, **I:** 3, 7
   first in Western hemisphere, **I:** 1
   "gag rule," **I:** 11
   and George Washington, **I:** 7
   impact of the cotton gin, **I:** 6
   landmarks, **I:** 186
   maroon communities, **I:** 3 **II:** 319
   and Mennonites and Quakers, **I:** 10, 112
   miscegenation, **II:** 323
   and music, **IV:** 921, 958–959
   naming practices, **II:** 323–324
   and Northwest Ordinance, **I:** 6
   in Northwest Territory, **II:** 325
   official approval, **I:** 1, 2
   owned by African Americans, **I:** 10
   population estimates, **I:** 1, 3, 4, 10 **III:** 543
   quarters for, **II:** *324*
   rationalizations for, **II:** 318, 329
   religious conversions, **III:** 671
   slave life, **II:** 322–323
   in West Indies and Latin America, **I:** 1 **II:** 239
   working on plantations, **I:** *7*
Slavery laws, **II:** 447–449, 472 *See also* Chapter 1
      for chronological look at court cases and
      legislation
Slaves, **IV:** 853
Slaves, free *See* Freed slaves
Slaves, runaway *See* Fugitive slaves
Sled dog racing
   African American firsts, **I:** 100
Sleet, Moneta, Jr., **I:** 98 **V: 1122–1123**
Sly and the Family Stone, **V:** 1040, 1042, 1075
Small Business Act Amendments, **III:** 579
Small Business Administration (SBA), **III:** 579
Smalls, Biggie *See* Notorious B.I.G.
Smalls, Mary J., **III:** 673
Smalls, Robert, **I:** 216 **III:** *533,* **533–534** **V:** 1209
Smiley, Carrie, **IV:** 769
Smiley, Tavis, **IV:** 775, **783**
Smith, Amanda Berry, **III: 703**
Smith and Gaston Funeral Directors, **III:** 587
Smith, Arthur Lee, Jr. *See* Asante, Molefi K.
Smith, Barbara, **IV: 783**
Smith, Bennett, Sr., **III:** 690

Smith, Bessie, **IV:** 968 **V:** 984, *985*, 1023, **1026**
    landmarks, **I:** 100
Smith, Bragg, **I:** 192
Smith, Chelsi, **I:** 105
Smith Court, **I:** 198
Smith, David L., **III:** 666
Smith, Denver A., **I:** 50
Smith, Emmitt, **V:** 1171
Smith, Freeman M., **III:** 579
Smith, Gerritt, **I:** 13, 207, 211
Smith, Hale, **IV:** **952**
Smith, Hughie Lee, **V:** 1094
Smith, James Webster, **I:** 107
Smith, Jane E., **I:** 81 **II:** 406
Smith, Jessie Carney, **III:** 666
Smith, Jimmy, **V:** 981
Smith, Karen, **V:** 1109
Smith, Lee, **V:** 1170
Smith, Lillian, **IV:** 900
Smith, Mamie, **IV:** 968 **V:** 984
Smith, Orlando "Tubby," **I:** 105, 108, *108*
Smith, Patricia, **I:** 81
Smith, Preston, **I:** 46
Smith Robertson Museum and Cultural Center,
    V: 1131
Smith, Tommie, **V:** 1175
Smith v. Allwright, **I:** 27 **II:** 458
Smith, Will, **IV:** 837
Smith, Willi, **V:** *1122*, **1123**
Smith, William French, **I:** 55, 56
Smith, William Kennedy, **II:** 483
Smith, Willie Mae Ford, **IV:** 961, 966, **969**
Smith, Wilson "Thunder," **V:** 1008
Smithsonian Institute, **I:** 188
Smithsonian Institute, National Museum of African
    Art, **V:** 1129
Smoking, cigarette, **III:** 608
SNCC *See* Student Non-Violent Coordinating
    Committee (SNCC)
Snead, W.T., **III:** 690
Snipes, Wesley, **III:** 602, 736 **IV:** **871**, *872*, 899
Snoop Doggy Dogg, **V:** 1045, 1053
Snow, Hank, **V:** 1038
Snyder, James, **IV:** 758
Sobhuza, II, King, **II:** 277
Social Gospel movement, **III:** 676
Social justice organizations, **II:** 429
Social welfare *See* Welfare
Social work and social workers, **II:** 405
Society for the Propagation of the Gospel in Foreign
    Parts, **III:** 621
Society of California Pioneers, **I:** 182
Society of Friends *See* Quakers
Sociology and sociologists, **I:** 20 **II:** 423 **III:** 640, 645
Socrates, **III:** 629

Sojourner-Douglass College, **III:** 656
A Soldier's Play, **III:** 725
A Soldier's Story, **III:** 725 **IV:** 853
Solicitors General
    African American firsts, **I:** 36
Solomons, Gus, Jr., **IV:** 895
Somalia, **II:** **273–274**
Some Considerations on the Keeping of Negroes, **I:** 4
Sommer, Helmut, **V:** 1081
Song of Solomon, **I:** 80
Songs, map *See* Map songs
Sonic booms, **V:** 1143
Sons of Liberty, **I:** 209
Sons of the American Revolution, **I:** 184
Soper Library (Morgan State University), **I:** 198
Sophisticated Gents, **IV:** 853
Sophisticated Ladies, **V:** 1062
Sororities, **II:** 400 *See also* Fraternities; Honor
        societies
    African American firsts, **I:** 89
    founded on white campuses, **II:** 400
Sosa, Sammy, **V:** 1188
Soul City, North Carolina, **I:** 52 **II:** 410
Soul Food, **IV:** 853
Soul music and musicians, **V:** 1039–1043, 1046–1085
        See also Music and musicians
Soul of the Game, **IV:** 853
Soul Stirrers, **V:** 1052
Soul Train, **I:** 75 **IV:** 768
Soulah, Sister *See* Sister Soulah
The Souls of Black Folks: Essays and Sketches, **I:** 157
Sounder, **IV:** 853
South Africa, **II:** **274–276**
    economic sanctions against, **I:** 60, 61
    leaders for racial equity, **I:** *63* **III:** 704
    literature, **II:** 233
    nationalist organizations, **II:** 227–228
South America, **II:** *238 See also* name of specific
        country, e.g., Brazil
South Carolina
    African American firsts, **I:** 18
    African American museums and galleries, **V:** 1134
    African American radio stations, **IV:** 822–823
    commending of slaves, **I:** 4
    education of African Americans, **I:** 10
    first Africans, **I:** 1
    landmarks, **I:** 216–217
    list of African American newspapers, **IV:** 804–805
    race riots, **I:** 40
    slavery issues, **I:** 3, 8
South Carolina Human Affairs Commission, **II:** 373
South Carolina State University, **III:** 656
South Carolina v. Katzenbach, **II:** 459
South Central, **IV:** 854
South Dakota, **I:** 18

landmarks, **I:** 217
South Dakota Attorney General's Office, **II:** 373
South View Cemetery, **I:** 192
Southall, Patricia, **IV:** 908
Southampton Insurrection *See* Nat Turner's slave
    insurrection
Southern Christian Leadership Conference (SCLC), **I:**
    180, 191 **II:** 361, 413, **443**
    formation, **I:** 30 **II:** 350, 397
    leaders, **I:** 9, 80 **II:** 350, 397
Southern Coalition for Educational Equity, **II: 443**
Southern Commercial Convention, **I:** 15
Southern Development Foundation National Black
    Survival Fund, **II: 437**
Southern Education Foundation, **I:** 221 **III:** 625, 626
Southern, Eileen, **IV:** 924
Southern Negro Leaders Conference *See* Southern
    Christian Leadership Conference (SCLC)
Southern Poverty Law Center, **I:** 179 **II: 444**
Southern Regional Council, **II: 444**
Southern United States *See* American South
Southern University (Baton Rouge, Louisiana),
    III: 656
Southern University (New Orleans, Louisiana),
    III: 656
Southern University (Shreveport, Louisiana), **III:** 656
Southwestern Christian College, **III:** 656
Sovine, Red, **V:** 1074
Soyer, Raphael, **V:** 1115
Soyinka, Wole, **III:** 640
Space exploration and explorers, **I:** 52 **V:** 1142–1143,
    1151–1152, 1157, 1162, 1163
    African American firsts, **I:** 100, 102, 104, 105 **V:**
        1142, 1143, 1151, 1157, 1162
    African American women's firsts, **I:** 103 **V:**
        1143, 1159
    first Russian-American mission, **V:** 1143, 1152
Space shuttles *See* name of shuttle, e.g., *Challenger*
    (Space shuttle)
Spanish Civil War, **I:** 25
Spanish-American War, A-13 **I:** 20 **V:** 1210–1212, 1212
Spaulding, Asa T., **I:** 212
Spaulding, Charles Clinton, **I:** 212
Special law enforcement forces *See* Law enforcement
    officers and administrators
Spectographs, **V:** 1152
Spector, Phil, **V:** 1041, 1081
Speech at Liberty Hall, **I:** 151–154
Speech on Lynch Law in All its Phases, **I:** 145
Speech on Presidential Impeachment Proceedings,
    I: 172
Speech on Woman Suffrage, **I:** 143, 144
Speeches *See also* name of specific speech, e.g., *I*
    Have a Dream speech
    African American women's firsts, **II:** 378

Spelman College, **I:** 191 **III:** 624, 656
Spencer, Anne, **I:** 222
Spencer, Jon Michael, **III:** 666
Spencer, Margaret Beale, **III:** 666
Spencer, Peter, **III:** 672, 687
Spielberg, Steven, **IV:** 891
Spies, **II:** 339
Spingarn, Joel, **I:** 22
Spingarn Medals, A-9–A-11 **I:** 21 **V:** 1139
Spinks, Leon, **V:** 1180
Spinks, Michael, **V:** 1189
Spirit Catcher: The Art of Beyte Saar, **V:** 1120
Spirit of Freedom Statue, **I:** 189
Spirituals (Music), **IV:** 958–960
Sports, **V: 1169–1204** *See also* name of specific
    sport, e.g., Baseball and baseball players
    biographical profiles of athletes, **V:** 1178–1204
    web sites, **V:** 1150
    women's issues, **V:** 1177–1178
Sports franchises
    African American firsts, **V:** 1174
Sports Illustrated, **I:** 106
Spottswood, Stephen Gill, **III: 703,** *703*
Sprewell, Latrell, **V:** 1174
St. Andrew's African Methodist Episcopal Church
    (Sacramento, California), **I:** 183
St. Augustine's College Art Gallery, **V:** 1133
St. George's Episcopal Church (New York City, New
    York), **I:** 210
St. John, Bishop the Divine *See* Hickerson, John
St. John, Keith, **III:** 603
St. Joseph's Hospital, **I:** 219
St. Luke Building, **I:** 222
St. Luke's Episcopal Church (District of Columbia), **I:**
    189 **II:** 386
St. Peter's Cemetery, **I:** 194
Stack, Carol, **III:** 595
Stackpole, Ralph, **V:** 1111
Stallings, George A., Jr., **I:** 67 **III:** 682, 684–685, **703–**
    704, *704*
Stamps, postage *See* Postage stamps
Stance, Emanuel, **V:** 1210
Standardized tests *See* Proficiency tests
Standing committees (Congress)
    African American firsts, **III:** 494
Stanford, John, **I:** 105
Stanley, Murray, **II:** 450
Stanton, Elizabeth Cady, **I:** 143 **II:** 329
Stanton, Robert, **I:** 80, 107
STARZ!3 *See* Black Entertainment Television (BET)
State agencies, **II:** 371–374
State courts *See* Courts (State)
State government officials *See* Government
    officials (State)
State legislators, **II:** 434

African American firsts, **I:** 18, 86
African American women's firsts, **I:** 25, 90
State of the Union messages
African American firsts, **I:** 109
State songs, **I:** 26
Stations, radio *See* Radio networks and stations
Stations, television *See* Television networks and
stations
Statistics *See* specific subject area, e.g., Family
Statues *See also* Chapter 4 for statues by city
and state; name of specific statue e.g.,
Emancipation Statue
African American firsts, **I:** 198
Staupers, Mabel K., **II: 415 V: 1165**
Stax/Volt record company, **V:** 1040, 1041
Steele, Claude M., **III:** 667
Steele, Shelby, **III: 648–649,** *649*
Steer wrestling, **I:** 214 *See also* Calf ropers
Steichen, Edward, **V:** 1105
Steinberg, Benjamin, **IV:** 923
Steinbrenner, George, **V:** 1189
Steinburg, Lewis, **V:** 1076
Stengstacke, John H., **I:** 79
Stephney, Bill, **V:** 1075
Stereotypes, racial, **IV:** 831–832 *See also* Racial
prejudice
Sterling, Scott *See* LaRock, Scott
Stevens, Nelson, **V: 1123–1124**
Stevens, Sandra Lee, **III:** 519
Stevens, Thaddeus, **I:** 215
Stevenson, Mickey, **V:** 1041
Steward, Susan McKinney, **V:** 1140
Stewardesses *See* Flight attendants
Stewart, Bennett, **I:** *55*
Stewart, Maria, **II:** 378 **III:** 673
Stewart, Sylvester, **V:** 1040
Still, William Grant, **I:** 89 **IV:** 924, **952–953,** *953*
Stillman College, **III:** 656
Stimson, Henry L., **V:** 1222
Stock exchanges, **III:** 565
African American firsts, **I:** 98 **III:** 588 **IV:** 837
Stockbrokers
African American firsts, **I:** 108
organizations and associations, **II:** 433
Stokes, Carl B., **I:** 43, 97 **III:** 495
Stokes, Louis, **III: 534**
Stone, Christopher, **I:** 83
Stone, Chuck, **III:** 667 **IV: 783–784**
Stone, Lyle "Toni," **I:** 94 **V:** 1178
Stone, W. Clement, **III:** 589
Stoner, J.B., **I:** 53
Stono River slave revolt, **I:** 217
Stormy Weather, **IV:** 854
Storytelling organizations, **II:** 432
Stotts, Carl, **II:** 473

Stoutt, Juanita Kidd, **I:** 102
Stowe, Harriet Beecher, **I:** 13, 198, 214 **II:** 339, 341
III: 728
landmarks, **I:** 213, *213*
Stowers, Freddie, **I:** 103 **V:** 1215
Stowkowski, Leopold, **IV:** 931
Strader, Jacob, **II:** 472
Strader v. Graham, **II:** 472
Stradford, J.B., **I:** 78
Straight Out of Brooklyn, **IV:** 854
Strait, George, **IV:** 759
Strauder v. West Virginia, **I:** 19, 22 **II:** 449, 466
Strayhorn, William "Billy," **V: 1026**
Streater, Angela, **V:** 1115
Street Knowledge, **V:** 1063
Streetcar conductors *See* Conductors (Streetcar)
Streets *See* name of specific street, e.g., Pearl Street
Stribling, T.S., **III:** 725
Strickland, Dorothy S., **III:** 667
String Society of Los Angeles, **IV:** 943
Strong, Barret, **V:** 1058
Stuart, Carol, **II:** 348
Stuart, Charles, **II:** 349
Student body presidents
African American firsts, **III:** 644
Student Non-Violent Coordinating Committee
(SNCC), **I:** 31 **II:** 364, 398, 400
Students, university and college *See* University and
college graduates and students
Studio Museum in Harlem, **V:** 1133
Suarez, Xavier, **I:** 64
Suburbanization, **III:** 549 *See also* Inner cities;
Urbanization
Sudan, **II: 276**
Sudie and Simpson, **IV:** 854
Suffrage *See* Voting and voting rights
Sugar Hill, **IV:** 854
Sugar Hill Gang, **V:** 1044
Sugar Hill, Harlem, **I:** 211
Sugar industry, **I:** 1, 197
significant inventions, **V:** 1137, 1165
Sullivan Awards, A-11
African American women's firsts, **V:** 1188
Sullivan, John L., **I:** 181
Sullivan, Leon H., **I:** *63* **II: 367–368 III: 704**
Sullivan, Louis W., **I:** 66 **III: 534,** *535*
Sumlin, Hubert, **V:** 1009
Summer, Donna, **V:** 1043, **1081**
Summits, **I:** 66
Summitt, Pat, **V:** 1188
Sumner, Charles, **I:** 183
Sumner Elementary School, **I:** 196
Sunday School Helper, **IV:** 777
Sunday School Publishing Board of the National
Baptist Convention, USA, **IV:** 750

Sundiata, Sekou, **V:** 983

Super Bowl football championships
  African American firsts, **I:** 99, 102

Superfly, **IV:** 854 **V:** 1072

Superintendents, school *See* Education and educators

Supermodels *See* Models (Fashion)

Suppression of the African Slave Trade, **I:** 20

Supreme Beauty Products, **IV:** 773

Supreme Court decisions *See also* Supreme Court of
    the United States
  education, **II:** 460–464
  employment and affirmative action, **II:** 464–
      466, 472–475
  interracial marriage, **II:** 469
  jury selection and duty, **II:** 466–467
  requirements for legislative membership, **II:** 470
  right of sale and restrictive covenants, **II:** 470–471
  sentencing and incarceration, **II:** 471–472
  slavery, **II:** 472
  voting rights, **II:** 457–459

Supreme Court justices *See* Judges and justices
    (United States Supreme Court)

Supreme Court of the United States, **II:** 454 *See also*
    name of specific cases, e.g., *Brown v. Board of
    Education of Topeka, Kansas;* Supreme Court
    decisions
  African American firsts, **II:** 452

The Supremes, **V:** 1078, 1082, 1083–1084

Surgeons General of the United States
  African American women's firsts, **I:** 104

Surgery and surgeons, **V:** 1150–1167 *See also*
    Medicine and medical doctors
  African American firsts, **I:** 86, 88, 99, 107, 193, 194
    V: 1140, 1161, 1166

Suriname, **II:** **311–312**

Surveyors, **V:** 1151, 1158

Sutton, Percy E., **III:** **593** **IV:** 754, 784

Sutton, Pierre Monte, **IV:** **784**

Swain, John, **I:** 181

*Swann v. Charlotte Mecklenburg Board of
    Education*, **II:** 462

Swanson, Howard, **IV:** **953**

Swayne Hall (Talladega College), **I:** 180

Swaziland, **II:** **276–277**

Sweatt, Herman Marion, **II:** 460 **III:** 627

Sweatt v. Painter, **I:** 155 **II:** 460 **III:** 627

Sweet Auburn Historic District, **I:** 192

Sweet Charity, **IV:** 884

Sweet Honey in the Rock, **IV:** 963

Sweet Sweetback's Baadasssss Song, **IV:** 833,
    854, 873

Swimming and swimmers
  African American firsts, **I:** 100

Swing music *See* Jazz and jazz musicians

Swygert, H. Patrick, **I:** 76 **III:** **649**

Symphonies *See* Orchestras and orchestra directors

Symphony of the New World, **IV:** 923, 941

Syphilis, **V:** 1158 *See also* Tuskegee Syphilis Study

T

Taft, William Howard, **III:** 733

Tagliabue, Paul, **III:** 538

Take 6, **IV:** 963

Take a Giant Step, **IV:** 854

Take My Hand, Precious Lord, **IV:** 961

Talbert, Florence Cole, **II:** 400

Talent agents
  African American firsts, **III:** 582

Talk shows, television *See* Television and
    television shows

Talladega College, **I:** 180 **III:** 656

Tambo, Oliver, **II:** 228

Tandy, Vertner Woodson, **I:** 211

Taney, Roger Brook, **I:** 115, 131, 205 **II:** 449, 472
  excerpt from *Dred Scott v. Sanford* ruling,
      I: 131–133

Tanner, Benjamin Tucker, **I:** 100

Tanner, Henry Ossawa, **I:** 106, 180 **V:** 1090, 1100,
    1124, 1128
  landmarks, **I:** 216
  works by, **V:** *1123*

Tanzania, **II:** **277–278**

Tarus Production Company, **V:** 1085

Tarver, Charles W.B., IV, **III:** 602

Tate, Earnest L., **I:** 107

Tatum, Arthur Art, **V:** **1027**

Taverns *See* name of specific tavern, e.g.,
    Fraunces Tavern

Taylor, Cecil, **V:** 980, **1027–1028**

Taylor, Charlie, **V:** 1171

Taylor, Eddie, **V:** 1024

Taylor, Gardner C., **III:** 678, *679*, **705**

Taylor, John Baxter, Jr., **I:** 89 **V:** 1175

Taylor, Koko, **V:** 984, **1027**

Taylor, Lawrence, **V:** 1171, **1202**

Taylor, Marshall, **V:** 1177, **1202**

Taylor, Robert "Pops," **V:** 1027

Taylor, Ruth Carol, **I:** 96

Taylor, Susan L., **IV:** 755, *784*, **784–785**

Taylor, Timothy D., **V:** 1038

Taylor, William "Billy," Jr., **V:** **1028,** *1028,* 1083

Teachers *See* Education and educators

Teamsters v. United States, **II:** 465

Technology *See* Science and technology

Teenage pregnancy, **III:** 562, 603–604, 616–617 *See
    also* Family and marriage; Population

Television and television shows, **IV:** **829–875,** 968
      See also Actors and actresses; Films and

filmmakers; Television directors and producers;
Television hosts and anchors
 advertising, **IV:** 759–760
 and affirmative action, **IV:** 759
 African American firsts, **IV:** 835, 861, 919, 949
 African American women's firsts, **I:** 100 **IV:**
  768, 773, 786
 court cases, **IV:** 764, 787
 early years, **IV:** 835
 first acceptance of African Americans, **IV:** 836
 first racial comedy, **IV:** 836
 future, **IV:** 838
 growth of networks, **IV:** 837
 longest-running programs, **IV:** 765, 768
 reaction to 1960s, **IV:** 835–836
 web sites, **V:** 1149
Television, cable *See* Cable networks and television
Television commercials
 African American women's firsts, **III:** 592
Television directors and producers, **IV:** 762–787 *See
 also* Actors and actresses; Television and
 television shows
 African American firsts, **I:** 100
 African American women's firsts, **IV:** 786
Television hosts and anchors, **IV:** 762–787 *See
 also* Actors and actresses; Television and
 television shows
 African American firsts, **I:** 91, 98, 100, 105
  IV: 758, 779
Television networks and stations, **II:** 432 **IV:** 826–827,
 837 *See also* Radio networks and stations;
 Television and television shows
 African American firsts, **I:** 99 **IV:** 757, 760, 774, 837
Television, public *See* Public television
Temple, Lewis, **I:** 201 **V:** 1138, **1165**
Temple of Islam, **I:** 24
Temple of Kawaida, **III:** 718
Temple, Shirley, **IV:** 913, *913*
The Temptations, **V:** 1042, 1068
Ten Week War *See* Spanish-American War
Tennessee, **I:** 41, 47
 admission into Union, **I:** 7
 African American museums and galleries, **V:**
  1134–1135
 African American newspapers, **IV:** 805
 African American radio stations, **IV:** 823
 African American television stations, **IV:** 827
 landmarks, **I:** 218–219
Tennessee Human Rights Commission, **II:** 373
Tennessee State University, **III:** 657
Tennessee State University Institute for African
 Studies, **V:** 1135
Tennis and tennis players, **II:** 421 **V:** 1175 *See also*
 name of specific tournament, e.g., Wimbleton
 tennis tournament

African American firsts, **I:** 95, 98 **V:** 1175,
 1180, 1187
African American women's firsts, **V:** 1177
biographical profiles, **V:** 1180–1181, 1186–
 1187, 1204
Tennis championships, **I:** 84
Teno, Jean-Marie, **II:** 233
10th Cavalry Regiment, **V:** 1209, 1211
Tenure (Educators)
 African American firsts, **V:** 1139
Terminator X, **V:** 1075
Terrell, Mary E. Church, **I:** 187, 188 **II:** 337,
 368, 395, 400
 landmarks, **I:** 189
Terrell, Robert H., **I:** 187, 188 **II:** 368, **488**
Terrell, Tammi, **V:** 1046, 1057
Terry, Lucy, **I:** 4 **III: 742**
Tests, proficiency *See* Proficiency tests
Texaco Inc., **I:** 78
Texas, **I:** 46
 admission into Union, **I:** 12
 African American firsts, **I:** 76
 African American museums and galleries, **V:** 1135
 African American newspapers, **IV:** 805–806
 African American radio stations, **IV:** 824
 African American television stations, **IV:** 827
 landmarks, **I:** 220
Texas Attorney General's Office, **II:** 373
Texas College, **III:** 657
Texas Rangers (Baseball team), **III:** 586
Texas Southern University, **III:** 657
A Thanksgiving Sermon (Alexander Crummell)
 title page, **II:** *379*
Tharp, Twyla, **IV:** 894
Tharpe, Rosetta, **IV: 969**
Theater and theater performers, **IV: 877–920** *See
 also* name of specific theater, e.g., African
 Grove Theatre
 1890 to 1920, **IV:** 879–880
 African American firsts, **I:** 96 **IV:** 877, 879, 930
 African American women's firsts, **IV:** 912
 biographical profiles, **IV:** 890–920
 early plays, **IV:** 877
 in Europe, **IV:** 880
 twentieth century, **IV:** 880–883
 web sites, **V:** 1149
Theater and theater performers (Musical), **IV:**
 890–920
 African American firsts, **IV:** 879, 915, 930
 twentieth century, **IV:** 883–885
Theater awards *See* name of specific award, e.g.,
 Tony Awards
Theology and theologians, **III:** 694–695, 705
There is Confusion, **III:** 725

They Came Before Columbus: The African Presence in Ancient America, **III:** 649

Thiele, Bob, **V:** 983

Thigpen, Lynne, **IV: 915**

Think and Grow Rich: A Black's Choice, **III:** 589

Third World Press, **III:** 737 **IV:** 751

Thirteenth Amendment to the United States Constitution, **I:** 19, 136 **II:** 333, 344, 449, 455
  excerpt from, **I:** 136
  passage, **I:** 17
  ratification, **I:** 17

This is Your Life, **III:** 643

Thomas, Alma W., **V: 1124**

Thomas, Carla, **V:** 1060, 1076

Thomas, Clarence, **I:** 68, 70, 71 **II:** 454, *455*, 482, **488**
  Anita Hill controversy, **I:** 73 **II:** 454, 480–481

Thomas, Debi, **I:** 101 **V:** 1177, **1202**

Thomas, Dylan, **III:** 747 **IV:** 907

Thomas, Isiah, **I:** 84

Thomas, James Joshua, **I:** 94

Thomas, Vivien, **V: 1165–1166**

Thompson, Allen, **I:** 59

Thompson, Bennie G., **III:** 498

Thompson, Bob, **V: 1124**

Thompson, Frank, **I:** 88

Thompson, Jacqueline, **I:** 107 **III:** 603

Thompson, John, Jr., **I:** 100 **V:** 1173, **1202–1203,** *1203*

Thompson, Linden, **I:** 107 **III:** 603

Thompson, Malachi, **V:** 983

Thompson, Myron, **I:** 63

Thompson sextuplets, **I:** 107 **III:** 603

Thompson, Virgil, **IV:** 949

Thompson, William, **V:** 1222

Thomson, Gerald E., **III:** 667

Thornburg v. Gingles, **II:** 459

369th Infantry Regiment, **V:** 1213–1214, 1237

369th Veteran's Association, **II: 444**

Three Tenors concert, **V:** 1056

Thriller, **V:** 1065

The Thunderbirds (Flight team), **I:** 99

Thurman, Howard, **III: 705**

Thurman, Wallace H., **III:** 732, **742–743**

Thurmond, Strom, **V:** 1222

Tidal Basin Bridge, **I:** 189

Tilden, Samuel J., **II:** 336

Till, Emmett, **I:** 29

Tillman, George, **III:** 534

A Time to Kill, **IV:** 854

Timucuan Ecological and Historic Preserve, **I:** 190

Tindley, Charles Albert, **III:** 676 **IV:** 960, **970**

Tindley Temple (Philadelphia, Pennsylvania), **IV:** 960

To Kill a Mockingbird, **IV:** 854

To Secure These Rights, **I:** 27 **II:** 397

To Sir, with Love, **IV:** 854

To Sleep with Anger, **IV:** 854

Tobago, **II:** 312

The *Today* show, **I:** 100 **IV:** 771

Togo, **II: 278–279**

Tolbert, Margaret E. M., **V: 1166**

Tolton, Augustine, **I:** 194

The Tom Joyner Morning Show, **IV:** 775

Tomassi, Leone, **I:** 218

Tomb guards
  African American women's firsts, **I:** 106

Tomoko Missions, **III:** 633

Tony Awards, A-11–A-12
  African American firsts, **I:** 93

Tony Brown's Black Journal, **IV:** 765

Toomer, Jean, **III:** *743*, **743–744**

Torrence, Ridgely, **IV:** 880

Tougaloo College, **III:** 657

Toure, Kwame, **I:** 37 **II: 352–353,** *353*, 383, 398 **IV:** 775

Toure, Sekou, **II:** 382

Toussaint, François, **II:** 237

Toussaint, Pierre, **III:** 673

Towne, Laura, **I:** 217

Towns *See* Human settlements and towns

Towns, Edolphus, **III:** 498

Townsend, Robert, **IV:** 834, **871**

Townsend, Ronald, **IV:** 758

Track and field athletes, **V:** 1175, 1178–1204
  African American firsts, **I:** 89, 93, 95 **V:** 1175
  African American women's firsts, **I:** 96, 102 **V:** 1177, 1183

Track and Field Hall of Fame *See* National Track and Field Hall of Fame

Trade, slave *See* Slave trade and traders

Trade unions *See* Labor and labor unions

Trafficante v. Metropolitan Life Insurance, **II:** 471

Trail, William, **I:** 194

Trails *See* name of specific trail, e.g., Beckwourth Trail

TransAfrica, **II:** 399, 412, 413, **444 III:** 495

TransAfrica Forum, **II: 444**

Transplants, kidney *See* Kidney transplants

Tranzlator Crew *See* The Fugees

Travel literature *See also* Literature
  African American firsts, **III:** 720

Travis, Betty, **V:** 1084

Travis, Dempsey, **IV:** 751

Treasurers
  African American firsts, **I:** 106

A Treatise on the Intellectual Character and Political Condition of the Colored People of the United States, **I:** 11

Treaty of Guadalupe Hidalgo, **II:** 325

Treemonisha, **IV:** 941

Trenholm State Technical College, **III:** 657

Trenton, North Carolina
  African American firsts, **I:** 83
"Trial of the Century" *See* Simpson, O.J.
A Tribe Called Quest, **V:** 984, 1044
Trim-Away Figure Contouring, **III:** 590
Trinidad and Tobago, **II: 312**
Trip to Coontown, **IV:** 879
Triumph the Church and Kingdom of God in Christ,
  III: 691
Trolleys, railway, **I:** 88
Trotter, James Monroe, **IV:** 924
Trotter, William M., **I:** 201 **II:** 337, **368–369 IV:** 753
Truman Committee on Civil Rights, **I:** 27
Truman, Harry S, **I:** 28, 189 **II:** 363, 397 **III:** 541
  V: 1223
  desegregation of military, **I:** 27, 154 **III:** 494
    V: 1222
Trustees, university *See* University trustees
Truth, Sojourner, **I:** 13, 128, *129* **II: 341 III:** 673
  V: 1209
  excerpt from *Book of Life*, **I:** 128
  landmarks, **I:** 201, *202*
Try Us Resources, **II: 445**
Tsongas, Paul, **III:** 505
Tubman, Harriet, **I:** 13, *13* **II:** 329, **341 IV:** 959
  V: 1209
  landmarks, **I:** 207
Tubman, John, **II:** 341
Tucker, C. Delores, **I:** 77
Tucker, Lemuel, **IV:** 758, **785,** *785*
Tucker, Sophie, **IV:** 893
Tucker, William, **I:** 85 **II:** 317
Tunisia, **II: 279**
Tunnell, Emlen, **I:** 97 **V:** 1171
Turead v. Board of Supervisors, **II:** 461
Turks and Caicos Islands, **II: 312–313**
Turner, Darwin T., **III:** 744
Turner, Henry McNeal, **I:** 86 **II: 391,** *391* **III:**
    491, 673, 675
  and African Methodist Episcopal Church, **II:** 379
    III: 673
Turner, Ike, **V:** 1037, 1081
Turner, Nat, **I:** 10 **II:** 329, **341 III:** 673
Turner, Tina, **V:** 1037, **1081,** *1082*
Turner v. Fouche, **II:** 467
Turner v. Murray, **II:** 467
Turnham, Edythe, **V:** 984
Turpin, Randy, **V:** 1200
Tuskegee Airmen, **I:** 93, 203 **II:** 411 **V:** *1218*
The Tuskegee Airmen (Film), **IV:** 854
Tuskegee, Alabama, **I:** 31
Tuskegee Institute *See* Tuskegee University
Tuskegee Syphilis Study, **I:** 50, 79 **III:** 605–606
  victims, **III:** *607*

Tuskegee University, **I:** 180 **II:** 411 **III:** 624, 657
    IV: 750
  chapels, **I:** *181*
  classrooms, **III:** *623*
  founding, **I:** 19, 211, 222 **II:** 345
Tuskegee University Press, **IV:** 750
Tutu, Desmond, **I:** 60, 61 **II:** 413 **V:** 1183
Twentieth Century Club of Boston, **III:** 634
25th Infantry Regiment, **I:** 20 **V:** 1209, 1211
24th Infantry Regiment, **I:** 27 **V:** 1209, 1211,
    1212, 1222
Twenty-Fourth Amendment to the United States
    Constitution, **I:** 34, 37, 164
Tyler, John, **II:** 325
Tympany Five, **V:** 1067
Tyner, McCoy, **V: 1029**
Typhoid, **V:** 1211
Tyson, Cicely, **I:** 99 **IV:** 836, *837*, **871–872**
Tyson, Mike, **I:** 76, 80 **II:** 483 **V:** 1173, 1189
Tyus, Wyomia, **V:** 1177

U

Uganda, **II: 279–281**
Uggams, Leslie, **IV:** 884, **915–916,** *916*
Ulanowsky, Paul, **IV:** 925
Umkhonto we Sizwe, **II:** 228
UNCF *See* United Negro College Fund (UNCF)
Uncle Noname Cookie Company, **III:** 583
Uncle Remus Museum, **V:** 1130
Uncle Tom *See* Henson, Josiah
Uncle Tom's Cabin (Book), **I:** 13, *14*
Uncle Tom's Cabin (Film), **IV:** 855
Uncle Tom's Cabin (Landmark), **I:** 198
Uncle Tom's Children, **III:** 747
Underground Railroad, **I:** 13 **II:** 329 *See also*
    Abolition and abolitionists; Slavery and slaves
  maps, **II:** *331*
  markers, **I:** 194, 195, 201, 203
  slaves who traveled, **II:** *332*
  stations, **I:** 194, 198, 206, 207, 214, 223, 224
Unemployment *See* Employment
UNIA *See* Universal Negro Improvement
    Association (UNIA)
Union Army, **I:** 16, 190, 199 **II:** 332–333 *See also*
    American Civil War; Confederate Army
Union Bethel African Methodist Episcopal Church
    (District of Columbia), **I:** 188
Union of Black Episcopalians, **II: 445**
Union Tavern *See* Yellow Tavern
Unions, labor *See* Labor and labor unions
Unitarian Universalist Association Black Concerns
    Working Group, **II: 445**
Unitarian Universalist Church, **II:** 445
United African movement, **II:** 366

United Black Church Appeal, **II: 445** *See also* Churches; Religion

United Church of Christ, **II:** 401, 445 *See also* Churches; Religion

United Church of Christ Commission for Racial Justice, **II: 445**

United Church of Jesus Christ, **III:** 691

United House of Prayer for All People, **III:** 697

United Machining Company, **I:** 201

United Methodist Church *See also* Churches; Religion African American women's firsts, **III:** 699

United Nations delegates *See* Delegates (United Nations)

United Negro College Fund (UNCF), **I:** 26 **II:** 411, 412, **430, 445 III:** 647

United States Amateur Boxing Inc., **I:** 107

United States Amateur Golf Championship, **I:** 105

United States Coast Guard, **I:** 84

United States Colored Troops (USCT), **V:** 1207–1209

United States Commission for the Relief of the National Freedmen, **III:** 623

United States Commission on Civil Rights, **I:** 158 **II:** 371 **III:** 494

United States Constitution *See* Constitution of the United States of America

United States Department of Labor, Women's Bureau, **III:** 644

United States Department of the Interior, **V:** 1145

United States Figure Skating Championship, **I:** 108

United States House of Representatives members *See* Members of Congress (United States House of Representatives)

United States Justice Department, **I:** 107

United States Military Academy (USMA) at West Point, **V:** 1229
  African American firsts, **I:** 83, 87, 107 **V:** 1210, 1232

United States Naval Academy (USNA) at Annapolis African American firsts, **I:** 87, 93, 107 **V:** 1222

United States Navy Women's Reserves (WAVES), **I:** 91

United States of America *See also* name of specific state or city, e.g., Virginia historic maps, **II:** *326, 333*

United States Open (Tennis), A-14 African American firsts, **V:** 1186

United States Radio, **IV:** 759, 772

United States Secretary of Labor, **I:** 107

United States Steel Workers of America v. Brian Weber, **I:** 52 **II:** 472–473

United States Supreme Court *See* Supreme Court of the United States

United States Surgeons General second African American, **V:** 1156

United States v. Cruikshank, **I:** 19

United States v. Fordice, **I:** 72 **II:** 464

United States v. Hamilton See Civil Rights Cases

United States v. Nichols See Civil Rights Cases

United States v. Paradise, **II:** 474

United States v. Reese, **II:** 457

United States v. Ryan See Civil Rights Cases

United States v. Singleton See Civil Rights Cases

United States v. Stanley See Civil Rights Cases

United States Volunteer Infantry (United States No. V.I.), **V:** 1211

Unity Broadcasting Network, **IV:** 773

Unity Fellowship Church, **III:** 693

Univerity of Texas Law School, **I:** 77

Universal Foundation for Better Living, Inc., **III:** 694

Universal Negro Improvement Association (UNIA), **I:** 21, 151–154 **II:** 388–389, 399 **IV:** 751

Universities and colleges, **I:** 65 **III:** 624, 627–628, 650–658 *See also* Education and educators; name of specific school, e.g., Howard University
  African American firsts, **I:** 14, 87, 180, 196, 214 **III:** 546, 624
  African American women's firsts, **I:** 109 **II:** 482
  court cases, **I:** 28, 71, 72
  desegregation issues, **I:** 60, 72
  enrollment statistics, **I:** 71 **III:** 627
  publishing enterprises, **IV:** 750
  racial composition, **III:** 628

University and college graduates and students, **III:** *625 See also* Doctoral degrees; Professional degrees; Universities and colleges
  African American firsts, **I:** 85, 97 **II:** 476 **III:** 649 **V:** 1139, 1153, 1161

University and college presidents *See* Presidents (Universities and colleges)

University and college professors *See* Education and educators

University chairs (Endowed) *See* Chairpersons (Endowed)

University of Arkansas (Pine Bluff), **III:** 657

University of California (Berkeley), **I:** 82

University of California (Davis), **I:** 76

University of California v. Bakke, **I:** 52
  demonstrations protesting decision, **I:** *53*

University of Islam, **III:** 628

University of Maryland, Eastern Shore, **III:** 657

University of Michigan Art Museum, **V:** 1131

University of Mississippi, **I:** 33

University of Pennsylvania, **I:** 74

University of the District of Columbia, **I:** 188 **III:** 657

University of the Virgin Islands, **III:** 657

University trustees
  African American firsts, **I:** 98

Uni-World, **IV:** 867

Upper Volta *See* Burkina Faso

Upshaw, Gene, **V: 1203**

Uptight, **IV:** 855
Uptown Records, **V:** 1060
Uptown Saturday Night, **IV:** 855
Urban Research Press, **IV:** 751
Urbanization, **II:** 427, 441, 442 **III:** 548–549 *See also*
    Inner cities; Suburbanization
Uridin, Jalal, **V:** 1044
Uruguay, **II: 313–314**
US (Organization), **III:** 644
US3, **V:** 984
USMA *See* United States Military Academy (USMA)
    at West Point
USNA *See* United States Naval Academy (USNA) at
    Annapolis
USS Harmon (Ship), **I:** 91, *92*
USS Maine (Ship), **V:** 1210
USS Miller (Ship), **V:** 1239
Utah
    African American museums and galleries, **V:** 1135
    African American radio stations, **IV:** 824
Utah Attorney General's Office, **II:** 373
Utah Museum of Fine Arts, **V:** 1135

V

Valiente, Juan, **II:** 236
Van Gogh, Vincent, **V:** 1112
Van Peebles, Mario, **IV:** 873
Van Peebles, Melvin, **IV: 872–873**
Vanderhorst, Richard, **III:** 688
VanDerZee, James, **V:** 1092, 1102, **1124–1125,** *1125*
    photographs by, **II:** *381* **V:** *1092*
Vandross, Luther, **IV:** 903 **V: 1082,** *1082*
Vanilla Ice, **V:** 1069
Vanzant, Iyanla, **III:** 678, 682, **705**
Vareen, Ben A., **IV: 916**
Varèse, Edgard, **IV:** 952
Varick, James, **I:** 9 **III:** 672, 686, **705**
Vassa, Gustavus *See* Equiano, Olaudah
Vaughan, Sarah Lois, **V: 1029**
Vaughn Cultural Center, **V:** 1131
Vaughn, Sarah, **V:** 1046, 1049
Vechten, Carl van, **I:** 23
Venereal disease, **V:** 1158
Venezuela, **II: 314**
Vermont, **I:** 6
Vermont Attorney General's Office, **II:** 373
Vernell, Rose, **I:** 103 **III:** 704
Verret, Harrison, **V:** 1052
Verrett, Shirley, **IV: 953–954,** *954*
Vesey, Denmark, **I:** 9 **II:** 325, **342,** 378 **III:** 673
    landmarks, **I:** 217
Vessels (Ships) *See* Ships
Veterans (War), **II:** 425, 444
Veterans Affairs Department, **III:** 496

Veterinary medicine and veterinarians, **II:** 411
    III: 624
Veverka, Charles, **I:** 54
Viacom, Inc., **IV:** 759
Vibe, **V:** 1067
Vice Presidential nominations
    African American firsts, **III:** 503
Victoria Falls, Zimbabwe, **II:** *282*
Victory Monument, **I:** 194
Vietnam War, A-14 **V:** 1224–1225
    African American firsts, **I:** 193
Vigilance Committee, **I:** 209
Villa Lewaro, **I:** 211
Villella, Edward, **IV:** 894
Vinson, Fred M., **II:** 460
Vinson, Michelle, **II:** 465
Violence, racial *See* Racial violence
Violin and violinists *See* Classical music and
    musicians
Virgin Islands (British), **II: 314–315**
Virgin Islands (United States), **II: 315**
Virginia, **I:** 2, 49, 61
    African American firsts, **I:** 61
    African American museums and galleries, **V:** 1135
    African American newspapers, **IV:** 806
    African American radio stations, **IV:** 824–825
    African Americans firsts, **III:** 538
    landmarks, **I:** 220–223
    laws for free African Americans, **I:** 3, 7, 13
    slavery issues, **I:** 1, 2, 3, 4, 10, 15
    state song, **I:** 26
Virginia Human Rights Council, **II:** 373
Virginia Key, Virginia, **III:** 548
Virginia Randolph Fund *See* Southern Education
    Foundation
Virginia Seminary and College, **III:** 657
Virginia State University, **III:** 657
Virginia Union University, **III:** 657
Virginia v. Rives, **II:** 466
Visual and applied arts and artists, **V: 1087–1135** *See
    also* Art collections and exhibits
    African American firsts, **I:** 97, 98 **V:** 1089, 1097,
        1111, 1116, 1121, 1123
    African American women's firsts, **V:** 1096, 1109,
        1114, 1122
    African legacy, **V:** 1088–1090
    African roots, **V:** 1087–1088
    biographical profiles, **III:** 732 **V:** 1099–1128
    Black Aesthetic and Afrocentrist movements, **V:**
        1094–1096
    contemporary, **V:** 1096–1097
    depiction of African American culture, **V:** 1090
    early America, **V:** 1089
    early compensation, **V:** 1089
    exploration of modernistic art forms, **V:** 1094

formation and principles, **V:** 1088
of landmarks, **I:** 189, 194, 198, 209
"New Negro" era, **V:** 1091–1092
organizations and associaitons, **II:** 429
related support professionals, **V:** 1097
rise of professional artists, **V:** 1089–1090
studying in Europe, **V:** 1090
twentieth century, **V:** 1091–1097
web sites, **V:** 1149–1150
Vlach, John Michael, **V:** 1098
Voice of the Children, Inc., **III:** 733
Voinovich v. Quilter, **I:** 73
Volleyball and volleyball players *See also* Sports
    African American firsts, **I:** 101
Volunteer Slavery: My Authentic Negro Experience,
    IV: 769
Von Lipsey, Roderick K., **V: 1242–1243**
Voodooism, **III:** 682, 686
Voorhees College, **III:** 657
Voter participation organizations, **II:** 425, 439
Voting and voting rights, **I:** 20, 35, 52, 73, 76 **II:** *456*,
    457–459 *See also* Civil rights and Civil Rights
    movements
    for all United States citizens, **I:** 18
    and Civil Rights Acts, **I:** 31, 159, 165
    demonstrations, **I:** *38*, 57
    denial of, **I:** 10, 17
    and fraud charges, **I:** 57
    grandfather clauses, **I:** 20
    increased rights, **I:** 73
    intimidation of African Americans, **I:** 19, 25
    landmarks, **I:** 180, 183
    literacy tests, **I:** 35
    reasons for not voting, **I:** 48
    and Septima Clark, **III:** 636
    states granting suffrage, **I:** 18
    statistics (1940), **I:** 25
    voter qualifications, **I:** 27
Voting Rights Act (1957) *See* Civil Rights Act (1957)
Voting Rights Act (1964), **I:** 58
Voting Rights Act (1965), **I:** 56, 69, 168, 180 **II:** 356
    amendment, **II:** 456
    excerpt from, **I:** 168
    landmarks, **I:** 180
    signing, **I:** 36
Voting Rights Act (1982), **I:** 60
Voucher programs (Education), **III:** 631 *See also*
    Education and educators
Vrdolyak, Edward R., **I:** 62
Vuono, Carl E., **I:** 64
Vytacil, Vaclav, **V:** 1115

W

WACS *See* Women's Army Corps (WACS)

Waddles, Charleszetta, **III: 612–613**
Waddles, Payton, **III:** 612
Wade, Banjamin, **V:** 1140
Wade in the Water, **IV:** 958
Wade-Gayles, Gloria, **III:** 667
Wagner, Richard, **IV:** 929, 936
Wagner, Wolfgang, **IV:** 936
Wagstaff, Lonnie H., **III:** 667
Waiting to Exhale, **III:** 736 **IV:** 855 **V:** 1062
Walcott, Joe, **V:** 1171, 1194
Walder College *See* Philander-Smith College
Walk, Leonard, **IV:** 756
Walker, Albertina, **IV: 970**
Walker, Albertina Scholarship Foundation, **IV:** 970
Walker, Alice, **I:** 190 **III:** 602, **744,** *744*
Walker and Williams *See* Walker, George;
    Williams, Bert
Walker, Armstead, **III:** 593
Walker Beauty College, **I:** 195
Walker, Charles T., **I:** 192
Walker, C.J., **I:** 195, 211 **V:** 1138
Walker College of Hair Culture, **III:** 578
Walker, David, **I:** 10 **II: 342,** 378
Walker, Dorothy, **I:** 107
Walker, Edward G., **I:** 86
Walker, George, **IV:** 879, 883, 885, 918, 930, **954**
    Pulitzer Prizes, **I:** 106
Walker, Madame C.J., **III:** 578, *578,* **593**
    landmarks, **I:** 211, *211*
Walker, Maggie Lena, **I:** 88, 222 **III: 593–594**
Walker, Margaret A., **III:** 728, **745,** *745*
Walker, Moses Fleetwood, **I:** 88 **V:** 1169
Walker, Robert S., **I:** 55
Walker, Sheila S., **III:** 667
Walker, T-Bone, **V:** 975, 989, 1025, **1029–1030,** 1038
Walker, William, **V:** 1207
Walker's Appeal, **II:** 342, 379
The Walking Dead, **IV:** 855
Wall Street *See also* Businesses and business
    professionals; Stock exchanges; Stockbrokers
    African American firsts, **III:** 589
Wallace, Christopher *See* Notorious B.I.G.
Wallace, George, **I:** 34, 180
Wallace, Henry A., **III:** 541 **V:** 1222
Waller, Thomas "Fats," **IV:** 884 **V: 1030,** *1030*
Walling, William English, **II:** 396
The Walls of Jericho, **III:** 725
Wally Amos Presents. . . Chip & Cookie, **III:** 583
War correspondents *See* Journalism and journalists
War of 1812, **I:** 190 **V:** 1206
War veterans *See* Veterans (War)
Ward, Billy, **V:** 1036
Ward, Bridget, **II:** 350
Ward, Clara, **IV:** 966
Ward, Douglas Turner, **IV:** 882

Ward, Frederick, **II:** 409
Ward, Jerry W., Jr., **III:** 667
Ward, Robert, **IV:** 948
Ward, Samuel R., **I:** 11, 12, 13
Wardlow, Alvia, **V:** 1099
Wards Cove Packing Co. Inc. v. Antonio, **I:** 67, 68, 69
    II: 348, 465–466
Ware, Charles, **IV:** 958
Warfield, Nima, **I:** 104
Warfield, William C., **IV:** 949, **954–955**, *955*
Warhol, Andy, **V:** 1100
Waring, Laura Wheeler, **V: 1125**
Warner, Isiah M., **III:** 667
Wars *See* Military; name of specific war, e.g.,
    American Civil War
Warwick, Dionne, **V:** 1060, 1061, 1069
Washington (State)
    African American newspapers, **IV:** 806
    African American radio stations, **IV:** 825
    landmarks, **I:** 223
Washington, Alonzo, **IV:** 752
Washington, Booker T., **II:** 337, *369*, **369–370**, 388
    III: 492, 643 **IV:** 750
    and *Atlanta Compromise* speech, **I:** 20, 146–148
    on Boley, Oklahoma, **III:** 547
    as civil rights activist, **II:** 345
    coins commemmorating, **I:** 90, 91
    critics, **I:** 20, 21, 201 **II:** 369, 379 **III:** 697
    former secretaries, **IV:** 830
    influences, **II:** 488
    landmarks, **I:** 211, 221, *222*, 222–223
    and National Negro Business League, **I:** 20 **II:** 395
    III: 576 **IV:** 769
    and Tuskegee Institute, **I:** 19, 180, 222 **III:** 624, 625
    V: 1154
Washington, Denzel, **III:** 602, 739 **IV:** *849*, **873**, *873*
Washington, Dinah, **V:** 984, **1030–1031**, *1031*, 1036,
    1038, 1049
Washington, Ford "Buck," **IV:** 894
Washington, Fredi, **IV:** 880, **917**
Washington, George (Former slave), **I:** 223
Washington, George (President), **I:** 4, 5, 7, *119* **II:**
    339 **III:** 746 **V:** 1205
    association with Samuel Fraunces, **I:** 209
    last will and testament, **I:** 119
Washington, Harold, **I:** 57, *58*, 62, 64, 100 **III: 534–**
    535, *536*
Washington Human Rights Commission, **II:** 374
Washington, Joe, **V:** 1177
Washington, Kenny, **V:** 1171
Washington, Lula, **IV:** 890
Washington, MaliVai, **V:** 1175
Washington Office on Africa, **II: 445**
Washington Research Project of the Southern Center
    for Public Policy *See* Children's Defense Fund

Washington Urban League, **II:** 407
Washington, Walter E., **I:** 97, 187
Washington, Warren, **V:** 1145
Watergate scandal, **I:** 50, 76
Watermelon Man, **IV:** 855
Waters, Ethel, **III:** 590 **IV:** 835, 859, 881, **917**
Waters, Maxine, **III:** 498, 521, **535–536**, *537*
Waters, Muddy, **V:** *975*, 996, 1025, **1031**, 1038, 1047
Watkins, Levi, Jr., **I:** 99 **V: 1166**
Watson, Clara, **II:** 465
Watson, James L., **III:** 530
Watson v. Fort Worth Bank and Trust, **II:** 465
Watt, Melvin L., **III:** 498
Wattleton, Faye, **II: 415–416**, *416*
Watts, André, **IV:** *955*, 955–956
Watts, J.C., Jr., **I:** 109, *109* **III:** 496, 517, **536–537**
Watts race riot, **I:** 36, *41 See also* Slave insurrections
    and insurrectionists
WAVES *See* United States Navy Women's
    Reserves (WAVES)
Wayans, Damon, **IV:** 886, **917–918**
Wayans, Keenan Ivory, **IV:** 837, 886, **918**, *918*
Wayne County Community College, **III:** 657
Weatherpersons *See* Meteorology and meteorologists
Weatherspoon Art Gallery, **V:** 1133
Weaver, Robert C., **I:** 26, 36, 97, *98* **III:** **537**
W.E.B. Du Bois Academy, **III:** 530
W.E.B. Du Bois Institute of Afro-American Research,
    III: 663
Web sites *See* The Internet
Webb, Chick, **V:** 999, 1067
Webb, Clifton, **IV:** 917
Webb, Wellington, **III: 538**
Webb, William, **I:** 201
Weber, Brian, **II:** 472
Weber v. Kaiser Aluminum and Chemicla Corp.,
    I: 57
Webster, Benjamin Francis Love "Ben," **V: 1031**
Webster, William H., **I:** 53
Webster-Ashburton Treaty, **I:** 12
The Wedding, **III:** 746
Weems, Carrie Mae, **V:** 1096, **1125**
Weight lifters *See* Bodybuilders
Wein, George, **II:** 389
Weiner, Nina, **IV:** 909
Welburn, Edward T., **V: 1125**
    cars designed by, **V:** *1126*
Weld, Theodore D., **I:** 123
Welfare, **III:** 562, 564–565
Wells, Ebenezer, **III:** 742
Wells, James Lesesne, **V: 1126–1127**
Wells, Mary, **V:** 1057, **1082–1083**
Wells, Orson, **III:** 748 **IV:** 866
Wells-Barnett, Ida, **I:** 19, 145, *145*, 194 **II:** 344, **370–**
    371

Welsch, Mary McKelvey, **III:** 667
Wendell Street Gallery, **V:** 1131
Werblin, Sonny, **V:** 1100
Wesley, Charles, **II:** 400
Wesley, Cynthia, **I:** 179
Wesley, John, **III:** 672
West, Ben, **II:** 364
West, Christopher, **IV:** 936
West, Clifton L., Sr., **III:** 705
West, Cornel, **III:** 667, **705–706**
West, Dorothy, **III: 745–746,** *746*
West Fairmount Park, **I:** 216
West Indies, **I:** 1, 25 **II:** 236–240, 444 *See also* name
    of specific country, e.g., Trinidad and Tobago
    African American women's firsts, **II:** 296
    emigration, **I:** 180 **II:** 240
    maps, **II:** *239*
    most Anglicized island, **II:** 286
West Point Military Academy *See* United States
    Military Academy (USMA) at West Point
West, Togo D., Jr., **V:** 1226
West Virginia
    African American newspapers, **IV:** 806
    landmarks, **I:** 223–224
West Virginia Human Rights Commission, **II:** 374
West Virginia State College, **III:** 657
Westerfield, Louis, **I:** 105
Western hemisphere, **I:** 1 **II:** 236–240, 283–315, 290
    See also specific region or country, e.g., Canada
Western United States *See* American West
Westinghouse, George, **V:** 1138
Weston, Kim, **V:** 1057
Westside Preparatory School, **III:** 628, 637
Wexler, Jerry, **V:** 1035, 1055
WGPR-TV (Detroit, Michigan), **I:** 99 **IV:** 763
Whaling industry, **I:** 201 **V:** 1165
Wharton, Clifton R., Jr., **I:** 73 **III: 649–650,** *650*
Whatcha Lookin 4, **IV:** 967
What's Love Got to Do With It?, **IV:** 855, 856
Wheat Street *See* Sweet Auburn Historic District
Wheatley, Phillis, **I:** 5, 200, 213 **III:** 709, **746 V:** 1089
Wheatley, Susannah, **III:** 746
*When and Where I Enter: The Impact of Black
    Women on Race and Sex in America,* **III:** 612
Whipple, Prince, **I:** 5
Whitaker, Forest, **III:** 736
Whitaker, Mark, **I:** 109
White, Barry, **V:** 1043
White, Bill, **I:** 103 **V:** 1170, 1184, **1203**
White, Charles, **V: 1127**
White Citizens Councils, **I:** 28
White, Clarence Cameron, **IV: 956**
White Eagle Monument, **I:** 214
White House fellows
    African American women's firsts, **I:** 99 **III:** 695

White, John, **IV:** 930
White, Jonathan Jasper, **II:** 453
White, Joseph, **IV:** 946
White, Loray, **IV:** 859
White, Michael R., **I:** 67 **III: 538**
White, Ronnie, **V:** 1084
White Sea Islands, South Carolina, **III:** 547
White supremacists, **I:** 63 *See also* Racial prejudice
White v. Regester, **II:** 459
White, Walter, **I:** 187 **II:** 396, **416,** 417
Whitefield, George, **III:** 672
Whitfield, Fred, **I:** 109
Whitfield, Lynn, **I:** 103 **IV:** *847*
Whitfield, Thomas, **IV:** 964
Whitman, Walt, **I:** 215
Whitney (Music record), **V:** 1061
Whitney, Eli, **I:** 6 **II:** 322
Whitten, Charles, **V:** 1145
WHUR-FM (District of Columbia), **IV:** 756
Wideman, John Edgar, **III: 746–747**
Wilberforce University, **I:** 214, *215* **III:** 624, 658
Wilberforce, William, **I:** 214 **III:** 624
Wilder, Gene, **IV:** 834, 912
Wilder, Julia, **I:** 57
Wilder, L. Douglas, **I:** 61, 65, 67, 70, 103, *103* **III:**
    538–539
Wiley College, **III:** 658
Wilkes, Sybil, **IV:** 775
Wilkins, Ernest, **I:** 28
Wilkins, Lenny, **I:** 105 **V:** 1174, **1203–1204,** *1204*
Wilkins, Roger W., **III:** 667
Wilkins, Roy, **I:** 51, 56 **II:** 397, 406, **416–417,** *417*
    landmarks, **I:** 211
Wilks, Gertrude, **III:** 628
Will Mastin Trio, **IV:** 859
William Christopher Handy Park, **I:** 218
William Monroe Trotter Institute, **III:** 663
William Morris Agency, **III:** 582
Williams, Ann, **IV:** 890
Williams, Bert, **IV:** 879, *879,* 883, 885, **918–919,** 930
Williams, Billy Dee, **IV:** 834, **874,** *874*
Williams, Camilla, **I:** 91
Williams, Charlie, **I:** 104
Williams, Cootie, **IV:** 892
Williams, Daniel Hale, **I:** 20, 88, 193 **V:** 1140, *1141,*
    1155, **1166–1167**
    landmarks, **I:** 194
Williams, Delores W., **III:** 667, 677
Williams, Doug, **I:** 102 **V:** 1171
Williams, Eric, **V:** 1077
Williams, Evelyn, **II: 488–489**
Williams, Frances, **I:** 85
Williams, Hank, **V:** 1047
Williams, Henry Sylvester, **II:** 380
Williams, James H., Jr., **III:** 667

Williams, Joe, **V:** 983
Williams, John, **I:** 46 **V:** 1032, 1122
Williams, Lucie Campbell, **III:** 676
Williams, Mary Lou, **V:** 984, **1032**
Williams, Montel, **IV: 785–786,** *786*
Williams, O.S., **V:** 1143, **1167**
Williams, Paul, **V:** 1067
Williams, Paul T., **V: 1127**
Williams, Preston Noah, **III:** 667
Williams, Richard, **V:** 1204
Williams, Robert F., **II: 391–392**
Williams, Serena, **I:** 84 **V:** 1175, 1177, **1204**
Williams, Vanessa, **I:** 100, *102* **IV: 874**
Williams, Venus, **I:** 84, *84* **V:** 1175, 1177, **1204**
Williams, Walter A., **III:** 667
Williams, Walter Edward, **II:** 403
Williams, William T., **V: 1127**
Williams, Willie, **II:** 487
Williamson, Lisa *See* Sister Soulah
Williamson, "Sonny Boy," **V: 1032**
Williard, Jess, **V:** 1191
Willie, Charles V., **III:** 667
Willis, Deborah, **V:** 1099
Willis, George, **II:** *470*
Willis, Jan, **III:** 667
Willis, Sylvia, **I:** 83
Wills *See* Last wills and testaments
Wills, Maury, **V:** 1182
"Wilmington 10," **II:** 401
Wilmington race riot (1898), **II:** 337
Wilmot, David, **II:** 325
Wilmot Proviso, **II:** 325
Wilson, August, **III: 747 IV:** *883*, 913
Wilson Brown Gallery, **V:** 1128
Wilson, Flip, **IV:** 836, 886, **919**, *919*
Wilson, Harriet E., **I:** 87 **III:** 640
Wilson, Jackie, **V:** 1056, 1058, **1083,** *1083*
Wilson, James, **II:** 415
Wilson, John S., **IV:** 856 **V: 1127–1128**
Wilson, Lionel, **I:** 99 **II:** 385, 411
Wilson, Llewelyn, **IV:** 893
Wilson, Margaret Bush, **I:** 58, 59, *59*
Wilson, Mary, **V:** 1078, **1083–1084**
Wilson, Nancy, **V:** 1046, **1084**
Wilson, Olly Woodrow, **IV: 956**
Wilson, Pete, **I:** 71
Wilson, Phill, **III: 613,** *613*
Wilson, Teddy, **V:** 978, **1032–1033**
Wilson, William Julius, **III:** 667
Wilson, Woodrow, **I:** 21 **II:** 369
Wimbledon tennis tournaments, A-15
    African American firsts, **V:** 1187
The Winans, **IV: 970–971,** *971*
Winans, Angie, **IV:** 971
Winans, Benjamin, **IV:** 970

Winans, Carvin, **IV:** 970
Winans, Cecelia, **IV:** 970
Winans, David, Sr., **IV:** 970
Winans, Debbie, **IV:** 971
Winans, Marvin, **IV:** 970
Winbush, Raymond, **III:** 667
Winchester, Jesse, **V:** 1039
Wind, Timothy E., **I:** 74
Windham Brothers Construction Company, **I:** 179
Winfield, Hemsley, **IV:** 887
Winfield, Paul, **IV: 875**
Winfrey, Oprah, **I:** 100 **III:** 715, 744, 746 **IV:** 759, *786*,
    786–787
    court cases, **IV:** 787
    earnings, **I:** 78
Winful, Herbert Graves, **III:** 667
Wingate, Livingston, **III:** 530
Winslow, Sydney W., **V:** 1164
Winston-Salem State University, **III:** 658
Winter, Marian Hannah, **IV:** 878
Wiretapping, **I:** 44, 51
Wisconsin
    African American newspapers, **IV:** 806
    African American radio stations, **IV:** 825
    African American television stations, **IV:** 827
    landmarks, **I:** 224
Wisconsin Attorney General's Office, **II:** 374
The Wiz, **IV:** 855, 884
WLIB-AM (New York, New York), **IV:** 756
WNBA *See* Women's National Basketball
    Association (WNBA)
Wolcott, Louis Eugene *See* Farrakhan, Louis
Wolfe, George C., **IV:** 884, **919–920**
Womack, Bobby, **V:** 1083
Womack, Cecil, **V:** 1083
The Women of Brewster Place, **IV:** 855
Women's Army Corps (WACS), **I:** 90
Women's Auxiliary Army Corps (WAAC)
    African American women's firsts, **V:** 1231
Women's Exchange and Girls' Home, **III:** 638
Women's health, **II:** 438 **III:** 609
Women's Leadership Institute, **III:** 663
Women's National Basketball Association (WNBA)
    African American firsts, **I:** 83
Women's Research and Resource Center, **III:** 663
Women's rights and women's rights activists, **II:** 355,
    425 **III:** 611–612, 681 *See also* Feminism and
    feminists
Women's suffrage, **I:** 143–144
Wonder, Stevie, **I:** 98 **II:** 413 **V: 1084–1085,** *1085*
Wonder, Stevie/SAP Vision Awards, **V:** 1085
The Wood, **IV:** 855
Wood, Roy, **IV:** 756
Wood, Willie, **V:** 1171
Woodruff, Hale, **I:** 180 **V: 1128**

Woodruff, Judy, **IV:** 782

Woods, Granville T., **V:** 1138

Woods, Johnnie, **IV:** 880

Woods, Love B., **I:** 210

Woods, Tiger, **I:** 79, *80*, 105, 106 **V:** *1176*, 1177, **1204**

Woodson, Carter G., **I:** 23 **II: 417–418 III:** *627*, **650**
   and Association for the Study of African American
      Life and History, **I:** 21, 89 **III:** 626 **IV:** 751
   landmarks, **I:** 189

Woodson, Charles, **I:** 107

Woodward, Alfre, **IV:** 899, 913

Woodward, Lynette, **V:** 1177

Woodward, Michael D., **III:** 575, 581

Woolman, John, **I:** 4

Wordlaw, Gary, **IV:** 759

Work, John W., **I:** 219 **IV:** 750

Work, Monroe N., **IV:** 750

Workplace discrimination, **II:** 347, 348 *See also*
   Employment; Equal employment opportunity
   and affirmative action
   effects, **III:** 558
   lawsuits, **I:** 67, 69 **III:** 560
   public policy, **III:** 559
   studies, **I:** 69

WorkPlace Integrators, **III:** 588

Work's Progress Administration (WPA), **V:** 1093–1094

World Class Records, **V:** 1055

World Class Wreckin' Cru, **V:** 1053

World Figure Skating Championship, **I:** 101

World News Tonight, **IV:** 779

World Series (Baseball)
   African American firsts, **I:** 104

The World, the Flesh, and the Devil, **IV:** 855

World War I, **V:** 1213–1215 *See also* Military
   African American firsts, **V:** 1237
   contributions of women, **V:** 1215
   group of sailors, **V:** *1214*
   highest ranking officer, **I:** 214
   landmarks, **I:** 194, 195
   Medals of Honor recipients, A-13
   soldiers leaving for, **I:** *23*
   training camps, **I:** 22

World War II, **I:** 27 **V:** 1215–1221 *See also* Military
   African American firsts, **V:** 1239
   belated recognition of heroes, **V:** 1221
   Medals of Honor recipients, A-13 **I:** 79
   propaganda films, **IV:** 832

World Wide Web *See* The Internet

Worrell, Richard, **I:** 112

Wreckx-N-Effect, **V:** 1077

Wright, Beryl J., **V:** 1099

Wright, J. Skelly, **I:** 39

Wright, Jonathan Jasper, **I:** 88 **II:** 334

Wright, Louis T., **II:** 415 **V:** 1141

Wright, Richard, **I:** 24 **III:** 711, *712*, 723, **747–748**

Wright v. City of Emporia, **II:** 463

Wright, Will, **IV:** 759

Wygant v. Jackson Board of Education, **I:** 61
   II: 473–474

Wylke, May L., **III:** 667

Wynn, Albert R., **III:** 498

Wyoming Attorney General's Office, **II:** 374

X

X, Malcolm, **I:** 34 **II:** 382–383, *384*, 390, *392*, **392–393 IV:** 898 **V:** 1044
   assassination, **I:** 35 **II:** 364
   family of, **I:** 76, 80
   and FBI, **I:** 50
   influence on authors, **III:** 727, 747
   influence on religious movements, **III:** 677, 692
   landmarks, **I:** 210
   and Nation of Islam leaders, **II:** 387, 390
   stance on Vietnam War, **V:** 1224

Xavier College, **III:** 624

Xavier University of Louisiana, **III:** 658

Xernona Clayton Show, **IV:** 768

Xuma, Alfred B., **II:** 228

Y

Yardbird Publishing Co., Inc., **III:** 740

Yarde, Richard, **V: 1128**

Yella, **V:** 1053

Yellow fever, **V:** 1211

Yellow Tavern, **I:** 212

Yerby, Frank, **I:** 192

Yo Yo (Musician), **V:** 1063

Yorkin, Bud, **IV:** 836

Yorktown, Battle of *See* Battle of Yorktown

Yorty, Sam, **I:** 50

Yoruba priestesses, **III:** 682, 705

Young, Andrew, **I:** 49, 51, 52 **III:** 495, *539*, **539–540,** 676
   resignation, **I:** 52

Young Black Programmers Coalition, **II: 446**

Young, Charles A., **I:** 214 **V:** 1210, 1213

Young Chicago Authors, **IV:** 769

Young, Coleman A., **I:** 67, 99 **III:** 499, *540*, **540–541 IV:** 778
   successor to, **I:** 75

Young Ideas, **III:** 540

Young, Lester, **V:** 988, 1031, **1033**

Young Negroes Cooperative League, **II:** 351

Young, Otis B., Jr., **V:** 1142

Young, Perry H., **V:** 1142

Young, Steve, **V:** 1198

Young, Thomas W., **I:** 91

Young, Whitney M., Jr., **I:** 197 **II:** 397, 408, **418,** *418*

Young, Whitney M., Sr., **I:** 196
Young Women's Leadership School, **III:** 631
Your Heritage House, **V:** 1131
Youth organizations, **II:** 438
Yucca Plantation *See* Melrose Plantation
Yugen, **III:** 717

Z

Zambia, **II:** 281
Zane, Arnie, **IV:** 907
Zebrahead, **IV:** 855
Zeely, **III:** 728

Zefferelli, Franco, **V:** 1077
Zeta Phi Beta (Sorority), **II:** 400, **446**
Zimbabwe, **II: 281–283**
Zimmerman, Fred, **IV:** 934
Zion Investment Associates, **II:** 367
Zoology and zoologists, **V:** 1161
Zooman, **IV:** 855
Zora Neale Hurston Memorial Park and Marker,
    I: 190
Zuni Pueblo, **I:** 207
Zydeco music, **V:** 991 *See also* Blues and blues
    musicians